Frommer's

Argentina & Chile

3rd Edition

*by Haas Mroue, Kristina Schreck
& Michael Luongo*

D0110179

Here's what the critics say about Frommer's:

"Amazingly easy to use. Very portable, very complete."
—*Booklist*

"Detailed, accurate, and easy-to-read information for all price ranges."
—*Glamour Magazine*

"Hotel information is close to encyclopedic."
—*Des Moines Sunday Register*

"Frommer's Guides have a way of giving you a real feel for a place."
—*Knight Ridder Newspapers*

WILEY

Wiley Publishing, Inc.

Published by:

Wiley Publishing, Inc.

111 River St.
Hoboken, NJ 07030-5774

ISBN-13: 978-0-7645-8439-8
ISBN-10: 0-7645-8439-1

Editor: Kendra L. Falkenstein
special thanks to Marc Nadeau and Stephen Bassman
Production Editor: Bethany André
Cartographer: Liz Puhl
Photo Editor: Richard Fox
Production by Wiley Indianapolis Composition Services

Front cover photo: Patagonia, Chile: Torres del Paine National Park
Back cover photo: A tango demonstration in the San Telmo district of Buenos Aires

Contents

17 The Carretera Austral   393

18 Patagonia, Tierra del Fuego & Antarctica   425

Index   487

List of Maps

About the Authors

Haas Mroue (chapters 1, 2, 4, 5, 6, 7, 8, 9, 10, and 18) is a freelance travel writer based in the United States. His short stories, poems, and travel pieces have appeared in a variety of publications—including the *Michigan Quarterly Review*, the *Literary Review*, Berlitz and National Geographic guides, among many others—and his work has been broadcast on the BBC World Service and Starz! cable channel. He is the author of *Frommer's Memorable Walks In Paris*, *Frommer's Paris from $95 a Day*, Frommer's *Amsterdam Day by Day*, and is a contributor to *Frommer's South America*, *Frommer's Gay & Lesbian Europe*, and *Frommer's Europe from $85 a Day*.

Kristina Schreck (chapters 1, 11, 12, 13, 14, 15, 16, 17, and 18) spends an endless amount of time on the road, but is happiest when back in Santiago, Chile, where she lives. She has traveled widely around the globe, and has lived in Argentina and Chile for nearly a decade, working as a freelance writer, an outdoor guide, and the marketing manager of Portillo ski resort. Currently, she is a public relations consultant for a variety of tourism-related entities. She is the former managing editor of *Adventure Journal* magazine, and is co-author of the first edition of *Frommer's Argentina & Chile*.

Michael Luongo (chapters 1, 3, and 4) has written on Argentina for the *New York Times*, the *Chicago Tribune*, *Frommer's Budget Travel*, *National Geographic Traveler*, *Town & Country Traveler*, the *Advocate*, *Out Traveler*, and numerous other publications. Having been to more than 75 countries and all 7 continents, Luongo considers Argentina to be one of his all-time favorites, and the first time he was in Buenos Aires, he cried when he had to leave. Living in Buenos Aires like a "real native" in order to write for Frommer's was like living a dream. His only regret is being a bad tangoer—even though he loves watching other people do the dance.

Acknowledgments

Haas Mroue would like to thank Ines Segarra at the Argentina Government Tourist Office in New York. He'd also like to thank Charlie O'Malley, Kelly Thornhill, and Kai Renk in Mendoza; and Mario in Patagonia for his exceptional driving skills on the endless miles of gravel roads. He'd like to extend special thanks to the team at the Secretaria de Turismo in Salta for their invaluable assistance.

Kristina Schreck would like to thank Mark Rawsthorne, Felipe Pumarino, and Amy Wilson for their help in updating this guide.

Michael Luongo: I want to give a big thanks to my editor Kendra for having the patience to work with me. Thanks to Ines and Deborah and Ricardo in New York, and to Luis, Lawrence, and Marcos in Buenos Aires for all of your help. I am sure I am missing many people, but please know you're loved and appreciated!

An Invitation to the Reader

In researching this book, we discovered many wonderful places—hotels, restaurants, shops, and more. We're sure you'll find others. Please tell us about them, so we can share the information with your fellow travelers in upcoming editions. If you were disappointed with a recommendation, we'd love to know that, too. Please write to:

Frommer's Argentina & Chile, 3rd Edition
Wiley Publishing, Inc. • 111 River St. • Hoboken, NJ 07030-5774

An Additional Note

Please be advised that travel information is subject to change at any time—and this is especially true of prices. We therefore suggest that you write or call ahead for confirmation when making your travel plans. The authors, editors, and publisher cannot be held responsible for the experiences of readers while traveling. Your safety is important to us, however, so we encourage you to stay alert and be aware of your surroundings. Keep a close eye on cameras, purses, and wallets, all favorite targets of thieves and pickpockets.

Other Great Guides for Your Trip:

Frommer's South America

Frommer's Peru

Frommer's Adventure Guides: South America

Frommer's Star Ratings, Icons & Abbreviations

Every hotel, restaurant, and attraction listing in this guide has been ranked for quality, value, service, amenities, and special features using a **star-rating system.** In country, state, and regional guides, we also rate towns and regions to help you narrow down your choices and budget your time accordingly. Hotels and restaurants are rated on a scale of zero (recommended) to three stars (exceptional). Attractions, shopping, nightlife, towns, and regions are rated according to the following scale: zero stars (recommended), one star (highly recommended), two stars (very highly recommended), and three stars (must-see).

In addition to the star-rating system, we also use **seven feature icons** that point you to the great deals, in-the-know advice, and unique experiences that separate travelers from tourists. Throughout the book, look for:

Finds	Special finds—those places only insiders know about
Fun Fact	Fun facts—details that make travelers more informed and their trips more fun
Kids	Best bets for kids and advice for the whole family
Moments	Special moments—those experiences that memories are made of
Overrated	Places or experiences not worth your time or money
Tips	Insider tips—great ways to save time and money
Value	Great values—where to get the best deals

The following **abbreviations** are used for credit cards:

AE	American Express	DISC	Discover	V	Visa
DC	Diners Club	MC	MasterCard		

Frommers.com

Now that you have the guidebook to a great trip, visit our website at **www.frommers.com** for travel information on more than 3,000 destinations. With features updated regularly, we give you instant access to the most current trip-planning information available. At Frommers.com, you'll also find the best prices on airfares, accommodations, and car rentals—and you can even book travel online through our travel booking partners. At Frommers.com, you'll also find the following:

- Online updates to our most popular guidebooks
- Vacation sweepstakes and contest giveaways
- Newsletter highlighting the hottest travel trends
- Online travel message boards with featured travel discussions

What's New in Argentina & Chile

ARGENTINA

Tourism in Argentina is booming. The country is a terrific bargain for most travelers. The peso is still weak, almost 3 to a dollar, and with the euro even stronger, Europeans are flocking here in droves. Hotels, restaurants, and national parks are full of Spaniards and Italians. Increasingly, however, there are "foreign visitor" rates and "resident" rates (especially at hotels and national parks), which can be frustrating for the traveler on a budget. Hotel rates are frequently posted in U.S. dollars, though Argentines get unadvertised lower rates in pesos. Beware of hotels charging for sundries in U.S. dollars, which can be confusing, since the $ sign is also used for pesos. (Just remember that if it's in U.S. dollars, the $ sign should be followed with USD, for example: $USD.) It never hurts to always double-check what currency is being used. A bottle of water from your minibar may cost as much as $4.50. Make sure that it means pesos, not dollars, if you're watching your budget!

Foreign visitors pay three times as much as Argentine residents to enter national parks and some other sights. The only place where prices are usually strictly in pesos are the restaurants (except for a few hotel restaurants), where everything is in pesos and, therefore, quite affordable.

GETTING THERE Flights to Argentina are so full that more airlines are adding service. **Delta** (www.delta. com) began daily service from Atlanta to Buenos Aires in December 2004. **United Airlines** (www.ual.com) began flying a daily flight from Chicago in November 2004, in addition to the daily arrival from Washington Dulles. And **Aerolíneas Argentinas** (www. aerolineasargentinas.com) is expanding rapidly—adding more flights from New York, Miami, Sydney, and Auckland. In late 2005, Aerolíneas Argentinas will launch the first nonstop flights from the U.S. West Coast to Buenos Aires. Flights will depart from Los Angeles International airport two or three times a week.

GETTING AROUND Flying is the most efficient way of getting around the world's eighth-largest country. **Aerolíneas Argentinas** remains the leading carrier after gobbling up LAPA's routes (LAPA went bankrupt and shut down in 2003). Aerolíneas is currently upgrading its domestic fleet after completely overhauling its international aircraft. Newer Boeing 737s are being added throughout 2005. **Southern Winds** (www.sw.com.ar) is an excellent domestic carrier that is adding more routes and frequency every few months. **American Falcon** (www.americanfalcon.com.ar) flies older planes but offers some of the cheapest last-minute fares from Buenos Aires to Bariloche, Salta, Iguazú, and Puerto Madryn (gateway to the Peninsula Valdes).

BUENOS AIRES Travelers will find that Buenos Aires continues to be a bargain, now that the peso has stabilized at about 3 to the U.S. dollar. However, since the world has taken notice of Buenos Aires and her charms, tourism has boomed, without hotel construction keeping pace. Because of that, you will find that some hotels that were bargains in previous years have now gone up a notch in category as their prices rose. We have, however, included many new and previously unlisted three-star hotels and hostels to make sure you don't spend any more than you want to while in Buenos Aires. Restaurants continue to open at a breakneck pace in the Palermo Viejo neighborhood, so there will always be new places to eat. Plus, new museums are also opening throughout the city, so it's a very exciting time to be there.

Accommodations A brand new tower has opened for the **Crowne Plaza Pan Americano** (Carlos Pellegrini 551; © **11/4348-5115**), more than doubling its capacity. This hotel, on Avenida 9 de Julio overlooking the Obelisco, has one of the best locations in the city. Its rooftop gym, in a glass box on the roof of the tower, gives the impression of exercising or swimming in mid-air, and has to be seen to be believed. The **Four Seasons Hotel** (Posadas 1086/88; © **11/4321-1200**) is upgrading its already luxurious property, completing a conversion from being a Hyatt until just a few years ago. Along with room renovations, the spa has been completely rebuilt, using a native Argentine theme. To keep pace with all the tourists coming in, many locals have decided to open their own minihotels and hostels. Among them is Palermo Viejo's **Casa Jardin** (Charcas 4416; © **11/4774-8783**). It was opened as an arts hotel and often has exhibits by local artists as well as the owner herself, Nerina Sturgeon.

Dining The peso crisis has lead to an explosion in new places to dine out and for young Argentine chefs to test out their skills. Palermo Viejo and nearby Las Cañitas continue to be the main neighborhoods for these new restaurants, many of which continue

to pay homage to beef, the main ingredient in any Argentine dish. **El Estanciero** (Báez 202; © **11/4899-0951**) in Las Cañitas offers an alternative to some of the more chic locations surrounding it. It's all about the beef here, arguably the best in the neighborhood, and there is rarely a crowd. A great bargain choice with wonderful beef is **Juana M** (Carlos Pellegrini 1535; © **11/4326-0462**), near the La Recova area of Recoleta, where Avenida 9 de Julio hits Libertador. Here, for less than $5, you get something from the *parrilla,* a drink, and unlimited access to the salad bar, all surrounded by some of the city's most expensive real estate.

Exploring Buenos Aires Maybe it is hard for visitors to Buenos Aires to believe, but it took more than 50 years after Evita's death for Argentina to finally have a museum in her honor. The **Museo Evita** (Calle Lafinur 2988; © **11/4807-9433**) is located in a Palermo mansion where she once opened a halfway house for single mothers. See her hats, dresses, shoes, and many other personal effects and items from the era here. Be aware that if renovations continue on schedule, 2005 may be the last year that you can see a show or visit the inside of the spectacular **Teatro Colón** (Calle Libertad 621; © **11/4378-7100**) until 2008. An intense renovation is ongoing, and will eventually move to the interior of the theater, meaning shows and visits will be impossible.

MENDOZA Mendoza's newest hotel and the city's best bargain is the elegant and affordable **Hotel Argentino,** Espejo 455, 5500 Mendoza (© **261/405-6300;** www. argentino-hotel.com). Opened in mid-2004, it commands a perfect location facing the Plaza de la Independencia, steps from the ritzy Park Hyatt at a third of the price: Doubles go for $50.

THE WINE COUNTRY Touring the Wine Country New in 2005 are Familia Zuccardi's (© **261/441-0000; turismo@familiazuccardi.com**) "Come To Harvest" wine excursions from February to April. For $67, you'll get a crash course on grape harvesting followed by 2 hours out in the fields picking grapes. Lunch and a tasting follow.

Where to Stay in the Wine Country Club Tapiz, Pedro Molina Ruta 60, Maipu (© **261/490-0202;** www. newage-hotels.com), opened in 2004 and is the most elegant place to stay in the Wine Country. There's a pristine pool, a spa, and a fantastic restaurant. Rates begin at $77 for a double.

CORDOBA The city's newest hotel opened in 2004 and commands a great downtown location. The **King David,** General Paz 386, 5000 Córdoba (© **351/570-3528;** www.king david.com.ar), is an all-suite hotel with fully equipped kitchens, spacious bathrooms, and living rooms with sofas. Rates are $60 for a double.

SALTA What to See & Do Salta's newest museum opened in November 2004. The **Museo de Arqueológia de Alta Montaña (Andean Archaeological Museum),** Mitre 77 (© **387/ 437-0499**), was built to house the three incredibly preserved 500-year-old mummies that were found buried in the ice on a nearby volcanic mountain. The locals have taken to affectionately calling it the "museo de las momias," although the mummies are still not on display. They soon will be. Until then, there's a good documentary showing the amazing discovery.

Where to Stay The **Casa Real Hotel,** Mitre 669, 4400 Salta (© **387/ 421-5675;** www.hotelcasareal.com.ar), is Salta's newest downtown hotel. Opened in 2004, it has spacious, modern rooms and large-screen TVs. There's a nice indoor pool and a good restaurant, too. Doubles begin at $87.

The **House of Jasmines,** Camino al Encon, La Merced Chica, 4407 Salta (©/fax **387/497-2002;** www. houseofjasmines.com), was opened in late 2004 by American actor Robert Duvall and his Argentine wife, who own this gorgeous farmhouse a short drive from the center of Salta. Surely destined to be featured in some of the world's leading design magazines, this hotel gives you a taste of *estancia* living without compromising on luxury. The antique-filled rooms with four-poster beds, plush mattresses, and fluffy duvets are filled with roses and jasmine (from the farm's private gardens) prior to a guest's arrival. The talented chef uses local ingredients to create delicious, healthy meals served on the pristine patio overlooking 120 hectares (300 acres) of lush grounds.

Where to Dine What may very well be Northwest Argentina's most talked-about restaurant opened in Salta in 2004, serving Andean cuisine with modern flair. **Jose Balcance,** Mitre and Necochea (© **387/421-1628**), is where you can sample llama carpaccio or llama filets in an elegant, refined setting. Main courses begin at $6.

PENINSULA VALDES New in this edition is our coverage of Atlantic Patagonia and the Peninsula Valdes, which has recently become a UNESCO World Heritage site.

THE ARGENTINE LAKE DISTRICT San Carlos de Bariloche Bariloche's newest hotel is the breathtaking **Design Suites,** Av. Bustillo Km 2.5 (© **11/4814-8700** for reservations in Buenos Aires; www.design suites.com), opened in 2004. If you stay here, expect minimalist luxury, attentive service, and a hip and happening youngish clientele hailing from Europe and Brazil. There's a fantastic spa and a great restaurant here, too. Doubles begin at $125.

PATAGONIA & TIERRA DEL FUEGO El Calafate The Southern Hemisphere summer (Dec–Mar) of 2005 has proven to be a record-breaker for visitor arrivals in this blessedly beautiful area of Patagonia. Flights have been so heavily booked that **Aerolíneas Argentinas (℃ 0810/ 222-86527;** www.aerolineasargetinas. com) has just announced the addition of twice-weekly 747-400 (the largest aircraft flying now) flights nonstop from Ezeiza to El Calafate. This is the first time Aerolíneas has used their largest wide-body jets on a domestic route. Not only are the flights full, but hotels are heavily booked, too, so I advise making your reservations as early as possible. Avoid Patagonia from mid-December to early March (when the hordes arrive), and come instead in the relative calm of October or November, or from mid-March to early May.

EL CHALTEN Finally, a deluxe accommodations option in Chalten. Opening in mid-2005 is the intimate **Los Cerros (℃ 11/4814-3934;** info@ loscerrosdelchalten.com), a small boutique inn built by the owners of the celebrated Los Notros (which overlooks Perito Moreno Glacier). Expect rustic luxury and exquisite service. Two-, 3-, and 4-day packages include your choice of treks, hikes, and 4×4 rides, in addition to gourmet meals.

CHILE

The **weak dollar** has made Chile more expensive than in previous years. In 2003, the peso hit a high of 720 to the dollar, but by 2004 it dropped to a low of 560. This book has converted prices at 600 pesos to the dollar; this is the rate at the time of publication.

The Chilean tourism industry lost a lot of business to neighboring Argentina when prices there hit rock bottom, but now most upscale Argentine hotels list their rates in dollars, meaning lodging prices in Chile are now more or less comparable. Also, Chile's pristine landscapes and adventure-travel opportunities are incomparable to those of its Andean neighbor—the reason Chile has grown wildly in popularity over the past five years. As a result, the country's tourism infrastructure continues to improve with new hotels, a focus on refining service, and easier trip planning.

The entry fee at Customs has remained at $100 per traveler, regardless of age, but it's good for the life of the visitor's passport and travelers can now pay the fee with a credit card instead of U.S. dollars only. This fee is intended as a reciprocity fee for the U.S. government's $100 visa application fee for Chileans.

It's comical how fast telephone numbers in Chile change and how these telephone numbers are immediately reassigned to a residence. All numbers in this book have been meticulously updated; however, do not be surprised if, occasionally, a Juan Doe answers without any idea of what you're talking about. Have your hotel help you find any updated numbers. Thankfully, nearly every business in tourism now has an e-mail address and/or website, and really there are only a few hotels mentioned in the book that still do not have a reservation system via the Internet. The Internet has proven invaluable to travelers planning their trip, especially in getting around the language barrier.

GETTING AROUND By Plane Lan Airlines (℃ 866/435-9526 in the U.S., or 600/526-2000 in Chile; www. lan.com), which recently upgraded its image by dropping the "Chile" from its title and designing a new logo, is no longer the only airline to offer domestic service. The Chilean-owned **Sky Airlines (℃ 2/353-3169;** www.sky airline.cl) now offers daily service to all major cities at cheaper prices; however, their website is largely useless (though this should change soon). Another airline new to the scene is the Argentine-owned **Aerolineas del Sur** (© 2/210-9000) with daily service from Santiago to Punta Arenas, and flight packages for multiple destinations within Patagonia. New competition for Lan means the company has lowered its prices slightly.

SANTIAGO Accommodations

Clean streets, a stable economy, and a modern infrastructure have recently put Santiago in the number two spot in Latin America for business travel. Nevertheless, competition has kept hotel rates constant over the past few years. When searching for a hotel room, don't be afraid to investigate rates for hotels that might seem well beyond your budget, as these hotels often advertise incredible bargains, especially for multiple-day stays.

South America's first **Ritz-Carlton** hotel, at El Alcalde 15 (© 800/241-3333 from the U.S., or 2/470-8500; www.ritzcarlton.com), which opened in 2003, is now generally considered the finest hotel Santiago has to offer for its bountiful amenities and the hotel chain's trademark service. It has also benefited from a more central location than the previous favorite, the Hyatt Regency.

Dining   Dining out in Santiago has never been so enjoyable. The capital city's culinary revolution seemingly sees no end, with the dozens of new hip, innovative eateries and improvements in food quality and atmosphere in classic restaurants. Diners now find wonderful updates on Chilean cuisine and international options from Czech to sushi, to Mexican. Now if only the rest of the country would follow suit.

VALPARAISO   Valparaíso's recent

UNESCO designation as a World Heritage Site, and the success of the nonprofit *Fundación Valparaíso* (which is leading renovation projects of the city's historical buildings), has sparked a renewed interest in this port town.

In years past, only backpackers and the more bohemian travelers could stomach the city's hostels and seedy hotels (choosing Viña del Mar for lodging instead), but the recent inauguration of two new boutique hotels has turned Valparaíso into an exciting overnight destination. The trendy design hotel **Ultramar,** Calle Pérez 173 (© 32/210000) and its hip, postmodern design suits younger tastes, and the antique splendor of the **Hotel Casa Thomas Somerscales,** San Enrique 446 (© 32/331006), provides discriminating travelers with elegant interiors and personalized service. Now it seems that every antique-home owner has converted his or her property into a "hostel" or "residencial," but be forewarned that a pretty exterior often belies shabby conditions within. On the restaurant scene, traditional restaurants such as the **Café Turri** are losing clout to new bistros such as the divine **Pasta e Vino** (© 32/496187), Templeman 352.

THE CENTRAL VALLEY   Chile's

wine industry is mushrooming, and as a result, many wineries have banded together to offer "wine routes" led by a tour guide or open to independent travelers with their own vehicle. But what's really news is that most top wineries have opened proper wine-tasting facilities for the public; just five years ago, it was next to impossible to set up a tour of a winery. There are five wine routes, though only a few, such as the tour through the Napa/Sonoma–like **Colchagua Valley** (© 72/823199; www.colchaguavalley.cl), have worked out the bugs. You're probably better off with a tour of these wine routes (try **Liz Caskey, Inc.,** tours at © 2/681-1799; www.lizcaskey.com), but adventurous travelers should have no difficulty renting a vehicle and setting a tasting date with any of the major wineries.

Several new gourmet restaurants have opened in wine country, too, making this a hot destination for travelers to Chile. Two new standout restaurants, both on the road to Valparaíso in the Casablanca Valley, are the **House of Morandé,** just off Highway 68, Km 61 (© **2/270-8900;** www. morande.cl), a stylish eatery with reinvented Chilean dishes, and **Restaurante Indómita,** Ruta 68, Km 63 (© **32/743869;** www.indomita.cl), a sophisticated eatery with a renowned chef who lends a modern flair to Chilean dishes.

PATAGONIA & TIERRA DEL FUEGO Explora (© 2/395-2533; www.explora.com) has added 20 new guest rooms to its hotel in Torres del Paine National Park. The good news is that it is far easier to get a reservation here during the high season; the bad news is that the ambience is slightly less intimate than it was previously. The **Hotel Altiplanico,** a cheaper alternative to Explora Hotel in San Pedro de Atacama, will open a new hotel in Puerto Natales in September 2005, and it is expected to be one of the town's top hotels. The Hotel Altiplanico will be located just outside of town. Feeling the onset of competition, the **Hotel CostAustralis** (© 61/ 412000; www.australis.com), Pedro Montt 262, the finest hotel in Puerto Natales, has completely renovated its waterfront lobby and restaurant. For a slightly more economical stay, the midrange **Aquaterra** hotel (© 61/ 412239; www.aquaterrapatagonia. com), Av. Bulnes 299, opened in

2004, filling the need for cozy, contemporary accommodations that are a step above the town's plethora of low-cost hostels.

The luxury small cruise company **Skorpios** (© 2/231-1030; www. skorpios.cl) has expanded with a base in Puerto Natales and now offers multiple-day journeys to the largest glacier in the Southern Hemisphere, the Pio XI, and a sailing path that takes passengers through the southern fjords with a stop in the remote village of Puerto Eden. Skorpios also sails to Chiloé and the Carretera Austral area from their other base in Puerto Montt.

Also in 2005, the **old road from Puerto Natales to Torres del Paine will reopen,** shaving more than an hour off the journey to the park's administration center.

Good news for travelers to Torres del Paine who can't or don't want to hike yet would like to see Glacier Grey up close: The **Hostería Lago Grey** (© 61/229512; www.austrohoteles.cl) now offers half-day boat rides to the face of the glacier and past the lake's floating icebergs, and their summer schedule allows enough time for travelers to take part in **Bigfoot Expeditions Glacier Walk** (© 61/414611; www.bigfootpatagonia.com) without having to spend the night at the Refugio Grey or hike 4 hours to the commencement site. This also means visitors can cross Lake Pehoé by catamaran, walk the 4 hours to the glacier lookout point, and then return by the *hostería* boat.

1

The Best of Argentina & Chile

Argentina and Chile—separated by the serrated peaks of the Andes Mountains—combine to blanket the southern half of South America; the distance from Chile's northern tip to the southern tail of Argentina's Tierra del Fuego spans almost 4,830km (2,995 miles). And the scope of experiences you can find here is no less grand: from the cosmopolitan bustle of Buenos Aires to the desolate moonscape of Chile's Atacama Desert, from the tropical jungles and thunderous falls of Iguazú to the tundra and glaciers of Torres del Paine National Park. Whether you've come to meander the quiet towns of Chile's Lake District or dance the night away in a smoky, low-lit Argentine tango bar, your trip to the Southern Hemisphere won't disappoint. In this chapter, we've selected the best that Argentina and Chile have to offer—museums, outdoor adventures, hotels, and more.

1 The Most Unforgettable Travel Experiences

- **Learning to Dance Tango in Buenos Aires:** *Salones de baile,* as tango salons are called, blanket the city; the most famous are in San Telmo. In these salons, you can watch traditional Argentine tango danced by all generations, and most offer lessons before the floor opens up to dancers. You won't find many novices on the dance floor after midnight, however. See chapter 3.
- **Visiting the Recoleta Cemetery:** This beautiful cemetery in Buenos Aires houses enormous, expensive mausoleums competing for grandeur—a place where people can remain rich, even after death. Among the only nonaristocrats buried here is Eva Perón, or "Evita." See p. 65.
- **Wandering the Caminito Pedestrian Walkway in La Boca:** Capture the flavor of early Buenos Aires on this short historic street, which is also considered an outdoor museum. The Caminito is famous for the brightly colored sheet-metal houses that border it and for the sculptures, paintings, and wall murals you'll find along the street. Performers and dancers are here every day. See p. 62.
- **Bronzing in Punta del Este in Summer:** As Porteños (residents of Buenos Aires) will tell you, anyone who has a peso left to travel on heads to Punta del Este for summer vacation. This glitzy Atlantic coast resort in Uruguay is packed with South America's jet set from December to February and offers inviting beaches and outstanding nightlife. See chapter 4.
- **Visiting Iguazú Falls:** One of the world's most spectacular sights, Iguazú boasts over 275 waterfalls fed by the Iguazú River. In addition to the falls, Iguazú encompasses a marvelous subtropical jungle with extensive flora and fauna. See chapter 5.
- **Riding the "Train to the Clouds":** The *Tren a las Nubes* is

one of the world's great railroad experiences. The journey through Argentina's Northwest takes you 434km (269 miles) through tunnels, turns, and bridges, culminating in the breathtaking La Polvorilla viaduct. You will cross magnificent landscapes, making your way from the multicolored Lerma valley through the deep canyons and rugged peaks of the Quebrada del Toro, and on to the desolate desert plateau of La Puña. See p. 110.

- **Traveling the Wine Roads of Mendoza:** Less commercialized than their European and American counterparts, Mendoza's wineries are free to visit and easily accessible along roads known locally as *los Caminos del Vino.* There are about 80 wineries that formally offer tours and tastings. See chapter 8.

- **Sailing Through the Andes Between Chile & Argentina:** Why fly or drive when you can sail through the Andes? Two companies work together to provide boat journeys between Ensenada, Chile, and Bariloche, Argentina. It's a very low-key affair and a cruise that's worth the journey only on a clear day and if a traveler has ample time to spare. The cruise takes visitors through the emerald waters of Lago Todos los Santos and the rugged peaks and rainforest of Vicente Pérez Rosales National Park in Chile, and in Argentina across Lake Nahuel Huapi to Puerto Blest. The trip can be done in 1 or 2 days. See "Essentials" under "San Carlos de Bariloche," on p. 154, and "Frutillar, Puerto Octay, Puerto Varas, Lago Llanquihue, Ensenada, Parque Nacional Vicente Pérez Rosales & the Lake Crossing to Argentina" on p. 353.

- **Seeing a Million Penguins Guarding Their Nests:** Every autumn, over a million penguins return to mate on a hillside overlooking the Atlantic, in a remote area of Patagonia. At Punta Tombo National Reserve, you can walk among these friendly creatures and, if you're lucky, get to see them guarding the babies in their nests. See p. 434.

- **Waking Up in Santiago After a Rainstorm:** Santiago is a magnificent city, but it's usually hidden under a blanket of smog that would make even Paris look like Detroit. If you're lucky enough to catch Santiago after a rainstorm has cleared the skies, try to make it to the top of Cerro San Cristóbal for a breathtaking view of the city spread below the towering, snow-capped Andes. Few cityscapes in the world compare. See "Barrio Bellavista & Parque Metropolitano" under "Seeing the Sights," on p. 248.

- **Exploring the Madcap Streets of Valparaíso:** The ramshackle, colorful, and sinuous streets of Valparaíso offer a walking tour unlike any other. Apart from the picturesque Victorian mansions and tin houses that seem cut into every shape possible, terraced walkways wind around the various hills that shoot up from downtown, and there are plenty of antique funiculars to lift you to the top. Great restaurants and cafes can be found at every turn to rest aching feet. Plus, Valparaíso's faded remains of this once-thriving port town are receiving a much-needed face-lift. See chapter 13.

- **Catching a Full Moon or Stargazing in the Valle de la Luna:** Nothing could be more appropriate, or dreamier, than an evening under the glow of a full moon in the Valley of the Moon.

This region of the Atacama Desert was named for its otherworldly land formations and salt-encrusted canyons that supposedly resemble the surface of the moon, a comparison that is hard to dispute, especially when these formations are cast under an eerie nighttime glow. Days later, when the moon has waned, the Atacama's unusually clear night skies provide one of the best stargazing opportunities in the world. See chapter 14 for tours of the area.

- **Sailing or Kayaking the "Emerald City," the Fjords of Southern Chile:** This far-flung region of pristine fjords is Chile's most remote territory, and it is accessible only by kayak or boat—but it is an adventure open to all ability levels and pocketbooks. You can take a 3-day sail aboard a passenger and cargo ferry from Puerto Montt to Puerto Natales. Alternatively, two luxury ships lead cruises through the southern fjords and directly to the face of the Laguna San Rafael Glacier. But travelers who are in good shape will find the most enjoyment from paddling a kayak and quietly savoring the solitude and exotic rainforest that blankets these dramatic fjords, said by travelers to be more impressive than those in Norway. See chapter 15.

- **Soaking in Hot Springs:** The volatile Andes not only build volcanoes, but they also produce steaming mineralized water that is used to fill hot-springs complexes from the desert north to the Aisén region. Chileans often take to these waters to relieve arthritis and rheumatism problems, but most take a soothing soak just to relax. These hot springs seem to have been magically paired by nature with outdoor adventure spots, making for a thankful way to end a day of activity. The Lake District is a noted "hot spot," especially around Pucón (don't miss Termas Geométricas). See chapter 15.

- **Driving the Carretera Austral:** It's a tough, crunchy drive along 1,000km (620 miles) of gravel road, but that is precisely why Chile's "Southern Highway" has kept the crowds at bay. This natural wonderland, saturated in green and hemmed in by jagged, snow-capped peaks, offers a journey for those seeking to travel through some of Chile's most remote and stunning territory. It can be done in a variety of directions and segments, but you'll need a rental car to experience it right. There are plenty of great stops along the way, including rainforest walks, the idyllic mountain valley of Futaleufú, the wet primeval forest of Parque Quelat, Puyuhuapi and its luxury thermal spas, and the city of Coyhaique. See chapter 17.

2 The Best Charming Small Towns

- **Colonia del Sacramento, Uruguay:** Just a short ferry trip from Buenos Aires, Colonia is Uruguay's best example of colonial life. The Old Neighborhood contains brilliant examples of colonial wealth and many of Uruguay's oldest structures. Dating from the 17th century, this beautifully preserved Portuguese settlement makes a perfect day trip. See chapter 4.

- **Salta, Argentina:** Salta sits in the Lerma valley of Argentina's Northwest, with an eternal springlike climate, and boasts Argentina's best-preserved colonial architecture. It's surrounded by the fertile valley of the provincial capital, the polychrome canyons of Cafayate, and the desolate plateau of La Puña. See chapter 6.

- **Villa Carlos Paz, Argentina:** A quick getaway from Córdoba, Villa Carlos Paz surrounds the picturesque Ebalse San Roque. Although it's actually a reservoir, vacationers treat San Roque like a lake, swimming, sailing, and windsurfing in its gentle waters. Year-round, people come to Carlos Paz to enjoy outdoor activities by day and party by night. See chapter 7.

- **La Falda, Argentina:** An excellent base from which to explore the Punilla, La Falda lies between the Valle Hermoso (Beautiful Valley) and the Sierras Chicas. Argentines come here for rest and relaxation, not wild entertainment. Crisp, clean air; wonderful hikes; and quiet hotels are the draw. See chapter 7.

- **San Martín de los Andes, Argentina:** City planners in San Martín had the sense to do what Bariloche never thought of: to limit building height to two stories and to mandate continuity in the town's alpine architecture. The result? Bariloche is crass, whereas San Martín is class, and the town is a year-round playground, to boot. Relax, swim, bike, ski, raft, hunt, or fish—this small town has it all. See chapter 9.

- **Villa La Angostura, Argentina:** Villa La Angostura has everything its neighbor Bariloche has and more. This is where you go to escape the crowds and savor the sense of exclusivity. Great restaurants go hand in hand with cozy lodging here. The town is spread along one street and along the shore of Nahuel Huapi Lake, with plenty of hiking, biking, and boating nearby; there's a great little ski resort here, too. The wood-heavy construction is eye-catching, and

the location is sumptuous. See chapter 9.

- **San Pedro de Atacama, Chile:** Quaint, unhurried, and built of adobe brick, San Pedro de Atacama has drawn Santiaguinos (residents of Santiago) and expatriates the world over to experience the mellow charm and New Age spirituality that wafts through the dusty roads of this town. Its location in the driest desert in the world makes for starry skies and breathtaking views of the weird and wonderful land formations that are just a stone's throw away. See chapter 14.

- **Pucón, Chile:** Not only was Pucón bestowed with a stunning location at the skirt of a smoking volcano and the shore of a glittering lake, but it's also Chile's self-proclaimed adventure capital, offering a plethora of outdoor activities. But Pucón also has plenty of low-key activities if your idea of a vacation is plopping yourself down on a beach. You'll find everything you want and need without forfeiting small-town charm (that is, if you don't come with the Jan–Feb crowds). Wood-hewn restaurants, pubs, and crafts stores fill downtown, blending harmoniously with the forested surroundings. See chapter 15.

- **Frutillar & Puerto Varas, Chile:** Built by German immigrants who settled here in the early 1900s, these neighboring towns bear the clear stamp of Prussian order and workmanship, from the crisp lines of trees to the picturesque, shingled homes and tidy plazas ringed with roses. If you're lucky, you can still catch a few old-timers chatting in German over coffee and *kuchen* (a dense cake). Both towns feature a glorious view of the Volcán Osorno volcano and a lakefront address, a picture-postcard location that makes for an excellent boardwalk stroll. If that isn't enough, both towns also offer above-par lodging and a few of the best restaurants in the country. See chapter 15.

- **Futaleufú, Chile:** Nestled in a green valley surrounded by an amphitheater of craggy, snow-encrusted peaks, Futaleufú is made of colorful clapboard homes and unpaved streets, and is without a doubt one of the prettiest villages in Chile. The population of 1,200 swells during the summer when the hordes descend for rafting adventures on the nearby Class V river, but it hasn't changed the town's fabric too dramatically, and locals rarely saunter past a visitor without a tip of the hat and a *"Buenas tardes."* See chapter 17.

3 The Best Outdoor Adventures

- **Discovering Iguazú Falls by Raft:** A number of tour companies operate rafts that speed toward the falls, soaking their awestruck passengers along the way. This is the best way to experience the sound and fury of Iguazú's magnificent *cataratas*. See chapter 5.

- **Traveling Beyond the Falls into the Iguazú Jungle:** This is a place where birds like the great dusky swift and brilliant morpho butterflies spread color through the thick forest canopy. You can easily arrange an outing into the forest once you arrive in Iguazú. See chapter 5.

- **Raging Down the Mendoza River:** Mendoza offers the best white-water rafting in Argentina, and during the summer months, when the snow melts in the Andes and fills the Mendoza River, rafters enjoy up to Class IV and V rapids here. Rafting is possible year-round, but the river is colder and calmer in winter months. See chapter 8.

- **Skiing Las Leñas:** One of South America's top ski destinations, Las Leñas boasts more slopes than any single resort in the Americas, with 40 miles of runs, excellent snow, and typically small crowds. Las Leñas also offers an active nightlife in winter. See chapter 8.

- **Climbing Aconcagua:** At 6,960m (22,272 ft.), Cerro Aconcagua is the highest peak in the entire Western Hemisphere. Those hoping to reach the top must buy a 20-day permit, which costs $200 (including emergency medical insurance). The climb is not technically difficult, but it demands strength and endurance. See chapter 8.

- **Whale-Watching off the Peninsula Valdes:** From April to December, the giant Southern whales come very close to shore off this barren peninsula. You can jump on a boat in the morning for an up-close and personal view of these awesome mammals. If you're lucky, a baby whale swimming with its mother will circle your boat, giving you the thrill of a lifetime. See chapter 10.

- **Rafting or Horseback Riding in the Cajón de Maipo:** Okay, it's not even close to rafting the Futaleufú, but the Maipo River whips up enough exciting rapids for a thrill, and, best of all, it's just a 45-minute drive from Santiago. The Maipo River winds through the Cajón del Maipo, a hemmed-in, alpine valley that is so fragrant and pleasant it seems worlds away from the smoggy metropolis. To get deep into the Andes, saddle up for a full- or half-day horseback ride. Beginners and kids are welcome, too. Contact **Cascada Expediciones** in Santiago, at ⓒ 2/ 861-1303, or the friendly **Altué Expeditions,** at ⓒ 2/232-1103. See chapter 13.

- **Skiing or Snowboarding Portillo:** It's been around for 54 years, and the steep chutes of **Portillo** still raise fear in the hearts of those about to make the descent on a pair of skis or snowboard. This is where the speed-skiing record was broken, where Fidel Castro spent the night, and where a Who's Who of northern ski lovers come in search of the endless winter. The grand yet rustic hotel is a single, all-inclusive destination, much like a cruise ship in the sky: no lift lines, a stunning location, great nightlife, a warm social ambience, and lots for kids to do, too. Call ⓒ 800/829-5325 from the United States or 2/263-0606 in Santiago. See p. 293.

- **Summiting a Volcano:** There's something more thrilling about summiting a volcano than any old mountain, especially when the volcano threatens to blow at any given time. Chile is home to a large share of the world's volcanoes, some of which are perfectly conical and entirely feasible to climb, such as Volcán Villarrica in Pucón and Volcán Osorno near Puerto Varas. Active Villarrica is a relatively moderate climb to the gaseous crater, followed by a slide on your rear down a human toboggan chute. Osorno offers a more technical climb, roping up for a crampon-aided walk past glacier crevasses and caves. Don't miss the electrifying views from the top of Volcano Osorno, from the ocean and into Argentina. For Volcán Villarrica, contact **Outdoor Experience** (ⓒ 09/7843139) or **Politur** (ⓒ 45/441373); for Volcán Osorno, contact **Tranco**

Expediciones (ⓒ 65/311311). See chapter 15.

- **Rafting or Kayaking the Futaleufú River:** With churning river sections that are frightening enough to be dubbed "Hell" and "The Terminator," the Class V Futaleufú River, or the "Fu," as it's known, is solemnly revered by rafting and kayaking enthusiasts around the world as one of the most difficult to descend. A little too much excitement for your nerves? Rafting companies offer short-section rafting trips on the Futaleufú and down the tamer, crystalline waters of the neighboring Espolón River—kayak schools use this stretch, too. The scenery here redefines mountain beauty. Contact **Expediciones Chile** (ⓒ 800/488-9082 in the U.S.) or **Earth River Expeditions** (ⓒ 800/ 643-2784 in the U.S.). See chapter 17.

- **Getting Face to Face with Perito Moreno Glacier:** Few natural wonders in South America are as magnificent or as easily accessed as Perito Moreno Glacier. You can drive right up to it, park, and descend a series of walkways that take you directly to the 48m-plus (160-ft.) wall of turquoise ice—an unforgettable experience. To get really close, strap on a pair of crampons and take a walk across the glacier's surface to admire the sculpted walls, caves, and changing tonal variety of blues. Nearly all travel agencies in Calafate book this excursion. See chapter 18.

- **Trekking in Torres del Paine:** This backpacking mecca has exploded in popularity, and it's no wonder why. Torres del Paine is one of the most spectacular national parks in the world, with hundreds of kilometers of trails through ever-changing landscapes of jagged peaks and one-of-a-kind granite spires; undulating meadows; milky, turquoise lakes and rivers; and mammoth glaciers. The park suits all budgets with a well-organized system of *refugios* and campgrounds, and several hotels, one of which is one of the best in Latin America. Visitors can access the park's major highlights on a day hike, too. See chapter 18.

4 The Best Hotels

- **Alvear Palace Hotel,** Buenos Aires (© 11/4808-2100): The most exclusive hotel in Buenos Aires and one of the top hotels in the world, the Alvear reflects the Belle Epoque era in which it was designed. Luxurious bedrooms and suites have private butler service, and the hotel's guest list reflects the top names in Argentina and visitors from abroad. See p. 50.

- **Four Seasons Hotel,** Buenos Aires (© 11/4321-1200): In 2002, the Four Seasons took over what was already one of the city's most luxurious properties. There are two parts to this landmark hotel—the 12-story Park Tower, housing the majority of the guest rooms, and the turn-of-the-20th-century French-rococo La Mansión, with seven elegant suites and a handful of private event rooms. See p. 51.

- **Marriott Plaza Hotel,** Buenos Aires (© 11/4318-3000): This historic hotel was the grande dame of Buenos Aires for much of the 20th century, a gathering place of Argentine politicians, foreign dignitaries, and international celebrities. It remains one of the city's most impressive hotels. See p. 44.

- **Radisson Montevideo Victoria Plaza Hotel,** Montevideo (© 02/902-0111): Montevideo's centerpiece hotel is situated next to Plaza Independencia in the heart of downtown. Spacious guest rooms boast French-style furnishings and upgraded amenities, and the hotel's restaurant, Arcadia, is outstanding. See p. 88.

- **Conrad Resort & Casino,** Punta del Este (© 042/491-111): This resort dominates social life in Punta del Este. Luxurious rooms have terraces overlooking the beach, and there's a wealth of outdoor activities, from tennis and golf to horseback riding and watersports. Nightlife centers on the Conrad's 24-hour casino, nightclub, and theater performances. See p. 92.

- **Sheraton Internacional Iguazú,** Puerto Iguazú (© 0800/888-9180 local toll-free, or 3757/491-800): If you visit Iguazú Falls, the Sheraton International Iguazú enjoys the best location by far. It's the only hotel on the Argentine side of the falls situated within the national park. From here, half the rooms overlook the falls, and guests are within easy walking distance of the waterfall circuits. See p. 102.

- **Park Hyatt Mendoza,** Mendoza (© 261/441-1234): Peering majestically over the Plaza de la Independencia, the new Park Hyatt is the top hotel from which to explore the region's wineries. Sweeping columns of granite and stone showcase the lobby, and an impressive collection of Mendocino art pays tribute to local culture. See p. 141.

- **Llao Llao Hotel & Resort,** near Bariloche (© 02944/448530): If you're looking for a memorable evening and your pocketbook can afford it, this is the place you should go. The world-renowned Llao Llao Hotel & Resort's style was influenced by Canadian-style mountain lodges, and the hotel's magnificent alpine setting is one of the best in the world. Antler chandeliers, pine-log walls, and Oriental rugs set the mood, and the "winter garden" cafe overlooking Lake Nahuel Huapi is divine. The hotel boasts every amenity imaginable, including its own golf course, and service is impeccable. See p. 165.

- **Ritz-Carlton,** Santiago (② **800/ 241-3333** or 2/470-8500): South America's first Ritz-Carlton has given other Santiago five-star hotels a run for their money. The Las Condes address is ultraconvenient for tourists and businesspeople alike. Though the bland brick exterior makes the Ritz virtually indistinguishable from its surrounding office buildings, the glittering, glass-enclosed rooftop gym; intricate Mediterranean decor; personal service that goes well beyond a guest's expectations; and one of Santiago's only wine bars makes this hotel the obvious choice for discriminating travelers. See p. 232.

- **Hotel Orly,** Santiago (② **2/231-8947**): The Hotel Orly is an ideal little inn for those who look for personal service and intimate accommodations to compensate for the overwhelming hustle and bustle of Santiago. The hotel is inside a converted French-style mansion, and there's a compact interior garden patio and bar. It's located smack-dab in the middle of everything in Providencia. See p. 230.

- **Hacienda Los Lingues,** near San Fernando (② **2/235-5446**): Step back in time to the 17th century with a visit to one of Chile's oldest hotels, located in the rural heartland of the central valley south of Santiago. Los Lingues has been in the same family hands for more than 400 years, and each venerable

room has been lovingly and individually decorated with personal touches such as family antiques, photos, and other collectibles. Like all haciendas, Los Lingues wraps around a plant-filled patio and fountain, but you'll also find a small chapel, a stately main building, and one of the country's finest horse-breeding farms on premises. The hotel also offers day visits that include lunch in the hacienda's grand wine cellar. See p. 284.

- **Hotel Ultramar,** Valparaíso (② **32/210000**): This brand-new hotel is one of Chile's best, and it is the first (and only) "design" boutique hotel in the country. The Ultramar really shows what can be accomplished when an architect puts imagination into the renovation of Chile's historic buildings—the exception in this country, not the rule. The hotel is fashioned out of the remains of a 1907 mansion, and it sits high above the city, with a breathtaking panorama of the city. Whimsically adorned with an eclectic, postmodern decor, the Ultramar is as trendy as it is fun. See p. 270.

- **Hotel Explora** in San Pedro de Atacama (② **55/851110,** local and 2/395-2533 in Santiago for reservations) and **Hotel Explora Salto Chico** in Torres del Paine (② **2/395-2533**): Few hotels (www.explora.com for both) have generated as much press in Latin America as the two all-inclusive Explora lodges in San Pedro de Atacama and Torres del Paine. A dynamite location has helped, of course, but great service, cozy rooms with out-of-this-world views, interiors that are equally elegant and comfortable, and guided outdoor trekking, horseback riding, and biking excursions are what really put these hotels above par. The lodges were designed by several of Chile's top architects, built of native materials, and decorated with local art. See p. 310 and 452.

- **Hotel Antumalal,** Pucón (© 45/441011): This low-slung, Bauhaus-influenced country inn is one of the most special places to lodge in Chile. Located high above the shore of Lake Villarrica and a sloping, terraced garden, the hotel literally sinks into its surroundings, offering a cozy ambience and an excellent view of the evening sunset. A warm welcome and a room with no lock are all part of making you feel at home. The inn has outstanding cuisine, too. See p. 328.
- **Termas de Puyuhuapi Spa & Hotel,** near Puyuhuapi (©/fax 22/256489): This is arguably the best hotel/thermal spa facility in Chile. Spread across a remote cove on the Ventisquero Sound, this one-of-a-kind resort is nestled in pristine rainforest and is reachable only by boat. The hotel itself has become the region's top attraction, drawing day visitors who come for a soak in one of the handful of indoor or outdoor pools, or treatments in the state-of-the-art spa. The accommodations are wonderfully comfortable and the food is outstanding. Many overnighters opt for the hotel's package trips with an additional trip to the Laguna San Rafael Glacier. See p. 421.
- **Los Notros,** Perito Moreno Glacier, near Calafate (© 11/4814-3934 in Buenos Aires): Location is everything at the Los Notros hotel, which boasts a breathtaking view spanning one of Argentina's great wonders, Perito Moreno Glacier. The hotel blends contemporary folk art with a range of colorful hues, and this, along with immaculately clean rooms that come with a dramatic view of the electric-blue tongue of the glacier, make this lodge one of the most upscale, unique lodging options in Argentina. The hotel arranges excursions around the area and occasional informative talks, and there are plenty of easy chairs and lounges for sitting and contemplating the glorious nature surrounding you. See p. 465.
- **Hotel José Nogueira,** Punta Arenas (© 61/248840): Originally the home of one of Punta Arenas's wealthiest families, the Nogueira offers the chance to spend the night in a historic landmark, the principal rooms of which have been preserved as a museum to give visitors a look at the outlandish luxury that must have seemed dramatically out of place in the Patagonia of the early 1900s. The upper floors have been converted into handsome, classically designed rooms that come with marvelously high ceilings. The mansion's glass-enclosed patio now houses the hotel's excellent restaurant, La Pérgola, and the cellar is now an evening pub. See p. 436.

5 The Best Dining Experiences

- **Cabaña las Lilas,** Buenos Aires (© 11/4313-1336): Widely considered the best *parrilla* (grill) in Buenos Aires, Cabaña las Lilas is always packed. The beef comes exclusively from the restaurant's private *estancia* (ranch), and the steaks are outstanding. See p. 54.
- **Catalinas,** Buenos Aires (© 11/4313-0182): This is without doubt the most recognized international restaurant in Buenos Aires, its kitchen a model of culinary diversity and innovation. In addition to Chef Pardo's enormous Patagonian toothfish steaks,

his grilled lamb chops—sprinkled with rosemary and fresh savory—are famous throughout Argentina. See p. 59.

- **Katrine,** Buenos Aires (© 11/4315-6222): One of the top dining choices in Buenos Aires, Katrine (named after the Norwegian chef-owner, who can be found every day in the kitchen) serves exquisite international cuisine in a loud and festive dining room. See p. 55.

- **1884,** Mendoza (© 261/424-2698): Inside Bodega Escorihuela, Francis Mallman has created Mendoza's top restaurant, his cuisine blending his Patagonian roots with his French culinary training. Dishes are prepared with matching wine selections, with Malbec and Syrah topping the list. You can easily combine a tour of the *bodega* in the same visit. See p. 143.

- **Jose Balcance,** Salta (© 387/421-1628): The best restaurant in Salta serves incredibly imaginative Andean cuisine in an elegant setting. Here's where you can try llama carpaccio or roasted llama medallions with prickly pear sauce, accompanied by Andean potatoes grown in the verdant hills on the outskirts of the city—all delicious. See p. 115.

- **La Bourgogne,** Buenos Aires and Punta del Este (© 11/4805-3857 in Buenos Aires, and 042/482-007 in Punta del Este): Jean-Paul Bondoux is the top French chef in South America, splitting his time between La Bourgogne in Punta del Este and its sister restaurant tucked inside the Alvear Palace Hotel in Buenos Aires. A member of Relais & Châteaux, La Bourgogne serves exquisite cuisine inspired by Bondoux's Burgundy heritage. See p. 55 and 94.

- **Agua,** Santiago (© 2/263-0008): Perhaps Santiago's most hip and innovative restaurant, Agua is *the* chic place to see and be seen. The minimalist design of concrete and glass is as fashionable and tasteful as the fusion cuisine. The young chef at Agua has catapulted to culinary fame in Santiago for his delicious creations, especially his extensive use of seafood in original dishes. You'll even find mahimahi imported from Easter Island on the menu, and there are outstanding meat and vegetarian dishes as well as an excellent wine list. See p. 240.

- **Astrid y Gastón,** Santiago (© 2/650-9125): Named for the Peruvian and German couple who own and run this wonderful restaurant with such care, Astrid y Gastón is one of the newest and most remarkable restaurants in Santiago—the reason you'll often need to make reservations days in advance. The chef uses the finest ingredients, combined so that each plate bursts with flavor and personality; here, you'll find French, Spanish, Peruvian, and Japanese influences, as well as impeccable service, an on-site sommelier, and a lengthy wine list. If you can afford it, don't miss dining here. See p. 238.

- **Europeo,** Santiago (© 2/208-3603): Europeo is named for its cuisine: central European–based cuisine expertly prepared by the restaurant's Swiss-born and -trained chef. In a word, the food is heavenly, and the offer of a more upscale main dining area and a more economical adjoining cafe makes the Europeo suitable for any budget. Not only are the entrees mouthwatering (try the leg of lamb in a merlot sauce served over polenta), but the Austrian-style desserts are heavenly. See p. 240.

- **The Bar Liguria bistros,** Santiago (© 2/231-1393): These two emblematic and lively restaurants are Providencia hot spots, and they consistently offer Santiago's best spots for dining and drinking. The new Liguria on Luis Thayer Ojeda is rollicking fun, but the restaurant near Manuel Montt has a vibrant scene as well, and both are packed by 9pm. The mix of actors, artists, businessmen, and locals makes for excellent people-watching here, and sharply dressed waiters provide entertaining and attentive service. They have good pisco sours and bistro dishes, too. See p. 239.

- **Aquí Está Coco,** Santiago (© 2/ 235-8649): This place is wildly popular with foreign visitors, with good reason: The kitsch atmosphere is as fun as the food is mouthwatering. The restaurant is spread over two levels of a 140-year-old home and festooned with oddball and nautically themed gadgets and curios. Arrive a little early and enjoy an aperitif in the cavelike, brick cellar lounge. Seafood is the specialty here. See p. 237.

- **Merlín,** Puerto Varas (© 65/ 233105): This little restaurant has the good sense to celebrate the bounty of fresh regional products available in the Lake District by offering creative, flavorful food that arrives at your table *prepared,* not just "cooked." Fresh fish and shellfish, meats, and vegetarian dishes are seasoned with flair here, using fresh herbs and spices. The restaurant occupies the first floor of an old home, with cozy, candlelit tables. See p. 263.

- **Latitude 42** at the Yan Kee Way Lodge, Ensenada (© 65/212030): Worth the drive from Puerto Varas, this gorgeous restaurant boasts superb views of the Osorno Volcano and delectable cuisine served in a beautiful dining room. The talented chef uses locally grown produce to create imaginative dishes that come as close to nouvelle cuisine as you're ever going to get in southern Chile. Service is impeccable, and there's a cigar bar and a cellar for wine tasting as well. See p. 367.

- **La Calesa,** Valdivia (© 63/ 225437): Don't overlook a Peruvian restaurant in Chile, especially La Calesa. The spicy, delectable cuisine here, brought to Valdivia by an immigrant family from Peru, is as enjoyable as the architecture of the 19th-century home in which the restaurant is housed. Soaring ceilings, antique furniture, great pisco sours at an old wooden bar, the river slowly meandering by . . . need we say more? See p. 349.

- **Remezón,** Punta Arenas (© 61/ 241029): You'll have to come to the end of Chile for some of the country's best and most exotic cuisine. This unassuming little restaurant consistently garners rave reviews by diners. Sumptuous dishes prepared with local king crab, lamb, and goose are the highlights here, as are the incredible desserts. Also on the menu are dishes made with beaver, guanaco, and the ostrichlike rhea, so come with an open mind. A warm welcome and personal contact with the chef will leave you feeling happy and well fed. See p. 438.

- **Kapué Restaurant,** Ushuaia (© 02901/422704): King crab features predominantly on the menu at the Kapué, in puff pastries, in soufflés, and fresh on the plate. Nearly every dish here is refined and delectable. The gracious, family-run service is as pleasant as the view of the Beagle Channel, and the restaurant's new wine bar really sets it apart from other eateries in town. See p. 478.

2

Planning Your Trip to Argentina

A little advance planning can make the difference between a good trip and a great trip. What do you need to know before you go? When should you go? What's the best way to get there? How much should you plan on spending? What safety or health precautions are advised? All the basics are outlined in this chapter—the when, why, and how of traveling to and around Argentina.

1 The Regions in Brief

Argentina is the world's eighth-largest country. To the north, it is bordered by Bolivia, Paraguay, Brazil, and Uruguay, the latter situated directly northeast of Buenos Aires. The Andes cascade along Argentina's western border with Chile, where the continent's highest peaks stand. The polychromatic hills and desert plateau of the nation's Northwest are as far removed from the bustling activity of Buenos Aires as are the flat grasslands of Las Pampas from the dazzling waterfalls and subtropical jungle of Iguazú. The land's geographic diversity is reflected in the people, too: Witness the contrast between the capital's largely immigrant population and the indigenous people of the Northwest. For me, Argentina's cultural distinction and geographic diversity make this South America's most fascinating travel destination.

Many people who spend at least a week in Argentina choose between traveling to Iguazú Falls and the Northwest. To see the spectacular falls of Iguazú from both the Argentine and Brazilian sides, you need at least 2 full days. A visit to the geographically stunning Northwest, where Argentina's history began and traces of Inca influence still appear, requires 3

or more days. If you choose to head south to the Lake District and Patagonia, you can do it in a week, but you'd spend a good chunk of that time just getting down there. Better to allot 2 weeks and allow time to savor the distinctive landscape.

BUENOS AIRES & THE PAMPAS
Buenos Aires, a rich combination of South American energy and European sophistication, requires at least several days (a week would be better) to explore. In addition to seeing the city's impressive museums and architectural sites, take time to wander its grand plazas and boulevards, to stroll along its fashionable waterfront, and to engage in its dynamic culture and nightlife. A thick Argentine steak in a local *parrilla* (grill), a visit to a San Telmo antiques shop, a dance in a traditional tango salon—these are the small experiences that will connect you to the city's soul.

The heartland of the country is the Pampas, an enormous fertile plain where the legendary gaucho (Pampas cowboy) roams. It includes the provinces of Buenos Aires, southern Santa Fe, southeastern Córdoba, and eastern La Pampa. The Pampas today contain many of the major cities,

Argentina

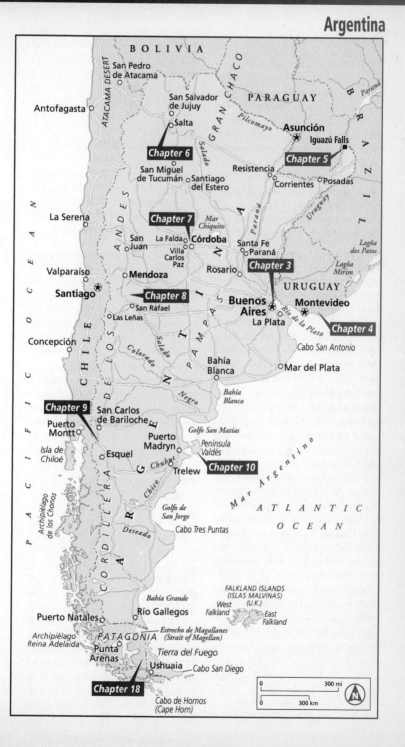

BOLIVIA

San Pedro
de Atacama

ATACAMA DESERT

Antofagasta

San Salvador
de Jujuy

Salta

GRAN CHACO

PARAGUAY

Pilcomayo

Asunción

Iguazú Falls

Chapter 6

Chapter 5

BRAZIL

Paraná

San Miguel
de Tucumán

Santiago
del Estero

Resistencia

Corrientes

Posadas

La Serena

ANDES

Mar
Chiquito

Córdoba

Chapter 7

La Falda

San
Juan

Villa
Carlos
Paz

Santa Fe

Paraná

Paraná

Chapter 3

Uruguay

Lagôa
dos Patos

Valparaíso

Mendoza

Rosario

Lagôa
Mirim

Santiago

Chapter 8

San Rafael

PAMPAS

Buenos
Aires

La Plata

URUGUAY

Montevideo

Río de la Plata

Chapter 4

CHILE

Las Leñas

Salado

Colorado

Cabo San Antonio

Concepción

CORDILLERA DE LOS ANDES

Negro

Bahía
Blanca

Mar del Plata

Bahía
Blanca

P A C I F I C   O C E A N

Chapter 9

San Carlos
de Bariloche

Puerto
Montt

Puerto
Madryn

Golfo San Matías

Península
Valdés

Mar Argentino

Isla de
Chiloé

Esquel

Chubut

Trelew

Chapter 10

A T L A N T I C

O C E A N

Archipiélago
de los Chonos

Chico

Golfo de
San Jorge

Deseado

Cabo Tres Puntas

ARGENTINA

Puerto Natales

Bahía Grande

Río Gallegos

FALKLAND ISLANDS
(ISLAS MALVINAS)
(U.K.)

West
Falkland

East
Falkland

Archipiélago
Reina Adelaida

PATAGONIA

Estrecho de Magallanes
(Strait of Magellan)

Punta
Arenas

Tierra del Fuego

Ushuaia

Cabo San Diego

Chapter 18

Cabo de Hornos
(Cape Horn)

0   300 mi

0   300 km

N

including the capital. One-third of Argentines live in greater Buenos Aires. For more, see chapter 3.

MISIONES   This small province of Mesopotamia enjoys a subtropical climate responsible for the region's flowing rivers and lush vegetation. The spectacular Iguazú Falls are created by the merger of the Iguazú and Parana rivers at the border of Argentina, Brazil, and Paraguay. For more, see chapter 5.

NORTHWEST   The Andes dominate the Northwest, with ranges between 4,877m and 7,010m (15,997 ft. and 22,993 ft.). It is here that South America's tallest mountain, Aconcagua, stands at 6,959m (22,826 ft.) above sea level. The two parallel mountain ranges are the Salto-Jujeña, cut by magnificent multicolored canyons called *quebradas*. This region is often compared with the Basin and Range region of the southwestern United States, and can be visited from the historic towns of Salta and Jujuy. For more, see chapter 6.

THE LAKE DISTRICT   Argentina's Lake District extends from Junín de los Andes south to Esquel—an alpine-like region of snowy mountains, waterfalls, lush forest, and, of course, glacier-fed lakes. San Martín de los Andes, Bariloche, and Villa La Angostura are the chief destinations here, but this isn't an area where you stay in one place for long. Driving tours, boating, skiing—you'll be on the move from the moment you set foot in the region. For more, see chapter 9. To avoid the crowds, I highly recommend that you plan a trip during the spring or fall (see "When to Go," below).

PATAGONIA   Also known as **Magallanes** or the **Deep South,** this dry, arid region at the southern end of the continent has soared in popularity over the past 5 years. We've grouped both Argentina and Chile in one Patagonia chapter because the majority of travelers visit destinations in both countries while here. Patagonia is characterized by vast, open Pampa; the colossal Northern and Southern Ice Fields and hundreds of glaciers; the jagged peaks of the Andes as they reach their terminus; beautiful emerald fjords; and wind, wind, wind. Getting here is an adventure—it usually takes 24 hours if coming directly from the United States or Europe. But the long journey pays off in the beauty and singularity of the region. El Calafate is a tourist-oriented village adjacent to Perito Moreno Glacier, which beckons visitors from around the world to stand face to face with its tremendous wall of ice. El Chaltén is a tiny village of 200 whose numbers swell each summer with those who come to marvel the stunning towers of mounts Fitz Roy, Cerro Torre, and Puntiagudo. This is the second-most-visited region of Argentina's Los Glaciares National Park and quite possibly its most exquisite, for the singular nature of the granite spires here that shoot up, torpedo-like, above massive tongues of ice that descend from the Southern Ice Field. For more, see chapter 18.

TIERRA DEL FUEGO   Even more south than the Deep South, this archipelago at the southern extremity of South America is, like Patagonia, shared by both Chile and Argentina. The main island, separated from the mainland by the Strait of Magellan, is a triangle with its base on the Beagle Channel. Tierra del Fuego's main town is Ushuaia, the southernmost city in the world. Many use the city as a jumping-off point for trips to Antarctica or sailing trips around the Cape Horn. As with the Argentine section of Patagonia, this region is outlined in chapter 18.

2 Visitor Information

IN THE U.S. The Argentina Government Tourist Office has offices at 12 W. 56th St., New York, NY 10019 (© 212/603-0443; fax 212/315-5545), and 2655 Le Jeune Rd., Penthouse Suite F, Coral Gables, FL 33134 (© 305/442-1366; fax 305/441-7029). For more details, consult Argentina's Ministry of Tourism website (see "Websites of Note," below).

IN CANADA Basic tourist information can be obtained from the Consulate General of Argentina, 2000 Peel St., Suite 600, Montreal, Quebec H3A 2W5 (© 514/842-6582; fax 514/842-5797; www.consargenmtl.com); for more details, consult Argentina's Ministry of Tourism website (see "Websites of Note," below).

IN THE U.K. For visitor information, contact the Embassy of Argentina in London (see "Entry Requirements & Customs," below) or consult Argentina's Ministry of Tourism website (see "Websites of Note," below).

WEBSITES OF NOTE

- **www.embajadaargentinaeeuu. org** Up-to-date travel information from the Argentine embassy in Washington, D.C.
- **www.turismo.gov.ar** This Ministry of Tourism site has travel information for all of Argentina, including a virtual tour of the country's tourist regions, shopping tips, links to city tourist sites, and general travel facts.
- **www.mercotour.com** A travel site focused on adventure and ecological excursions, with information on outdoor activities in both Argentina and Chile.
- **www.allaboutar.com** This well-written site is packed with practical information about the country including skiing, golfing, and *estancia* (ranch) stays.

You can also e-mail questions or requests for information to secturusa@turismo.gov.ar.

3 Entry Requirements & Customs

ENTRY REQUIREMENTS

Citizens of the United States, Canada, the United Kingdom, Australia, New Zealand, and South Africa require a passport to enter the country. No visa is required for citizens of these countries for tourist stays of up to 90 days. For more information concerning longer stays, employment, or other types of visas, contact the embassies or consulates in your home country.

IN THE U.S. Contact the Consular Section of the Argentine Embassy, 1718 Connecticut Ave. NW, Washington, DC 20009 (© 202/238-6460). For more information, try www.uic.edu/orgs/argentina.

IN CANADA Contact the Embassy of the Argentine Republic, Suite 910, Royal Bank Center, 90 Sparks St., Ottawa, Ontario K1P 5B4 (© 613/236-2351; fax 613/235-2659).

IN THE U.K. Contact the Embassy of the Argentine Republic, 65 Brooke St., London W1Y 4AH (© 020/7318-1300; fax 020/7318-1301; seruni@mrecic.gov.ar).

CUSTOMS
WHAT YOU CAN TAKE HOME FROM ARGENTINA

For **U.S. citizens,** contact the **U.S. Customs Service,** 1300 Pennsylvania Ave. NW, Washington, DC 20229 (© 877/287-8867), and request the free pamphlet *Know Before You Go.* It's also available on the Web at www.customs.gov. (Click on "Traveler Information," then "Know Before You Go.")

For a clear summary of **Canadian** rules, write for the booklet *I Declare,* issued by the **Canada Customs and Revenue Agency** (© 800/461-9999 in Canada, or 204/983-3500; www.ccra-adrc.gc.ca).

U.K. citizens should contact **HM Customs & Excise,** Passenger Enquiry Point, 2nd Floor Wayfarer House, Great South West Road, Feltham, Middlesex, TW14 8NP (© 0181/910-3744, or from outside the U.K. 44/181-910-3744), or consult its website at www.open.gov.uk.

4 Money

CASH & CURRENCY

The official Argentine currency is the **peso,** made up of 100 **centavos.** Money is denominated in notes of 2, 5, 10, 20, 50, and 100 pesos; and coins of 1, 2, and 5 pesos, and 1, 5, 10, 25, and 50 centavos. At the time this book went to press, the exchange rate was at just a few cents shy of 3 pesos to the dollar.

Prices have fallen across the board with the peso's devaluation in 2002, and Argentina is still a terrific bargain for foreign visitors. Often prices are only half what they were before the economic crisis. Prices quoted in this book continue to be quoted in U.S. dollars only, but realize that high inflation and volatile exchange rates will limit their accuracy. Hotels, especially, are guilty of wildly fluctuating rates. As more and more Europeans (mostly Spaniards and Italians) flock to Argentina, hotels are jacking up their prices since they know the euro is so strong.

EXCHANGING MONEY

U.S. dollars are widely accepted in Buenos Aires and can be used to pay taxis, hotels, restaurants, and stores. (In fact, many ATMs, in Buenos Aires and other major cities, dispense U.S. dollars as well as pesos.) Keep some pesos on hand, however, because you might run into spots where you'll need them. You'll find that U.S. dollars are less useful in rural areas (and places to exchange money less common), so plan ahead. Exchange American Express traveler's checks in Buenos Aires at **American Express,** Arenales 707 (© 11/4130-3135). It is difficult to exchange traveler's checks outside the capital. Therefore, I recommend that you carry sufficient pesos (or purchase traveler's checks in pesos) when you venture into small-town Argentina.

ATMs

ATMs (automated teller machines) are easy to access in Buenos Aires and other urban areas, but don't depend on finding them off the beaten path. Typically, they are connected to **Cirrus** (© 800/424-7787; www.mastercard.com/cardholderservices/atm) or **PLUS** (© 800/843-7587; www.visa.com/atms) networks. Check the back of your ATM card to see which network your bank belongs to. The toll-free numbers and websites will give you specific locations of ATMs where you can withdraw money while on vacation. You can withdraw only as much cash as you need every couple of days, which eliminates the insecurity of carrying around a wad of cash. Many ATMs also accept Visa and MasterCard.

One important reminder: Many banks now charge a fee ranging from 50¢ to $3 whenever non–account holders use their ATMs. Your own bank might also assess a fee for using an ATM that's not one of its branch locations. This means that, in some cases, you'll get charged *twice* just for using your bankcard when you're on vacation. And while an ATM card can be an amazing convenience when traveling in another country (put your card in the machine, and out comes foreign currency, at an extremely advantageous exchange rate), banks are also likely to slap you with a "foreign currency transaction fee."

CREDIT CARDS

If you choose to use plastic instead of cash, Visa, American Express, MasterCard, and Diners Club are commonly accepted. However, some establishments—especially smaller businesses—will give you a better price if you pay cash. Credit cards are accepted at most hotels and restaurants, except for the very cheapest ones. But note that you cannot use credit cards in many taxis or at most attractions (museums, trams, and so on).

5 When to Go

The seasons in Argentina are the reverse of those in the Northern Hemisphere. Buenos Aires is ideal in fall (Mar–May) and spring (Sept–Nov), when temperatures are mild. The beaches and resort towns are packed with vacationing Argentines in summer (Dec–Mar), while Buenos Aires becomes somewhat deserted (you decide if that's a plus or a minus—hotel prices usually fall here in summer). Plan a trip to Patagonia and the southern Andes in summer, when days are longer and warmer. Winter (June–Aug) is the best time to visit Iguazú and the Northwest, when the rains and heat have subsided; but spring (Aug–Oct) is also pleasant, as temperatures are mild and the crowds have cleared out.

CLIMATE Except for a small tropical area in northern Argentina, the country lies in the temperate zone, characterized by cool, dry weather in the South and warmer, humid air in the center. Accordingly, January and February are quite hot—often in the high 90s to more than 100°F (35°C–40°C)—while winter (approximately July–Oct) can be chilly.

HOLIDAYS Public holidays are January 1 (New Year's Day), Good Friday, May 1 (Labor Day), May 25 (First Argentine Government), June 10 (National Sovereignty Day), June 20 (Flag Day), July 9 (Independence Day), August 17 (Anniversary of the Death of General San Martín), October 12 (Día de la Raza), December 8 (Immaculate Conception Day), and December 25 (Christmas).

FESTIVALS & SPECIAL EVENTS Several holidays and festivals are worth planning a trip around; the best place to get information for these events is through your local Argentine tourism office (see "Visitor Information," above). **Carnaval (Mardi Gras),** the week before the start of Lent, is celebrated in many towns in Argentina, although to a much lesser extent than in neighboring Brazil. In Salta, citizens throw a large parade, including caricatures of public officials and "water bomb" fights. The **Gaucho Parade** takes place in Salta on June 16, with music by folk artists and gauchos dressed in traditional red ponchos with black stripes, leather chaps, black boots, belts, and knives.

Inti Raymi (Festival of the Sun) takes places in towns throughout the Northwest the night before the summer solstice (June 20) to give thanks for the year's harvest. **Día de Independencia (Independence Day)** is celebrated in Tucumán on July 9. **Exodo Jujeño (Jujuy Exodus)** takes place August 23 and 24, when locals re-enact the exodus of 1812. The **Batalla de Tucumán (Battle of Tucumán)** celebrates Belgrano's victory over the Spanish on September 24. And the **Fiesta Provincial del Turismo (Provincial Tourist Festival)** takes place in December in Puerto Iguazú.

6 Health & Insurance

HEALTH

Argentina requires no vaccinations to enter the country, except for passengers coming from countries where cholera and yellow fever are endemic. Some people who have allergies can be affected by the pollution in the city and the high level of pollen during spring. Because motor vehicle crashes are a leading cause of injury among travelers, walk and drive defensively. Avoid nighttime travel if possible, and always use a seat belt.

Most visitors find that Argentine food and water is generally easy on the stomach. Water and ice are considered safe to drink in Buenos Aires. Be careful with street food, especially in dodgy neighborhoods of Buenos Aires and in cities outside the capital.

ALTITUDE SICKNESS If you visit the Andes Mountains, beware of **altitude sickness.** Altitude sickness, known as *soroche* or *puna,* has symptoms that may include nausea, fatigue, headaches, shortness of breath, and sleeplessness. If you feel as though you've been affected, drink plenty of water, take aspirin or ibuprofen, and avoid alcohol and sleeping pills. To prevent altitude sickness, acclimatize your body by ascending gradually to allow time for your body to adjust to the high altitude.

AUSTRAL SUN The shrinking ozone layer in southern South America has caused an onset of health problems among the citizens who live there. If you are planning to travel to Patagonia, keep in mind that on "red alert" days (typically Sept–Nov), it is possible to burn in *10 minutes.* If you plan to be outdoors, you'll need to protect yourself with strong sunblock, a long-sleeved shirt, a wide-brimmed hat, and sunglasses.

WHAT TO DO IF YOU GET SICK AWAY FROM HOME

The medical facilities and personnel in Buenos Aires and the other urban areas in Argentina are very professional and comparable to United States standards. Argentina has a system of socialized medicine, where basic services are free. Private clinics are inexpensive by Western standards. If you worry about getting sick away from home, you may want to consider **medical travel insurance** (see the section on travel insurance below). In most cases, however, your existing health plan will provide all the coverage you need. Be sure to carry your identification card in your wallet.

TRAVEL INSURANCE

Check your existing insurance policies before you buy travel insurance to cover trip cancellation, lost luggage, medical expenses, or car rental insurance. You're likely to have partial or complete coverage. But if you need some, ask your travel agent about a comprehensive package. The cost of travel insurance varies widely, depending on the cost and length of your trip, your age and overall health, and the type of trip you're taking. Insurance for extreme sports or adventure travel, for example, will cost more than coverage for a cruise. Some insurers provide packages for specialty vacations, such as skiing or backpacking. More dangerous activities may be excluded from basic policies.

For information, contact one of the following popular insurers:

- **Access America** (© 866/807-3982; www.accessamerica.com)
- **Travel Guard International** (© 800/826-4919; www.travel guard.com)
- **Travel Insured International** (© 800/243-3174; www.travel insured.com)

• **Travelex Insurance Services** (℃ 888/457-4602; www.travelex-insurance.com)

MEDICAL INSURANCE

Most health insurance policies cover you if you get sick away from home—but check, particularly if you're insured by an HMO. With the exception of certain HMOs and Medicare/Medicaid, your medical insurance should cover medical treatment—even hospital care—overseas. However, most out-of-country hospitals make you pay your bills upfront, and send you a refund after you've returned home and filed the necessary paperwork. Members of **Blue Cross/Blue Shield** can now use their cards at select hospitals in most major cities worldwide (℃ 800/810-BLUE or www.bluecares.com for a list of hospitals).

If you require additional insurance, try one of the following companies:

• **MEDEX International,** 9515 Deereco Rd., Timonium, MD 21093-5375 (℃ **888/MEDEX-00** or 410/453-6300; fax 410/453-6301; www.medexassist.com).

• **Travel Assistance International** (℃ **800/821-2828;** www.travel assistance.com), 9200 Keystone Crossing, Suite 300, Indianapolis, IN 46240 (for general information on services, call the company's Worldwide Assistance Services, Inc., at ℃ **800/777-8710**).

Check your existing policies before you buy additional coverage. Also, check to see if your medical insurance covers you for emergency medical evacuation: If you have to buy a one-way same-day ticket home and forfeit your nonrefundable round-trip ticket, you may be out big bucks.

7 Specialized Travel Resources

FOR TRAVELERS WITH DISABILITIES

Argentina is not a very accessible destination for travelers with disabilities. Four- and five-star hotels in Buenos Aires often have a few rooms designed for travelers with disabilities—check with the hotel in advance. But once you get out of the city, services dry up pretty quickly.

Fortunately, there are several organizations in the United States that can help.

AGENCIES/OPERATORS
• **Flying Wheels Travel** (℃ **507/451-5005;** www.flyingwheels travel.com) offers escorted tours and cruises that emphasize sports and private tours in minivans with lifts.
• **Access Adventures** (℃ **716/889-9096**), an agency based in Rochester, New York, offers customized itineraries for a variety of travelers with disabilities.

• **Accessible Journeys** (℃ **800/TINGLES** or 610/521-0339; www.disabilitytravel.com) caters specifically to slow walkers and wheelchair travelers and their families and friends.

ORGANIZATIONS
• **The Moss Rehab Hospital** (℃ **215/456-9603;** www.moss resourcenet.org) provides friendly, helpful phone assistance through its **Travel Information Service.**
• **The Society for Accessible Travel and Hospitality** (℃ **212/447-7284;** fax 212/725-8253; www.sath.org) offers a wealth of travel resources for all types of disabilities and informed recommendations on destinations, access guides, travel agents, tour operators, vehicle rentals, and companion services. Annual membership costs $45 for adults, $30 for seniors and students.

PUBLICATIONS

- **Twin Peaks Press** (© 360/694-2462) publishes travel-related books for travelers with special needs.
- *Open World for Disability and Mature Travel* magazine, published by the Society for Accessible Travel and Hospitality (see above), is full of good resources and information. A year's subscription is $13 ($21 outside the U.S.).

FOR SENIORS

Argentines treat seniors with great respect, making travel for them easy. Discounts are usually available; ask when booking a hotel room or before ordering a meal in a restaurant. **Aerolíneas Argentinas** (© 800/333-0276 in the U.S.; www.aerolineas.com.ar) offers a 10% discount on fares to Buenos Aires from Miami and New York for passengers 62 and older; companion fares are also discounted. Both **American** (© 800/433-7300; www.americanair.com) and **United** (© 800/241-6522; www.united.com) also offer discounted senior fares.

Members of **AARP** (formerly known as the American Association of Retired Persons), 601 E St. NW, Washington, DC 20049 (© 800/424-3410 or 202/434-2277; www.aarp.org), get discounts on hotels, airfares, and car rentals. AARP offers members a wide range of benefits, including *AARP: The Magazine* and a monthly newsletter. Anyone over 50 can join.

The Alliance for Retired Americans, 8403 Colesville Rd., Suite 1200, Silver Spring, MD 20910 (© 301/578-8422; www.retiredamericans.org), offers a newsletter six times a year and discounts on hotel and auto rentals; annual dues are $13 per person or couple. *Note:* Members of the former National Council of Senior Citizens receive automatic membership in the Alliance.

AGENCIES/OPERATORS

- **Grand Circle Travel** (© 800/221-2610 or 617/350-7500; fax 617/346-6700; www.gct.com) offers package deals for the 50-plus market, mostly of the tour-bus variety, with free trips thrown in for those who organize groups of 10 or more.
- **Elderhostel** (© 877/426-8056; www.elderhostel.org) arranges study programs for those aged 55 and over (and a spouse or companion of any age) in the United States and in more than 80 countries around the world. Most courses last 5 to 7 days in the U.S. (2–4 weeks abroad), and many include airfare, accommodations in university dormitories or modest inns, meals, and tuition.
- **Interhostel** (© 800/733-9753; www.learn.unh.edu/interhostel), organized by the University of New Hampshire, also offers educational travel for seniors. On these escorted tours, the days are packed with seminars, lectures, and field trips, with sightseeing led by academic experts. **Interhostel** takes travelers 50 and over (with companions over 40), and offers 1- and 2-week trips, mostly international.

PUBLICATIONS

- *101 Tips for the Mature Traveler* is available from Grand Circle Travel (see above).
- *The 50+ Traveler's Guidebook* (St. Martin's Press).
- *Unbelievably Good Deals and Great Adventures That You Absolutely Can't Get Unless You're Over 50* (Contemporary Publishing Co.).

FOR GAY & LESBIAN TRAVELERS

Argentina remains a very traditional, Catholic society and is fairly closed-minded about homosexuality. Buenos

Aires is more liberal than the rest of the country; in particular, the Rosario neighborhood is gay- and lesbian-friendly.

The **International Gay & Lesbian Travel Association (IGLTA)** (✆ **800/ 448-8550** or 954/776-2626; fax 954/ 776-3303; www.iglta.org) links travelers up with gay-friendly hoteliers, tour operators, and airline and cruise-line representatives. It offers monthly newsletters, marketing mailings, and a membership directory that's updated once a year. Membership is $200 yearly, plus a $100 administration fee for new members.

AGENCIES/OPERATORS

- **Above and Beyond Tours** (✆ **800/397-2681;** www.above beyondtours.com) offers gay and lesbian tours worldwide and is the exclusive gay and lesbian tour operator for United Airlines.
- **Now, Voyager** (✆ **800/255- 6951;** www.nowvoyager.com) is a San Francisco–based gay-owned and -operated travel service.

PUBLICATIONS

- *Planetout.com* (✆ **800/929-2268** or 415/644-8044; www.planet out.com/travel) offers electronic guidebooks and an e-mail newsletter packed with solid information on the global gay and lesbian scene.
- *Spartacus International Gay Guide* and *Odysseus* are good annual English-language guidebooks focused on gay men, with some information for lesbians. You can get them from most gay and lesbian bookstores, or order them from **Giovanni's Room** bookstore, 1145 Pine St., Philadelphia, PA 19107 (✆ **215/923-2960;** www.giovannisroom.com).
- *Gay Travel A to Z: The World of Gay & Lesbian Travel Options at Your Fingertips,* by Marianne Ferrari (Ferrari Publications; Box 35575, Phoenix, AZ 85069), is a very good gay and lesbian guidebook series.

FOR WOMEN TRAVELERS

Female beauty is idealized in Argentina, and women seem constantly on display—both for each other and for Argentine men. Any looks and calls you might get are more likely to be flirtatious than harassing in nature. If you seek to avoid unwanted attention, don't dress skimpily (as many Porteñas do) or flash jewelry. Women should not walk alone at night.

8 Getting There

BY PLANE

Argentina's main international airport is **Ezeiza Ministro Pistarini (EZE)** (✆ **11/4480-9538**), located 35km (22 miles) outside Buenos Aires. You will be assessed a departure tax of approximately $19 upon leaving the country. For flights from Buenos Aires to Montevideo (in Uruguay), the departure tax is $6. Passengers in transit and children under 2 are exempt from this tax. However, visitors are advised to verify the departure tax with their airline or travel agent, as the exact amount changes frequently.

I have listed below the major airlines that fly into Argentina from North America, Europe, and Australia. They include Argentina's national airline, **Aerolíneas Argentinas** (✆ **800/333-0276** in the U.S., 0810/222-86527 in Buenos Aires, or 1800/22-22-15 in Australia; www. aerolineas.com.ar); **American Airlines** (✆ **800/433-7300** in the U.S., or 11/4318-1111 in Buenos Aires; www.americanair.com); **United Airlines** (✆ **800/241-6522** in the U.S., or 0810/777-8648 in Buenos Aires;

www.ual.com); **Air Canada** (© **888/ 247-2262** in Canada, or 11-4327- 3640 in Buenos Aires; www.air canada.ca); **British Airways** (© **0845/ 773-3377** in the U.K., or 11/4320- 6600 in Buenos Aires); and **Iberia** (© **0845/601-2854** in the U.K., or 11/4131-1000 in Buenos Aires).

FLYING FOR LESS: TIPS FOR GETTING THE BEST AIRFARE

Passengers within the same airplane cabin are rarely paying the same fare for their seats. Passengers who can book their ticket long in advance, who don't mind staying over Saturday night, or who are willing to travel on a Tuesday, Wednesday, or Thursday after 7pm usually pay a fraction of the full fare. Here are a few easy ways to save.

1. Check your newspaper for adver- tised discounts, or call the airlines directly and ask if any **promo- tional rates** or **special fares** are available. You'll almost never see a sale during peak travel times (Dec–Feb). If your schedule is flexible, ask if you can secure a cheaper fare by staying an extra day or by flying midweek. (Many airlines won't volunteer this infor- mation.) If you already hold a ticket when a sale breaks, it might even pay to exchange your ticket, which usually incurs a $100 to $150 charge.

   Note, however, that the lowest- priced fares are often nonrefund- able, require advance purchase of 1 to 3 weeks and a certain length of stay, and carry penalties for changing dates of travel.

2. **Consolidators,** also known as bucket shops, are a good place to find low fares. Consolidators buy seats in bulk from the airlines, then sell them back to the public at prices below even the airlines' dis- counted rates. Their small, boxed ads usually run in the Sunday

travel section at the bottom of the page. Before you pay, however, ask for a confirmation number from the consolidator, then call the air- line itself to confirm your seat. Be prepared to book your ticket with a different consolidator; there are many to choose from if the airline can't confirm your reservation. Also be aware that bucket shop tickets are usually nonrefundable or rigged with stiff cancellation penalties, often as high as 50% to 75% of the ticket price. (In addition, many air- lines won't grant frequent-flier miles on consolidator tickets.)

STA Travel (© 800/781-4040; www.statravel.com) caters espe- cially to young travelers, but its bargain-basement prices are avail- able to people of all ages. **Travel Bargains** (© 800/AIR-FARE; www.1800airfare.com) was for- merly owned by TWA but now offers the deepest discounts on many other airlines, with a 4-day advance purchase. Other reliable consolidators include **FlyCheap. com** (www.1800flycheap.com); **TFI Tours International** (© 800/ 745-8000 or 212/736-1140), which serves as a clearinghouse for unused seats; or "rebators" such as **Travel Avenue** (© 800/333-3335 or 312/876-1116) and the **Smart Traveller** (© 800/448-3338 in the U.S., or 305/448-3338), which rebate part of their com- missions to you.

3. **Surf the Net and save.** It's possi- ble to get some great deals on air- fare, hotels, and car rentals via the Internet. Grab your mouse and surf before you take off; you could save a bundle on your trip. Always check the lowest published fare, however, before you shop for flights online.

   Of course, we're a little biased, but we think **Frommers.com** is an excellent travel-planning resource.

You'll find indispensable travel tips, reviews, destination information, monthly vacation giveaways, and online booking. Full-service sites like **Travelocity** (www.travelocity. com) and **Microsoft Expedia** (www.expedia.com) offer domestic and international flight booking, hotel and car-rental reservations, late-breaking travel news, and personalized "fare watcher" e-mails that keep you posted on special deals for preselected routes.

If the thought of all that surfing and comparison shopping gives you a headache, try **Smarter Living** (www.smarterliving.com). Sign up for its newsletter service, and every week you'll get a customized e-mail summarizing the discount fares available from your departure city. Smarter Living tracks more than 15 different airlines, so it's a worthwhile time-saver. Another excellent way to take advantage of several Internet travel-booking services at once is to use **Qixo** (www.qixo.com). Qixo is a search engine that offers real-time airfare price comparisons for some 20 online booking sites (such as Travelocity) at once.

9 Getting Around

BY PLANE

The easiest way to travel Argentina's vast distances is by air. **Aerolíneas Argentinas** (see above) connects most cities and tourist destinations in Argentina, including Córdoba, Trelew, Iguazú, El Calafate, and Salta. Its competitor, **Southern Winds** (© 0810/ 777-7979), serves roughly the same routes. By American standards, domestic flights within Argentina are expensive. In Buenos Aires, domestic flights and flights to Uruguay (see chapter 4) travel out of **Jorge Newbery Airport** (© 11/4514-1515), 15 minutes from downtown.

If you plan to travel extensively in Argentina, consider buying the **Airpass Visit Argentina,** issued by Aerolíneas Argentinas. You must purchase the pass in your home country; it cannot be purchased once you are in Argentina. This pass offers discounts for domestic travel in conjunction with your international Aerolíneas Argentinas ticket. The average one-way fare is $125 (price depends on destination), and you can change your dates of travel as many times as you'd like. If you arrive in Argentina on an eligible airline other than Aerolíneas Argentinas, the price for the Visit Argentina coupons is higher—$165 to $225, depending on your destination. For more information, contact the Aerolíneas office in your home country, or www.aerolineas.com and click on "Special Offers" to view the Visit Argentina fares. Note that the Visit Argentina fares have to be issued in conjunction with an international ticket, and you have to show your passport at every domestic check-in point.

BY BUS

Argentine buses are comfortable, safe, and efficient. They connect nearly every part of Argentina, as well as bordering countries. In cases where two classes of bus service are offered (*común* and *diferencial*), the latter is more luxurious. Most long-distance buses offer toilets, air-conditioning, and snack/bar service. Bus travel is usually considerably cheaper than air travel for similar routes. In almost every instance, I believe travelers would prefer a more expensive 2-hour flight to a 20-plus-hour bus ride (see chart below). But taking a long-distance bus in South America is a singular cultural experience, so you might find it time well spent.

Among the major bus companies that operate out of Buenos Aires are

La Veloz del Norte (© 11/4315-2482), serving destinations in the Northwest, including Salta and Jujuy; Singer (© 11/4315-2653), serving Puerto Iguazú as well as Brazilian destinations; and T.A. Chevallier (© 11/4313-3297), serving Bariloche.

Sample Times & Fares for Travel in Argentina from Buenos Aires

From Buenos Aires to	Length of bus trip	Cost of a one-way bus ticket	Length of plane trip	Cost of a one-way plane ticket
Bariloche	23 hr.	$76	2¼ hr.	$100–$220
Puerto Iguazú	21 hr.	$50	2 hr.	$90–$220
Salta	22 hr.	$80	2 hr.	$110–$220

BY CAR

Argentine roads and highways are generally in good condition, with the exception of some rural areas. Most highways have been privatized and charge nominal tolls. In Buenos Aires, drivers are aggressive and don't always obey traffic lanes or lights. Wear your seat belt, as required by Argentine law. U.S. driver's licenses are valid in greater Buenos Aires, but you need an Argentine or international license to drive in most other parts of the country. Fuel is expensive, at about $1 per liter (or $4 per gal.). A car that uses gasoil (as the name implies, a hybrid fuel of gas and oil) is the cheaper option fuel-wise, about 15% cheaper than regular unleaded gasoline.

The **Automóvil Club Argentino (ACA),** Av. del Libertador 1850 (© 11/4802-6061), has working arrangements with international automobile clubs. The ACA offers numerous services, including roadside assistance, road maps, hotel and camping information, and discounts for various tourist activities.

CAR RENTALS Many international car-rental companies operate in Argentina with offices at airports and in city centers. Here are the main offices in Buenos Aires for the following agencies: Hertz, Paraguay 1122 (© 800/654-3131 in the U.S., or 11/4816-8001 in Buenos Aires); Avis, Cerrito 1527 (© 800/230-4898 in the U.S., or 11/4300-8201 in Buenos Aires); Dollar, Marcelo T. de Alvear 523 (© 800/800-6000 in the U.S., or 11/4315-8800 in Buenos Aires); and Thrifty, Av. Leandro N. Alem 699 (© 800/847-4389 in the U.S., or 11/4315-0777 in Buenos Aires). Car rental is expensive in Argentina, with standard rates beginning at about $50 to $60 per day for a subcompact with unlimited mileage (ask for any special promotions, especially on weekly rates). Check to see if your existing automobile insurance policy (or a credit card) covers insurance for car rentals.

BY TRAIN

Argentina's railroad network is very limited. There are trains from Buenos Aires to Bariloche and to Mar del Plata, but they are neither as comfortable nor as convenient as buses. One train service stands out, however. The tourist train called *Tren a las Nubes* **(Train to the Clouds)** begins in Salta and cuts an unforgettable swath through the Andes in Argentina's Northwest. The trip lasts approximately 14 hours and costs $63 per person. For more information, call © 387/431-4984 in Salta or © 11/4311-8871 in Buenos Aires, consult www.trenalasnubes.com.ar (a Spanish-language site), or see chapter 6 for more information.

Finding an Address

In Argentina and Chile, as in many South American countries, not all addresses have street numbers. This is especially true in rural areas. You'll know there's no number if the address includes the abbreviation "s/n," which stands for *sin número* (without number).

10 The Active Vacation Planner

Argentina encompasses so many climate zones, with such a wide variety of terrain, that it is a haven for outdoor activities of all kinds. There are numerous hiking and climbing opportunities in the Northwest. Activities around Iguazú Falls range from easy hiking along the waterfall circuits and on San Martín Island to speed-rafting along the river and trekking into the jungle. And of course, Argentine Patagonia is home to more kayaking, climbing, and trekking than you could possibly fit into one lifetime. Below, I have listed some recommended tour operators specializing in outdoor-themed vacations in Argentina.

ORGANIZED ADVENTURE TRIPS The advantages of traveling with an organized group are plentiful, especially for travelers who have limited time and resources. Tour operators take the headache out of planning a trip, and they iron out the wrinkles that invariably pop up along the way. Many tours are organized to include guides, transportation, accommodations, meals, and gear (some outfits will even carry gear for you, for example, on trekking adventures). Independent travelers tend to view organized tours as antithetical to the joy of discovery, but leaving the details to someone else does free up substantial time to concentrate on something else. Besides, your traveling companions are likely to be kindred souls interested in similar things.

Remember to be aware of what you're getting yourself into. A 5-day trek in the remote Patagonian wilderness may look great on paper, but are you physically up to it? Tour operators are responsible for their clients' well-being and safety, but that doesn't let you off the hook in terms of personal responsibility. Inquire about your guide's experience, safety record, and insurance policy. Remember, no adventure trip is 100% risk free.

RECOMMENDED OPERATORS The following U.S.-based adventure operators offer solid, well-organized tours, and they are backed by years of experience. Most of these operators are expensive, a few are exorbitant (remember that prices do not include airfare), but that usually is because they include luxury accommodations and gourmet dining. Most offer trips to hot spots like Patagonia, and operators with trips to that region are listed here for both Argentina and Chile.

- **Abercrombie & Kent,** 1520 Kensington Rd., Oak Brook, IL 60521 (© **800/323-7308;** www. abercrombiekent.com), is a luxury tour operator that offers a "Patagonia: A Natural Playground" trip that heads from Buenos Aires to Ushuaia for a 3-day cruise around Tierra del Fuego, followed by visits to Torres del Paine park, Puerto Varas, and Bariloche. Cost is $7,000 to $8,000 per person, double occupancy. This trip also features a 4-day extension to Iguazú Falls.
- **Butterfield and Robinson,** 70 Bond St., Toronto, Canada M5B 1X3 (© **800/678-1147;** www. butterfieldandrobinson.com), is another gourmet tour operator,

with a walking-oriented, 10-day trip to Patagonia starting in El Calafate, Argentina, and finishing in Punta Arenas, Chile. In between, travelers visit national parks Los Glaciares and Torres del Paine, with visits to Perito Moreno Glacier and lodging in fine lodges and ranches. Cost is roughly $6,300 per person, double occupancy.

- **Mountain-Travel Sobek,** 6420 Fairmount Ave., El Cerrito, CA 94530 (© **888/MTSOBEK** or 510/527-8100; fax 510/525-7718; www.mtsobek.com), are the pioneers of organized adventure travel, and they offer trips that involve a lot of physical activity. One of their more gung-ho journeys traverses part of the Patagonian Ice Cap in Fitzroy National Park for 21 days; a more moderate "Patagonia Explorer" mixes hiking with cruising. Prices run from $1,500 to $3,000 and more. Sobek always comes recommended for their excellent guides.

- **Backroads Active Vacations,** 801 Cedar St., Berkeley, CA 94710-1800 (© **800/GO-ACTIVE** or 510/527-1555; www.backroads.com), offers a biking tour through the lake districts of Chile and Argentina, with stops in Villa La Angostura and San Martín de los Andes; an afternoon of rafting is included. There's also a hiking trip through the same region, and a 9-day hiking trip in Patagonia that

begins in El Calafate and travels between the two countries. Guests lodge in luxury hotels and inns. Costs run from $3,800 to $5,300.

- **Wilderness Travel,** 1102 Ninth St., Berkeley, CA 94710 (© **800/368-2794** or 510/558-2488; www.wildernesstravel.com), offers a more mellow sightseeing/day-hiking tour around Patagonia, including Los Glaciares, Ushuaia, El Calafate, and Perito Moreno Glacier. The trip costs $4,600 to $5,200, depending on the number of guests (maximum 15).

- **Wildland Adventures,** 3516 NE 155th St., Seattle, WA 98155 (© **800/345-4453** or 206/365-0686; www.wildland.com), offers a few adventure tours of Argentina. The "Salta Trek Through Silent Valleys" tour takes in Salta, Jujuy, and the Andean plain. Two Patagonia tours are offered: "Best of Patagonia," which concentrates on Argentine Patagonia (including Península Valdés, Río Gallegos, Perito Moreno, and Ushuaia), and "Los Glaciares Adventure," which visits El Calafate, Fitzroy National Park, and Perito Moreno Glacier, among others. Accommodations range from hotels to camping to rustic park lodges. Ecotourism is an integral part of Wildland tours. Prices start at $1,500 for the 8-day Salta tour and continue upward of $4,350 for the 2-week Patagonia trip.

FAST FACTS: Argentina

American Express Offices are located in Buenos Aires, Bariloche, Salta, San Martín, and Ushuaia. In Buenos Aires, the Amex office is at Arenales 707 (© 11/4130-3135).

Business Hours Banks are open weekdays from 10am to 3pm. Shopping hours are weekdays from 9am to 8pm and Saturday from 9am to 1pm.

Shopping centers are open daily from 10am to 8pm. Some stores close for lunch.

Climate See "When to Go," earlier in this chapter.

Currency See "Money," earlier in this chapter.

Documents See "Entry Requirements & Customs," earlier in this chapter.

Driving Rules In cities, Argentines drive exceedingly fast and do not always obey traffic lights or lanes. Seat belts are mandatory, although few Argentines actually wear them. When driving outside the city, remember that *autopista* means motorway or highway, and *paso* means mountain pass. Don't drive in rural areas at night, as cattle sometimes overtake the road to keep warm and are nearly impossible to see.

Drugstores Ask your hotel where the nearest pharmacy *(farmacia)* is; they are generally ubiquitous in city centers, and there is always at least one open 24 hours. In Buenos Aires, the chain **Farmacity** is open 24 hours, with locations at Lavalle 919 (© **11/4821-3000**) and Av. Santa Fe 2830 (© **11/4821-0235**). Farmacity will also deliver to your hotel.

Electricity If you plan to bring any small appliance with you, pack a transformer and a European-style adapter because electricity in Argentina runs on 220 volts. Note that most laptops operate on both 110 and 220 volts. Luxury hotels usually have transformers and adapters available.

Embassies These are all in Buenos Aires: **U.S. Embassy,** Av. Colombia 4300 (© 11/4774-5333); **Australian Embassy,** Villanueva 1400 (© 11/4777-6580); **Canadian Embassy,** Tagle 2828 (© 11/4805-3032); **New Zealand Embassy,** Carlos Pellegrini 1427, 5th Floor (© 11/4328-0747); **United Kingdom Embassy,** Luis Agote 2412 (© 11/4803-6021).

Emergencies The following emergency numbers are valid throughout Argentina. For an **ambulance,** call © **107;** in case of **fire,** call © **1100;** for **police** assistance, call © **101.**

Information See "Visitor Information," earlier in this chapter.

Internet Access Cybercafes called "Locuturios" are found on every corner in Buenos Aires and in other cities and towns as well, so it won't be hard to stay connected while in Argentina. Access is reasonably priced (usually averaging just under $1 per hour) and connections are reliably good.

Mail Airmail postage for a letter 7 ounces or less from Argentina to North America and Europe is $1. Mail takes, on average, between 10 and 14 days to get to the U.S. and Europe.

Maps Reliable maps can be purchased at the offices of the **Automóvil Club Argentino,** Av. del Libertador 1850, in Buenos Aires (© **11/4802-6061** or 11/4802-7071).

Safety Petty crime has increased significantly in Buenos Aires as a result of Argentina's economic crisis. Travelers should be especially alert to pickpockets and purse snatchers on the streets and on buses and trains. Violent crime has increased in the suburbs of the capital and in Buenos Aires Province. Tourists should take care not to be overly conspicuous, walking in pairs or groups when possible. Avoid demonstrations, strikes, and other political gatherings. In Buenos Aires, do not take taxis off the street. You should call for a radio-taxi instead. Take similar precautions when traveling in Argentina's other big cities.

Smoking Smoking is a pervasive aspect of Argentine society, and you will find that most everyone lights up in restaurants and clubs. Most restaurants do, however, provide nonsmoking sections.

Taxes Argentina's value added tax (VAT) is 21%. You can recover this 21% at the airport if you have purchased local products totaling more than 70 pesos (per invoice) from stores participating in tax-free shopping. Forms are available at the airport.

Telephone The country code for Argentina is **54**. When making domestic long-distance calls in Argentina, place a 0 before the area code. For international calls, add 00 before the country code. Direct dialing to North America and Europe is available from most phones. International, as well as domestic, calls are expensive in Argentina, especially from hotels (rates fall 10pm–8am). Holders of AT&T credit cards can reach the money-saving **USA Direct** from Argentina by calling toll-free ℂ **0800/555-4288** from the north of Argentina or 0800/222-1288 from the south. Similar services are offered by **MCI** (ℂ **0800/555-1002**) and **Sprint** (ℂ **0800/555-1003** from the north of Argentina, or 0800/222-1003 from the south).

Public phones take either phone cards (sold at kiosks on the street) or coins (less common). Local calls cost 20 centavos to start and charge more the longer you talk. Telecentro offices—found everywhere in city centers—offer private phone booths where calls are paid when completed. Most hotels offer fax services, as do all Telecentro offices. Dial ℂ **110** for directory assistance (most operators speak English) and ℂ **000** to reach an international operator.

Time Argentina does not adopt daylight saving time, so the country is 1 hour ahead of Eastern Standard Time in the United States in summer and 2 hours ahead in winter.

Tipping A 10% tip is expected at cafes and restaurants. Give at least $1 to bellboys and porters, 5% to hairdressers, and leftover change to taxi drivers.

Water In Buenos Aires, the water is perfectly safe to drink. But if you are traveling to more remote regions of Argentina, it's best to stick with bottled water for drinking.

3

Buenos Aires

Buenos Aires is a city that does not know where or what it is at times. You may feel that you've been transplanted into Europe by the overwhelmingly Parisian architecture, but the warmth you find from the locals tells you something different is going on. The city was founded twice by the Spanish along the shores of the Rio de la Plata, unsuccessfully in 1536, and again for good in 1580. The late 19th and early 20th century saw a strong colonization by immigrants from Spain and Italy. Neighborhoods like Recoleta and Barrio Norte maintain the most European feel of all, and much of the city was transformed architecturally during the 1910 Independence Centennial period and the worldwide Ecole des Beaux-Arts architectural movement. The city has always looked outside of the country, rather than inside, for inspiration, and locals call themselves Porteños, forever associating themselves with the port that they have always used to communicate with the world.

Family and friendship are of the utmost importance to Porteños. It is a city where locals go outside to interact, lining the streets, packing cafe terraces, and strolling in parks and plazas. Things take a long time, and a simple interaction with a local—asking for mere directions—might lead to an afternoon coffee break.

While exploring Buenos Aires, you will find a city of contradictions. Immense wealth exists side by side with intense poverty, all the more so since the 2001 devaluation of the peso. Under a new government installed in 2003, the Argentine economy is quickly improving, but not for all. Still, hotels are packed to capacity, and new shops and restaurants are opening at a dizzying pace, particularly in the trendy Palermo district. Porteños seem self-assured, although the population is intensely image conscious and uncertain about its place in the global economy. Buenos Aires and its suburbs, where nearly a third of the country lives, is the country's face to the world, but it has little to do with the interior. All these elements demonstrate the complexity of a city searching for identity among its South American and European influences.

This search has become more prominent as ordinary Argentines reel from the country's economic meltdown of late 2001. Middle-class citizens watched their savings disappear in the wake of sharp currency devaluations, ending the peso's decade-long parity with the dollar and, with it, the illusion that Argentina was a rich nation. Weekend shopping, eating out, clubbing, and traveling to other countries—routine for many Porteños in the 1990s—ceased to be possible for everyone but the very rich. Homelessness, malnutrition, and street crime rose as a result of ongoing economic troubles, and foreign travelers must now exercise greater caution than they did in the past, especially in certain districts. But one of the few upsides of the country's financial woes, besides the fact that Argentina is a much, much cheaper country to visit

Buenos Aires

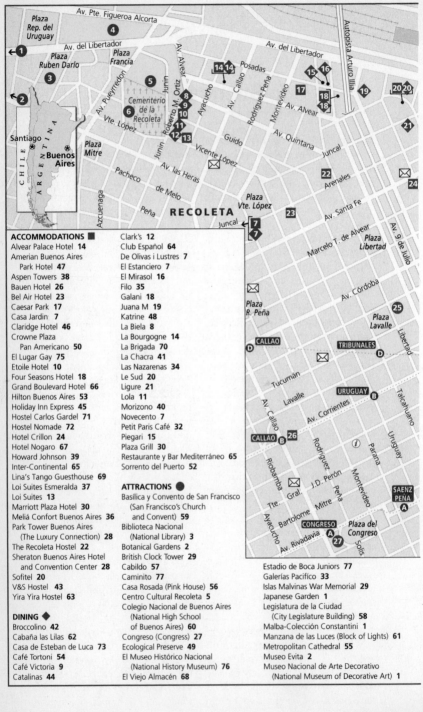

ACCOMMODATIONS ■

Alvear Palace Hotel **14**
Amerian Buenos Aires
  Park Hotel **47**
Aspen Towers **38**
Bauen Hotel **26**
Bel Air Hotel **23**
Caesar Park **17**
Casa Jardin **7**
Claridge Hotel **46**
Crowne Plaza
  Pan Americano **50**
El Lugar Gay **75**
Etoile Hotel **10**
Four Seasons Hotel **18**
Grand Boulevard Hotel **66**
Hilton Buenos Aires **53**
Holiday Inn Express **45**
Hostel Carlos Gardel **71**
Hostel Nomade **72**
Hotel Crillon **24**
Hotel Nogaro **67**
Howard Johnson **39**
Inter-Continental **65**
Lina's Tango Guesthouse **69**
Loi Suites Esmeralda **37**
Loi Suites **13**
Marriott Plaza Hotel **30**
Meliá Confort Buenos Aires **36**
Park Tower Buenos Aires
  (The Luxury Connection) **28**
The Recoleta Hostel **22**
Sheraton Buenos Aires Hotel
  and Convention Center **28**
Sofitel **20**
V&S Hostel **43**
Yira Yira Hostel **63**

DINING ◆

Broccolino **42**
Cabaña las Lilas **62**
Casa de Esteban de Luca **73**
Café Tortoni **54**
Café Victoria **9**
Catalinas **44**

Clark's **12**
Club Español **64**
De Olivas i Lustres **7**
El Estanciero **7**
El Mirasol **16**
Filo **35**
Galani **18**
Juana M **19**
Katrine **48**
La Biela **8**
La Bourgogne **14**
La Brigada **70**
La Chacra **41**
Las Nazarenas **34**
Le Sud **20**
Ligure **21**
Lola **11**
Morizono **40**
Novecento **7**
Petit Paris Café **32**
Piegari **15**
Plaza Grill **30**
Restaurante y Bar Mediterráneo **65**
Sorrento del Puerto **52**

ATTRACTIONS ●

Basílica y Convento de San Francisco
  (San Francisco's Church
  and Convent) **59**
Biblioteca Nacional
  (National Library) **3**
Botanical Gardens **2**
British Clock Tower **29**
Cabildo **57**
Caminito **77**
Casa Rosada (Pink House) **56**
Centro Cultural Recoleta **5**
Colegio Nacional de Buenos Aires
  (National High School
  of Buenos Aires) **60**
Congreso (Congress) **27**
Ecological Preserve **49**
El Museo Histórico Nacional
  (National History Museum) **76**
El Viejo Almacén **68**

Estadio de Boca Juniors **77**
Galerías Pacífico **33**
Islas Malvinas War Memorial **29**
Japanese Garden **1**
Legislatura de la Ciudad
  (City Legislature Building) **58**
Malba-Colección Constantini **1**
Manzana de las Luces (Block of Lights) **61**
Metropolitan Cathedral **55**
Museo Evita **2**
Museo Nacional de Arte Decorativo
  (National Museum of Decorative Art) **1**

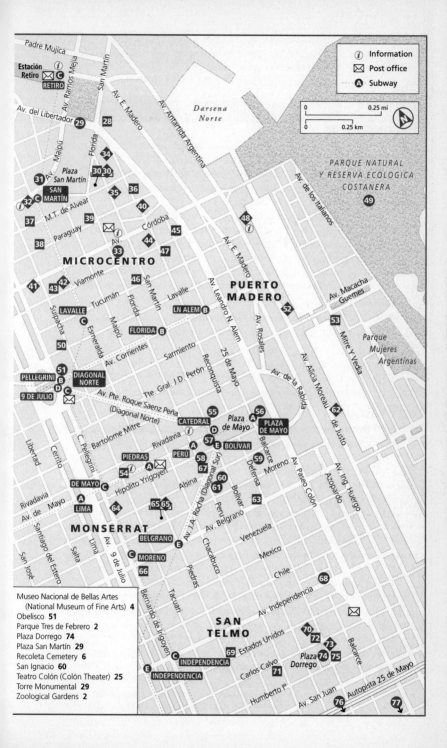

Padre Mujica

Estación Retiro (i) ⊠ Ⓒ
RETIRO

Av. del Libertador 29   28

Plaza San Martín 31   30 30
SAN MARTÍN   34
(i) 32   35   36
37   40

Florida

Av. E. Madero

Av. Antártida Argentina

Darsena Norte

PARQUE NATURAL Y RESERVA ECOLOGICA COSTANERA
49

M.T. de Alvear
39 ⊠ (i)
Paraguay   Córdoba
38   33   44   45
47

MICROCENTRO

48 (i)

Av. E. Madero

PUERTO MADERO

Av. de los Italianos

41   42 Viamonte   46 San Martín
43   Tucumán   Florida   Lavalle
LAVALLE Ⓒ   LN ALEM Ⓑ

Av. Macacha Guemes

52
53

Parque Mujeres Argentinas

50   Esmeralda   FLORIDA Ⓑ
Av. Corrientes   Sarmiento

Av. Leandro N. Alem

Av. Rosales

Maipú   25 de Mayo

51 Tte. Gral. J.D. Perón   Reconquista
PELLEGRINI Ⓑ DIAGONAL NORTE Ⓒ
9 DE JULIO Ⓓ ⊠
Av. Pte. Roque Saenz Peña
(Diagonal Norte)   CATEDRAL   55   56
Plaza de Mayo   PLAZA DE MAYO
Ⓓ (i)   Ⓔ
C. Bartolome Mitre   Rivadavia   57
PIEDRAS   PERÚ   58   BOLÍVAR
54 (i) Ⓐ ⊠   67   59
DE MAYO Ⓒ   Hipolito Yrigoyen   60   Moreno
61
Rivadavia   Alsina   63
LIMA Ⓐ   64   65 65

Av. de la Rábida

Av. Alicia Moreau de Justo

62

Av. Ing. Huergo

MONSERRAT

Av. 9 de Julio   BELGRANO Ⓔ
Santiago del Estero   MORENO Ⓒ
San José   66

Av. Belgrano   Venezuela   Mexico   Chile
68

Av. Paseo Colón   Azopardo

⊠

Av. Independencia

SAN TELMO

70
72
69 Estados Unidos   73
Plaza Dorrego   74 75
71
Carlos Calvo

Bernardo de Irigoyen

INDEPENDENCIA Ⓒ
INDEPENDENCIA Ⓔ

Tacuari

Humberto I°
Av. San Juan   Autopista 25 de Mayo
76   77

Information (i)
Post office ⊠
Subway Ⓐ

0   0.25 mi
0   0.25 km

now, is an increased recognition among Argentines that tourists provide oxygen for the economy. Do not let Argentina's economic situation keep you away: Buenos Aires remains a fascinating and welcoming city to visit.

1 Essentials

GETTING THERE

BY PLANE   International flights arrive at **Ezeiza International Airport** (© 11/4480-0224), located 34km (21 miles) west of downtown Buenos Aires. You can reach the city by shuttle or *remise* (private, unmetered taxi); you will see official stands with set fares in the airport once you clear Customs. Taxis from the airport to the center of town cost about $11 to $15.

Domestic airlines and flights to Uruguay use **Jorge Newbery Airport** (© 11/4514-1515), located only 15 minutes to the north along the river from downtown. Taxis and *remises* cost $5 to $10 to the city center. At both airports, take only officially sanctioned transportation and do not accept transportation services from any private individuals. **Manuel Tienda León** (© 11/4314-3636) is the most reliable transportation company, offering buses and *remises* to and from the airports.

BY BUS   The **Estación Terminal de Omnibus,** Av. Ramos Mejía 1680 (© 11/4310-0700), located near Retiro Station, serves all long-distance buses.

BY CAR   In Buenos Aires, travel by *subte* (subway), *remise,* or radio-taxi (radio-dispatched taxis, as opposed to street taxis) is easier and safer than driving yourself. Rush-hour traffic is chaotic, and parking is difficult. If you do rent a car, park it at your hotel or a nearby garage and leave it there.

CITY LAYOUT

Although Buenos Aires is a huge city, the main tourist neighborhoods are concentrated in a small, comparatively wealthy section hugging the Río de la Plata. The "Microcentro" of the city extends from Plaza de Mayo to the south and Plaza San Martín to the north, and from Plaza del Congreso to the west and Puerto Madero to the east. The neighborhoods of San Telmo, La Boca, Puerto Madero, Recoleta, and Palermo surround the Microcentro. The city layout follows a wobbly grid pattern; *avenidas* are the wide boulevards where most traffic flows and the subways lines are generally routed, *calles* are narrower one-way streets, and *diagonales* cut streets and avenues at 45-degree angles, providing beautiful vista points to many of the city's tourist sites. Each city block extends 100m (328 ft.), and building addresses indicate the distance on that street.

The **Microcentro** includes Plaza de Mayo (the political and historic center of Buenos Aires), Plaza San Martín, and Avenida Nueve de Julio, generally claimed to be the widest street in the world. *Note:* Addresses on this thoroughfare generally take on those of its parallel service streets, such as Carlos Pelligrini, Cerrito, and Bernardo de Irogoyen, which is important to note in order to avoid confusion when looking for a location. Most commercial activity is focused in this busy zone, as are the majority of hotels and restaurants. Next to the Microcentro, the newly renovated riverfront area called **Puerto Madero** boasts excellent restaurants and nightlife, as well as new commercial and residential zones. Farther south, **La Boca, Monserrat,** and **San Telmo** are the historic neighborhoods where the first immigrants arrived and *milonga* and tango originated. These areas are somewhat run-down and are considered by some locals to be

> **Tips   Websites for Your Trip**
>
> We have included useful websites for virtually every listing we can in this section. In addition, Buenos Aires's city government uses www.bue.gov.ar as its main tourist page, providing information and links for sites and businesses, and a calendar of events of interest to the tourist. For maps, check out www.dediosonline.com, the site of an Argentine company producing tourist maps. *Subte*, or subway, information is available through the interactive website www.subte.com.ar which offers maps, estimated times, and transfer information between stations. If your Spanish is excellent, use www.google.com.ar for some of the latest locally produced Web information on Buenos Aires.

dangerous at night. While they are beautiful and loaded with areas of interest to tourists, caution should be taken after sunset.

The city's most European neighborhood, **Recoleta,** offers fashionable restaurants, cafes, and evening entertainment on tree-lined streets. It's home to the city's cultural center, built into a former church, as well as the Recoleta Cemetery, where key personalities such as Evita and many former presidents are buried. **Barrio Norte** borders Recoleta and is famous for its Avenida Santa Fe shopping and nightlife. To the northwest, **Palermo** is a sprawling multicentered neighborhood of parks, mansions, and cobblestone streets lined with tiny stucco homes, and it has fast become the city's trendiest area. It is vastly wealthy in some parts and gracefully bohemian in others.

STREET MAPS   Ask the front desk of your hotel for a copy of "The Golden Map" and "QuickGuide Buenos Aires" to help you navigate the city. Before leaving town, you can also get great maps ahead of time from the Buenos Aires–based company **De Dios** (www.dediosonline.com), which has laminated street guides for helping you plan your trip.

GETTING AROUND

The Buenos Aires Metro—called the *subte*—is the fastest, cheapest way to get around. Buses are also convenient, though less commonly used by tourists. Get maps of Metro and bus lines from tourist offices and most hotels. (Ask for the "QuickGuide Buenos Aires.") In theory, all Metro stations should have maps, although they are rarely in good supply.

BY METRO   Five *subte* lines connect commercial, tourist, and residential areas in the city Monday through Saturday from 5am to 11pm, and Sunday and holidays from 8am to 11pm. The flat fare is 70 *centavos* (25 ¢), with tickets purchased at staffed windows at every station. You can also buy a *subte* pass for 7 pesos ($2.30), valid for 10 trips. The passes demagnetize easily and do not work well in intense humidity, which is most of the summer. Considering the low cost, buy extra cards as backup. See the inside back cover of this guide for a map. Although the *subte* is the fastest and cheapest way to travel in Buenos Aires, it gets crowded during rush hours and unbearably hot in summer. You should also make sure to ride the A line at least once, a tourist attraction in itself. This was the first line built, running along Avenida de Mayo, and it still uses the rickety old wooden trains. Peru station, in particular, retains most of the turn-of-the-last-century ornamentation and advertising.

Neither the Recoleta nor Puerto Madero neighborhoods have *subte* access. Most of Puerto Madero, however, can be reached via the L.N. Alem *subte* stop on the B line. (It's a 5- to 20-min. walk, depending on which dock you're going to: The Puerto Madero area is a renovated port district, so it is very long and stretches along the Rio de la Plata waterfront in the downtown area.) The D runs through Barrio Norte, which borders Recoleta. Visit www.subte.com.ar for maps before heading to Argentina. The interactive site also gives estimated times and transfer information between stations.

BY BUS   Some 140 bus lines operate in Buenos Aires 24 hours a day. The minimum fare is 80 *centavos* and goes up depending on distance traveled. Pay your fare inside the bus at an electronic ticket machine, which accepts coins only but gives change. Many bus drivers, provided you can communicate with them, will tell you the fare for your destination and help you with where to get off. The *Guia T* is a comprehensive guide to the buses, dividing the city up into various grids. Buy it at bookstores, newspaper kiosks, or on the *subte* from peddlers.

BY TAXI   The streets of Buenos Aires are crawling with taxis. Fares are low, with an initial meter reading of 1.60 pesos increasing 20 centavos every 200m (656 ft.) or each minute. *Remises* and radio-taxis are much safer than street taxis (see the "Traveling by Taxi" box below). Most of what the average tourist needs to see in the city is accessible for under $2. Radio-taxis, when hailed on the street, are recognized by the plastic lightboxes on their rooftops. Ordinary taxis, more likely to be run by members of Buenos Aires's infamous taxi mafia, do not have these special lights. A rarely enforced law means taxi drivers can stop only if their passenger side is facing the curb. If you're being ignored by cabs with the red word *libre* (available) flashing on their windshield, cross the other side of the street and hail again. To request a taxi by phone, consider **Taxi Premium** (© 11/4374-6666), which is used by the Four Seasons Hotel, or **Radio Taxi Blue** (© 11/4777-8888), contracted by the Alvear Palace Hotel.

BY CAR   This is not a place where you need a car, and rules are only marginally followed by most drivers in the city. The only one that seems to be heeded is no turn on red. It's a better idea to hire a *remise* or radio-taxi with the help of your hotel or travel agent. Though it is not recommended, if you must drive, international car rental companies rent vehicles at both airports. Most hotels can also arrange car rentals.

CAR RENTALS   Rental cars are available from **Hertz** (© 800/654-3131 in the U.S.), Paraguay 1122 (© 11/4815-6789); **Avis** (© 800/230-4898 in the U.S.), Cerrito 1527 (© 11/4326-5542); **Dollar** (© 800/800-6000 in the

---

Tips **Traveling by Taxi**

At the risk of sounding repetitive, we strongly recommend that if you need a taxi, you take only a *remise* or radio-taxi that has been called in advance. When taking taxis off the streets, use only those with plastic light boxes on their roofs, indicating that they are radio-taxis. There has been a sharp increase in the number of robberies by street taxi drivers since the economic crisis began. *Remises* are only marginally more expensive than street taxis, but far safer. Most hotels have contracts with *remise* companies and will be happy to call one for you. You should also call for a cab from restaurants, museums, and so on (see above for numbers).

U.S.), Marcelo T. de Alvear 523 (© 11/4315-8800); and **Thrifty** (© **800/847-4389** in the U.S.), Av. Leandro N. Alem 699 (© 11/4315-0777).

ON FOOT   You'll find yourself walking more than you planned in this pedestrian-friendly city. Most of the center is small enough to navigate by foot, and you can connect to adjacent neighborhoods by catching a taxi or using the *subte*. Based on the Spanish colonial plan, the city is a wobbly grid expanding from the Plaza de Mayo, so you are not likely to get too lost. Plazas and parks all over the city supply a wonderful place to rest, people-watch, and meet the locals.

VISITOR INFORMATION
Obtain tourist information for Argentina from the **Tourism Secretariat of the Nation,** Av. Santa Fe 883 (© **0800/555-0016,** or 11/4312-1132). It is open weekdays from 9am to 5pm, but the toll-free information line remains open daily from 8am to 8pm. There are branches at Ezeiza International Airport and Jorge Newbery Airport as well, open daily from 8am to 8pm.

The central office of the **City Tourism Secretariat,** responsible for all visitor information on Buenos Aires, is located at Calle Balcarce 360 in Montserrat but is not open to the general public (© 11/4313-0187). Instead, the city uses several kiosks spread in various neighborhoods, which have maps and hotel, restaurant, and attraction information. These are found at J.M. Ortiz and Quintana in Recoleta, Puerto Madero, the central bus terminal, Caminito in La Boca, and Calle Florida 100, where it hits Diagonal Norte. Most are open Monday through Friday from 10am to 5pm, although some open and close later. Others are also open on weekends as well, including the one in San Telmo at Defensa 1250. The center on Caminito in La Boca is open weekends only, usually Saturday and Sunday from 10am to 5pm. In addition, individual associations have their own tourist centers, providing a wealth of information, such as that for the Calle Florida Business Association in the shopping center Galerías Pacifico and where Calle Florida hits Plaza San Martín.

FAST FACTS: Buenos Aires

American Express   The enormous American Express building is located next to Plaza San Martín, at Arenales 707 (© **11/4312-1661**). The travel agency is open Monday through Friday from 9am to 6pm; the bank is open Monday through Friday from 9am to 5pm. In addition to card-member services, the bank offers currency exchange (dollars only), money orders, check cashing, and refunds.

Area Code   The city area code for Buenos Aires, known locally as a *"caracteristica,"* is **011**. Drop the 0 when combining from overseas with Argentina's country code, **54. 15** in front of a local number indicates a cellular phone. This will need the addition of the **011** when calling from outside of Buenos Aires.

Business Hours   Banks are generally open weekdays 10am to 3pm, with ATMs working 24 hours. Shopping hours are Monday through Friday from 9am to 8pm or 10pm, and Saturday from 10am to midnight. Shopping centers are open daily 7 days from 10am to 10pm. Most independent stores are closed on Sunday, and some close for lunch. Some kiosks, selling water, candy, and packaged food are open 24 hours. There is almost always a 24-hour pharmacy or *locutorio* in each neighborhood.

Currency Exchange Although American dollars are often accepted in major hotels and businesses catering to tourists, you will need Argentine pesos for ordinary transactions. Credit cards are widely used, although some businesses have suspended credit card services or charge a small additional fee. It's easiest to exchange money at the airport, your hotel, or an independent exchange house rather than at an Argentine bank. Traveler's checks can be difficult to cash: **American Express** (see above) offers the best rates on its traveler's checks and charges no commission. It offers currency exchange for dollars only. ATMs are plentiful in Buenos Aires, but you should use those only in secure, well-lit locations. At some ATMs, you can withdraw pesos or dollars. You can have money wired to **Western Union,** Av. Córdoba 917 (© **0800/800-3030**).

Embassies & Consulates See "Fast Facts: Argentina" in chapter 2.

Emergencies For an **ambulance,** call © **107;** in case of **fire,** call © **100;** for **police** assistance, call © **101;** for an English-speaking hospital, call **Clínica Suisso Argentino** (© **11/4304-1081**). The **tourist police** (© **11/4346-5770**) are located at Av. Corrientes 436.

Language Shops, hotels, and restaurants are usually staffed by at least one or two fluent English speakers, and many people speak at least a few words of English. A rule of thumb though is that less expensive venues will have fewer, if any, English speakers.

Post Office You never have to venture more than a few blocks to find a post office, open weekdays from 10am to 8pm and Saturday until 1pm. The main post office, or *Correo Central,* is at Av. Sarmiento 151 (© **11/ 4311-5040**). In addition, the post office works with some *locutorios,* which offer limited mailing services. The purple-signed and ubiquitous **OCA** is a private postal service.

Safety Crime in Buenos Aires—especially pickpocketing, robberies, and car thefts—has increased sharply in recent years as the economy has collapsed, although it's generally safe to walk around Recoleta, Palermo, and the Microcentro by both day and night. Some tourist areas deemed safe by day, such as La Boca, should be avoided at night. Be careful at night when in San Telmo and Monserrat, though these areas are becoming safer, with gentrification, than in years past. Tourists should take care not to be overly conspicuous, walking in pairs or groups when possible. Do not flaunt expensive possessions, particularly jewelry. Call for a radio-taxi or *remise* when leaving a place of business.

Taxes The 21% sales tax, or VAT, is already included in the sales price of your purchase. Foreign tourists are entitled to a VAT tax return for certain purchases over 70 pesos, but you must request a refund check at the time of purchase from participating shops (the shop should display a "Global Refund" logo). Before departing the country, present these refund checks (invoices) to Customs, and then your credit card will be credited for the refund or you will be mailed a check. Be aware when checking into hotels that the posted or spoken price may or may not reflect this tax, so make sure to ask for clarification.

Taxis See "Getting Around," above.

Telephone Unless you are calling from your hotel (which will be expensive), the easiest way to place calls in Buenos Aires is by going to a *locutorio* or *telecentro*, found on nearly every city block. Private glass booths allow you to place as many calls as you like dialing directly, after which you pay an attendant. A running meter tells you what you'll owe. Most *locutorios* also have fax machines and broadband Internet computers. Calls to the U.S. or Canada generally run about a peso or less per minute.

Although some coin-operated public phones still exist in Buenos Aires, most require a calling card, available at kiosks, which are specifically branded for the various communication companies. Local calls, like all others, are charged by the minute. Dial 🕻 **110** for information, 🕻 **000** to reach an international operator. To dial another number in Argentina from Buenos Aires, dial the area code first, then the local number, including with cellular numbers. *Note:* If you call someone's cellular phone in Argentina, the call is also charged to you and can cost significantly more than a standard landline.

Tipping A 10% to 15% tip is common at cafes and restaurants. Taxis do not require tips, but many people round up to the nearest peso or 50 centavo figure.

2 Where to Stay

Hotels in Buenos Aires often fill up in high season, so book ahead. Most of the best and most convenient hotels are found in Recoleta and the Microcentro. Recoleta is more scenic and not quite as noisy as the Microcentro, but you might spend more money on cabs, as it is not near the *subte* lines. Prices listed below are rack rates in high season and include the 21% tax levied on hotel rooms. Discounts are almost always available for weekends and low season, and may even be available in high season. Web packages and specials can also be found on various hotel sites. Most hotels charge about $4 a night for valet parking, or are close to self-parking facilities they can recommend. You should avoid parking long term on the street.

Buenos Aires accommodations have improved in recent years, following a series of renovations among many of the city's government-rated four- and five-star hotels. Most five- and four-star hotels in Buenos Aires offer in-room safes, cable TV, direct-dial phones with voice mail, and in-room modem access. Most hotels in this chapter are designated four or five stars.

Not all hotel prices are the bargains they once were immediately after the 2001 peso crisis, when rooms suddenly became a third of their original cost. Exponentially increasing numbers of tourists have made available hotel rooms a scarce commodity, and hotels are trending their rates up in accordance. Still, bargains can be had, especially with four-stars off the beaten path, as well among locally owned rather than international hotel chains.

BARRIO NORTE
INEXPENSIVE

Bauen Hotel   We're not recommending this hotel because you'll be impressed by the service, the upkeep of the rooms, or some of the other things that usually impress people when they stay in a hotel. The number one reason for staying in this hotel is that it gives you a glimpse as best a tourist can into a post–peso crisis phenomenon in Argentina: the development of the worker "Cooperativas" in which employees take over a failed business abandoned by the owners in order to keep their jobs. The Bauen, a disco-era hotel, never made a lot of money, and the peso crisis drove it under. The workers reacted by taking over and keeping it open. Virtually everything dates from its late-1970s opening: the lobby signs, the curves of the front desk, avocado Formica furniture, shiny globe-shape lamps, old televisions, and the *pièce de la resistance,* the underground disco lounge you expect John Travolta to be dancing in. Upper floors have fantastic views of the surrounding city. The staff is also exceptionally friendly and helpful.

Av. Callao 360 at Corrientes, 1022 Buenos Aires. ⓒ **11/4372-1932.** Fax 11/4372-3883. 220 units, including 18 suites. From $35 double; from $50 suite. Rates include continental breakfast. AE, MC, V. Metro: Callao. **Amenities:** Restaurant; bar; disco lounge; small health club; sauna; concierge; business center; room service; laundry service; theatre; convention center. *In room:* A/C, TV w/cable.

MICROCENTRO
VERY EXPENSIVE

Crowne Plaza Pan Americano 𝒜𝒜𝒜   The Crowne Plaza is an enormous hotel, facing both the Obelisco and the Teatro Colon, offering convenient access to tourist sites as well as virtually all of the *subte* lines that converge at this part of the city. The South Tower's rooms are a good size, but many are still in need of renovation, which is ongoing. The North Tower rooms are larger and better appointed and, for the small difference in price, worth asking for. Decor also varies here; some are fully carpeted; others offer elegant hardwood floors. Bathrooms are also larger, with whirlpool tubs and separate shower units, and marble counters and floors. Valet presses are also standard in the North Tower rooms. All rooms in both towers come with desks, extra side chairs, and ample closet space. The hotel's health club, spa, and sauna are perhaps the most amazing and magical in the city and must be experienced, if only for the view. They're in a three-level glass box on the top of the North Tower. Swimming in its heated pool, which is both indoors and outdoors, as well as working out on its various machines, gives the feeling of floating above Avenida Nueve de Julio. The health club's restaurant, **Kasuga,** becomes a sushi bar at night. Two other restaurants are located in the gracious and inspiring lobby with Greek frescoes and dark wood and marble accents. **Lucíernaga,** where breakfast is served, is enormous, but its niche-filled layout and Jacobean tapestry upholstered furniture offer an intimate feeling; it also serves as the main lobby bar. **Tomo I** has a modern decor, and both offer international, Argentine, and Italian cuisine.

Carlos Pellegrini 551, 1009 Buenos Aires. ⓒ **11/4348-5115.** Fax 11/4348-5250. www.buenosaires.crowne plaza.com. 386 units. $240 double; from $300 suite. Rates include sumptuous buffet breakfast. AE, DC, MC, V. Valet parking free. Metro: Lavalle, Diagonal Norte. **Amenities:** 3 restaurants; enormous health club with indoor-outdoor pool; exercise room; spa; sauna; concierge; business center; salon; room service; massage service; babysitting; laundry service; dry cleaning. *In room:* A/C, TV, dataport, minibar, coffeemaker, hair dryer, safe.

Marriott Plaza Hotel 𝒜𝒜   The historic Plaza was the grande dame of Buenos Aires for most of the 20th century, and the Marriott management has maintained much of its original splendor. (The hotel still belongs to descendants of the first owners from 1909.) The intimate lobby, decorated in Italian marble, crystal, and Persian carpets, is a virtual revolving door of Argentine politicians, foreign diplomats, and business executives. The veteran staff offers outstanding service, and the concierge will address needs ranging from executive business services to sightseeing tours. Although the quality of guest rooms is hit or miss while renovations continue, all are spacious and well appointed. Twenty-six overlook Plaza San

Martín, providing dreamlike views of the green canopy of trees in the spring and summer. The **Plaza Grill** (p. 60) remains a favorite spot for a business lunch and offers a reasonably priced multicourse dinner menu as well. The hotel's health club is one of the best in the city. In a unique gesture, guests whose rooms are not ready are provided access to a special lounge area in the health club where they can rest and shower. The value of this service cannot be overstated when arriving very early after overnight flights from North America.

Calle Florida 1005, 1005 Buenos Aires. ℂ **11/4318-3000.** Fax 11/4318-3008. www.marriott.com. 325 units. $210 double; from $260 suite. Rates include buffet breakfast. AE, DC, MC, V. Valet parking $23. Metro: San Martín. **Amenities:** 2 restaurants; cigar bar; excellent health club with outdoor pool; exercise room; sauna; concierge; business center; salon; room service; massage service; laundry service; dry cleaning. *In room:* A/C, TV, dataport, minibar, coffeemaker, hair dryer, safe.

Park Tower Buenos Aires (The Luxury Connection) 𝕬𝕬𝕬   One of the most beautiful, and expensive, hotels in Buenos Aires, the Park Tower is connected to the Sheraton next door. The hotel combines traditional elegance with technological sophistication and offers impeccable service. Common areas as well as private rooms feature imported marble, Italian linens, lavish furniture, and impressive works of art. The lobby, with its floor-to-ceiling windows, potted palms, and Japanese wall screens, contributes to a sense that this is the Pacific Rim rather than South America. Tastefully designed guest rooms are equipped with 29-inch color TVs, stereo systems with CD players, and cellphones. The rooms have stunning views of the city and the river. Guests also have access to 24-hour private butler service. The hotel boasts three restaurants, including Crystal Garden, serving refined international cuisine; El Aljibe, cooking Argentine beef from the grill; and Cardinale, offering Italian specialties. The lobby lounge features piano music, a cigar bar, tea, cocktails, and special liquors.

Av. Leandro N. Alem 1193, 1104 Buenos Aires. ℂ **11/4318-9100.** Fax 11/4318-9150. www.luxurycollection. com/parktower. 181 units. From $400 double. AE, DC, MC, V. Metro: Retiro. **Amenities:** 3 restaurants; snack bar; piano bar; 2 pools; putting green; 2 lighted tennis courts; fitness center with gym; wet and dry saunas; concierge; business center and secretarial services; room service; massage therapy; laundry service; dry cleaning. *In room:* A/C, TV/VCR, dataport, minibar, hair dryer, safe.

Sofitel 𝕬𝕬𝕬   The Sofitel opened in late 2002, the first in Argentina. This classy French hotel near Plaza San Martín joins two seven-story buildings to a 20-story neoclassical tower dating from 1929, with a glass atrium lobby bringing them together. The lobby resembles an enormous gazebo, with six ficus trees, a giant iron-and-bronze chandelier, an Art Nouveau clock, and Botticcino and black San Gabriel marble filling the space. Adjacent to the lobby, you will find an elegant French restaurant, **Le Sud** (p. 59), and the early-20th-century-style Buenos Aires Café. The cozy library, with its grand fireplace and dark woods, offers guests an enchanting place to read outside their rooms. These rooms vary in size, mixing modern French decor with traditional Art Deco styles; ask for one of the "deluxe" rooms or suites if you're looking for more space. Beautiful marble bathrooms have separate showers and bathtubs and feature Roger & Gallet amenities. Rooms above the 8th floor enjoy the best views, and the 17th-floor suite, *L'Appartement,* covers the whole floor. Many of the staff members speak Spanish, English, and French.

Arroyo 841/849, 1007 Buenos Aires. ℂ **11/4909-1454.** Fax 11/4909-1452. www.sofitel.com. 144 units. From $240 double; from $340 suite. AE, DC, MC, V. **Amenities:** Restaurant; cafe; bar; indoor swimming pool; fitness center; concierge; business center; room service; laundry service. *In room:* A/C, TV, dataport, minibar, hair dryer, safe.

EXPENSIVE

Claridge Hotel ⭐ The Claridge is living testimony to the once close ties between England and Argentina. The grand entrance with its imposing Ionic columns mimics a London terrace apartment, and the lobby was renovated in 2002 in a classical style with colored marbles. Guest rooms are spacious, tastefully decorated, and equipped with all the amenities expected of a five-star hotel. The restaurant's hunting-theme wood-paneled interior is a registered city landmark and offers a good-value menu with carefully prepared international food for as little as $8 and an inviting breakfast buffet included in the rates. Because it occasionally hosts conventions, the Claridge can become very busy. The rates at this hotel can go down significantly when booking promotions via the website, pushing it into the moderate category.

Tucumán 535, 1049 Buenos Aires. ℃ 11/4314-7700. Fax 11/4314-8022. www.claridge.com.ar. 165 units. $235 double; from $355 suite. Rates include buffet breakfast. AE, DC, MC, V. Metro: Florida. **Amenities:** Restaurant; bar; health club with heated outdoor pool; exercise room; sauna; concierge; business center; room service; massage service; laundry service; dry cleaning. In room: A/C, TV, minibar, safe.

Meliá Confort Buenos Aires ⭐⭐ Within easy walking distance of Plaza San Martín and Calle Florida, the Meliá Confort is among the best of the city's four-star hotels. Spacious guest rooms colored in soft earth tones feature overstuffed chairs, soundproof windows, and marble bathrooms. Large desks, two phone lines, and available cellphones make this a good choice for business travelers. The staff offers friendly, relaxed service. The Meliá has a small Spanish restaurant and bar.

Reconquista 945, 1003 Buenos Aires. ℃ 11/4891-3800. Fax 11/4891-3834. www.solmelia.com. 125 units. $120 double; from $190 suite. Rates include buffet breakfast. AE, DC, MC, V. Metro: San Martín. **Amenities:** Restaurant; bar; exercise room; concierge; business services; room service; laundry service; dry cleaning. *In room:* A/C, TV, dataport, minibar, hair dryer, safe.

Sheraton Buenos Aires Hotel and Convention Center ⭐ Situated in the heart of the business, shopping, and theater district, the Sheraton is an ideal location for business travelers and tourists. Guest rooms are typical of a large American chain—well equipped, but lacking in charm. What the hotel lacks in intimacy, however, it makes up for in the wide range of services offered to guests. It shares three restaurants with the neighboring Park Tower Buenos Aires (The Luxury Collection), and its "Neptune" pool and fitness center are among the best in the city.

Av. San Martín 1225, 1104 Buenos Aires. ℃ 11/4318-9000. Fax 11/4318-9353. www.sheraton.com. 741 units. $260 double; from $360 suite. AE, DC, MC, V. Metro: Retiro. **Amenities:** 3 restaurants; snack bar; piano bar; 2 pools; putting green; 2 lighted tennis courts; fitness center with gym; wet and dry saunas; concierge; activities desk; car-rental desk; business center; shopping arcade; salon; room service; massage therapy; babysitting; laundry service; dry cleaning. *In room:* A/C, TV, minibar, hair dryer, safe.

MODERATE

Amerian Buenos Aires Park Hotel ⭐⭐ *Finds* One of the best four-star hotels in the city, the modern Amerian is a good bet for tourists as well as business travelers, and it has become a bargain with the peso crisis, dropping to about half its original price. The warm atrium lobby looks more like California than Argentina, and the highly qualified staff offers personalized service. Soundproof rooms are elegantly appointed with wood, marble, and granite, and all boast comfortable beds, chairs, and work areas. The Argentine-owned hotel is just blocks away from Calle Florida, Plaza San Martín, and the Teatro Colón.

Reconquista 699, 1003 Buenos Aires. ⓒ **11/4317-5100.** Fax 11/4317-5101. www.amerian.com. 152 units. $96 double; from $145 suite. Rates include buffet breakfast. AE, DC, MC, V. Parking $4. Metro: Florida. **Amenities:** Restaurant and pub; exercise room; sauna; concierge; business center; room service; laundry service; dry cleaning. *In room:* A/C, TV, minibar.

Aspen Towers ⓕⓕ   Built in 1995, the Aspen Towers is one of the city's newer and more refined hotels. Its 13-floor tower is contemporary in design, with a light-filled atrium lobby, elegant restaurant, and inviting rooftop pool. Guest rooms are small but classically decorated, with faux-antique furniture and soft-colored linens. All rooms feature marble bathrooms with whirlpool baths—something you're unlikely to find anywhere in the city at this price. The hotel is popular with Brazilians, Chileans, and Americans, and lies within easy walking distance of downtown's attractions.

Paraguay 857, 1057 Buenos Aires. ⓒ **11/4313-1919.** Fax 11/4313-2662. www.aspentowers.com.ar. 105 units. $135–$175 double. Rates include buffet breakfast. AE, DC, MC, V. Metro: San Martín. **Amenities:** Restaurant; cafe; rooftop pool; exercise room; sauna; concierge; business center; room service; laundry service; dry cleaning. *In room:* A/C, TV, minibar.

Holiday Inn Express ⓕ   This hotel enjoys a convenient location next to Puerto Madero and its restaurants and nightlife. Although it lacks room service, concierge, or bellhop, the hotel is friendly, modern, and inexpensive. Guest rooms have large, firm beds; ample desk space; and 27-inch cable TVs. Half of them boast river views. Coffee and tea are served 24 hours, and the buffet breakfast is excellent. Pets are also allowed.

Av. Leandro N. Alem 770, 1057 Buenos Aires. ⓒ **11/4311-5200.** Fax 11/4311-5757. www.holiday-inn.com. 116 units. From $140 double. Children under 18 stay free in parent's room. Rates include buffet breakfast. AE, DC, MC, V. Metro: L.N. Alem. Free parking. **Amenities:** Deli; exercise room; whirlpool; sauna; business center. *In room:* A/C, TV.

Hotel Crillon ⓕ   This French-style hotel enjoys an outstanding location adjacent to Plaza San Martín, next to some of the city's best sights and shops. Having completed a renovation in 2002, the Crillon has become more comfortable, with guest rooms refitted with furniture and better linens. A business center, racquetball and squash courts, gym, and sauna have been added. The hotel is popular with European and Brazilian business travelers, and offers high-tech conveniences such as wireless Internet access and cellphones. Deluxe rooms enjoy views of calles Santa Fe and Esmeralda; the suites (with Jacuzzis) overlook Plaza San Martín. Stay away from interior rooms, which have no views. The hotel staff is extremely helpful.

Av. Santa Fe 796, 1059 Buenos Aires. ⓒ **11/4310-2000.** Fax 11/4310-2020. www.hotelcrillon.com.ar. 96 units. $95 double; $150 suite. Rates include buffet breakfast. AE, DC, MC, V. Metro: San Martín. **Amenities:** Restaurant; bar; concierge; business services; room service; laundry service; dry cleaning. *In room:* A/C, TV, wireless Internet access, minibar, hair dryer, safe.

Howard Johnson ⓕⓕ ⓥⓐⓛⓤⓔ   Having taken over from Courtyard by Marriott, this Howard Johnson's is an excellent choice for business travelers who don't require many special services. It has a great location off Calle Florida near Plaza San Martín, with access through a shopping and restaurant gallery in the hotel's ground level. Guest rooms resemble studio apartments, with king- or queen-size beds, sleeper chairs, large desks and dressers, and well-appointed bathrooms. Each room has two phones, and local calls and Internet use are free—a rarity in Buenos Aires. A small, airy cafe is in the lobby, but room service is not offered. The hotel also advertises extensively as gay-friendly accommodations.

Calle Florida 944, 1005 Buenos Aires. ✆ **11/4891-9200.** Fax 11/4891-9208. www.hojoar.com. 77 units. $90 double. Rates include buffet breakfast. AE, DC, MC, V. Metro: San Martín. **Amenities:** Restaurant; business services; laundry service. *In room:* A/C, TV, minibar, hair dryer, safe.

Loi Suites Esmeralda 🜲 *Kids* Previously a Comfort Inn, this Loi Suites (part of a small local chain) lies 3 blocks from Plaza San Martín and the pedestrian walking street Calle Florida. Spacious rooms can accommodate up to six people, making this a good choice for families traveling with children. Renovated in 2001, rooms are decorated in soft whites with kitchenettes and microwaves, and all come with cellphones. The hotel also offers complimentary access to a gym and swimming pool located off-property. A more upscale (five-star) Loi Suites is in Recoleta.

Marcelo T. de Alvear 842, 1058 Buenos Aires. ✆ **11/4131-6800.** Fax 11/4131-6888. 103 units. $120 double; $205 suite. Rates include buffet breakfast. AE, DC, MC, V. Metro: San Martín. **Amenities:** Restaurant; bar; room service; laundry service. *In room:* A/C, TV, dataport, minibar, safe.

INEXPENSIVE

V&S Hostel 🜲🜲 *Finds* Privately owned, but part of an Argentine network of hostels, V&S Hostel provides exceptionally friendly service in a convenient Microcentro location. The hostel is inside of a gorgeous turn-of-the-20th-century apartment building. The inexpensive rooms are accented by lavish touches like molded plaster, curved doorway entries, stained-glass ornamentation, and balconies. Five private bedrooms with attached shower-stall bathrooms are also available. A kitchen is available for making meals. A quiet library, a TV sitting room, and a patio dining area are some of the areas where guests can mingle. Several computers are also available for Internet access. This place is a great value. Atypical of hostels, there is air-conditioning.

Viamonte 887 at Maipu, 1053 Buenos Aires. ✆ **11/4322-0994.** Fax 11/4327-5131. www.hostelclub.com or www.argentinahostels.com. 60 bed spaces, including 10 in 5 bedrooms with attached bathroom. From $8 per bed; $23–$27 per private room. Rates include continental breakfast. No credit cards. Metro: Lavalle. **Amenities:** Concierge; Internet center; shared kitchen; lockers. *In room:* A/C, hair dryer.

MONSERRAT
MODERATE

Grand Boulevard Hotel 🜲 The Grand Boulevard offers a location similar to the Inter-Continental at a much lower price, while still offering a convenient set of services for both business and leisure travelers. Double-glazed German-made windows lock out noise from Avenida Nueve de Julio while offering incredible views of that street and the river in higher floors. The restaurant and bar is open 24 hours, and offers both international cuisine and a special spa menu of light, nutritious foods, explaining caloric content for health-conscious travelers. All rooms offer desks of varying sizes, and a single bedside panel controls all room lights. The Argentine queen-size beds are slightly larger than an American full and are comfortable, but not the firmest, and all rooms have large closets. Internet access is free in all rooms, as well as in the 24-hour business center. Subway access is easy, and with the autopista nearby, this is also the city's closest four-star hotel to the airport. The hotel can arrange babysitting, and some rooms have limited accessibility for travelers with disabilities. A small glassed-in meeting room space sits on the roof of the building.

Bernardo de Irogoyen 432, 1072 Buenos Aires. ✆ **11/5222-9000.** www.grandboulevardhotel.com. 85 units. $80 double; from $135 suite. AE, DC, MC, V. Free parking. Metro: Moreno. **Amenities:** Restaurant; bar; small health club with personal trainer; sauna; concierge; business center; 24-hr. room service; massage service; laundry service; dry cleaning. *In room:* A/C, TV, dataport, minibar, hair dryer, safe.

Hotel Nogaro ✦ Hotel Nogaro's grand marble staircase leads to a variety of guest rooms noteworthy for their comfort and quiet. Deluxe rooms boast hardwood floors and high ceilings, and small but modern bathrooms with whirlpool tubs in the suites. Standard rooms, while smaller, are pleasant, too, with red carpeting, large closets, and a bit of modern art. The hotel is a good bet for people who want to stay slightly outside the city center, although you should not walk in Monserrat at night. The staff will arrange sightseeing tours upon request. In keeping with the increasing pricing trend in Buenos Aires, this hotel is no longer the bargain it was, nearly tripling its older rates.

Av. Julio A. Roca 562, 1067 Buenos Aires. ✆ 11/4331-0091. Fax 11/4331-6791. www.nogarobue.com.ar. 140 units. From $132 double; from $145 suite. Rates include buffet breakfast. AE, DC, MC, V. Metro: Monserrat. **Amenities:** Restaurant; business center; room service; babysitting; laundry service. *In room:* A/C, TV, minibar.

Inter-Continental ✦✦✦ The Inter-Continental opened in 1994, and despite its modernity, this luxurious tower hotel was built in one of the city's oldest districts, Monserrat, and decorated in the Argentine style of the 1930s. The marble lobby is colored in beige and apricot tones, heavy black and brass metal accents, and handsome carved-wood furniture and antiques inlaid with agates and other stones. The lobby's small Café de las Luces sometimes offers evening tango performances. The Inter-Continental is also the only five-star in walking distance to the San Telmo tango district. The **Restaurante y Bar Mediterráneo** (p. 59) serves healthful, gourmet Mediterranean cuisine on an outdoor patio under a glassed in trellis. Stop by the Brasco & Duane wine bar for an exclusive selection of Argentine vintages. Guest rooms continue the 1930s theme, with elegant black woodwork, comfortable king-size beds, marble-top nightstands, large desks, and black-and-white photographs of Buenos Aires. Marble bathrooms have separate showers and bathtubs, and feature extensive amenities.

Moreno 809, 1091 Buenos Aires. ✆ **11/4340-7100.** Fax 11/4340-7119. www.buenos-aires.interconti.com. 312 units. $150 double; from $300 suite. AE, DC, MC, V. Parking $10. Metro: Moreno. **Amenities:** Restaurant; wine bar; lobby bar; health club with indoor pool; exercise room; sauna; concierge; business center; room service; massage service; laundry service; dry cleaning; executive floors; sun deck. *In room:* A/C, TV, dataport, minibar, hair dryer, safe.

INEXPENSIVE

Casa Jardin ✦ Owner Nerina Sturgeon wanted to create an "artist hostel" in the heart of Palermo Viejo, and she has succeeded in doing so. Built into an old house, this intimate hostel boasts extremely high ceilings, all the better to have more wall space to show off her own and other people's paintings throughout the space. The artist atmosphere is further highlighted by gallery events held here periodically, complete with rooftop parties on the garden-wrapped terrace overlooking the street. The guest rooms are accessed by old French doors, and each has just a few beds. In total, there are 10 bed spaces, including 1 as a single. As a woman-owned and -run business, this is also an ideal location for young women travelers to feel comfortable, even if alone. The only complaint would be the bathroom ratio, which is not enough. There is also no breakfast, but a 24-hour cafe sits across the street. A shared kitchen completes the picture. An Internet station is also in the living room.

Charcas 4416, 1425 Buenos Aires. ✆ 11/4774-8783. Fax 11/4891-9208. www.casajardinba.com.ar. 10 bed spaces, including 1 single unit. $9 per bed; $13 for single space. No credit cards. Metro: Plaza Italia. **Amenities:** Self-service drink station; concierge; free Internet; TV room; shared kitchen. *In room:* Lockers.

Yira Yira Hostel ✦ This place is perfect for young travelers and those seeking a bargain in a great location. Yira Yira takes its name from an old tango song, appropriate enough for a place that, though in Monserrat, puts you only blocks from the tango neighborhood of San Telmo. This is a very clean youth hostel, opened in May 2004, with excellent services, considering the price. A small portion of the funds goes to the Madres de Plaza de Mayo, so you can also feel that you're doing a social benefit by staying here. There is a main living room space, complete with a TV. Many young people gather here with friends, and a self-service bar even sells champagne. Breakfast is served in the morning, and the kitchen is available for public use. A small terrace sits outside of the living room area, with an *asado* where barbecues are often held. The staff is very helpful and proud of this new hostel. They arrange tours of Buenos Aires with the young and adventurous in mind, such as city biking trips. One bedroom with attached bath is available for up to four people. The remaining spaces all share bathrooms.

Defensa 377 at Belgrano, 1066 Buenos Aires. ⓒ 11/4311-4600. Fax 11/4311-3302. www.yirayirahostel. com.ar. 53 bed spaces, including 4 in 1 private room. From $7 per bed; $25 for room. Rates include continental breakfast. AE, MC, V. Metro: Bolivar. **Amenities:** Bar; small gym; sauna; concierge; laundry service; Internet; shared kitchen. *In room:* A/C, lockers.

PUERTO MADERO

There are no convenient Metro stops to this neighborhood.

EXPENSIVE

Hilton Buenos Aires 𝄞𝄞 The Hilton opened in mid-2000 as the first major hotel and convention center in Puerto Madero. It lies within easy walking distance of some of the best restaurants in Buenos Aires and is an excellent choice for steak and seafood gourmands. The strikingly contemporary hotel—a sleek silver block hoisted on stilts—features a seven-story atrium with more than 400 well-equipped guest rooms and an additional number of private residences. Spacious guest rooms offer multiple phone lines, walk-in closets, and bathrooms with separate showers and baths. Those staying on the executive floors receive complimentary breakfast and have access to a private concierge. Next to the lobby, the El Faro restaurant serves California cuisine with a focus on seafood. The hotel has an impressive on-site pool and fitness center, and the staff can also arrange access to golf, tennis, and other recreational activities.

Av. Macacha Güemes 351, 1106 Buenos Aires. ⓒ 11/4891-0000. Fax 11/4891-0001. www.buenos.hilton. com. 418 units. From $180 double; from $320 suite. AE, DC, MC, V. **Amenities:** Restaurant; bar; modern gym facility with open-air pool deck and a service of light snacks and beverages; concierge; business center and secretarial services; room service; babysitting; laundry service; dry cleaning; executive floors; 2 ballrooms; exhibition center. *In room:* TV, dataport, minibar, hair dryer, safe.

RECOLETA

There are no convenient Metro stops to this neighborhood.

VERY EXPENSIVE

Alvear Palace Hotel 𝄞𝄞𝄞 Located in the center of the upscale Recoleta district, the Alvear Palace is the most exclusive hotel in Buenos Aires and one of the top hotels in the world. A gilded classical confection full of marble and bronze, the Alvear combines Empire- and Louis XV-style furniture with exquisite French decorative arts. After a long process, the historically important facade was restored in 2004 to its original glory. The illustrious guest list has included Antonio Banderas, Donatella Versace, the emperor of Japan, and Robert Duvall, to name a few. Recently renovated guest rooms combine luxurious comforts, such as chandeliers, Egyptian cotton linens, and silk drapes, with modern conveniences. All rooms come with personal butler service, cellphones that can be activated on demand, fresh flowers and fruit baskets, and daily newspaper delivery.

Large marble bathrooms contain Hermès toiletries, and most have Jacuzzi baths. The formal hotel provides sharp, professional service, and the excellent concierge staff goes to great lengths to accommodate guest requestsIf it is your dream to stay here while in Buenos Aires, the website sometimes offers discounts when occupancy is low. The Alvear Palace is home to one of the best restaurants in South America (**La Bourgogne**, p. 55) and also offers an excellent, if expensive, Sunday brunch and afternoon tea in L'Orangerie. Kosher catering and dining is also available at the Alvear.

Av. Alvear 1891, 1129 Buenos Aires. ⓒ **11/4808-2100.** Fax 11/4804-0034. www.alvearpalace.com. 210 units, including 85 "palace" rooms and 125 suites. From $300 double; from $475 suite. Rates include luxurious buffet breakfast. AE, DC, MC, V. **Amenities:** 2 restaurants; bar; small health club; spa; concierge; elaborate business center; shopping arcade; room service; massage service; laundry service; dry cleaning; private butler service. *In room:* A/C, TV, dataport, minibar, hair dryer, safe.

Four Seasons Hotel ⭐⭐⭐ *(Kids)* In 2002, the Four Seasons took over the Park Hyatt, which was already one of the city's most luxurious properties. This landmark hotel consists of two parts—the 12-story "Park" tower housing the majority of the guest rooms, and the turn-of-the-last-century French-rococo "La Mansión," with seven elegant suites and a handful of private event rooms. A French-style garden and a pool separate the two buildings, and a well-equipped health club offers spa treatments, including a wine massage and facial. The spa was renovated in mid-2004, and renovations continue on all the rooms to convert them from Hyatt treatments to Four Seasons style. The hotel's restaurant, **Galani** (p. 56), serves excellent Mediterranean cuisine in a casual environment. Spacious guest rooms offer atypical amenities like walk-in closets, wet and dry bars, stereo systems, and cellphones. Large marble bathrooms contain separate water-jet bathtubs and showers. People staying on the club floors enjoy exclusive check-in and checkout; additional in-room amenities including a printer, fax machine, and Argentine wine; and complimentary breakfast and evening cocktails. The attentive staff will assist you in arranging day tours of Buenos Aires, as well as access to golf courses, tennis, boating, and horseback riding. Kids receive bedtime milk and cookies.

Posadas 1086/88, 111 Buenos Aires. ⓒ **11/4321-1200.** Fax 11/4321-1201. www.fourseasons.com. 165 units, including 49 suites (7 suites in La Mansión). $250 double; from $300 suite; $3,500 mansion suite. AE, DC, MC, V. **Amenities:** Restaurant; lobby bar; heated outdoor pool; exercise room; health club; sauna; concierge; multilingual business center; room service; massage service; babysitting; laundry service; dry cleaning. *In room:* A/C, TV/VCR, dataport, minibar, hair dryer, safe.

EXPENSIVE

Caesar Park ⭐ *(Overrated)* This classic hotel sits opposite Patio Bullrich, the city's most exclusive shopping mall. Guest rooms vary in size and amenities, but all have been tastefully appointed with fine furniture and elegant linens, marble bathrooms with separate bathtubs and showers, and entertainment centers with TVs and stereos. Larger rooms come with a fresh fruit basket on the first night's stay. The art collection in the lobby and on the mezzanine is for sale, and a few boutique shops are located on the ground level. Although the hotel, part of a larger international chain, is a member of The Leading Hotels of the World, service is formal and not particularly warm.

Posadas 1232/46, 1014 Buenos Aires. ⓒ **11/4819-1100.** Fax 11/4819-1121. www.caesar-park.com. 170 units. $180 double; from $400 suite. Buffet breakfast included. AE, DC, MC, V. Free valet parking. **Amenities:** Restaurant; 2 bars; small fitness center with indoor pool and sauna; concierge; business center; room service; laundry service; dry cleaning. *In room:* A/C, TV, dataport, minibar, hair dryer, safe.

Loi Suites 🌟🌟   Part of a small local hotel chain, the new Loi Suites Recoleta is a contemporary hotel with spacious rooms and personalized service. A palm-filled garden atrium and covered pool adjoin the lobby, which is bathed in various shades of white. Breakfast and afternoon tea are served in the "winter garden." Although the management uses the term *suites* rather loosely to describe rooms with microwaves, sinks, and small fridges, the hotel does, in fact, offer some traditional suites in addition to its more regular studio-style rooms. Loi Suites lies just around the corner from Recoleta's trendy restaurants and bars, and the staff will provide information on city tours upon request.

Vicente López 1955, 1128 Buenos Aires. 📞 **11/5777-8950.** Fax 11/5777-8999. www.loisuites.com.ar. 112 units. From $200 double; from $300 suite. Rates include buffet breakfast. AE, DC, MC, V. Parking $4. **Amenities:** Restaurant; indoor pool; exercise room; sauna; small business center; limited room service; laundry service; dry cleaning. *In room:* A/C, TV, dataport, minibar, fridge, hair dryer, safe.

MODERATE

Etoile Hotel 🌟 *Value*   Located in the heart of Recoleta, steps away from the neighborhood's fashionable restaurants and cafes, the 14-story Etoile is an older hotel with a Turkish flair. It's not as luxurious as the city's other five-star hotels, but it's not as expensive, either—making it a good value for Recoleta. Colored in gold and cream, guest rooms are fairly large—although they're not really "suites," as the hotel describes them. Executive rooms have separate sitting areas, large tile-floor bathrooms with whirlpool baths, and balconies. Rooms facing south offer balconies overlooking Plaza Francia and the Recoleta Cemetery.

Roberto M. Ortiz 1835, 1113 Buenos Aires. 📞 11/4805-2626. Fax 11/4805-3613. www.etoile.com.ar. 96 units. $110 double; from $160 suite. Rates include buffet breakfast. AE, DC, MC, V. Free parking. **Amenities:** Restaurant; rooftop health club with indoor pool; exercise room; concierge; executive business services; room service; laundry service; dry cleaning. *In room:* A/C, TV, minibar, hair dryer.

INEXPENSIVE

The Recoleta Hostel 🌟 *Finds*   This is a great inexpensive choice for young people who want to be close to everything and in a beautiful neighborhood, but can't ordinarily afford the prices associated with such a location. The accommodations are simple, with 22 bunk bed–filled rooms for 8 to 12 people each. Two double rooms with private bathrooms can also be rented, but they have bunk beds, too, so lovers wishing to cozy up will have to deal with such an arrangement. The rooms are simple, with bare floors and walls, beds, and a small wooden desk in the private rooms. The decor is reminiscent of a convent. Public areas have high ceilings, and there is a public kitchen, a TV room, laundry service, lockers, and an outdoor patio. Bring the laptop, too, because the hostel is a wi-fi hotspot.

Libertad 1216 at Juncal, 1012 Buenos Aires. 📞 11/4812-4419. Fax 11/4815-6622. www.trhostel.com.ar. 75 bed spaces, including 4 in 2 bedrooms with attached bathroom. From $12 per bed; $30 per private room. Rates include continental breakfast. No credit cards. Metro: Lavalle. **Amenities:** Concierge; Internet center; wi-fi; shared kitchen; outdoor patio; lockers. *In room:* Hair dryer.

SAN TELMO
INEXPENSIVE

El Lugar Gay 🌟   This is Buenos Aires's first exclusively gay hotel, but it is open only to men. It's located inside of a historical turn-of-the-last-century building less than a block from Plaza Dorrego, the heart of San Telmo. It has a homey feeling, with industrial chic well blended into a century-old interior. Nestor and Juan, the gay couple who own the building, operate with a friendly staff, but most don't speak much English. Ask for the rooms in the back with the beautiful views of the Church of San Telmo, which is just to the side of the building. The rooms are small and sparse, and some share bathrooms with adjacent rooms, but one group has a Jacuzzi. They do not provide shampoo or hair dryers in the bathroom, which is somewhat surprising for a place catering to gay men. Rooms do not have phones, but some have small desks or tables for use as work stations. Small in-room safes, TVs, and air conditioners complete the rooms. There is 24-hour free use of an Internet station. Several flights of narrow stairs leading to the hotel's lobby and the rooms might be a problem for people with limited mobility. The hotel becomes a de facto gay community center at times, with its small cafe and Sunday evening tango lessons from 5pm to 7pm done by the gay tango group La Marshall. These are open to the public, so even if you don't stay here, you can still visit this hotel when in town.

Defensa 1120 at Humberto I, 1102 Buenos Aires. © 11/4300-4747. www.lugargay.org. 7 rooms, some with shared bathrooms. From $35–$50 double. Rates include continental breakfast. No credit cards. Metro: Independencia. **Amenities:** Restaurant; bar; business center. *In room:* A/C, TV w/cable, small safe.

Hostel Carlos Gardel *🐟* If you can't get enough of Gardel in the tango clubs, then stay here, where a red wall full of his pictures is the first thing to greet you. This hostel is built into a renovated old house, and though it has been severely gutted, a few charming elements, like marble staircases, wall sconces, and stained-glass windows remain. The location is also very new, having opened in March 2004. Two rooms with private bath are available in this location, but at $43, they are expensive, considering the lack of amenities other than a bathroom. The staff is friendly, and a large TV room off the concierge area allows for chatting with them and other patrons. A shared kitchen and an *asado* on the rooftop terrace provide more spaces for interacting and sharing stories of your adventures in Buenos Aires. Towels and sheets are provided for guests, but of all the hostels, this seems to have the fewest bathrooms for the number of guests.

Carlos Calvo 579, 1102 Buenos Aires. © 11/4307-2606. www.hostelcarlosgardel.com.ar. 45 bed spaces, including 10 in 2 private rooms with bathroom. From $5 per bed; $43 for room. Rates include continental breakfast. No credit cards. Metro: Independencia. **Amenities:** Self-service drink station; concierge; TV room; free Internet; shared kitchen. *In room:* Lockers.

Lina's Tango Guesthouse *🐟🐟🐟* *Finds* If you really want to expose yourself to the tango scene, this is the place to stay. Owner Lina Acuña, who originally hails from Columbia, opened this charming little spot in 1997. She is herself a tango dancer and wanted to create a space where the tango community from around the world could come together, enjoy each other's company, and share in Buenos Aires's unique tango history. As a woman-owned space, it's also great for women traveling alone, and Lina often goes with her guests on informal trips to *milongas* of San Telmo and other neighborhoods, offering a unique inside view. Lina lives in the house, and its 1960s exterior hides the fact that the building dates from the turn of the last century. In the rooms off the back garden, the original doors and other elements remain. She has painted these in kitschy colors reminiscent of La Boca, and vines and trees add to the authentic Porteño atmosphere. Guests and Lina's friends gather here for conversation, impromptu help with each other's dance techniques, and *asados* on holidays and weekends. Three of the eight guest rooms share bathrooms, and the rooms come in different sizes but are adequate for sharing. Breakfast is included, and there is also a small kitchen guests can use to cook their own meals, and a washing machine for cleaning up clothes sweaty from a night of tango. Lina is most proud of the shelves she created in all the rooms for her guests' tango shoes. The downsides of the place are that it is not a full-service location, without Internet service or in-room phones. The TV is in the shared living room, and it can be noisy with people talking and dancing in the courtyard. Guests may also encounter the periodic barking of Lina's very friendly dog. No other pets but hers are allowed, however. But if you're all about tango, this is where you should stay.

Estados Unidos 780 at Piedras, 1011 Buenos Aires. © 11/4361-6817 and 11/4300-7367. www.tango guesthouse.com.ar. 8 units, 5 with bathrooms. From $20–$50. Rates include continental breakfast. No credit cards. Metro: Independencia. **Amenities:** Continental breakfast; self-service laundry; tango tours; self-service kitchen.

3 Where to Dine

Buenos Aires offers world-class dining, with a variety of Argentine, Italian, and international restaurants. With the collapse of the peso, fine Argentine dining has become marvelously inexpensive as well. Nothing in the world matches the meat from the Pampas grass-fed Argentine cows, and it is the focus of the dining experience throughout the city, from the humblest *parrilla*, or grill, to the finest business-class restaurant. Many kitchens have an Italian influence, and you'll find pasta on most menus. The city's most fashionable neighborhoods for eating out are all found in Palermo. Las Cañitas provides a row of Argentine and Nouvelle-fusion cuisine concentrated on Báez Street. Palermo Hollywood is quickly matching this, with even more trendy hotspots combining fine dining with a Bohemian atmosphere in small, renovated, turn-of-the-last-century houses. Additional top restaurants line the docks of Puerto Madero, along with a mix of chains and hit-or-miss spots. The Microcentro and Recoleta offer many outstanding restaurants and cafes, some of which have been on the map for decades. Smoky cafe life, where friends argue over coffee, is as sacred a ritual to Porteños as it is to Parisians.

Porteños eat breakfast until 10am, lunch between noon and 4pm, and dinner late—usually after 9pm, though some restaurants open as early as 7pm. Executive lunch menus are offered at many places at noon, but dinner menus are a la carte. Sometimes a small cover charge is applied for bread and other items placed at the table. In restaurants that serve pasta, the pasta and its sauce are sometimes priced separately. Standard tipping is 10% in Buenos Aires; leave more for exceptional service. When paying by credit card, you will often be expected to leave the *propina* (tip) in cash, since many credit card receipts don't provide a place to include it. Be aware that some new restaurants are not yet accepting credit cards, due to still resonating fears from the peso collapse. Many restaurants close between lunch and dinner, and some close completely on Monday.

To locate the following restaurants, see the map on p. 36.

PUERTO MADERO

There are no convenient Metro stops to this neighborhood.

EXPENSIVE

Cabaña las Lilas ✹✹✹ ARGENTINE   Widely considered the best *parrilla* in Buenos Aires, Cabaña las Lilas is always packed. The menu pays homage to Argentine beef, which comes from the restaurant's private *estancia* (ranch). The table "cover"—which includes dried tomatoes, mozzarella, olives, peppers, and delicious garlic bread—nicely whets the appetite. Clearly, you're here to order steak: The best cuts are the rib-eye, baby beef, and thin skirt steak. Order sautéed vegetables, grilled onions, or Provençal-style fries separately. Service is hurried but professional; ask your waiter to match a fine Argentine wine with your meal. The enormous eatery offers indoor and outdoor seating, and, in spite of its high price, is casual and informal. Patrons come in suits or shorts.

Alicia Moreau de Justo 516. (C) 11/4313-1336. Reservations recommended. Main courses $8–$12. AE, DC, V. Daily noon–midnight. Metro: L.N. Alem.

Katrine ☆☆☆ INTERNATIONAL   One of the top dining choices in Buenos Aires, Katrine (named after the restaurant's Norwegian chef-owner) serves exquisite cuisine. Yet for such an exclusive restaurant, the dining room is surprisingly loud and festive. You won't go wrong with any of the menu choices, but a couple of suggestions include marinated salmon Scandinavian style, followed by shrimp with vegetables and saffron, or thinly sliced beef tenderloin with portobello mushrooms, onions, and a cabernet sauvignon reduction. All of the pasta dishes are excellent, too. Katrine's modern dining room and outdoor terrace overlook the water. Service is outstanding.

Av. Alicia Moreau de Justo 138. (C) 11/4315-6222. Reservations recommended. Main courses $8–$15. AE, DC, MC, V. Mon–Fri noon–3:30pm and 8pm–midnight; Sat 8pm–12:30am. Closed Sun. Metro: L.N. Alem.

MODERATE

Sorrento del Puerto ☆☆ ITALIAN   The only two-story restaurant in Puerto Madero enjoys impressive views of the water from both floors. When the city decided to reinvigorate the port in 1995, this was one of the first five restaurants opened (today you'll find more than 50). The sleek modern dining room boasts large windows, modern blue lighting, and tables and booths decorated with white linens and individual roses. The outdoor patio accommodates only 15 tables, but the inside is enormous. People come here for two reasons: great pasta and even better seafood. Choose your pasta and accompanying sauce: seafood, shrimp scampi, pesto, or four cheeses. The best seafood dishes include trout stuffed with crabmeat, sole with a Belle Marnier sauce, Galician-style octopus, paella Valenciana, and assorted grilled seafood for two. A three-course menu with a drink costs $7. Sorrento has a second location in Recoleta at Posadas 1053 ((C) **11/4326-0532**).

Av. Alicia Moreau de Justo 430. (C) 11/4319-8731. Reservations recommended. Main courses $5–$9. AE, DC, MC, V. Mon–Fri noon–4pm and 8pm–1am; Sat 8pm–2am. Closed Sun. Metro: L.N. Alem.

RECOLETA
There are no convenient Metro stops in this neighborhood.

EXPENSIVE
La Bourgogne ☆☆☆ FRENCH   The only Relais Gourmand in Argentina, Chef Jean Paul Bondoux serves the finest French and international food in the city. *Travel and Leisure* rated La Bourgogne the number one restaurant in South America, and *Wine Spectator* gave it the distinction of being one of the "Best Restaurants in the World for Wine Lovers." Decorated in elegant pastel hues, the formal dining room serves the city's top gourmands. To begin your meal, consider a warm *foie gras* scallop with honey wine sauce, or perhaps the succulent *ravioli d'escargots*. Examples of the carefully prepared main courses include *chateaubriand béarnaise,* roasted salmon, veal steak, and lamb with parsley and garlic sauce. The kitchen's fresh vegetables, fruits, herbs, and spices originate from Bondoux's private farm. Downstairs, **La Cave** offers a slightly less formal dining experience, with a different menu but from the same kitchen as La Bourgogne. Wine tastings are offered Thursday in the restaurant's wine cellar; contact La Bourgogne directly for details.

Av. Alvear 1891 (Alvear Palace Hotel). © **11/4805-3857.** Reservations required. Jacket and tie required for men. Main courses $7–$12. AE, DC, MC, V. Mon–Fri noon–3pm and 8pm–midnight; Sat 8pm–midnight. Closed Sun and Jan. Free valet parking.

Lola ★★ *Overrated* INTERNATIONAL   Among the best-known international restaurants in Buenos Aires, Lola recently completed a makeover, turning its dining room into one of the brightest and most contemporary in the city. Caricatures of major personalities adorn the walls, and fresh plants and flowers give Lola's dining room a springlike atmosphere. A French-trained chef offers creative dishes such as chicken fricassee with leek sauce, grilled trout with lemon-grass butter and zucchini, and beef tenderloin stuffed with Gruyère cheese and mushrooms. The chef will prepare dishes for those with special dietary requirements. Although Lola remains among the city's most famous restaurants, some feel that its quality has slipped in recent years due to a number of management changes.

Roberto M. Ortiz 1805. © **11/4804-5959** or 11/4802-3023. Reservations recommended. Main courses $7–$12. AE, DC, MC, V. Daily noon–4pm and 7pm–1am.

Piegari ★★ ITALIAN   You would not think such a fine restaurant could be located where it is: under a highway overpass in a part of Recoleta dubbed La Recova. (La Recova literally means a place where small ships hide in a storm, and this location is so named since it's under an overpass and mimics a place where a ship would seek shelter.) Piegari has two restaurants located across the street from each other; the more formal focuses on Italian dishes, and the other (Piegari Vitello e Dolce) is a *parrilla*. Both restaurants are excellent, but visit the formal Piegari for outstanding Italian cuisine, with an emphasis on seafood and pastas. Homemade spaghetti, six kinds of risotto, pan pizza, veal scallops, and black salmon ravioli are just a few of the mouthwatering choices. Huge portions are made for sharing, and an excellent eight-page wine list accompanies the menu. If you decide to try Piegari Vitello e Dolce instead, the best dishes are the short rib roast and the leg of Patagonian lamb.

Posadas 1042. © **11/4328-4104.** Reservations recommended. Main courses $13–$23. AE, DC, MC, V. Daily noon–3:30pm and 7:30pm–1am.

MODERATE

El Mirasol ★★ ARGENTINE   One of the city's best *parrillas,* El Mirasol serves thick cuts of fine Argentine beef and is also located in La Recova. Its glassed dining area full of plants and trellises gives the impression of outdoor dining. Your waiter will guide you through the selection of cuts, among which the rib-eye, tenderloin, sirloin, and ribs are most popular. A mammoth 2½-pound serving of tenderloin is a specialty, certainly meant for sharing. El Mirasol is part of a chain, which first opened in 1967. The best dessert is an enticing combination of meringue, ice cream, whipped cream, *dulce de leche,* walnuts, and hot chocolate sauce. The wine list pays tribute to Argentina Malbec, Syrah, merlot, and cabernet sauvignon. El Mirasol, which is frequented by business executives and government officials at lunch and a more relaxed crowd at night, remains open throughout the afternoon (a rarity in a city where most restaurants close between lunch and dinner).

Posadas 1032. © **11/4326-7322.** www.el-mirasol.com.ar. Reservations recommended. Main courses $6–$45. AE, DC, MC, V. Daily noon–2am.

Galani ★★ MEDITERRANEAN   This elegant but informal bistro inside the spectacular Four Seasons Hotel serves Mediterranean cuisine with Italian and Asian influences. The executive lunch menu includes an antipasto buffet with seafood, cold cuts, cheese, and salads, followed by a main course and dessert. From the dinner menu, the aged Angus New York strip makes an excellent choice, and all grilled dishes come with béarnaise sauce or *chimichurri* (a thick herb sauce) and a choice of potatoes or seasonal vegetables. Organic chicken and fresh seafood join the menu, along with a terrific selection of desserts. Live harp music often accompanies meals, and tables are candlelit at night. Enjoy an after-dinner drink in Le Dôme, the split-level bar adjacent to the lobby featuring live piano music and occasional tango shows.

Posadas 1086 (Four Seasons Hotel). © 11/4321-1234. Reservations recommended. Main courses $5–$8; fixed-price lunch $10. AE, DC, MC, V. Daily 7–11am, noon–3pm, and 8pm–1am.

INEXPENSIVE

Café Victoria 🌀 CAFE   Perfect for a relaxing afternoon in Recoleta, the cafe's outdoor patio is surrounded by flowers and shaded by an enormous tree. Sit and have a coffee or enjoy a complete meal. The three-course express lunch menu offers a salad, main dish, and dessert, with a drink included. Afternoon tea with pastries and scones is served daily from 4 to 7pm. The cafe remains equally popular in the evening, when live music serenades the patio, providing excellent people-watching. This is a great value for the area—the Recoleta Cemetery and cultural center are located next door.

Roberto M. Ortiz 1865. © 11/4804-0016. Main courses $3–$5. AE, DC, MC, V. Daily 7:30am–11:30pm.

Clark's 🌀 INTERNATIONAL   The dining room here is an eclectic mix of oak, yellow lamps, live plants, and deer antlers. A slanted ceiling descends over the English-style bar with a fine selection of spirits; in back, a 3m-high (9¾-ft.) glass case showcases a winter garden. Booths and tables are covered with green-and-white checkered tablecloths and are usually occupied by North Americans. Specialties include tenderloin steak with goat cheese, sautéed shrimp with wild mushrooms, and sole with a sparkling wine, cream, and shrimp sauce. A number of pasta and rice dishes are offered as well. A large terrace attracts a fashionable crowd in summer.

Roberto M. Ortiz 1777. © 11/4801-9502. Reservations recommended. Main courses $4–$8. AE, DC, MC, V. Daily noon–3:30pm and 7:30pm–midnight.

Juana M 🌀🌀 *Value* ARGENTINE   This amazing little *parrilla* can be easily overlooked, but don't miss it. A family-owned affair, it takes its name from the owner and is known almost solely to Porteños, who want to keep this place all to themselves. Located in the basement of an orphanage that was once the city's Catholic University, the neoclassical building is one of the few saved from the highway demolition, which created the nearby La Recova area where Nueve de Julio intersects with Libertador. The cavernous industrial chic space is white and luminous by day, with seating for more than 210 patrons. At night, the space is lit only by candlelight and trendy young patrons flood in, chattering the night away. The menu is simple, of high quality, and amazingly inexpensive, with a free unlimited salad bar with several healthful options.

Carlos Pellegrini 1535 (basement). © 11/4326-0462. Main courses $3–$4. AE, MC, V. Daily noon–4pm and 8pm-12:30am.

La Biela 🌀🌀🌀 CAFE   Originally a small sidewalk cafe opened in 1850, La Biela earned its distinction in the 1950s as the choice rendezvous of race car champions. Black-and-white photos of these Argentine racers decorate the huge dining room. Today artists, politicians, and neighborhood executives (as well as a fair number of tourists) all frequent La Biela, which serves breakfast, informal lunch plates, ice cream, and crepes. The outdoor terrace sits beneath an enormous 19th-century gum tree opposite the church of Nuestra Señora del Pinar and the adjoining Recoleta Cemetery. This place ranks among the most important cafes in the city, with some of the best sidewalk viewing anywhere in Recoleta.

Quintana 600. ℭ 11/4804-0449. Main courses $3–$5. V. Daily 7am–3am.

PALERMO
MODERATE

De Olivas i Lustres ⭐⭐ MEDITERRANEAN   Located in Palermo Viejo, this magical restaurant is one of our favorites in Buenos Aires. The small, rustic dining room displays antiques, olive jars, and wine bottles, and each candlelit table is individually decorated—one resembles a writer's desk, another is sprinkled with seashells. The reasonably priced menu celebrates Mediterranean cuisine, with light soups, fresh fish, and sautéed vegetables the focus. The breast of duck with lemon and honey is mouthwatering; there are also a number of *tapeos*—appetizer-size dishes. For about $9 each, you and your partner can share 15 such dishes brought out individually (a great option, provided you have at least a couple of hours). Open only for dinner, this romantic spot offers low-key, subtle service.

Gascón 1460. ℭ 11/4867-3388. Reservations recommended. Main courses $3–$5; fixed-price menu $8. AE, V. Mon–Sat 7:30pm–1:30am. Metro: Scalabrini Ortiz.

El Estanciero ⭐ (Finds ARGENTINE   In most of the restaurants in the Las Cañitas section of Palermo, it's all about the glamour. Here in the *parrilla* El Estanciero, it's all about the beef, arguably the best in the neighborhood. The portions are not the largest, but the cuts are amazingly flavorful, with the right mix of fat to add tenderness. If you order the steak rare, or *jugoso,* they also have the sense here not to serve it nearly raw. The restaurant is on two levels, with sidewalk seating at the entrance and a covered terrace above. Both floors have a subtle gaucho-and-rope-braid-accented decor that doesn't overwhelm the senses. Never as crowded as the other restaurants lining the street, this is a great option when the lines are too long at the adjacent see-and-be-seen hotspots.

Báez 202. ℭ 11/4899-0951. Main courses $5–$10. AE, MC, V. Daily noon–4pm and 8pm–1am (8pm–2am weekends). Metro: Ministro Carranza.

Novecento ⭐⭐⭐ INTERNATIONAL   With a sister restaurant in New York's SoHo, Novecento was one of the pioneer restaurants of Palermo's Las Cañitas neighborhood. Fashionable Porteños pack the New York–style bistro by 11pm, clinking wine glasses under a Canal Street sign or opting for the busy outdoor terrace. Waiters rush to keep their clients happy, with dishes like salmon carpaccio and steak salad. The pastas and risotto are mouthwatering, but you may prefer a steak *au poivre* or a chicken brochette. Other wonderful choices include filet mignon, grilled Pacific salmon, and penne with wild mushrooms. Top it off with an Argentine wine. With its candle lighting, this makes a romantic choice for couples looking for something special in the city. A separate but slightly sterile nonsmoking room is also available for seating.

Báez 199. ℭ 11/4778-1900. Reservations recommended. Main courses $4–$7. AE, DC, MC, V. Daily noon–4pm and 8pm–2am; Sunday brunch 8am–noon. Metro: Ministro Carranza.

MONSERRAT
MODERATE

Club Español ⭐⭐ SPANISH   This Art Nouveau Spanish club, with its high, gilded ceiling and grand pillars; bas-relief artwork; and original Spanish paintings, boasts the most magnificent dining room in Buenos Aires. Despite the restaurant's architectural grandeur, the atmosphere is surprisingly relaxed and often celebratory; don't be surprised to find a table of champagne-clinking Argentines next to you. Tables have beautiful silver place settings, and tuxedo-clad waiters offer formal service. Although the menu is a tempting sample of Spanish cuisine—including the paella and Spanish omelets—the fish dishes are the best.

Bernardo de Yrigoyen 180. ⓒ 11/4334-4876. Reservations recommended. Main courses $4–$8. AE, DC, MC, V. Daily noon–4pm and 8pm–midnight. Metro: Lima.

Restaurante y Bar Mediterráneo 𝆠𝆠 MEDITERRANEAN   The Inter-Continental Hotel's exclusive Mediterranean restaurant and bar were built in colonial style, resembling the city's famous Café Tortoni. The downstairs bar, with its hardwood floor, marble-top tables, and polished Victrola playing a tango, takes you back to Buenos Aires of the 1930s. A spiral staircase leads to the elegant restaurant, where subdued lighting and well-spaced tables create an intimate atmosphere. Mediterranean herbs, olive oil, and sun-dried tomatoes are among the chef's usual ingredients. Carefully prepared dishes might include shellfish bouillabaisse; black hake served with ratatouille; chicken casserole with morels, fava beans, and potatoes; or duck breast with cabbage confit, wild mushrooms, and sautéed apples. Express menus (ready within minutes) are available at lunch.

Moreno 809. ⓒ 11/4340-7200. Reservations recommended. Main courses $6–$9. AE, DC, MC, V. Daily 7–11am, 11:30am–3:30pm, and 7pm–midnight. Metro: Moreno.

MICROCENTER
EXPENSIVE

Catalinas 𝆠𝆠𝆠 MEDITERRANEAN/INTERNATIONAL   Since 1979, Galician-born Ramiro Rodríguez Pardo has impressed gourmands from Argentina and abroad, his kitchen defined by culinary diversity and innovation. The colorful yet classic dining room—adjacent to the Lancaster hotel—has three open salons, each painted by one of Argentina's most famous "plastic" artists: Polesello, Beuedit, and Rovirosa. A Venetian crystal chandelier shines on the center dining room, created by the same artist who arranged the chandeliers in the lobby of New York's Plaza Hotel. Tables are large, decorated with white linens, fresh flower arrangements, and porcelain. A three-course, prix-fixe menu, including two bottles of Argentina's finest wines, is offered at lunch and dinner—an excellent value for such an elegant restaurant. The menu changes seasonally but always includes impeccable lobsters, T-bone steaks, and steaks of Patagonian tooth fish. Pardo's grilled lamb chops are famous throughout Argentina.

Reconquista 850. ⓒ 11/4313-0182. Reservations recommended. Main courses $7–$10; fixed-price menu $15. AE, DC, MC, V. Mon–Fri noon–3pm and 8pm–1am; Sat 8pm–1am. Closed Sun. Metro: San Martín.

Le Sud 𝆠𝆠 FRENCH/MEDITERRANEAN   Executive Chef Thierry Pszonka earned a gold medal from the National Committee of French Gastronomy and gained experience at La Bourgogne before opening this gourmet restaurant in the new Sofitel Hotel. His simple, elegant cooking style embraces spices and olive oils from Provence to create delicious entrees, such as the stewed rabbit with green pepper and tomatoes, polenta with Parmesan and rosemary, and spinach with lemon ravioli. Le Sud's dining room offers the same sophistication as its cuisine, a contemporary design with chandeliers and black marble floors, tables of Brazilian rosewood, and large windows overlooking Calle Arroyo. Following dinner, consider a drink in the adjacent wine bar.

Arroyo 841/849 (Sofitel Hotel). ⓒ 11/4131-0000. Reservations recommended. Main courses $10–$20. AE, DC, MC, V. Daily 6:30–11am, 12:30–3pm, and 7:30pm–midnight. Metro: San Martín.

Plaza Grill 🍴🍴 INTERNATIONAL For nearly a century, the Plaza Grill dominated the city's power-lunch scene, and it remains the first choice for government officials and business executives. The dining room is decorated with dark oak furniture, a 90-year-old Dutch porcelain collection belonging to the owners, Indian fans from the British Empire, and Villeroy & Boch china place settings. Tables are well spaced, allowing for intimate conversations. Order a la carte from the international menu or off the *parrilla*—the steaks are perfect Argentine cuts. Marinated filet mignon, thinly sliced and served with gratinéed potatoes, is superb. The "po parisky eggs" form another classic dish—two poached eggs in a bread shell topped with a rich mushroom-and-bacon sauce. The restaurant's wine list spans seven countries, with the world's best Malbec coming from Mendoza.

Marriott Plaza Hotel, Calle Florida 1005. ✆ **11/4318-3070.** Reservations recommended. Main courses $7–$10. AE, DC, MC, V. Daily noon–4pm and 7pm–midnight. Metro: San Martín.

MODERATE

Broccolino 🍴 ITALIAN Taking its name from New York's Italian immigrant neighborhood—notice the Brooklyn memorabilia filling the walls and the mural of Manhattan's skyline—this casual trattoria near Calle Florida is popular with North Americans (Robert Duvall has shown up three times). Many of the waiters speak English, and the restaurant has a distinctly New York feel. Three small dining rooms are decorated in quintessential red-and-white checkered tablecloths, and the smell of tomatoes, onions, and garlic fills the air. The restaurant is known for its spicy pizzas, fresh pastas, and, above all, its sauces (*salsas* in Spanish). The restaurant also serves 2,000 pounds per month of baby calamari sautéed in wine, onions, parsley, and garlic.

Esmeralda 776. ✆ **11/4322-7652.** Reservations recommended. Main courses $3–$5. No credit cards. Daily noon–4pm and 7pm–1am. Metro: Lavalle.

La Chacra 🍴 ARGENTINE Your first impression will be either the stuffed cow begging you to go on in and eat some meat, or the open-fire spit grill glowing through the window. Professional waiters clad in black pants and white dinner jackets welcome you into what is otherwise a casual environment, with deer horns and wrought-iron lamps adorning the walls. Dishes from the grill include sirloin steak, T-bone with red peppers, and tenderloin. Barbecued ribs and suckling pig call out from the open-pit fire, as do a number of hearty brochettes. Steaks are thick and juicy. Get a good beer or an Argentine wine to wash it all down.

Av. Córdoba 941. ✆ **11/4322-1409.** Main courses $4–$6. AE, DC, MC, V. Daily noon–1:30am. Metro: San Martín.

Las Nazarenas 🍴 ARGENTINE This is not a restaurant, an old waiter will warn you; it's an *asador*. More specifically, it's a steakhouse with meat on the menu, not a pseudo-*parrilla* with vegetable plates or some froufrou international dishes for the faint of heart. You have two choices: cuts grilled on the *parrilla* or meat cooked on a spit over the fire. Argentine presidents and foreign ministers have all made their way here. The two-level dining room is handsomely decorated with cases of Argentine wines and abundant plants. Service is unhurried, offering you plenty of time for a relaxing meal.

Reconquista 1132. ✆ **11/4312-5559.** Reservations recommended. Main courses $4–$6. AE, DC, MC, V. Daily noon–1am. Metro: San Martín.

Ligure 🍴🍴 *(Finds* FRENCH Painted mirrors look over the long rectangular dining room, which since 1933 has drawn ambassadors, artists, and business leaders by day and a more romantic crowd at night. A nautical theme prevails, with fishnets, dock ropes, and masts decorating the room; captain's wheels substitute for chandeliers. Portions are huge and meticulously prepared—an unusual combination for French-inspired cuisine. Seafood options include the Patagonian tooth fish sautéed with butter, prawns, and mushrooms, or the trout glazed with an almond sauce. If you're in the mood for beef, the chateaubriand is outstanding, and the *bife de lomo* (filet mignon) can be prepared seven different ways (pepper sauce with brandy is delightful, and made at your table).

Juncal 855. (C) 11/4393-0644 or 11/4394-8226. Reservations recommended. Main courses $4–$6. AE, DC, MC, V. Daily noon–3pm and 8–11:30pm. Metro: San Martín.

INEXPENSIVE

Café Tortoni *Moments* CAFE   You cannot come to Buenos Aires and not visit this important Porteño institution. This historic cafe has served as the artistic and intellectual capital of Buenos Aires since 1858, with guests such as Jorge Luis Borges, Julio de Caro, Cátulo Castillo, and José Gobello. Wonderfully appointed in woods, stained glass, yellowing marble, and bronzes, the place tells more about its history by simply existing than any of the photos hanging on its walls. This is the perfect place for a coffee or a small snack when wandering along Avenida de Mayo. Twice nightly tango shows in a cramped side gallery where the performers often walk through the crowd are worth taking the time for. What makes the Tortoni all the more special is that locals and tourists seem to exist side by side, one never overwhelming the other. Do not, however, expect great service: Sometimes only jumping up and down will get the staff's attention, even when they are a few feet from you.

Av. de Mayo 825. (C) 11/4342-4328. Main courses $2–$7. AE, DC, MC, V. Mon–Thurs 8am–2am; Fri–Sat 8am–3am; Sun 8am–1am. Metro: Av. de Mayo.

Filo *Finds* PIZZA   Popular with young professionals, artists, and anyone looking for cause to celebrate, Filo presents its happy clients with mouthwatering pizzas, delicious pastas, and potent cocktails. The crowded bar has occasional live music, and tango lessons are offered downstairs a few evenings per week.

San Martín 975. (C) 11/4311-0312. Main courses $2–$5. AE, MC, V. Daily noon–4pm and 8pm–2am. Metro: San Martín.

Morizono *Value* JAPANESE   A casual Japanese restaurant and sushi bar, Morizono offers such treats as dumplings stuffed with pork, shrimp and vegetable tempuras, salmon with ginger sauce, and a variety of sushi and sashimi combination platters. Morizono also has locations in Palermo at Paraguay 3521 ((C) 11/4823-4250) and Lacroze 2173, in Belgrano ((C) 11/4773-0940).

Reconquista 899. (C) 11/4314-0924. Reservations recommended. Main courses $3–$6. AE, DC, MC, V. Mon–Fri 12:30–3:30pm and 8pm–midnight; Sat 8pm–1am. Closed Sun. Metro: San Martín.

Petit Paris Café *SNACKS/AFTERNOON TEA   Marble-top tables with velvet-upholstered chairs, crystal chandeliers, and bow tie–clad waiters give this cafe a European flavor. Large windows look directly onto Plaza San Martín, placing the cafe within short walking distance of some of the city's best sights. The menu offers a selection of hot and cold sandwiches, pastries, and special coffees and teas. Linger over your coffee as long as you like—nobody will pressure you to move.

Av. Santa Fe 774. (C) 11/4312-5885. Main courses $2–$4. AE, DC, MC, V. Daily 7am–2am. Metro: San Martín.

SAN TELMO
MODERATE
La Brigada ★★★ ARGENTINE   The best *parrilla* in San Telmo is reminiscent of the Pampas, with memorabilia of gauchos (Pampas cowboys) filling the restaurant. White linen tablecloths and tango music complement the atmosphere, with an upstairs dining room that faces an excellent walled wine rack. The professional staff makes sure diners are never disappointed. Chef-owner Hugo Echevarrieta, known as *el maestro parrillero*, carefully selects meats. The best choices include the *asado* (short rib roast), *lomo* (sirloin steak, prepared with a mushroom or pepper sauce), baby beef (an enormous 850g/30 oz., served for two), and the *mollejas de chivito al verdero* (young goat sweetbreads in a scallion sauce). The Felipe Rutini merlot goes perfectly with baby beef and chorizo. Service is outstanding.

Estados Unidos 465. ℂ 11/4361-5557. Reservations recommended. Main courses $4–$8. AE, DC, MC, V. Daily noon–3pm and 8pm–midnight. Metro: Constitución.

INEXPENSIVE
Casa de Esteban de Luca ★ ARGENTINE   This historic house, once inhabited by Argentina's beloved poet and soldier Esteban de Luca (who wrote the country's first national anthem, the *Marcha Patriótica*), was built in 1786 and declared a national historic monument in 1941. Today it's a popular restaurant serving pasta and meat dishes. Come on Thursday, Friday, or Saturday night after 9pm for the fun-spirited piano show.

Calle Defensa 1000. ℂ 11/4361-4338. Main courses $4–$6. AE, DC, MC, V. Tues–Sun noon–4pm and 8pm–1am. Metro: Constitución.

4 What to See & Do

Buenos Aires is a wonderful city to explore and is fairly easy to navigate. The most impressive historical sites surround Plaza de Mayo, although you will certainly experience Argentine history in neighborhoods such as La Boca and San Telmo, too. Don't miss a walk along the riverfront in Puerto Madero or an afternoon among the plazas and cafes of Recoleta or Palermo. Numerous sidewalk cafes offer respite for weary feet, and good public transportation is available to carry you from neighborhood to neighborhood.

Your first stop should be one of the city tourism centers (see "Visitor Information," earlier in this chapter) to pick up a guidebook, city map, and advice. You can also ask at your hotel for a copy of "The Golden Map" and "QuickGuide Buenos Aires" to help you navigate the city and locate its major attractions.

NEIGHBORHOODS TO EXPLORE
LA BOCA

La Boca, on the banks of the Río Riachuelo, developed originally as a trading center and shipyard. This was the city's first Little Italy, giving the neighborhood the distinct flavor it maintains today. La Boca is most famous for giving birth to the tango in the numerous bordellos, known as *quilombos,* which once served the largely male population.

The focus of La Boca is the **Caminito,** a pedestrian walkway, named ironically after a tango song about a rural village. The walkway is lined with humorously sculpted statues and murals explaining its history. Surrounding the cobblestone street are corrugated metal houses painted in a hodge-podge of colors, recalling a time when the poor locals decorated with whatever paint was left over from ship maintenance in the harbor. Today many artists live or set up their studios in these houses. Along the Caminito, art and souvenir vendors work side by side with tango performers. This Caminito "Fine Arts Fair" is open daily from 10am to 6pm. La Boca is, however, a victim of its own success and has become an obscene tourist trap. While the area is historically important, most of what you will find are overpriced souvenir and T-shirt shops and constant harassment from people trying to hand you flyers for mediocre restaurants. In the summer, the smell from the heavily polluted river becomes almost overbearing. Come to this area because you have to, but if you are short on time, don't let the visit take up too much of your day.

What remains authentic in the area is off the beaten path, whether art galleries or theaters catering both to locals and to tourists, or the world-famous **Estadio de Boca Juniors,** 4 blocks away in a garbage-strewn lot at the corner of Calles Del Valle Iberlucea and Brandsen. This is the home of the *futbal* or soccer club Boca Juniors, the team of Argentine legend Diego Maradona, who, like his country, went from glory to fiery collapse rather quickly. Go on game day, when street parties and general debauchery take over the area. For information on football (soccer) games, see the *Buenos Aires Herald* sports section. Wealthy businessman Mauricio Macri, president of the Boca Juniors Futbal Club, recently opened a museum in the stadium, part of his unsuccessful bid to woo Porteños into electing him the city's mayor.

Use caution when straying too far from the Caminito, however, as the less patrolled surrounding areas can be unsafe. The police here are not for protecting the locals, but for tourists. Once the shopkeepers go home, so do they. Still, at dusk and away from the Camenito is where you will have the most interesting interactions with the neighborhood residents, who quietly reclaim the streets and stroll along the waterfront. Most come not from Italy now, but from the poor interior provinces of the country. *Caution:* Avoid La Boca at night.

SAN TELMO

Buenos Aires's oldest neighborhood, San Telmo originally housed the city's elite. When yellow fever struck in the 1870s—aggravated by substandard hygienic conditions in the area—the aristocrats moved north. Poor immigrants soon filled the neighborhood, and the houses were converted to tenements, called *conventillos*. In 1970, the city passed regulations to restore some of San Telmo's architectural landmarks. Still, gentrification has been a slow process, and the neighborhood maintains a gently decayed, very authentic atmosphere, reminiscent of Cuba's old Havana. It's a bohemian enclave, attracting tourists, locals, and performers 7 days a week on its streets. The collapse of the peso has also meant that a glut of antiques, sold for ready cash, are available for purchase and export. The best shops and markets line **Calle Defensa.**

After Plaza de Mayo, **Plaza Dorrego** is the oldest square in the city. Originally the site of a Bethlehemite monastery, the plaza is also where Argentines met to reconfirm their Declaration of Independence from Spain. On Sunday from 10am to 5pm, the city's best **antiques market** ✶✶✶ takes over the square. You can buy leather, silver, handicrafts, and other products here along with antiques, and tango and *milonga* dancers perform on the square. The tall, darkly handsome dancer nicknamed *El Indio* is the star of the plaza.

San Telmo is full of tango clubs; one of the most notable is **El Viejo Almacén** ✶ (at Independencia and Balcarce). An example of colonial architecture, it was built in 1798 and was a general store and hospital before its reincarnation as the quintessential Argentine tango club. Make sure to go for a show at night (see "Buenos Aires After Dark," later in this chapter). If you get the urge

for a beginner or refresher tango course while you're in San Telmo, look for signs
advertising lessons in the windows of clubs.

PALERMO
Palermo Neighborhoods

Palermo ✷✷✷ is a catchall term for a rather nebulous and large chunk of
northern Buenos Aires. It encompasses **Palermo** proper, with its park system;
Palermo Chico; Palermo Viejo, which is further divided into **Palermo Soho**
and **Palermo Hollywood;** and **Las Cañitas,** which is just to the side of the city's
world-famous polo field.

Palermo Chico is an exclusive neighborhood of elegant mansions off of
Avenida Libertador, whose prices were seemingly unaffected by the peso crisis.
Other than the beauty of the homes and a few embassy buildings, this small set
of streets, tucked behind the Malba museum, has little of interest to the tourist.

Palermo is a neighborhood of parks filled with magnolias, pines, palms, and
willows, where families picnic on weekends and couples stroll at sunset.
Designed by French architect Charles Thays, the parks take their inspiration
from London's Hyde Park and Paris's Bois de Boulogne. Take the Metro to Plaza
Italia, which lets you out next to the **Botanical Gardens** ✷ (© **11/4831-2951**)
and **Zoological Gardens** ✷ (© **11/4806-7412**), open dawn to dusk. Stone
paths wind their way through the botanical gardens, where a student might
escape hurried city life to study on a park bench. Flora from throughout South
America fills the garden, with over 8,000 plant species from around the world
represented. Next door, the city zoo features an impressive diversity of animals,
including indigenous birds and monkeys, giant turtles, llamas, elephants, and a
polar bear and brown bear habitat. The eclectic kitschy architecture housing the
animals, some designed as exotic temples, is as much of a delight as the inhabitants. Peacocks and some of the small animals are allowed to roam free, and
feeding is allowed with special food for sale at kiosks, making it a great place for
entertaining kids.

Parque Tres de Febrero ✷✷, a 400-hectare (1,000-acre) paradise of trees,
lakes, and walking trails, begins just past the Rose Garden off Avenida
Sarmiento. In summer, paddleboats are rented by the hour. The Jardin Botan-
ico, located off Plaza Italia, is another paradise, with many South American
plants specially labeled. It is famous for its population of abandoned cats, tended
by little old ladies from the neighborhood—a delight for kids to watch. Nearby,
small streams and lakes meander through the **Japanese Garden** ✷✷ (© **11/
4804-4922;** open daily 10am–6pm; admission $1), where children can feed the
fish (*alimento para peces* means "fish food") and watch the ducks. Small wood
bridges connect classical Japanese gardens surrounding the artificial lake. A simple restaurant offers tea, pastries, sandwiches, and a few Japanese dishes such as
sushi and teriyaki chicken. You'll also find notes posted for various Asian events
throughout the city.

Palermo Viejo, once a run-down neighborhood of warehouses, factories, and
tiny decaying stucco homes few cared to live in as recently as 15 years ago, has
been transformed into the city's chicest destination. Palermo Viejo is further
divided into **Palermo Soho** to the south and **Palermo Hollywood** to the north,
with railroad tracks and Avenida Juan B. Justo serving as the dividing line. The
center of Palermo Hollywood is Plazaleto Jorge Cortazar, better known by its
informal name, Plaza Serrano, a small oval park at the intersection of Calle Serrano and Calle Honduras. Young people gather here late at night in impromptu
singing and guitar sessions, sometimes fueled by drinks at the myriad of funky

bars and restaurants that surround the plaza. On weekends, there is a crafts festival, but you'll always find someone selling bohemian jewelry and leather goods, no matter the day. The neighborhood gained its name because many Argentine film studios were initially attracted to its once cheap rents and easy parking. Palermo Soho is better known for boutiques owned by local designers, with some restaurants mixed in.

Las Cañitas was once the favored location of the military powers during the dictatorship, and the area remains the safest and most secure of all of the central Buenos Aires neighborhoods. While the military powers no longer control the country, their training base, hospital, high school, and various family housing units still remain and encircle the neighborhood. Today the area is far better known among the hip, trendy, and nouveau riche as the place to dine out, have a drink and party, and be seen along the fashionable venues built into converted low-rise former houses on Calle Báez. Located near the polo grounds, it's a great place for enthusiasts to catch polo stars dining on the sidewalks in season.

RECOLETA

The city's most exclusive neighborhood, La Recoleta wears a distinctly European face. Tree-lined avenues lead past fashionable restaurants, cafes, boutiques, and galleries, many housed in French-style buildings. Much of the activity takes place along the pedestrian walkway Roberto M. Ortiz and in front of the Cultural Center and Recoleta Cemetery. This is a neighborhood of plazas and parks, a place where tourists and wealthy Argentines spend their leisure time outside. Weekends bring street performances, art exhibits, fairs, and sports.

The **Recoleta Cemetery** ✦✦✦ (© 11/4804-7040 or 11/7803-1594), open daily from 8am to 6pm, pays tribute to some of Argentina's historical figures and is a lasting place where the elite can show off their wealth. Once the garden of the adjoining church, the cemetery was created in 1822 and is the oldest in the city. You can spend hours wandering the grounds that cover 4 city blocks, adorned with works by local and international sculptors. More than 6,400 mausoleums form an architectural free-for-all, including Greek temples and pyramids. The most popular site is the tomb of Eva "Evita" Perón, which is always heaped with flowers and letters from adoring fans. To prevent her body from being stolen as it had been many times, she has been buried in a concrete vault 8.1m (27 ft.) underground. Many other rich or famous Argentines are buried here as well, including a number of Argentine presidents whose tomb names you'll recognize matching some of the streets of the city. The dead are not the only residents of the cemetery—about 75 cats roam among the tombs. The cats here are plumper than most strays, since a few women from the area come to feed them at 10am and 4pm. The cats gather in anticipation at the entrance, and this is a good time to bring children who might otherwise be bored in the cemetery. Weather permitting, free English guided tours take place every Tuesday and Thursday at 11am from the cemetery's Doric-columned entrance at Calle Junin 1790.

Adjacent to the cemetery, the **Centro Cultural Recoleta** ✦ (p. 77) holds permanent and touring art exhibits along with theatrical and musical performances. Designed in the mid–18th century as a Franciscan convent, it was reincarnated as a poorhouse in 1858, serving that function until becoming a cultural center in 1979. The first floor houses an interactive children's science museum where it is "forbidden not to touch." Next door, Buenos Aires Design Center features shops specializing in home decor. Among the best is Puro Diseno Argentina, featuring high-quality items, designed and manufactured strictly in Argentina.

PLAZA DE MAYO

Juan de Garay founded the historic core of Buenos Aires, the Plaza de Mayo, in 1580. The plaza's prominent buildings create an architectural timeline: the Cabildo, Pirámide de Mayo (Pyramid of May), and Metropolitan Cathedral are vestiges of the colonial period (18th and early 19th c.), while the seats of national and local government reflect the styles of the late 19th and early 20th centuries. In the center of the plaza, you'll find palm trees, fountains, and benches. Plaza de Mayo remains the political heart of the city, serving as a forum for protests. The mothers of the *desaparecidos,* victims of the military dictatorship's war against left-ists, have demonstrated here since 1976. You can see them march, speak, and set up information booths every Thursday afternoon at 3:30pm.

The Argentine president, whose actual residence is now located in Los Olivos in the suburbs, goes to work at the **Casa Rosada (Pink House)** ⟨⟨⟨. It is from a balcony of this mansion that Eva Perón addressed adoring crowds of Argentine workers, and former President Carlos Menem allowed Madonna to use it for the 1996 movie. Most Argentines now, however, associate the balcony with military dictator Leopoldo Galtieri's ill-fated declaration of war against the United King-dom over the Falkland Islands, known here as the *Islas Malvinas.* You can watch the changing of the guard in front of the palace every hour on the hour, and around back is the **Presidential Museum** (© 11/4344-3802), with information on the history of the building and items owned by various presidents over the centuries. It's open Monday through Friday from 10am to 6pm; admission is free.

The original structure of the **Metropolitan Cathedral** ⟨⟨ (© 11/4331-2845) was built in 1745; it was given a new facade with carvings telling the story of Jacob and his son Joseph, and was designated a cathedral in 1836. Inside lies a mausoleum containing the remains of Gen. José de San Martín, South Amer-ican liberator regarded as the Father of the Nation. (San Martín fought success-fully for freedom in Argentina, Peru, and Chile.) His body was moved here in 1880 to become a symbol of Argentina's unification and rise to greatness when Buenos Aires became the capital of Argentina at the end of a civil war. The tomb of the unknown soldier of Argentine independence is also here.

The **Cabildo** ⟨, Bolívar 65 (© 11/4334-1782), was the original seat of city government established by the Spaniards. Completed in 1751, the colonial building proved significant in the events leading up to Argentina's declaration of independence from Spain in May 1810. Parts of the Cabildo were demolished to create space for Avenida de Mayo and Diagonal Sur. The remainder of the building was restored in 1939 and is worth a visit. The small informal museum offers paintings and furniture from the colonial period, and its ledges and win-dows offer some of the best views of the Plaza de Mayo open to the public (museum open Tues–Fri 12:30–7pm, Sun 2–6pm; admission $1). The Cabildo is the only remaining public building dating back to colonial times. On Thurs-day and Friday, the Cabildo's back patio is home to a crafts fair (11am–6pm).

A striking neoclassical facade covers the **Legislatura de la Ciudad (City Leg-islature Building),** at Calle Perú and Hipólito Yrigoyen, which houses exhibi-tions in several of its halls. Ask about tours, offered on an informal basis in English or Spanish. Legend has it that the watchtower was made so high so that the city could keep on eye on the nearby president in the Casa Rosada. In front of the Legislatura, you'll see a bronze statue of Julio A. Roca. He is considered one of Argentina's greatest presidents and generals, but one of his legacies is the slaughtering of tens of thousands of Indians in the name of racial purity within the province of Buenos Aires. He is why, unlike most of Latin America, Argentina is a largely white rather than mestizo society.

Farther down Calle Perú are the **Manzanas de las Luces (Blocks of Lights)** 𝒜𝒜, Calle Perú 272, which served as the intellectual center of the city in the 17th and 18th centuries. This land was granted in 1616 to the Jesuits, who built **San Ignacio**—the city's oldest church—still standing at the corner of calles Bolívar and Aslina. San Ignacio has a beautiful altar carved in wood with baroque details. It is currently under renovation after years of neglect and was nearly destroyed in the revolution that took Perón out of power in 1955, which also sought to reduce the power of the Catholic church. Also located here is the **Colegio Nacional de Buenos Aires (National High School of Buenos Aires).** Argentina's best-known intellectuals have gathered and studied here, and the name "block of lights" recognizes the contributions of the National School's graduates, especially in achieving Argentina's independence in the 19th century. Tours are usually led on Saturday and Sunday at 3 and 4:30pm, and include a visit to the Jesuits' system of underground tunnels, which connected their churches to strategic spots in the city (admission $2). Speculation remains as to whether the tunnels also served a military purpose or funneled pirated goods into the city, and their full extent is still unknown. *Ratear se,* the Argentine slang for playing hooky, which literally means becoming a rat, comes from the tunnels, as this is where students hid when they did not want to go to class. In addition to weekend tours, the Comisión Nacional de la Manzana de las Luces organizes a variety of cultural activities during the week, including folkloric dance lessons, open-air theater performances, art expositions, and music concerts. Call ℰ **11/4331-9534** for information.

PUERTO MADERO

Puerto Madero became Buenos Aires's second major gateway to trade with Europe when it was built in 1880, replacing in importance the port at La Boca. By 1910, the city had already outgrown it. The Puerto Nuevo (New Port) was established to the north to accommodate growing commercial activity, and Madero was abandoned for almost a century. Urban renewal saved the original port in the 1990s with the construction of a riverfront promenade, apartments, and offices. Bustling and businesslike during the day, the area attracts a fashionable, wealthy crowd at night. It's lined with elegant restaurants serving Argentine steaks and fresh seafood specialties, and there is a popular cinema showing Argentine and Hollywood films, as well as several dance clubs such as **Opera Bay** and **Asia de Cuba.** The entire area is rapidly expanding, with high-rise luxury residences making this a newly fashionable, if somewhat isolated and artificial, neighborhood to live in. Of note is that all of the streets in Puerto Madero are named for important women in Argentine history. Look for the Buenos Aires City Tourism brochure "Women of Buenos Aires" to learn more about some of them. At sunset, take a walk along the eastern, modern part of the renovated area, and watch the water shimmer in brilliant reds as the city forms a backdrop.

As you walk out from the port, you'll also come across the **Ecological Preserve** 𝒜𝒜. This area is an anomaly for a modern city and exists as proof that nature can regenerate from an ecological disaster. In the 1960s and 1970s, demolished buildings and debris were dumped into the Rio de la Plata after the construction of the *autopista* or highway system. Over time, sand and sediment began to build up, plants and grasses grew, and birds now use it as a breeding ground. Ask travel agents about bird-watching tours. In the summer, adventurous Porteños use it as a beach, but the water is too polluted to swim in and you must be careful of jagged debris and the homeless who set up camp here. In spite of limited protection, Puerto Madero development is slowly creeping onto the preserve.

PLAZA SAN MARTÍN AND SURROUNDING MICROCENTRO AREA

Plaza San Martín 🌟🌟🌟, a beautiful park at the base of Calle Florida in the Retiro neighborhood, acts as the nucleus of what's considered the city's *Microcentro*. In summer months, Argentine businesspeople flock to the park on their lunch hour, loosening their ties, taking off some layers, and sunning for a while amid the plaza's flowering jacaranda trees. A monument to Gen. José de San Martín towers over the scene. The park is busy at all hours, and even the playground will be teeming with kids and their parents out for a post-midnight stroll. Plaza San Martín was once the location of choice for the most elite families at the beginning of the twentieth century. The San Martín Palace, now used by the Argentine Ministry of Foreign Affairs; the Circulo Militar, once the home of the Paz family who own the *La Prensa* newspaper; and the elegant Plaza Hotel testify to this former grandeur. The construction of the modern American Express building unfortunately destroyed this once completely classical area.

Plaza San Martín cascades gently down a hill, at the base of which sits the **Islas Malvinas War Memorial,** a stark circular wall engraved with the names of the nearly 750 dead and an eternal flame, overseen by guards from the various branches of the military. The memorial directly faces the Elizabethan-style **British Clock Tower,** since renamed the **Torre Monumental,** though most locals still use the old name. It was a gift from the British, who built and ran the nearby Retiro train station complex. Oddly, it remained unscathed during the war but was attacked by a mob years later, which also toppled an accompanying statue of George Canning, the British Foreign Secretary who recognized Argentina's independence from Spain. The tower is open to the public and provides a view to the city and river.

Calle Florida 🌟🌟🌟 is the main pedestrian thoroughfare of Buenos Aires and a shopper's paradise. The busiest section, extending south from Plaza San Martín to Avenida Corrientes, is lined with boutiques, restaurants, and record stores. It extends all the way through Avenida de Mayo to the south, forming into **Calle Peru,** where many international banks have retail branches. Day and night, street performers walk on glass, tango, and offer comedy acts. You'll find the upscale Galerías Pacífico fashion center here where it intersects Calle Viamonte (see "Shopping," below). Most of the shopping on the street itself, however, is middle of the road. Leather stores abound, so compare prices and bargain by stopping into a few before finalizing your purchase. Florida intersects with **Calle Lavalle,** a smaller version of itself. You'll find even more stores, most of lesser quality, and some inexpensive *parrillas* worth visiting. The street is also home to numerous video and electronic game arcades, so it's a good place for teenagers to hang out in while you shop around.

Avenida Corrientes 🌟 is a living diary of Buenos Aires's cultural development. Until the 1930s, Avenida Corrientes was the favored hangout of tango legends. When the avenue was widened in the mid-1930s, it made its debut as the Argentine Broadway, and Evita's first apartment was here. Today Corrientes, lined with Art Deco cinemas and theaters, pulses with cultural and commercial activity day and night. It is also home to many bookstores, from the chains that sell bestsellers and offer English-language guidebooks, to independent bargain outlets and rare booksellers. The **Obelisco,** Buenos Aires's defining monument, marks the intersection of Corrientes with **Nueve de Julio.** Whenever locals have something to celebrate, this is where they gather.

MUSEUMS

Note that several of these museums are in the Recoleta area, which has no Metro stations.

El Museo Histórico Nacional (National History Museum) 🐾🐾 Argentine history from the 16th through the 19th centuries comes to life in the former Lezama family home. The expansive Italian-style mansion houses 30 rooms with items saved from Jesuit missions, paintings illustrating clashes between the Spaniards and Indians, and relics from the War of Independence against Spain. The focal point of the museum's collection is artist Cándido López's series of captivating scenes of the war against Paraguay in the 1870s.

Calle Defensa 1600. 🕐 11/4307-1182. Free admission. Tues–Sun noon–6pm. Closed Jan. Metro: Constitución.

Malba-Colección Constantini 🐾🐾🐾 The airy and luminescent Museo de Arte Latinoamericano de Buenos Aires (Malba) houses the private art collection of Eduardo Constantini. One of the most impressive collections of Latin American art anywhere, its temporary and permanent exhibitions showcase names like Antonio Berni, Pedro Figari, Frida Kahlo, Cândido Portinari, Diego Rivera, and Antonio Siguí. Many of the works confront social issues and explore questions of national identity. Even the benches are modern pieces of art, and the enormous atrium offers access to the various floors under a metal sculpture of a man doing pushups over the escalator bay. In addition to the art exhibitions, Latin films are held Tuesday through Sunday at 2pm and 10pm. This wonderful museum, which opened in late 2001, is located in Palermo Chico.

Av. Figueroa Alcorta 3415. 🕐 11/4808-6500. www.malba.org.ar. Admission $1.75. Free admission Wed. Wed–Mon noon–8pm. Closed Tues.

Museo Evita 🐾🐾🐾 It is almost impossible for non-Argentines to fathom that it took 50 years from the time of her death for Evita, the world's most famous Argentine, to finally get a museum. The Museo Evita opened July 26, 2002, in a mansion where her charity, the Eva Perón Foundation, once housed single mothers with children. While the museum treats her history fairly, looking at both the good and the bad, it is obvious that love is behind the presentation, and Evita's grandniece Cristina Álvarez Rodríguez is often in the building meeting with the staff. The museum divides Evita's life into several parts, looking at her childhood; her arrival in Buenos Aires to become an actress; her assumption as Evita, First Lady and unofficial saint to millions; and finally her death and legacy. You will be able to view her clothes, remarkably preserved by the military government, which took power after Perón. Other artifacts of her life include her voting card, as only through Evita did Argentine women gain the right to vote. There are also toys and schoolbooks adorned with her image, given to children to indoctrinate them with the Peronist ideology. The most touching artifact of all though is a smashed statue of Evita hidden for decades by a farmer in his barn, despite of the possibility of being jailed for housing it. Whether you hate, or love, or are indifferent to Evita, this is a museum that no visitor to Argentina should miss. Digesting the exhibits in this museum will help you truly understand why she remains such a controversial figure within the Argentine psyche.

Calle Lafinur 2988. 🕐 11/4807-9433. www.evitaperon.org. Admission $2. Tues–Sun 2–7:30pm. Closed Mon. Metro: Plaza Italia.

Museo Nacional de Arte Decorativo (National Museum of Decorative Art) ⚔

French architect Rene Sergent, who designed some of the grandest mansions in Buenos Aires, envisioned and developed this museum. The building's 18th-century French design provides a classical setting for the diverse decorative styles represented within. Breathtaking sculptures, paintings, and furnishings round off the collection, and themed shows rotate seasonally. The **Museo de Arte Oriental (Museum of Eastern Art)** displays art, pottery, and engravings on the first floor of the building. The building is itself a work of art and gives an idea of the incredible mansions that once lined the avenue, overlooking the extensive Palermo park system.

Av. del Libertador 1902. ℂ 11/4801-8248. Admission $1. Mon–Fri 2–8pm; Sat–Sun 11am–7pm.

Museo Nacional de Bellas Artes (National Museum of Fine Arts) ⚔⚔

This building that formerly pumped the city's water supply metamorphosed into Buenos Aires's most important art museum in 1930. The museum contains the world's largest collection of Argentine sculptures and paintings from the 19th and 20th centuries. It also houses European art dating from the pre-Renaissance period to the present day. The collections include notable pieces by Renoir, Monet, Rodin, Toulouse-Lautrec, and van Gogh, as well as a surprisingly extensive collection of Picasso drawings.

Av. del Libertador 1473. ℂ 11/4803-0802. Free admission. Tues–Sun 12:30–7:30pm.

OTHER ATTRACTIONS

Basílica y Convento de San Francisco (San Francisco's Church and Convent) ⚔

The San Roque parish is one of the oldest in the city. A Jesuit architect designed the church in 1730, but a final reconstruction in the early 20th century added a German baroque facade, along with statues of Saint Francis of Assisi, Dante, and Christopher Columbus. Inside you'll find a tapestry by Argentine artist Horacio Butler, along with an extensive library.

Calle Defensa and Alsina. ℂ 11/4331-0625. Free admission. Hours vary. Metro: Plaza de Mayo.

Biblioteca Nacional (National Library) ⚔

Opened in 1992, this modern architectural oddity stands on the land of the former Presidential Residence in which Eva Perón died. With its underground levels, the library's 13 floors can store up to five million volumes. Among its collection, the library stores 21 books printed by one of the earliest printing presses, dating from 1440 to 1500. Visit the reading room—occupying two stories at the top of the building—to enjoy an awe-inspiring view of Buenos Aires. The library also hosts special events in its exhibition hall and auditorium.

Calle Aguero 2502. ℂ 11/4807-0885. Free admission. Mon–Fri 9am–9pm; Sat–Sun noon–8pm.

Congreso (Congress) ⚔

The National Congress towers over Avenida de Mayo, forming the end of the Avenida de Mayo processional route, which begins at the president's Casa Rosada down the street. The capitol building, built in 1906, combines elements of classical Greek and Roman architecture and is topped with an immense central dome modeled after its counterpart in Washington, D.C. Today the building cannot accommodate the entire congressional staff, some of whom have spilled over into neighboring structures.

Plaza Congreso was designed in 1910 to frame the congress building and memorialize the centennial of a revolutionary junta that helped overthrow Spanish rule in Argentina. Stroll around the square and its surroundings to see a number of architectural landmarks, theaters, sidewalk cafes, and bars.

Plaza Congreso. Free hourly tours 11am–4pm. Metro: Congreso.

Teatro Colón (Colón Theater) ☆☆☆ *Moments*   Buenos Aires's golden age of prosperity gave birth to this luxurious opera house, which is one of the crowning visual delights of Nueve de Julio, though its true entrance faces a park on the opposite side of the building. Over the years, the theater has been graced by the likes of Enrico Caruso, Luciano Pavarotti, Julio Bocca, Maria Callas, Plácido Domingo, Arturo Toscanini, and Igor Stravinsky. Work began in 1880 and took close to 18 years to complete, largely because the first two architects died during the building process. The majestic building opened in 1908 and combines a variety of European styles, from the Ionic and Corinthian capitals and stained-glass pieces in the main entrance to the Italian marble staircase and French furniture, chandeliers, and vases in the Golden Hall. In the main theater—which seats 3,000 in orchestra seats, stalls, boxes, and four rises—an enormous chandelier hangs from the domed ceiling painted by Raúl Soldi in 1966 during a previous renovation. The theater's acoustics are world-renowned. In addition to hosting visiting performers, the Colón has its own philharmonic orchestra, choir, and ballet company. Opera and symphony seasons last from February to late December. **Guided tours,** which let you view the main theater, backstage, and costume and underground stage-design workshops, take place hourly between 11am and 3pm weekdays, and from 9am to noon Saturday. Call © 11/ 4378-7130 for information. Currently, tickets for events cannot be purchased more than 2 days in advance, but the management claims it will change this policy in 2005. The building is undergoing an ongoing renovation in preparation for its 100th anniversary and will be closed to the public for various periods in 2006 and 2007.

Calle Libertad 621 or Calle Toscanini 1180. © 11/4378-7100. www.teatrocolon.org.ar. Tour admission $2.50. Seating for events $2–$45. Metro: Tribunales.

SPECTATOR SPORTS & OUTDOOR ACTIVITIES

GOLF   Argentina has more than 200 golf courses. Closest to downtown are **Cancha de Golf de la Ciudad de Buenos Aires,** Av. Torquist 1426 and Olleros (© 11/4772-7261), 10 minutes from downtown with great scenery and a 71-par course; and **Jockey Club Argentino,** Av. Márquez 1700 (© 11/4743-1001), in San Isidro, which offers two courses (71 and 72 par) designed by Allister McKenzie.

HORSE RACING   Over much of the 20th century, Argentina was famous for its thoroughbreds. It continues to send prize horses to competitions around the world, although you can watch some of the best right here in Buenos Aires. Races take place at two tracks: **Hipódromo de San Isidro,** Av. Márquez 504 (© 11/4743-4010), and **Hipódromo Argentino de Palermo,** Av. del Libertador 4205 (© 11/4778-2839), in Palermo. Check the *Buenos Aires Herald* for race information.

POLO   Argentina has won more international polo tournaments than any other country, and the **Argentine Open Championship,** held late November through early December, is the world's most important polo event. Argentina has two seasons for polo: March through May and September through December, held at the **Campo Argentino de Polo,** Avenida del Libertador and Avenida Dorrego (© 11/4576-5600). Tickets can be purchased at the gate. Contact the **Asociación Argentina de Polo,** Hipólito Yrigoyen 636 (© 11/4331-4646 or 11/4342-8321), for information on polo schools and events. **La Martina Polo Ranch** (© 11/4576-7997), located 60km (37 miles) from Buenos Aires near the town of Vicente Casares, houses more than 80 polo horses, as well as a guest-house with a swimming pool and tennis courts.

SOCCER   One cannot discuss soccer in Argentina without paying homage to Diego Armando Maradona, Argentina's most revered player and one of the sport's great (if fallen) players. Any sense of national unity dissolves when Argentines watch their favorite clubs—River Plate, Boca Juniors, Racing Club, Independiente, and San Lorenzo—battle on Sunday. Passion for soccer could not run hotter, and you can catch a game at the **Estadio Boca Juniors,** Brandsen 805 (© **11/4362-2260**), in San Telmo, followed by raucous street parties. Ticket prices start at $3 and can be purchased in advance or at the gate.

5 Shopping

Porteños like to consider their city one of the fashion capitals of the world. Although the wealthiest Argentines still fly to Miami for their wardrobes, Buenos Aires boasts many of the same upscale stores you would find in New York or Paris. Do not expect to find a city full of indigenous textiles and crafts as you would elsewhere in Latin America; Hermès, Louis Vuitton, Versace, and Ralph Lauren are more on the mark in wealthy districts like Recoleta or Palermo. The European boutiques also sell much better-quality clothes than their Argentine counterparts, with the exception of furs, wool, and some leather goods, which are excellent across the country.

STORE HOURS & SHIPPING

Most stores are open weekdays from 9am to 8pm and Saturday from 9am until midnight, with some still closing for a few hours in the afternoon. You might find some shops open Sunday along Avenida Santa Fe, but few will be open on Calle Florida. Shopping centers are open daily from 10am to 10pm.

Certain art and antiques dealers will crate and ship bulky objects for an additional fee; others will tell you it's no problem to take that new sculpture directly on the plane. If you don't want to take any chances, contact **UPS** at © **800/222-2877** or **Federal Express** at © **810/333-3339.** Various stores participate in a tax-refund program for purchases over 70 pesos. In such a case, ask for a special receipt, which can entitle you to refund of the hefty 21% tax (IVA) when you leave the country.

GREAT SHOPPING AREAS

MICROCENTRO   Calle Florida, the pedestrian walking street in the microcenter, is home to wall-to-wall shops from Plaza San Martín past Avenida Corrientes. The **Galerías Pacífico** mall is located at Calle Florida 750 and Avenida Córdoba (© **11/4319-5100**), with a magnificent dome and stunning frescoes painted by local artists. Over 180 shops are open Monday through Saturday from 10am to 9pm and Sunday from noon to 9pm, with tango and folk-dancing shows held on Thursday at 8pm. As you approach Plaza San Martín from Calle Florida, you find a number of well-regarded shoe stores, jewelers, and shops selling leather goods.

RECOLETA   Avenida Alvear is Argentina's response to the Champs-Elysées, and—without taking the comparison too far—it is indeed an elegant, Parisian-like strip of European boutiques and cafes. Start your walk from Plaza Francia and continue from Junín to Cerrito. Along Calle Quintana, French-style mansions share company with upscale shops. Nearby **Patio Bullrich,** Av. del Libertador 750

(© **11/4814-7400**), is one of the city's best malls. Its 69 elegant shops are open daily from 10am to 9pm.

AVENIDA SANTA FE   Popular with local shoppers, Avenida Santa Fe offers a wide selection of clothing stores and more down-to-earth prices. You will also find bookstores, cafes, ice-cream shops, and cinemas. The **Alto Palermo Shopping Center,** Av. Santa Fe 3253 (© **11/5777-8000**), is another excellent shopping center, with 155 stores open daily from 10am to 10pm.

SAN TELMO & LA BOCA   These neighborhoods offer excellent antiques as well as artists' studios and arts and crafts celebrating tango. Street performers and artists are omnipresent. La Boca should be avoided at night.

OUTDOOR MARKETS

The **antiques market in San Telmo** 𝄢𝄢, which takes place every Sunday from 10am to 5pm at Plaza Dorrego, is a vibrant, colorful experience that will delight even the most jaded traveler. As street vendors sell their heirlooms, singers and dancers move amid the crowd to tango music. Among the 270-plus vendor stands, you will find antique silver objects, porcelain, crystal, and other antiques.

Plaza Serrano Fair is at the small plaza at the intersection of Calle Serrano and Honduras, which forms the heart of Palermo Hollywood. Bohemian arts and crafts are sold here while dread-headed locals sing and play guitars. Officially, it's held Saturday and Sunday from 10am to 6pm, but impromptu vendors set up at night, too, when the restaurants are crowded.

Recoleta Fair 𝄢𝄢, which takes place Saturday and Sunday in front of Recoleta Cemetery from 10am until sunset, offers every imaginable souvenir and craft, as well as food. This has become the city's largest fair, completely taking over all the walkways in the area—even the Iglesia Pilar gets involved. Live bands sometimes play on whatever part of the hill is not taken over by vendors.

La Boca Fair is open every day from 10am to 6pm or sundown. It's the most touristy of all the fairs, and most of the items are terribly overpriced. Still, if you need tacky souvenirs in a hurry, you can get all of your shopping done here quickly. Besides, tango singers and other street performers will keep your mind off the inflated prices. When the vendors start leaving at the end of the day, you should, too, for safety reasons.

SHOPPING A TO Z

Almost all shops in Buenos Aires accept credit cards. However, you will often get a better price if you offer to pay with cash. You won't be able to use credit cards at outdoor markets.

ANTIQUES

Throughout the streets of San Telmo, you will find the city's best antiques shops; don't miss the antiques market that takes place all day Sunday at Plaza Dorrego (see "Outdoor Markets," above). A number of fine antiques stores are scattered along Avenida Alvear in Recoleta, including a collection of boutique shops at **Galería Alvear,** Av. Alvear 1777.

Tips **Shopping Tip**

Most antiques stores will come down 10% to 20% from the listed price if you try to bargain.

Galería El Solar de French Built in the early 20th century in a Spanish colonial style, this is where Argentine patriot Domingo French lived. Today it's a gallery, with antiques shops and photography stores depicting the San Telmo of yesteryear. Calle Defensa 1066. Metro: Constitución.

Pallarols Located in San Telmo, Pallarols sells an exquisite collection of Argentine silver and other antiques. Calle Defensa 1015. © 11/4362-5438. Metro: Constitución.

ART GALLERIES
Galería Ruth Benzacar This avant-garde gallery, in a hidden underground space at the start of Calle Florida next to Plaza San Martín, hosts exhibitions of local and national interest. Among the best-known Argentines who have appeared here are Alfredo Prior, Miguel Angel Ríos, Daniel García, Graciela Hasper, and Pablo Siguier. Calle Florida 1000. © 11/4313-8480. Metro: San Martín.

FASHION & APPAREL
Palermo Soho is fast becoming the place for boutiques showcasing young designers who seem to have done well in spite of, or perhaps because of, the peso crisis. Women's fashion as a whole is flirty, fun, and, above all, feminine, made for a thin figure. You will find the city's top international fashion stores along Avenida Alvear and Calle Quintana in Recoleta, including **Gianni Versace** (Av. Alvear 1901), **Polo Ralph Lauren** (Av. Alvear 1780), and **Emporio Armani** (Av. Alvear 1750).

Ermenegildo Zegna The famous Italian chain sells outstanding suits and jackets made of light, cool fabrics. If you've landed in Buenos Aires without your suit, this is among your best options. Av. Alvear 1920. © 11/4804-1908.

Escada You can find casual and elegant selections of women's clothing combining quality and comfort in this boutique shop. Av. Alvear 1516. © 11/4815-0353.

JEWELRY
The city's finest jewelry stores are in Recoleta and inside many five-star hotels. You can find bargains on gold along Calle Libertad, near Avenida Corrientes.

Cousiño Jewels Located along the Sheraton hotel's shopping arcade, this Argentine jeweler features a brilliant collection of art made of the national stone, the rhodochrosite, or Inca Rose. In the Sheraton Buenos Aires Hotel, Av. San Martín. © 11/4318-9000. Metro: Retiro.

H.Stern This upscale Brazilian jeweler, with branches in major cities around the world, sells an entire selection of South American stones, including emeralds and the unique imperial topaz. It's the top jeweler in Latin America. Branches in the Marriott Plaza (© 11/4318-3083) and the Sheraton (© 11/4312-6762).

LEATHER
With all that beef in the restaurants, Argentina could not be anything but one of the world's best leather centers. If you're looking for high-quality, interestingly designed leather goods, especially women's shoes, accessories, and handbags, few places beat Buenos Aires's selection. Many leather stores will also custom-make jackets and other items for interested customers, so do ask if you see something you like in the wrong size or want to combine ideas from pieces.

Casa López Widely considered the best *marroquinería* (leather goods shop) in Buenos Aires, Casa López sells an extensive range of Argentine leather products. The Patio Bullrich Mall has another branch. Marcelo T. de Alvear 640. © 11/4312-8911. Metro: San Martín.

El Nochero All the products sold at El Nochero are made with first-rate Argentine leather and manufactured by local workers. Shoes and boots, leather goods and clothes, and native silverware (including *mates*) decorate the store. Posadas 1245, in the Patio Bullrich Mall. (℃ 11/4815-3629.

Louis Vuitton The famous Parisian boutique sells an elite line of luggage, purses, and travel bags. It's located alongside Recoleta's most exclusive shops. Av. Alvear 1751. (℃ 11/4813-7072.

Rossi & Caruso This store offers the best leather products in the city and is the first choice for visiting celebrities—the king and queen of Spain and Prince Philip of England among them. Products include luggage, saddles and accessories, leather and chamois clothes, purses, wallets, and belts. The Galerías Pacífico Mall contains another branch. Av. Santa Fe 1601. (℃ 11/4811-1965. Metro: Bulnes.

WINE SHOPS

Argentine wineries, particularly those in Mendoza and Salta, produce some excellent wines. Stores selling Argentina wines abound, and three of the best are **Grand Cru,** Av. Alvear 1718; **Tonel Privado,** in the Patio Bullrich Shopping Mall; and **Winery,** which has branches at L.N. Alem 880 and Av. Del Libertador 500, both downtown.

6 Buenos Aires After Dark

From the Teatro Colón (Colón Theater) to dimly lit tango salons, Buenos Aires offers an exceptional variety of nightlife. Porteños eat late and play later, with theater performances starting around 9pm, bars and nightclubs opening around midnight, and no one showing up until after 1am. Thursday, Friday, and Saturday are the big going-out nights, with the bulk of activity in Recoleta, Palermo, and Costanera. Summer is quieter because most of the town flees to the coast.

Performing arts in Buenos Aires are centered on the highly regarded Teatro Colón, home to the National Opera, National Symphony, and National Ballet. In addition, the city boasts nearly 40 professional theaters (many located along Av. Corrientes between Nueve de Julio and Callao and in the San Telmo and Abasto neighborhoods) showing Broadway- and off-Broadway-style hits, Argentine plays, and music reviews, although most are in Spanish. Buy tickets for most productions at the box office or through **Ticketmaster** (℃ 11/4321-9700). The **British Arts Centre,** Suipacha 1333 (℃ 11/4393-0275), offers productions in English.

For current information on after-dark entertainment, consult the *Buenos Aires Herald* (in English) or any of the major local publications. The "QuickGuide Buenos Aires" also has information on shows, theaters, and nightclubs.

THE PERFORMING ARTS
OPERA, BALLET & CLASSICAL MUSIC

Luna Park Once the home of international boxing matches, the Luna is the largest indoor stadium in Argentina and hosts the biggest shows and concerts in Buenos Aires. Many of these are classical music concerts, and the National Symphonic Orchestra often plays here. Av. Corrientes and Bouchard. (℃ 11/4311-1990. Metro: L.N. Alem.

Teatro Colón Known across the world for its impeccable acoustics, the Colón has attracted the world's finest opera performers—Luciano Pavarotti, Julio Bocca, Maria Callas, Plácido Domingo, and Arturo Toscanini among them. Opera season runs from April to November, and the Colón has its own

Moments   Tango: Lessons in the Dance of Seduction & Despair

It seems impossible to imagine Argentina without thinking of tango, its greatest export to the world. Tango originated with a guitar and violin toward the end of the 19th century and was first danced by working-class men in La Boca, San Telmo, and the port area. Combining African rhythms with the *habanera* and *candombe*, it was not the sophisticated dance you know today—rather, the tango originated in brothels, known locally as *quilombos*. It was considered too obscene for women, and as they waited their turn, men would dance it with each other in the brothel lounges.

Increasing waves of immigrants added Italian elements and helped the tango make its way to Europe, however, and the dance was internationalized in Paris. With a sense of European approval, the Argentine middle and upper classes began to accept the newly refined dance as part of their cultural identity, and the form blossomed under the extraordinary voice of Carlos Gardel, who brought tango to Broadway and Hollywood, and is nothing short of legendary among Argentines. Astor Piazzola further internationalized the tango, elevating it to a more complex form incorporating classical elements.

Tango may be played by anywhere from two musicians to a complete orchestra, but a piano and *bandoneón*—an instrument akin to an accordion—are usually included. If there is a singer, the lyrics might come from one of Argentina's great poets, such as Jorge Luis Borges, Homero Manzi, or Horacio Ferrer. Themes focus on a downtrodden life or a woman's betrayal, making it akin to American jazz and blues, which developed at the same time. The dance itself is improvised rather than standardized, although it consists of a series of long walks and intertwined movements, usually in eight-step. In the tango, the man and woman glide across the floor as an exquisitely orchestrated duo with early flirtatious movements giving way to dramatic leads and heartfelt turns, with the man always leading the way. These movements, such as

philharmonic orchestra, ballet, and choir companies. The main theater seats 2,500. Calle Libertad 621. (© **11/4378-7100.** Metro: Tribunales.

THEATERS & EXHIBITIONS

The city's best theater takes place at the **Teatro Nacional Cervantes,** Calle Libertad 815 (© **11/4816-4224**). **Teatro Opera,** Av. Corrientes 860 (© **11/4326-1335**), has been adapted for Broadway-style shows. The **Teatro Municipal General San Martín,** Av. Corrientes 1530 (© **0800/333-5254**), has three theaters offering drama, comedy, ballet, music, and children's plays. In Recoleta, **Teatro Coliseo,** Marcelo T. de Alvear 1125 (© **11/4816-5943**), presents classical music productions. **Teatro Presidente Alvear,** Av. Corrientes 1659 (© **11/4374-6076**), features tango and other music shows. The majority of foreign and national music concerts are held at the **Teatro Gran Rex,** Av. Corrientes 857 (© **11/4322-8000**).

the kicks which simulate knife movements, or the sliding, shuffled feet that mimic the walk of a gangster silently walking up to murder someone, belie the dance's rough roots even though the tango you will see performed today is undeniably beautiful.

Learning to dance the tango is an excellent way for a visitor to get a sense of what makes the music—and the dance—so alluring. Entering a tango salon—called a *salon de baile*—can be intimidating for the novice. The style of tango danced in salons is more subdued than "show tango." Most respectable dancers would not show up before midnight, giving you the perfect opportunity to sneak in for a group lesson, offered at most of the salons starting around 8 or 9pm. They usually cost between $1 and $3 for an hour; you can request private instruction for between $10 and $20 per hour, depending on the instructor. In summer, the city of Buenos Aires promotes tango by offering free classes in many locations. Visit the nearest tourist information center for updated information.

For additional advice on places to dance and learn tango, get a copy of *B.A. Tango* or *El Tangauta,* the city's dedicated tango magazines. One of the best spots to learn is **Gricel,** La Rioja 1180 (© **11/4957-7157**), which offers lessons Monday through Friday at 8pm and opens its doors to the city's best dancers on Saturday and Sunday nights. **La Galería,** Boedo 722 (© **11/4957-1829**), is open Thursday, Saturday, and Sunday and attracts excellent dancers, many of whom compete professionally. **Café Ideal,** Suipacha 384 (© **11/4326-1081**), has tango shows on Monday, Wednesday, and Friday afternoons. The dancers here come in all ages and have varied abilities. Ongoing evening lessons are also offered at the **Academia Nacional de Tango,** located above Café Tortoni at Av. de Mayo 833 (© **11/4345-6968**), which is an institute rather than a tango salon.

Centro Cultural Recoleta (Recoleta Cultural Center) ☞   The distinctive building—originally designed as a Franciscan convent—hosts Argentine and international art exhibits, experimental theater works, occasional music concerts, and an interactive science museum for children called Museo de Tocar, where children are encouraged to touch and play with the displays. The Hard Rock Cafe is located behind the Cultural Center in the Recoleta Design Shopping Center. Junín 1930. © **11/4803-1041.**

THE CLUB & MUSIC SCENE
TANGO CLUBS
In Buenos Aires, you can *watch* the tango or *dance* the tango. You'll have many opportunities to see the dance during your visit: Tango and *milonga* dancers frequent the streets of La Boca and San Telmo, some hotels offer tango shows in their lobbies and bars, and tango salons blanket the city. The most famous (besides Café Tortoni) are in San Telmo and combine dinner and a show. Have

a radio-taxi or *remise* take you to San Telmo, La Boca, or Barracas at night rather than taking the Metro or walking.

Café Tortoni High-quality yet inexpensive tango shows are held in the back room of the Café Tortoni and do not include dinner. Shows are every day at 9pm except Tuesday. Av. de Mayo 829. ℭ **11/4342-4328.** Metro: Plaza de Mayo.

El Querandí El Querandí offers the best historically based tango show in the city, showing it from its early bordello roots when only men danced it, to its current leggy, sexy style. You'll also get a great slab of beef and a glass of wine with the show. Open Monday through Saturday; dinner begins at 8:30pm, followed by the show at 10:15pm. Perú 302. ℭ **11/4345-0331.**

El Viejo Almacén The most famous of the city's tango salons, the Almacén offers what some consider the city's most authentic performance. Shows involve traditional Argentine-style tango (many other shows feature international-style tango). Sunday through Thursday shows are at 10pm; Friday and Saturday shows are at 9:30 and 11:45pm. Dinner is served each night before the show starts in the three-story restaurant across the street (guests may opt for dinner-show or show only). Transportation is offered from some hotels. Independencia and Balcarce. ℭ **11/4307-6689.**

Esquina Carlos Gardel One of the most elegant tango spots, Esquina Carlos Gardel lies in the same location where "Chanta Cuatro"—a restaurant where Carlos Gardel used to dine with his friends—was located, though it is actually a new building built from the ground up. The luxurious old-time-style dining room features high-tech acoustics and superb dancers, creating a wonderful tango environment. Doors open at 8pm. Carlos Gardel 3200. ℭ **11/4876-6363.**

Señor Tango This enormous theater is more akin to a Broadway production hall than a traditional tango salon, but the dancers are fantastic and the owner, who clearly loves to perform, is a good singer. The walls are decorated with photos of what appear to be every celebrity who's ever visited Buenos Aires—and all seem to have made it to Señor Tango! Diners choose among steak, chicken, or fish for dinner, and, despite the huge crowd, the food quality is commendable. Have dinner or come only for the show (dinner is at 8:30pm; shows start at 10pm). Vieytes 1653. ℭ **11/4303-0212.**

OTHER DANCE CLUBS

Dancing in Buenos Aires is not just about tango; the majority of the younger population prefers salsa and European beats. Of course, nothing in life changes quite so fast as the "in" discos, so ask around for the latest hot spots. The biggest nights out are Thursday, Friday, and Saturday. Here are some of the hottest clubs as this book went to press: **Opera Bay,** Cecilia Grierson 225 in Puerto Madero (no phone), boasts the top spot among the city's clubs, attracting an affluent and fashionable crowd. Built along the waterfront and resembling the Sydney opera house, Opera Bay features an international restaurant, tango show, and disco. The city's best salsa dancers head to **Salsón,** Av. Alvarez Thomas 1166 (ℭ **11/4637-6970**), which offers lessons on Wednesday and Friday at 9pm. In Palermo, **Buenos Aires News,** Av. del Libertador 3883 (ℭ **11/4778-1500**), is a rocking late-night club with Latin and European mixes. **Chicharron Disco Bar,** Bartolomo Mitre 1849 (ℭ **11/4373-4884**), is a wild Dominican salsa club that mostly packs in locals who have relocated to Buenos Aires from the Caribbean. **Tequila,** Costanera Norte and La Pampa (ℭ **11/4788-0438**), is packed every night. A number of popular discos are also nearby. Ladies who just want to dance and avoid lechery should head to **Mambo,** Báez 243 (© 11/4778-0115), in Las Cañitas where most patrons are groups of friends. The most popular gay and lesbian club is **Amerika,** Gascón 1040 (© **11/4865-4416;** www.mambo bar.com.ar), which has three floors of dance music and all-you-can-drink specials on Friday and Saturday. Straight Porteños come often too, claiming it has the city's best music. **Palacio,** Alsina 934, is giving it a run for the money but is open only on Friday.

THE BAR SCENE

Buenos Aires has no shortage of popular bars, and Porteños need little excuse to party. The following are only a few of many bars and pubs worthy of recommendation. Strolling along, you'll find plenty on your own.

Chandon Bar   This intimate champagne lounge serves bottles and flutes of Chandon, produced in both France and Argentina. Located in Puerto Madero adjacent to some of the city's best restaurants, Chandon is perfect for a before- or after-dinner drink. Light fare is offered as well. Av. Alicia Moreau de Justo 152. © 11/4315-3533. Metro: L.N. Alem.

Gran Bar Danzon   A small, intimate bar, Danzon attracts a fashionable crowd. An excellent barman serves exquisite cocktails, and a small selection of international food is offered as well. Smart, relaxing lounge music is played at night. Libertad 1161. © 11/4811-1108.

Henry J. Beans   A favorite of the expat-American community and visiting foreigners, this casual Recoleta bar serves burgers, sandwiches, and nachos, along with cocktails and beer. Old Coca-Cola ads, Miller and Budweiser neon signs, and model airplanes hang from the ceilings. The waiters do occasional impromptu dances, and the place is packed after midnight. A number of other popular restaurants, bars, and discos are strung along Junín. Junín 1749. © 11/4801-8477.

The Kilkenny   This trendy cafe-bar is more like a rock house than an Irish pub, although you will still be able to order Guinness, Kilkenny, and Harp draft beers. It's packed with both locals and foreigners; you are as likely to find people in suits and ties as in jeans and T-shirts. The Kilkenny offers happy hour from 6 to 8pm and live bands every night after midnight; it stays open until 5am. Marcelo T. de Alvear 399. © 11/4312-9179 or 11/4312-7291. Metro: San Martín.

Plaza Bar   Nearly every Argentine president and his cabinet have come here, in addition to visiting celebs such as the queen of Spain, the emperor of Japan, Luciano Pavarotti, and David Copperfield. The English-style bar features mahogany furniture and velvet upholstery, where guests can sip martinis and smoke Cuban cigars. Tuxedo-clad waiters recommend a fine selection of whiskeys and brandies. Marriott Plaza Hotel, Calle Florida 1005. © 11/4318-3000. Metro: San Martín.

Plaza Dorrego Bar ⚓   Representative of a typical Porteño bar from the 19th century, Plaza Dorrego displays portraits of Carlos Gardel, antique liquor bottles in cases along the walls, and anonymous writings engraved in the wood. Stop by on Sunday, when you can catch the San Telmo antiques market on the plaza in front and the crowd spills onto the street. Calle Defensa 1098. © 11/4361-0141. Metro: Constitución.

The Shamrock   The city's best-known Irish pub is somewhat lacking in authenticity; you're more likely to hear hot Latin rhythms than soft Gaelic music here. That said, it remains hugely popular with both Argentines and foreign visitors, and is a great spot to begin the night. Rodríguez Peña 1220. © 11/4812-3584. Metro: Callao.

4

Side Trips from Buenos Aires

1 Mar del Plata, Argentina

400km (248 miles) south of Buenos Aires

Argentina's most popular beach resort is a sleepy coastal town until mid-December, when Porteños flock here through March for summer vacation. Although not as luxurious as Uruguay's Punta del Este—the beach favorite of many jet-setting Argentines—Mar del Plata is closer to Buenos Aires and far cheaper to stay in. Its long, windy coastline offers beaches crowded with tanned bodies and quieter seaside coves, as well as beautiful landscapes farther inland leading to the Pampas. Within Mar del Plata, a number of high-rise developments, products of the Perón era, sadly have replaced much of the city's earlier charm. However, some of the magnificent French-style residences, which housed Argentina's summer elites in the early 20th century, have been meticulously preserved as museums. Mar del Plata offers excellent nightlife in summer, when independent theater companies from Buenos Aires travel to this seaside resort and nightclubs open their doors to passionate Latin party-goers.

ESSENTIALS

GETTING THERE   You can reach Mar del Plata by plane, bus, car, train, or boat. The airport lies 10 minutes from downtown and is served by **Aerolíneas Argentinas** (jets) and **Aerovip** (prop planes). The RN 2 is the main highway from Buenos Aires; it takes about 4 to 5 hours to drive to Mar del Plata. More than 50 bus companies link the city with the rest of the country. Buses to Buenos Aires, which leave from the central bus terminal at Alberti 1602 (© **223/451-5406**), are comfortable and cost under $15 each way. A train also connects Mar del Plata with Buenos Aires and is only slightly more expensive than buses. Purchase tickets at the train station, located at Avenida Luro and Italia (© **223/475-6076**). Both bus and train trips take about 4 to 5 hours.

VISITOR INFORMATION   The **Centro de Información Turística,** Bulevar Marítimo P.P. Ramos 2270, at the Casino building (© **223/495-1777**), has a knowledgeable, helpful staff offering maps and suggested itineraries. It is open daily from 10am to 5pm (until 8pm in summer). A branch can also be found at the airport. You can visit their website at www.mardelplata.gov.ar.

GETTING AROUND   La Rambla marks the heart of the city, the seaside walk in front of the Casino and main city beach. Farther south, the Los Tronces neighborhood houses the city's most prominent residences as well as Playa Grande (the main beach), the Sheraton hotel, and the Mar del Plata Golf Club. Mar del Plata has 47km (29 miles) of Atlantic coastline, so if you plan to leave your hotel area, you'll need to take a taxi or rent a car. **Avis** (© **223/470-2100**) rents cars at the airport.

WHAT TO SEE & DO

People come first and foremost to Mar del Plata for the beaches, the best of which is **Playa Grande.** A long cluster of cliffs and dunes lead to more serene southern beaches. With long, slow breaks, **Waikiki** is the best spot for surfing. The coastline is nice, but you should not come expecting to find the Caribbean—the Atlantic remains fairly cold, even during summer. Once you've brushed off the sand, visit the **fishing harbor,** where hundreds of red and yellow boats unload their daily catches. The harbor houses a colony of about 800 male sea lions that come to bathe on the rocky shores. Next to the colony lies an ugly but intriguing boat graveyard, where rusty boats have been left to rest. The harbor also offers the town's best seafood restaurants. In the Los Troncos neighborhood, **Villa Victoria,** at Matheu 1851 (𝄐 223/492-0569), showcases the early-20th-century summer house—all of which came from England—of a wealthy Argentine writer, Victoria Ocampo. Some of Argentina's greatest authors have stayed here, including Jorge Luis Borges. In summer, musical and theatrical performances are held in the gardens. Nearby, **Villa Ortiz Basualdo,** Av. Colón 1189 (𝄐 223/486-1636), resembles a Loire castle and is decorated with exquisite Art Nouveau furniture from Belgium. In the same neighborhood, the **Museo del Mar,** Av. Colón 1114 (𝄐 223/451-9779), shelters a collection of 30,000 seashells. Twenty minutes from the city center, **De los Padres Lake and Hills** is a picturesque forest with wide parks surrounding the lake, perfect for an afternoon picnic. Nearby, the **Zoo el Paraíso,** Route 266, Km 16.5 (𝄐 223/463-0347), features a wonderful collection of flora and fauna, including plants and trees from all over Argentina, as well as lions, pumas, monkeys, llamas, and other animals. For information on surfing, deep-sea fishing, mountain biking, horseback riding, trekking, and other adventure sports, contact the tourism office.

WHERE TO STAY

Sheraton 𝄐𝄐   It may not be the most modern Sheraton, but it is the city's best hotel by far. Built on a golf course, the Sheraton faces the ocean and is a quick hop to Mar del Plata's best beach, Playa Grande. The fishing harbor is also just down the road. A full-scale heath club leads out to the beautiful pool, next to which is a small outdoor cafe. Rooms are light-filled and well-equipped; suites have Jacuzzi tubs. The staff will help you arrange outdoor activities, including a tee time, upon request.

Alem 4221, 7600 Mar del Plata. 𝄐 0800/777-7002 or 223/499-9000. Fax 223/499-0009. 193 units. $129 double with city view; $150 double with ocean view. Rates include buffet breakfast. AE, DC, MC, V. **Amenities:** Restaurant; bar; health club with heated outdoor pool; golf; concierge; business center; room service; massage; babysitting; laundry service; dry-cleaning service. *In room:* A/C, TV, minibar, hair dryer, safe.

WHERE TO DINE

La Marca 𝄐𝄐 ARGENTINE   A few times a year, the chefs here cook an entire cow for a mesmerized dining room. The rest of the year, La Marca simply acts as the town's best *parrilla,* serving thick rump steaks, tenderloins, barbecued ribs of beef, flanks, and every other cut of meat you can think of. The tender filet mignon with mushroom sauce is delicious. Pork chops, sausages, sweetbread, black pudding, and other delights are on the menu as well. An extensive salad bar allows you to eat something other than protein. Service is polite and unhurried. Make sure to try the *dulce de leche* before you leave.

Almafuerte 253. 𝄐 223/451-8072. Main courses $3–$6. AE, DC, MC, V. Daily noon–3pm and 8:30pm–1am.

MAR DEL PLATA AFTER DARK

Nightlife follows closely behind beaches as Mar del Plata's biggest draw. In summer, theater companies leave Buenos Aires to perform in this coastal resort; ask the tourism office for a schedule of performance times and places. The city's most popular bars are located south of Plaza Mitre. The best dance clubs are along Avenida Constitución, 3km (2 miles) from downtown, including **Chocolate,** Constitución 4451 (© **223/479-4848**). The other top clubs are: **Divino Beach,** Paseo Costanero Sur Presidente Illia (© **223/467-1506**); **Go!,** Av. Constitución 5780 (© **223/479-6666**); and **Sobremonte,** Av. Constitución 6690 (© **223/479-7930**). **Amsterdam,** Castilli 3045 (© **15/527-8606**), is the best gay disco. **Coyote,** Av. Constitución 6670 (© **223/479-7930**), is a favorite local bar which breaks into salsa and merengue as the night goes on.

2 An Introduction to Uruguay

Just across the Rio de la Plata from Buenos Aires lies the second-smallest nation in South America. But while Uruguay is a little place, it certainly makes a big impression. With an impressive living standard, high literacy rate, large urban middle class, and excellent social services—including the best medical care system in South America—it has become a model for other developing countries in the region. Despite its homogeneous population (mostly of European descent), Uruguay reveals splendid contrasts. This is a land of dusty colonial towns and sparkling beach resorts, of rough-and-ready gauchos and subtle artists and festive plazas. Uruguay is a place where soccer *(fútbol)* is worshipped without reserve, where the sun shines brightly and the air stays warm, where few question the dignity of their homeland. And despite the economic troubles of recent years, Uruguay remains a proud and peaceful nation.

Porteños (as residents of Buenos Aires are called) take the ferry over to Montevideo for the day to shop and to dine. Montevideo is the cultural heartland of Uruguay, a vibrant city where you can discover the bold accomplishments of Uruguay music, art, and literature. Outside the capital, pastureland and rolling hills draw your attention to a softer, quieter life. But this rural lifestyle stops at the coast, where world-class resorts centered around glitzy Punta del Este lure the continent's rich and famous. Porteños by the thousands descend on Punta during summer weekends. For a grander, quieter side trip, consider lovely Colonia del Sacramento, a UNESCO World Heritage City, only an hour away from Buenos Aires.

ENTRY REQUIREMENTS & CUSTOMS

Citizens of the United States, the United Kingdom, Canada, and New Zealand need only a passport to enter Uruguay (for tourist stays of up to 90 days). Australian citizens must get a tourist visa before arrival.

URUGUAYAN EMBASSY LOCATIONS

In the U.S.: 2715 M St. NW, 3rd Floor, Washington, DC 20007 (© **202/331-1313;** fax 202/331-8142; www.embassy.org/uruguay).

In Canada: 130 Albert St., Suite 1905, Ottawa, ON K1P 5G4 (© **613/234-2727;** fax 613/233-4670; www.iosphere.net/~uruott).

In the U.K.: 140 Brompton Rd., 2nd Floor, London SW3 1HY (© **207/589-8835**).

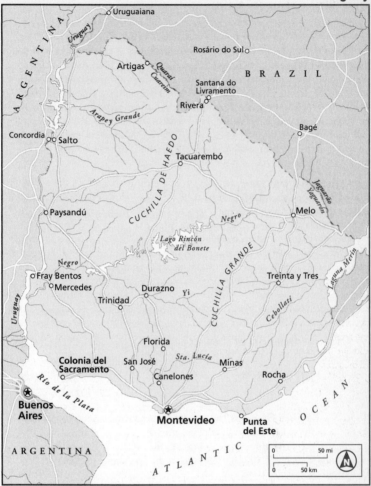

MONEY

The official currency is the **Uruguayan peso** (designated NP$, $U, or simply
$); each peso is comprised of 100 **centavos.** Uruguayan pesos are available in
$10, $20, $50, $100, $200, $500, $1,000, and $5,000 notes; coins come in 10,
20, and 50 centavos, and 1 and 2 pesos. The Uruguayan currency devalued by
half in July 2002, and the exchange rate as this book went to press was approximately 26 pesos to the dollar. The value of the peso fluctuates greatly with inflation, so all prices in this chapter are quoted in U.S. dollars.

3 Montevideo

210km (130 miles) east of Buenos Aires

Montevideo, the southernmost capital on the continent, is home to half the
country's population. On the banks of the Río de la Plata, Montevideo first
existed as a fortress of the Spanish Empire and developed into a major port city
in the mid–18th century. European immigrants, including Spanish, Portuguese,

French, and British, influenced the city's architecture, and a walk around the capital reveals architectural styles ranging from colonial to Art Deco. Indeed, the richness of Montevideo's architecture is unrivaled in South America.

Although Montevideo has few must-see attractions, its charm lies in wait for the careful traveler. A walk along La Rambla, stretching from the Old City to the neighborhood of Carrasco, takes you along the riverfront past fishermen and their catch to parks and gardens where children play and elders sip *mate* (a tealike beverage). Restaurants, cafes, bars, and street performers populate the port area, where you will also discover the flavors of Uruguay at the afternoon and weekend Mercado del Puerto, or Port Market. Many of the city's historic sites surround Plaza Independencia and can be visited in a few hours.

ESSENTIALS
GETTING THERE
International flights and those from Buenos Aires land at **Carrasco International Airport** (*©* **02/604-0386**), located 19km (12 miles) from downtown Montevideo. Uruguay's national carrier is **Pluna,** Colonia and Julio Herrera (*©* **0800/118-811** or 02/604-4080), which operates several flights daily from Aeroparque. **Aerolíneas Argentinas** (*©* **02/901-9466**) connects both Aeroparque and Ezeiza with Montevideo; the flight takes 50 minutes. The fare ranges between $140 and $220 round-trip, depending on how far in advance you make reservations.

A taxi or *remise* (private, unmetered taxi) from the airport to downtown costs about $15.

BY BOAT OR HYDROFOIL   The most popular way to get to Montevideo, **Buquebús,** Calle Río Negro 1400 (*©* **02/916-8801**), operates three to four hydrofoils per day from Buenos Aires; the trip takes about 2½ hours and costs about $90 round-trip. Montevideo's port is about 1.5km (1 mile) from downtown.

BY BUS   **Terminal Omnibus Tres Cruces,** General Artigas 1825 (*©* **02/409-7399**), is Montevideo's long-distance bus terminal, connecting the capital with cities in Uruguay and throughout South America. Buses to Buenos Aires take about 8 hours. **COT** (*©* **02/409-4949**) offers the best service to Punta del Este, Maldonado, and Colonia.

ORIENTATION
Montevideo is surrounded by water on three sides, a testament to its earlier incarnation as an easily defended fortress for the Spanish Empire. The Old City begins near the western edge of Montevideo, found on the skinny portion of a peninsula between the Rambla Gran Bretaña and the city's main artery, Avenida 18 de Julio. Look for the Plaza Independencia and the Plaza Constitución to find the center of the district. Many of the city's museums, theaters, and hotels reside in this historic area, although a trip east on Avenida 18 de Julio reveals the more modern Montevideo with its own share of hotels, markets, and monuments. Along the city's long southern coastline runs the Rambla Gran Bretaña, traveling 21km (13 miles) from the piers of the Old City past Parque Rodó and on to points south and east, passing fish stalls and street performers along the way.

GETTING AROUND
It's easy to navigate around the center of Montevideo on foot or by bus. Safe, convenient buses crisscross Montevideo if you want to venture outside the city

Montevideo

ATTRACTIONS ●
Catedral **3**
El Cabildo **4**
Museo de Arte
  Contemporáneo **10**
Museo Municipal
  de Bellas Artes
  "Juan Manuel Blanes" **12**
Palacio Salvo **8**
Palacio Taranco **2**
Plaza Independencia **5**

ACCOMMODATIONS ■
Belmont House **14**
Days Inn Obelisco **13**
Holiday Inn **7**
Radisson Montevideo **6**
Victoria Plaza Hotel
Sheraton Montevideo **15**

DINING ◆
Arcadia **5**
El Fogón **11**
El Viejo y El Mar **16**
Las Brasas **9**
Río Alegre **1**

(ℹ) Information

Río de la Plata

0.25 mi
0.25 km

center (for less than $1 per trip). Taxis are safe and relatively inexpensive but can be difficult to hail during rush hour. One recommended company is **Remises Carrasco** (© **09/440-5473**). To rent a car, try **Thrifty** (© **02/204-3373**). For roadside emergencies or general information on driving in Uruguay, contact the **Automóvil Club de Uruguay,** Av. Libertador 1532 (© **02/902-4792**), or the **Centro Automovilista del Uruguay,** E.V. Haedo 2378 (© **02/408-2091**).

VISITOR INFORMATION

Uruguay's **Ministerio de Turismo** is at Av. Libertador 1409 and Colonia (© **02/ 908-9105**). It assists travelers with countrywide information and is open daily from 8am to 8pm in winter, from 8am to 2pm in summer. There's also a branch at Carrasco International Airport and Tres Cruces bus station. The **municipal tourist office,** Explanada Municipal (© **1950**), offers city maps and brochures of tourist activities and is open weekdays from 11am to 6pm, weekends from 10am to 6pm. It also organizes cultural city tours on weekends.

FAST FACTS: Montevideo

Area Code The country code for Uruguay is **598**; the city code for Montevideo is **2**.

ATMs ATMs are plentiful; look for **Bancomat** and **Redbrou** banks. Most have access to the Cirrus network.

Currency Exchange To exchange money, try **Turisport Limitada** (the local Amex representative), San José 930 (© **02/902-0829**); **Gales Casa Cambiaria,** Av. 18 de Julio 1046 (© **02/902-0229**); or one of the airport exchanges.

Embassies & Consulates United States Embassy, Lauro Muller 1776, Montevideo 11100 (© **02/408-7777**); British Embassy, Marco Bruto No. 1073, P.O. Box 16024, Montevideo 11300 (© **02/622-3630**); Canadian Embassy, Edificio Torre Libertad, Plaza Cagancha 1335, Office 1105, Montevideo 11100 (© **02/902-2030**).

Hospital The **British Hospital** is located at Av. Italia 2420 (© **02/487-1020**) and has emergency room services.

Internet Access Internet cafes appear and disappear faster than discos, but you won't walk long before coming across one in the city center. Reliable cybercafes include **El Cybercafé,** Calle 25 de Mayo 568; **Arroba del Sur,** Guayabo 1858; and **El Cybercafé Softec,** Santiago de Chile 1286. The average cost is $2 per hour of usage.

Post Office The main post office is at Calle Buenos Aires 451 (© **0810/444- CORREO**) and is open weekdays from 9am to 6pm.

Safety Although Montevideo remains very safe by big city standards, street crime has risen in recent years. Travelers should avoid walking alone, particularly at night, in Ciudad Vieja, Avenida 18 de Julio, Plaza Independencia, and the vicinity around the port. Take a taxi instead.

WHAT TO SEE & DO

Catedral ⍟   Also known as Iglesia Matriz (Matriz Church), the cathedral was the city's first public building, erected in 1804. It houses the remains of some of

Uruguay's most important political, religious, and economic figures, and is distinguished by its domed bell towers.

Calle Sarandí at Ituzaingó. Free admission. Mon–Fri 8am–8pm.

El Cabildo (Town Hall) ⚘   Uruguay's constitution was signed in the old town hall, which also served as the city's jailhouse in the 19th century. Now a museum, the Cabildo houses the city's historic archives as well as maps and photos, antiques, costumes, and artwork.

Juan Carlos Gómez 1362. ℭ 02/915-9685. Free admission. Tues–Sun 2:30–7pm.

Museo de Arte Contemporáneo (Museum of Contemporary Art) ⚘ Opened in 1997, this museum is dedicated to contemporary Uruguayan art and exhibits the country's biggest names. To promote cultural exchange across the region, a section of the museum has been set aside for artists who hail from various South American countries.

Av. 18 de Julio 965, 2nd floor. ℭ 02/900-6662. Free admission. Daily noon–8pm.

Museo Municipal de Bellas Artes "Juan Manuel Blanes" (Municipal Museum of Fine Arts) ⚘   The national art history museum displays Uruguayan artistic styles from the beginning of the nation to the present day. Works include oils, engravings, drawings, sculptures, and documents. Among the great Uruguayan artists exhibited are Juan Manuel Blanes, Pedro Figari, Rafael Barradas, José Cúneo, and Carlos Gonzales.

Av. Millán 4015. ℭ 02/336-2248. Free admission. Tues–Sun 2–7pm.

Palacio Salvo (Salvo Palace) ⚘   Often referred to as the symbol of Montevideo, the Salvo Palace was once the tallest building in South America. Although its 26 stories might not impress you, it remains the city's highest structure.

Plaza Independencia.

Palacio Taranco (Taranco Palace) ⚘   Now the decorative arts museum, the Taranco Palace was built in the early 20th century and represents the trend toward French architecture during that period. The museum displays Uruguayan furniture, draperies, clocks, paintings, and other cultural works.

Calle 25 de Mayo 379. ℭ 02/915-1101. Free admission. Tues–Sat 10am–6pm.

Plaza Independencia ⚘⚘   Originally the site of a Spanish citadel, Independence Square marks the beginning of the Old City and is a good point from which to begin your tour of Montevideo. An enormous statue of Gen. José Gervasio Artigas, father of Uruguay and hero of its independent movement, stands in the center. His ashes are displayed in a mausoleum under the monument.

Bordered by Av. 18 de Julio, Florida, and Juncal.

Teatro Solís ⚘⚘   Montevideo's main theater and opera house, opened in 1852, completed an extensive renovation a few years back. It hosts Uruguay's most important cultural events and is the site of the **Museo Nacional de Historia Natural (National Museum of Natural History).**

Calle Buenos Aires 652. ℭ 02/916-0908. Free admission. Museum Mon–Fri 2–6pm.

SHOPPING
MARKETS   The **Villa Biarritz fair** at Parque Zorilla de San Martín-Ellauri takes place Saturday from 9:30am to 3pm and features handicrafts, antiques, books, fruit and vegetable vendors, flowers, and other goodies. The **Mercado**

del Puerto (Port Market) ✿ opens afternoons and weekends at Piedras and Yacaré, letting you sample the flavors of Uruguay, from small empanadas to enormous barbecued meats. Saturday is the best day to visit. **Tristán Narvaja,** Avenida 18 de Julio in the Cordón neighborhood, is the city's Sunday flea market (6am–3pm), initiated more than 50 years ago by Italian immigrants. **De la Abundancia/Artesanos** is a combined food and handicrafts market. It takes place Monday through Saturday from 10am to 8pm at San José 1312.

WHERE TO STAY

Note that a 14% tax will be added to your bill. Parking is included in the rates of most Uruguay hotels.

EXPENSIVE

Belmont House ✿✿ *Finds*   A boutique hotel in Montevideo's peaceful Carrasco neighborhood, Belmont House offers its privileged guests intimacy and luxury. Small elegant spaces with carefully chosen antiques and wood furnishings give this hotel the feeling of a wealthy private home. Beautiful guest rooms feature two- or four-poster beds; rich, colorful linens; and marble bathrooms with small details like towel warmers and deluxe toiletries. Many of the rooms feature balconies overlooking the pretty courtyard and pool, and two of the rooms have Jacuzzis. Belmont House is a skip and a jump away from the beach, golf, and tennis. Gourmands will find an excellent international restaurant, afternoon tea, and a *parrilla* (grill) open weekends next to the pool. The gracious staff assists guests with outdoor activities and local itineraries.

Av. Rivera 6512, 11500 Montevideo. © 02/600-0430. Fax 02/600-8609. www.belmonthouse.com.uy. 28 units. $160 double; from $186 suite. Rates include gourmet breakfast. AE, DC, MC, V. **Amenities:** Restaurant; tea room; bar; beautiful outdoor pool; discounts for tennis and golf; small fitness center; sauna; business center; babysitting; laundry service; dry cleaning. *In room:* A/C, TV, minibar, hair dryer.

Radisson Montevideo Victoria Plaza Hotel ✿✿   The Victoria Plaza has long been one of Montevideo's top hotels. Standing in the heart of the financial district, this European-style hotel makes a good base from which to do business or explore the capital. Its convention center and casino also make it the center of the city's business and social activity. Ask for a room in the new tower, built in 1995, which houses spacious guest rooms and executive suites with classic French-style furnishings and panoramic city or river views. The busy hotel has a large multilingual staff that attends closely to guest needs. Inquire about weekend spa packages. Plaza Victoria is famous for its casino, with French roulette tables, blackjack, baccarat, slot machines, horse races, and bingo. There are two lobby bars, in addition to the casino bars. **Arcadia** (see "Where to Dine," below), on the 25th floor, is the city's most elegant dining room.

Plaza Independencia 759, 11100 Montevideo. © 02/902-0111. Fax 02/902-1628. www.radisson.com/montevideouy. 254 units. $175 double; from $210 suite. Rates include breakfast at rooftop restaurant. AE, DC, MC, V. **Amenities:** Restaurant; cafe; 2 bars; excellent health club with skylit indoor pool; fitness center; aerobics classes; Jacuzzi; sauna; concierge; travel agency; business center with high-speed Internet access; room service; massage service; laundry service; dry cleaning; executive floors. *In room:* A/C, TV, dataport, minibar, hair dryer, safe.

Sheraton Montevideo ✿✿   Opened in 1999, the Sheraton Montevideo has replaced Plaza Victoria as Montevideo's most luxurious hotel. A walkway connects the hotel to the Punta Carretas Shopping Center, one of the city's best malls. Spacious guest rooms have imported furniture, king-size beds, sleeper chairs, marble bathrooms, 25-inch televisions, and works by Uruguayan artists. Choose among views of the Río de la Plata, Uruguay Golf Club, or downtown

Montevideo, with views from the 20th through 24th floors being the most impressive. Rooms on the top two executive floors feature Jacuzzis and individual sound systems. Hotel service is excellent, particularly for guests with business needs. The main restaurant, Las Carretas, serves Continental cuisine with a Mediterranean flair—don't miss the dining room's spectacular murals by contemporary Uruguayan artist Carlos Vilaro. Next door, the lobby bar is a popular spot for casual business meetings and afternoon cocktails.

Calle Víctor Soliño 349, 11300 Montevideo. (C) 02/710-2121. Fax 02/712-1262. www.sheraton.com. 207 units. From $180 double; from $215 suite. Rates include buffet breakfast. AE, DC, MC, V. **Amenities:** Restaurant; bar; indoor pool; deluxe health club with fitness center; sauna; concierge; car-rental desk; business center and secretarial services; room service; massage service; babysitting; laundry service; dry cleaning; executive floors; emergency medical service. In room: A/C, TV, dataport, minibar, hair dryer, safe.

MODERATE

Holiday Inn ⭐ This colorful Holiday Inn is actually one of the city's best hotels, popular both with tourists and business travelers. It's situated in the heart of downtown, next to Montevideo's main square. A bilingual staff greets you in the marble lobby, which is attached to a good restaurant and bar. Guest rooms have simple, contemporary furnishings typical of an American chain. Because the hotel doubles as a convention center, it can become very busy. On the flip side, rooms are heavily discounted when the hotel is empty; be sure to ask for promotional rates, which can be as low as $50 per night.

Colonia 823, 11100 Montevideo. (C) 02/902-0001. Fax 02/902-1242. www.holidayinn.com.uy. 137 units. From $90 double. Rates include buffet breakfast. AE, DC, MC, V. **Amenities:** Restaurant; bar; heated indoor pool; fitness center; sauna; business center; room service; laundry service; dry cleaning. In room: A/C, TV, minibar, safe.

INEXPENSIVE

Days Inn Obelisco 𝘝𝘢𝘭𝘶𝘦 This modern Days Inn caters to business travelers looking for good-value accommodations. The hotel is located next to the Tres Cruces bus station and is not far from downtown or the airport. Rooms are comfortable and modern, if not overly spacious. Free local calls are permitted.

Acevedo Díaz 1821, 11800 Montevideo. (C) 02/400-4840. Fax 02/402-0229. www.daysinn.com. 60 units. From $45 double. Rates include buffet breakfast. AE, DC, MC, V. **Amenities:** Coffee shop; small health club; business center; room service. In room: A/C, TV, minibar, hair dryer.

WHERE TO DINE

Restaurants in Montevideo serve steak—just as high in quality as Argentine beef—and usually include a number of stews and seafood selections as well. You will find the native barbecue, in which beef and lamb are grilled on the fire, in any of the city's *parrilladas* (as *parrillas* are called in Uruguay). Sales tax on dining in Montevideo is a whopping 23%. There's usually a table cover charge, called the *cubierto,* as well—usually about $1 per person.

MODERATE

Arcadia ⭐⭐ 𝘔𝘰𝘮𝘦𝘯𝘵𝘴 INTERNATIONAL Virgil and Homer wrote that Arcadia was a quiet paradise in ancient Greece; this elegant restaurant atop the Plaza Victoria is a quiet paradise and the best restaurant in Montevideo. Tables are nestled in semiprivate nooks with floor-to-ceiling bay windows. The classic dining room is decorated with Italian curtains and crystal chandeliers; each table has a fresh rose and sterling silver place settings. Creative plates such as terrine of pheasant marinated in cognac are followed by grilled rack of lamb glazed with mint and garlic, or duck confit served on a thin strudel pastry with red cabbage.

Plaza Independencia 759. (C) 02/902-0111. Main courses $6–$11. AE, DC, MC, V. Daily 7pm–midnight.

El Fogón ✦ URUGUAYAN   This brightly lit *parrillada* and seafood restaurant is popular with Montevideo's late-night crowd. The extensive menu includes calamari, salmon, shrimp, and other fish, as well as generous steak and pasta dishes. Food here is priced well and prepared with care. The express lunch menu comes with steak or chicken, dessert, and a glass of wine.

San José 1080. ⓒ 02/900-0900. Main courses $6–$9. AE, DC, MC, V. Daily noon–4pm and 7pm–1am.

El Viejo y el Mar ✦ SEAFOOD   Resembling an old fishing club, El Viejo y el Mar is located on the riverfront near the Sheraton hotel. The bar is made from an abandoned boat, while the dining room is decorated with dock lines, sea lamps, and pictures of 19th-century regattas. You'll find every kind of fish and pasta on the menu, and the restaurant is equally popular for evening cocktails. An outdoor patio is open most of the year.

Rambla Gandhi 400. ⓒ 02/710-5704. Main courses $5–$8. MC, V. Daily noon–4pm and 8pm–1am.

Las Brasas ✦✦ URUGUAYAN   Hillary Clinton once visited this restaurant; a picture of her with the staff hangs proudly on the wall. This casual *parrillada* resembles one you'd find in Buenos Aires—except that this restaurant also serves an outstanding range of *mariscos* (seafood) such as the Spanish paella or *lenguado Las Brasas* (a flathead fish) served with prawns, mushrooms, and mashed potatoes. From the *parrilla*, the *filet de lomo* is the best cut—order it with Roquefort, mustard, or black pepper sauce. The restaurant's fresh produce is displayed in a case near the kitchen.

San José 909. ⓒ 02/900-2285. Main courses $5–$8. AE, DC, MC, V. Daily 11:45am–3:30pm and 7:30pm–midnight.

INEXPENSIVE

Río Alegre ✦ *Value* SNACKS   This casual, inventive lunch stop specializes in quick steaks off the grill. Ribs, sausages, and most cuts of beef are cooked on the *parrilla* and made to order. Río Alegre is a local favorite because of its large portions, good quality, and cheap prices.

Calle Pérez Castellano and Piedras, at the Mercado del Puerto, Local 33. ⓒ 02/915-6504. Main courses $2–$4. No credit cards. Daily 11am–3pm.

MONTEVIDEO AFTER DARK

As in Buenos Aires, nightlife in Montevideo means drinks after 10pm and dancing after midnight. For earlier entertainment, ask at your hotel or call the **Teatro Solís,** Calle Buenos Aires 652 (ⓒ **02/916-0908**), the city's center for opera, theater, ballets, and symphonies, for performance information. **SODRE,** Av. 18 de Julio 930 (ⓒ **02/901-2850**), is the city's "Official Radio Service," which hosts classical music concerts from May to November. Gamblers should head to the **Plaza Victoria Casino,** Plaza Independencia (ⓒ **02/902-0111**), a fashionable venue with French roulette tables, blackjack, baccarat, slot machines, horse races, and bingo. It opens at 2pm and keeps going through most of the night. **Mariachi,** Gabriel Pereira 2964 (ⓒ **02/709-1600**), is one of the city's top bars and discos, with live bands or DJ music Wednesday to Sunday after 10pm. **Café Misterio,** Costa Rica 1700 (ⓒ **02/600-5999**), is another popular bar, while **New York,** Calle Mar Artico 1227 (ⓒ **02/600-0444**), mixes a restaurant, bar, and dance club under one roof and attracts a slightly older crowd. Montevideo's best tango clubs are **La Casa de Becho,** Nueva York 1415 (ⓒ **02/400-2717**), where composer Gerardo Mattos Rodríguez wrote the famous "La Cumparsita," and **Cuareim,** Zelmar Michelini 1079, which offers both tango and *candombe,* a lively dance indigenous to the area. La Casa de Becho is open Friday and Saturday after 10:30pm; Cuareim, Wednesday, Friday, and Saturday after 9pm. The tourist office can give you schedule information for Montevideo's other tango salons.

4 Punta del Este

140km (87 miles) east of Montevideo

Come late December, Punta del Este is transformed from a sleepy coastal village into a booming summer resort. For 2 months, there seem to be more Porteños (as residents of Buenos Aires are called) in "Punta" than in Buenos Aires itself. Without a doubt, this coastal strip that juts into the southern Atlantic is the favorite summer getaway for Argentines, a resort with beautiful white-sand beaches and perfect swimming, world-class hotels and restaurants, and an inexhaustible list of outdoor activities—including golf, tennis, horseback riding, biking, bird-watching, and numerous watersports. The shopping here is world class as well, you'll have no problem finding an excellent restaurant for dinner, and nightlife in Punta del Este beats just about anywhere else in South America in summer.

ESSENTIALS
GETTING THERE

BY PLANE   **Pluna** (© **0800/118-881** or **042/490-101**) and **Aerolíneas Argentinas** (© **042/444-343**) fly between Buenos Aires and Punta. The flight takes 50 minutes. **Aeropuerto Internacional de Laguna del Sauce** is 24km (15 miles) east of Punta del Este. A taxi or *remise* from the airport into town will run about $15.

BY FERRY & BUS   The **Terminal de Buses Punta del Este,** Rambla Artigas and Calle Inzaurraga (© **042/489-467**), has buses connecting to Montevideo and Colonia that connect with the **Buquebus** (see the "Getting There" section under Montevideo on p. 84) ferry to Buenos Aires. **COT** (© **042/486-810,** or 02/409-4949 in Montevideo) offers the best bus service. The trip takes 1½ hours to Colonia and 2 hours to Montevideo, and the fare is about $16 to $20 round-trip.

ORIENTATION

Punta del Este is both the name of the famous resort city and the broader region taking in Punta Ballena and Maldonado. The Rambla Artigas is the coastal road that winds its way around the peninsula past the enticing beaches (see "Outdoor Activities," below). Avenida Gorlero is the main street running through the center of Punta, where you find most of the city's restaurants, cafes, and boutiques.

GETTING AROUND

If you want to explore the region by car, you can visit **Avis** at the airport (© **042/559-065**) or at Calle 31 and Calle Gorlero (© **042/442-020**). **Budget** also has a branch at the airport. **Hertz** rents cars at the airport (© **042/559-032**) and in the Conrad Hotel (© **042/492-109**).

VISITOR INFORMATION

The **Oficina de Turismo** is at Parada 24 (© **042/230-050**) and is open daily from 9am to 10pm (shorter hours in winter). You should also be able to obtain visitor information from your hotel staff and from the **Centro de Hoteles y Restaurantes de Punta del Este,** Plaza Artigas on Avenida Gorlero (© **042/440-512**).

WHAT TO SEE & DO
OUTDOOR ACTIVITIES

In Punta itself, the main beaches are **Playa Mansa** (on the Río de la Plata) and **Playa Brava** (on the Atlantic). The two beaches are separated by a small peninsula only a few blocks wide. **La Barra del Maldonado,** a small resort 5km (3 miles) east of Punta del Este, also boasts clean, beautiful beaches.

In summer, you will find vendors offering watersports from parasailing and windsurfing to water-skiing and snorkeling on both Playa Mansa and Playa Brava. For boating or fishing expeditions, contact the **Yacht Club Punta del Este,** Puerto de Punta del Este (© 042/441-056).

Golf courses include **Club de Golf** (© 042/482-127) in Punta itself, and **Club del Lago** (© 042/578-423) in Punta Ballena. Horseback riding can be arranged through **Hípico Burnett,** Camino a La Laguna, Pinares 33 (© 042/230-375). Tennis fans should call **Médanos Tennis,** Avenida Mar del Plata and Avenida Las Delicias (© 042/481-950).

SHOPPING

Punta has world-class shopping, with Uruguayan shops and European boutiques lining **Calle Gorlero,** the principal street bisecting this resort town. **Punta Shopping Mall,** Avenida Roosevelt at Paradas 6 and 7, has 100 stores on three levels and a 12-screen cinema. A weekend crafts market takes place from 5pm to midnight at Plaza Artigas.

WHERE TO STAY

Prices listed below are for summer peak season and are often half that in the off season. Christmas Eve to New Year's Eve is the busiest, most expensive week. Reserve well ahead of your visit, as all of Buenos Aires seems to flee to Punta del Este during summer vacation. Parking is free and available at all hotels in Punta.

VERY EXPENSIVE

Conrad Resort & Casino 🎞🎞🎞   The spectacular Conrad dominates social life in Punta del Este. It's the first choice of the international jet set that descends on this Atlantic resort in summer. The hotel's elegance stands in stark contrast to the city's other hotels, and guests here look as though they've dressed for an afternoon on Rodeo Drive rather than the beach. Luxurious rooms have terraces overlooking Playa Mansa and Playa Brava, and the professional staff is highly attentive to guest needs. Personal trainers can assist you with your favorite sport, from tennis to golf to horseback riding. The outdoor pool and gardens are gorgeous, and there's an excellent health club for the truly motivated. The Conrad's casino and showrooms are focal points for Punta nightlife.

The Conrad offers nonstop entertainment, from fashion shows and Las Vegas–style reviews to music, dance, magic shows, and an enormous casino. There are five restaurants, from refined dining to poolside barbecues. Two excellent beaches are located in front of the resort. Be sure to inquire about promotional rates and packages when making your reservations, especially in the off season.

Parada 4, Playa Mansa, 20100 Punta del Este. © 042/491-111. Fax 042/489-999. www.conrad.com.uy. 302 units. From $280 double (high season). AE, DC, MC, V. **Amenities:** 5 restaurants; temperate-water pool; golf; 2 lit tennis courts; deluxe health club with fitness center; sauna; concierge; business center and secretarial services; room service; massage; laundry service; dry cleaning; executive floors; water-skiing; scuba diving; horseback riding. *In room:* A/C, TV, dataport, minibar, hair dryer, safe.

Mantra Resort Spa & Casino 🎞🎞🎞 *(Finds* Punta's newest and most exclusive hotel is nestled in a quiet neighborhood, a 5-minute drive from the center of town and a short walk from the beach. If you like small, intimate hotels with high-quality service, then this should be your first choice—if your budget allows. Rooms are very modern and comfortable, bordering on minimalist style with dark wood furnishings, snow-white linens with a high thread count, and spacious marble baths. Many of the rooms have good views out to the sea, but the suites boast the prime views and come with fireplaces and large private terraces. The spa menu is huge and offers a myriad of treatments, including half- and 1-day packages. The health club offers spinning, yoga, and pilates classes, a rarity in hotel gyms. If you'd rather not walk to the beach, you can have a golf cart whisk you the short distance.

Ruta 10 Km 162, Calle Publica, 20100 Punta del Este. ⓒ 042/771-000. Fax 042/771-302. www.mantra resort.com. 100 units. $250–$350 double; $450–$950 suite. AE, DC, MC, V. **Amenities:** 2 restaurants; bar; lounge; spectacular outdoor pool and smaller indoor pool; 2 lit tennis courts; health club; immense spa with 16 treatment rooms; concierge; meeting rooms; room service; babysitting; laundry service; dry cleaning. *In room:* A/C, TV, dataport, minibar, hair dryer, safe.

EXPENSIVE

L'Auberge ⓡⓡ   This exclusive boutique hotel lies in the quiet residential neighborhood of Parque de Golf, 2 blocks from the beach. Formerly an 18th-century water tower, the hotel houses beautiful guest rooms decorated with antiques. The dedicated staff is committed to warm, personalized service. The staff can help you arrange horseback riding, golf, tennis, or other outdoor sports in the surrounding parks. The sophisticated resort has an elegant European tea-room overlooking the gardens, famous for its homemade waffles. An evening barbecue is offered by the pool.

Barrio Parque del Golf, 20100 Punta del Este. ⓒ **042/482-601.** Fax 042/483-408. www.lauberge.com.uy. 40 units. From $175 double; from $320 suite. Rates include continental breakfast. AE, DC, MC, V. **Amenities:** Outdoor pool; golf; tennis court; fitness center; spa; concierge; business center and secretarial services; room service; babysitting; laundry service; dry cleaning; horseback riding; barbecue; garden. *In room:* TV, minibar, hair dryer, safe.

MODERATE

Best Western La Foret ⓡ *Kids*   Opened in 2000, La Foret offers spacious guest rooms 1 block from Playa Mansa. The amenities are impressive given the price, and the hotel is a nice option for families (children under 17 stay free, and there's a children's playground and babysitting services). There's also a good international restaurant and coffee shop, with a multilingual staff.

Calle La Foret, Parada 6, Playa Mansa, 20100 Punta del Este. ⓒ **042/481-004.** Fax 042/481-004. www.best western.com. 49 units. From $70 double. Rates include buffet breakfast. AE, DC, MC, V. **Amenities:** Restaurant; bar/lounge; outdoor pool; exercise room; hot tub; sauna; concierge; business services; babysitting; playground. *In room:* TV, minibar, dataport, hair dryer, safe.

Days Inn Punta del Este ⓡⓡ *Value*   This atypical Days Inn sits on the waterfront. It's an excellent value for its location, featuring simple but modern rooms, many with ocean views. The Conrad Resort & Casino is next door, along with restaurants, cinemas, and excellent beaches. This is the best midrange hotel in Punta.

Rambla Willman, Parada 3, Playa Mansa, 20100 Punta del Este. ⓒ **042/484-353.** Fax 042/484-683. www. daysinn.com. 38 units. From $81 double, including buffet breakfast. AE, DC, MC, V. **Amenities:** Bar/lounge; indoor heated and outdoor pool; room service; babysitting; laundry services. *In room:* TV, minibar, dataport, hair dryer, safe.

WHERE TO DINE

Punta's dining scene is seasonal, with restaurants packed in summer and fairly dead in winter. Restaurant hours vary depending on the season, and some establishments close altogether from April to October.

EXPENSIVE

La Bourgogne 🌟🌟 *(Moments)* FRENCH   Jean-Paul Bondoux is the top French chef in South America, splitting his time between La Bourgogne in Punta del Este and its sister restaurant in Buenos Aires (p. 55). You'll have an unforgettable dining experience at this Relais & Châteaux member. Traditional main courses such as rack of lamb, breast of duck, rabbit with mustard sauce, and veal cutlet are the chef's favorites, while fresh vegetables, fruits, herbs, and spices from the owner's private farm accentuate the menu. Delicious French bread, baked in-house, is available for takeout from the restaurant's small bakery. Ask for a table inside the elegant dining room or amid the jasmine-scented garden. Service is impeccable, as is the wine list featuring French and South American labels.

Pedragosa Sierra (Maldonado). ℂ **042/482-007.** Main courses $15–$26. AE, DC, MC, V. Nov–Mar daily 8pm–11:30pm; Apr–Oct Thurs–Sun 8pm–11:30pm.

MODERATE

Andrés 🌟🌟 INTERNATIONAL   This father-son establishment enjoys an excellent reputation. Its setting along the Rambla, with most tables outside, makes for a perfect summer night out. Dishes, ranging from grilled meats to baked fish and fresh vegetable soufflés, are prepared with considerable care. Service is friendly and professional; ask for assistance matching a South American wine with your meal.

Edificio Vanguardia, Parada 1. ℂ **042/481-804.** Main courses $8–$15. AE, MC, V. Dec–Mar Thurs–Sun 8pm–midnight. Closed Apr–Nov.

Lo de Tere 🌟 *(Finds)* URUGUAYAN   This cozy establishment has a staff that makes you feel at home, offering graceful, cheerful service. Lo de Tere sits right on the water, with a beautiful view of the harbor. The specialties are fresh fish and pasta, which vary depending on the catch and the chef's inspiration. The restaurant transforms from festive and relaxed at lunch to more refined at dinner. Three-course menus are available for $16 to $32.

Rambla del Puerto and Calle 21. ℂ **042/440-492.** Main courses $8–$15. AE, DC, MC, V. Nov–Mar daily 12:30–6pm and 9pm–3am; Apr–Oct daily noon–3:30pm and 8pm–midnight.

Yacht Club Uruguayo 🌟 URUGUAYAN   This popular restaurant, with tables inside and on the outdoor terrace, looks across the water to Gorriti Island. The dining room's marine theme prepares you for an evening of seafood, with octopus, hake, and swordfish among the favorites. Waiters, dressed in proud white shirts, offer attentive service.

Rambla Artigas and Calle 8. ℂ **042/441-056.** Main courses $8–$20. AE, DC, MC, V. Nov–Mar daily noon–2am; Apr–Oct daily noon–3:30pm and 7:30pm–midnight.

INEXPENSIVE

Los Caracoles 🌟 *(Value)* URUGUAYAN   The town's most recommended *parrillada* also serves excellent seafood, including Spanish-style paella. A good salad bar accompanies the hearty selection of meats and fish, and there are a number of homemade pastas to choose from as well. Packed with 70 tables, the rustic dining room is casual and boisterous.

Calle Gorlero 20. (✆ **042/440-912**. Main courses $5–$8. AE, DC, MC, V. Nov–Mar daily noon–6pm and 8pm–3am; Apr–Oct daily noon–4pm and 7pm–1am.

PUNTA DEL ESTE AFTER DARK

The **Conrad Resort & Casino,** Parada 4, Playa Mansa (✆ **042/491-111**), is the focal point for evening entertainment in Punta, featuring Las Vegas–style reviews and other music, dance, and magic shows—sometimes around the torch-lit swimming pools. The enormous 24-hour casino has 450 slots and 63 tables for baccarat, roulette, blackjack, poker, dice, and fortune wheel.

Bars and discos come and go with considerable frequency in Punta. The concierge at Conrad Resort & Casino (see "Where to Stay," above) is a good source for what's hot in town. The best bar is **Moby Dick,** located at Rambla de la Circunvalación (✆ **042/441-240**), near the yacht harbor. Punta's bronzed Latin bodies then make their way to **Gitane** and **La Plage** (✆ **042/484-869**), two discos next to each other on Rambla Brava, Parada 12. The Conrad Hotel's own disco, **La Boite,** is another upscale club free for hotel guests and $10 to enter for outsiders (this $10 can be redeemed for chips in the casino).

5 Colonia del Sacramento

242km (150 miles) northwest of Montevideo

The tiny gem of Colonia del Sacramento, declared a World Heritage City by UNESCO, appears untouched by time. Dating from the 17th century, the old city boasts beautifully preserved colonial artistry down its dusty streets. A leisurely stroll into the **Barrio Histórico (Historic Neighborhood)** leads you under flower-laden windowsills to churches dating from the 1680s, past exquisite single-story homes from Colonia's time as a Portuguese settlement, and on to local museums detailing the riches of the town's past. The Barrio Histórico contains brilliant examples of colonial wealth and many of Uruguay's oldest structures. A mix of lovely shops and delicious cafes makes the town more than a history lesson.

ESSENTIALS
GETTING THERE

The easiest way to reach Colonia from Buenos Aires is by ferry. **FerryLíneas** (✆ **02/900-6617**) runs a fast boat that arrives in 45 minutes, and a 3-hour bus, **Buquebús** (✆ **02/916-1910**), also offers two classes of service. Prices range from $18 to $40 each way.

Colonia can also easily be visited from Montevideo and is a good stopping-off point if you're traveling between Buenos Aires and Montevideo. **COT** (✆ **02/409-4949** in Montevideo) also offers bus service from Montevideo and from Punta del Este.

VISITOR INFORMATION

The **Oficina de Turismo,** General Flores and Rivera (✆ **052/27000** or 052/27300), is open daily from 8am to 8pm. Speak with someone at the tourism office to arrange a guided tour of the town.

WHAT TO SEE & DO
A WALK THROUGH COLONIA'S BARRIO HISTORICO

Your visit to Colonia will be concentrated in the **Barrio Histórico (Old Neighborhood),** located on the coast at the far southwestern corner of town. The sites, which are all within a few blocks of each other, can easily be visited on foot in a few hours. Museums and tourist sites are open daily (except Tues–Wed) from 11:30am to 5:45pm. For less than $1, you can buy a pass at the Portuguese or Municipal museums that will get you into all the sites.

Start your tour at **Plaza Mayor,** the principal square that served as the center of the colonial establishment. To explore Colonia's Portuguese history, cross the Calle Manuel Lobo on the southeastern side of the plaza and enter the **Museo Portugués (Portuguese Museum),** which exhibits European customs and traditions that influenced the town's beginnings. Upon exiting the museum, turn left and walk to the **Iglesia Matriz (Matriz Church),** among the oldest churches in the country and an excellent example of 17th-century architecture and design.

Next, exit the church and turn left to the **Ruinas Convento San Francisco (San Francisco Convent Ruins).** Dating from 1696, the San Francisco convent was once inhabited by Jesuit and Franciscan monks, two brotherhoods dedicated to preaching the gospel to indigenous people. Continue up Calle San Francisco to the **Casa de Brown (Brown House),** which houses the **Museo Municipal (Municipal Museum).** Here, you will find an impressive collection of colonial documents and artifacts, a must-see for history buffs.

For those with a more artistic bent, turn left on Calle Misiones de los Tapes and walk 2 blocks to the **Museo del Azulejo (Tile Museum),** a unique museum of 19th-century European and Uruguayan tiles housed in a gorgeous 300-year-old country house. Then stroll back into the center of town along Calle de la Playa, enjoying the shops and cafes along the way, until you come to the **Ruinas Casa del Gobernador (House of the Viceroy Ruins).** The House of the Viceroy captures something of the glorious past of the city's 17th- and 18th-century magistrates, when the city's port was used for imports, exports, and smuggling. Complete your walk with a visit to the **UNESCO–Colonia** headquarters, where exhibits on the city's newly acquired Historic Heritage of Humanity status will place your tour in the larger context of South American history.

WHERE TO STAY & DINE

Few people stay in Colonia, preferring to make a day trip from Buenos Aires or a stop along the way to Montevideo. If you'd rather get a hotel, however, your best bets are the colonial-style **Hotel Plaza Mayor,** Calle del Comercio 111 (© **052/23193**), and **Hotel La Misión,** Calle Misiones de los Tapes 171 (© **052/26767**), whose original building dates from 1762. Both hotels charge from $80 for a double. For dining, **Mesón de la Plaza,** Vasconcellos 153 (© **052/24807**), serves quality international and Uruguayan food in a colonial setting, while **Pulpería de los Faroles,** Calle Misiones de los Tapes 101 (© **052/ 25399**), in front of Plaza Mayor, specializes in beef and bean dishes and homemade pasta.

5

Iguazú Falls

A dazzling panorama of cascades whose power overwhelms the sounds of the surrounding jungle, Las Cataratas del Iguazú (Iguazú Falls) refers to the spectacular canyon of waterfalls fed by the Río Iguazú. Declared a World Heritage Area by UNESCO in 1984, these 275 waterfalls were shaped by 120 million years of geological history and form one of Earth's most unforgettable sights. Iguazú Falls are shared by Argentina and Brazil, and are also easily accessible from nearby Paraguay. Excellent walking circuits on both the Argentine and Brazilian sides allow visitors to peek over the tops of or stare at the faces of raging sheets of water, some with sprays so intense it seems as though geysers have erupted from below. Although a five-star hotel overlooking the falls exists in both the Argentine and Brazilian national parks, visitors looking for less expensive accommodations often stay in the towns of Puerto Iguazú in Argentina or Foz do Iguaçu in Brazil.

While Iguazú is best known for its waterfalls, consider including the surrounding subtropical jungle in your itinerary (see "Behind the Falls and into the Iguazú Jungle," below). Here, *cupay* trees (South American hardwoods) tower over the various layers of life that compete for light, and the national park is known to contain 200 species of trees, 448 species of birds, 71 species of mammals, 36 species of reptiles, 20 species of amphibians, and more than 250 species of butterflies. Iguazú's climate also provides for the flowering of plants year-round, lending brilliant color to the forest, and since spray from the waterfall keeps the humidity levels over 75%, there's a tremendous growth of epiphytes (plants that grow on other plants without taking nutrients from their hosts).

You can visit the waterfalls on your own, but you will most certainly need a tour operator to explore the jungle. Allow at least 1 full day to explore the waterfalls on the Argentine side, another to visit the Brazilian side, and perhaps half a day for a jungle tour.

1 Puerto Iguazú

1330km (825 miles) northeast of Buenos Aires

This sedate town serves as the main base from which to explore Iguazú National Park, 18km (11 miles) north. It is smaller and safer than its Brazilian counterpart, Foz do Iguaçu, and the hotels and restaurants here are inexpensive and commendable. Foz do Iguaçu, however, offers better nightlife and is much more vibrant.

ESSENTIALS
GETTING THERE
BY PLANE   Aerolíneas Argentinas (© 3757/420-194), **Southern Winds** (© 0810/777-7979), and **American Falcon** (© 0810/222-3252) offer up to six to seven daily flights from Buenos Aires to **Aeropuerto Internacional Cataratas del Iguazú;** the trip takes 1½ hours. Round-trip fares range from about $85 to $240, depending on whether any specials are offered. Aerolíneas Argentinas occasionally offers flights to Iguazú out of Ezeiza international airport, usually on Saturday or Sunday. Catch a taxi (for about $9) or one of the shuttle buses from the airport to town ($2), a 20-minute drive.

BY BUS   The fastest bus service from Buenos Aires is with **Vía Bariloche** (© 011/4315-4456 in Buenos Aires), which takes 16 hours and costs $83 to $116 one-way, depending on the seat you choose. (The more expensive fare lands you a fully reclining "cama" seat.) Less pricey but longer (21 hr.) are **Expreso Singer** (© 011/4313-3927 in Buenos Aires) and **Expreso Tigre Iguazú** (© 011/4313-3915 in Buenos Aires), which both run about $80 one-way.

VISITOR INFORMATION
In Puerto Iguazú, obtain maps and park information from the **Parque Nacional** office at Victoria Aguirre 66 (© 3757/420-722), open Monday through Friday from 8am to 2pm. For information on the town, contact the **municipal tourist office,** at Victoria Aguirre and Brañas (© 3757/420-800). It's open daily from 8am to 8pm. Visitor information is also available near the national park entrance (see below).

In Buenos Aires, get information about Iguazú from **Casa de la Provincia de Misiones,** Av. Santa Fe 989 (© 011/4322-0686), open Monday through Friday from 10am to 5pm.

GETTING AROUND
El Práctico local buses run every 45 minutes from 7am to 8pm between Puerto Iguazú and the national park, and cost $1. **Parada 10** (© 3757/421-527) provides 24-hour taxi service. You can rent a car at the airport, although this is much more a luxury than a necessity. Within both Puerto Iguazú and the national park, you can easily walk.

VISITING THE NATIONAL PARK ☆☆☆
Your first stop will likely be the recently opened (and environmentally friendly) **visitor center,** where you can get maps and information about the area's flora and fauna. The visitor center is located .8km (½ mile) from the park entrance, close to the parking lot and footbridges for the waterfall circuits. Adjacent to the visitor center, you will find a restaurant, snack shops, and souvenir stores. A natural gas train takes visitors to the path entrance for the Upper and Lower Circuits and to the footbridge leading to Devil's Throat. (If you'd rather walk, footpaths are available, but note that the walk to Devil's Throat is about 3km/1¾ miles). The visitor center is staffed with a number of English-speaking guides, available for individual and private tours—you may opt to see the falls on your own or with an experienced local guide. A guide is not really necessary unless you're limited for time or want to ask detailed questions about the region's geography and fauna. There is a $10 entrance fee (which covers the train ride) for non-Argentines to enter the national park. The national park is open from 8am to 7pm in summer, and 8am until 6pm in winter.

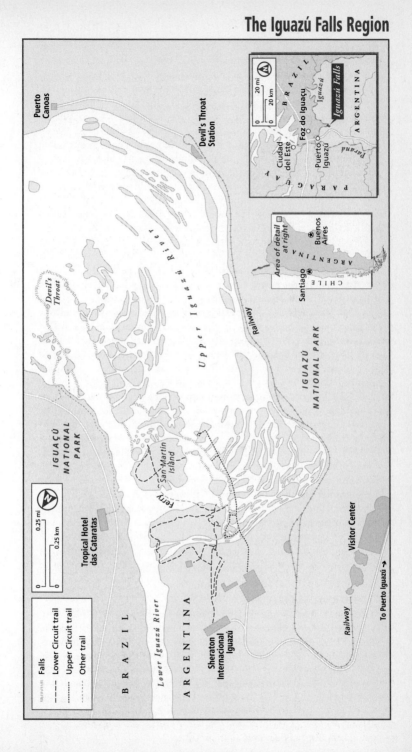

Falls
- - - Lower Circuit trail
· · · Upper Circuit trail
····· Other trail

0   0.25 mi
0   0.25 km

Tropical Hotel
das Cataratas

San Martín
Island

Ferry

Devil's
Throat

Puerto
Canoas

Devil's Throat
Station

Upper Iguazú River

Railway

Lower Iguazú River

BRAZIL

ARGENTINA

IGUAÇU
NATIONAL
PARK

IGUAZÚ
NATIONAL PARK

Sheraton
Internacional
Iguazú

Visitor Center

Railway

To Puerto Iguazú →

20 mi
20 km
0
0

BRAZIL

Foz do Iguaçu

Iguazú Falls

Iguazú

ARGENTINA

Ciudad
del Este

Puerto
Iguazú

Paraná

PARAGUAY

Area of detail
at right

Buenos
Aires

ARGENTINA

CHILE

Santiago

The two main paths to view the waterfalls are the **Circuito Superior (Upper Circuit)** and the **Circuito Inferior (Lower Circuit)** , both of which begin within walking distance (less than .8km/½ mile) from of the visitor center. However, you may want to save your energy and catch the train to the path entrance. There's a small snack shop near the beginning of the trails. The Upper Circuit winds its way along the top of the canyon, allowing you to look down the falls and see the area's rich flora, including cacti, ferns, and orchids. The Lower Circuit offers the best views, as magnificent waterfalls come hurtling down before you in walls of silvery spray. The waterfalls are clearly marked by signs along the way.

The best time to walk the **Upper Circuit** is early in the morning or late in the afternoon, and rainbows often appear near sunset. This .9km (½-mile) path takes 1 to 2 hours depending on how many stops you make, starting at the viewing tower and leading past **Dos Hermanos (Two Brothers), Bossetti, Chico (Small), Ramírez,** and **San Martín** (the park's widest) falls. You can come right to the edges of these falls and look over them as they fall as far as 60m (197 ft.) below. Along your walk, you can also look across to San Martín Island and the Brazilian side, and you'll pass a number of small streams and creeks.

The 1.8km (1¼-mile) **Lower Circuit** takes 2 hours to walk, leading you first past **Lanusse** and **Alvar Núñez** falls, then along the Lower Iguazú River past the raging **Dos Mosqueteros (Two Musketeers)** and **Tres Mosqueteros (Three Musketeers)** falls. The trail winds its way toward **Ramírez, Chico,** and **Dos Hermanos** falls. Here, you'll find an inspiring view of the **Garganta del Diablo (Devil's Throat)** and **Bossetti** falls. From the Salto Bossetti waterfall, a small pathway leads down to a small pier where you can catch a free boat to **San Martín Island.**

Once on the island, climb the stairs and walk along clearly marked trails for remarkable views of the surrounding *cataratas* (falls)—to the left, you see the enormous **Garganta del Diablo, Saltos Brasileros (Brazilian Falls),** and **Ventana;** to the right, you overlook the mighty **Salto San Martín,** which sprays 30m (98 ft.) high after hitting the river below. This panoramic view looks out at dozens of falls forming an arch before you. San Martín Island also has a small, idyllic beach perfect for sunbathing and swimming.

Garganta del Diablo is the mother of all waterfalls in Iguazú, visible from observation points from both the Brazilian and Argentine parks. You'll notice that the water is calm as it makes its way down the Iguazú River, then begins to speed up as it approaches the gorge ahead. In front of you, Mother Nature has created a furious avalanche of water and spray that is the highest waterfall in Iguazú and one of the world's greatest natural spectacles. You might want to bring a raincoat—you *will* get wet.

OUTDOOR ACTIVITIES

The area's main tour operator is **Iguazú Jungle Explorer** (© 3757/421-696; **www.iguazujunglexplorer.com**), located both inside the national park and in the Sheraton Internacional Iguazú. This company offers a "Nautical Adventure" ($10) that visits the falls by inflatable raft, an "Ecological Tour" ($5) that takes you to Devil's Throat and lets you paddle rubber boats along the Upper Iguazú Delta, and the *Gran Aventura* (Great Adventure) tour ($23). This last tour begins with an 8km (5-mile) safari ride along the Yacoratia Path, the original dirt road that led through the forest and on to Buenos Aires. During the ride, you'll view the jungle's extensive flora and might catch a glimpse of some of the region's indigenous wildlife (see the "Behind the Falls and into the Iguazú Jungle," below). You will then be let off at Puerto Macuco, where you'll hop into an inflatable boat with

Behind the Falls and into the Iguazú Jungle

Dawn in Iguazú brings the first rays of light through the forest canopy, as orchids, butterflies, frogs, lizards, parrots, and monkeys wake and spread color and life through the forest. Binoculars in hand, step softly into this wonderland, where most sounds are masked by the roar from the falls.

You'll see parakeets long before entering the jungle. Their green bodies and loud song make them easy to spot; macaws, parrots, and toucans are other feathered residents. Look and listen carefully for the great dusky swift, which nests near the waterfalls, and the great kiskadee, whose family name—*Tyrannidae*—tells much about this yellow-breasted bird's hunting prowess. Look below the canopy to observe the other flying wonders of the park—an enormous population of butterflies. Brilliant blue flyers known as morpho butterflies flit between deciduous trees and above lines of leaf-cutter ants, along with beautiful red, black, and yellow species of butterflies.

It's close to impossible to walk through the park without running across some of the area's indigenous reptiles. The ubiquitous tropidurus lizards, which feed on bird eggs, scamper everywhere, while colorful tree frogs hop and croak the nights away. Larger and rarer creatures, such as the 1.5m-long (5-ft.) tegu lizard and the caiman, a crocodile-like reptile, are discovered only by the patient and persistent visitor.

Warm-blooded creatures share this forest as well. Coatis—aardvark-like mammals that travel in groups searching for insects and fruit—are frequent and fearless visitors to the trails. Swinging above the footpaths are brown capuchin monkeys, whose chatter and gestures make them seem more human than most primates. The predators of this warm-blooded group range from vampire bats to endangered jaguars and pumas. For your safety, stay on the walking paths and, when in the jungle, with your tour operator.

An array of subtropical flora surrounds Iguazú's resident animals and insects. Bamboo, ficus, fig, and ancient rosewood trees—up to 1,000 years old—are but a few of the trees that grow near the river and compete for light, and there is also a proliferation of epiphytes (plants growing on others) such as bromeliads, güembés, and orchids. Eighty-five species of orchid thrive in the park, mostly close to the damp and well-lit waterfalls.

your tour group and navigate 6.5km (4 miles) along the lower Iguazú River, braving 1.6km (1 mile) of rapids as you approach the falls in Devil's Throat Canyon. After a thrilling and wet ride, the raft lets you off across from San Martín Island—from there, catch a free boat to this island with excellent hiking trails and a small beach for swimming and sunbathing. You can combine the Ecological Tour and Great Adventure by buying a full-day Pasaporte Verde for $27.

If you want to arrange a private adventure tour for your specific interests, the best outfit is **Explorador Expediciones,** with offices in the Sheraton Internacional

Iguazú and in Puerto Iguazú at Puerto Moreno 217 (© **3757/421-632**). The guides are experts on life in the Iguazú jungle.

WHERE TO STAY

Peak season for hotels in Iguazú extends through January and February (summer holiday) and also includes July (winter break), Semana Santa (Holy Week, the week before Easter), and long weekends. On the Argentine side, the Sheraton Internacional Iguazú is the only hotel inside the national park; the rest lie in Puerto Iguazú, 18km (11 miles) away. You can usually find discounts in the off season.

EXPENSIVE

Hotel Cataratas ⭐ *Kids*   Although it's not located next to the falls, Hotel Cataratas, on the outskirts of town, deserves consideration for its excellent service, from the helpful receptionists to the meticulous housekeepers. None of the stuffiness you sometimes feel at luxury hotels is evident here. Despite the hotel's unimpressive exterior, rooms are among the most modern and spacious in the area—especially the 30 "master rooms" that feature two double beds, handsome wood furniture, colorful artwork, large bathrooms with separate toilet rooms, in-room safes, and views of the pool or gardens (these rooms are only slightly more than the standard rooms—called "superior"—and the staff is often willing to offer promotional rates). The hotel's many facilities, including outdoor pool, spa, tennis and volleyball courts, putting green, playroom, and gymnasium, make this a great choice for families. The Cataratas restaurant offers a fine selection of regional and international dishes, and you can dine inside or out. The hotel lies 4km (2½ miles) from the center of Puerto Iguazú and 17km (11 miles) from the national park entrance. Bus service is available.

Ruta 12, Km 4, 3370 Misiones. © **3757/421-100**. Fax 3757/421-090. www.hotelcataratas.com.ar. 111 units. $83 double superior; from $150 suite. Rates include buffet breakfast. AE, DC, MC, V. **Amenities:** Restaurant; outdoor pool; putting green; tennis court; spa; Jacuzzi; sauna; game room; concierge; conference room; secretarial services; room service; massage; laundry service. *In room:* A/C, TV, minibar, hair dryer, safe.

Sheraton Internacional Iguazú ⭐⭐   Once the famous Internacional Cataratas de Iguazú, the Sheraton enjoys a magnificent location inside the national park (and it's the only hotel inside the park). Guests have little need to leave the resort, a self-contained sanctuary overlooking the falls. The hotel lies only steps from the Upper and Lower Circuit trails, and half of the guest rooms have direct views of the water (the others have splendid views of the jungle). The only drawback to the rooms is that they are fairly standard Sheraton decor. There are three restaurants, including the stunning Garganta del Diablo that peers over Devil's Throat and serves outstanding, if pricey, international dishes.

Parque Nacional Iguazú, 3370 Misiones. © **0800/888-9180** local toll-free, or 3757/491-800. Fax 3757/491-848. www.sheraton.com. 180 units. $145–$185 double with jungle view; $199–$230 double with view of waterfalls; from $285 suite. Rates include buffet breakfast. AE, DC, MC, V. **Amenities:** 3 restaurants; outdoor pool; 2 tennis courts; fitness center; concierge; car-rental desk; conference rooms; shopping arcade; room service; babysitting; laundry service. *In room:* A/C, TV, minibar, hair dryer, safe.

MODERATE

Hotel Saint George ⭐ *Finds*   A modest hotel in the heart of Puerto Iguazú, the Saint George features colorful rooms with single beds, an inviting pool surrounded by lush vegetation, and a commendable international restaurant that serves tasty fish from the local river. The friendly and enthusiastic staff will answer questions about the national park and help arrange tours, if requested.

Av. Córdoba 148, 3370 Puerto Iguazú. © 3757/420-633. Fax 3757/420-651. 56 units. $49 double. Rates include buffet breakfast. AE, DC, MC, V. **Amenities:** Restaurant; pool. *In room:* A/C, TV, minibar.

INEXPENSIVE

Los Helechos *(Value* Los Helechos is a great bargain for those seeking comfortable, inexpensive accommodations in Puerto Iguazú. Located in the city center, this intimate hotel offers simple rooms, many of which surround a plant-filled courtyard and offer a sense of sleeping near the jungle. If you dislike humid nights, be sure to splurge for a room with air-conditioning (request it at the time of booking and be ready to cough up an additional $10).

Paulino Amarante 76, 3370 Puerto Iguazú. ©/fax **3757/420-338.** 54 units. $19 double without A/C or TV; $29 with A/C and TV. AE, DC, MC, V. **Amenities:** Restaurant; bar; pool. *In room:* A/C, TV (in some rooms only).

WHERE TO DINE

Dining in Puerto Iguazú is casual and inexpensive, provided you're looking for a meal outside your hotel. Argentine steaks, seafood, and pasta are common on most menus. The Sheraton Internacional Iguazú, inside the national park, has the area's best (and most expensive) restaurant.

EXPENSIVE

Garganta del Diablo *✹✹* INTERNATIONAL   Located inside the national park at the Sheraton Internacional Iguazú, this restaurant serves excellent international and regional dishes. Open for nearly 25 years, the restaurant is best known for its magnificent view of Devil's Throat. Enjoy a romantic table for two overlooking the falls, and consider the grilled *suribí* (a mild fish from the river in front of you) or *bife de chorizo* (a New York strip steak).

Parque Nacional Iguazú. © **3757/491-800.** Main courses $9–$13. AE, DC, MC, V. Daily noon–3pm and 7–11pm.

INEXPENSIVE

El Charo *(Finds* ARGENTINE   Superficially, El Charo seems to be in shambles: Its sagging roof is missing a number of wood beams, pictures hang crooked on the walls, and the bindings on the menus are falling apart. Consider it part of the charm, however, since this casual, cozy restaurant offers cheap, delicious food and is tremendously popular with both tourists and locals. Among the main dishes, you'll find breaded veal, sirloin steaks, pork chops, catfish, and items from the *parrilla* (grill). Also available are salads and pastas such as ravioli and cannelloni.

Av. Córdoba 106. © **3757/421-529.** Main courses $3–$4. No credit cards. Daily 11am–1am.

La Rueda *✹ (Finds* ARGENTINE   Nothing more than a small A-frame house with an outdoor patio, La Rueda is a delightful place to eat. Despite the casual atmosphere, tables have carefully prepared place settings, waiters are attentive and friendly, and the food—served in large portions—is very good. The diverse menu features pasta, steaks, and fish dishes. Try the *serubi brochette,* a local whitefish prepared with bacon, tomatoes, onions, and peppers, and served with green rice and potatoes.

Av. Córdoba 28. © **3757/422-531.** Main courses $3–$5. No credit cards. Daily noon–4pm and 7pm–1am.

PUERTO IGUAZU AFTER DARK

Puerto Iguazú offers little in the way of nightlife, although the major hotels—including the Sheraton Internacional Iguazú and Hotel Cataratas—often have live music and other entertainment during peak seasons. Try **La Reserva,** a popular bar-restaurant, or **La Baranca** (© 3757/423-295), a pub with nightly live music. Both are located next to each other at Avenida Tres Fronteras and Costanera.

2 The Brazilian Side: Foz do Iguaçu ⋆⋆⋆

A visit to the Brazilian side of Iguazú Falls affords a dazzling perspective of the waterfalls. Although the trails here are not as extensive as on the Argentine side, the views are no less spectacular. In fact, many people find Brazil's unobstructed panoramic view of Iguazú Falls even more inspiring.

If you decide to stay on the Brazilian side, the Tropical das Cataratas Hotel and Resort (see "Where to Stay," below) is a spectacular hotel at the foot of the national park, overlooking the falls. Alternatively, you could stay in Foz do Iguaçu—the Brazilian counterpart to Puerto Iguazú. Foz is a slightly larger town 25km (16 miles) from Iguaçu National Park with numerous hotels, restaurants, and shops (along with a slightly larger incidence of poverty and street crime).

ESSENTIALS
GETTING THERE
BY PLANE   **Varig** (© 045/523-2111) and **Vasp** (© 045/523-2212) fly from Rio de Janeiro and other major Brazilian cities to Foz do Iguaçu Airport. The airport lies 11km (6¾ miles) from Foz do Iguaçu. Public buses make frequent trips to the national park and into town for a small fee.

FROM THE ARGENTINE SIDE   Crossing the border is fairly easy (make sure you bring your passport). The most convenient way to get from the Argentine to the Brazilian side is by taxi (about $30 round-trip). Buses are considerably less expensive, but less convenient, too. **Tres Fronteras** and **El Práctico** buses make the half-hour trip to Foz do Iguaçu 15 times per day ($1) from the Puerto Iguazú bus terminal; to visit the national park, ask the bus driver to let you off just after the border check, then catch the national park bus.

BY CAR   To avoid border hassles and international driving issues, it's best to take a bus or taxi to the Brazilian side.

VISITOR INFORMATION
Foz do Iguaçu's **municipal tourism office,** at Praça Getúlio Vargas (© 045/523-8581), is open weekdays from 7am to 11pm. **Teletur** (© 0800/451-516) is a toll-free information service.

SEEING THE BRAZILIAN SIDE OF THE FALLS
The national park entrance to the **Cataratas do Iguaçu** is at Km 17, Rodovía das Cataratas, and the entrance fee is $3. Park your car or get off the bus here and pay your entry fee; private vehicles (except for taxis and guests of the Tropical) are not allowed in the park. From here, you board a shuttle bus bound for the falls. The waterfall path begins just in front of the Tropical das Cataratas Hotel and Resort, which is 11km (6¾ miles) from the national park entrance (if you are taking a taxi, have your driver bring you directly to the Tropical das Cataratas hotel and jump onto the trail from here). You will catch your first sight of the falls from a small viewpoint at the foot of the hotel lawn, from which the path begins. The trail zigzags down the side of the gorge and trundles along the cliff face for about 2km (1¼ miles) past **Salto Santa María, Deodoro,** and **Floriano** falls. There are 275 separate waterfalls with an average drop of 60m (197 ft.). The last catwalk plants you directly in front of the awesome **Garganta do Diablo (Devil's Throat),** and, once again, you will get wet (there's a small store

in front where you can buy rain gear and film, if you need it). Back on the main trail, a tower beckons visitors to take an elevator to the top for an even broader panoramic view of the falls. This circuit takes about 2 hours.

WHERE TO STAY

As with the hotels on the Argentine side, peak season is January and February (summer holiday), July (winter break), Semana Santa (Holy Week, the week before Easter Sunday), and all long weekends. Rates are often substantially discounted in the off season.

EXPENSIVE

Bourbon Foz do Iguaçu *Kids*   A full-service resort hotel, the Bourbon is located 2.5km (1½ miles) out of town on the road to the falls. All rooms are colorfully appointed; standard rooms in the original wing have light colors and look out over the front of the hotel, while superior rooms have verandas with views over the pool and lawn. The newer wing houses "master" suites with modern furnishings and huge windows. But don't count on spending a lot of time in your room; the real draw of the Bourbon is its leisure space. There's a 1.3km (¾-mile) trail in the woods behind the hotel; keep an eye out for toucans, parakeets, and the colorful butterflies in the aviary. The vast outdoor pool area includes three large pools, one especially for children with lots of play equipment. In high season, activity leaders organize all-day children's activities in the pool or in the Tarzan house, tucked away in the forest.

Rodovía das Cataratas, Km 2.5, Foz do Iguaçu, 85863-000 PR. ©️ **0800/451-010** or 045/523-1313. www. bourbon.com.br. 311 units. $116–$144 Standard, Superior, or Master double; $29–$36 extra person. Bus: Parque Nacional or Cataratas. **Amenities:** 3 restaurants; huge pool complex (3 outdoor pools, 1 small indoor pool); outdoor tennis courts lit for evening play; sauna; children's programs; game room; concierge; tour desk; car-rental desk; business center; shopping arcade; salon; room service; massage; laundry service; nonsmoking rooms. *In room:* A/C, TV, dataport (master suites only), minibar, fridge, hair dryer, safe.

Tropical das Cataratas Hotel and Resort   The Portuguese colonial hotel (called Hotel das Cataratas for most of its existence), built in 1958 and ideally located in the Brazilian national park, is a UNESCO-declared World Heritage Site. The meticulously kept pink and white buildings, on a cliff above the Brazilian falls, have hosted an impressive list of princes and princesses, presidents and ministers, artists and celebrities. The hotel is often fully booked, but if you can get a reservation, its spacious corridors and quiet courtyards promise a relaxing vacation. Deluxe and superior rooms, fitted with two-poster beds, granite- or marble-top tables, and hardwood floors, are far better than standard rooms; make sure you ask for one that's been refurbished so you don't get stuck with a more than 50-year-old bathroom. Only the presidential suite has direct views of the falls; other rooms stare at trees. The trail to the Brazilian falls is just steps from the hotel entrance; when there's a full moon, magical night hikes are arranged. The hotel has two commendable restaurants serving Brazilian and international food. Restaurante Itaipu is the more formal choice, while the outdoor Ipe Bar & Grill offers evening entertainment. Although the national park closes to the public after 7pm, people wanting to come for dinner at the hotel can get a special after-hours pass at the park entrance.

Parque Nacional do Iguaçu, Foz do Iguaçu, 85863-000 PR. ©️ **0800/150-006** or 045/521-7000. www.tropcal hotel.com.br. 200 units. $148–$177 double superior; $207 double deluxe. Children under 10 stay free in parent's room. AE, DC, MC, V. Take the road to Iguaçu Falls, go straight towards the gate, do not turn left into the visitor's area. Identify yourself at the gate. **Amenities:** 2 restaurants; bar; large outdoor pool; tennis court; game room; concierge; tour desk; business center (24-hr. Internet access); shopping arcade; salon; room service; laundry service. *In room:* A/C, TV, minibar, fridge, hair dryer, safe.

MODERATE

Continental Inn 🌟 *Finds* Recently renovated, the Continental Inn is a real gem. All rooms have been redone and are quite comfortable, but the suites are truly outstanding, well worth the extra money. The regular suites have beautiful hardwood floors, modern blond-wood furniture, a separate sitting area, a desk, a table, and a bathroom with a large round tub. The best rooms in the house are the master suites: hardwood floors, king-size bed, fancy linens, a large desk, a separate sitting area, a walk-in closet, and a bathroom with a Jacuzzi tub and a view over the city of Iguaçu. The amenities are top-notch, too: large pool with children's play area, sauna, and game room with video games. Rooms for travelers with disabilities are also available.

Av. Paranà 1089, Foz do Iguaçu, 85852-000 PR. ⓒ 045/523-5000. www.continentalinn.com.br. 113 units, 102 rooms showers only. $56 double; $75 suite; $100 master suite. In low season 30% discount. Children under 5 stay free in parent's room, 5 and over $14 extra. AE, DC, MC, V. **Amenities:** Restaurant; large pool; exercise room; sauna; game room with video arcade; car-rental desk; business center; room service; laundry service. *In room:* A/C, TV, dataport, minibar, fridge, hair dryer, safe.

WHERE TO DINE

You will find a number of pleasant restaurants in Foz do Iguaçu. **Avenida Brasil,** a main artery of the town, is a good place to wander for food stalls, coffee bars, and hearty home-style Brazilian fare.

EXPENSIVE

Restaurante Itaipu—Tropical das Cataratas 🌟 BRAZILIAN The best *feijoada* (a Brazilian black bean dish) in town is served here, only on Saturday afternoons, in this elegant colonial-style restaurant in the Tropical das Cataratas. A large feast is put out, with white rice, *farofa* (a manioc meal, a very Brazilian ingredient—a bit like tapioca, a bit like corn meal, it is the most authentic accompaniment to *feijoada*), fried banana, green cabbage, orange slices, and all the *feijoada* you can eat. The big clay dishes of beans and meat are clearly labeled (a vegetarian version is also available). Desserts are sweet and rich; try the various caramelized fruits with coconut.

In the Tropical das Cataratas Hotel and Resort, Km 28, Parque Nacional do Iguaçu. ⓒ 045/574-1688. Main courses $7–$15. AE, DC, MC, V. Daily 11:30am–2pm and 6–11pm. *Feijoada* is served Sat 11:30am–3pm. No public transit, easiest to combine eating here with a visit to the falls; the park shuttle will leave you in front of the Tropical.

MODERATE

Clube Maringá 🌟 SEAFOOD One of the most popular seafood restaurants for locals is Clube Maringá. It can be a bit tricky to find, on a dead-end road that leads to the Brazilian border across from Argentina and Paraguay. The food is excellent. The menu is all fish and mostly local. Try the *piapara* fish grilled in a banana leaf or the barbecued *dourado*. Other dishes include *surubi* sautéed in butter, tilapia skewers, cod pastries, and *surubi a milanesa* (breaded and fried). Even the *sashimi* is made with local tilapia and piapara.

Av. Dourado (just off Av. General Meira s/n, by the Policia Militar). ⓒ 045/527-3472. Main courses $9–$13. MC, V. Mon–Sat 5–10pm. Call ahead for lunch hours; these vary by season. A taxi is recommended.

FOZ DO IGUAÇU AFTER DARK

The best bars and clubs line Avenida Jorge Schimmelpfeng. Try **Tass Bier and Club,** Av. Jorge Schimmelpfeng 450 (ⓒ 045/523-5373), which acts as a pub during the week and disco on weekends. The **Teatro Plaza Foz,** BR (National Rd.) 277, Km 726 (ⓒ 045/526-3733), offers evening folkloric music and dance shows celebrating Brazilian, Argentine, and Paraguayan cultures.

6

The Northwest

Far removed from the urban noise of Buenos Aires, Argentina's Northwest feels like a different country altogether. Here you'll find a land rich in history, influenced by an age of pre-Hispanic civilization—a place more culturally similar to Chile and Bolivia (which border the region) than to the federal capital. Here, you'll notice a different pace to life among the old country houses and farms scattered across the land. It also has wildly diverse terrain ranging from the cold peaks of the Andes to the subtropical air of its fertile valleys.

The Northwest incorporates one of Argentina's oldest settled regions, inhabited largely by Quechuan

Indians, an Inca-influenced tribe that descended from Peru in 1450. The Spaniards arrived in the early 16th century under explorers Pizarro and Diego de Almagro, and colonized the area with forts in Salta, San Salvador de Jujuy, Tucumán, and San Luis. The Diaguita tribes (living here before the Quechuans arrived) were agricultural people whom the Spaniards forced into slavery while extending their empire into the New World. Archaeological sites throughout the region reveal traces of precolonial life, including Indian settlements with terraced irrigation farming in the subtropical valleys.

EXPLORING THE REGION

The most fascinating way to discover the Northwest is aboard the **Tren a las Nubes (Train to the Clouds)** ✪, an all-day trip that takes you from Salta toward the Chilean border, climbing through breathtaking Andean landscapes and on to the magnificent La Puña Desert. For more, see the box "Riding the Train to the Clouds," below.

Even if you don't find time for that 15-hour locomotive adventure, you can still witness the rich history and flavor of the Northwest in its principal towns of **Salta** and **San Salvador de Jujuy.** Keep your eyes open for cultural festivals or religious celebrations to glimpse just how alive the Northwest's traditions remain. Three days at a minimum to 5 days should allow you to thoroughly experience the flavor of the region. The easiest way to visit the Northwest is to rent a car, take a bus, or hire a tour guide.

1 Salta ✪

90km (56 miles) south of San Salvador de Jujuy, 1,497km (928 miles) north of Buenos Aires; 1,268km (786 miles) north of Mendoza

One of Argentina's largest provinces, Salta is bordered by Chile, Bolivia, and Paraguay and is characterized by vastly diverse terrain, ranging from the fertile valley of the provincial capital to the polychrome canyons of Cafayate and the desolate plateau of La Puña. The provincial capital, also called Salta, sits in the Lerma valley with an eternal springlike climate. It is a town boasting Argentina's best-preserved colonial architecture. Wandering its narrow streets and charming plazas, you will get a sense of how Salta has existed for centuries—quietly, graciously, and reservedly. Salta, however, loses its quietude during *Carnaval* (Mardi Gras), when thousands of Salteños come out for a parade of floats celebrating the region's history; water balloons are also tossed from balconies with great aplomb. Without doubt, however, the Tren a las Nubes is Salta's main attraction (see the "Riding the Train to the Clouds" box, below).

ESSENTIALS
GETTING THERE
I don't recommend making the long-distance drive to Argentina's Northwest; it's safer and much easier to either fly or take the bus.

BY PLANE   Flights land at **Aybal International Airport,** RN 51 (© 387/424-2904), 10km (6¼ miles) from the city center. **Aerolíneas Argentinas** (© 0810/222-86527), **Southern Winds** (© 0810/777-7979), and **American Falcon** (© 0810/222-3253) fly from Buenos Aires (some flights make a stop in Córdoba). Nonstop flights from Buenos Aires take 2 hours and cost between $55 and $100 each way, depending on the season and availability. **LAB Aero Boliviano** (© 387/431-0320) flies twice a week from Santa Cruz, Bolivia, the sole international arrival. A shuttle bus travels between the airport and town for about $1 one-way; a taxi into town will run about $3.

BY BUS   The **Terminal de Omnibus,** or central bus station, is at Avenida H. Yrigoyen and Abraham Cornejo (© 387/431-5227). Buses arrive from Buenos Aires (22 hr., $40) and travel to San Salvador de Jujuy (2½ hr., $2) and other cities in the region. **Chevalier** (© 387/431-2819) and **La Veloz del Norte** (© 387/431-7215) are the main bus companies.

VISITOR INFORMATION
The tourism office, **Secretaría de Turismo de Salta,** Buenos Aires 93 (© 387/431-0950 or 387/431-0640; www.turismosalta.gov.ar), will provide you with maps and information on dining, lodging, and sightseeing in the region. It can also help you arrange individual or group tours. It's open weekdays 8am to 9pm and weekends 9am to 8pm. In Buenos Aires, obtain information about Salta from the **Casa de Salta en Bs. As.,** Sáenz Pena 933 (© 011/4326-2426).

FAST FACTS: SALTA
Currency Exchange   Exchange money at the airport, at **Dinar Exchange,** Mitre and España (© 387/432-2600), or at **Banco de La Nación,** Mitre and Belgrano (© 387/431-1909). Open 8:30am to 2pm.

Emergency   Dial © 377/431-9000 for police, © 377/421-2222 for fire.

Hospital   Saint Bernard Hospital, Dr. M. Boedo 69 (© 387/421-4926).

Tour Operators   Arrange a tour of the region with **Saltur Turismo,** Caseros 525 (© 387/421-2012). The tourist office can also recommend English-speaking tour guides.

GETTING AROUND
Salta is small and easy to explore by foot. The **Peatonal Florida** is Salta's pedestrian walking street—a smaller version of Calle Florida in Buenos Aires—where most of the city's shops are. The main sites are centered on **Plaza 9 de Julio,** where a monument to General Arenales stands in the center and a beautiful baroque cathedral stands at its edge. Built in 1858, the **Catedral** is considered

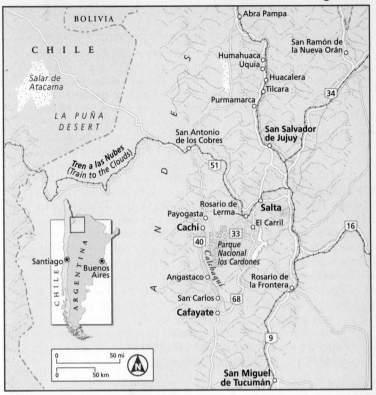

Argentina's best-preserved colonial church. All the other attractions here—except the **Salta Tram** and the **Tren a las Nubes**—are within easy walking distance.

RENTING A CAR   Rent a Truck 4×4 and Car, Buenos Aires 1 Local 6 Caseros 489 (© **387/431-0740**), has subcompacts and four-wheel drives. **Hertz** is at Caseros 374 (© **387/421-7553**) and **Avis** is at the airport (© **387/424-2289**). Following the currency evaluation, cars have become more affordable to rent here, ranging from $35 to $45 per day.

SEEING THE SIGHTS

Most museums in the Northwest don't have formal admission fees; instead, they request small contributions, usually $1 or less.

El Cabildo/Museo Histórico del Norte (Historic Museum of the North)

First erected in 1582 when the city was founded, the Cabildo has since reinvented itself a number of times. The latest town hall was completed in 1783 and is typical of Spanish construction—two levels and a tower built around interior patios. The building houses the Museo Histórico del Norte (Historic Museum of the North), with 15 exhibition halls related to the Indian, colonial, and liberal periods of Salteño history. Here you will see religious and popular art, as well as works from the Jesuit period and from Upper Peru.

Caseros 549. © **387/421-5340.** Museum Tues–Sat 9:30am–1:30pm and 3:30–8:30pm; Sun 9:30am–1:30pm.

Riding the Train to the Clouds

The **"train to the clouds"** ✿ is one of the world's great railroad experiences—a breathtaking ride that climbs to 4,220m (13,842 ft.) without the help of cable tracks. The journey takes you 434km (269 miles) through tunnels, turns, and bridges, culminating in the stunning La Polvorilla viaduct. You will cross magnificent landscapes, making your way from the multicolored Lerma valley through the deep canyons and rugged peaks of the Quebrada del Toro and on to the desolate desert plateau of La Puña. The train stops at the peak, where your tour guide (there's one in each car) will describe the region's topography and check that everyone is breathing fine and not suffering from altitude sickness. In the small town of San Antonio de los Cobres, you'll have a chance to buy handicrafts, ponchos, and other textile goods from the indigenous people. The 14½-hour ride includes a small breakfast, lunch (additional), and a folkloric show with regional music and dance. A restaurant, post office, communications center, and infirmary are among the first-class passenger cars. The ride makes for a fascinating experience, but be prepared for a very long day.

The ticket office for *Tren a las Nubes* (Train to the Clouds) is at Mitre and España (© **387/432-2600**). The train operates April to November and departs Salta's General Belgrano Station most Saturdays at 7:10am and returns that night at 9:50pm, making one stop. In July there are additional trains every Tuesday and Thursday.

The cost in first class is **$68**, not including lunch.

Iglesia San Francisco (San Francisco Church) ✿✿   Rebuilt in 1759 after a fire destroyed the original building, the Iglesia San Francisco is Salta's most prominent postcard image. The terra-cotta facade with its 53m (174-ft.) tower and tiered white pillars was designed by architect Luis Giorgi. The belfry—the tallest in the Americas—holds the *Campaña de la Patria*, a bronze bell made from the cannons used in the War of Independence's Battle of Salta. A small museum exhibits a variety of 17th- and 18th-century religious images.

Córdoba and Caseros. No phone. Daily 8am–noon and 4–8pm.

Museo de Arqueológia de Alta Montaña (Andean Archaeological Museum) ✿✿   The MAAM, as it has fast become known in Salta, opened its doors on the main plaza in November 2004 to much fanfare. A beautifully restored historic building, the MAAM houses a good collection of Andean textiles woven over the years. This museum is also home to a large research library dedicated to Andean culture and anthropology. The main focus of the museum is its film screen, which shows the recent excavations at Mount Llullaillaco, the highest volcanic peak in Argentina, near the Chilean border. There, three amazingly preserved Andean mummies (over 500 years old) were found in 1999 by a *National Geographic* team of archaeologists, and MAAM was designed for their display. The mummies are still being studied by scientists but will soon be on exhibit here, although at press time there is no exact date available. Over 100 other objects were found with the mummies—gold statues and other objects dating back to the Inca era, which will also slowly be featured over the coming years. Already, the locals are affectionately calling this place the mummy museum (*museo de las momias*). Plan to spend an hour here if you want to watch the 30-minute documentary; longer, of course, if the mummies are finally on display.

Mitre 77. (✆) **387/437-0499**. Admission $1. Tues–Sun 9am–1pm and 4–8pm.

Museo Histórico José Evaristo Uriburo (★) José Evaristo Uriburo's family, which produced two of Argentina's presidents, bought this simple adobe house with a roof of reeds and curved tiles in 1810. An entrance from the street leads directly to the courtyard, characteristic of homes of this era. Exhibits include period furniture and costumes, as well as documents and objects belonging to the Uriburos and General Arenales.

Caseros 179. (✆) **387/421-5340**. Tues–Sat 9:30am–1:30pm and 3:30–8:30pm; Sun 9:30am–1:30pm.

Museo Provincial de Bellas Artes de Salta (Museum of Fine Arts) (★) Colorfully decorated tapestries and other regional works fill this 18th-century Spanish house, which houses a permanent collection of colonial art upstairs and religious and contemporary art downstairs. Noteworthy pieces include a portrait of Francisco de Uriburo by Spanish painter Joaquín Sorolla y Bastida and a painting of Salta by Italian Carlo Penutti.

Florida 20. (✆) **387/421-4714**. Mon–Fri 8:30am–12:30pm and 4:30–8:30pm; Sat 9am–7pm.

San Bernardo Convent (★★) This is the oldest religious building in Salta, declared a Historical National Monument in 1941. It's worth a walk by to admire the city's most impressive example of colonial and indigenous art (only Carmelite nuns are allowed to enter). The entrance was carved from a carob tree by aborigines in 1762.

Caseros near Santa Fe.

Teleférico (Salta Tram) (★) This Swiss-made cable car has been in operation since 1987 and takes tourists to the top of San Bernardo Hill, 300m (984 ft.) over Salta, where there's not much to do other than enjoy the panoramic view of the Lerma valley and grab a snack at the casual restaurant. If you miss the last tram, a cheap taxi will return you to the city center.

At the intersection of avenidas H. Yrigoyen and San Martín. (✆) **387/431-0641**. Admission $3 adults, $2 children. Daily 10am–7:30pm.

OUTDOOR ACTIVITIES & TOUR OPERATORS

The bounty of nature around Salta is staggering. Since most of the landscape is untouched and there are gorges and canyons and volcanic peaks to negotiate, **trekking** is the most popular outdoor activity in the area. **Adventure Life Journeys** (1655 S. 3rd St. W., Missoula, MT 59801; (✆) **800/344-6118** or 406/541-2677; www.adventure-life.com) offers some of the best-organized treks in the region, usually beginning and ending in Buenos Aires. Their popular 9-day Northwest trek through Salta, Cafayate, and Cachi runs about $1,695 per person, everything included.

Ecotourism is gaining popularity in the area due to the abundance of wildlife. One- to 4-day safaris and bird-watching expeditions are organized by **Clark Expediciones** (Caseros 121, Salta; (✆) **387/421-5390;** www.clarkexpediciones.com.ar), an excellent local outfitter. Their bird-watching trips run from half a day to 2 days, and the highlight is usually seeing the immense Andean Condor soaring over the mountains.

Rafting, windsurfing, and other **watersports** are becoming popular in the Dique Cabra Corral, 70km (43 miles) south of Salta. For more information,

contact **Salta Rafting** (Buenos Aires 88; ✆ **387/401-0301;** info@saltarafting.
com) and **Active Argentina** (Zuviria 982; ✆ **387/4311-1868**).

SHOPPING

The Secretary of Tourism of the province of Salta does a great job controlling
their handmade products—from textiles to bamboo and wood ornaments—and
they are sold (after certification) only at the **Mercado Artesanal,** San Martín
2555 (no phone), open from 9am to 9pm daily. Here, you'll find authentic
products from leather goods to candles made throughout Salta Province by local
craftsmen and women. The price is controlled, too, so you don't have to worry
about bargaining here. You'll also find beautiful jewelry and silver.

WHERE TO STAY

Until the new Marriott resort opens in 2006, Salta will not have a truly luxurious hotel. But there are good options both in and outside the city center. Staying in the city center gives you a chance to walk everywhere. But if you're after
some peace and quiet, consider staying in the nearby village of San Lorenzo or
at a ranch just outside the city center.

IN THE CITY CENTER
Expensive

Casa Real Hotel 🏵🏵 *Value*   The most luxury you can get in Salta for under
$100 per room is at this new hotel, opened in 2004, right in the center of town.
Rooms are very spacious and comfortable, with big picture windows (some overlooking the mountains), large-screen TVs, and firm, comfortable beds. Bathrooms are also large and very clean. The Casa Real boasts a decent-size exercise
room and a good-size indoor pool, as well as an attractive restaurant and bar.
The staff is friendly and can help in arranging transportation and tours.

Mitre 669, 4400 Salta. ✆ 387/421-5675. www.hotelcasareal.com.ar. 83 units. $87–$97 double; from $107
suite. Rates include buffet breakfast. AE, DC, MC, V. **Amenities:** Restaurant; bar; lounge; indoor pool; exercise room; sauna; business center with free Internet; meeting rooms; room service; laundry service; dry cleaning. *In room:* A/C, TV, minibar, hair dryer, safe.

Gran Hotel Presidente 🏵   This contemporary hotel has attractive guest
rooms splashed in rose and apple green with sparkling white-tile bathrooms. The
chic lobby features black and white marble with Art Deco furniture and leop-
ard-skin upholstery. The pleasant international restaurant is located on the
upstairs mezzanine, and there's a spa with a heated indoor pool, a sauna, a fitness room, and a solarium.

Av. de Belgrano 353, 4400 Salta. ✆/fax 387/431-2022. 96 units. $110 double; $170 suite. Rates include buffet breakfast. AE, DC, MC, V. **Amenities:** Restaurant; small indoor pool; exercise room; sauna; meeting rooms;
room service; laundry service; dry cleaning. *In room:* A/C, TV, minibar, hair dryer, safe.

Hotel Solar de la Plaza 🏵🏵🏵 *Finds*   This absolutely charming hotel used to
be the residence of one of Salta's well-known families, Patron Costas. In 2000, a
new wing was built behind the main house and the hotel opened its doors. The
four rooms in the older section were the actual bedrooms of the family members. They have been meticulously transformed into comfortable hotel rooms
while retaining their old-world feel—hardwood floors, Jacuzzi tubs, and
wrought-iron floor lamps (handmade in Salta). The rooms in the newer wing
sport the same decor but with a slightly more modern feel, including marble
pedestal sinks in the bathrooms and writing desks made from local wood. Service is gracious and refined, and the public areas are incredibly elegant, from the
rooftop pool with its adjoining sun deck to the attractive restaurant serving

regional specialties with a nouvelle twist. The competent and English-speaking staff can arrange many outdoor activities, including hiking, horseback riding, and bird-watching at the Patron Costas nearby ranch.

Juan M. Leguizamon 669, 4400 Salta. ©/fax 387/431-5111. www.solardelaplaza.com.ar. 30 units. $120–$140 double; $190 suite. Rates include continental breakfast. AE, DC, MC, V. **Amenities:** Restaurant; bar; lounge; small outdoor pool; exercise room; sauna; business center; limited room service. *In room:* A/C, TV, minibar, safe.

Moderate

Hotel Salta ⭐ *(Moments*   Popular with Europeans, this neoclassical hotel sits in the heart of Salta—facing Plaza 9 de Julio—and makes an excellent base from which to explore the city. Opened in 1890, these are hardly the most modern accommodations you'll find, but the hotel's wood balconies and arabesque carvings, peaceful courtyard, refreshing pool, and beautiful dining room overlooking the plaza considerably increase its appeal. At $10 more, "A" rooms are larger than standard rooms and have bathtubs, as opposed to just showers. The friendly staff will arrange horseback riding, golf, and other outdoor activities upon request.

Buenos Aires 1, 4400 Salta. ©/fax 387/431-0740. www.hotelsalta.com. 98 units. From $47 double; from $95 suite. Rates include buffet breakfast. AE, DC, MC, V. **Amenities:** Restaurant; bar; pool; sauna; small business center; meeting rooms; room service; massage; laundry service. *In room:* A/C, TV, minibar, safe.

Portezuelo Hotel *(Overrated*   The Portezuelo Hotel stands on top of Cerro San Bernardo, a hill just outside the city center. Guest rooms have A-frame ceilings and simple wood decor; unfortunately, they are a bit shabby and drab, and are not well maintained. The tiny bathrooms desperately need some care. At $10 more, VIP rooms are slightly larger than standard ones and have work desks and safe deposit boxes, but offer no luxury. Stay here only if the other hotels are full.

Av. Turística 1, 4400 Salta. © 387/431-0104. Fax 387/431-4654. www.portezuelohotel.com. 63 units. From $44 double; from $62 suite. Rates include buffet breakfast. AE, DC, MC, V. **Amenities:** Restaurant; bar; outdoor pool; room service; laundry service. *In room:* TV, minibar, hair dryer, safe.

Inexpensive

Victoria Plaza   If your purpose in Salta is sightseeing rather than hotel appreciation, then the Victoria Plaza should do just fine. Rooms are stark and simple but also clean, comfortable, and cheerfully maintained. Those on the seventh floor and above enjoy better views for a few dollars more. The hotel has an excellent location next to the main plaza, the *cabildo* (town hall), and the cathedral. The cafeteria-like restaurant is open 24 hours, and the hotel offers free airport transfers.

Zuviría 16, 4400 Salta. ©/fax 387/431-8500. 96 units. From $24 double. Rates include buffet breakfast. AE, DC, MC, V. **Amenities:** Tiny exercise room; sauna; meeting room; laundry service. *In room:* A/C, TV, fridge.

OUTSIDE THE CITY CENTER
Very Expensive

House of Jasmines ⭐⭐⭐ *(Moments*   American actor Robert Duvall and his Argentine wife bought this pristine farmhouse on 120 hectares (300 acres) and converted it into a fantastic inn in 2004, worthy of a spread in *House & Garden*. A large photograph of the actor hangs over the beautiful fireplace in the main living room as you enter the house. Each of the seven rooms is different, but all are exquisitely decorated in keeping with the colonial feel of the house—four-posted beds, antique furniture, and fluffy duvets. Fresh roses (and jasmines in season) will fill your room with a glorious scent. Bathrooms are sparkling and new. Most guests opt to dine in the elegant dining room, and the chef prepares everything from scratch—even the bread is baked on the premises. There are

miles of trails and open fields surrounding a magnificent swimming pool and a
rose garden. You are a guest here, not a customer, and the staff will do everything
to help make you feel at home. Although the owners are American, the staff does
not speak English. The farmhouse is located close to Salta's airport, about a 15-
minute drive from the city center.

Camino al Encon, La Merced Chica, 4407 Salta. ℂ/fax **387/497-2002**. www.houseofjasmines.com. 7 units.
$130–$260. Rates include continental breakfast. MC, V. **Amenities:** Restaurant; lounge; pristine outdoor
pool; room service; laundry service.

Moderate

El Castillo 𝘊𝘊 *Finds*   A 10-minute drive from downtown Salta, this lovely
hideaway feels like it's 100 miles away. Built in the late 1800s as a summer home
in the style of an Italian "Castello" by Italian immigrant Luigi Bartoletti, it was
bought some 20 years ago by John Johnston from Alabama who has lovingly
restored it to its turn-of-the-20th-century glory. The rooms are different but all
are comfortable and furnished with antiques. Room no. 3 has a Jacuzzi tub and
large windows with views of the lush grounds. The two-story suite comes with
a fireplace and a giant candelabra. The restaurant serves excellent regional specialties. There are also countless outdoor activities in the area that the friendly
English-speaking staff will be happy to arrange for you.

Camino a la Quebrada, Villa San Lorenzo, 4193 Salta. ℂ/fax **387/492-1052**. www.hotelelcastillo.com.ar. 8
units. $42–$58 double; $87 suite. Rates include continental breakfast. MC, V. **Amenities:** Restaurant; lounge;
beautiful outdoor pool; room service. *In room:* TV.

WHERE TO DINE

The Northwest has its own cuisine influenced by indigenous cooking. *Locro*
(a corn and bean soup), *humitas* (a sort of corn and goat cheese soufflé), tamales
(meat and potatoes in a ground corn shell), empanadas (a turnover filled with
potatoes, meat, and vegetables), *lechón* (suckling pig), and *cabrito* (goat) occupy
most menus. Traditional Argentine steaks and pasta dishes usually are available,
too. In addition to the locations listed below, the Mercado Central, at Florida
and San Martín, has a number of inexpensive eateries serving regional food.

MODERATE

Café van Gogh 𝘊 CAFE   "Our mission is to make everyone feel at home, no
matter where they're from," says one staff member, who proudly displays a collection of coffee cups from Argentina, Europe, and North America. This cheeky
cafe, surrounded by little white lights on the outside and decorated with van
Gogh prints inside, serves pizzas, sandwiches, meats, hot dogs, and empanadas.
Come evening, the cafe-turned-bar becomes the center of Salta nightlife, with
live bands playing Wednesday through Saturday after midnight. Café van Gogh
is also a popular spot for breakfast.

España 502. ℂ **387/431-4659**. Main courses $3–$4. AE, DC, MC, V. Mon–Thurs 7am–2am; Fri–Sat 24 hr.;
Sun 7am–1am.

El Solar del Convento 𝘊𝘊 ARGENTINE   Ask locals to point you to Salta's
best "typical" restaurant—the word used to describe places serving traditional
Argentine fare—and they won't hesitate with their answer. This former Jesuit
convent has long been an outstanding *parrilla* (grill) serving quality steaks (the
mixed grill for two is a deal at $4) and regional specialties like empanadas,
tamales, and *humitas*. The 10-page menu also includes beef brochettes, grilled
salmon, chicken with mushrooms, and large, fresh salads. There are two dining
rooms connected by an A-frame thatched roof, and a medieval-style chandelier

hangs from the ceiling. The atmosphere is festive and even late on a Sunday night, expect the restaurant to be packed.

Caseros 444. ℂ **387/439-3666.** Main courses $3–$6. AE, DC, MC, V. Daily 11am–3pm and 8pm–midnight.

Jose Balcance ★★★ (*Finds*) INTERNATIONAL/REGIONAL   Salta's newest and most elegant restaurant opened in 2004 and is destined to become one of the most talked-about eateries in Northwestern Argentina. Everything here is done right. From the exposed stone walls to the exquisite lighting and elegant dark wood tables to the very efficient service, you'll feel you have definitely come to a very special place. Andean cuisine with a modern flair is the specialty at Jose Balcance. Here's where you can try roasted llama meat served with Andean potatoes or quinoa. Or llama medallions with prickly pear sauce. Local goat cheese is served drizzled over a "tower" of grilled aubergines and olive tapenade. You can even have llama carpaccio if you're feeling truly adventurous, although simpler dishes are always available, such as fresh trout roasted with butter and ginger, or chicken curry with vegetables. The menu changes very often, and different world cuisines, in addition to the Andean, are featured occasionally. Order a well-chilled Torrontes white wine to round out your meal.

Mitre and Necochea. ℂ **387/421-1628.** Reservations recommended. Main courses $6–$9. AE, DC, MC, V. Mon–Thurs 9pm–midnight; Fri–Sat 9pm–1am.

Restaurante del Portezuelo Hotel REGIONAL   This restaurant in the Portezuelo Hotel offers good views, and the intimate dining room, with large windows overlooking the Lerma valley, is decorated with regional artwork and tables topped with white linens and silver candles. You won't go wrong with any of the creative entrees, such as trout stuffed with shrimp and cheese, sirloin steak with scalloped potatoes, or grilled chicken with mustard and tarragon. The restaurant also serves regional specialties like *locro, pastel de choclo* (corn-and-meat pie), empanadas, *humitas,* and tamales. Jazz music occasionally accompanies dinner. Consider a table on the veranda in warm weather.

Av. Turística 1. ℂ **387/431-0104.** Reservations recommended. Main courses $4–$7. AE, DC, MC, V. Daily noon–3pm and 8pm–1am.

Santana ★ INTERNATIONAL   This is one of the few international restaurants in Salta with a classic rather than rustic style. The enticing menu features chicken with white-wine cream sauce, lobster with chimichurri sauce, and homemade ravioli with various cheeses. There is a rich selection of Argentine wines; ask for a bottle from San Juan or Mendoza.

Mendoza 208. ℂ **387/432-0941.** Reservations recommended. Main courses $3–$5. AE, DC, MC, V. Daily noon–3:30pm and 8pm–midnight.

Viejo Jack II (*Kids*) (*Value*) ARGENTINE   An inexpensive local *parrilla* frequented by locals, Viejo Jack II (Viejo Jack I is at Av. Virrey Toledo 145) serves succulent steaks and fresh pastas. Kids have access to a play area as well.

Av. Reyes Católicos 1465. ℂ **387/439-2802.** Main courses $2–$4. DC, MC, V. Daily noon–3:30pm and 8:30pm–1am.

2 A Driving Tour of the Calchaquíes Valley via Cachi & Cafayate

The landscape surrounding Salta resembles the southwestern United States, with polychromatic hills keeping watch over the Lerma valley. Tobacco, tropical fruits, and sugar cane are the main agricultural products here, and you will see tobacco "ovens" off the side of the road (Marlboro grows Virginia tobacco here through a subsidiary). Heading south from Salta on RN 68 for 38km (24 miles) will bring you to **El Carril,** which is a typical small town of the valley, with a central plaza and botanical garden displaying 70% of the region's flora.

Although you can reach **Cafayate** more quickly by continuing south on RN 68, it is far more interesting to go west on RP 33 for about 2.7km (1¾ miles) after El Carril to **Cabaña de Cabras, La Flor del Pago** (© 387/499-1093), one of the principal goat farms and cheese factories in Argentina. Ducks, geese, and hundreds of goats roam the scenic property, and there is a small dining room and cheese shop in the proprietors' home where you can sample the delicious chèvre. A bread and jam snack costs only 40¢; a cheese sandwich is $1.50, and a glass of local wine is $1.25. (The kind owners will prepare a multicourse lunch or dinner with advance reservations.)

While the region surrounding El Carril is characterized by dense vegetation, the land quickly becomes dry as you climb RP 33 toward **Piedra del Molino (Mill Rock).** The road narrows from pavement to dirt 10km (6¼ miles) west of El Carril—watch closely for oncoming cars. A small shrine to Saint Raphael (a patron saint of travelers) indicates your arrival at Mill Rock (3,620m/11,874 ft. elevation) and the entrance to **Parque Nacional los Cardones,** a semiarid landscape filled with cacti, sage, and limestone rock formations.

Ten kilometers (6¼ miles) before Cachi lies **Payogasta,** an ancient Indian town on the path of the Inca Road that once connected an empire stretching from Peru to Northern Argentina. **Cachi** (see below) is another precolonial village worth a visit for its Indian ruins. From Cachi, take RN 40 south past Brealito to Molinos, a 17th-century town of adobe homes and dusty streets virtually unchanged from how it must have appeared 350 years ago. Continuing south, consider stopping 9km (5½ miles) before Angastaco at the **Estancia Carmen** (© 368/1569-3005), which boasts spectacular views of the Calchaquíes valley and its long mountain canyon. Between 9am and 6pm, you can visit the ranch's Inca ruins, rent horses, and peek inside the private church in back, where two 300-year-old mummies rest in peace.

Continue south on RN 40 to **Angastaco**—this may be a good place to spend the night. **Hostería Angastaco,** Avenida Libertad (© 3868/1563-9016), lies 1km (about ½ mile) west of the village and is popular with European travelers. The simple hotel offers live folkloric music each evening. The staff will help arrange regional excursions and horseback riding. From Angastaco to San Carlos, you will pass the **Quebrada de las Flechas (Arrows Ravine),** with its stunning rock formations that appeared in *The Empire Strikes Back*. People often stop their cars at the side of the road and climb a bit. Jesuits settled in **San Carlos,** and the church is a national historic monument. **Cafayate** (see below) marks the southern end of this circuit.

Return to Salta along RN 68 heading north, which takes you through the **Río Calchaquíes valley** and on to the **Quebrada del Río de las Conchas (Canyon of the River of Shells).** Among the most interesting crimson rock formations you should stop at are Garganta del Diablo (Devil's Throat), El Anfiteatro (the Ampitheater), and Los Castillos (the Castles), which are all indicated by road signs. Salta is 194km (120 miles) from Cafayate along RN 68, and it shouldn't take more than a few hours to drive.

CACHI ✦

Home of the Chicoanas Indians before the Spaniards arrived, Cachi is a tiny pueblo of about 5,000 people, interesting for its Indian ruins, colonial church, and archaeological museum. The Spanish colonial **church,** built in the 17th century and located next to the main plaza, has a floor and ceiling made from cactus wood. The **archaeological museum** is the most impressive museum of its kind in the Northwest, capturing the influence of the Incas and Spaniards on the region's indigenous people. Located next to the main plaza, its courtyard is filled with Inca stone engravings and pre-Columbian artifacts. Wall rugs, ponchos, and ceramics are sold at the **Centro Artesanal,** next to the tourist office, on the main plaza (the people of Cachi are well respected for their weaving skills, and the ponchos they sell are beautiful). **La Paya,** 10km (6¼ miles) south of Cachi, and **Potrero de Payogasta,** 10km (6¼ miles) north of Cachi, hold the area's most important archaeological sites.

GETTING THERE Cachi lies 157km (97 miles) west of Salta on RP 33. **Empresa Marcos Rueda** offers two buses daily from Salta; the trip takes 5 hours and costs $5.

VISITOR INFORMATION You can pick up maps, excursion information, and tips on restaurants and hotels at the **Oficina de Turismo,** Avenida General Güemes (© **3868/491053**), open Monday through Saturday from 9am to 8pm.

WHERE TO STAY
Hostal La Paya ⟁ Opened in 2000 on a 19th-century *estancia* (ranch), this rustic inn looks out to the Calchaquíes valley and is a quiet place to walk, read, and relax. Guest rooms have adobe walls and wood-beam ceilings, llama-wool rugs, and mattresses laid on stone frames. You can have your meals here, if you like—all the produce (except the meat) comes from this farm. The owners will also arrange excursions to the nearby mountains, valley, and river.

8km (5 miles) from Cachi, on RN 40 to Molinos. ©/fax **3868/491139.** 10 units. From $52 double. Rates include breakfast. No credit cards. **Amenities:** Restaurant; pool; outdoor excursions.

WHERE TO DINE
Confitería y Comedor del Sol REGIONAL When you walk into this village restaurant, locals are likely to cease their conversations and stare for a minute. Not to worry—they will quickly return to their business once you sit down; many are engaged in the afternoon's current soap opera. The menu is simple, consisting of pastas, *milanesas* (breaded meat cutlets), empanadas, and tamales. This is a great place to have lunch on your way to Molinos.

Ruiz de los Llanos. © **15/6055-149.** Main courses $1–$4. No credit cards. Daily 8am–1am.

CAFAYATE ⟁⟁
Cafayate is a picturesque colonial town nestled in the Río Calchaquíes valley and famous for its wine production. Popular with Argentine tourists, Cafayate's streets are lined with baroque-style houses built in the late 19th century. The main tourist attractions, in addition to the two major vineyards just outside town, are the Regional and Archaeological Museum and the Museum of Grapevines and Wine (see below). You can find regional arts and crafts of excellent quality at shops surrounding the main plaza.

GETTING THERE Cafayate lies 194km (120 miles) southwest of Salta on RN 68. **Empresa El Indio** (© **387/432-0846**) offers three buses daily from Salta; the trip takes 3½ hours and costs about $5.

VISITOR INFORMATION The **tourist office** (© **3868/421470**) is located on the main plaza and provides maps, bus schedules, and lodging recommendations. Open hours are Monday through Saturday from 10am to 6pm.

SEEING THE SIGHTS

Though there are quite a few vineyards to visit in the area, some unexpectedly shut down their guided visits for extended periods for renovations or for other inexplicable reasons. When I visited Cafayate in November 2004, roughly half the *bodegas* were not open to the public. The most popular months to visit are February to early April, when the harvest occurs. Most wineries are open daily except Sunday during that time. I've listed below the wineries most likely to be open year-round. Most museums in this area are free or request a small donation, usually no more than $1.

Bodegas Etchart 🍷   Owned by the French giant Pernod-Ricard, this is one of the region's most important vineyards, producing 6,000 bottles of wine per hour—including chardonnay (for which this *bodega* is best known), cabernet sauvignon, Tannat, Torrontes, and Malbec. The *bodega* exports its wine to more than 30 countries. One-hour guided tours and wine tastings are offered Monday through Friday from 9am to 3pm, and Saturday from 9am to noon.

Finca La Rosa, 3km (1¾ miles) from Cafayate on RN 40. 🕐 **3868/421310.**

Finca Las Nubes 🍷🍷🍷 *Finds*   One of Argentina's smallest vineyards is strictly family run and produces some young but excellent wines. This is the last frontier of winemaking, a few kilometers up a dirt road from the center of town. Jose and Mercedes Mounier started their tiny operation 8 years ago, producing 2,000 bottles. In 2004, they produced 30,000 bottles of Cabernet-Malbec, Rose de Malbec, and Torrontes. They use no fertilizer on their vines—so the wine is almost organic. If you call ahead, the Mouniers will arrange for lunch and dinner to be served on their lovely terrace overlooking the vineyard. During visiting hours, you'll see the tiny operation up close and personal (including the labeling of bottles and boxes of wine being readied for shipment). A wine and cheese tasting is the highlight of the 1-hour visit. The Mouniers have a comfortable *cabaña* for rent next to the house overlooking the fields for $40 per night, including breakfast. Wine tours and tastings are offered free of charge Monday to Saturday 9am to 5pm; call for an appointment outside of these hours or to arrange for a meal.

El Divisadero, Alto Valle de Cafayate, 5km (3 miles) from Cafayate (ask for directions from town). 🕐 **3868/422129.** Japmounier@yahoo.com.ar. Mon–Sat 9am–5pm.

Michel Torino Bodega La Rosa 🍷🍷   This medium-size *bodega,* open since 1892, produces roughly 10 million liters of wine per year (10,000 bottles per hour), with Malbec (a dry red), cabernet sauvignon, merlot, chardonnay, and "Michael Torino" Torrontes (a Muscadet-like white) the main products. The Don David reserve is the vineyard's top selection. Guided tours in Spanish only are offered Monday through Thursday from 9am to 5pm, and Friday from 9am to 4pm. The *bodega* also has a small guesthouse with charming rustic rooms.

Finca La Rosa, 3km (1¾ miles) from Cafayate on RN 40. No phone. Mon–Thurs 9am–5pm; Fri 9am–4pm.

Museo de Vitivinicultura (Museum of Grapevines and Wine) 🍷🍷   Part of the Bodega Encantada winery, this museum tells the story of grape-growing and wine-making in and around Cafayate. The 19th-century building houses old-fashioned machinery and more modern equipment, as well as agricultural implements and documentary photographs.

RN 40, at Av. General Güemes. 🕐 **3868/421125.** Mon–Fri 10am–1pm and 5–9pm.

Travel Tip: He who finds the best hotel deal has more to spend on facials involving knobbly vegetables.

Hello, the Roaming Gnome here. I've been nabbed from the garden and taken round the world. The people who took me are so terribly clever. They find the best offerings on Travelocity. For very little cha-ching. And that means I get to be pampered and exfoliated till I'm pink as a bunny's doodah.

travelocity

1-888-TRAVELOCITY / travelocity.com / America Online Keyword: Travel

Plan your vacation

- flights, hotels, car rentals
- cruises & vacation packages
- destination guides
- fare alerts
- go to yahoo.com, click travel

**Museo Regional y Arqueológico Rodolfo Bravo (Regional and Archae-
ological Museum)** ⊛   This small museum displays ceramics, textiles, and
metal objects discovered over a 66-year period by Rodolfo Bravo. These archaeological finds celebrate the heritage of Diaguita-Calchaquíes and Inca tribes in
the region and cover a period between the 4th and 15th centuries.

Colón 191. ✆ 3868/421054. Hours vary.

Vasija Secreta ⊛   At the entrance of town, this large *bodega* also houses a
small but interesting museum with wine-making equipment dating back to
1857. A good collection of black-and-white photos depicts life at the *bodega* in
the late 1800s. There are also huge oak barrels (ca. 1900) from Nancy, France,
and barrels made from local wood that ruined the wine and thus were not used
much. The 1-hour tour ends with a tasting of the various wines, most of them
sold to restaurants around Argentina. Vasija Secreta, unlike other *bodegas,* markets heavily for the local market.

RN 40, Valle Calchaquies. ✆ 3868/421850. Mon–Sat 9am–4pm.

WHERE TO STAY

A much-needed deluxe hotel, a Design Suites, is under construction and will
open in 2006. Until then, there is no luxury to be found in Cafayate—just bare
accommodations warranting only a speedy overnight stay. For more charm and
character, book the comfortable Cabaña at Finca Las Nubes (see above), and
you'll have lovely views of the vineyards and a chance to mingle with Jose
Mounier, a seasoned winemaker, and his wife, Mercedes, who own the *bodega.*

Gran Real   This terribly modest hotel has quiet rooms with very simple furnishings. These rooms, some with pleasant mountain views, are considerably
more enticing than the gloomy downstairs lobby and cafe. Popular with Argentine visitors, the Gran Real has an attractive pool and barbecue area, which is its
saving grace. Service is friendly. TVs are available, on request, for an additional
$3 per night.

Av. General Güemes 128, 4427 Cafayate. ✆ 3868/421231. Fax 3868/421016. 35 units. $20 double. Rates
include continental breakfast. MC, V. **Amenities:** Restaurant; lounge; nice outdoor pool. *In room:* TV on request.

Hostal Killa ⊛ *(Value*   Opened in mid-2004, this pleasant hostal is very well
maintained and is a short walk from the main plaza. Set back from the street,
the rooms face a small courtyard and are very basic but charming, with wood
furnishings made from local trees. Bathrooms are tiny but adequate and
sparkling clean. Room no. 7 has a larger stone and marble bathroom and a hallway with two handmade wooden chairs. There's an upstairs apartment, with a
small kitchen, that sleeps four. A pleasant garden with an olive tree and a barbecue area is also on the premises.

Colon 47, 4427 Cafayate. ✆ 3868/422254. Hostalkillacafayate@hotmail.com. 8 units. $27 double; $50
apartment for 4. Rates include continental breakfast. No credit cards. **Amenities:** Small lounge.

WHERE TO DINE

El Rancho ⊛ ARGENTINIAN   This is the best restaurant on the main plaza
and is less touristy than La Carreta (below). When locals go out to eat, they come
here. The expansive dining room has an authentic bamboo roof, and the fans
overhead keep things cool in the summer months. Start with freshly made
empanadas, *humitas*, or tamales and a salad, and move on to oven-baked *cabrito*
(young goat) with roasted potatoes. Pastas are made on the premises here and
served with a variety of meat dishes, including tenderloin, if you're after something

simple. They have decent house wines, served in small jugs, and a short wine list featuring local wines.

Vicario Toscano 4. © **3868/421256.** Main courses $3–$6. MC, V. Daily noon–3:30pm and 8–11:30pm.

La Carreta de Don Olegario REGIONAL   Popular with foreign visitors, this restaurant has a pleasant dining room that lacks elegance, but the kitchen serves up an authentic selection of regional dishes, including *cabritos*. Service is unhurried, so plan to enjoy a leisurely lunch or dinner if you come here. Folkloric shows take place in the evenings.

Av. General Güemes 20. © **3868/421004.** Main courses $2–$3. MC, V. Daily noon–3pm and 8–11pm.

3 San Salvador de Jujuy

1,620km (1,004 miles) northwest of Buenos Aires; 90km (56 miles) north of Salta

The regional capital of Jujuy, San Salvador—commonly called Jujuy—was established by the Spaniards in 1592 as their northernmost settlement in Argentina. In 1812, during the wars of independence, General Belgrano evacuated residents of the city before Spanish troops arrived—an event celebrated each July known as *éxodo jujeño* (Jujuy Exodus). The well-preserved colonial town is smaller than Salta and doesn't have a great deal to offer, although there are a few interesting museums and a beautiful cathedral surrounding Plaza Belgrano. The Indian market across from the bus terminal offers a good sense of daily life here, with many vendors dressed in traditional costumes selling food, indigenous crafts, and textiles. Jujuy is also the best base from which to explore the Quebrada de Humahuaca (Humahuaca Gorge), which extends to the north (see the "Driving the Quebrada de Humahuaca [Humahuaca Gorge]" section below). The circuit includes the Cerro de los Siete Colores (Hill of the Seven Colors), the artists' haven Tilcara, and La Garganta del Diablo (Devil's Throat) gorge.

ESSENTIALS

GETTING THERE   Jujuy's airport (© 388/491-1109) is 35km (22 miles) from town. **Aerolíneas Argentinas** (© 0810/222-86527) and **Southern Winds** (© 0810/777-7979) fly from Buenos Aires. Flights from Buenos Aires cost between $80 and $200, depending on the season and availability.

The **Terminal de Omnibus,** or main bus station, is located at Dorrego and Iguazú (© 388/422-1375). Buses arrive from Buenos Aires and travel to Salta, Tucumán, Catamarca, and other cities in the region. **Empresa Balut** (© 387/432-0608) makes the 2½-hour trip to Humahuaca (see "Driving the Quebrada de Humahuaca [Humahuaca Gorge]" section below), as well as to other cities throughout the region.

If you opt to rent a car, there are a few independent companies located at the airport.

VISITOR INFORMATION & FAST FACTS   The **regional visitor center** is located at Urquiza 354 (© 388/424-9501), in the old train station. It is open weekdays from 7am to 9pm and weekends from 9am to 9pm.

You can arrange regional tours at **Grafitti Turismo,** Belgrano 601 (© 388/423-4033). They will exchange money here, too.

Citibank, located at the corner of España and Balcare, has a 24-hour ATM and change machine. The bank is open weekdays from 9am to 2pm.

GETTING AROUND   Easy to explore on foot, Jujuy is more compact than Salta, and its major attractions can be visited in a few hours. The bulk of commercial activity takes place around **Plaza Belgrano,** where the Casa de Gobierno, the cabildo (town hall), and the cathedral are located. Built in 1750, the **Cate-dral** has a baroque pulpit carved in wood by the indigenous people and should not be missed. Shopping in Jujuy is concentrated along **Calle Belgrano.**

SEEING THE SIGHTS

Most museums in this area are free or request a small donation, usually no more than $1.

Catedral (Cathedral) ⊛ Successor to an earlier cathedral dating from the 17th century, this beautiful updated version, built in 1763, salvaged the original wood pulpit characteristic of Spanish baroque. The cathedral towers over bustling Plaza Belgrano, where a pottery market takes place during the day.

West side of Plaza Belgrano. No phone. Daily 8am–noon and 5–8:30pm.

Museo Arqueológico Provincial (Provincial Archaeological Museum) ⊛⊛ Archaeological finds here represent over 2,500 years of life in the Jujuy region, including a 2,600-year-old ceramic goddess, a lithic collection of arrowheads, the bones of a child from 1,000 years ago, and two mummified adults. Objects from the Yavi and Humahuaca cultures are also exhibited.

Lavalle 434. © 388/422-1315. Daily 9am–noon and 3–8pm.

Museo Histórico Provincial (Provincial Historical Museum) ⊛ This was the house in which General Lavalle was killed in 1841, and the large door through which he was shot is on display, right next to an enormous bust of the Argentine hero. Other exhibits include war materials and documents used during the 25-year struggle for independence in Jujuy.

Lavalle 252. © 388/422-1355. Mon–Fri 8am–12:30pm and 4–8pm; Sat–Sun 9am–1pm and 4–8pm.

WHERE TO STAY

Accommodations in the Northwest have become more reasonably priced following the peso's devaluation, but their quality has not improved much. The places we list are the best you will find, but in many cases that's not saying much. Yet you're here to see the sights, not to linger in the confines of your hotel. Note that accommodations in San Salvador quickly fill up in July during the *éxodo jujeño* (Jujuy Exodus) celebration.

Altos de la Viña ⊛ *Kids* This is the best hotel in Jujuy, located on a hill 3km (1¾ miles) from the city center. A wealth of outdoor activities on the sprawling property includes volleyball, miniature golf, tennis, and swimming in the outdoor pool. Half of the guest rooms have balconies with terrific views of the city; bathrooms have phones, hair dryers, and good amenities. The best rooms are "VIPs" (only $15 more)—they feature classic furniture, impressive woodwork, and linens decorated with country French colors. The hotel has an excellent restaurant and a very friendly staff.

Av. Pasquini López 50, 4600 Jujuy. © 388/426-2626. 70 units. From $80 double; $120 suite. Breakfast included. AE, DC, MC, V. **Amenities:** Restaurant; outdoor pool; tennis; volleyball; children's games; room service; massage; babysitting; laundry service. *In room:* A/C, TV, minibar, hair dryer.

Jujuy Palace Hotel ⊛ If lobbies are any indication of a hotel's quality, then the modern and comfortable furnishings you'll find upon entering the Jujuy Palace prove that the management is committed to maintaining a good face. Guest rooms have been remodeled and are modern and inviting, with locally made lamps. Fluffy pillows and new black-and-white bedspreads have been added. Both the rooms and the bathrooms are rather small. If you'd like space, splurge for the suite, with its separate living area and spacious bathroom. The restaurant is attractive and serves excellent steaks. The hotel is centrally located in front of the cathedral.

Calle Belgrano 1060, 4600 Jujuy. ©/fax **388/423-0433**. jpalace@imagine.com.ar. 52 units. $44 double; $62 suite. Rates include buffet breakfast. AE, DC, MC, V. **Amenities:** Restaurant; gym; sauna; room service. In room: A/C, TV.

WHERE TO DINE

Chung King ✦ REGIONAL   Despite the misleading name, Chung King is a longtime regional favorite in Jujuy, serving *humitas,* tamales, empanadas, *picante de pollo,* and *pollo al ajillo* (both local chicken and vegetable dishes). On Saturday evenings, local artists perform traditional Northwestern dances here and the atmosphere is very fun and festive. A pizzeria is located next door serving delicious oven-baked pizzas.

Alvear 627. © **388/422-8142.** Main courses $3–$6. AE, DC, MC, V. Daily 11:30am–4pm and 7pm–3am.

Krysys ✦ *Finds* REGIONAL   A giant Coke sign outside marks the entrance to Jujuy's best *parrilla,* serving juicy Argentine steaks. The international menu also has a number of pasta and chicken selections, and the trout is excellent. This is a festive restaurant, where locals come to celebrate good times and special occasions.

Balcarce 272. © **388/423-1126.** Main courses $3–$5. AE, DC, MC, V. Daily noon–3:30pm and 8pm–2am (Sun only for lunch).

La Royal Confitería SNACKS   One of the few places you can eat any time of day in Jujuy, La Royal offers pizzas, empanadas, sandwiches, and other light snacks. An old grandfather clock ticks along undisturbed by the modern American rock playing over speakers. Black-and-white photos of American actors decorate the walls of this casual but popular cafeteria, which is packed at breakfast.

Calle Belgrano 766. © **388/422-6202.** Main courses $2–$3. MC, V. Daily 7:30am–midnight.

Manos Jujeñas ✦ *Value* REGIONAL   Tables are normally packed at this delightful restaurant specializing in regional dishes like empanadas, *humitas,* and tamales. The small, two-level dining room is decorated with local crafts and costumes, and soft Andean music plays in the background. You will have an excellent and very inexpensive meal here: Consider the trout from the nearby Yala River or one of the homemade pastas served weekends only. A tall glass of orange juice is only a peso. When it's crowded, be prepared to wait a bit for your food.

Senador Pérez 222. © **388/422-2366.** Main courses $2–$4. No credit cards. Mon–Sat noon–3pm and 8pm–2:30am (Sun only for lunch).

Restaurante del Hotel Altos de la Viña ✦ INTERNATIONAL   This is as elegant as Jujuy gets. You'll have to leave the city center to reach this hilltop hotel restaurant, with splendid views of the town below. Folkloric groups occasionally serenade the dining room at dinner, and there are candlelit tables outside in summer. The extensive menu focuses on seafood and homemade pastas: The *trucha rellena*—trout stuffed with shrimp, mushrooms, cognac, and white wine—is among the best choices, as are the pastas, *humitas,* and empanadas. Plan to stay for a long meal, as you'll want to linger over one of the mouthwatering desserts.

Av. Pasquini López 50. © **388/426-2626.** Reservations recommended. Main courses $3–$6. AE, DC, MC, V. Daily 11am–3pm and 7:30pm–midnight.

Need a Break?
Heladería Pinguino, Belgrano 718 (© 388/422-7247), has 50 flavors of ice cream and frozen yogurt to cool you down. The small cafe is open daily from 9am to midnight.

4 Driving the Quebrada de Humahuaca (Humahuaca Gorge)

For the first 30 or 40 minutes as you head north on RN 9 from San Salvador de Jujuy, undulating hills reveal fields rich with tobacco and corn and expose the rural economy of Argentina's Northwest. Quechuan women wearing colorful ponchos walk with babies strapped to their backs, while horses, cows, and goats graze on the surrounding vegetation. Look closely and you might spot a gaucho charging after his herd.

As you climb along the Río Grande to Purmamarca, 71km (44 miles) from the region's capital, the land becomes increasingly dry and gives way to striking rock formations. When you arrive at the junction of RP 52 and RN 9, head west for a few kilometers to reach the small colonial hamlet. Framing Purmamarca like a timeless painting, the **Cerro de los Siete Colores (Hill of the Seven Colors)** reflects its beauty onto the pueblo's quiet streets and dusty adobe homes. Try to arrive early—9am is best—when the morning sun shines brightly on the hill's facade and reveals its tapestry of colors.

Heading back to RN 9 and continuing 20km (12 miles) north, you will arrive at the artist's haven of **Tilcara**, with a pre-Hispanic fortress called a *pucará*. Here you will find spectacular panoramic views of the Humahuaca valley as well as a trapezoid-shape monument marking the Tropic of Capricorn. To visit **La Garganta del Diablo (Devil's Throat)**—a steep gorge with a small walkway leading along the rock's edge—leave RN 9 and head east of Tilcara for a short distance. Be careful walking here, as there is only a small rope separating you from the depths below.

Continue north along RN 9, where you will pass the small adobe villages of Huacalera and Uquia. About 42km (26 miles) north of Tilcara lies **Humahuaca,** a sleepy yet enchanting village of only a couple of thousand Indian residents. Its relaxed pace will make Buenos Aires seem light-years away. Note that at an elevation of 2,700m (8,856 ft.), you will feel a little out of breath here, and nights are quite cold. Although the nearby Inca ruins of **Coctaca** are best explored with a tour guide, you can visit them on your own or with a taxi ($5 round-trip, including driver wait time) by following a dirt road about 10km (6¼ miles) out of Humahuaca. Coctaca is a large Indian settlement that the Spaniards discovered in the 17th century. Although the ruins are hard to distinguish from the rocks and debris, you can make out outlines of the terraced crop fields for which the Incas were famous. The site is surrounded by cactus and provides excellent photo opportunities.

From San Salvador de Jujuy, you can travel this circuit by bus or by car. If you decide you'd like to stay the night in Humahuaca (126km/78 miles north of San Salvador), a simple but hospitable option is the **Posta del Sol,** Martín Rodríguez at San Martín (© 388/499-7157), which will arrange horseback and 4×4 excursions into the surrounding area. Otherwise, the Humahuaca circuit can easily be completed in a day. There are several restaurants within walking distance serving Andean cuisine. I recommend that you ask the manager at Posta del Sol for the best place to dine in town.

7

Córdoba

Situated in the center of Argentina, Córdoba's diverse regional landscapes range from undulating hills and forest mountains to water-filled valleys and long green plains. Córdoba is both the capital of this province and the intellectual heart of the nation. Allow for at least 1 or 2 days to visit the old city, where you will discover Córdoba's Jesuit roots and university tradition. Then get out and explore the mountains, which you can do in a day trip or turn into a longer retreat.

The core of Córdoba's tourist area is the Punilla Valley, peacefully set between the Sierras Chicas to the

north and east, and the Sierras Grandes to the west. The valley is filled with reservoirs created by the Cosquín and San Antonio rivers, and the San Roque reservoir in Villa Carlos Paz attracts water-lovers with sailing, swimming, windsurfing, and other lake activities. The sleepier village of La Falda to the north attracts a slower-paced crowd longing for quiet and fresh mountain air. Adventure companies in both towns arrange horseback riding, trekking, and camping in the surrounding mountains, as well as driving tours to the province's many *estancias* and colonial sights.

1 Córdoba

713km (442 miles) northwest of Buenos Aires; 721km (447 miles) northeast of Mendoza

Córdoba, Argentina's second-largest city, with 1.3 million inhabitants, was created as a stop for Spaniards traveling between Peru and the Atlantic coast. It was founded in 1573 by Jerónimo Luis de Cabrera, who honored his wife's family by naming this South American city after their Spanish home. The Jesuits arrived at the end of the 16th century, opening Córdoba's university in 1613 and financing their projects by establishing six large *estancias* throughout the region. Today you can follow the "road of the Jesuit *estancias*" by arranging a tour with a local travel agent.

Built at the bottom of what is essentially a hole, Córdoba was once plagued by flooding. As a result, a small stream called La Cañada was created with walls around it to capture the water, and today La Cañada is one of the city's symbols. Moving into downtown, Córdoba's most important historical sights line up around Plaza San Martín, including the Cabildo, cathedral, Marqués de Sobre Monte's residence, and the Jesuit Block. The Manzana Jesuítica, as the Jesuit Block is called in Spanish, developed not just as a place of worship, but also as an intellectual and cultural center that produced Argentina's top doctors and lawyers. It includes the Jesuit churches, the university, and a prestigious secondary school. In 2000, it was declared a UNESCO World Heritage Site and became a historic museum. The city still serves as an intellectual center, although the economic crisis and dispersion of universities throughout the country has lessened some of Córdoba's luster. There is so much else of more interest to see in Argentina that I do not recommend Córdoba unless you are going with a specific

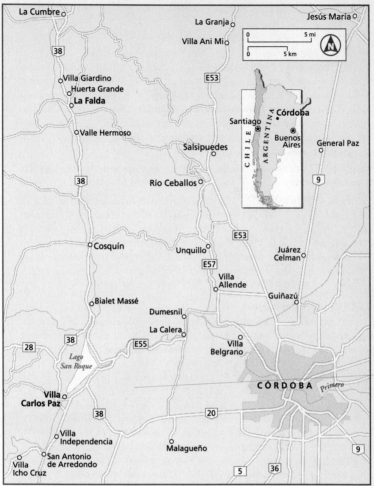

interest in mind, such as the history of the Jesuits, for example. That said, many people opt to study Spanish and Spanish literature here instead of in Buenos Aires, since Córdoba is a midsize city, vibrant and intellectual, but still of manageable size.

ESSENTIALS

GETTING THERE

BY PLANE Córdoba is most easily reached by air, and there are numerous daily flights from Buenos Aires, including one morning departure from Ezeiza International Airport. **Aeropuerto Internacional Ing. Ambrosio Taravella** (also called Pajas Blancas; ℂ **351/434-8390**) sits 11km (6¾ miles) outside town. **Aerolíneas Argentinas** (ℂ **0810/222-86527**), **Southern Winds** (ℂ **0810/ 777-7979**), and **LanChile** (ℂ **351/475-9555**), operate here, with flights to Buenos Aires, Iguazú, Mendoza, Salta, and Santiago de Chile. **Varig** (ℂ **351/ 426-3315**) also flies once daily from Rio de Janeiro and Sao Paulo, Brazil. **LAB**

Lloyd Aero Boliviano (© **351/421-6458**) has two weekly flights from Santa Cruz, Bolivia.

Taxis from the airport to downtown cost between $3 and $4.

BY BUS The **Terminal de Omnibus,** or central bus station, is located at Bulevar Perón 380 (© **351/433-1980**). Numerous companies serve destinations throughout Argentina. Travel times are approximately 10 hours to Buenos Aires, 12 hours to Mendoza, 30 minutes to Villa Carlos Paz, and 2 hours to La Falda. A one-way ticket from Buenos Aires should cost no more than $19; promotions are constantly being offered and companies change their prices frequently. I recommend you check with the tourism office or directly with the bus station before booking your ticket.

BY CAR The drive from Buenos Aires takes approximately 10 hours on RN 9, which is a good road.

VISITOR INFORMATION Córdoba's **Centro de Información Turística,** in the Cabildo (© **351/428-5856**), offers limited hotel and restaurant information and has small city maps. It's open daily from 8am to 9pm in summer, with shorter hours in winter. There are also branches at the airport and bus station. The **provincial tourist board** (provides information and maps on the entire region, such as La Falda, not just on Córdoba), located on Carcano, facing the stadium (© **351/434-1545**), is open daily from 8am to 2pm.

GETTING AROUND

The old city of Córdoba is easily explored by foot, with 24 blocks of pedestrian walking streets located near the Cabildo. The heart of the old city spreads out around Plaza San Martín, situated in the southeast quadrant of Córdoba. Most of the historical sights lie in this area. Avenida Colón, which becomes Avenida Olmos, is the city's main street. As a general rule, you should not walk alone in big cities at night. In Córdoba, this is especially true anywhere along the river.

Driving is difficult in the city, and parking almost impossible downtown. If you do rent a car, try **Hertz,** at Pajas Blancas airport (© **351/4475-0581**). Cheaper, but less known, is **AI Rent a Car,** Entre Ríos 70 (© **351/422-4867**). City buses are cheap and abundant, but only *cospeles*—80¢ tokens available at kiosks around town—are accepted. In Córdoba, taxis are colored bright yellow, while the safer and similarly priced *remises* (private, unmetered taxis) are colored light green. As is the case throughout Argentina, it is always safer to hire a *remise* and not flag a taxi on the streets. This is just an extra measure of security for the visitor—locals have no problems with flagging taxis on the street.

FAST FACTS: Córdoba

Area Code 351.

ATMs & Currency Exchange ATMs and currency-exchange houses have been plagued by long lines and limited cash since the beginning of the economic crisis. Two reliable exchange houses are Maguitur, 25 de Mayo 122, and Barujel, Rivadavia 97. There is also an exchange booth at the airport. Citibank is located at 25 de Mayo and Rivadavia.

Emergency For a medical emergency, dial © **107**; for police, dial © **101** or 351/428-7000; in case of fire, dial © **100**.

Hospital The Hospital de Urgencias (emergency hospital; ℭ 351/421-5008) is located at Catamarca and Salta.

Internet Access Telefónica, with a branch on almost every corner downtown, provides Internet access for less than $1 per hour.

Pharmacy Farmacia Virtual, 27 de Abril 99 (ℭ 351/411-1101), is open daily until midnight.

Post Office The main post office, Correo Argentino, is located at Av. General Paz 201.

Seasons Córdoba can be visited any time of year, although you should expect hot temperatures and big crowds in January and February, and fairly cold temperatures June through August. In addition to peak summer season, tourist destinations also fill up during Easter week.

WHAT TO SEE & DO

City bus tours operated by **Córdoba City Tour** (ℭ 351/424-6605) explore the main tourist spots. The tour lasts 1½ hours, visiting 40 sights, so it is especially good if you're spending only a short time in Córdoba—you'll see a lot on this tour in under 2 hours. The double-decker red buses leave from Plaza San Martín, and you should go to the tourist office or call directly for departure times. The tour costs $3. The tourism office also arranges 2-hour **walking tours** of the city departing at 9:30am and 4:30pm, which cost $2. Call in advance to arrange a tour in English (ℭ 351/428-5600). In addition to the sights listed below, an excellent antiques and handicrafts fair, **Feria Artesanal del Paseo de las Artes,** opens at Achaval Rodríguez and La Cañada on Saturday and Sunday (3–10pm in winter, 6–11pm in summer).

Catedral ⋆ Construction of the cathedral, situated next to the Cabildo, began in 1577 and took nearly 200 years to complete. No wonder, then, that the structure incorporates such an eclectic mix of styles, heavily influenced by baroque. On each of the towers, next to the bells, you will see Indian angels created by—and in the image of—indigenous people of this region. The dome was painted by Emilio Carrafa, one of Córdoba's best-remembered artists. Visitors are free to enter the church but should respect the Masses that take place at various times during the day.

Independencia 72, at Plaza San Martín. ℭ 351/422-3446. Mon–Sat 8am–noon and 4:30–8pm; hours vary on Sun.

Manzana Jesuítica ⋆⋆⋆ *Moments* The Jesuit Block, which includes the Society of Jesus's Church, the Domestic Chapel, the National University of Córdoba, and the National School of Monserrat, has been the intellectual center of Argentina since the early 17th century. Today the entire complex is a historic museum, although the churches still hold Masses, the cloisters still house priests, and the schools still enroll students.

The **Domestic Chapel,** completed in 1668, was used throughout much of its history for private Masses and religious studies of the Jesuits. Having practiced their building skills on the Domestic Chapel, the Jesuits finished the main church, called the **Compañía de Jesús,** in much the same style in 1676. Built in the shape of a Latin cross, the Compañía de Jesús is the oldest church in Argentina. Its nave was designed by a Belgian shipbuilder in the shape of an inverted hull, which was the best way to make use of the short wood beams available for construction at the time. The dome is all wood—no iron is found anywhere—and the beams remain fastened with raw cowhide. The gilded altarpiece was carved in Paraguayan cedar, indicative of baroque design. At each of the church's wings stands a chapel, one of which has often been used for university graduation ceremonies.

In 1613, the Jesuits founded the **National University of Córdoba,** the oldest university in Argentina and one of the continent's longtime academic centers. With most of the university (including the medical and law schools) having moved elsewhere in the city, the majority of rooms here now form part of the historic museum. You can visit the Hall of Graduates, the main university library, and the exquisite Jesuit library holding roughly 1,000 books dating back to the 17th century. The books are in Latin, Greek, and Spanish, and there's a complete Bible from 1645 written in seven languages. Many of the original books in the library disappeared when the Jesuits were first expelled from the Americas, but some are slowly returning from Buenos Aires, where they were hiding.

The Jesuit library leads to the **National College of Monserrat,** which opened in 1687 and quickly became one of the country's top public secondary schools. Walking around the cloisters, you can see the classrooms as well as exhibits of early science machines used for mechanics, electronics, magnetics, color, and sound. During the academic year, you will also find students at work here. You can enter the Compañía de Jesús, the university patio, and the Colegio Nacional de Monserrat free of charge, and if you pay $1, you can also visit the Domestic Chapel and the Hall of Graduates.

Obispo Trejo 242. ✆ 351/433-2075. Free admission to most sites; $1 to see Domestic Chapel and Hall of Graduates. Tues–Sun 9am–1pm and 4–8pm. Guided tours in English and Spanish at 10am, 11am, 5pm, and 6pm.

Museo Histórico Provincial Marqués de Sobre Monte ✹✹   The largest colonial house to survive intact in Argentina, this historical museum was used as the 18th-century home and office of the first Spanish governor of Córdoba. Completed in 1772, the house showcases the town's early colonial history. The governor's commercial and office rooms were downstairs, with the more intimate family rooms upstairs. An amazing collection of period furniture fills the bedrooms; public spaces display religious paintings, military uniforms, a rifle collection, early saddles and other leatherwear, plus an 18th-century chamber organ.

Rosario de Santa Fé. ✆ 351/433-1661. Admission $1. Tues–Sun 9am–1pm and 3–7pm.

Plaza San Martín and the Cabildo ✹   The 4-century-old plaza orients the city, with General San Martín facing the direction of Mendoza (from which his army crossed into Chile and later Peru to liberate them from Spanish rule). Exhibitions, fairs, and impromptu markets are frequent events on the plaza. The **Cabildo** stands on the plaza's west side. During the military dictatorship of the late 1970s and early 1980s, the Cabildo functioned as police headquarters and was used, as acknowledged by a small sign along Pasaje Santa Catalina, as a clandestine detention, torture, and death center. Today the Cabildo is a friendlier place, used mainly for cultural exhibitions and events.

The Cabildo is located at Deán Funes and Independencia. ✆ 351/428-5856.

OUTDOOR ACTIVITIES

A number of tour and adventure companies offer excursions into the Sierras de Córdoba, where it is possible to mountain-climb, hike, mountain-bike, horseback-ride, hang-glide, and fish. Try **Estación Uno** (✆ 354/349-2924), **Explorando Sierras de Córdoba** (✆ 354/343-7901), or **Aventur** (✆ 351/474-4595), all of which offer discovery tours into the mountains and overnight camping trips as well. To visit the province's Jesuit *estancias,* you should contact the tourist office or a local travel agent, such as **Stylo Viajes,** Chacabuco 321 (© **351/424-6605**).

Golf is big in Córdoba, with six world-class 18-hole courses scattered around the city, and an additional two a half-hour drive away. The Jockey Club and the Córdoba Golf Club are the most popular. Log onto www.golfencordoba.com to get detailed course and address information. The site is available in both English and Spanish.

WHERE TO STAY

Córdoba offers a wide variety of hotels, with no stellar choices directly downtown. Hotels sometimes charge different prices for foreigners than Argentines, so make sure you confirm the price before you book. Prices listed below do not include the 19% tax. Parking is usually free for hotel guests.

Holiday Inn ✦ *Value* One of the city's favorite hotels, this newer Holiday Inn is similar in quality but substantially less expensive than the Sheraton (see below). Okay, there's definitely less marble, but the service is comparable. The hotel lies between the airport and downtown, next to a large shopping complex and near the posh neighborhood of Cerro de las Rosas. Standard rooms are colorful, bright, and airy, with slightly larger rooms on the executive floor. The gorgeous pool is complemented by a fitness center, sauna, and state-of-the-art massage facility. The helpful staff will arrange airport transfer, regional excursions, and sports activities upon request. You'll need to take a taxi or *remise* to the city center, located about 10 minutes away. The hotel also functions as a convention center.

Centro Comercial Libertad: Fray Luis Beltrán and M. Cardenosa, 5008 Córdoba. © **351/477-9100.** Fax 351/477-9101. www.holidayinncba.com.ar. 144 units. $50 double; from $75 suite. Rates include buffet breakfast. AE, DC, MC, V. **Amenities:** Restaurant; bar; heated outdoor pool; fitness center; sauna; business center; room service; babysitting; laundry service; dry cleaning. *In room:* A/C, TV, minibar, hair dryer, safe.

King David ✦✦ *Value* Córdoba's newest hotel, opened in mid-2004, offers 110 modern and comfortable apartment-suites in the heart of downtown, just a short walk from all the main attractions. This is, hands down, Córdoba's best value. Every room is a mini-apartment with separate living area with TV and sofa, a small but fully equipped kitchen with microwave and stove, and a spacious marble bathroom next to the smallish bedroom. The decor is contemporary, with light wood and large windows overlooking the city. The staff is friendly and can help in arranging transportation and tours. When making reservations, be sure to ask for promotional rates. In late 2004, the hotel was offering rates as low as $30 per apartment per night for arrivals Sunday through Thursday.

General Paz 386, 5000 Córdoba. © **351/570-3528.** Fax 351/570-3535. www.kingdavid.com.ar. 110 units. From $60 apt for 2; $103 apt for 3; $121 apt for 4. Rates include buffet breakfast. AE, DC, MC, V. **Amenities:** Restaurant; bar; tiny outdoor pool; small exercise room; business center with free Internet; room service; laundry service. *In room:* A/C, TV, minibar, safe.

Sheraton ✦✦ Just outside the city center next to a fashionable shopping mall, this five-star Sheraton is widely considered Córdoba's best hotel. Elevators shoot up the center of the 16-floor atrium lobby, which is decorated with rose-colored marble, California palms, and paintings by national artists. Spacious, well-appointed guest rooms have marble tables and desks, large bathtubs, and views of either the city or mountains. Service is first-rate, although the hotel gets crowded when its convention center is booked. The restaurant is fairly standard, offering a la carte or buffet dining, but the piano bar is good evening fun. The

Sheraton offers the most extensive list of amenities of any hotel in Córdoba. Be sure to check their website for Internet-only rates as low as $86 for a double room.

Av. Duarte Quirós 1300, 5000 Córdoba. ℂ 351/526-9000. Fax 351/526-9150. www.sheraton.com/cordoba. 188 units. $119–$190 double; from $280 suite. Rates include buffet breakfast. AE, DC, MC, V. **Amenities:** Restaurant; piano bar; heated outdoor pool; tennis court; fitness center; sauna; business center; room service; laundry service; dry cleaning. *In room:* A/C, TV, minibar, hair dryer, safe.

Windsor Hotel & Tower ⭐   This centrally located hotel is the best of hotel choices near Plaza San Martín, having added a new tower with modern, comfortable rooms. Ask for a room in this tower rather than in the "classic" section. King-size-bed rooms are larger than those with two twins. Also new are the rooftop pool, fitness room, and sauna. The fifth-floor Oxford restaurant enjoys an impressive view of the city, with good international cuisine. Piano music fills the lobby after 9pm, and the hotel staff will organize city tours and mountain excursions.

Buenos Aires 214, 5000 Córdoba. ℂ/fax 351/422-4012. www.windsortower.com. 82 units. $42–$58 double; from $78 suite. Rates include buffet breakfast. AE, DC, MC, V. **Amenities:** 2 restaurants; piano bar; small outdoor pool; fitness center; sauna; business center; room service; laundry service; dry cleaning. *In room:* A/C, TV, minibar, hair dryer, safe.

WHERE TO DINE

In addition to the restaurants listed below, the most elegant *parilla* in town is **Al Corta,** Figueroa Alcorta 330 (ℂ 351/424-7452), serving the best cuts of beef in the city for $6 to $8 for main courses. The best Italian restaurant is **La Momma,** at Santa Rosa and La Canada (ℂ 351/421-2212), with homemade pastas, veal escalopes, and an incredible lasagna (main dishes cost $3–$7).

Elegon's ⭐ *Moments* ARGENTINE   President Sarmiento once said that Córdoba has more churches than houses, and it is from Elegon's seventh-floor perspective that his words seem most true. This unpublicized restaurant inside the Colegio de Escibanos has panoramic windows overlooking the cathedral, Basílica Santo Domingo, Santa Catalina de Siena Church, Teresa's Church and Convent, and the Manzana Jesuítica. With only a dozen tables and a couch, the dining area resembles a small European tearoom. Open solely during the day, it offers lunchtime choices of a *milanesa* (the best choice, topped with ham, cheese, and tomatoes) or a beefsteak. There are also a variety of salads and sandwiches. Many people just opt to come here between meals for tea or coffee and to relax while taking in the awesome view.

Obispo Trejo 104, 7th floor. ℂ 351/423-2912. Reservations suggested. Main courses $3–$5; 3-course prix-fixe lunch $3.50. No credit cards. Weekdays 8am–5pm.

La Alameda *Value* ARGENTINE   The city's best empanada shop is decorated with jokes posted all over its walls. This very casual eatery with wood benches for tables serves food typical of Argentina's Northwest, including *locro, humitas,* and, of course, a selection of empanadas. Food is quick, cheap, and no-nonsense. Post a joke before you leave.

Obispo Trejo 170. ℂ 156/562-757. Main courses $1–$3. No credit cards. Mon–Sat noon–5am; Sun 8pm–5am.

L'America ⭐⭐ *Finds* INTERNATIONAL   In a beautifully restored 16th-century building, this elegant restaurant has been serving some of the best international dishes in Córdoba since 2000. The young chef at L'America was trained in the United States (thus the name) and loves to combine Argentine ingredients with North American and international flavors, such as the smoked baby back ribs with barbecue sauce, served with jasmine rice. The smoked pork loin wrapped in pancetta is a masterpiece. There's also a good selection of salads and delicious appetizers. The menu changes every 3 months, and the wine list has over 175 labels. The chef, a big wine aficionado, hopes to have over 400 bottles by 2006.

Caseros 67. © 351/421-0476. Main courses $4–$7. AE, DC, MC, V. Mon–Sat noon–3:30pm; Tues–Sat 8:30pm–midnight.

Mandarina ⟨⟨ ITALIAN   This eclectic and not-altogether-sane restaurant, located along the pedestrian walkway Obispo Trejo, is a cornucopia of surreal and occasionally sexual artwork. The city's cultural crowd comes for salads, pizzas, calzones, and pastas, and later for wines, whiskeys, and wacky cocktails. Freshly baked breads and jams prepared with fresh fruits add to Mandarina's appeal.

Obispo Trejo 171. © 351/426-4909. Main courses $3–$6; 3-course prix-fixe lunch $3.50. No credit cards. Mon–Sat 11am–3:30pm and 8:30pm–12am.

CORDOBA AFTER DARK

The **Cabildo** serves as a cultural center, with occasional evening events including tango on Friday evenings. For $2, you can get a crash lesson in tango at 9:30pm every Friday and then try to dance the rest of the night away. **Teatro Libertador San Martín,** Vélez Sársfield 365 (© **351/433-2319**), is the city's biggest theater, hosting mostly musicals and concerts. The smaller **Teatro Real,** San Jerónimo 66 (© **351/433-1669**), presents more traditional theater. You can pick up current theater, comedy, and special events information in the "Espectáculos" section of the daily paper, *La Voz del Interior.* **El Arrabal,** Belgrano 899 at Fructuoso Rivera (© **351/460-2990**), is a bar that hosts excellent tango, milonga, salsa, and folkloric shows most nights. One of the best bars is **Rock & Fellers,** Av. Hipólito Yrigoyen 320 (© **351/424-3960**), which serves typical American food and has '60's style rock-'n'-roll music. Happy hour takes place weekdays from 7 to 9pm. The most popular disco is **Carreras,** Avenida Cárcano and Piamonte (© **15/6762-767**), found in the Chateau Carreras neighborhood, where a number of other upscale discos are located. The rest of the city's nightlife is concentrated along Bulevar Guzmán in the north of the city and in Nueva Córdoba along Avenida Hipólito Yrigoyen.

2 Villa Carlos Paz ⟨★

36km (22 miles) west of Córdoba

A quick getaway from Córdoba, Villa Carlos Paz surrounds the picturesque Ebalse San Roque, which, although it's actually a reservoir, vacationing Cordobese and Porteño families treat like a lake, swimming, sailing, and windsurfing in its gentle waters. Year-round, people come to Villa Carlos Paz to enjoy outdoor activities by day and partying by night, with disco-bound buses transporting the youth of Córdoba back and forth. The city of 40,000 inhabitants really comes alive in January and February, when more than 200,000 tourists visit each month. Live theater, comedy shows, music, and dancing fill the night air, and no one seems to sleep. Yet you don't have to be a nocturnal animal to enjoy Villa Carlos Paz—quiet lakeside resorts offer a more serene alternative, if you're interested.

ESSENTIALS

GETTING THERE   The N20 is a fast, new highway (with a 1-peso toll) that goes directly from Córdoba to Villa Carlos Paz. The drive takes no more than

40 minutes except on Sunday evenings, when Cordobese vacationers return home from the mountains. Bus transportation to Villa Carlos Paz is frequent and reliable. Public bus companies running to and from Córdoba in about 50 minutes are **El Serra** and **Ciudad de Córdoba,** both costing under $1. **Fero Bus** and **Caru** travel slightly faster but less often and cost about $1. **Chevallier** buses to Buenos Aires take about 10 hours.

VISITOR INFORMATION The local **tourism office,** adjacent to the bus station at San Martín 400 (© **351/421-624** or **0810/888-2729**), is open in summer from 7am to 9pm and winter from 7am to 11pm. The staff provides information on hotels, restaurants, and tourist circuits around the city.

GETTING AROUND Villa Carlos Paz is small and easily explored by foot. The city is safe to walk in, although, as in other places, you should not walk alone at night. If you want to rent a car, various rental agencies are located at the bus station.

WHAT TO SEE & DO

There are no special sights in the city, save a 7m-high (23-ft.) cuckoo clock that, for no good reason, has become the city's symbol. Daytime activities focus on the lake and excursions into the surrounding hills. Although it's not clear why the city allows so many water activities in what is actually a reservoir, swimming, sailing, windsurfing, trout fishing, and—at least, for now—jet skiing are all possible. Villa Carlos Paz is also well positioned for the many driving circuits that explore the Punilla Valley and go into the mountains. These include treks to waterfalls, Jesuit ruins, and mountain *estancias.* Check with **El Rosario** (© **351/451-257**) or one of the other tourist agencies open at the bus station for more information. In summer, two buses dressed as trains offer city tours, including **Tren de Turismo La Porteñita y del Ensueño** (© **351/431-692**) and **Trencito Turismo Lago San Roque** (© **351/421-521**). You can call directly for departure times and points, or ask at the tourism office. These are worth it if you have no time to meander on your own; they're also a good way to get to know the town.

WHERE TO STAY

Hipocampus Resort *(Kids)* A bumpy back road leads to this hidden retreat, a white colonial house that resembles an old Spanish mission. Its two pools sit perched on a cliff overlooking the lake, and each of the guest rooms has a balcony with a beautiful water view. Rooms are uniquely decorated, and many have hardwood floors and colorful linens. Bathrooms are small, with showers only, however. The hotel offers a cozy fireside sitting room, as well as a small library and TV area. The restaurant serves regional dishes as well as afternoon tea, and the gracious staff makes this feel more like a B&B than a hotel. Excursions, horseback riding, and hiking trips can all be arranged at reception.

Calle Brown 240, 5152 Villa Carlos Paz. © **351/421-653.** www.hipocampusresort.com. 50 units. $62 double. Rates include buffet breakfast. AE, DC, MC, V. **Amenities:** Restaurant; 2 outdoor pools; kids' pool; minigolf; gym; sauna. *In room:* A/C, TV, fridge, hair dryer, safe.

Portal del Lago Hotel *(★)* The striking wood-frame lobby here leads directly out to the main pool and spacious grounds bordering the lake. The hotel forms a half-moon shape along the banks of the lake, and most of the rooms have water views. Brick walls and dark woods give you the sense of being deep in the mountains, and there are many sitting areas for relaxing. Guest rooms vary in size, although all bathrooms are small; some rooms have two levels and multiple beds to accommodate families. A warm therapeutic pool, sauna, and gym are on the top floor, and a lake-view restaurant extends along the mezzanine of the lobby. The hotel houses a convention center and can become crowded in summer months. The hotel's many stairs prevent access to those with disabilities.

Gdor. Alvarez, at J.L. Cabrera, 5152 Villa Carlos Paz. © 351/424-931. Fax 351/424-932. www.portal-del-lago.com. 110 units. $66 double. Rates include buffet breakfast. AE, DC, MC, V. **Amenities:** Restaurant; bar; 3 outdoor pools; gym; sauna; room service. *In room:* A/C, TV, safe.

WHERE TO DINE

Let's just say that fine dining is not the reason people come to Villa Carlos Paz. However, there are a number of good, casual eateries in the city's center. The two best *parrillas* in town are **Carilo,** Yrigoyen 44 (© 351/431-346), and **La Volanta,** San Martín 1262 (© 351/422-954). The latter is easy to spot—look for loud green and yellow paint and the carriage sitting on the roof. For excellent Italian dishes, try **Il Gato Trattoria,** at Libertad and Belgrano (© 351/439-500), and **Covadonga,** Carcano 2825 (© 351/427-477), both of which offer fish and meat dishes, too.

VILLA CARLOS PAZ AFTER DARK

Many young—and even not-so-young—people come to Villa Carlos Paz from Córdoba for drinking and dancing, and some of the discos arrange private caravans from the city. Expect a late night out—dancing begins after 2am and continues past dawn. By far, the most famous disco is **Keop's,** R.S. Peña and Seneca (© 351/433-553), with **Zebra Restobar Disco,** Bernardo D'Elia 150 (© 351/427-130), placing second. For something tamer, visit the **Punta Hidalgo** piano bar at the corner of Uruguay and Hidalgo (© 351/421-127). **Casino Carlos Paz** is located at Liniers and Uruguay (© 351/425-772).

3 La Falda ⭐

81km (50 miles) northwest of Córdoba

An excellent base from which to explore the Punilla Valley, La Falda (literally, "lap of the mountain") lies between the Valle Hermoso (Beautiful Valley) and the Sierras Chicas. Argentines come here for rest and relaxation, not wild entertainment. Crisp, clean air; wonderful hikes; and quiet hotels are the draw. The city's main tourist site is the once-prestigious (but now decrepit) Hotel Edén, which entertained international celebrities in the early 20th century.

ESSENTIALS

GETTING THERE   Frequent buses travel from both Córdoba and Villa Carlos Paz, the most comfortable of which is **TranSierras** (© 351/424-666), costing about $3. If you are driving, you have the option of first going to Villa Carlos Paz and then on to La Falda via the N38, or you can bypass Carlos Paz by taking the new A73, which branches off from the N20 a few miles before Carlos Paz. The trip takes 2 hours from Córdoba.

VISITOR INFORMATION   The **tourist office** is located inside the old train station at Av. Buenos Aires 50 (© 351/423-007). Open daily from 8am to 11pm, it provides city and regional maps as well as hotel, restaurant, and tourist information.

GETTING AROUND   You can walk around the small center, but you will probably want to hire a driver, rent a car, or sign up with a tour operator to explore the Sierras Chicas (although you can always hike). La Falda's main road is Avenida Edén, which extends from the town center to the old Hotel Edén.

WHAT TO SEE & DO

You come here first and foremost to relax. Once that's accomplished, visit the once prestigious **Hotel Edén** (east end of Av. Edén), which during the first half of the 20th century hosted the likes of Albert Einstein, the Duke of Savoy, two presidents of Argentina, and the country's high society. The hotel quickly fell out of favor after World War II because its owners had been Nazi sympathizers. Boarded up by 1960, the castlelike hotel was left to ruin, and the insides have been completely gutted, although, amazingly, the entrance fountain still operates. Guided tours are offered daily between 10am and 6pm, and there's a bar adjacent to the ghost lobby with pictures of the grand old dame in its day. Outside the city, various adventure agencies offer horseback riding, trekking, mountain-biking, hang-gliding, and 4×4 excursions into the Sierras Chicas. Contact **Purehuek Turismo Aventura,** Av. Edén 338 (© **351/423-690**), for details. You might also considering taking an inexpensive taxi (all taxis are inexpensive here) toward La Cumbre, where numerous handicrafts shops and stands dot the artesian road.

WHERE TO STAY

Hostal L'Hirondelle ✿ Never mind the term "hostal"; in this case, it's an architectural distinction rather than a reference to a budget traveler's dormitory. The house looks like a French chalet, surrounded by gardens and the Sierras Chicas. Each individually decorated room takes a poet's name, as a tribute by the owner to his poet son. On the second floor, Walt Whitman enjoys a corner view of the pool, courtyard, and nearby mountains. French prints and old bottles and spices decorate the long wood dining room, where guests enjoy half-board (breakfast and dinner) in summer months. Breakfast includes tea, croissants, fruit, cereal, homemade sweets, and fresh juice. For city folks unaccustomed to clear, starry nights, the owner has set up a telescope for celestial viewing. The staff will help you arrange outdoor activities, including hiking and horseback riding, as well as airport transfer upon request.

Av. Edén 861, 5172 La Falda. © **351/422-825.** hostallhirondelle@digitalcoop.com.ar. 21 units. $92 double in summer, including half-board; ½ that price in winter with breakfast only. AE, DC, MC, V. **Amenities:** Restaurant; outdoor pool; video and game room; babysitting; laundry. *In room:* TV.

WHERE TO DINE

La Parrilla de Raúl ✿ ARGENTINE A popular *parrilla* with a distinctive family atmosphere, Raúl's menuless system works like this: First, help yourself to the salad bar, an assortment of mixed vegetable dishes, cabbages, stuffed eggs, candied sweet potatoes, and other delights. As you finish your salad, the first meat course will land on your plate, likely a tender slice of pork with a *cerveza* (yes, beer) sauce. Next comes thick *chorizo* and a rich piece of *morcilla* (blood pudding). No stopping here—*costilla* (a beef rib) is next. Ready for more? Following the rib is *matambre,* another delicious morsel of beef. At this point, you can politely request that they stop bringing you meat, or you can wave on more. Request a large soda, and they will bring you a 1.25-liter bottle to help wash it all down. Finish your meal with a trip to the dessert bar, an enticing table of flans, fruits, creams, and the obligatory *dulce de leche.* Then go hit the gym.

Av. Buenos Aires 111. © **351/421-662.** Main courses $3–$5. No credit cards. Daily noon–3pm and 8:30pm–midnight.

8

Mendoza

"**A**nd so you are traveling to the land of *sol y vino,*" my taxi driver says with a smile, capturing the two great temptations of a region showered with sun and flowing with wine. Boasting nearly 300 annual days of sun and three-fourths of the nation's wine production, Mendoza seems destined for the distinction of Napa South. Few might imagine, however, that the sweet, voluptuous grapes coloring the province grow on inhospitable desert land brought to life only through a vast network of irrigation canals dating back to the Incas. The canals extend not just through the diverse vineyards, but also into the streets of Mendoza itself.

This picturesque city lies at the heart of the Cuyo, the name of the region that comprises the provinces of Mendoza, San Juan, and San Luis. It was founded in 1561 by Spanish colonialists, and retains an idyllic serenity that has carried over from centuries past.

Los Caminos del Vino refers to the seven wine roads that wind their way through the most important wineproducing zones of Mendoza. You should spend at least 1 or 2 days exploring Mendoza—discovering the old city, visiting the plazas, and wandering about Parque General San Martín—before heading for the wine route. Choose your own pace when touring the *bodegas* (wineries); two or

three visits are possible in half a day. Keep in mind that the *bodegas,* which offer free tours with tastings, are open only on weekdays. But a journey into the magnificent mountains is possible anytime, and the best circuit is Alta Montaña, which follows parts of the old Inca trail and Andes railroad to the border with Chile. Travelers are best off choosing Mendoza as their base for exploring the region, although small lodgings and *fincas* (private homes opened to guests) do dot the province.

Mendoza also offers a wealth of outdoor activities, ranging from Class III, IV, and V white-water rafting in the Mendoza River to horseback riding, mountain biking, and trekking in the Andes. Tour operators in Mendoza will arrange an itinerary according to your preferences, from part-day outings to multiple-day excursions.

Las Leñas is a world-class ski resort in the south of the province—playground of Porteños escaping the capital for a snowy retreat—while Los Penitentes offers decent runs closer to Mendoza. For the bold and the brave, Aconcagua Mountain provides an irresistible challenge, its 6,960m (22,829 ft.) towering above all other peaks in the Western Hemisphere. With a good bit of endurance, money, and time on your hands, the mountain can be conquered.

1 Mendoza ⋆⋆⋆

710km (440 miles) northwest of Buenos Aires; 721km (447 miles) southwest of Córdoba

Mendoza is an artificial oasis. It receives no more than 5 days of rain per year; the tree-lined boulevards, plazas with trickling fountains, and enormous city park exist only thanks to a centuries-old roadside canal system. Ask a local what she likes best about Mendoza, and she is likely to tell you *"La tranquilidad,"* the tranquillity of what must be Argentina's loveliest city. You'll want to linger about these streets and parks before rushing to the countryside, where a seductive journey along Los Caminos de Vino (see "Touring the Wineries," later in this chapter) awaits.

ESSENTIALS
GETTING THERE
BY PLANE Mendoza's international airport, **Francisco Gabrielli** (© 261/ 520-6000), lies 8km (5 miles) north of town on Ruta 40. **Aerolíneas Argentinas** (© 0810/222-86527) and **Southern Winds** (© 0810/777-7979) offer up to seven daily arrivals from Buenos Aires (one flight of which departs from Ezeiza International Airport) and a daily arrival from Córdoba. **LanChile** (© 261/ 425-7900) operates here with two daily flights from Santiago, Chile, one in the morning and one in the evening, making a day trip from Santiago possible.

BY BUS The **Terminal del Sol** (© 261/431-3001), or central bus station, lies just east of central Mendoza. Buses travel to Buenos Aires (12–14 hr., $20); Córdoba (12 hr., $9); Santiago, Chile (7 hr., $10); Las Leñas (7 hr., $5); and other cities throughout the region. **Chevallier** (© 261/431-0235), **Expreso Uspallata** (© 261/438-1092), and **Andesmar** (© 261/431-0585) are the main bus companies.

BY CAR The route from Buenos Aires is a long (10 hr.) but easy drive on either the RN 7 or the RN 8. Mendoza is more easily reached by car from Santiago, Chile, along the RN 7, although the 250km (155-mile) trek through the Andes can be treacherous (and requires chains) in winter.

VISITOR INFORMATION Mendoza's **Subsecretaría Provincial de Turismo,** Av. San Martín 1143 (© 261/420-2357), is open daily from 9am to 9pm. The helpful staff will provide you with tourist information on the entire province, including maps of the wine roads and regional driving circuits. **Municipal tourist offices,** called Centros de Información, are located at Garibaldi near San Martín (© 261/423-8745), 9 de Julio 500 (© 261/449-5185), and Las Heras 340 (© 261/429-6298). Open daily from 9am to 9pm, they provide city maps, hotel information, and brochures of tourist activities. You will find small visitor information booths at the airport and bus station as well. Information and permits for Aconcagua Provincial Park are available at the **Centro de Informes del Parques,** located in Mendoza's Parque San Martín (© 261/420-5052). Permits to climb to the summit cost $200. In addition, several websites offer useful tourist information: www.turismo.mendoza.gov.ar, www.aconcagua.mendoza.gov.ar, www.culturamendoza.com.ar, and www.mendoza.com.ar.

GETTING AROUND You can easily explore central Mendoza by foot, although you will want to hire a driver or rent a car to visit the wine roads and tour the mountains. Taxis and *remises* (private, unmetered taxis) are inexpensive: Drivers cost no more than $10 per hour. Travelers should be wary of walking alone, especially at night. Although traditionally one of Argentina's safest cities, Mendoza has experienced an increase in crime resulting from the economic crisis. Have your hotel call a *remise* or radio-taxi, rather than flagging down a taxi on your own. For a *remise*, try **La Veloz Del Este** (© 261/423-9090), **Mendozar** (© 261/431-3689), or **Remises-Transporte** (© 261/429-8734). For a taxi, call **Radiotaxi** (© 261/437-1111).

Mendoza

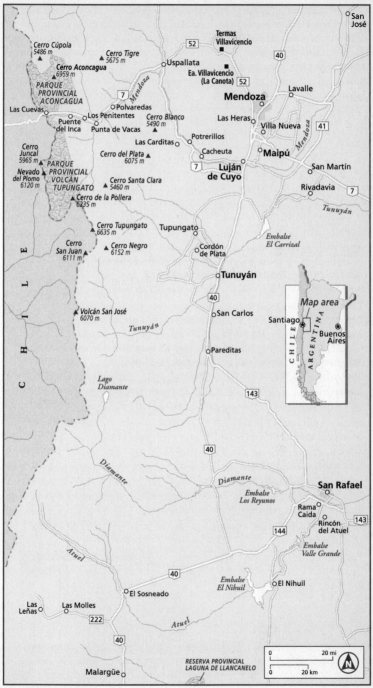

San José

Cerro Cúpola
5486 m
Cerro Tigre
5675 m
Cerro Aconcagua
6959 m

Termas
Villavicencio

PARQUE
PROVINCIAL
ACONCAGUA

Uspallata

Ea. Villavicencio
(La Canota)

Mendoza

Lavalle

Las Cuevas
Puente
del Inca
Polvaredas
Los Penitentes
Punta de Vacas
Cerro Blanco
5490 m

Las Heras

Villa Nueva

Cerro
Juncal
5965 m
Cerro del Plata
6075 m
Las Carditas
Potrerillos
Cacheuta

Maipú

Nevado
del Plomo
6120 m
PARQUE
PROVINCIAL
VOLCÁN
TUPUNGATO
Cerro Santa Clara
5460 m

Luján
de Cuyo

San Martín

Rivadavia

Cerro de la Pollera
6235 m

Tunuyán

Cerro Tupungato
6635 m
Tupungato

Embalse
El Carrizal

Cerro
San Juan
6111 m
Cerro Negro
6152 m
Cordón
de Plata

Tunuyán

C H I L E

Volcán San José
6070 m
Tunuyán

San Carlos

Map area

Santiago

Buenos
Aires

Pareditas

CHILE
ARGENTINA

Lago
Diamante

Diamante

Diamante

San Rafael

Embalse
Los Reyunos
Rama
Caida
Rincón
del Atuel

Embalse
Valle Grande

Atuel

Embalse
El Nihuil
El Nihuil

Las
Leñas
Las Molles
El Sosneado

Atuel

Malargüe

RESERVA PROVINCIAL
LAGUNA DE LLANCANELO

0   20 mi
0   20 km

If you do rent a car, parking is easy and inexpensive inside the city, with paid parking meters and private lots clearly marked. Easy to navigate, the city spreads out in a clear grid pattern around Plaza Independencia. Avenida San Martín is the city's main thoroughfare, Paseo Sarmiento is the pedestrian walking street that extends from Plaza Independencia to Avenida San Martín, and Avenida Emilio Civit is the posh residential avenue leading to the entrance of Parque San Martín. Outside the city, road signs are sometimes missing or misleading, and you should pay careful attention to road maps. Both **Avis** (*©* **261/447-0150**) and **Hertz** (*©* **261/448-2327**) rent cars at Mendoza's airport. Expect to pay about $52 per day for a compact car with insurance and 200km (124 miles) included. If you reserve the car before arriving in Argentina, you can usually negotiate a similar rate, but with unlimited mileage. **Hertz** also has a new office downtown, close to the Plaza de la Independencia, at Espejo 415 (*©* **261/423-0225**). If you are off to explore the wine country, they have a 3-day package with 1,200km (744 miles) free and insurance for $155.

FAST FACTS: Mendoza

Area Code **261.** The country code for Argentina is **54.**

ATMs & Currency Exchange ATMs and currency-exchange houses have been plagued by long lines and limited cash since the beginning of the economic crisis. Two reliable exchange houses, both at the corner of San Martín and Catamarca, are **Maguitur** (*©* **261/425-3405**) and **Cambio Santiago** (*©* **261/420-0277**). They are open Monday through Friday from 8:30am to 1pm and 5 to 8:30pm, and Saturday from 9:30am to 1pm. **Citibank,** Av. Sarmiento 20 (*©* **261/49-6519**), has an ATM with Cirrus and PLUS access.

Emergency For an **ambulance,** dial *©* **107** or 261/428-0000; for **police,** dial *©* **101** or 261/423-8710; in case of **fire,** dial *©* **100.**

Hospital **Hospital Central** (*©* **261/428-0600**) is near the bus station at Salta and Alem.

Internet Access Internet access in most places costs a meager 1 or 2 pesos (35¢–65¢) per hour. There are a number of cybercafes along Avenida Sarmiento; try **Mundo Internet,** Sarmiento 107 (*©* **261/420-3795**), open daily from 8:30am to 1am. **Official Telefónica** and **Telecentro** offices, located all over town, also offer Internet use.

Pharmacy **Farmacia del Puente,** Av. Las Heras 201 (*©* **261/425-9209**), operates 24 hours.

Post Office The main post office, **Correo Argentino** (*©* **261/429-0848**), located at the corner of Avenida San Martín and Colón, is open weekdays from 8am to 8pm.

WHAT TO SEE & DO

Museo Fundacional ★★   This museum, located 3km (1¾ miles) from downtown, displays what remains of the old city, which was ravaged by an 1861 earthquake. Chronicling the early history of Mendoza, the museum begins by looking at the culture of the indigenous Huarpes and continues with an examination of the city's development through Spanish colonization to independence. An underground chamber holds the ruins of the aqueduct and fountain that once provided Mendoza's water supply. Near the museum, the **Ruinas de San Francisco** represent a Jesuit church and school that were used until the Jesuits were expelled from the continent in 1767 and later occupied by the Franciscan Order. Videla Castillo between Beltrán and Alberdi. ℂ **261/425-6927**. Admission 50¢. Tues–Sat 8am–8pm; Sun 3–8pm.

Museo Histórico General San Martín ⭐ Adjacent to the "Alameda," a beautiful promenade under white poplars, the San Martín Library and Museum stands in the spot where General San Martín had hoped to make his home. The museum's small collection of artifacts pays homage to Argentina's beloved hero, who prepared his liberation campaigns from Mendoza. Remedios Escalada de San Martín 1843. ℂ **261/425-7947**. Admission $1. Mon–Fri 9am–1pm.

Parque General San Martín ⭐⭐⭐ Almost as big as the city itself, this wonderful park, designed in 1896 by Carlos Thays (who also designed the Palermo parks in Buenos Aires), extends over 350 hectares (865 acres) with 17km (11 miles) of idyllic pathways and 300 species of plants and trees. A tourist office, located near the park's main entrance, provides information on all park activities, which include walking, jogging, bicycling, boating, horseback riding (outside the park's perimeters), and hang-gliding. A national science museum and zoo (open daily 9am–6pm) are located inside the park, and you can also camp here. The best hike leads to the top of Cerro de la Gloria, which offers a panoramic view of the city and surrounding valley, as well as a bronze monument to the men who liberated Argentina, Chile, and Peru. You can hang-glide from the top of the other hill, Cerro Arco. Main entrance at Av. Emilio Civit and Bologne sur Mer. Free admission. Always open.

Plaza Independencia ⭐⭐ The plaza marks the city center, a beautiful square with pergolas, fountains, frequent artesian fairs, and cultural events. Following the 1861 earthquake, the new city was rebuilt around this area. Four additional plazas, San Martín, Chile, Italia, and España, are located 2 blocks off each corner of Independence Square. Surrounding the square you will find the Julio Quintanilla Theater, the National School, the Independencia Theater, the Provincial Legislature, and the small Modern Art Museum. Art Museum. ℂ **261/425-7279**. Admission $1. Mon–Sat 9am–1pm and 4–9pm.

TOUR OPERATORS & OUTDOOR ACTIVITIES

Aymara Adventures & Expeditions, 9 de Julio 1023 (ℂ **261/420-2064;** www.aymara.com.ar), is the leading tour operator in the region. They can organize everything from horseback-riding trips to Aconcagua, to mountain treks and wine tours. They have licensed tour guides with many years of experience under their belts.

HIKING   Huentata, Las Heras 680, Mendoza (ℂ **261/425-3108**), arranges single- or multiple-day hiking trips. Two-hour treks offered by **Argentina Rafting Expediciones,** Ruta 7 s/n, 5549 Potrerillos (ℂ **262/448-2037**), extend from Potrerillos to the waterfall at la Quebrada del Salto, where rappelling is possible. The 2-hour trek costs $12, while a full-day hike with lunch included is $24.

HORSEBACK RIDING   Juan Jardel (ℂ **262/448-3030**) offers horseback-riding trips of various lengths and also coordinates with Argentina Rafting Expediciones. A day trip involving rafting in the morning and horseback riding in the afternoon can easily be arranged. **Argentina Rafting Expediciones** (see above) and **Ríos Andinos,** Ruta 7 Km 64, 5549 Potrerillos (© **261/431-6074**), offer 2-hour horseback rides for $15.

MOUNTAIN BIKING In February, cyclists from around the world participate in **La Vuelta Ciclista de Mendoza,** a mini–Tour de France around Mendoza province. **Argentina Rafting Expediciones** (see above) and **Ríos Andinos** (see above) offer 2-hour mountain bike adventures for $15.

SKIING The best place to ski, not just in Argentina but also in South America, is **Las Leñas** (see box on p. 151). Closer to Mendoza, the small resort of **Los Penitentes** (see "The Alta Montaña Driving Circuit" section beginning on p. 148) offers 23 downhill slopes as well as cross-country skiing. **Portillo** is a much larger and better-equipped ski resort just on the other side of the Chilean border. Eighty kilometers (50 miles) south, **Vallecitos** is the smallest and closest ski resort to Mendoza but can be difficult to reach in heavy snow conditions. Obtain information on the province's ski areas from Mendoza's **Subsecretaría Provincial de Turismo** (see "Essentials," earlier in this chapter).

WHITE-WATER RAFTING Mendoza offers the best white-water rafting in Argentina, and during the summer months when the snow melts in the Andes and fills the Mendoza River, rafters enjoy up to Class IV and V rapids. Rafting is possible year-round, but the river is colder and calmer in winter months. Potrerillos, 53km (33 miles) west of Mendoza, has two professional tour operators offering half-day, whole-day, and 2-day trips on the Mendoza River, with direct transfers provided from Mendoza. These are **Argentina Rafting Expediciones** (see above) and **Ríos Andinos** (see above). Be sure to bring an extra pair of clothes and a towel because you are guaranteed to get soaked. Children under 12 are not allowed to raft. Argentina Rafting has a small restaurant and bar where you can eat and defrost following your soaking in the river. Rafting starts at $12 for 1 hour, and both agencies also offer kayaking ($14 for 1 hr., single or double kayaks available), horseback riding, trekking, and mountain biking. The 2-day, 60km (37-mile) rafting trip is a Class III and IV excursion offered November through April. It costs $68 and includes all meals, camping gear, and transfer from Mendoza.

SHOPPING

On Friday, Saturday, and Sunday, an outdoor **handicrafts market** takes place during the day on Plaza Independencia. Regional shops selling handicrafts, leather goods, gaucho paraphernalia, and *mate* are located along Avenida Las Heras, two of which are **Las Veñas,** Av. Las Heras 399 (© **261/425-0498**), and **Los Andes,** Av. Las Heras 445 (© **261/425-6688**). More mainstream stores line Avenida San Martín. The city's best shopping mall is **Palmares Open Mall,** located on Ruta Panamericana 2650 in Godoy Cruz (© **261/413-9100**). Most shops close from 1 to 4pm each day for siesta. You can also buy Mendocine wines at many shops, the least expensive costing no more than a few dollars a bottle and premiums going for $25 to $80. The Park Hyatt, Chile 1124 (© **261/441-1234**), has an excellent wine shop with a knowledgeable sommelier, and prices are not overly inflated for a hotel shop.

WHERE TO STAY

Mendoza has recently opened a few new hotels, which have substantially boosted the city's lodging quality. However, after the Park Hyatt, the level of hotel service quickly drops and the star classification posted at local accommodations is not reliable. In addition to the hotels listed below, a couple up-and-coming, modestly priced accommodations worth looking into are the **Microtel,** outside the city center at Acc. Sur and Lamadrid (℗ **261/432-0503**), and a bed-and-breakfast called **Quinta Rufino,** Rufino Ortega 142 (℗ **261/420-4696**). Prices quoted are for high season, which in Mendoza is February through March, July, and September through November. Hotel rates are often discounted 15% to 20% in the off season. Prices listed below do not include the 21% tax.

EXPENSIVE

Park Hyatt Mendoza ★★★   Peering majestically over the Plaza de la Independencia, the Park Hyatt opened in 2001 after restoring the original facade of the 19th-century Plaza Hotel and building a seven-floor tower for guest rooms. Sweeping columns of granite and stone showcase the lobby, and an impressive collection of Mendocino art pays tribute to local culture. A landscaped courtyard separates different sections of the hotel, leading past water fountains and an outdoor dining area to a warm, inviting pool. Guest rooms could stand to lose a bit of the wood paneling but are nevertheless spacious and contemporary. Fluffy duvets and feather pillows blanket the beds, and white-marble bathrooms have separate bathtubs and showers with crystal washbasins. The exquisite spa deserves special mention because of its uniqueness: A professional team of masseurs from Bangkok give wonderful Thai massages, and the spa incorporates Mendocino wines in a variety of its body treatments (for example, shampoo based on wine acids or grape-seed-oil body lotion). A well-equipped fitness room, Jacuzzi, sauna, and steam bath are here, too. Hotel guests benefit from frequent cultural events, ranging from jazz and music shows to Spanish festivals and flamenco dances. Some events take place in Bistro M (see "Where to Dine," below), an excellent international restaurant boasting one of South America's first open kitchens. Bar Uvas is the city's premier wine bar, and the Regency Casino is Mendoza's try at Las Vegas. Be sure to check the hotel's website for Internet-only rates that come with a 10% discount.

Chile 1124, 5500 Mendoza. ℗ **261/441-1234.** Fax 261/441-1235. www.mendoza.park.hyatt.com. 186 units. $164 double; from $184 suite. Rates include a beautiful buffet breakfast. AE, DC, MC, V. **Amenities:** Restaurant; wine bar; sports bar; heated outdoor pool; nearby golf; excellent health club and spa; concierge; business center; room service; babysitting; laundry service; dry cleaning. *In room:* A/C, TV, minibar, hair dryer, safe.

MODERATE

Hotel Argentino ★★ (Value   The best value in all of Mendoza is just cater-cornered from the lavish Park Hyatt (see above), and also overlooks the Plaza de la Independencia. Opened in the spring of 2004, the Argentino offers elegance and comfort at very affordable rates. As expected from a brand-new hotel, rooms are in perfect condition, furnished with light-wood and black-wood writing desks and chairs, satiny bed covers, and small but sparkling marble bathrooms (with shower only). There's also an airy restaurant in the bright and expansive lobby and an adjacent bar. The business center offers free Internet access for hotel guests. If you're traveling alone, be sure to ask about their single rates at about 10% off the regular rates. Note that this hotel's rates include all taxes, making it even more of a bargain.

Espejo 455, 5500 Mendoza. ℗ **261/405-6300.** www.argentino-hotel.com. 46 units. $50 double; $60 triple. Rates include buffet breakfast. AE, DC, MC, V. **Amenities:** Restaurant; bar; lounge; small outdoor pool; business center; room service; laundry service. *In room:* A/C, TV, hair dryer, safe.

Hotel NH Cordillera ★   The Spanish hotel chain NH (New Hotel) caters to business travelers, and this Mendoza property is no different. Opened in late 2002, the NH has four floors of crisp, compact rooms, half of which face Plaza

San Martín. The staff describes the hotel's style as minimalist, which fairly well describes their approach to service as well. Yet the NH stands heads and shoulders above most of the city's other self-proclaimed luxury hotels, and guest rooms offer every modern convenience. Stay here because of the hotel's newness and central location, but don't expect many thrills. The restaurant offers a good selection of salads, fresh fish, and meat but is closed on Sunday. A computer with free Internet access is available for guests next to the bar.

Av. España 1324, 5500 Mendoza. © 261/441-6464. Fax 261/441-6450. www.nh-hotels.com. 105 units. $100 double; from $140 suite. Rates include small buffet breakfast. AE, DC, MC, V. **Amenities:** Restaurant; bar; miniscule outdoor pool; tiny exercise room; sauna; room service; laundry service; dry cleaning. *In room:* A/C, TV, minibar, hair dryer, safe.

Park Suites Apart Hotel 🏕   A stylish newer hotel 2 blocks from Plaza Independencia, the Park Suites attracts businesspeople during the week and tourists on weekends. Single rooms are called "suites," ranging in size from junior to grand, while those with more than one room are called "apartments," accommodating up to six people. All have hardwood floors, kitchenettes, firm mattresses, stereo systems, and light, modern decor, although bathrooms are on the small size. Ask for a room with a mountain view. The staff is small but friendly.

Mitre 753, 5500 Mendoza. © **261/413-1000.** Fax 261/413-1019. www.parksuitesmza.com.ar. 56 units. $50 and up double. AE, DC, MC, V. **Amenities:** Restaurant; bar; pool; sauna; fitness room. *In room:* A/C, TV, minibar, fridge, hair dryer, safe.

INEXPENSIVE

Winca's Hostel *Value*   This newish hostel opened in late 2003 and is perfectly located just steps from the Plaza de la Independencia on a street filled with cafes and restaurants. There are eight rooms, five of them with bunk beds and shared en-suite bathrooms. The three double rooms with private bathrooms are simple but attractive, with wood-paneled ceilings and small, clean bathrooms. There's a tiny pool in the private backyard and a barbecue area for guests to use. The manager is very laid-back and friendly, and can help in arranging excursions—from rafting to wine tasting. There are several good bikes for rent for $2.75 per day. There's also a computer with Internet access for a small fee. The hearty breakfast included in your stay comes with fresh fruit and cereal (a rarity in Argentina).

Sarmiento 717, 5500 Mendoza. © **261/425-3804.** www.wincashostel.com.ar. 8 units, 5 with shared bathroom. $17 double with private bathroom; $6.50 per person with shared bathroom. Rates include buffet breakfast. No credit cards. **Amenities:** Outdoor pool; laundry; Internet access. In room: A/C, TV (in nonshared rooms).

WHERE TO DINE
EXPENSIVE

Bistro M 🏕🏕🏕 REGIONAL/INTERNATIONAL   An international restaurant with French overtones but using regional ingredients, Bistro M created the first open kitchen in South America. Busy chefs attend to the wood-burning oven while crisp waiters attend to you; the most interesting dishes include marinated goat with *chimichurri* (chile and garlic sauce), grilled trout with artichokes and tomato slices, and veal spareribs. The filet mignon served with a drizzle of Malbec reduction is exquisite. A spiral staircase climbs past a two-floor wine gallery housing over 2,500 selected regional wines, some of which are available by the glass. The sommelier will help guide you toward a selection, but don't be surprised if you're steered toward a Malbec. At $60 a bottle, the Alta Vista "Alta 1999" is an exquisite, if expensive, choice; a glass of Alta Vista

> ## *Tips* Join the Club
>
> If you're in Mendoza on a Sunday afternoon, join a group of expatriates who have recently formed **The Grapevine Wine Club.** The group meets in various locations throughout the city every Sunday afternoon from 5 to 8pm to taste a variety of local wines. Call Charlie, Kai, or Kelley at © **261/ 429-2931** or 261/423-3350 for directions and further information, or you can e-mail them at ask@thegrapevine-argentina.com. It's a good place to meet knowledgeable folks who have the lowdown on the best *bodegas* to visit and the best local wines to drink, and also firsthand information on the current hip and happening eateries, cafes, and bars around town.

Grande Reserve will run you $6. Bistro M has large windows looking out to Plaza Independencia, and an outdoor terrace open in warm weather. Cultural events, such as a Mexican festival or Spanish flamenco, are occasionally offered on weekend nights.

Park Hyatt Hotel, Chile 112. © **261/441-1234.** Reservations recommended. Main courses $7–$12. AE, DC, MC, V. Daily 6:30–11am, 12:30–3:30pm, and 8pm–midnight.

1884 *★★★* INTERNATIONAL   Francis Mallman has created Mendoza's top restaurant inside Bodega Escorihuela, known, among other things, for housing the biggest wine barrel in the province. With fine Argentine meats and fresh local produce, his carefully presented cuisine combines his Patagonian roots with his French culinary training. Dishes are prepared with matching wine selections, with Malbec and Syrah topping the list. You can easily combine in the same visit a meal here with a tour of the *bodega,* which also has an art gallery. Tours are offered weekdays every hour from 9:30am to 3:30pm.

Belgrano 1188, Godoy Cruz. © **261/424-2698.** Reservations recommended. Main courses $9–$17. AE, DC, MC, V. Daily 6:30–11am, 12:30–3:30pm, and 8pm–midnight.

MODERATE

Azafran *★ Finds* INTERNATIONAL   This charming eatery is set behind an attractively decorated all-wood wine store. Needless to say, wines are big here, and they have over 300 different labels for you to choose from. The food is imaginative, fresh, and eclectic. You may start with a warm spinach and asparagus salad or a platter of smoked meats and cheeses. The rabbit ravioli in champagne sauce is delicate and unusual, and the vegetables and tofu baked in a puff pastry will please any vegetarian. Even the steak here is served with a twist —in this case, with sweet potato pureed in a light cream sauce. The service is convivial, and the wood tables and vintage checkered floors give you a sense of dining in an old farmhouse. In the warmer months, there are a few lovely tables outside on the sidewalk for alfresco dining.

Sarmiento 765. © **261/429-4200.** Reservations recommended. Main courses $4–$7. AE, MC, V. Mon–Sat 11am–1am.

Don Mario ARGENTINE   Next door to La Marchigiana, Don Mario serves the best Argentine steaks in town. Don't let the soothing country house atmosphere fool you—this is a serious Argentine *parrilla.* The *bife de chorizo* (strip steak) served *a punto* (medium rare) is the top selection, but any of the meats are outstanding. The "Don Mario brochette" includes sirloin, chicken, tomatoes, onions, and peppers on one delicious skewer. Non–meat eaters can choose from pizza, pasta, or one of the fish dishes. Two shelves of Mendoza wines beg to be disturbed, and the expert waitstaff will help guide you to a selection.

Palmares Open Mall. © 261/439-4838. Main courses $4–$7. AE, DC, MC, V. Daily noon–3pm and 8pm–midnight.

La Marchigiana 🗶🗶 ITALIAN   Known to nearly everyone in town, Maria Theresa arrived from Italy in 1950 to open what's become Mendoza's top Italian kitchen. The restaurant's own history book details 50 years of experience in Mendoza and reveals some of the recipes of its famed homemade pastas. Octopus-like chandeliers hang from the familial A-frame dining room, where guests can easily hear the creative voices of the kitchen. You could start with a seasonal salad, but I recommend a hearty bowl of minestrone sprinkled with fresh Parmesan. Spaghetti, tagliatelli, ravioli, cannelloni, and lasagna are among the pasta choices, with a diverse selection of sauces to choose from (mushrooms in a light Provençal sauce being one). Never mind the North American tradition of drinking white wine with your pasta; a polite waiter is sure to steer you toward a *vino tinto* (red wine). Three pages of meat and fish follow on the menu, but you well may not have room after the minestrone and pasta. An extensive selection of desserts seals the menu—maybe a rich ricotta with chocolate pudding? The restaurant has a second location at Av. España 1619 (© **261/423-0751**).

Palmares Open Mall. © 261/439-1961. Main courses $4–$7. AE, DC, MC, V. Daily noon–3pm and 8pm–midnight.

INEXPENSIVE

Estancia La Florencia 𝘝𝘢𝘭𝘶𝘦 ARGENTINE   This casual eatery pays homage to the legendary gaucho, and its two levels mimic a traditional *estancia*. Ask one of the waiters, none of whom is under 50, for a recommended plate and he is likely to tell you, *"Una comida sin carne no es comida"* (a meal without meat isn't a meal). So choose one of the many varieties of steaks, the *lomo* being the most tender, or order a half grilled chicken served with a lemon slice. Just remember that a plate of meat is a plate of meat, uncorrupted by green vegetables or anything but potatoes (usually fries). Other accouterments must be ordered separately. Food is served promptly and without fanfare, and the bill may be one of the lowest you will ever find.

Sarmiento and Perú. © 261/429-9117. Main courses $2–$5. AE, DC, MC, V. Mon–Wed noon–5pm and 8pm–2am; Thurs–Sun noon–2am.

MENDOZA AFTER DARK

Mendoza nightlife is substantially more subdued than in Buenos Aires or Córdoba, but there is still a fair selection of bars and nightclubs that capture a night owl's attention. Thursday through Sunday are the biggest nights, with people getting started around midnight. The Park Hyatt Mendoza **Bar Uvas,** Chile 1124 (© **261/441-1234**), begins a bit earlier and offers a complete selection of Mendocine wines, with jazz and bossa nova groups playing most nights. Wine tastings are offered every Thursday at 9pm. **Apeteco,** at San Juan and Barraquero, has live music and dancing most nights, but locals tend to flock there mostly on Thursday nights.

The city's best bars line Aristides Villanueva street in the center of town, and many people begin here with a drink before heading to a disco along Ruta Panamericana, located roughly 10km (6¼ miles) from the town center. **Runner** and **El Diablo** are the top discos in this area. There are a few tango bars in

Mendoza, two of which are **C'Gastón,** Lavalle 35 (② **261/423-0986**), and **Abril Café,** Las Heras 346 (② **261/420-4224**).

The locals flock to **La Reserva,** Rivadavia 32 (② **261/420-3531**), on weekend nights for the drag show at midnight. The **Blah Blah Bar,** Paseo Peatonal Alameda, Escalada 2301 Maipu (no phone), is great for a late-night drink if you're not heading out to the discos.

For you gamblers, the **Regency Casino,** Chile 1124 (② **261/441-1234**), is substantially better than the Casino Provincial, offering blackjack, roulette, poker, and slots. Table bets are $1 to $50.

2 Touring the Wineries ★★★

Less commercialized than their European and American counterparts, Mendoza's wineries are free to visit and easily accessible along wine roads known locally as Los Caminos del Vino. These roads are as enticing as the wine itself, weaving and winding through tunnels of trees to vast dry valleys dominated by breathtaking views of the snowcapped Andes. Some roads climb as high as 1,524m (4,999 ft.) in the High Zone surrounding the Mendoza River, while others lead to lower-level vineyards in the south. Mendoza's wine region is divided into four zones: the High Zone, Mendoza East, Uco Valley, and Mendoza South. Different wine roads branch out through these zones and can be driven in part or total, allowing you to tour as many of Mendoza's *bodegas* as you like. There are presently 632 functioning wineries, 75 of which formally offer tours.

The **High Zone** ★★★ that surrounds the Mendoza River includes Luján de Cuyo and parts of Las Heras, Guaymallén, Luján, and Maipú. This first zone is best regarded for its production of Malbec, although cabernet sauvignon, Chenin, merlot, chardonnay, and Syrah are all bottled as well. Many of the *bodegas* in this zone lie within 1 hour's drive of Mendoza.

The **Mendoza East Region** is the second zone, comprised of Junín, Rivadavia, San Martín, Santa Rosa, and La Paz. This is the province's largest wine-producing area, where vineyards irrigated by the Tumuyán and Mendoza rivers harvest Malbec, merlot, sangiovese, and Syrah, among others. South of

---

⌒ *Tips* Book Ahead!

As tourism to this area is increasing rapidly, the wineries have begun to accept visitors by appointment only. This makes a Napa-like drive a bit difficult unless you call ahead and make appointments. Your name must be with the guard at the *bodega*'s gate for them to even allow you access to the reception area. I suggest you call a few days ahead, or at least a day before, and make appointments after plotting out your desired stops. They are not strict about keeping your allotted time (remember, this is Argentina), but making an appointment gets your name on the list and that's all that the guards care about.

If you need help planning your trip, contact Kelly at **The Grapevine Wine Tours** (② **261/429-2931;** ask@thegrapevine-argentina.com), a small British company based in Mendoza that specializes in personalized wine tours. They organize half-day, full-day, or multiple-day tours of the *bodegas* with a car and a guide. A 1-day tour costs $50 to $85 per person (depending on where lunch is eaten and what vintages are sampled). Every trip is tailored to meet your needs.

Mendoza, the **Uco Valley Region,** including Tunuyán, Tupungato, and San Carlos, produces excellent Malbec, Semillon (a white), and Torrontés (another white, very floral, like a Muscadet, more common in Salta). Allow at least 2 hours to reach this area. The final zone is the **Mendoza South Region,** between San Rafael and General Alvear. Fed by the Atuel and Diamante rivers, its best varieties are Malbec, Bonarda, and cabernet sauvignon. You will need at least a day to visit this region.

Throughout your drive, you will stumble upon wineries old and new, some producing on a large scale and exporting internationally, others small and focused on the local market. It is difficult to say which *bodegas* excel over others, as each has its own focus and success. Among some of the best-known in Lujan are Bodega Catena Zapata (© 261/490-0214); Alta Vista (© 261/496-4684); Chandon (© 261/490-9900), a subsidiary of France's Moet & Chandon; Norton (© 261/488-0480); Nieto Senetiner (© 261/498-0315); Etchart (© 261/488-0211); Dolium (© 261/490-0200); Cavas de Weinert (© 261/496-4684); Lagarde (© 261/498-3522); and Terrazas (© 261/488-0058).

In Maipú: La Rural (© 261/497-2013), which produces the enormously popular Rutini labels; Trapiche (© 261/497-3679); San Telmo (© 261/499-0050); and Familia Zuccardi (© 261/441-0000).

In Tunuyán: Lurton (© 262/249-2078) and Salentein (© 262/242-9000).

Bodega La Rural has a small winery museum that exhibits Mendoza's earliest wine-production methods. Dolium is one of the only *bodegas* producing underground to allow for natural cooling. As at most *bodegas,* a tasting follows a tour of the laboratory and winery, and there is little pressure to buy. As Italian owner Mario Giadorou proudly states, "We offer an institutional show, not a sales show."

You can pick up a map of the wine routes, as well as information on individual *bodegas,* from any of the tourist offices listed earlier in this chapter. The wineries are generally open Monday to Friday 9am to 5pm, and Saturday 10am to 3pm. Appointments are suggested and are fast becoming a requirement. Admission to all the wineries (including those with museums) is still free. But there is talk of asking an admission or tasting fee in the future.

The protocol for tasting a wine that is not featured in the visit is to ask to buy a bottle. They will open it then and there for you to sample, but, of course, you have to pay for the entire bottle (which is not always much less than the market price). If you have your heart set on tasting a certain vintage, be sure to bring cash.

Each March, the wine season culminates with the **Fiesta Nacional de la Venimia (National Wine Harvest Festival),** which includes a parade, folk dancing, and coronation of the festival's queen. This is the busiest time in Mendoza and the wine region.

Tips Come to Harvest

If you're in Mendoza between February and April, Familia Zuccardi invites you to come pick some grapes. This new program gives the wine aficionado a hands-on morning at the vineyards. After a short tutorial, you are given scissors and a basket and are expected to work for 2 hours. Afterward, a fantastic lunch is served (with ample wine), followed by a tour and tasting. The cost is $67 per person and includes transportation to and from your hotel, lunch, tour, and tasting. Reservations are accepted by e-mail at turismo@familiazuccardi.com or by calling © **261/441-0000.**

The Story of Mendoza's Wine

Blessed by rich sunlight and a panorama of snow-filled mountains, Mendoza dominates Argentina's wine-making industry and is one of the most successful wine regions on Earth. Surrounding the beautiful city of Mendoza and lying just to the east of the towering Andes, the province accounts for over 70% of the nation's wine production and is the world's sixth-largest producer of grapes.

The Spanish began cultivating Mendoza's wild American vines in the 16th century, and wine production soon dominated the region's economy. They were able to harvest this semiarid land—which receives little natural rainfall—by using a vast irrigation system originally developed by the Incas and extended by the Huarpes, indigenous people from the region. A series of artificial irrigation ditches and canals divert water from the Mendoza, Diamante, Tunuyán, and Atuel rivers, which fill as snow melts in the Andes to nourish the land.

The development of Mendoza's wine industry ebbed and flowed. Wine production stalled in the late 18th century as Spain restricted grape growing to prevent competition with its colonies. The industry was renewed following national independence, as European experts introduced French grapevine stocks and wineries to the region. However, the earthquake of 1861 destroyed most of the existing wineries, and it was not until the opening of a railroad in 1884 that wine production resumed on a significant scale. The railway brought with it many of the founding families of today's wineries, who carried new wine-making techniques and varietals from Italy, France, and Spain. A series of economic crises plagued the industry in the first half of the 19th century, and Mendoza's wines seldom made it farther than the common Argentine table. Some of the wines were so low in quality that soda water was needed to help wash them down, a tradition that continues in some places today (although no longer because of poor quality).

In the past decade, wine from Mendoza has finally reached beyond the common table to the international stage. Argentina's National Wine Growing Institute has regulated the country's wine industry and spearheaded quality improvements, increasingly focusing on the international market. New production techniques, state-of-the-art machinery, advanced irrigation processes, and better grape varieties have combined to bring Mendoza international acclaim. The region's dry, sandy soil; low humidity; and rich sun combine to create wines of high alcohol content and rich fruity character, the most important of which is Malbec, characterized by a powerful fruit bouquet with sweet, dense tannins. Mendocine vineyards grow numerous other varietals, including cabernet sauvignon, Syrah, Barbera, chardonnay, and sauvignon blanc.

WHERE TO STAY & DINE

Club Tapiz ★★★ is the best place to stay in the heart of the wine country, a small inn (Pedro Molina Ruta 60, Maipu; © 261/490-0202; www.newage-hotels.com) that opened in late 2004 and offers seven luxurious rooms in a meticulously restored 1800s farmhouse, minutes from many vineyards. There's a pristine outdoor pool, a spa, and a fantastic restaurant. The backyard is ringed with olive trees, and there's a well-stocked cellar beneath the lovely living room. Rooms have their original bamboo ceilings, but everything else is spanking new. Be sure to request one of the three rooms that look out onto the back garden. There's a wine tasting nightly. Celebrated Argentine chef Max Casa, whose creations range from escargots in puff pastry to vegetable tartare with duck confit, heads the inn's restaurant, TerrUno. Other specials include lamb risotto and young goat baked in Malbec wine. The wine list, needless to say, is exhaustive, with almost every award-winning Mendoza *bodega* featured. Rooms here run $77 to $90 for a double. Main courses at the restaurant will set you back $6 to $8.

Finca Adalgisa ⚘, Pueyrredon 2222, Chacras de Coria (© **261/496-0713**), is an old *bodega* in the midst of a small village. The old house has three bedrooms behind an enormous kitchen. In the lush backyard, facing the pool, there's a stone house that sleeps four and two additional rooms. The pleasant double rooms go for $92, and the stone house for four is $177 per night. Guests have the opportunity to taste wines and have meals at the tiny *bodega* adjacent to the old house. A small quantity of wine (6,000 bottles) is still produced at the winery, but it is not marketed. If you're not staying here, you may call ahead to arrange for a meal or a wine tasting and a visit. Meals run $18 to $23.

Many of the region's *bodegas* have delightful dining areas overlooking the vineyards. None of them accepts walk-in customers, though, so you must call ahead for reservations if you are hoping to have lunch at any of the *bodegas* you intend to visit. **Familia Zuccardi** ⚘, RP 33, Maipu (© **261/441-0000**), is the sole *bodega* to offer afternoon tea in addition to a fantastic lunch. Either will run you $17 per person; the tea service is quite substantial, with sandwiches, cheeses, cakes, and pastries. Lunch here is lovely, with an outdoor oven where empanadas are baked daily and an assado where the meat is freshly grilled.

Another good choice for lunch is **Bodega Nieto Senetiner** ⚘, Guardia Vieja, Lujan de Cuyo (© **261/498-0315**). Unlike many other wineries, they are open on Sunday. Expect to pay $16 to $20 per person for a meal here, which will probably include homemade empanadas, salads, and a variety of grilled chicken and cuts of beef. Wine is included in the price and is usually both white and red.

3 The Alta Montaña Driving Circuit

Climbing the mountains on the way to the Chilean border, this excellent driving circuit leads past the magnificent vineyards of Mendoza to breathtaking vistas of the Andes. It is an all-day excursion (it would take at least 5 hr. with no stops) that leads past the Uspallata Valley up to nearly 3,000m (9,840 ft.) at Las Cuevas and the entrance of Aconcagua Park. There are two routes you can take: The easier drive takes you past Potrerillos on the RN 7—a small area along the Mendoza River popular for its white-water rafting—while a more challenging drive (due to winding dirt roads) takes you through the gorgeous natural-springs town of Villavicencio. (We recommend you go Villavicencio on the way and return via Potrerillos on the RN 7.) Whichever route you choose, the roads come together in Uspallata, where the circuit continues to Las Cuevas on the RN 7. You can do this tour on your own, but it is easier with a driver who knows the roads. Note that a 4×4 is preferable, although not obligatory, for the route to Villavicencio. Expect temperatures to drop significantly as you climb the mountains.

HEADING TO USPALLATA VIA VILLAVICENCIO

Although it takes a couple hours longer than heading straight north on RN 7, driving the Ruta 52 takes you to the natural springs of Villavicencio, the source of Argentina's well-known mineral water. Leaving Mendoza to the north through Las Heras, you'll be driving on the old international road to Chile. After 34km (21 miles), you'll pass the **Monumento Canota,** the spot where generals San Martín and Las Heras split to confront the Spanish at different fronts in 1817. After Canota, you will begin to climb the Villivicencio Valley, and by 40km (25 miles), the road turns to gravel and becomes winding (the road here is known locally as the Caracoles de Villavicencio, or "the snails of Villavicencio"). A small **ranger station** at 50km (31 miles) offers information on the Villavicencio natural reserve, including sources of the mineral water and the region's flora and fauna. Eagles, condors, pumas, mountain cats, foxes, ostriches, guanacos, flowering cacti, and many plants and trees occupy the area.

VILLAVICENCIO

French-owned Danone purchased the rights to this land and its mineral water, and it is working hard to preserve the integrity of the springs. This explains why the **Hotel Termas Villavicencio,** frequented by Argentina's high society until its closing in 1980, has not reopened. Yet the lush gardens of the Normandy-style hotel, seen on the label of Villavicencio bottles, can still be toured by foot. Perched against the foothills with oaks and poplars, trickling streams, and wildflowers surrounding it, the hotel's location represents a little paradise in the Andes. A small chapel, opened in 1941, lies just behind it. Next to the hotel, you can stop at the Hostería Villavicencio for lunch or a drink.

THE USPALLATA VALLEY

Continuing along the Ruta 52, you will follow the path that San Martín used for his liberation campaign. The dirt road zigzags its way up the canyon, dotted with silver mines exploited by the Spaniards in the 18th century. When you get 74km (46 miles) from Mendoza, you will have climbed to the 3,000m (9,840-ft.) summit. From here, you'll have a magnificent view of Aconcagua and the mountains, and the road begins to improve.

The road from the summit to Uspallata is a breathtaking 28km (17-mile) drive through the **Uspallata Valley.** You will descend into the valley through a small canyon, and when the valley emerges, you'll be treated to one of the most beautiful sights in Argentina. The polychromatic mountains splash light off Aconcagua to your left and the "Tiger Chain" ahead, with occasional clouds painting shadows on some mountains and allowing sun to pour light on others. The curious rock formations surrounding you were filmed for the dramatic setting of *Seven Years in Tibet,* starring Brad Pitt. Just before you arrive in Uspallata, 2km (1¼ miles) north of town, you will see **Las Bovedas**—peculiar egg-shape mud domes built in the 18th century to process gold and silver for the Spaniards.

HEADING TO USPALLATA VIA POTRERILLOS

This drive is significantly easier than the route through Villavicencio, taking you along the RN 7 through the Precordillera mountains. Potrerillos is a small stop along the Río Mendoza, where tour companies arrange white-water rafting, horseback riding, and trekking. **Argentina Rafting Expediciones** (see "Tour Operators & Outdoor Activities" on p. 140) operates a small restaurant and bar off the RN 7. The drive continues 49km (30 miles) alongside the Mendoza River directly to Uspallata.

USPALLATA

With only 3,500 inhabitants, Uspallata is a pretty sleepy place. But this small Andean town offers a variety of outdoor activities and makes an excellent base from which to explore the mountains. You can obtain limited visitor information from the **tourist information booth,** open daily from 9:30am to 8:30pm and located at the corner of RN 7 and Ruta 52. Gustavo Pizarro is the area's best tour guide, and his **Pizarro Expediciones,** RN 7 (*© 262/442-0261*), organizes horseback riding, mountain biking, climbing, and white-water rafting. If you want to stop for lunch while doing the Circuito Alta Montaña, do it in Uspallata, the last real town before the Chilean border.

WHERE TO STAY & DINE

Hotel Valle Andino ⚘   Given the town's limited selection of hotels, this is probably the best choice. The hotel's greatest merit is its beautiful grounds stretching toward the Andes. A true mountain retreat, the dimly lit wood lodge is popular with backpackers and hiking groups, and the staff can organize horseback-riding trips from the hotel. Rooms are stark but modern, some accommodating up to five people. The recreation room has a fireplace and pool table.

Ruta 7 s/n. *©* 262/442-0033. www.hotelguia.com/hoteles/valleandino. 26 units. $28 double. Rates include breakfast. No credit cards. **Amenities:** Restaurant; bar; indoor pool.

La Estancia de Elias ARGENTINE   A simple, friendly *parrilla* across from the Shell station, La Estancia de Elias is less touristy than other restaurants located along RN 7. The empanadas are fresh and fluffy, and the *bife de chorizo* is enormous. There are also salads and pastas, or you could try the grilled *chivito* (goat), which is the specialty of the region. Heck, it's cheap enough you could probably order one of each.

Ruta 7, Km 1146. *©* 262/442-0165. Main courses $2–$4. No credit cards. Daily 9am–2am.

HEADING TO ACONCAGUA FROM USPALLATA

Continuing along the RN 7, you'll drive through the wide U-shape valley carved from ancient glaciers and loaded with minerals like iron, sulfur, talc, and copper. As you climb the canyon, you will see the first signs of the atrophying **Andes railway** to your left, an old, narrow track from 1902 that lifted an early-20th-century steam train up the mountains. The railroad was abandoned in 1980 due to a political dispute between Chile and Argentina, and has never been reopened. When you get 20km (12 miles) from Uspallata, you'll come to **Puente Pichueta,** a stone bridge over the Pichueta River that was commissioned by Fernando VII in 1770 to allow messengers to travel from Argentina to Chile. The road leading to the bridge forms part of the old Inca trail.

LOS PENITENTES

About 165km (102 miles) past Mendoza, you will hit **Los Penitentes,** a small resort for downhill and cross-country skiing. There are 23 slopes accommodating all ski levels, as well as a ski school for instruction. Keep in mind, however, that **Portillo** (p. 140) is a much larger and better-equipped ski resort just on the other side of the Chilean border. If you decide to stay in Los Penitentes, **Ayelan,** Ruta 7, Km 165 (*© 261/427-1123*), sits across the street from the ski resort with basic rooms looking toward the mountains. Doubles cost roughly $65, including breakfast, and the rustic dining room serves quality regional dishes (although the selection is limited).

PUENTE DEL INCA

Puente del Inca is a natural stone bridge used by the Incas to cross the Río de las Cuevas; it's about 6km (3¾ miles) past Los Penitentes. Under the bridge you will see the remains of an old spa that once belonged to a hotel. That hotel was destroyed in an avalanche, but, in what many consider a miracle, the adjacent church went unscathed. Natural hot springs still flow through here, and you can don your bathing suit and take a dip. Near the spa, vendors sell handicrafts.

PARQUE PROVINCIAL ACONCAGUA

Just after Puente del Inca, you will come to the entrance of **Aconcagua Provincial Park.** At 6,960m (22,829 ft.), Cerro Aconcagua is the highest peak not just in South America, but also in the entire Western Hemisphere. From RN 7, you

---

Hitting the Slopes in Las Leñas

One of South America's top ski destinations, with more slopes than any single resort in the Americas, Las Leñas boasts 64km (40 miles) of runs, excellent snow, and typically small crowds. The summit reaches 3,430m (11,250 ft.), with a 1,230m (4,034-ft.) vertical drop. There are 30 runs, with approximately 8% set aside for beginners, 22% for intermediates, and 70% for advanced skiers. The resort's 11 lifts can transport up to 9,200 skiers per hour, which is far more capacity than the town has in accommodations. Consequently, you seldom have to wait in line to get to the top.

Las Leñas attracts wealthy Porteños as well as international skiers, and it has an active nightlife in winter. Snow season runs from June to mid-October. In summer, Las Leñas offers mountain biking, trekking, rafting, and fishing, and hotel prices drop significantly. The resort is most easily reached by taking a 90-minute flight from Buenos Aires to Malargüe, followed by a 1-hour bus to Las Leñas (68km/42 miles). Alternatively, you can travel by car or bus from Mendoza, which is a 4- to 5-hour drive (399km/247 miles).

While maybe not quite the five-star hotel the sign proclaims, **Pisces Club Hotel** ⭐⭐ is by far the best place to stay in Las Leñas. Many people arriving at the hotel, as elsewhere in Las Leñas, come on week-long ski packages. Well-equipped rooms accommodate up to three people, and the stay includes breakfast and dinner. Following a day of skiing, the hotel provides hot drinks and warming by the fireplace, and the indoor pool, Jacuzzi, and sauna should reinvigorate the remaining cold parts of your body. The hotel also offers ski instruction and children's activities, as well as adult activities in the casino and nightclub.

Las Leñas lies in the southwest of Mendoza province, near the city of Malargüe and close to the Chilean border. To drive from Mendoza, take the RN 40 to the PR222. One tour operator offering packages from the United States is **Holidaze Ski Tours,** www.holidaze.com. In Buenos Aires, try **Rotamund,** Av. Roque Sáenz Peña 846, Piso 2 (© **4321-5100;** www.rotamund.com).

Lift tickets run about $40 per day, with multiple-day passes available. A weekly pass, for example, will run you $215.

can see the summit on clear days. To enter the park, however, you must first obtain a permit from the park's "attention center" called Edificio Cuba (© **261/ 425-2031**), inside Mendoza's Parque San Martín. The location where you can buy permits changes periodically, so check with Mendoza's tourism office for additional details. Two-day, 7-day, and 20-day permits are available. With one of the shorter-duration permits, you can hike to the base camps without climbing to the summit. Those hoping to reach the top must buy a 20-day permit, which costs $200 (including emergency medical insurance). The climb is not technically difficult, but it demands strength and endurance. The south face, which gets little sun, is the most treacherous climb. The normal route is along the west side. You can get more information by checking the following website: www.aconcagua.com.

After visiting the park, we recommend you continue on to Las Cuevas and return to Mendoza via Potrerillos on the RN 7.

9

The Argentine Lake District

The Lake District is Argentina's premier vacation destination, a ruggedly beautiful jewel of a region characterized by snowcapped mountains, waterfalls, lush forest, the area's namesake lakes, and trout-filled, crystalline rivers. The region stretches from north of Junín de los Andes to the south of Esquel, incorporating small villages, ranches, several spectacular national parks, and the thriving city of Bariloche. Visitors here often liken the Lake District to Alpine Europe, as much for the landscape as for the clapboard architecture influenced by Swiss and German immigration. Although it is considered part of Patagonia (see chapter 18), the Lake District has little in common with its southern neighbors, especially now that increased migration from cities such as Buenos Aires continues to urbanize the region.

The allure of the Lake District is that it offers something for everyone year-round, from hiking to biking, fishing to hunting, sightseeing to sunbathing, summer boating to winter skiing. The region is also well known for its food—venison, wild boar, trout, smoked cheeses, wild mushrooms, sweet marmalades, chocolates, and more. Tourism is the principal economic force here, which means that prices soar as the swarming masses pour into this region from mid-December to early March and during the month of July. We highly recommend that you plan a trip during the off season, especially in November or April, when the weather is still pleasant, although it is possible to escape the crowds even during the middle of summer.

Considering the enormous, flat Pampa that separates Buenos Aires from the Lake District, and the region's proximity to the international border with Chile, many visitors opt to include a trip to Chile's Lake District while here. (For more on Chile's Lake District, see chapter 15.) This can be done by boat aboard the popular "Lake Crossing" through Puerto Blest to Lago Todos los Santos near Ensenada, or by vehicle. For general information about this region on the Web, try **www.interpatagonia.com**.

EXPLORING THE REGION

In this chapter, we have focused on the most scenic and accessible destinations in the Lake District: San Carlos de Bariloche (usually called simply Bariloche), Villa La Angostura, and San Martín de los Andes. This coverage includes the area's many national parks, as well as driving tours and boat trips that take in the best of the stunning lakeside scenery. The best way to view this region is to base yourself in one of these towns and strike out and explore the surrounding wilderness. All of the towns described in this chapter offer enough outdoor and sightseeing excursions to fill 1 or even 2 weeks, but 4 to 5 days in one location is ample time for a visit. An interesting option for travelers is to make a detour into Chile via the lake crossing from Bariloche, or to organize a boat-bus combination that loops from Bariloche and Villa La Angostura in Argentina, then crosses the border into Chile and stops in Puyehue, continuing on south to Puerto Varas or Puerto Montt, then crossing back into Argentina and Bariloche via the Lake Crossing. Another option is to cross from San Martín de los Andes to Pucón, Chile. All this takes some intricate planning; see chapter 15 for more information.

1 San Carlos de Bariloche ★★

1,621km (1,005 miles) southwest of Buenos Aires; 180km (112 miles) south of San Martín de los Andes

San Carlos de Bariloche, or simply Bariloche, is the winter and summer playground for vacationing Argentines and the second-most-visited destination in the country. The city sits in the center of Nahuel Huapi National Park and is fronted by an enormous, irregularly shaped lake of the same name. Bariloche's grand appeal is in its many outdoor activities, sightseeing drives, boat trips, great restaurants, and shopping opportunities here. Visitors could easily occupy themselves for a week, regardless of the season.

The city itself embodies a strange juxtaposition: an urban city plopped down in the middle of beautiful wilderness. Unfortunately, Argentine migrants fleeing Buenos Aires, an ever-growing tourism industry, and 2 decades of unchecked development have left a cluttered mess in what once was an idyllic mountain town. Bits and pieces of the charming architecture influenced by German, Swiss, and English immigration are still in evidence. But visitors to Bariloche are sometimes overwhelmed by the hodgepodge of ugly apartment buildings, clamorous discos, and the crowds that descend on this area, especially from mid-December until the end of February and during ski season in July. Yet drive 10 minutes outside town, and you'll once again be surrounded by thick forests, rippling lakes, and snowcapped peaks that rival those found in Alpine Europe. If you're looking for a quiet vacation, you'd be better off lodging outside the city center, on the road to the Llao Llao Peninsula or in the town of Villa La Angostura (p. 171). On the flip side, Bariloche offers a wealth of services.

ESSENTIALS
GETTING THERE

BY PLANE The **Aeropuerto Bariloche** (© 02944/426162) is 13km (8 miles) from downtown. Buses to the city center are timed with the arrival of flights and can be found outside at the arrival area; some are run by the airlines themselves. A taxi costs about $10. **Aerolíneas Argentinas/Austral,** Quaglia 238 (© 02944/422425; www.aerolineasargentinas.com), has at least three daily flights from Buenos Aires and in summer operates three weekly flights from El Calafate. **Southern Winds** (© 0810/777-7979) and **American Falcon** (© 02944/425200) fly from Buenos Aires, while **LADE,** Quaglia 238 #8 (© 02944/423562), serves small destinations in the area such as Neuquen and Esquel. **Lan-Chile** (© 11/4312-8161) offers the only scheduled international flights, from both Puerto Montt and Santiago.

BY BUS The **Terminal de Omnibus** (© 02944/432860) is at Av. 12 de Octubre 2400; a dozen companies serve most major destinations in Argentina and Chile. **TAC** (© 02944/431521) has three daily arrivals from Buenos Aires and daily service from El Bolsón, Esquel, Mendoza, and Córdoba. **Vía Bariloche** (© 02944/435770) has three daily arrivals from Buenos Aires (the trip lasts about 20 hr.) and one daily trip from Mar del Plata. **Andesmar** (© 02944/422140) has service from Mendoza, Río Gallegos, and Neuquén, and service from Osorno, Valdivia, and Puerto Montt in Chile. In addition, there's a daily

Argentina's Lake District

Mafil
Panguipulli
Lago Panguipulli
Lago Huechulafquén
Río Aluminé

Río Calle Calle
Riñihue
Lago Riñihue
Valdivia
Los Lagos

PARQUE NACIONAL LANIN
Junin de los Andes

Lago Pirehuico

Lago Maihué
Lago Lolog

Santiago
CHILE
ARGENTINA
Buenos Aires

Lago Ranco
Lago Lacar
San Martín de los Andes
▲ Cerro Chapelco 2394 m.

Lago Ranco

PARQUE NACIONAL
Río Caleufú

PARQUE NACIONAL PUYEHUE
Lago Puyehue
Lago Trafiul
Cerro Bayo
NAHUEL

Termas de Puyehue
■ **Aguas Calientes**
Entre Lagos
HUAPI

Rio Negro
Lago Rupanco
■ Antillanca
Villa La Angostura

Purranque
Piedras Negras
Lago Nahuel Huapi

Pt. Octay
Lago Todos los Santos
■ Llao Llao

Frutillar
Lago Llanquihue
PARQUE NACIONAL V. PEREZ ROSALES
▲ Monte Tronador 3478 m.
▲ Cerro Catedral 2388 m.
San Carlos de Bariloche

Lllanquihue
Ensenada

Río Maullín

Puerto Montt
Lago Chapo
■ Cascada los Alerces

Seno de Reloncaví
PARQUE NACIONAL ALERCE ANDINO
○ Rio Villegas

Calbuco
Caleta La Arena
Puelo
CHILE
ARGENTINA
Norquinco

Isla Puluqui
Caleta Puelche
Río Puelo
El Bolsón

Hornopiren
El Maitén

Golfo de Ancud
Lago Puelo

Fiordo Comau
PARQUE NACIONAL LAGO PUELO
Río Chubut

Península Huequi
Lago Cholila
Leleque

Fiordo Reñihue
Leptepú
Lago Menéndez

Caleta Gonzalo
Lago Futalaufquen
Río Percey
Esquel

✈ Airport
🎿 Ski Area
▲ Mountain
PARQUE NACIONAL LOS ALERCES
Lago Amutui Quimei
Trevelin

0   20 mi
0   20 km
N
Río Yelcho
Futaleufú

service from San Martín de los Andes via the scenic Siete Lagos (Seven Lakes) route (only during the summer); from Villa La Angostura, try **Ko-Ko** (© **02944/ 423090**). For more on the Siete Lagos route, see chapter 15.

BY CAR   Bariloche can be reached from San Martín via several picturesque routes. The 200km (124-mile) scenic Siete Lagos route from San Martín de los Andes follows Ruta 234, 231, and 237 (not recommended when it's raining, as the dirt roads turn to mud); the 160km (99-mile) Paso Córdoba takes Ruta 234, 63, and 237; the longest, yet entirely paved (unlike the other routes described), 260km (161-mile) Collón Curá route follows Ruta 234, 40, and 237 and is recommended for night driving or when the weather is crummy. To get to El Bolsón, follow Route 258 south; continue down 40 to get to Esquel. To cross into Chile, take the Puyehue Pass via Route 231 (through Villa La Angostura); during periods of heavy snowfall, chains are required.

TRAVELING BY BOAT TO CHILE   **Catedral Turismo** offers a spectacular journey to the Lake District in Chile that operates as a boat-and-bus combination that terminates in Lago Todos los Santos near Ensenada and Puerto Varas. If you're planning to visit Chile, this is a superb option that really allows you to take in the beauty of the Andes and the volcanoes, rivers, and waterfalls in the mountain range; however, this journey is not recommended on days with heavy rain. The trip can be done in 1 long day or in 2 days, with an overnight in the Hotel Peulla in Chile (see the "Frutillar, Puerto Octay, Puerto Varas ★★, Lago Llanquihue, Ensenada, Parque Nacional Vicente Pérez Rosales & the Lake Crossing to Argentina" section beginning on p. 353 of chapter 15 for more information). The trip costs $178 per person for the boat trip (including lunch), and an average of $85 double for an overnight at the Hotel Peulla. Book at any travel agency or from Catedral Turismo's offices in Bariloche at Moreno 238 (© **02944/425443;** www.crucedelagos.cl).

GETTING AROUND
BY FOOT   The city is compact enough to explore by foot. However, most visitors spend just a few hours touring the city, and instead use Bariloche as a base to explore surrounding areas.

BY CAR   A rental car is how most savvy travelers visit this area; you'll want one here if you're staying outside the city center and also to drive through the region's sinuous roads that pass through exceptionally scenic landscapes, such as the Circuito Chico. All travel agencies offer excursions to these areas, which is another option. Rental agencies, including Budget, Dollar, Hertz, and Avis, have kiosks at the airport, and many downtown offices: **Budget,** Mitre 106 (© **02944/ 422482**); **AI Rent a Car,** Av. San Martín 235 (© **02944/422582**); **Dollar,**

⌒Tips Taking a Car into Chile

If you're hoping to do a Lake District circuit combining both the Argentine and Chilean lake districts, be warned that you'll need additional insurance and written permission from the car-rental agency to take the vehicle across the border. We suggest using Avis rental car for these trips, as it's the only company that has offices in numerous towns in both countries and can offer roadside assistance and get a replacement car to you quickly if you run into any problems.

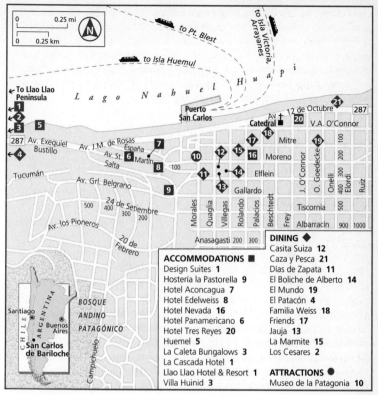

ACCOMMODATIONS ■

Design Suites **1**
Hostería la Pastorella **9**
Hotel Aconcagua **7**
Hotel Edelweiss **8**
Hotel Nevada **16**
Hotel Panamericano **6**
Hotel Tres Reyes **20**
Huemel **5**
La Caleta Bungalows **3**
La Cascada Hotel **1**
Llao Llao Hotel & Resort **1**
Villa Huinid **3**

DINING ◆

Casita Suiza **12**
Caza y Pesca **21**
Días de Zapata **11**
El Boliche de Alberto **14**
El Mundo **19**
El Patacón **4**
Familia Weiss **18**
Friends **17**
Jauja **13**
La Marmite **15**
Los Cesares **2**

ATTRACTIONS ●

Museo de la Patagonia **10**

Villegas 285 (© **02944/430333**); **Hertz,** Quaglia 165 (© **02944/434543**); **Bariloche Rent a Car,** Moreno 115 (© **02944/427638**); **Localiza,** Av. San Martín 463 (© **02944/424767**); and **A Open Rent a Car,** Mitre 171 #15 (© **02944/426325**).

When navigating the streets of Bariloche, do not confuse two streets with similar names: V.A. O'Connor runs parallel to the Costanera, and J. O'Connor bisects it.

VISITOR INFORMATION

The **Secretaría de Turismo,** in the stone-and-wood Civic Center complex between calles Urquiza and Panzoni (© **02944/426784;** securismo@bariloche. com.ar), has general information about Bariloche and is an indispensable source for accommodations listings, especially during the high season. It also operates an information stand in the bus terminal. It's open Monday through Friday from 8am to 9pm, Saturday and Sunday from 9am to 9pm. For information about lodging and attractions surrounding Bariloche, try the **Secretaría de Turismo de Río Negro,** Av. 12 de Octubre 605, at the waterfront (© **02944/426644**); it's open Monday through Friday from 9am to 2pm.

A good website for all sorts of up-to-date travel information is www. bariloche.org.

The **Club Andino Bariloche,** Av. 20 de Febrero 30 (© **02944/422266;** fax 02944/424579; transitando@bariloche.com.ar), provides excellent information about hiking, backpacking, and mountaineering in the area. They sell maps and provide treks, mountain ascents, and ice walks led by guides from the Club Andino, as well as rafting, photo safaris, and horseback rides; open daily from 9am to 1pm and 6 to 9pm during winter, daily from 8:30am to 3pm and 5 to 9pm during summer. For general info about **Nahuel Huapi National Park,** head to the park's headquarters in the Civic Center (© **02944/424111**), open Monday through Friday from 8:30am to 12:30pm.

FAST FACTS: Bariloche

Banks & Currency Exchange Most banks exchange currency, including **Banco de Galicia,** Moreno and Quaglia (© **02944/427125**), and **Citibank,** Mitre 694 (© **02944/436301**). Try also **Cambio Sudamérica,** Mitre 63 (© **02944/434555**).

Hospital **Hospital Privado Regional** is located at 20 de Febrero 594 (© **02944/423074**).

Internet Access Internet cafes are on just about every corner—and almost every hotel has Internet access, which is usually free for guests. Try **Cyber-mac Café,** Rolando 217, #12 (no phone), or **Net & Cappuccino,** Quaglia 220 (© **02944/426128**). The cost is less than $1 per hour.

Laundry There are two reliable laundromats here: **Marva Lavematic,** at San Martín 325 (© **02944/426319**) and **Lavematic,** located on Beschtedt 180 (© **02944/433022**).

Pharmacy The three main pharmacies in the city center are **Angel Gallardo,** A. Gallardo 701 (© **02944/427023**); **Zona Vital,** Moreno and Rolando (© **02944/420752**); or **Nahuel,** Moreno 238 (© **02944/422490**).

Police For emergencies, dial **101.** For other matters, call © **02944/423434.**

Post Office The central post office (no phone) is in the Civic Center, next to the tourist office.

WHAT TO SEE & DO IN BARILOCHE

Bariloche's **Civic Center,** Avenida Juan Manuel de Rosas and Panzoni, is a charming stone-and-wood complex that houses most municipal offices and tourism services, such as the information center and national park headquarters. The complex, built in 1940, was inspired by the architecture of Bern, Switzerland. Here you'll find the **Museo de la Patagonia Perito Moreno** (© **02944/422309**), open Tuesday through Friday from 10am to 12:30pm and 2 to 7pm, Monday from 10am to 1pm; closed Sunday. Admission is $1. The museum has five salons dedicated to the natural science, history, and ethnography of the Bariloche region. The well-tended displays here are intriguing, notably the stuffed and mounted local fauna, such as *pudú* (miniature deer), puma, condor, and more. The second floor has displays of Mapuche artifacts, such as weapons, art, and jewelry, and other artifacts from the colonial period. A small gift shop sells postcards, books, and crafts.

SHOPPING You'll find everything and anything along Bariloche's main street, Mitre, including shops selling souvenirs and Argentine products such as *mate* (tea), gourds, and leather goods. For the region's famous smoked meats and cheese, and other regional specialties such as trout pâté, try the renowned

Familia Weiss, Mitre 360 ((©) **02944/424829**), or **Del Turista,** Av. San Martín 252 or Mitre 239 (no phone). Del Turista also has an enormous array of chocolates and candy, as do other confectioneries up and down Calle Mitre, such as **Abuela Goye,** Mitre 258 ((©) **02944/423311**) and Quaglia 221 ((©) **02944/ 422276**); **Bari,** Mitre 339 ((©) **02944/422305**); **Mexicana,** Mitre 288 ((©) **02944/ 422505**); and **Mamuschka,** Mitre 216 ((©) **02944/423294**). Stop by the visitor center for a map of Avenida Bustillo and the Llao Llao Peninsula, along which are dozens of shops selling regional specialties. Note that food items such as smoked meats wrapped in plastic are generally not permitted outside Argentina.

TOUR OPERATORS

A plethora of travel agencies offer everything under the sun along the streets of Bariloche. Most tours do not include lunch, and some charge extra for a bilingual guide. The best of the lot includes **Catedral Turismo,** Moreno 238 ((©) **02944/425443**), with a wide variety of land excursions to El Bolsón, Cerro Tronador, and circuit sightseeing routes. **Tom Wesley Viajes de Aventura,** Mitre 385 ((©) **02944/435040**), specializes in horseback riding but offers everything else, too, even sightseeing tours and an adventure camp. **Cumbres Patagonia,** Villegas 222 ((©) **02944/423283;** cumbres@bariloche.com.ar), has easy sightseeing trips and more adventurous excursions, including trekking, fishing, and 4×4 trips. Also try **Ati Viajes,** V.A. O'Connor 335 ((©) **02944/426782**); **Barlan Travel,** Mitre 340 #68 ((©) **02944/426782**); or **Viajes Danneman,** Mitre 86 ((©) **02944/428793**).

PARQUE NACIONAL NAHUEL HUAPI ✸✸

Nahuel Huapi is Argentina's oldest and most popular national park, offering just about everything for any interest or physical level. The park surrounds the city of Bariloche, and its headquarters are downtown in the Civic Center (see "Visitor Information," above). The park's main feature is the 3,500m (11,480-ft.) extinct volcano **Tronador (Thunderer),** named for the rumbling produced by ice falling from the mountain's peak. But the park is also known for the glacial-formed Lake Nahuel Huapi and its lovely forested peninsulas and waterways that often provoke comparison to the channels of southern Patagonia or the fjords of Norway. During summertime, visitors can take part in day hikes or backpacking trips along one of the park's several trails or boat out to one of the lake's islands.

The park also has plenty of other outdoor activities, such as rafting, horseback riding, and fishing; during the winter, the park's other dominant peak, **Cerro Catedral,** is a popular ski resort. Easy access to all regions of the park makes Nahuel Huapi popular with visitors seeking mellower activities, such as sightseeing drives and cable cars to magnificent lookout points. The following information is for all attractions within Nahuel Huapi and around Bariloche.

THE ROAD TO THE LLAO LLAO PENINSULA ✸✸✸

The Cerro Campanario provides possibly the best lookout point in the region, with exceptional views of Nahuel Huapi and Perito Moreno lakes, as well as the ravishing beauty of the Llao Llao Peninsula and the peaks surrounding it. The lookout point is accessed by a 7-minute cable car ride located 17km (11 miles) outside Bariloche on the road to Llao Llao, meaning you'll have to arrange transportation with a tour, drive a rental car, or take a bus. Or you can inquire about transfer shuttles from downtown at the Cerro Campanario cable car company's Bariloche office. A restaurant here offers panoramic views. The office is at Belgrano 41 #B ((©) **02944/427274**) and is open daily from 9am to noon and 2 to 6pm; the cost for the cable car is $5.

The Cerro Campanario is along a popular 60km (37-mile) drive around the Llao Llao Peninsula, commonly known as the **Circuito Chico.** This drive offers spectacular views of Nahuel Huapi and Perito Moreno lakes and the snow-capped peaks of Cerro Otway and Catedral that tower over them. The drive begins 18km (11 miles) from Bariloche on Avenida Bustillo, which changes into Route 237, loops around the peninsula as Route 77, and meets back at Route 237 and eventually Bustillo, all the while meandering through dense forest and picturesque bays with outstanding lookout points. Visitors will find *parrilla* (grill) and fondue-style restaurants along the way, as well as the world-renowned **Llao Llao Hotel & Resort** (see later in this chapter). Stop by the visitor center to pick up a detailed Circuito Chico map highlighting restaurants and shops along the way. Again, most tour operators offer this excursion.

CERRO OTTO 𝓡𝓡

Walk, bike, drive, or ride a cable car to the top of **Cerro Otto** for sweeping views of Lake Nahuel Huapi, the Llao Llao Peninsula, and the high peaks of Catedral and Tronador, as well as for an assortment of diversions, including paragliding, trekking, rock climbing, and, during the winter, skiing and dog-sledding. The road up to Cerro Otto takes visitors through a thick forest of pine, beech, and *alerce* (larch) populated with charming chalets. To walk (2–3 hr.) or bike, take Avenida Los Pioneros for about 1km (about ½ mile) and follow the signs to Cerro Otto. Or take the free shuttle bus that leaves from Mitre and Villegas; it runs daily every hour from 10:30am to 4:30pm. The **cable car** (𝓒 **02944/ 441035**) costs $8 per person and runs January through February and July through August daily from 9:30am to 6pm; the rest of the year, it runs daily from 10am to 6pm. Atop the summit, you'll also find a revolving restaurant (𝓒 **02944/441035**). About a 20-minute walk from the restaurant **Club Andino** runs a cafe (see "Visitor Information," earlier in this chapter).

A DRIVING TOUR: CERRO TRONADOR, LOS ALERCES WATERFALL & VENTISQUERO NEGRO

This wonderful, full-day excursion takes visitors through lush forest and past hidden lakes such as the picturesque Lago Mascardi, waterfalls, and beaches to a trail head that leads to the face of Ventisquero Negro (Black Glacier). You'll need a vehicle to drive the 215km (133-mile) round-trip road, including a detour to Cascada Los Alerces (Los Alerces Waterfall); it's 170km (105 miles) without the detour. Plan to stop frequently at the various lookout points along the road. Most tour agencies offer this excursion for about $12 to $14 per person.

Leaving Bariloche on Onelli Street headed south, continue along Route 258 toward El Bolsón, passing Lake Gutierrez and several tea houses and smokeries that sell regional specialties. After about 35km (22 miles), you'll reach Villa Mascardi. From here it is possible to take a full-day sailing excursion aboard the *Victoria II* that takes riders across Lake Mascardi to the Hotel Tronador for lunch, followed by a bus ride up the valley to Pampa Linda and Los Ventisqueros for a trail walk. Visitors return the same way. This excursion can be booked at any travel agency and usually includes transportation from Bariloche, leaving at 9am and returning at 8pm (Nov–Mar only), or you can leave directly from the dock if you have your own vehicle. The cost, including transportation from Bariloche, is $15 per person.

If you're not taking the sailing excursion, continue past Villa Mascardi and take the road that branches off to the right. At the Río Manso bridge, a road heads left to the Los Alerces Waterfall. A 300m (984-ft.) walk takes you to a vista point looking out at the waterfall. After doubling back, you reach the bridge again, where you head left, continuing along the shore of Lake Mascardi until reaching the Hotel Tronador. The charming log cabin hotel, built in 1929 by a Belgian immigrant family, is backed by high peaks and makes a good spot for lunch. The road continues up the valley of the Río Manso Superior, winding through alpine scenery until arriving at Pampa Linda and eventually ending at a stunning cirque (a steep valley containing a lake) draped with vegetation and waterfalls. From here a trail leads to Black Glacier, named for the debris that colors the ice at its terminus. Return to Bariloche the same way you came.

BOAT EXCURSIONS

Several boat excursions are available from Puerto San Carlos or Puerto Pañelo at Llao Llao. Cost fluctuates between $9 and $16 per person; to obtain exact prices for any of the following trips and make a reservation, stop by any travel agency, or call © **02944/426109** for more information.

An enjoyable full-day excursion takes you to **Isla Victoria** and the **Bosque Arrayanes** (see also "Villa La Angostura," later in this chapter) by boat from Puerto San Carlos or Puerto Pañuelo. The excursion begins with a 30-minute sail to Isla Victoria, where passengers can disembark for a walk through a conifer forest or ascend to a lookout point atop Cerro Bella Vista via chair lift. The second stop is Península Quetrihué and the Bosque Arrayanes, famous for its concentration of the unusual terra cotta–colored *arrayán* tree. These handsome trees (which are really bushes) have an odd, slick trunk that is cool to the touch. From Puerto Pañuelo to Isla Victoria, trips leave at 10am and return at 5:30pm; from Puerto San Carlos, trips leave at 9am and return at 6:30pm.

Boat trips are also offered to **Puerto Blest.** These excursions sail through classic fjords and exuberant vegetation known as the Valdivian Forest, until reaching Puerto Blest. From this point, there is an optional bus ride to Laguna Frías followed by a boat ride to Puerto Frías, then back to Puerto Blest. The return trip to Puerto Pañuelo includes a stop at Los Cántaros Waterfall. Visitors can dine at the restaurant at Puerto Blest or can bring a picnic lunch. These trips are very crowded in the summer. From Puerto Pañuelo, trips to Puerto Blest leave at 10am and return at 5pm; trips from Puerto San Carlos leave at 9am and return at 6pm.

The new sailing trip to the well-organized, auto-guided trail at **Isla Huemul** gives visitors a chance to walk through native forest and visit a now-abandoned nuclear fusion study center. Six sailings depart daily from Puerto Pañuelo; the round-trip journey takes 3 hours.

OUTDOOR ACTIVITIES

BIKING   Mountain bike rental and information about bike trails and guided trips in Nahuel Huapi are available from **Bike Way,** V.A. O'Connor 867 (© **02944/424202**); **Bariloche Mountain Bike,** Gallardo 375 (© **02944/ 462397**); and **Dirty Bikes,** V.A. O'Connor 681 (© **02944/425616**).

FISHING   This region provides anglers with excellent fly-fishing on the Manso, Traful, and Machico rivers, and trolling on Lake Nahuel Huapi for introduced species such as brown trout, rainbow trout, and landlocked salmon. You can pick up information and fishing licenses at the **Club Caza y Pesca** on the coast at Onelli and Avenida 12 de Octubre (© **02944/421515**), open Monday through Friday from 9am to 1pm, or the office of the Parque Nacional Nahuel Huapi in the Civic Center. The **Patagonia Fly-Shop** and its owner-guide Ricardo Ameijeiras offer great fly-fishing expeditions, multiple-day programs in lodges, and day tours with bilingual guides. They can be found at Quichahuala 200 (© **02944/441944;** flyshop@bariloche.com.ar). Tour agencies such as **Cumbres Patagonia,** Villegas 222 (© **02944/423283**), offer half-day and full-day fly-casting and trolling fishing excursions.

HIKING The Nahuel Huapi National Park has a well-developed trail system that offers day hikes, multiple-day hikes, and loops that connect several back-country *refugios,* some of which offer rustic lodging. The national park office in the Civic Center provides detailed maps and guides to difficulty levels of trails. Another great source for information is the **Club Andino,** Av. 20 de Febrero 30 (© **02944/422266;** www.clubandino.com.ar), which also has trails, guided trekking, ice walks, and climbing trips on Cerro Tronador.

HORSEBACK RIDING Horseback rides in various areas of the park are offered by **Tom Wesley Viajes de Aventura,** Mitre 385 (© **02944/435040**), which also has a kid-friendly adventure camp. Rides cost an average of $10 for 2 hours and $15 for 3 hours. **Cumbres Patagonia,** Villegas 222 (© **02944/423283**), has trips to Fortín Chacabuco for $18 per half-day and $30 per full day, including lunch.

RAFTING Various companies offer river rafting on the Río Manso in both Class III and Class IV sections, either half-day or full-day trips. The average cost for a half-day is $23 to $28, and full day, $35 to $42. Easier floats down the Class I Río Limay are also available, for about $15 for a half-day. Excursions include all equipment, transportation, and a snack or lunch (full-day trips). Try **Cumbres Patagonia,** Villegas 222 (© **02944/423283**); **Transitando lo Natural,** Mandisoví 72 (© **02944/423918**); or **Rafting Adventure,** Mitre 161 (© **02944/432928**).

SKIING & SNOWBOARDING Bariloche's main winter draw is the ski resorts at Cerro Catedral. The resort is divided in two, with separate tickets for Robles and Catedral (it's possible to buy a more expensive ticket accepted by both resorts). Robles's bonus is that it is typically less crowded, with excellent open-bowl skiing. Catedral offers more advanced lift services, but its runs are usually packed. Lift tickets cost $15 to $20 for adults and $8 to $12 for kids, depending on high and low seasons. Bariloche suffers from a continually ascending snowline level, so the bottom portion is often patchy or bald. Both resorts are well liked by families and beginners for their abundance of intermediate terrain, but there's plenty of advanced terrain, too.

The season runs from about June 15 to September 30. Every August the resorts host the **National Snow Party,** with torchlight parades and other events (contact the Catedral ski resort for more information). The bustling Villa Catedral is at the base of the resorts, with a jumble of shops, rental stores, and several lodging options. **Alp Apart Hotel** has fully furnished apartments for two to six guests, with lodging and ticket combinations that run about $65 to $80 per person per evening (© **02944/460105;** alp_uno@bariloche.com.ar). **Cabañas Autu Pukem** has cabins for six to eight guests; consult them directly for prices (© **02944/460074;** norconde@ciudad.com.ar).

WHERE TO STAY
If you're looking for luxury, you'll find the most options along the main road outside town that runs parallel to the lake and leads to the Llao Llao Peninsula. The larger hotels in the city (such as the Panamericano) tend to cater to tour groups and aren't especially luxurious or service oriented, but their advantage is

location; staying in town puts you steps from the many excellent restaurants and shops in this tiny metropolis in the mountains. If you're planning to rent a car, then by all means stay outside the city and drive in at your convenience.

A handful of hotels in and around Bariloche are owned by unions and offer discounts to members. These hotels, such as Argentina Libre, Curu Leuvu, Puente Perón, and the larger hotels on Avenida Bustillo toward Llao Llao, including the Amancay and Panamericano (not to be confused with the Panamericano that's downtown), can take on a clubby workers' atmosphere not usually desired by most visitors. Avoid completely hotels owned by the several tour groups that bring thousands of energetic teens to Bariloche from June to December every year (these hotels are identifiable by the blue logo AUSTONIA). A few hotels are subcontracted to lodge students, such as the Hotel Bella Vista. During the high season (Dec 15–Feb 28 and Easter week), prices double. Many hotels consider the months of July and August to be midseason, with midrange prices to match, but some hotels charge high-season rates (July is especially busy).

The cheapest rates are from March 1 to June 30 and September 1 to December 15. Dates vary; inquire before booking and always ask for promotions or discounts for multiple-day stays.

WITHIN THE CITY CENTER
Expensive

Hotel Edelweiss *✿*   This hotel offers reliable service and huge double bedrooms, and is a solid choice in downtown Bariloche in this price category (but don't expect much luxury). Double superiors come with two full-size beds, bay windows, and lake views, as do the suites. The double standards are smaller, with a single full-size bed or two twins and a view of a building in the back, but they are just as comfortable and $10 cheaper. All rooms and bathrooms have recently been updated. The design is pleasant but very run-of-the-mill for a hotel that deems itself a five-star. The suites deserve mention for their gargantuan size, with separate living areas and small bars; suite bathrooms have hydromassage tubs. An aging penthouse pool with glass walls affords views of Lake Nahuel Huapi. The lounge area has polished floors, leather couches, and fresh flowers; a computer with Internet access is available for a nominal fee. The hotel offers several attractive packages and promotional rates, so be sure to ask when making your reservations.

Av. San Martín 202, San Carlos de Bariloche. © **02944/426165;** in the U.S. 800/207-6900; in the U.K. 08705/300-200; in Australia 800/221-176. Fax 02944/425655. www.edelweiss.com.ar. 100 units. $80–$160 double superior; from $170 suite. Rates include buffet breakfast. AE, DC, MC, V. Valet parking. **Amenities:** 2 restaurants; bar; indoor pool; sauna; game room; room service. *In room:* TV, minibar, safe.

Hotel Nevada   Centrally located and welcoming with an appealing mint-green-and-wood facade, the Nevada underwent a complete renovation in 1993, a date it now posts in large numbers outside in contrast to its real date of construction, 1952, when it was one of the few hotels in the city. The hotel is billed as traditional, although its rooms and lobby are slick and modern. A cream-and-maroon restaurant/lounge has a bar offset with pillars painted to appear marble, and loud music often plays in the background. The rooms are agreeable, with varnished wood paneling, but are average size for the price. Two rooms can be connected to make an apartment, but there isn't really any advantage, apart from giving parents an open door to their kids' bedroom. For $10 to $15 more, you can book a brighter double superior with a tiny seating area and large windows that overlook the street. Most guests are South American and traveling individually, so you get fewer busloads of tourists traveling on package tours here.

Rolando 250, San Carlos de Bariloche. © **02944/522778.** Fax 02944/527914. www.nevada.com.ar. 89 units. $62–$105 double standard; from $115 junior suite. Rates include continental breakfast. AE, DC, MC, V. **Amenities:** Restaurant; lounge; small exercise room; sauna; business center; room service; laundry service. *In room:* TV, minibar.

Hotel Panamericano (Overrated)

Hotel Panamericano *(Overrated)* The Hotel Panamericano has long coasted on its reputation as one of Bariloche's premier accommodations, boasting a casino, a lake view, a range of amenities, and a downtown branch of the popular El Patacón restaurant (see "Where to Dine," below). Its deluxe rating is exaggerated, however, especially when compared to rivals such as the Llao Llao Hotel & Resort (see below). The rooms are spacious and comfortable, but the design needs a face-lift and everything seems rather aging and tired. The lake views are available only above the fifth floor; in fact, the hotel rarely books rooms on the bottom floors unless they're hosting a convention, although they have plenty of tour groups that keep the hotel busy year-round. The back rooms face an ugly building but are cheaper. The junior suites are quite nice, and really a better deal than the regular suites—although just a tad smaller, they come with plant-filled balcony patios and outdoor table and chairs, as well as a fireplace and a living area setup the staff will arrange to your liking. A double comes with two full-size beds or a king-size. Inside the lobby, a faux waterfall trickles in the background, and a bar/lounge regularly has live piano music. You can laze around the steamy penthouse pool or exercise in a glass-enclosed exercise room while savoring the lake view; a personal trainer is on hand to offer special ski-oriented workouts in the winter. The hotel has another 100 or so rooms and a casino on the other side of the street, connected by an aerial walkway.

Av. San Martín 536, San Carlos de Bariloche. ©/fax **02944/425846.** www.panamericanobariloche.com. 306 units. $110 double; from $185 suite. Rates include buffet breakfast. AE, DC, MC, V. Valet parking. **Amenities:** 2 restaurants; bar; lounge; indoor pool; exercise room; sauna; room service; massage; laundry service; dry cleaning service. *In room:* TV, dataport, minibar, coffeemaker, safe.

Moderate

Hotel Tres Reyes Located directly on the Costanera, just a few minutes' walk from the civic center, this venerable hotel is often overlooked, but it's difficult to understand why. It has a tremendous amount of stark, Scandinavian style preferred by the Belgian immigrant who built the hotel in 1950, and perhaps that does not appeal to everyone. Nevertheless, the hotel has been superbly maintained, with architectural details such as wood ceilings and beechwood paneling, and the vast lounge area has dozens of chairs and a velvet couch to sink into while you gaze out over the lake. The backyard has a path that meanders through a pleasant garden. All the rooms have been renovated within the past year, with new bedding, paint, curtains, and carpet, and all are warm and come with sparkling bathrooms. Lake-view rooms are more expensive, but they might not be as desirable, as loud traffic speeds by well into the night. During the 1960s, the hotel's red-leather bar was the "in" spot for Bariloche's fashionable set, and it hasn't been altered in the slightest. The service is very friendly.

Av. 12 de Octubre 135, San Carlos de Bariloche. © **02944/426121.** Fax 02944/424230. www.hoteltresreyes. com. 75 units. $48–$92 double garden view; $54–$103 double lake view; from $102 suite. Rates include continental breakfast. AE, DC, MC, V. **Amenities:** Restaurant; bar; room service; laundry service. *In room:* TV, safe.

Inexpensive

Hostería La Pastorella This cozy little hotel was one of the first in Bariloche, built in the 1930s. Its gingerbread style harks back to the German family who first ran the establishment. The Pastorella is entirely comfortable, with a dining area and a sunny lounge and bar that open up onto a lush garden. The rooms are a bit tired, but for the price, they're a good value. Some rooms have an extra seating area, although the funny futonlike chairs do nothing to beckon you to take a seat. Try to get a room that looks out over the garden. The hotel is run by a friendly Argentine couple who have recently installed a sauna ($3 extra). Note that this hotel does not accept children.

Belgrano 127, San Carlos de Bariloche. ℂ **02944/424656.** Fax 02944/525984. lapastorella@bariloche. com.ar. 12 units. $24–$38 double. Rates include continental breakfast. AE, MC, V. **Amenities:** Bar; sauna.

Hotel Aconcagua *Value*   This small, well-kept, but older hotel is one of the best values in Bariloche. The establishment runs like clockwork, a carry-over from the German immigrant who built the hotel and whose design influence can be found throughout the lobby and lounge area. The rooms are nothing to go wild over, with average beds and a late 1960s design, but a few have lake views, and doubles with a full-size bed are spacious (doubles with 2 twins are not, however). The bathrooms are aging but impeccable; the showers do not have stalls, just a shower curtain. Within the lounge is a cowhide bar with leatherette chairs surrounding a fireplace. The included "American" breakfast is quite good, and the dining area is pleasant and sunny. The receptionists are friendly and try hard to help with directions; but be patient, as they don't speak much English.

Av. San Martín 289, San Carlos de Bariloche. ℂ **02944/424718.** Fax 02944/424719. aconcagua@infovia. com.ar. 32 units. $22–$36 double. Rates include continental breakfast. AE, MC, V. **Amenities:** Lounge; room service. *In room:* TV.

OUTSIDE THE CITY CENTER, ON THE ROAD TO THE LLAO LLAO PENINSULA

As we go to press, the newest luxury hotel in Bariloche is opening its doors. **Design Suites,** Av. Bustillo Km 2.5 (ℂ **11/4814-8700** for reservations in Buenos Aires; www.designsuites.com), caters to a young, hip, and upscale crowd. Just a couple of kilometers outside of town, this very contemporary hotel has spacious suites with lovely hardwood floors, light-wood furnishings, and large-screen TVs. Many of the suites look out onto the lake. A restaurant, wine bar, health club, spa, and art gallery are on the premises. Rates begin at $125 for a double standard, $150 to $220 for a junior suite with a lake view, and from $210 for one- and two-bedroom suites. Rates include buffet breakfast.

Very Expensive

Llao Llao Hotel & Resort ★★★ *Kids*   The internationally renowned Llao Llao Hotel & Resort is one of the finest hotels in Latin America, as much for its magnificent location as its sumptuous, elegant interiors and refined service. Situated on a grassy crest of the Llao Llao Peninsula and framed by rugged peaks, this five-star hotel was modeled after the style of Canadian mountain lodges, taking cues such as cypress and pine-log walls, stone fireplaces, antler chandeliers, and barn-size salons. This is the place to spend the night if you're willing to splurge for a special evening. The hotel was first built in 1938 but burned to the ground and was rebuilt again in 1939; since its inception, it has been scrupulously maintained. A driveway winds up to the hotel, where a discreet security guard monitors traffic: The hotel tries to keep gawkers at a distance, although visitors may come for a drink, afternoon tea, or a meal. The lounge has glossy wood floors carpeted with Oriental rugs, coffee-colored wicker furniture, and soft lights, and is the site of frequent teas and special appetizer hours. The nearby Club House has a daily tea from 4 to 7pm.

From the lobby, every turn leads to another remarkable room, including a "winter garden" cafe whose expansive glass walls look out onto a large patio, the hotel's golf course, and Lake Nahuel Huapi beyond. A monumental hallway adorned with paintings from local artists leads to the rooms, all of which have been decorated in a rustic country design and come with gleaming white bathrooms—nice, but the style is not as exceptional as one would expect from a hotel of this caliber. Standard rooms are comfortable but quite small; superior suites are split into bedroom and living areas and come with a wraparound deck and fireplace; a lovely two-bedroom cabin with a splendid view of Lake Moreno is also available. The hotel has a handful of unadvertised inside standard double rooms that come without a view. Those are reserved for drop-ins who inquire at reception for the cheapest accommodations (no prior reservations accepted for these rooms). The spa offers views that are nothing less than panoramic, with treatment rooms affording breathtaking lake and mountain vistas. Included in the price of the rooms is a myriad of daily activities, from watercolor painting classes for adults to games and events for kids.

The hotel's fine-dining restaurant, Los Cesares, is the best in the Bariloche area (see "Where to Dine," below), and the business center has free Internet access available for registered guests.

Av. Bustillo, Km 25. © 02944/448530. Fax 02944/445789. Reservations (in Buenos Aires): © 11/4311-3434; fax 11/4314-4646. www.llaollao.com. 159 units. $175–$375 double; $360–$1,770 suite; $415–$695 cottage. Rates include buffet breakfast. AE, DC, MC, V. **Amenities:** 2 restaurants; bar; lounge; small indoor heated pool; on-property golf course; tennis courts; exercise room; fabulous spa; Jacuzzi; extensive watersports equipment; children's center; video arcade; tour and car-rental desk; business center; shopping arcade; salon; room service; massage; babysitting; laundry service; dry cleaning. *In room:* TV, safe.

Expensive

La Cascada Hotel ⊕ La Cascada's prize feature is a lovely garden with a frothing waterfall that gives the hotel its name. The property has an uneven style but is comfortable and pleasant, and its location 6km (3¾ miles) from town ensures a quiet connection with nature. The hotel has hosted its share of luminaries, notably Argentine ex-president Carlos Ménem and, more recently, Sarah Ferguson, the Duchess of York. The hotel seems like someone's stately home. Although the property was totally renovated in 1988, many design details hark back to the hotel's founding in 1950, such as the Scandinavian-style dining area and the classic English "Imperial" suites. Each guest room and common area seems to come from a different school of design, such as the early '80s purple disco or the country-style, wood-walled standard doubles with gingham bedspreads. The "Gris" suites are perhaps the best in the hotel; fresh, clean interiors feature two glass-enclosed nooks and an abundance of sunlight. A double with a lake view costs $20 more than rooms with a view of the surrounding vegetation. Doubles have bay windows, and a few have king-size beds, but you'll have to ask for one. Outside is a grassy slope that leads to a private beach, and a short nature trail winds around the hotel's 3-hectare (7½-acre) property. A taxi to town costs about $2.

Av. Bustillo, Km 6. © 02944/441088. Fax 02944/441076. www.lacascada.com. 24 units. $120–$155 double; from $185 suite. Rates include full breakfast. AE, DC, MC, V. **Amenities:** Restaurant; bar; heated indoor pool; exercise room; sauna; game room. *In room:* TV, safe.

Villa Huinid ⊕⊕ *Finds* The country-style, luxurious cabins and suites that make up the newer and very modern Villa Huinid, 2.5km (1½ miles) from the city center, are top-notch choices for travelers looking for independent accommodations outside town. The complex faces the lake, where it has a private beach, and is backed by a thick forest with a walking trail. Each cabin is hand-crafted of knotty cypress, with stone fireplaces, lovely decks with a full-size bar-becue, and a handsome decor of floral wallpaper, plaid bedspreads, craftsy furniture, and other accents such as dried flowers and iron lamps. The units come as four-, six-, and eight-person *cabañas* with fully stocked kitchens and cozy living areas; however, there are also five suites with minibar and cof-feemaker, but no kitchen or separate seating area. The suites might seem a bit lonely, as the villa has no lobby to relax in. All accommodations come with daily maid service. The bathrooms are sumptuous, with wooden sinks and hydro-massage baths, and the cabins come with one-and-a-half bathrooms. The serv-ice provided by the gracious owners of the Villa Huinid is one of this hotel's highlights, as are the property's well-manicured grounds, which are offset by a trickling stream that meanders through the property. Behind the rooms are sev-eral aromatic gardens, a greenhouse, and a dense forest. The Huinid has its own transfer van to get you into town or to the ski areas in winter.

Av. Bustillo, Km 2.5. ℂ/fax 02944/5235234. www.villahuinid.com.ar. 18 units. $40–$90 suite; $67–$168 2- to 4-person *cabaña*. AE, DC, MC, V. **Amenities:** Laundry service. *In room:* TV, fridge, coffeemaker, safe.

Moderate

La Caleta Bungalows *(Value* These two- to seven-person bungalows are a deal for those seeking the independence of kitchen facilities and a location close to town, without actually being in it. Run by an amicable British expatriate, the rooms are not the most luxurious on the shore, but they are entirely comfortable and have knockout views of Nahuel Huapi. Each bungalow is nestled among winding, flower-filled walkways, and the principal room has a large dining table and a basic, open kitchen. The interiors are made of white stucco and feature a combination of one full-size bed and bunk beds, depending on the size. The bedrooms that sit behind the dining area have large, one-way mirrored windows that allow guests to see out toward the view. Each unit comes with a central fire-place. La Caleta has a private beach across the road, and the owner has a wealth of tourist information and offers excursions. Downtown is a 25-minute walk or $1 taxi ride away.

Av. Bustillo, Km 5.7, San Carlos de Bariloche. ℂ/fax 02944/441837. bungalows@bariloche.com.ar. 13 units. $28–$80 *cabaña* for 2. No credit cards. **Amenities:** Tour desk. *In room:* TV, kitchen.

Inexpensive

Huemel *(Value* *(Kids* This wood-and-stone lodge sits right on the edge of a cliff, affording magnificent views of the lake from most of its expansive public areas. A 100-year-old cypress tree towers over the entire structure. Originally built in the late 1940s, the rambling building has seen several additions, including a restaurant and lounge on the lower floor, closer to the water, where you feel as if you're aboard a ship heading out to sea. Rooms are very basic, with white bed-spreads, wooden shelves, and tiny, clean bathrooms. Many of the rooms have a window looking directly out onto the water, though beware that some have only partial lake views. Ask to see the room, if possible, before accepting it. This is the best bargain in Bariloche for budget accommodations with lake views, so be sure to make your reservations early if you're arriving during the high season. On the flip side, during the low season, a single room can go for as low as $11, including both tax and breakfast, so do not hesitate to bargain.

Av. Bustillo 1500, San Carlos de Bariloche. ℂ/fax 02944/424066. Huemel@bariloche.com.ar. 78 units. $25–$38 double. Rates include continental breakfast. No credit cards. **Amenities:** Restaurant; bar; lounge; game room; laundry service. *In room:* TV.

WHERE TO DINE

The best restaurants are located on the road to the Llao Llao Peninsula. El Patacón and Los Cesares are the region's top restaurants. Unlike hotels, however, the restaurants in downtown Bariloche are an excellent value, and even if you're not staying in town, you'll probably find yourself coming here to dine. The best value in Patagonia might very well be the El Boliche de Alberto Steakhouse, where you can get a tender cut of Argentine steak, salad, and potatoes for less than $6. For value and quality, Bariloche restaurants are quite superb. Service, however, is not a highlight here. We've found the starred restaurants below to offer the best overall service, quality, and variety in the city. But remember to be patient with the waitstaff at the rest of the establishments listed below, and always allow plenty of time for lunch (2 hr.) and dinner (3 hr.).

WITHIN THE CITY CENTER
Moderate

Casita Suiza SWISS   The Casita Suiza lives up to its name with a menu of Swiss dishes, such as smoked pork, sauerkraut, and apple strudel, but it also offers a wide variety of international meat and fish dishes. The restaurant is owned by the children of Swiss immigrants; the owner's mother still bakes fresh cakes and tarts daily using old family recipes. The Casita Suiza's ambience is slightly more cozy than its competitor, the Rincón Suiza, and the service is impeccable. Fondues are an excellent value, at $6 per person. If you're interested in a diner-participation meal, choose instead the *pierrade,* a platter of various meats, sauces, and potatoes that you grill at the table, for $7 per person. Call ahead to see if they're open for lunch, as their daytime hours are erratic.

Quaglia 342. © 02944/426111. Main courses $4–$8. AE, DC, MC, V. Daily 8pm–midnight.

Caza y Pesca REGIONAL   Like the name ("Hunting and Fishing") suggests, this panoramic restaurant on the waterfront has a hunting lodge atmosphere with rough-hewn interiors made of knotty cypress tree trunks, a crackling fireplace, and deer antler chandeliers. The chef here whips up tasty regional specialties and international dishes such as trout in garlic, tomatoes, and wine; salmon ravioli; and steak with a pepper sauce, but the restaurant also makes a suitable spot for a drink and an appetizer platter. The restaurant has great views during the day and a warm, candlelit ambience in the evening, at least until around 11pm, when they drop a giant TV screen and begin playing music videos and concerts.

Av. 12 de Octubre and Onelli. © 02944/435963. Main courses $4–$6. AE, MC, V. Year-round daily 7pm–2am; Nov–Feb daily 11am–4pm.

Días de Zapata MEXICAN   Bariloche's only Mexican restaurant is surprisingly good. You'll find the usual tacos, fajitas, and nachos on the menu, but you'll also find dishes that stay true to Mexican cooking, such as chicken *mole* (a spicy sauce made with chocolate), Veracruz conger eel, and spicy enchiladas. Every evening from 7 to 9pm, the restaurant has a happy hour, with buy-one-get-one-free drinks. The warm brick walls and Mexican folk art make for a cozy atmosphere; the service is very friendly, too.

Morales 362. © 02944/423128. Reservations recommended for dinner on weekends. Main courses $3–$6. MC, V. Daily noon–3pm and 7pm–midnight.

Familia Weiss ⟨ (Kids) (Value) REGIONAL   The Weiss family is well known all over the region for their outstanding smoked meats and cheeses, which they've been selling from their shop at Mitre 360 for decades. They've also run a tiny restaurant up the street for years, and in 2000 they opened this new restaurant near the waterfront that is so architecturally unique you really should at least stop in for one of the locally brewed beers and to view the handsome interiors. The decor includes cypress trunks that form pillars rising from a mosaic floor also made of cypress. Each wall is a patchwork of wood, brick, and ceramic, except the front area, which has large picture windows looking out onto the lake. Details such as papier-mâché lamps and folk art lend character.

As for the food, a lot is on offer here, all of it very good. Start off with an appetizer of the smoked meats, seafood, and cheese the Familia Weiss is known for. There's cheese and beef fondue with five dipping sauces; large, leafy salads; stewed venison with spaetzle; grilled meats with fresh vegetables; homemade pastas; local trout served with ratatouille; and much, much more. A good wine list and a kids' menu make the Familia Weiss hard to beat.

Corner of Palacios and V.A. O'Connor. (©) **02944/435789.** Main courses $3–$6. AE, DC, MC, V. Daily 11:30am–1am.

Jauja ★★ REGIONAL   Jauja is one of the best restaurants in Bariloche, for both its extensive menu and its woodsy atmosphere. You'll find just about everything on offer here, from regional to German-influenced dishes, including grilled or stewed venison, goulash with spaetzle, stuffed crepes, homemade pastas, barbecued meats, and trout served 15 different ways. The semicasual dining area is made entirely of wood, with wooden tables and lots of glass, plants, basket lamps, and candles. A glass-and-wood wall divides smoking and nonsmoking sections. The Jauja's fresh salads and desserts are quite good, especially the poached pears and apple mousse. Food is available to go.

Quaglia 366. (©) **02944/422952.** Main courses $4–$6. AE, MC, V. Daily 11:30am–3pm and 7:30pm–midnight.

La Marmite SWISS   La Marmite is very similar to the Casita Suiza; it's not as cozy in the evening, but it has a more extensive menu. The Swiss-inspired decor includes ruby-red tablecloths and carved wooden beams stained black and stenciled with flowers. The menu offers fondue ($8–$10 for 2) and *raclette,* but the main dishes are a better bet, especially regional specialties such as hunter's hare stew or wild boar steeped in burgundy wine with mushrooms. You'll also find grilled tenderloin beef and exquisite tarts and cakes.

Mitre 329. (©) **02944/423685.** Main courses $3–$6. AE, DC, MC, V. Daily noon–3:30pm and 7:30–11:30pm.

Inexpensive
El Boliche de Alberto ★★ (Value) STEAKHOUSE   If you're in the mood for steak, this is your place. El Boliche de Alberto is our favorite *parrilla* in Bariloche, and everyone else's too, it seems. Some regulars have been coming back for 20 years, and some make the crossing from Chile to have an inexpensive, delicious meal here. The quality of meat is outstanding, and the prices are extremely reasonable. The menu is brief: several cuts of beef, chicken, and sausages, with salads and side dishes such as french fries. The dining area is unpretentious and brightly lit, with wooden tables. The charismatic owner, Alberto, has plastered an entire wall with photos of regulars and luminaries who have paid a visit, along with notes thanking him for a wonderful meal. Alberto will usually take your order. A typical *bife de chorizo* steak is so thick you'll need to split it with your dining partner; if you're alone, they can do a half-order for $2.50. The Boliche de Alberto has a very good pasta restaurant at Elflein 163 ((©) **02944/431084**).

Villegas 347. (©) **02944/431433.** Main courses $4–$5. AE, MC, V. Daily noon–3:30pm and 8pm–midnight.

El Mundo PIZZERIA   El Mundo serves up crispy pizza in more than 100 varieties, as well as empanadas, pastas, and salads. The sheer number of pies makes the menu a little overwhelming. The pasta is fresh, and they deliver. A large seating area makes El Mundo a good spot for groups.

Mitre 759. ℂ 02944/423461. Main courses $2.50–$5. AE, DC, MC, V. Daily noon–midnight.

Friends *Kids* CAFE   Friends is worth a mention more than anything because it is open 24 hours a day and is popular with families with kids. The cafe is embellished with hundreds of antique toys and trinkets, which hang from the ceiling and fill every corner. The menu serves grilled meats and fish, crepes, sandwiches, soups, and salads. There's also pan-fried trout served several different ways and a huge selection of rich, sugary desserts, too.

Corner of Mitre and Rolando. ℂ 02944/423700. Main courses $2–$4. AE, MC, V. Daily 24 hr.

OUTSIDE THE CITY CENTER/ON THE ROAD TO THE LLAO LLAO PENINSULA
Expensive

El Patacón *Finds* ARGENTINE/REGIONAL   This superb restaurant is a 7km (4¼-mile) drive from the city center. El Patacón's unique architecture and mouthwatering cuisine are so appealing that it was chosen as the dining spot for Bill Clinton and Argentina's Carlos Ménem during a presidential meeting several years back, a fact the restaurant is more than happy to advertise. The building is made of chipped stone inlaid with polished, knotty tree trunks and branches left in their natural shape, which form zany crooked beams and pillars. The tables and chairs were handcrafted from cypress driftwood also kept in its natural form.

Start your meal with a platter of five provolone cheeses served crispy warm off the grill, and follow it with venison ravioli or goulash, trout in a creamy leek sauce with puffy potatoes, wild boar in wine, or mustard chicken. A *parrilla* serves grilled meats and daily specials, and a *bodega* offers an excellent selection of wines. The restaurant recently inaugurated an adjoining bar, a fascinating medieval-style lounge with iron chandeliers and a tremendous fireplace with a tree-trunk mantel. If you're staying in the city center, you can opt to dine at the downtown branch of this restaurant, located at the Hotel Panamericano (see "Where to Stay," earlier in this chapter), where the menu is identical but the decor is not nearly as enticing as this location's.

Av. Bustillo, Km 7. ℂ 02944/442898. Reservations recommended on weekends. Main courses $7–$13. AE, DC, MC, V. Daily noon–3pm and 8pm–midnight.

Los Cesares *Moments* PATAGONIAN FINE DINING   This enchantingly romantic restaurant offers the only fine-dining experience in the Bariloche area. Located in the luxurious Llao Llao Hotel & Resort (see "Where to Stay," earlier in this chapter), the refined and slightly formal setting comes complete with fireplace, antiques, white tablecloths, and ultracomfortable chairs with armrests. The restaurant prides itself on using the highest-quality ingredients grown locally—from wild game for the main courses to the wild berries for dessert. Specialties include grilled venison with blackberry sauce, almond-crusted local trout (from the nearby lake), and a good selection of Argentine steaks. The excellent wine list features many regional wines for under $18. Service is superb, and when you finally get the bill, you'll be pleasantly surprised at how affordable it really is for such an exquisite place.

Av. Bustillo, Km 25. In the Llao Llao Hotel & Resort. ℂ 02944/448530. Reservations required. Main courses $9–$18. AE, DC, MC, V. Daily 7:30–11:30pm.

BARILOCHE AFTER DARK

Bariloche is home to a handful of discos catering to the 20- to 30-year-old crowd. These discos adhere to Buenos Aires nightlife hours, beginning around midnight or 12:30am, with the peak of the evening at about 3 or 4am. The cover charge is usually $3 to $4 per person, and women often enter for free. Try **Roket,** J.M. de Rosas 424 (© **02944/431940**), or **Cerebro,** J.M. de Rosas 405 (© **02944/424965**). The Hotel Panamericano runs Bariloche's **Casino,** Av. San Martín 570 (© **02944/425846**), open from 9am to 5am. The Casino hosts live shows every evening. Guests must be over 18 years old; entrance is free. The local cinema can be found at Moreno 39 (© **02944/422860**).

2 Villa La Angostura ⋆⋆

81km (50 miles) north of Bariloche; 44km (27 miles) east of the Chilean border

Villa La Angostura (Narrow Village) takes its name from the slender isthmus that connects the town's center with the Quetrihué Peninsula. The town was founded in 1934, when it was a collection of simple farmers with small plots of land. These farmers were eventually usurped by out-of-towners who chose this lovely location for their summer homes. Increased boating activity, the paving of the road to Bariloche, increased tourism with Chile (whose border crossing is just 20 min. from town), and the inauguration of several exclusive hotels and a handful of bungalow complexes have converted Villa La Angostura into a popular tourist destination—although the tiny enclave still sees only a fraction of visitors to the region, unlike Bariloche. This picturesque village is for visitors seeking to get away from the crowds. Most lodging options are tucked away in the forest on the shore of the Lake Nahuel Huapi, providing beautiful views and quiet surroundings. Like Bariloche, Villa La Angostura is located within the borders of Parque Nacional Nahuel Huapi.

GETTING THERE   By Plane   For airport and flight information, see "Getting There," under "San Carlos de Bariloche," earlier in this chapter. To get to Villa La Angostura from the airport, take a taxi or transfer service (about $55–$75). The drive takes about an hour.

By Bus   Algarrobal Buses (© **02944/494360**) leave for Villa La Angostura from Bariloche's Terminal de Omnibus about every 3 hours from 8am to 9pm. The trip takes about 1½ hours.

VISITOR INFORMATION   The Secretaría de Turismo is at Av. Siete Lagos 93 (© **02944/494124**), open daily from 8am to 8pm. It offers accommodations listings and prices, and information about excursions around the area. For information about Nahuel Huapi National Park or Parque Nacional Bosque Arrayanes, try the **Bosques y Parques Provinciales Oficína de Turismo** at the pier (© **02944/494157**), open Monday through Friday from 11am to 4pm, Wednesday until 2pm, Saturday and holidays from 2:30 to 5pm; closed Sunday.

WHAT TO SEE & DO
PARQUE NACIONAL BOSQUE ARRAYANES ⋆

The Parque Nacional Bosque Arrayanes is home to the only two *arrayán* forests in the world (although the *arrayán* can be found throughout this region, including in Chile), one of which can be visited at the tip of Península Quetrihué. This fascinating bush grows as high as 20m (66 ft.) and to the untrained eye looks like a tree, with slick cinnamon-colored trunks that are cool to the touch. They are especially beautiful in the spring when in bloom.

The peninsula itself offers a pleasant 24km (15-mile) round-trip moderate hiking and biking trail to the *arrayán* forest. Most visitors either walk (2–3 hr.) or bike (1–2 hr.) half of the trail and boat to or back from the park; you can also take the boat both ways (trip time 2½ hr.). **Paisano** (© 02944/494459) has an 18-passenger launch with a cafeteria and daily trips leaving at 3pm. They offer four to five trips during the summer, depending on demand; cost for adults is $10 round-trip, kids 6 to 12 $6 round-trip; $5 for all ages one-way. **Bettanso Excursiones** has a 50-person boat with daily departures at 2:30pm, and six to seven trips during the summer for the same price as Paisano (© 02944/495024). Bettanso also offers excursions to Isla Victoria and Puerto Blest, a trip that is described in "Boat Excursions," earlier in this chapter.

OTHER OUTDOOR ACTIVITIES

BIKING   Ian Bikes, Topa Topa 102 (© 02944/495047; ianbikes@hot mail.com), has a large selection of rental bikes for $1 per hour, $4 up to 6 hours, and $5 for a full day. They also supply trail information.

FISHING   Anglers typically head to the renowned Río Correntoso for rainbow and brown trout, reached just before crossing the bridge just outside town on Route Nacional 231, from the Siete Lagos road. **Banana Fly Shop,** at Arrayanes 282 (© 02944/494634), sells flies and gear, and they have information and can recommend guides. You may pick up a **fishing license** here or at the Bosques y Parques Provinciales office at the port (© 02944/494157); open Monday through Friday from 11am to 4pm, Wednesday until 2pm, Saturday and holidays from 2:30 to 5pm; closed Sunday.

SKIING   Villa La Angostura is home to a little gem of a ski resort, **Cerro Bayo,** located about 9km (5½ miles) from downtown. It's a smaller resort than the one at Cerro Catedral, but the crowds are thinner and the view is wonderful—for those reasons, we almost prefer it. There are 250 skiable acres, with 40% of the terrain intermediate and about 35% advanced. To get to it, you'll need to take a long lift from the base up to the summit; during the summer, this same chair lift provides access to an excellent short hike and lookout point. Cerro Bayo has ski and snowboard rental and instruction; the season runs from mid-June to mid-September, although it can get fairly patchy toward the end of the season.

To get to Cerro Bayo, ask your hotel to arrange transportation or hire a taxi for the short ride. Tickets are $8 to $20 for adults, $5 to $12 for kids, depending on the season. Kids under 6 and adults over 65 ski free. Half-day tickets, 3-day tickets, and weekly passes are also available. For more information, call © 02944/494189 or visit www.puertomanzano.com.

WHERE TO STAY

Hostal Las Nieves 🌟🌟 *Value*   The very friendly and energetic Marita Miles owns and runs this lovely lodge located 5 minutes from the center of town behind exquisitely manicured gardens (Marita is an avid gardener and has won many awards for her landscaping). The rooms are rustic, simple, and comfortable, with white-washed walls, red checkered bedspreads, and handmade wooden side tables. The gleaming bathrooms are small but adequate. Apartments are on the upper level and come with kitchenettes, slanted roofs, and wood furniture, including a pair of charming cypress chairs in each unit. There's an outdoor pool in the lovely back garden, and overlooking the front garden is a lounge with a roaring fireplace where you can order drinks from the bar. The ample breakfast buffet is served from 8am onward (until the last guest has been served), and the restaurant serves both lunch and dinner in high season. The tiny "spa" offers shiatsu and other massage options, as well as facials.

Av. Siete Lagos 980. Ⓒ/fax **02944/494573**. www.lasnieves.com. 12 units. $25–$56 double; from $34–$62 apt. Rates include buffet breakfast. MC, V. **Amenities:** Restaurant; bar; lounge; heated outdoor pool; miniscule exercise room; Jacuzzi; sauna; massage. In room: TV, fridge (in apts only).

La Posada ⒡ ⒦ⁱᵈˢ Ⓕⁱⁿᵈˢ This attractive country inn packs a punch with a magnificent view of the rippling waters of Lago Nahuel Huapi from its west-facing rooms. La Posada's cozy country decor features plaid and oak-wood furnishings. The junior suites don't seem any larger than the doubles. Doubles that face the lake come with bay windows and are substantially better than those that don't, but this might not matter if you plan to spend the entire day outdoors. The beds are very comfortable, and the decor handsome, with striped furnishings and wooden ceilings. Outside, a terraced walkway leading through the award-winning garden to the dock has tables and lounge chairs set among fragrant flowers. Another walkway leads to the hotel's outdoor pool overlooking the lake. The hotel has its own private dock and during the summer sets out kayaks and small boats for guests; in the evening, the dock is lit up with twinkling lights. The hotel is near the Río Correntoso, which offers excellent fishing. The new spa offers a variety of massages and facials. Note that La Posada is usually closed the entire month of June.

Route Nacional 231. Ⓒ **02944/494368**. Fax 02944/494450. www.hosterialaposada.com. 20 units. $66–$99 double with view; $46–$85 double without view; $68–$115 suite. Rates include continental breakfast. AE, MC, V. Closed June. **Amenities:** Restaurant; bar; lounge; small heated outdoor pool; spa; Jacuzzi; room service; laundry. In room: TV, safe.

Las Balsas ⒡ ⒪ᵛᵉʳʳᵃᵗᵉᵈ Part of the Relais & Châteaux group, this hideaway sits directly on the shore of Lago Nahuel Huapi, with its own private dock, spa, and superb gourmet restaurant (see below). While the location is ideal, the rooms are far too small to warrant more than a speedy overnight stay—there's hardly room to open a suitcase or move around without bumping into the wall or the bed. That said, all the rooms do come with views of the lake and the evening sunset, and each is thematically different, from romantic to folksy. A nice touch are the peek-a-boo windows in the extra-small bathrooms, leading to views of the room and the lake. A cozy attic loft (read: really tiny) is popular with honeymooning couples. If you really want to spend the night here, you must splurge for a suite. Ask for the upstairs unit, which comes with polished wood floors, larger-than-king-size beds, rectangular desks with fax and stereo, bathrooms nearly as large as the standard doubles, and wraparound floor-to-ceiling windows that allow the sun to cascade in.

Downstairs, the lounge area abounds with couches and chairs to sink into for reading, gazing at the roaring fire, or enjoying conversation among guests. Next door, a minimalist river rock–and–wood "spa" has an exquisite indoor/outdoor heated pool separated by a wall of windows, and a massage room built like a temple of relaxation. This is one of the few Relais & Châteaux hotels to welcome children, and although kids are required to dine upstairs, they usually love it, as the room doubles as a play/TV area. A computer with free Internet access is available for guests. The hotel offers inflatable rafts, paddle boats, and kayaks to guests, as well as a fleet of mountain bikes. If you're arriving between mid-August and mid-November, always ask for any promotional rates on offer. A slew of promotional "spa packages" are also on offer during the low season that include all your meals and spa treatments.

Bahía Las Balsas. ℂ/fax **02944/494308.** www.lasbalsas.com.ar. 15 units. $300 double; $400 suite. Rates include continental breakfast. AE, MC, V. **Amenities:** Exquisite restaurant; bar; lounge; indoor/outdoor heated pool; spa; sauna; watersports equipment; room service; massage; babysitting; laundry service.

WHERE TO DINE

Many *parrillas* and cafes line the town's sole main street. The best, however, are on side streets or are a few minutes' drive from town.

La Macarena ⊛ CONTEMPORARY ARGENTINE   Don't be fooled by the semicasual atmosphere at La Macarena—the food is divine. Chef Pablo Tejeda whips up a creative take on regional cooking, with mouthwatering cuisine such as polenta with a ragout of wild mushrooms, venison goulash, and rack of lamb steeped in merlot and sautéed vegetables. His recipe for wild hare in a sauvignon blanc sauce was chosen as northern Patagonia's representative dish in the Certamen Nacional Cucarón cooking competition in 2000. There's also fresh pasta with a choice of 10 different sauces, as well as several Chinese and Mexican dishes.

Cerro Bayo 65. ℂ **02944/495120.** Main courses $3.50–$6. MC, V. Tues–Sun noon–3pm and 8–11:30pm.

Las Balsas ⊛⊛ *Moments* PATAGONIAN/INTERNATIONAL   A 10-minute drive from town, this enchanting restaurant is on the ground floor of the Las Balsas inn (see "Where to Stay," above) and boasts large picture windows overlooking the lake. With only a few tables and both the quality of the food and the service top-notch, this is a fine place to sample the authentic local flavors. Using only local ingredients, Chef Pablo Campoy seamlessly blends together Patagonian and international cuisines to create dishes such as the deer carpaccio with whipped cream cheese, and local greens served with a delicate fresh raspberry dressing. For a main course, trout from the lake is always available, along with usually a wild game dish such as venison, wild boar, or *guanaco* (a Patagonian animal similar to the llama), grilled and served with a side such as pureed garbanzo and quinoa. Desserts are exquisite—try the stewed cherries and strawberries with homemade vanilla ice cream and a chocolate brownie. The wine list is extensive and offers regional wines for under $20. Las Balsas is not easy to find; be sure to ask for detailed directions when making reservations.

Bahía Las Balsas. ℂ/fax **02944/494308.** Reservations required. Main courses $9–$16. AE, MC, V. Daily 8–10:30pm.

Parrilla Cancahue ⊛ *Value* STEAKHOUSE   Two kilometers out of town, you'll find this gem of a place, opened in the fall of 2002. It's a very basic and very good Argentine steakhouse that is steadily gaining a local following. In the large, unassuming dining room with large windows and tables with checkered tablecloths, the menu is short and simple: several different kinds of salads and several different kinds of steak grilled to order. The *bife de chorizo* is excellent here and, at $2.50 per order, is an incredible bargain. There's also grilled chicken, if you prefer, and homemade french fries. If you order a house red wine to accompany your meal and a mixed salad, you'll walk away paying less than $7 per person, plus tip.

Av. Siete Lagos 727. ℂ **02944/494922.** Main courses $3–$5. No credit cards. Daily 12:30–4pm and 8:30pm–midnight. Closed Wed in low season.

Rincón Suiza SWISS/REGIONAL   This little restaurant comes with all the usual trappings of a Swiss-style restaurant, from Alpine interiors to a menu offering everything from fondue to pork chops with sauerkraut. The owner is of Swiss descent and strives to "rescue the traditional flavors of the Swiss and regional Argentine kitchens." Also on the menu are venison marinated in beer and served with spaetzle, lamb brochettes, and a trout dish served with caper sauce, Roquefort cheese, and almonds. Some of the richest, most flavorful items on the menu are the desserts, including the *Torta Rincón Suiza* made of chocolate, peaches, and cream, as well as the apple strudel.

Av. Arrayanes 44. ©/fax **02944/494248.** Main courses $4–$7. AE, MC, V. Daily noon–3pm and 8–11:30pm. Apr–Sept closed Wed.

Waldhaus SWISS/REGIONAL   If you think the Rincón Suiza has gone overboard with the Swiss theme, try this little restaurant, whose gingerbread eaves, notched furniture, and woodsy location will make you feel like you're dining in the Black Forest. The location 6km (3¾ miles) from downtown makes the Waldhaus less convenient than the Rincón Suiza, but the food is slightly better here. In addition to nightly specials, typical menu offerings include wild mushroom soup, beef fondue, venison marinated in burgundy wine, and typical Tyrolean dishes such as spaetzle with ham.

Route Nacional 231, Km 61. © **02944/495123.** Main courses $4–$6. MC, V. Daily noon–3:30pm and 8pm–midnight.

3 San Martín de los Andes ★★

1,640km (1,017 miles) southwest of Buenos Aires; 200km (124 miles) north of San Carlos de Bariloche

San Martín de los Andes is a charming mountain town of 15,000 nestled on the tip of Lago Lácar between high peaks. The town is considered the tourism capital of the Neuquen region, a claim that's hard to negate, considering the copious arts-and-crafts shops, gear-rental shops, restaurants, and hotels that constitute much of downtown. San Martín has grown considerably in the past 10 years but, thankfully, hasn't succumbed to the whims of developers as Bariloche has, owing to city laws that limit building height and regulate architectural styles. The town is quieter than Bariloche and decidedly more picturesque, thanks to its timber-heavy architecture and Swiss Alpine influence. San Martín overflows with activities including biking, hiking, boating, and skiing. The town is also very popular for hunting and fishing—and, believe it or not, some do come just to relax. The tourism infrastructure here is excellent, with every lodging option imaginable (except the ultraluxurious) and plenty of great restaurants.

ESSENTIALS
GETTING THERE
BY PLANE   Aeropuerto Internacional Chapelco (© **02972/428388**) sits halfway between San Martín and Junín de los Andes (see later in this chapter) and, therefore, serves both destinations. **Aerolíneas Argentinas/Austral,** Capitán Drury 876 (© **02972/427003**), and **Southern Winds** (© **0810/777-7979**) fly from Buenos Aires. **LADE,** Av. San Martín 915 (© **02972/427672**), has seasonal service to Buenos Aires, Bariloche, and Neuquen. A taxi to San Martín costs about $7; transfer services are also available at the airport for $2 per person. A taxi to Junín de los Andes costs $8; transfer services are $2 per person. By Mich Rent a Car and Avis both have auto rental kiosks at the airport.

BY BUS   The **Terminal de Omnibus** is at Villegas and Juez del Valle (© **02972/427044**). Daily bus service to San Martín de los Andes from Buenos Aires (a 19-hr. trip) is offered by **El Valle** (© **02972/422800**). **Ko-Ko Chevalier** (© **02972/427422**) also offers service to and from Buenos Aires, and serves Villa La Angostura and Bariloche by the paved or by the scenic Siete Lagos route. **Centenario** (© **02972/427294**) has service to Chile and also offers daily service to Buenos Aires; Villarrica- and Pucón-bound buses leave Monday through Saturday, and those for Puerto Montt, Tuesday through Thursday. **Albus** (© **02972/428100**) has trips to Bariloche via the Siete Lagos route (about 3 hr.). Bus service can vary due to season, and it's best to evaluate a coach's condition and services before buying a ticket, especially for trips to and from Buenos Aires.

BY CAR San Martín de los Andes can be reached from San Carlos de Bariloche following one of three routes. The popular 200km (124-mile) Siete Lagos route takes Ruta 234, 231, and 237, and sometimes closes during the winter. The 160km (99-mile) Paso Córdoba route takes Ruta 234, 63, and 237; the longest, yet entirely paved 260km (161-mile) Collón Curá route follows Ruta 234, 40, and 237. If driving at night, take the paved route. To get to Neuquén (420km/260 miles), take Ruta 234, 40, and 22. From Chile, take the Tromen Pass (132km/82 miles from Pucón) to Route 62, taking you to Route 234 and through Junín de los Andes; note that a large portion of this route is on unpaved roads.

GETTING AROUND

San Martín is compact enough to explore by foot. For outlying excursions, tour companies can arrange transportation. **Avis** car rental has an office at Av. San Martín 998 (© **02972/427704;** fax 02972/428500), as well as a kiosk at the airport; **ICI Rent-A-Car** is at Villegas 590 (© **02972/427800**); **Nieves Rent-A-Car** is at Villegas 725 (© **02972/428684**); **Localiza/El Claro** is at Villegas 977 (© **02972/428876**); and **By Mich Rent a Car** is at Av. San Martín 960 (© **02972/427997**) and at the airport.

Note that two main streets have similar names and can be confusing: Perito Moreno and Mariano Moreno.

VISITOR INFORMATION

San Martín's excellent **Oficina de Turismo** offers comprehensive accommodations listings with prices and other tourism-related info, and the staff is friendly and eager to make your stay pleasurable. They can be found at Rosas and Avenida San Martín at the main plaza and are open Monday to Sunday 8am to 11pm (©/fax **02972/427347** and 02972/427695). The **Asociación Hotelero y Gastronomía** (© **02972/427166**) also offers lodging information, including photographs of each establishment. It's open Monday through Sunday from 9am to 1pm and 3 to 7pm, and during high season Monday through Sunday from 9am to 10pm, but this service is not as efficient as the Oficina de Turismo.

A new website chock-full of valuable information is www.sanmartindelos andes.com.

FAST FACTS: San Martín de los Andes

Banks & Currency Exchange **Andina International,** Capitán Drury 876, exchanges money; banks such as **Banco de la Nación,** Av. San Martín 687; **Banco de la Provincia Neuquén,** Belgrano and Obeid; and **Banco Río Negro,** Perito Moreno and Elordi, have automatic tellers and money exchange. All banks are open Monday through Friday from 10am to 3pm.

Emergency Dial © **107.**

Hospital **Hospital Regional Ramón Carrillo** is at Avenida San Martín and Coronel Rodhe (© **02972/427211**).

Laundry The most convenient laundromats are **Marva,** Capitán Drury and Villegas ((*C* **02972/428791**); **Laverap Plus,** Villegas 972 ((*C* **02972/427500**); and **Lácar,** Elordi 839 ((*C* **02972/427317**).

Police For emergencies, dial (*C* **101.** The federal police station is at Av. San Martín 915 ((*C* **02972/428249**); the provincial police station is at Belgrano 635 ((*C* **02972/427300**).

Post Office **Correo Argentino** is at the corner of General Roca and Coronel Pérez ((*C* **02972/427201**).

Telephone & Internet The fastest computers are at **Cooperativa Telefónica,** Capitán Drury 761, open from 9am to 11pm, where you can also make phone calls. Half an hour of Internet use costs less than $1.

WHAT TO SEE & DO

San Martín de los Andes is heavily geared toward tourism, and, accordingly, its streets are lined with shops selling arts and crafts, wonderful regional specialties such as smoked meats and cheeses, outdoor gear, books, and more. Visitors will find most of these shops on **Avenida San Martín** and **General Villegas.** For regional specialties and/or chocolates, try **Ahumadero El Ciervo,** General Villegas 724 ((*C* **02972/427450**); **El Turista,** Belgrano 845 ((*C* **02972/428524**); or **Su Chocolate Casero,** Villegas 453 ((*C* **02972/427924**). For arts and crafts, try **Artesanís Neuquinas,** J.M. de Rosas 790 ((*C* **02972/428396**).

San Martín is a mountain town geared toward outdoor activities. If you're not up to a lot of physical activity, take a stroll down to the lake and kick back on the beach. Alternatively, rent a bike and take a slow pedal around town. Pack a picnic lunch and head to Hua Hum (described below).

TOUR OPERATORS & TRAVEL AGENCIES

Both **Tiempo,** Av. San Martín 950 ((*C*/fax **02972/427113;** tiempopatagonico@ usa.net), and **Pucará,** Av. San Martín 943 ((*C* **02972/427218;** pucara@ smandes.com.ar), offer similar tours and prices, and also operate as travel agencies for booking plane tickets. Excursions to the village Quila Quina, via a sinuous road that offers dramatic views of Lago Lácar, cost $7; a longer excursion including Chapelco and Arrayán is $10. Excursions to the hot springs Termas de Lahuenco are $12; scenic drives through the Siete Lagos route are $12 (to Villa La Angostura) and $15 (to Bariloche). A gorgeous circuit trip to Volcán Lanín and Lago Huechulafquén goes for $15. Tours do not include lunch, which must be brought along or arranged ahead of time.

OUTDOOR ACTIVITIES

BIKING San Martín is well suited for biking, and shops offer directions and maps. Bike rentals are available at **Enduro Kawa & Bikes,** Belgrano 845 ((*C* **02972/427093**); **HD Rodados,** Av. San Martín 1061 ((*C* **02972/427345**); and **Mountain Snow Shop,** Av. San Martín 861 ((*C* **02972/427728**).

BOATING **Naviera Lácar & Nonthué** ((*C* **02972/428427**), at the Costanera and main pier, offers year-round boat excursions on Lago Lácar. A full-day excursion to Hua Hum includes a short navigation through Lago Nonthué. The cost is $14 adults, $7 kids 6 to 12 and seniors, plus park entrance fees ($5); there's a restaurant in Hua Hum, or you can bring a picnic lunch. Naviera also operates a ferry service to the beautiful beaches of Quila Quina (which are packed in the summer) for $5 adults, $3 kids 6 to 12 and seniors. Naviera also rents kayaks for $2 per hour.

To raft the Hua Hum River, get in contact with Tiempo Tours or Pucará (see "Tour Operators & Travel Agencies," above).

FISHING INFORMATION & LICENSES **Jorge Cardillo Pesca,** General Roca 636 (© **02972/428372;** cardillo@smandes.com.ar), is a well-stocked fly-fishing shop that organizes day and overnight fishing expeditions to the Meliquina, Chimehuín, and Malleo rivers, among other areas. The other local fishing expert is **Alberto Cordero** (© **02972/421453;** acordero@smandes. neuquen.com.ar), who will arrange fishing expeditions around the area. He speaks fluent English; for more information, visit his website at www.ffandes. com. You can pick up a fishing guide at the **Oficina Guardafauna,** General Roca 849 (© **02972/427091**).

MOUNTAINEERING Víctor Gutiérrez and his son Jano Gutiérrez are the top climbing and mountaineering guides in the region (Víctor has more than 40 years' experience), and offer climbing and orientation courses, ascents of Volcán Lanín and Volcán Domuyo, and treks, climbs and overnight trips in Lanín and Nahuel Huapi national parks. Both have cellphones; Víctor can be reached at © **02944/15-61-0440;** victorg11@latinmail.com. Jano can be reached at © **02944/15-63-3260;** janoclif@latinmail.com. Both speak passable English.

SKIING The principal winter draw for San Martín de los Andes is **Cerro Chapelco,** one of the premier ski resorts in South America. Just 20km (12 miles) outside town, Cerro Chapelco is known for its plentiful, varying terrain and great amenities. Although popular, the resort isn't as swamped with skiers as Bariloche is. The resort sports one gondola (which takes skiers and visitors to the main lodge), five chair lifts, and five T-bars. The terrain is 40% beginner, 30% intermediate, and 30% advanced/expert. Chapelco offers excellent bilingual ski instruction, ski and snowboard rental, and special activities such as dog-sledding. The resort has open-bowl skiing and tree skiing, and numerous restaurants. To get here without renting a car, ask your hotel to arrange transportation or hire a *remise* (private taxi).

To drive to the resort from town, follow Route 234 south along Lago Lácar; it's paved except for the last 5km (3 miles). Lift tickets are quite reasonable and vary from low to high season. A 3-day ticket runs $24 to $60 for adults, and $18 to $35 for kids. During the summer, the resort is open for hiking and sightseeing, with lift access. For more information, call © **02972/427460** or visit www. sanmartindelosandes.com. The road is usually passable, but you may need chains during heavy snowfall; check before heading up to the resort.

WHERE TO STAY

One thing that is lacking in San Martín is a luxury hotel. Although visitors will find plenty of excellent *hosterías* and *cabañas,* if it's luxury you're looking for, you'd be better off spending the bulk of your time in the Bariloche area. This is a very laid-back, rugged, outdoorsy town, and its hotels reflect that.

MODERATE

La Cheminée ⚜ Warm, attentive service and snug accommodations make La Cheminée a top choice, which is why so many foreign travel groups book a few nights here. The Alpine-Swiss design popular in San Martín is in full swing here, with carved and stenciled woodwork and other touches that have been meticulously well maintained. Spacious rooms are carpeted and feature wood ceilings and a pastel, country design with thick cotton floral bedspreads and striped wall-paper. The room they call a double *hogar* includes a fireplace for $8 more. The best room is the top-floor unit with wood-beamed ceilings. The bathrooms are rather small in all units. The fern-filled lobby's wooden floors are softened by fluffy rugs, and the walls are adorned with oil paintings by local artists; a small gallery has paintings for sale. The hotel is known for its delicious breakfast, adding trout pâté, caviar, and fresh bread to the usual offerings; a restaurant also serves lunch and dinner. It's conveniently located but a block away from the hubbub. Ask for multiple-day discounts. Although this hotel has stopped accepting credit cards, this may change if the financial situation improves in Argentina; inquire when making reservations.

General Roca and Mariano Moreno, San Martín de los Andes. © **02972/427617**. Fax 02972/427762. www.hosterialacheminee.com.ar. 19 units. $45–$75 double. Rates include full breakfast. No credit cards. **Amenities:** Restaurant; bar; lounge; outdoor pool; Jacuzzi; sauna; room service; laundry service. *In room:* TV, minibar.

Le Chatelet Le Chatelet's spacious bedrooms, charming Swiss design, and full-service amenities are its strength. The classically designed lobby/lounge area is not as cozy as those in other hotels, but the bedrooms are wonderful, with fire-places and queen-size beds. All rooms have wooden ceilings, triangular windows, lace curtains, and a tremendous amount of walking room; suites are twice the size of doubles. The hotel offers free use of VCRs and stocks a video and book library in the lobby. Suites come with CD players. The hotel is 2 blocks from downtown on a quiet residential street, and also sports an enclosed backyard with an outdoor pool. Le Chatelet often offers ski and summer package deals; inquire when making a reservation. They'll also help you organize excursions. A generous breakfast is served each morning; the restaurant boasts a roaring fire in the evenings and makes a good place to unwind after a day of outdoor activity. Internet access is available for registered guests.

Villegas 650, San Martín de los Andes. © **02972/428294**. www.hotellechatelet.com.ar. 32 units. $68–$115 double; $85–$130 suite. Rates include full breakfast. No credit cards. **Amenities:** Lounge; outdoor pool; exercise room; sauna; game room; room service; laundry service. *In room:* TV.

Le Village This Alpine Swiss–style hotel is similar to La Cheminée and Le Chatelet in design, and is popular during the off season for its slightly lower prices. The ambience leans toward family style; the staff is extremely friendly, knowledgeable, and eager to help you plan activities. Rooms are average size and carpeted; a few come with a small balcony. Several lounge areas, including a reading area and library, felt-covered game table, and TV/VCR, help entertain guests. Le Village also has five *cabañas* with queen-size and twin beds and spacious living areas, although they are not particularly bright. Note that *cabañas* for six means two will sleep on a sofa bed in the living room. All guests have use of the sauna. An ample breakfast features specialties such as deer and trout and comes served in a pleasant eating area. A *quincho,* or separate barbecue/dining area for groups, allows guests to throw dinners for friends not staying at the hotel. A computer gives 1 hour of free Internet access to guests.

General Roca 816, San Martín de los Andes. ©/fax **02972/427698**. www.hotellevillage.com.ar. 23 units, 5 *cabañas*. $33–$66 double; $45–$78 *cabaña* for 4. Rates include full breakfast. AE, MC, V. **Amenities:** Restaurant; bar; sauna; game room; room service; library. *In room:* TV, minibar.

Patagonia Plaza *(Overrated* San Martín's only full-service four-star hotel feels like a bland, generic motel. Although the public areas are expansive with lots of windows overlooking the street, a feeling that everything is fading already pervades the place. Rooms are comfortable and fairly modern, with colorful bedspreads and large windows overlooking the street. Bathrooms are sparkling clean and adequate. There's a small indoor heated pool and sauna, and an ample breakfast buffet every morning. This is a good place for a hassle-free overnight stay just steps from all the shops and restaurants, but don't expect much luxury or charm.

Av. San Martín and Rivadavia. © 02972/422280. Fax 02972/422284. 78 units. $68–$120 double. Rates include buffet breakfast. AE, DC, MC, V. **Amenities:** Restaurant; bar; lounge; indoor heated pool; sauna; tour desk; limited room service; massage; laundry service. *In room:* TV.

Rincón de los Andes *(Kids)*   Rincón de los Andes is part of the timeshare operation Interval, but rents many of its apartments to travelers who are not part of the program. The sizeable resort abuts a steep, forested mountain slope, and is recommended for both the smartly decorated apartments and the wealth of activities offered—especially for families. Set up like a town-house complex and centered on a large, airy restaurant with outdoor deck, the apartments range in size to accommodate two to eight guests. All come with fully stocked kitchens and spacious bedrooms. The new units are set up for two guests. One features a large living room and kitchen; the neighboring unit has a breakfast nook and kitchenette. You can connect the two to form a larger apartment. The grassy grounds include a driving range, a paddle court, and a heated pool in a glass-enclosed building. The complex is about a 5-block walk to downtown.

Juez de Valle 611, San Martín de los Andes. © 02972/428583. www.rinconclub.com.ar. 100 units. Apts $44–$112 double. AE, MC, V. **Amenities:** Restaurant; lounge; indoor pool; sauna; game room; tour desk; room service; massage; laundry service. *In room:* TV, kitchen.

INEXPENSIVE

Hostería Anay *(Value)*   A convenient location, economical price, and simple yet comfortable accommodations make the Anay a good value in San Martín. The rooms come with a double bed or two twins, and triples and apartments are available for four and five guests. All rooms come with wooden ceilings and ruby-red bedspreads, a lamp here and there, and nothing else, but are all clean and neat. The bathrooms are older, yet they have huge showers (no bathtubs). Downstairs, the lobby has a large fireplace, a felt-covered game table, and plenty of plants. The sunny, pleasant eating area is a nice spot for breakfast. The hotel is owner-operated, with direct and professional service.

Capitán Drury 841, San Martín de los Andes. ©/fax 02972/427514. anay@smandes.com.ar. 15 units. $20–$25 double. Rates include continental breakfast. No credit cards. **Amenities:** Lounge; limited room service; babysitting; laundry service. *In room:* TV.

Hostería del Chapelco   Just about every kind of unit is available at this *hostería*, including new hotel rooms and *cabañas*, and cheaper, older duplex and A-frame units. Although it sits on the lakeshore, the rooms do not benefit from the view, but a bright lobby takes advantage of the location with giant picture windows. The hotel rooms and the six attached *cabañas* are spanking new, with stark, modern furnishings and tile floors; the *cabañas* have open living/kitchen areas. The duplex units are more economical, but they feel like family rumpus rooms, and the interiors could use new carpet and fresh paint. Las Alpinas houses the oldest units, six small but decent A-frame detached *cabañas*. The wood and whitewashed walls of the hotel are pleasant but lend little character to the place. The lobby's fireside chairs and wraparound banquette are a nice place to watch the rippling lake. Quality, size, and character of the units differ, so it's best to view all of them if you have the opportunity to do so before booking.

Almirante Brown 297, San Martín de los Andes. ℂ **02972/427610.** Fax 02972/427097. 14 units, 22 *cabañas*. $19–$24 double. AE, MC, V. **Amenities:** Bar; limited room service. *In room:* TV, microwave (in *cabañas* only).

Hostería La Casa de Eugenia ⟨ *Finds* Built in 1927, this lovely old building with bright blue trim used to house the local historical society; now it's a bed-and-breakfast. The charming living room with its large fireplace, piano, and colorful sofas leads to five bedrooms, named by color. The *verde* (green) has a skylight keeping it bright throughout the day; all the rooms come with comfortable beds with down comforters, gleaming white bathrooms, and little else. Breakfast is served in the bright dining room overlooking a small park, and the friendly managers can help you plan excursions in and around San Martín.

Colonel Díaz 1186. ℂ **02792/427206.** www.lacasadeeugenia.com.ar. 5 units. $22–$36 double. Rates include continental breakfast. No credit cards. **Amenities:** Lounge; room service. *In room:* No phone.

Hostería La Posta del Cazador ⟨ *Value* The *hostería* that bills itself as "the only lodge with a view of the lake" actually affords views to only half the guests; the other half have a view of a parking lot. Either way, proximity to the lakeshore is a bonus during the summer months, and the street on which the hotel sits is quiet and wooded. La Posta del Cazador (The Hunting Lodge) comes with the de rigueur deer antlers and the like, but it feels more like a castle, thanks to an enormous circular iron chandelier, a floor-to-ceiling stone fireplace, stained glass, and walls adorned with battle swords and crosses-of-arms. Rooms are slightly cramped, but they are exceptionally clean and comfortable, with wood furniture and flowery bedspreads; interiors feature wavy white plaster walls, dark wood, and chiffon curtains. The *hostería* is owner run and patrolled by a friendly cat. The breakfast features homemade breads and pastries.

Av. San Martín 175, San Martín de los Andes. ℂ/fax **02972/427501.** www.postadelcazador.com.ar. 19 units. $26–$44 double; from $40 suite. Rates include full breakfast. AE, DC, MC, V. **Amenities:** Bar; lounge. *In room:* TV.

La Raclette The design of this appealing hotel is a cross between something you'd find in Morocco and Switzerland—molded white stucco interiors set off by carved wooden shutters and eaves. It might also be described as a Hobbit House—anyone over 1.8m (6 ft.) tall might have to stoop, the ceilings upstairs are so low. On a quiet street, La Raclette has a cozy seating area and a bar and restaurant downstairs. The public areas and the rooms have nooks and crannies and a haphazard design, and lots of charisma, but they're slightly cramped (especially the attic apartments), and the beds are nothing more than thick foam mattresses. The hotel exudes a lot of warmth in the evening, but the service can be harried and distracted during the day.

Coronel Pérez 1170, San Martín de los Andes. ℂ/fax **02972/427664.** aspen@smandes.com.ar. 9 units. $21–$27 double. MC, V. **Amenities:** Restaurant; bar. *In room:* TV.

Residencial Italia This little hotel, run by a sweet, elderly woman, is simple and kept scrupulously clean; indeed, it is doubtful you'll find a speck of dust anywhere. It's a good value, given that the price for doubles does not fluctuate during the year. Rooms are modestly decorated in 1950s style; downstairs rooms are slightly darker—book the sunnier upstairs double or one of the two apartments. The apartments are for four and six people, with fully stocked kitchens, and both have large dining tables. There's a tiny eating area for breakfast (for guests only). The sole single room is not recommended due to its Lilliputian size. In the spring and summer, beautiful roses frame the *residencial*.

Coronel Pérez 799 (at Obeid), San Martín de los Andes. © **02972/427590.** 7 units. $26 double; $46–$68 apt. Rates include full breakfast. No credit cards. **Amenities:** Laundry. *In room:* TV.

CABAÑAS

San Martín has over three dozen *cabaña* complexes, ranging from attached units to detached A-frames. The quality varies somewhat; generally, the real difference between each is size, so always ask if a cabin for four means one bedroom and two fold-out beds in the living room. *Cabañas* are a great deal for parties of four to six, as they're usually less expensive and come with small kitchens. During the off season, couples will find reasonably priced *cabañas;* however, many places charge a full six-person price during the high season.

On the upscale end (with doubles priced at around $24 during low season and high season at $90), try the following: **Claro del Bosque** ⚲, Belgrano 1083 (© **02972/427451;** fax 02972/428434; www.clarodelbosque.com.ar), is a Swiss Alpine–style building tucked away at the end of a street on a wooded lot. The managers are very friendly and accommodating. If they're full here (which happens frequently), they also operate a brand-new complex of charming apartments nearby. **Appart Niwen** ⚲, G. Obeid 640 (© **02972/425888;** www. niwen.com.ar), has similar accommodations and rates, though a tad less charming than the *cabañas* above.

If you'd like to get out of town, try **Paihuén's** beautiful stone-and-mortar attached *cabañas* in a forested lot at Route Nacional 234, Km 48 (©/fax **02972/ 428154;** www.paihuen.com.ar). **Aldea Misonet,** Los Cipreses 1801 (©/fax **02972/421821;** aldeamisonet@smandes.com.ar), has wood-and-stone attached units that sit at the edge of town; some units look out onto a gurgling stream, as does a pleasant terrace. **Terrazas del Pinar,** Juez de Valle 1174 (©/fax **02972/ 429316;** www.7lagos.com/terrazasdelpinar), is near the lakeshore, and it has a children's play area.

Cabañas with doubles ranging from a low-season price of $18 to $45 in the high season include the following: **El Ciervo Rojo,** Almirante Brown 445 (©/fax **02972/427949;** cabanaselciervorojo@smandes.com.ar), has nice wooden cabins; cheaper units have open second-story sleeping areas. **Del Lácar,** Coronel Rohde 1144 (©/fax **02972/427679;** cabanasdellacar@smandes.com. ar), has several large, detached wooden cabins. **Las Rosas,** Almirante Brown 290 (©/fax **02972/422002;** lrosas@ciudad.com.ar), has pretty whitewashed units half a block from the shore. **Hostería del Chapelco** and **Le Village** both offer *cabañas* in addition to their regular hotel rooms (see "Where to Stay," above).

On the edge of town, **Cabañas Arique** ⚲ (© **02972/429262;** www.arique. com) are extremely charming, with lots of local wood, fireplaces, modern kitchens; there's also a small barbecue area and a heated outdoor pool. Cabins are $18 to $48 double, $24 to $58 for four people.

Note: Prices fluctuate wildly according to who makes the reservation (Spanish speakers always seem to get a lower rate). Feel free to bargain when making your reservations. Make your final offer if you find the price too high—the owners may very well take whatever you offer—especially in low season.

WHERE TO DINE

San Martín has several excellent restaurants. For sandwiches and quick meals, try **Peuma Café,** Av. San Martín 851 (© **02972/428289**); for afternoon tea and delicious cakes and pastries, try **La Casa de Alicia,** Capitán Drury 814, #3 (© **02944/616215**).

EXPENSIVE

Avataras (k) *(Finds)* INTERNATIONAL   Exceptionally warm, friendly service and a marvelous variety of international dishes from Hungary to China to Egypt make this restaurant an excellent, if slightly expensive, choice in San Martín. The chefs, youngish transplants from Buenos Aires, whip up exquisite items, such as Indian lamb curry, wild boar with juniper-berry sauce, Malaysian shrimp sambal, and filet mignon with four-pepper sauce. The appetizer menu features Scandinavian gravlax and Caribbean citrus shrimp. What stands out, however, is Avataras's willingness to please its guests. Although they officially do not serve dinner until 8:30pm, give them 15 minutes' notice, and they'll open earlier for parties as small as two (they'll also open for lunch if you call ahead). The decor includes light beechwood, ferns, Japanese paper lanterns, and an acoustic ceiling made of beige linen. With smoking and nonsmoking sections, the restaurant even sells cigars, which diners may smoke on the premises. Avataras sometimes hosts live jazz music.

Teniente Ramayón 765. (C) **02972/427104**. Reservations recommended. Main courses $9–$17. AE, DC, MC, V. Daily 8:30pm–midnight.

MODERATE

La Pierrade (k)(k) *(Finds)* INTERNATIONAL   This is the town's most modern and sleek eatery. A giant stone fireplace and a long bar are on the ground floor, with two cozy dining areas on the floor above. Soothing and romantic lighting gives the place a very relaxing atmosphere. Fluffy red pillows are strewn around the fireplace so you can unwind with your predinner drink. Once you've been seated, the young waitstaff will take extra-good care of you. Begin with the very unusual rabbit pudding with green salad and dried tomatoes, a delicate deer carpaccio, or a tasting of Patagonian pâtés; then move on to the exquisite pumpkin cannelloni with a mushroom ragout or the grilled steak encrusted in sesame seeds and served with tomato and basil risotto. A fish or shrimp specialty is usually available, along with a choice of wild game. For dessert, the tiramisu is divine, and so is the homemade ice cream. You can round out your evening with a Cuban cigar from the restaurant's collection and a glass of Argentine port.

Mariano Moreno and Villegas. (C) **02972/421421**. Reservations recommended. Main courses $6–$9. No credit cards. Daily 8pm–1am.

La Reserva (k) *(Moments)* ARGENTINE   This lovely stone-and-wood house was transformed into one of the most romantic restaurants in Patagonia with a stone fireplace, elegant cloth-covered tables, soothing music, and superb service. La Reserva is run by the talented chef Rodrigo Toso, who is influenced by many ethnic cuisines while using mostly Patagonian ingredients. Begin with a cold glass of Argentine champagne to go with an order of tapas—a tasting of cheeses and dried meats. Then move on to grilled trout fresh from the nearby lake, tender venison with fresh berry sauce, or chicken breast stuffed with feta cheese and herbs. Excellent regional wines are available for under $10 a bottle, and the desserts, a selection of homemade fruit tarts and ice creams, are divine.

Belgrano 940. (C) **02972/428734**. Reservations recommended. Main courses $6–$10. AE, DC, MC, V. Daily noon–3pm and 8pm–midnight.

La Tasca (k) REGIONAL   La Tasca is a solid choice for its fresh, high-quality cuisine and extensive wine offerings. Regional specialties are the focus, such as venison flambéed in cognac and blueberries, saffron trout, and raviolis stuffed with wild boar. All meats are hand-picked from local ranches by the chef-owner, and the organic cheese is made at a local German family's farm. Mushroom lovers will savor the fresh, gourmet varieties served with appetizers and pasta. Appetizer platters are a specialty here. The cozy restaurant is festooned with hanging hams, bordered with racks of wine bottles, and warmed by a few pot-bellied iron stoves. It's a bit too bright for a romantic dinner, but great for families, as they have several large tables.

Mariano Moreno 866. ℂ 02972/428663. Reservations recommended. Main courses $5–$8. AE, MC, V. Daily noon–3:30pm and 7pm–1am.

INEXPENSIVE

El Tata Jockey *(Value* PARRILLA/PASTA   This semicasual restaurant is popular for its grilled meats and pastas at reasonable prices. It's possible to order a *parrilla* of assorted barbecued meats and sausages for two; the price is $6 for enough food for three diners. The homemade pastas are also a good bet, as is the trout al Jockey, served with seasonal vegetables and a smoked bacon and cream sauce. Owned and operated by a friendly, enthusiastic mountaineer, the restaurant is decorated with photos and tidbits taken from his various exploits around the area; the long, family-style tables have checkered tablecloths. El Tata Jockey also offers special menus for groups.

Villegas 657. ℂ 02972/427585. Main courses $3–$6. No credit cards. Daily noon–2:30pm and 8pm–midnight.

La Costa del Pueblo *(Kids* INTERNATIONAL   A lake view and an extensive menu with everything from pastas to *parrilla* make this restaurant a good bet. The establishment operated as a cafe for 20 years until new owners expanded to include a dozen more tables, a cozy fireside nook, and a children's eating area separate from the main dining room, complete with mini tables and chairs. La Costa offers good, homemade pasta dishes such as cannellonis stuffed with ricotta and walnuts, grilled meats, pizzas, and sandwiches. A kids' menu and vegetarian sandwiches help please any crowd. The restaurant is also a good spot for a cold beer and an appetizer platter of smoked cheeses and venison while watching the lake lap the shore. Service can be really slow.

Av. Costanera and Obeid. ℂ 02972/429289. Main courses $2–$5. No credit cards. Daily 11am–1am.

La Nonna Pizzería PIZZA   La Nonna's pizza, calzones, and empanadas are so good, they're sold packaged and ready-to-bake at the supermarket. Toppings generally run the repetitive gamut of ham and onion, ham and pineapple, ham and hearts of palm, but there are a few deviations, such as anchovy, Roquefort, and Parmesan, and, oddly enough, mozzarella with chopped egg. La Nonna also offers specialty regional pizzas with trout, wild boar, and deer, and calzones with fillings such as chicken, mozzarella, and bell pepper. La Nonna also delivers.

Capitán Drury 857. ℂ 02972/422223. Pizzas $1.50–$3 small, $2–$5 large. No credit cards. Daily noon–3:30pm and 7:30pm–midnight.

Pura Vida VEGETARIAN   San Martín's only vegetarian restaurant serves a few chicken and trout dishes, too (the curried chicken is excellent). This home-spun, tiny restaurant has about seven tables, and features meatless dishes such as vegetable chop suey, soufflés, soy and eggplant *milanesas* (breaded filets), and rich flan. The vegetarian offerings are not really extensive, but what they do offer is fresh and good. Pastas are not only homemade, but are made from scratch the moment you order, which can mean a long wait.

Villegas 745. © **02972/429302.** Main courses $3–$6. No credit cards. Daily 12:30–3:30pm and 8:30pm–midnight.

4 Junín de los Andes

41km (25 miles) north of San Martín de los Andes

The tiny town of Junín de los Andes does not hold much interest unless you're a fly-fishing fanatic. The sport has caught on so well here that now even the street signs are shaped like fish. Junín is spread out in a grid pattern, a fertile little oasis along the shore of the Río Chimehuín, surrounded by dry Pampa. You'll pass through Junín if you're crossing into Argentina from the Pucón area in Chile.

ESSENTIALS

GETTING THERE   By Plane   See "Getting There" under "San Martín de los Andes," earlier in this chapter.

By Bus   Ko-Ko Chevalier (© **02972/427422**) has service from San Martín de los Andes and Buenos Aires. Ko-Ko also has service to Lago Huechulafquén.

GETTING AROUND   Most visitors find that the only real way to get around is to rent a car, especially if you've come to fly-fish. Car-rental agencies can be found at the airport and in San Martín (see "Getting Around" under "San Martín de los Andes," earlier in this chapter).

VISITOR INFORMATION   The **Secretaría Municipal de Turismo** is located at Padre Milanesio 596 (© **02972/491160**); it's open daily from 8am to 9pm, from 8am to 11pm during the summer.

WHAT TO SEE & DO

Puerto Canoa is the central entrance to the splendid **Parque Nacional Lanín,** 30km (19 miles) from Junín. Here, you'll find a 30-minute interpretive trail and the departure spot for catamaran excursions across Lago Huechulafquén, which looks out onto the snowcapped, conical Volcán Lanín. Río Chimehuín begins at the lake's outlet and offers outstanding fishing opportunities. Several excellent hiking and backpacking trails traverse the area, as well as a few rustic backcountry huts; you can pick up information at the ranger station at Puerto Canoa. If you're in San Martín de los Andes, stop by the park's headquarters, the **Intendencia Parque Nacional Lanín,** Emilio Frey 749 (© **02972/427233**).

Visitors can book a tour or rent a car for the 132km (82-mile) drive to the hot springs **Termas de Epulafquen,** winding through volcanic landscape and past Lake Curruhue. For tours, try Huiliches Turismo, Padre Milanesio 570, Local B (© **02972/491670**), or ask at the visitor center.

FISHING INFORMATION & LICENSES   Licenses can be obtained at the **Tourism Office,** the office of the Guardafauna (© **02972/491277**), open Monday to Friday 8am to 3pm; The Fly Shop, Pedro Illera 378 (© **02972/491548**); Bambi's Fly Shop, Juan Manuel de Rosas 320 (© **02972/491167**); or Patagonia Fly Fishing, Laura Vicuña 135 (©/fax **02972/491538**).

WHERE TO STAY & DINE

Junín de los Andes has a few lodges that specialize in fly-fishing, such as the **Hostería de Chimehuín,** Suarez and Avenida 21 de Mayo, on the shore of the Chimehuín River (© **02972/491132; $12 double**). Accommodations are basic, including rooms with balconies and apartments, but the atmosphere is friendly and homey, and it has a good breakfast. An excellent fly-fishing lodge is the **San Humberto Lodge,** located on a privately owned stretch of the Malleo River (© **02972/491238**), which charges $68 for a double. The San Humberto consists of six chalets with twin beds, units that are separate from an enormous rustic lodge. The restaurant is excellent, and so are the fishing guides. **Cerro los Pinos,** Brown 420 (© **02972/427207**), is a charming family ranch with close access to the Chimehuín River. Doubles are $12 to $28; they'll arrange a fishing guide. Dining options are limited here; try the **Ruca Hueney,** Milanesio 641 (© **02972/491113**), which serves pasta dishes and, of course, trout.

10

Peninsula Valdes

In the middle of Atlantic Patagonia in the vast province of Chubut lies the remote and barren Peninsula Valdes that became a UNESCO World Heritage Site in 1999.

The bays and shores on this peninsula that jut out into the Atlantic serve as a marine-life preserve for sea elephants. Sea lions are also plentiful, as are the enormous southern whales, which come in from April to December. Visitors come here to see the whales and walk on the beaches to view the unusual sea elephants up-close. Diving trips are also common.

Other animals that run wild here include guanacos (similar to llamas), maras (large wild rabbits), and a bevy of birds and smaller animals.

The area is very well controlled—in fact, in some areas, beach access is restricted unless you are with a certified "naturalist guide." When the whales are in the bays (which is most of the year), beach activities are not allowed. This, after all, is a natural preserve, not a playground. Kayaks are allowed from late December to March only, when the whales are gone. Diving is allowed offshore throughout the year, but only on certified boats with government-sanctioned guides. Most visitors come here in small groups on day tours from nearby Puerto Madryn.

On the peninsula itself (the entire area is a national park), the tiny village of **Puerto Piramides** (100km/62 miles from Puerto Madryn) is the departure point for all the whale-watching and diving trips. Here, some visitors opt to stay overnight. But most of the tourist infrastructure is in **Puerto Madryn,** a small, laid-back, beachside city of 70,000 people. It's the most pleasant place (the town went from a tiny, sleepy hamlet of 6,000 people to a bustling small city, a center for industrial products in Eastern Patagonia) for visitors to base themselves, a jumping-off point for day trips to the peninsula and to **Punta Tombo** (2 hr. south), where the Magellan penguins come to mate every year.

The capital of Chubut province is the nearby residential town of **Rawson** (only 20,000 inhabitants), where there's not much to see. Nearby, the bigger city of **Trelew** serves as a gateway to the area with an airport capable of handling bigger jets. Trelew has a good museum and a few hotels, but is not of much interest to the visitor. The Welsh town of **Gaiman** is much more interesting and makes for an excellent afternoon excursion. Settled in 1865 to 1870, this is one of the few places outside of Wales where Welsh is still spoken. The houses here are reminiscent of the English countryside. A handful of tea houses offer real English tea, and Princess Diana visited in 1995.

1 Puerto Madryn

1,374km (852 miles) south of Buenos Aires; 62km (38 miles) north of Trelew; 1,798km (1,115 miles) north of Ushuaia

A laid-back city of 70,000, Puerto Madryn's population boom came in the mid-1970s. Until then, the city had only 6,000 inhabitants, but the "Aloar" aluminum factory completely changed the town when it opened its doors here in 1973. Now, there are tile, fish, and ceramic factories on the outskirts of town. And "Aloar" is still expanding. The coastal road, Avenida Roca, is mostly used by foreign visitors (locals tend to patronize establishments at least one block inland) and is lined with restaurants, bars, and hotels. Across the street, the wide beach is great, with frequently calm waters making swimming possible from mid-December to mid-March. The streets a few blocks inland are buzzing with locals. Here you'll find inexpensive clothing stores and cafes and bars catering more to the residents rather than to the tourists. Very few visitors take the time to walk around here, but meandering in the locals' neighborhood is worth at least an hour of your time. There's an easygoing and relaxed feeling about Puerto Madryn, and you may want to spend an extra day here just relaxing before continuing your journey.

ESSENTIALS
GETTING THERE
BY PLANE   Only **American Falcon,** Roca 536 (© **2965/453637**), has regularly scheduled jet flights from Buenos Aires to Puerto Madryn's **Aerodromo El Tehuelche** (© **2965/451909**). Three flights weekly make the 2-hour journey at a cost of $60 to $160 each way, depending on the seasons and how far in advance you make your reservations. **LADE Lineas Aereas del Estado,** Roca 119 (© **2965/451256** or 0810/810-5233), has two weekly flights from Buenos Aires aboard small commuter jets (the flights makes one or two stops along the way). The fare is $71 each way.

A taxi from the airport to the center of Puerto Madryn, 10km (6¼ miles) away, should cost no more than $3 for the 10-minute ride.

Most visitors to this region fly into Trelew Airport, **Aeropuerto de Trelew** (© **2965/433443**), 62km (38 miles) away. **Aerolíneas Argentinas** (© **0810/222-86527**) has three to four daily flights to Trelew from Buenos Aires and several weekly flights from Bariloche, El Calafate, and Ushuaia.

A taxi or *remise* from Trelew airport to Puerto Madryn costs $17 to $22, and the trip takes 40 minutes.

BY BUS   The **Terminal de Omnibus** is on Garcia and Independencia. The fastest bus from Buenos Aires takes 19 hours aboard **Andesmar** (© **2965/473764**). The least expensive one-way fare is $30, but for $5 more you can travel in a reclining *"cama"* chair. Andesmar also has daily services to Mendoza ($38 one-way) and Bariloche ($24 one-way). Other reputable bus companies to try are **QueBus** (© **2965/455805**), **Mar y Valle** (© **2965/472056**), and **Ruta Patagonia** (© **2965/454572**).

VISITOR INFORMATION
You can pick up maps and detailed park information from the **Puerto Madryn Secretaria de Turismo (Tourist Office),** located at Roca 223 (© **2965/453504;** www.turismo.madryn.gov.ar). Their office is open daily from 8am to 8pm.

GETTING AROUND
Puerto Madryn is compact enough that you can pretty much walk everywhere. However, taxis are available if you need them. A trip within the city center

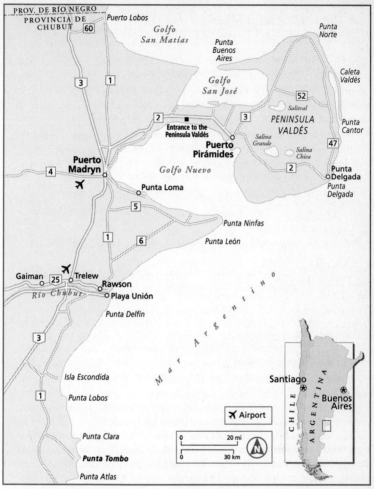

should cost no more than $2 or $3. Taxis are lined up near the Plaza San Martín, or you can call one at © 2965/472214. A reputable *remise* company is **Remise Madryn** (España 1560; © 2965/453444).

28 de Julio buses (© 2965/472056) depart every hour for the 45-minute journey to Trelew. The cost is $2 one-way. Unfortunately, bus service to Puerto Piramides in the Peninsula Valdes National Park, is spotty. Currently, there's only one bus twice a week (Tues and Sun) in either direction. The cost is $3.50 each way. Inquire at the Tourist Office for the most up-to-date information.

You can rent a car at Trelew Airport or from the center of Puerto Madryn. **Avis,** Av. Roca 493 (© 2965/475422), and **Hertz,** Av. Roca 331 (© 2965/436-005), have similar rates of about $50 per day for a small car. If you think you'll want a car, it's best to book it before leaving home to get a lower rate. If not, try bargaining at either **Localiza,** Roca 45 (© 2965/458044), or Fiorassi, Av. Roca 165 (© 2965/456300), two local companies that offer lower rates if they have cars available.

FAST FACTS: Puerto Madryn

ATMs There are quite a few ATMs around town. **Banco Galicia,** Mitre 25 (*©* **2965/452323**), and **Bansud,** corner of R. Saenz Pena and Marcos A. Zar (*©* **2965/451489**), are the most conveniently located.

Currency Exchange The Casa de Cambio at Roca 497 (*©* **2965/455858**) is open until at least 10pm every night.

Emergency Dial *©* **101** or 451449 for police; *©* **100** for fire.

Internet You'll find many Internet cafes around town. The **telecommunications center,** at Roca 742 (*©* **2965/452021**), has the fastest connections, at under $1 per hour. They are open Monday to Saturday from 8am to midnight, and Sunday from 9am to midnight.

Hospital The **Hospital Subzonal** is at R. Gomez 383 (*©* **2965/451999**).

Laundry The laundromat at 2040 Roca (*©* **2965/456-969**) is open Monday to Saturday from 10am to 9pm.

Pharmacy **FarMadryn,** corner of Roca and Belgrano (*©* **2965/474555**), is open 24 hours.

Post Office The main post office for Correo Argentino (the official name of the Argentine postal service) is located at Belgrano and Maiz (no phone).

WHAT TO SEE & DO

There's not much to see in Puerto Madryn itself, apart from a couple of museums. Most visitors are here because of the town's proximity to the Peninsula Valdes. The Oceanographic Museum is closed for remodeling until further notice.

Ecocentro ★★ The newest museum in the region is more like an interactive learning center. This is where you can educate yourself on the marine ecosystems of Atlantic Patagonia. I recommend coming to Ecocentro on your first day in Puerto Madryn, before heading out to the Peninsula Valdes. Not only is the view of the ocean exquisite from this lovely modern building, but the nautical and topographical maps really give you a deep insight into this region. There's even a tank that re-creates a tidal pool where you can see species that inhabit the coastal areas. A soundtrack plays the different sounds that whales make. There's also a good movie about the Peninsula Valdes, details about the Magellan penguins in Punta Tombo, and a bunch of other interesting facts about the elephant seals and sea lions in this area.

You'll need about 2 hours to visit Ecocentro, and there's a very pleasant cafe where snacks are served.

Julio Verne 3784. *©* 2965/457470. www.ecocentro.org.ar. Admission $5. Daily 10am–7pm.

VISITING THE PENINSULA VALDES NATIONAL PARK ★★★

Most visitors to the national park come for the day on guided excursions, aboard small nine-passenger vans. If you choose to drive on your own, remember that the only gas station is in Puerto Piramides and that the peninsula is very isolated and barren. Sometimes you can go for hours and not see another soul. All the roads on the peninsula are gravel, and driving is hazardous.

Just past the entrance to the national park (which is about an hour's drive northeast of Puerto Madryn), there's a small museum, **Museo Regional Puerto San Jose,** open from 8am to 8pm daily. Admission is free. It's a tiny museum showing the history of the Peninsula Valdes, with some good maps and bones and skulls of Tehuelches aborigines. There's also a huge skeleton of a whale and an interesting collection of stuffed animals—a guanaco and a Patagonian fox.

Another hour's drive heading east on Ruta 2 from the park entrance, and you'll reach the tiny village of Puerto Piramides (pop. 202), which is only 2 blocks wide. This is the main launching spot for the whale-watching boats that depart from here from April to late December. Whale-watching trips cost $17 per person and last about 1½ hours.

During the other months, which happen to be the warmest months here, the town becomes more of a beach town, with snorkelers, kayakers, and swimmers enjoying the wide, sandy beach.

The southern whales come to these bays just off the peninsula to mate from April to December. They each weigh 35 to 40 tons and are about 17m (56 ft.) long. About 800 whales show up every year, after spending 3 months feeding in Antarctica.

From Puerto Piramides, if you continue east on RP 2, you'll reach **Punta Delgada,** a stretch of beach favored by elephant seals from mid-June to late December.

Heading north on RP 47 will bring you to **Caleta Valdes,** which has a cafeteria on the bluff overlooking the ocean. This is where most visitors on excursions have their lunch. The stairs leading down to the beach take you to another stretch of sand that is full of (usually sleeping) elephant seals.

At the northeastern tip of the peninsula is Punta Norte, where from January to June hundreds of sea lions congregate. Orcas can also sometimes be seen off this point, attracted by the sea lions—their favorite snack.

Since the peninsula is barren and dry, you'll be able to spot guanacos (animals reminiscent of small llamas that are only found in Patagonia). However, because they are so shy, they usually run in the opposite direction when they see a car coming. There's not much else to see as you drive around the peninsula. One day is sufficient for visiting the park, though you may want to opt to spend the night in Puerto Piramides (see later in this chapter) if you are interested in taking diving trips.

PUNTA TOMBO NATIONAL RESERVE

Most visitors spend a day on the Peninsula Valdes and then a day at Punta Tombo National Reserve, the second-most-visited attraction in Atlantic Patagonia. Punta Tombo is 248km (154 miles) south of Puerto Madryn and is the largest sanctuary for the Magellan penguins. Every year from September to April (the park is closed May–Aug), up to a million of these penguins return to Punta Tombo to mate. Visitors are able to walk just a few feet away from hundreds and thousands of penguins guarding their nests. Baby penguins are visible in December and January.

The drive from Puerto Madryn is on a highway until you pass Trelew; then you head south on RP 1, a monotonous gravel road that seems to go on forever. The entrance to the national reserve is clearly marked, and the entrance fee is $7. Be sure to observe all the posted signs (stopping your car is strictly prohibited except in the designated parking lots). There are walkways and handrails to point you in the right direction as you explore. Veering off the trail is prohibited, and going down onto the beach is also not allowed.

You'll need about 2 hours to visit the Reserve and observe the penguins, and it takes over 2 hours to get here from Puerto Madryn.

Tips **When to Visit**

Coming to this region at the right time is crucial. Forget coming here between May and August if you want to see the penguins. And don't come here mid-December to April if you're hoping to see the whales. The most ideal time to visit Atlantic Patagonia is in November. The penguins have laid their eggs and are guarding their nests, the whales are happily swimming in the bays with their offspring, and schools in Argentina are still in session, so crowds are thin.

TOUR OPERATORS

Flamenco Tour, Av. Roca 331 (© **2965/455505;** www.flamencotour.com), is the most reputable operator in the area. Here, the friendly agents can help you plot out the itinerary that best suits your needs. They have a fleet of brand-new nine-passenger vans, with several different excursion options to the Peninsula Valdes, Punta Tombo, and Gaiman. They can also arrange car rentals, air transportation, biking trips, and diving trips in the area.

The 1-day guided tour to the Peninsula Valdes lasts from 7:30am to 7pm and includes a stop at the museum, a chance to go on a whale-watching cruise, and guided walks on the Punta Delgada beach and Caleta Valdes to view the elephant seals.

One-day tours of the Peninsula Valdes start at $30 per person, not including the whale-watching trip (an additional $17) or lunch.

OUTDOOR ACTIVITIES

Biking   Ecobikes, 25 de Mayo 309 (© **2965/454411;** www.ecobikes.com.ar), offers a 3-hour guided excursion around Puerto Madryn for $15 per person. Longer guided excursions are also available. A 1-day bike rental will cost $7.

Diving   Aquatours, Av. Roca 550 (© **2965/451954**), offers a variety of diving trips in the bay off Puerto Madryn and also off the Peninsula Valdes.

Fishing   Call **Raul Diaz (© **2965/450812**), a seasoned fisherman who will be happy to take visitors out with him on a fishing trip.

Golf   The **Puerto Madryn Golf Club (http://golf.madryn.com) is on Ruta 4, on the road to the airport. Call the club manager, Juan Gonzalez (© **15/530110**), to arrange your tee times and get detailed information on the rates.

WHERE TO STAY

Puerto Madryn desperately needs a luxury hotel. In 2003, a giant luxury resort was being built when design problems halted the construction. The enormous structure sits empty and half-built on the shore and is visible from everywhere in town. Most visitors to Puerto Madryn spend only 2 or 3 nights here. They visit the peninsula one day and Punta Tombo the next, and then fly out. Parking is free at hotels in Puerto Madryn.

EXPENSIVE

Hotel Peninsula Valdes ☟ This is the most expensive hotel in Puerto Madryn, but not necessarily the best. It's the only hotel with air-conditioning, but its rooms are a bit tired and resemble a roadside motel you may find in the United States. They are adequate but far too pricey for the quality. The charge for "panoramic" rooms with sea views is 20% extra (though it never hurts to ask at check-in for a free upgrade). The panoramic rooms have king-size beds and flatscreen TVs. The rest of the rooms are fairly spacious but come with tiny baths. The most annoying thing about this hotel is the charge for the use of the sauna ($14) and not-very-attractive indoor Jacuzzi ($10). They do, however, offer free Internet access for guests from the tiny business center, and the staff is efficient, if a bit snotty. By late 2005, all the rooms will come with their own safes. Until then, a safe is available at the front desk. If you don't care about air-conditioning, for half the price (and albeit slightly smaller but more charming rooms), stay at the Hotel Bahia Nueva (see below).

Av. Roca 155, 9120 Puerto Madryn. ℂ 2965/471292. Fax 2965/452584. www.hotel-peninsula-valdes.com. 70 units. $121 double; $146 triple. Rates include buffet breakfast. AE, DC, MC, V. **Amenities:** Bar; lounge; sauna; Jacuzzi; small business center with free Internet; room service; massage; laundry service. *In room:* A/C, TV, hair dryer.

MODERATE

Hotel Bahia Nueva ✦✦ *Value*   This is Puerto Madryn's best-kept hotel. The staff is friendly and helpful, and they take great pride in maintaining a spick-and-span hotel. The rooms are pleasant, with wood furnishings and nice tiled baths. Four rooms have sea views; ask at check-in if one is available, and you'll be upgraded at no extra cost. The full breakfast buffet may very well be the best in town, served in a cheerful dining room on the second floor. The buffet includes fresh fruit and eggs—a rarity in these parts. On the ground-level bar area, there's a pool table and a lovely fireplace in the cozy lounge. The staff is knowledgeable about the area and can help arrange excursions.

Av. Roca 67, 9210 Puerto Madryn. ℂ/fax 2965/451677. www.bahianueva.com.ar. 40 units. $44 double; $55 triple. Rates include excellent buffet breakfast. AE, MC, V. **Amenities:** Bar; lounge; game room; small business center with free Internet; laundry service. *In room:* TV.

INEXPENSIVE

Aguas Mansas *Overrated*   The location is nice, a few minutes' walk from the center of town on a residential street lined with fancy houses, half a block from the beach. It's a quiet and pleasant area, but once inside the hotel, there's a feeling that time has stood still. The humorless front desk staff seem perpetually tired. The rooms are aging and do not warrant the almost-deluxe status the tourist office has given them. Carpets are worn, the tiny bathrooms are leaky and noisy, and the beds and pillows lumpy. Why stay here? The price is good and the location is excellent, and, if everything else is full, this will do fine. The cable TV works well and the rooms are very quiet, except for the occasional loud bangs from the lounge area (where the frustrated receptionists also double as bartenders). Stay here with caution and have low expectations.

J. Hernandez 51, 9120 Puerto Madryn. ℂ 2965/473103. 18 units. $30 double. Rates include buffet breakfast. MC, V. **Amenities:** Bar; lounge. *In room:* TV.

Hotel Muelle Viejo ✦ *Value*   This is an excellent bargain—one of the best in town. Having remodeled its rooms in late 2004, the Muelle Viejo now stands head and shoulders above the other inexpensive hotels in the city. Half a block off the main drag, the location is ideal. Most of the rooms now have hardwood floors, TVs, and brand-new fixtures in the bathrooms. The new bedcovers are blindingly white. A few rooms remain to be overhauled, but the owner insists that the work will be done by mid- to late summer 2005. But just to make sure, ask for a "special" room when making your reservations, to make sure you land a remodeled one. Breakfast is also a bargain—an extra $1.25 per person, if you choose to take it.

Hipolito Yrigoyen 38–42, 9120 Puerto Madryn. ℰ/fax **2965/471284**. www.muelleviejo.com. 27 units. $27 double; $30 triple. MC, V. **Amenities:** Bar; lounge; laundry service. *In room:* TV.

WHERE TO DINE

Fish is big in Puerto Madryn. The fishermen go out into the bay every morning and fish for white salmon, cod, and sole. Meat is double the price here than in Buenos Aires, since everything has to be flown or trucked in.

If you are craving meat, the best place to have it is with the locals at the simple **Estella Parilla,** R.S. Pena 17 (ℰ **2965/451973**). For $6 to $9, you can have tenderloin or filet mignon and a salad. A variety of sausages is also available, as well as chicken on the grill. They're open Monday to Saturday from 8pm to midnight and Sunday from noon to 11pm.

MODERATE

Mar y Meseta 🏖🏖 SEAFOOD/INTERNATIONAL   This is the most elegant seafood restaurant in town. Service is top-notch, and the chef uses Patagonian ingredients whenever possible to create his masterpieces. Start with a bottle of cold Argentine sparkling wine with the chef's appetizer platter, consisting of steamed mussels, smoked mackerel, fried cod fingers, and pickled carrots and cauliflower. Move on to what may very well be the most creative dish in Puerto Madryn: fresh local cod baked with Patagonian honey, served on a bed of toasted cinnamon sticks and sweet-potato chips. There's a variety of other seafood dishes and a daily selection of fresh grilled fish filets (depending on what the fishermen brought in). The seafood stew is a hearty meal on a cold evening. There's also a good selection of Patagonian and Mendoza wines to round out your meal.

Av. Roca 485. ℰ **2965/458740**. Main courses $6–$9. AE, MC, V. Daily 11am–3pm and 7pm–midnight.

Nativo Sur 🏖🏖 *(Kids* REGIONAL/INTERNATIONAL   This is the best restaurant in town that is directly on the beach. There's a small playground for kids facing the pleasant patio area. The main dining room is very rustic, furnished in a purely Patagonian motif with dark local-wood tables and chairs. Even the plates are ceramic and made in Patagonia.

The large windows overlooking the bay give the entire place a very airy and relaxed feel. The owners, a husband-and-wife team, work here every day and make sure that every ingredient used is of the highest quality. Not only is the fish bought daily from a local fisherman, but even the vegetables are trucked in from a nearby farm. The focus here is fish—whatever is fresh (usually white salmon, sole, or cod), made to order. The fresh grilled calamari is tender and yummy. The best appetizer on the menu is a "salad" of roasted eggplant, onion, and tomatoes with mozzarella, served with half a head of butter lettuce drizzled with balsamic. This is a wonderfully laid-back place where you can have a long, leisurely dinner. Service is very friendly and unhurried.

Tips Call Ahead

Although reservations are not required anywhere in Puerto Madryn, you can usually score a better table and a warmer greeting if you call ahead. Even if you don't arrive exactly on time, the mere fact that your name is on a "list" gives you a bit more leeway with the waitstaff. If you see a table you like (by a window, for example) and you have a reservation, they are more likely to give it to you.

Corner of Brown and Humphreys. © **2965/457403**. Main courses $6–$9. MC, V. Tues–Fri 8–11:30pm; Sat–Sun noon–3:30pm and 8–11:30pm.

Placido ☞ INTERNATIONAL   Puerto Madryn's fanciest restaurant has a great location in the center of town. An airy, expansive dining room with plenty of windows, large wine glasses, crisp white tablecloths, and heavy silverware set the stage for an elegant evening. Unfortunately, the management is a bit too overzealous in attracting a stream of foreign visitors, which has made the cuisine schizophrenic, at best. Paella, cod in hollandaise sauce, white salmon with three-colored rice, and shrimp in curry sauce with white rice are just a few of the many main courses available. The wine list is impressive and service is very refined. If only the food could be simpler and more regional. Stick with simply prepared fresh fish or prawns or the good selection of homemade pastas (the vegetarian tagliattele with wild mushrooms is delicious), and you'll have a memorable meal. Call ahead and reserve a table by a window, overlooking the bay.

Av. Roca 506. © **2965/455991**. Reservations recommended. Main courses $4–$11. AE, DC, MC, V. Daily noon–3pm and 7:30pm–midnight.

INEXPENSIVE
Ambigu ☞ *Value* INTERNATIONAL   Elegant but very affordable, Ambigu serves a mélange of dishes from chicken curry to beef chop suey and all kinds of pizzas. The most interesting is the asparagus and provolone pizza with black olives. It's a fun, boisterous, and informal place that is busy every night. Service can be spotty when they're swamped, but nobody's ever in a rush here. Order a bottle of Mendoza Malbec to go with your meal, then sit back and watch all the people walking by on the Avenida Roca.

On the corner of Roca and Roque Saenz Pena. © **2965/472541**. Main courses and pizzas $4–$7. MC, V. Daily 7:30pm–midnight.

PUERTO MADRYN AFTER DARK
This is a very subdued town at night. As most of the visitors usually get up at the crack of dawn to head out to the Peninsula Valdes, Puerto Madryn shuts down early. The best place for a late-night drink (and light snacks such as pizza and hamburgers for $3–$5, served until 1am) is **Margarita Pub,** R.S. Pena 15 (© **2965/450454;** open daily 5pm–3am; no credit cards), an attractive wood-and-tile lounge with a large bar. All the locals who work as guides during the day come here on weekends—this place is hopping from midnight to 3am on Friday and Saturday.

On the weekends, the locals also go out to **El Clasico,** 25 de Mayo and 28 de Julio (no phone), a sports bar and restaurant that is loud and fun.

2 Puerto Piramides
100km (62 miles) northeast of Puerto Madryn

The only village inside the Peninsula Valdes National Park, Puerto Piramides is tiny—about 4 blocks. It's the sole launching point for the many whale-watching trips that depart from here from April to late December. During the day, the beach here is mobbed with day-trippers. Some travelers choose to stay here overnight instead of in Puerto Madryn (see above), especially if they have their own transportation. You can venture to other parts of the park much quicker from here than from Puerto Madryn, and you can have the stretch of beach all to yourself in the evening when the tourists have left. Most of the visitors who opt to stay here more than 1 night are on diving trips.

ESSENTIALS
GETTING THERE
See "Getting There" under "Puerto Madryn," earlier in this chapter.

By Car You can rent a car in Puerto Madryn or in Trelew. From Puerto Madryn, the trip is 100km (62 miles) and takes about an hour and a half. There's only one road here: Ruta 2.

By Bus Unfortunately, bus service to Puerto Piramides is spotty. Currently, there's only one bus twice a week from Puerto Madryn (Tues and Sun) in either direction. The cost is $3.50 each way. Inquire at the tourist office for the most up-to-date information.

A taxi or *remise* from Puerto Madryn should cost no more than $75; from Trelew, the cost is $84.

WHAT TO SEE AND DO
See "Visiting the Peninsula Valdes National Park," earlier in this chapter.

Since Puerto Piramides is the only town on the peninsula, it's entirely tourist oriented and, therefore, very expensive. The only gas station on the peninsula is located here. Basically, this is a stopover point for people who are visiting the park. Diving trips leave from here, and the few hotels here are frequently filled with groups of divers from Europe. From late December to late March, when the whales leave the bay, it becomes possible to kayak and swim, but the main draw of coming here is to see the whales on whale-watching trips. The cost is about $10 per person for these trips, but if you're staying overnight, I encourage you to bargain with Captain Pinino (see below) and see if you can get your own excursion arranged.

Captain Pinino at **Pinino Aquatours** (© 2965/495015; capitanpinino@infovia.com.ar) has the newest boat around and is fun and very experienced. There's usually a group whale-watching trip around 10:30am daily, but he can arrange private trips later in the day as well.

For diving trips and kayaking (in the summer), try either **Hydrosport** (© 2965/495065) or **Moby Dick** (© 2965/495122). Sand boarding is becoming popular on a hillside overlooking the town, and you can inquire here for sand boards (much like snow boards). Mountain bikes are also available.

WHERE TO STAY
In addition to the two places below, there's a new hotel in town, **The Paradise** (© 2965/495030; www.hosteriaparadise.com.ar), a pleasant option, though expensive for the quality. Double rooms are $120, and dinner is $15 per person at the hotel's restaurant. The friendly owners can arrange for whale-watching trips and mountain bikes.

Motel Puerto Piramides *Value* The name says it all, and this is an excellent value if you're just here for a speedy overnight stay. The single-story building surrounds a parking lot, and many of the bedrooms have windows overlooking the sea on the other side. The very basic rooms are well looked after by the affable manager, Mario. The small bathrooms are tiled and very clean. There's also a pleasant dining room where meals are served.

1st right turn as you enter the village. © 2965/495004. www.piramides.net. 16 units. $28 double. Rates include continental breakfast. MC, V. **Amenities:** Restaurant; bar. *In room:* TV.

Patagonia Franca *Finds* The best and most expensive hotel in the region has 12 rooms, 8 of which are oceanfront with fantastic views. If you're lucky, you might even spot a whale from your private patio. The modern two-story structure is reminiscent of Laguna Beach or La Jolla, and inside the airy lobby and adjacent dining room with its exposed stone, everything is understated elegance and very pleasant. Rooms have tiled floors, wooden beds, wrought-iron lamps, ceiling fans, and sliding French doors that overlook the ocean or the village. I highly recommend you splurge for the sea view—the other rooms are darker and less cheery. Marble bathrooms have bathtubs. The friendly front-desk staff can arrange your excursions and help with transportation. The hotel has one computer with an Internet connection available for guests' use. This is the only Internet access in the entire village! The restaurant here is the best in town, with a daily selection of fresh fish.

Primera Bajada al Mar, Puerto Piramides. © 2965/495101. www.patagoniafranca.com. 12 units. $133–$174 double. Rates include breakfast and either lunch or dinner. AE, MC, V. **Amenities:** Restaurant; bar; tour desk; room service; laundry service. *In room:* Minibar, hair dryer.

WHERE TO DINE

Patagonia Franca (see above) has the best restaurant in the village.

El Refugio ⚤ The owner of this quirky restaurant-bar is a fisherman, so you can be assured that what you're eating is fresh from local waters. Ask what he found that day, and order that. The small dining room is filled with antiques and has a very cozy feel to it. Just behind the restaurant are two snug cabins for rent, $26 for a double; they each have tiny kitchenettes, a small but clean bathroom, and a double bed.

Puerto Piramides. © 2965/495031. Main courses $3.50–$8. No credit cards. Daily noon–11pm.

La Estacion ⚤ A very pleasant patio area makes this place a great choice for lunch on a warm day. Fresh seafood is the focus, but they also have homemade pastas, salads, and some grilled meats. Note that the restaurant is closed the last week in December.

Puerto Piramides. © 2965/495047. Main courses $3.50–$10. No credit cards. Daily 10am–11pm.

3 Trelew

67km (42 miles) south of Puerto Madryn

Trelew's airport is the gateway to the region, and, therefore, many travelers pass through here on their way to and from the Peninsula Valdes. The largest city in the region (pop. 100,000), Trelew has a pleasant square and an excellent paleontological museum, but little else of interest. The nearby Welsh town, Gaiman, is worth an afternoon visit.

ESSENTIALS
GETTING THERE

Aerolíneas Argentinas (© 0810/222-5627) is the sole operator at **Almirante Zar** airport, 5km (3 miles) from the city center. They fly at least twice daily from Buenos Aires, with extra flights on weekends. Aerolíneas also has several weekly flights from Bariloche, El Calafate, and Ushuaia.

28 de Julio buses (© 2965/472056) arrive every hour from Puerto Madryn at the OmniBus Station, located at 100 Urquiza (© 2965/420121). The cost is $2 one-way.

Buses from Buenos Aires take 20 hours and cost $30 one-way.

11

Planning Your Trip to Chile

Pristine landscapes and a solid tourism infrastructure have made Chile, especially Patagonia and the Lake District, a hot destination for international travelers. But with so many destinations to choose from and a hotel industry with a fluctuating price-vs.-quality factor, it can be difficult to decide where to go and stay. Much of your Chile trip can be planned on your own, but if you are not the savviest of planners or if you don't have the time or patience to organize your own trip, there are many tour operators who can do it for you. The following information should answer all the questions you might encounter when planning your trip to Chile.

1 The Regions in Brief

Sandwiched between the Andes and the Pacific Ocean, Chile's lengthy, serpentine shape at first glance seems preposterous: nearly 3,000 miles of land stretching from the arid northern desert to the wild desolation of Patagonia, and a width that averages 180km (112 miles). Chile encompasses such a breathtaking array of landscapes and temperate zones (the only zone not found here is tropical), it is hard to believe such variation can exist in just one country. In order to help you plan your visit here, we've divided the country into four zones: the North, the Central Valley, the Lake District (including Chiloé), and Patagonia (including the Carretera Austral and Tierra del Fuego).

NORTHERN CHILE This region claims the world's driest desert, a beautiful "wasteland" set below a chain of purple and pink volcanoes and high-altitude salt flats. The most popular destinations here, including the Atacama Desert, sit at altitudes of 2,000m (6,560 ft.) and up. The extreme climate and the geological forces at work in this region have produced far-out land formations and superlatives such as the highest geyser field in the world. The earth here is parched, sun-baked, and unlike anything you've ever seen, but it gives thing you've ever seen, but it gives relief through many of its tiny emerald oases, such as San Pedro de Atacama. See chapter 14.

SANTIAGO & CENTRAL CHILE The central region of Chile, including Santiago and its environs, features a mild, Mediterranean climate, which reminds many of California. This is Chile's breadbasket, with fertile valleys and rolling fields that harvest a large share of the country's fruit and vegetables; it also is the site of world-famous Chilean wineries. Santiago's proximity to ski resorts, beach resorts, and the idyllic countryside with its campestral and ranching traditions and colonial estates offers a distinct variety of activities that make the Central Valley an excellent destination. See chapters 12 and 13.

LAKE DISTRICT Few destinations in the world rival the lush scenery of Chile's Lake District, and for that reason it's the most popular destination for foreigners visiting Chile. This region is packed with a

VISITOR INFORMATION   The tourist office is located on the Plaza San Martín, at 387 Mitre (© **2965/420139;** www.trelew.gov.ar). The English-speaking agents are very helpful and have lots of maps and information about the Peninsula Valdes and the region. The office is open from 8am to 8pm daily.

GETTING AROUND

A taxi or *remise* from the airport to the city center will cost no more than $3.50.

From Puerto Madryn to Trelew, a taxi or *remise* will cost no more than $24. And a taxi from Puerto Piramides is $85.

Fiorasi Rent-A-Car has offices at the airport and at Urquiza 31 (© **2965/435344**) in the city center. **Hertz** has an office only at the airport (© **2965/436-005**). The average cost for a compact car is $50 per day.

WHAT TO SEE & DO

There's not much to see here except for one museum, but if you have a bit of extra time, you may want to take a walk around the pleasant San Martín square.

MEF, Museo Paleontologico Egidio Feruglio (Paleontological Museum Edigio Feruglio) ✶✶   The MEF, as it is widely known, is one of the best paleontological museums in South America. It's a brand-new building (opened in 2000) to house an amazing collection of fossils and dinosaur bones. Inside the museum (and visible when you visit) is a working lab where a team of scientists studies and cleans fossils. Try to come here during the week when the scientists are at work (Mon–Fri), and you'll get a sense of how much work they do to study just one fossil. An amazing skeleton of a titonausaurus (that walked on this land 70 million years ago) fills one room. Other rooms take you through a chronological order of dinosaur discoveries over the years, from past to present. There's also a good movie with English subtitles showing sea fossils found in Patagonia. You'll need about an hour and a half to visit the museum, and there's a gift shop and a snack bar in the lobby.

Av. Fontana 140. © 2965/420012. Admission $5. Daily 10am–6pm.

WHERE TO STAY & DINE

The best and most centrally located hotel is **The Rayentray,** San Martín 101 (© **2965/434702;** www.cadenarayentray.com.ar), just steps from the main plaza. The modern building has 110 rooms that are comfortable but neither luxurious nor elegant. There's a small indoor pool, massage available, a restaurant, and a bar. Cable TV is in each of the rooms. American Express, MasterCard, and Visa are accepted. The cost is $37 to $42 for a double.

Up the hill from the main plaza is the older but slightly grander **Hotel Libertador,** Rivadavia 31 (© **2965/420220;** www.hotellibertadortw.com.ar). The aging rooms with very 1970s mustard-colored drapes and bedcovers have a tiny bit of charm, but not that much; superior rooms are slightly brighter, with off-white curtains and bedcovers. The small bathrooms are clean but in desperate need of a remodel. Doubles are $32 to $46. MasterCard and Visa are accepted.

The best Parilla in town is **Quijote,** Rivadavia 457 (© **15/402937**), with an excellent selection of grilled sausages, beef, chicken, and lamb. They also have interesting vegetable dishes, such as crepes with vegetables, and eggplant roasted on skewers and beans marinated in garlic sauce. Main courses cost $5 to $9. No credit cards are accepted. They are open from noon to 3pm and from 8 to 11:30pm daily.

High Tea in Gaiman

Just a 10-minute drive west of Trelew, you'll find the Welsh town of Gaiman, settled in 1870 by immigrants from Wales. It's a pleasant place to take a walk, admiring the very English-looking houses. The Welsh museum, **Museo Historico Regional Gales,** at the corner of Rivadavia and Sarmiento streets (no phone), is an interesting place to get the lowdown on the town and its origins. The Welsh immigrants built the Chubut railway, and the museum is housed in the old railway station. It contains some interesting documents and relics from the late 1800s and early 1900s. Admission is $1.

Most visitors come to Gaiman to have real English tea. Even Princess Diana enjoyed tea here in 1995 when she made an official visit. The chair she sat on is on display inside a lovely house that has become one of the best tea houses in Gaiman: **Ty Te Caerdydd,** Finca 202 (© **2965/491510**), serves English tea complete with sandwiches, cakes, and lemon pie every day from 2 to 8pm. The cost is $6 per person.

Chile

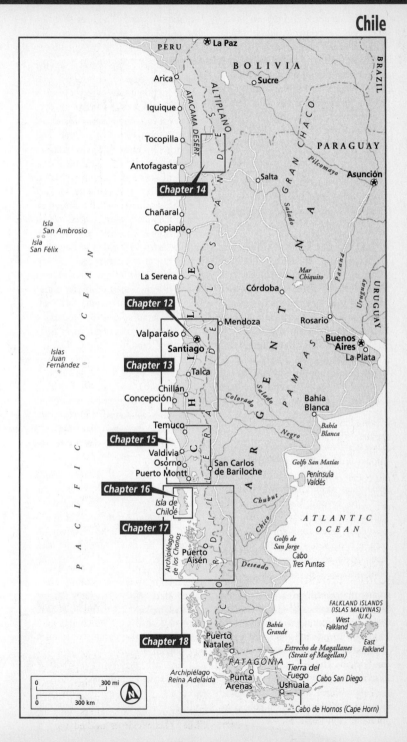

PERU

★ **La Paz**

B O L I V I A

Arica○

○ **Sucre**

ATACAMA DESERT

ALTIPLANO

A N D E S

Iquique○

Tocopilla○

G R A N   C H A C O

Pilcomayo

PARAGUAY

Antofagasta○

Chapter 14

Salta○

Asunción ★

Chañaral○

Salado

Copiapó○

Isla
San Ambrosio

Isla
San Félix

L O S

A N D E S

Mar
Chiquito

Paraná

URUGUAY

La Serena○

Córdoba○

Uruguay

Chapter 12

Mendoza○

Rosario○

O C E A N

Valparaíso○

★

**Buenos
Aires** ★

Islas
Juan
Fernández ○

Santiago

La Plata○

Chapter 13

○Talca

A R G E N T I N A

P A M P A S

Chillán○

Concepción○

Colorado

Salado

Bahía
Blanca○

C O R D I L L E R A   D E   L O S   A N D E S

Temuco○

Negro

Bahía
Blanca

Chapter 15

Valdivia○

Osorno○

Puerto Montt○

San Carlos
de Bariloche○

Golfo San Matías

Península
Valdés

Chapter 16

Isla de
Chiloé

Chubut

A T L A N T I C
O C E A N

Chapter 17

C O R D I L L E R A   D E L   S U R

Archipiélago
de los Chonos

Puerto
Aisén○

Chico

Golfo de
San Jorge

Deseado

Cabo
Tres Puntas

P A C I F I C

O C E A N

FALKLAND ISLANDS
(ISLAS MALVINAS)
(U.K.)

West
Falkland

East
Falkland

Chapter 18

Bahía
Grande

Puerto
Natales○

Estrecho de Magallanes
(Strait of Magellan)

P A T A G O N I A

Tierra del
Fuego

Cabo San Diego

Archipiélago
Reina Adelaida

Punta
Arenas

Ushuaia○

Cabo de Hornos (Cape Horn)

0 _____ 300 mi

0 _____ 300 km

N

chain of conical, snowcapped volcanoes; glacier-scoured valleys; several national parks; thick groves of native forest; hot springs; jagged peaks; and, of course, many shimmering lakes. Temperatures during the summer are idyllic, but winter is characterized by months of drizzling rain. It's an outdoor-lover and adventure-seeker's paradise, especially in Pucón and Puerto Varas, offering biking, hiking, kayaking, rafting, fly-fishing, and more, but it is also a low-key destination for those who just want to kick back and enjoy the marvelous views. See chapter 15.

CHILOE   The island of **Chiloé** is as attractive for its emerald, rolling hills and colorful wooden churches as it is for the unique culture that developed after 300 years of geographic isolation. Picturesque fishing hamlets and views that stretch from the Pacific to the Andes make for fine sightseeing drives, and Chiloé National Park offers ample opportunity for hiking along the island's untamed coastal rainforest. See chapter 16.

THE CARRETERA AUSTRAL Across the sound from Chiloé sits Chile's "frontier" highway, commonly known as the **Carretera Austral,** a dirt road that stretches nearly 1,000km (620 miles) from Puerto Montt in the north to beyond Coyhaique in the south. Along the way, this relatively new road passes through virgin territory visited by few travelers: tiny villages speckled among thick virgin rainforest, rugged peaks from which waterfalls descend. This area could be one of Chile's best-kept secrets. See chapter 17.

PATAGONIA   Also known as the **Magallanes Region,** this region has soared in popularity over the past 5 years, drawing visitors from all over the world to places such as Torres del Paine National Park in Chile and Argentina's Perito Moreno Glacier. We've grouped both Argentina and Chile in one Patagonia chapter because many travelers like to visit destinations in both countries when here. Patagonia is characterized by vast open Pampa, the colossal Northern and Southern Ice Fields and hundreds of mighty glaciers, the peaks of the Andes as they fade into the southern Pacific Ocean at their terminus, emerald fjords, and wind, wind, wind. Getting here is an adventure—it usually takes 24 hours if coming directly from the United States or Europe, but the singular beauty of the region renders the journey worth it. Cruise through emerald fjords, walk across a glacier, stroll through frontierlike immigrant towns such as Puerto Natales, and, without a doubt, visit Chile's national jewel, Torres del Paine. For more, see chapter 18.

TIERRA DEL FUEGO   South America's largest island sits across the Strait of Magellan and is shared by both Chile and Argentina. There is a major city here, Ushuaia, in Argentina; the rest of the island is populated with more beavers than people. See chapter 18 for more information.

2 Visitor Information

You'll find a municipal tourism office in nearly every city and a **Sernatur (National Tourism Board)** office in major cities. The quality of service and availability of maps and brochures varies from office to office. A good place to begin your research is the tourism board's helpful website at www.visit-chile.org, which has general regional information in Spanish and English. In the U.S., for consular and visa information, dial ℭ 202/ 530-4104; for an information kit sent by e-mail or tourism information, facts, and tips answered by phone, call ℭ 866/YESCHILE. The tourism might even spot a whale from your private patio. The modern two-story structure is reminiscent of Laguna Beach or La Jolla, and inside the airy lobby and adjacent dining room with its exposed stone, everything is understated elegance and very pleasant. Rooms have tiled floors, wooden beds, wrought-iron lamps, ceiling fans, and sliding French doors that overlook the ocean or the village. I highly recommend you splurge for the sea view—the other rooms are darker and less cheery. Marble bathrooms have bathtubs. The friendly front-desk staff can arrange your excursions and help with transportation. The hotel has one computer with an Internet connection available for guests' use. This is the only Internet access in the entire village! The restaurant here is the best in town, with a daily selection of fresh fish.

Primera Bajada al Mar, Puerto Piramides. ⓒ 2965/495101. www.patagoniafranca.com. 12 units. $133–$174 double. Rates include breakfast and either lunch or dinner. AE, MC, V. **Amenities:** Restaurant; bar; tour desk; room service; laundry service. *In room:* Minibar, hair dryer.

WHERE TO DINE
Patagonia Franca (see above) has the best restaurant in the village.

El Refugio ⚡ The owner of this quirky restaurant-bar is a fisherman, so you can be assured that what you're eating is fresh from local waters. Ask what he found that day, and order that. The small dining room is filled with antiques and has a very cozy feel to it. Just behind the restaurant are two snug cabins for rent, $26 for a double; they each have tiny kitchenettes, a small but clean bathroom, and a double bed.

Puerto Piramides. ⓒ 2965/495031. Main courses $3.50–$8. No credit cards. Daily noon–11pm.

La Estacion ⚡ A very pleasant patio area makes this place a great choice for lunch on a warm day. Fresh seafood is the focus, but they also have homemade pastas, salads, and some grilled meats. Note that the restaurant is closed the last week in December.

Puerto Piramides. ⓒ 2965/495047. Main courses $3.50–$10. No credit cards. Daily 10am–11pm.

3 Trelew

67km (42 miles) south of Puerto Madryn

Trelew's airport is the gateway to the region, and, therefore, many travelers pass through here on their way to and from the Peninsula Valdes. The largest city in the region (pop. 100,000), Trelew has a pleasant square and an excellent paleontological museum, but little else of interest. The nearby Welsh town, Gaiman, is worth an afternoon visit.

ESSENTIALS
GETTING THERE
Aerolíneas Argentinas (ⓒ 0810/222-5627) is the sole operator at **Almirante Zar** airport, 5km (3 miles) from the city center. They fly at least twice daily from Buenos Aires, with extra flights on weekends. Aerolíneas also has several weekly flights from Bariloche, El Calafate, and Ushuaia.

   28 de Julio buses (ⓒ 2965/472056) arrive every hour from Puerto Madryn at the OmniBus Station, located at 100 Urquiza (ⓒ 2965/420121). The cost is $2 one-way.

   Buses from Buenos Aires take 20 hours and cost $30 one-way.

VISITOR INFORMATION The tourist office is located on the Plaza San Martín, at 387 Mitre (© **2965/420139;** www.trelew.gov.ar). The English-speaking agents are very helpful and have lots of maps and information about the Peninsula Valdes and the region. The office is open from 8am to 8pm daily.

GETTING AROUND

A taxi or *remise* from the airport to the city center will cost no more than $3.50.

From Puerto Madryn to Trelew, a taxi or *remise* will cost no more than $24. And a taxi from Puerto Piramides is $85.

Fiorasi Rent-A-Car has offices at the airport and at Urquiza 31 (© **2965/ 435344**) in the city center. **Hertz** has an office only at the airport (© **2965/ 436-005**). The average cost for a compact car is $50 per day.

WHAT TO SEE & DO

There's not much to see here except for one museum, but if you have a bit of extra time, you may want to take a walk around the pleasant San Martín square.

MEF, Museo Paleontologico Egidio Feruglio (Paleontological Museum Edigio Feruglio) ★★ The MEF, as it is widely known, is one of the best paleontological museums in South America. It's a brand-new building (opened in 2000) to house an amazing collection of fossils and dinosaur bones. Inside the museum (and visible when you visit) is a working lab where a team of scientists studies and cleans fossils. Try to come here during the week when the scientists are at work (Mon–Fri), and you'll get a sense of how much work they do to study just one fossil. An amazing skeleton of a titonausurus (that walked on this land 70 million years ago) fills one room. Other rooms take you through a chronological order of dinosaur discoveries over the years, from past to present. There's also a good movie with English subtitles showing sea fossils found in Patagonia. You'll need about an hour and a half to visit the museum, and there's a gift shop and a snack bar in the lobby.

Av. Fontana 140. © 2965/420012. Admission $5. Daily 10am–6pm.

WHERE TO STAY & DINE

The best and most centrally located hotel is **The Rayentray,** San Martín 101 (© **2965/434702;** www.cadenarayentray.com.ar), just steps from the main plaza. The modern building has 110 rooms that are comfortable but neither luxurious nor elegant. There's a small indoor pool, massage available, a restaurant, and a bar. Cable TV is in each of the rooms. American Express, MasterCard, and Visa are accepted. The cost is $37 to $42 for a double.

Up the hill from the main plaza is the older but slightly grander **Hotel Libertador,** Rivadavia 31 (© **2965/420220;** www.hotellibertadortw.com.ar). The aging rooms with very 1970s mustard-colored drapes and bedcovers have a tiny bit of charm, but not that much; superior rooms are slightly brighter, with off-white curtains and bedcovers. The small bathrooms are clean but in desperate need of a remodel. Doubles are $32 to $46. MasterCard and Visa are accepted.

The best Parilla in town is **Quijote,** Rivadavia 457 (© **15/402937**), with an excellent selection of grilled sausages, beef, chicken, and lamb. They also have interesting vegetable dishes, such as crepes with vegetables, and eggplant roasted on skewers and beans marinated in garlic sauce. Main courses cost $5 to $9. No credit cards are accepted. They are open from noon to 3pm and from 8 to 11:30pm daily.

High Tea in Gaiman

Just a 10-minute drive west of Trelew, you'll find the Welsh town of Gaiman, settled in 1870 by immigrants from Wales. It's a pleasant place to take a walk, admiring the very English-looking houses. The Welsh museum, **Museo Historico Regional Gales,** at the corner of Rivadavia and Sarmiento streets (no phone), is an interesting place to get the lowdown on the town and its origins. The Welsh immigrants built the Chubut railway, and the museum is housed in the old railway station. It contains some interesting documents and relics from the late 1800s and early 1900s. Admission is $1.

Most visitors come to Gaiman to have real English tea. Even Princess Diana enjoyed tea here in 1995 when she made an official visit. The chair she sat on is on display inside a lovely house that has become one of the best tea houses in Gaiman: **Ty Te Caerdydd,** Finca 202 (© 2965/ **491510),** serves English tea complete with sandwiches, cakes, and lemon pie every day from 2 to 8pm. The cost is $6 per person.

11

Planning Your Trip to Chile

Pristine landscapes and a solid tourism infrastructure have made Chile, especially Patagonia and the Lake District, a hot destination for international travelers. But with so many destinations to choose from and a hotel industry with a fluctuating price-vs.-quality factor, it can be difficult to decide where to go and stay. Much of your Chile trip can be planned on your own, but if you are not the savviest of planners or if you don't have the time or patience to organize your own trip, there are many tour operators who can do it for you. The following information should answer all the questions you might encounter when planning your trip to Chile.

1 The Regions in Brief

Sandwiched between the Andes and the Pacific Ocean, Chile's lengthy, serpentine shape at first glance seems preposterous: nearly 3,000 miles of land stretching from the arid northern desert to the wild desolation of Patagonia, and a width that averages 180km (112 miles). Chile encompasses such a breathtaking array of landscapes and temperate zones (the only zone not found here is tropical), it is hard to believe such variation can exist in just one country. In order to help you plan your visit here, we've divided the country into four zones: the North, the Central Valley, the Lake District (including Chiloé), and Patagonia (including the Carretera Austral and Tierra del Fuego).

NORTHERN CHILE This region claims the world's driest desert, a beautiful "wasteland" set below a chain of purple and pink volcanoes and high-altitude salt flats. The most popular destinations here, including the Atacama Desert, sit at altitudes of 2,000m (6,560 ft.) and up. The extreme climate and the geological forces at work in this region have produced far-out land formations and superlatives such as the highest geyser field in the world. The earth here is parched, sun-baked, and unlike anything you've ever seen, but it gives relief through many of its tiny emerald oases, such as San Pedro de Atacama. See chapter 14.

SANTIAGO & CENTRAL CHILE The central region of Chile, including Santiago and its environs, features a mild, Mediterranean climate, which reminds many of California. This is Chile's breadbasket, with fertile valleys and rolling fields that harvest a large share of the country's fruit and vegetables; it also is the site of world-famous Chilean wineries. Santiago's proximity to ski resorts, beach resorts, and the idyllic countryside with its campestral and ranching traditions and colonial estates offers a distinct variety of activities that make the Central Valley an excellent destination. See chapters 12 and 13.

LAKE DISTRICT Few destinations in the world rival the lush scenery of Chile's Lake District, and for that reason it's the most popular destination for foreigners visiting Chile. This region is packed with a

Chile

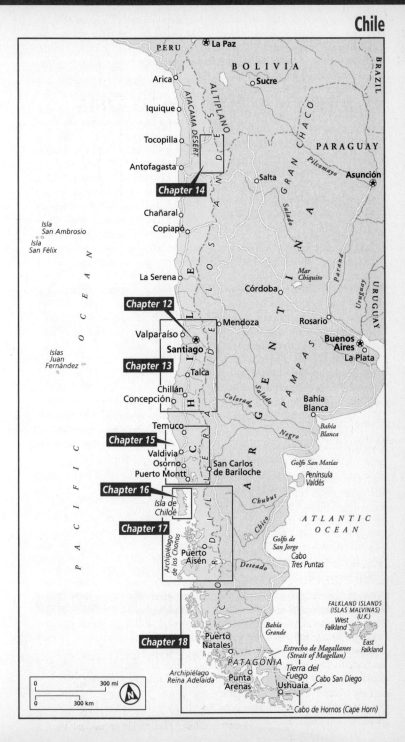

chain of conical, snowcapped volcanoes; glacier-scoured valleys; several national parks; thick groves of native forest; hot springs; jagged peaks; and, of course, many shimmering lakes. Temperatures during the summer are idyllic, but winter is characterized by months of drizzling rain. It's an outdoor-lover and adventure-seeker's paradise, especially in Pucón and Puerto Varas, offering biking, hiking, kayaking, rafting, fly-fishing, and more, but it is also a low-key destination for those who just want to kick back and enjoy the marvelous views. See chapter 15.

CHILOE   The island of **Chiloé** is as attractive for its emerald, rolling hills and colorful wooden churches as it is for the unique culture that developed after 300 years of geographic isolation. Picturesque fishing hamlets and views that stretch from the Pacific to the Andes make for fine sightseeing drives, and Chiloé National Park offers ample opportunity for hiking along the island's untamed coastal rainforest. See chapter 16.

THE CARRETERA AUSTRAL   Across the sound from Chiloé sits Chile's "frontier" highway, commonly known as the **Carretera Austral,** a dirt road that stretches nearly 1,000km (620 miles) from Puerto Montt in the north to beyond Coyhaique in the south. Along the way, this relatively new road passes through virgin territory visited by few travelers: tiny villages speckled among thick virgin rainforest, rugged peaks from which waterfalls descend. This area could be one of Chile's best-kept secrets. See chapter 17.

PATAGONIA   Also known as the **Magallanes Region,** this region has soared in popularity over the past 5 years, drawing visitors from all over the world to places such as Torres del Paine National Park in Chile and Argentina's Perito Moreno Glacier. We've grouped both Argentina and Chile in one Patagonia chapter because many travelers like to visit destinations in both countries when here. Patagonia is characterized by vast open Pampa, the colossal Northern and Southern Ice Fields and hundreds of mighty glaciers, the peaks of the Andes as they fade into the southern Pacific Ocean at their terminus, emerald fjords, and wind, wind, wind. Getting here is an adventure—it usually takes 24 hours if coming directly from the United States or Europe, but the singular beauty of the region renders the journey worth it. Cruise through emerald fjords, walk across a glacier, stroll through frontierlike immigrant towns such as Puerto Natales, and, without a doubt, visit Chile's national jewel, Torres del Paine. For more, see chapter 18.

TIERRA DEL FUEGO   South America's largest island sits across the Strait of Magellan and is shared by both Chile and Argentina. There is a major city here, Ushuaia, in Argentina; the rest of the island is populated with more beavers than people. See chapter 18 for more information.

2 Visitor Information

You'll find a municipal tourism office in nearly every city and a **Sernatur (National Tourism Board)** office in major cities. The quality of service and availability of maps and brochures varies from office to office. A good place to begin your research is the tourism board's helpful website at www.visit-chile.org, which has general regional information in Spanish and English. In the U.S., for consular and visa information, dial © 202/ 530-4104; for an information kit sent by e-mail or tourism information, facts, and tips answered by phone, call © 866/YESCHILE. The tourism

Recommended Websites for Chile

It seems that nearly every general information website about Chile that existed in the past has converted itself into a for-profit travel-booking site, so the best site is the tourism board's website (see below). A few destinations have their own websites: Try **www.pucon. com**, **www.chiloe.cl**, **www.sanpedroatacama.com**, or **www.santiago.cl**. I have put a few of the best sites below; unfortunately, many of them are Spanish-only.

- **www.visit-chile.org**   The *Corporación Promoción Turística* produces a site with general information in English about Chile, including travel and information about hotels, restaurants, and tour companies. This is a good overall view of top sites in Chile.
- **www.chip.cl**   The "Chile Information Project" is the most comprehensive site out there and includes a general information site, a link to the English-language newspaper the *Santiago Times,* and a travel agency. The general information offered is excellent. Start your research on Chile here.
- **www.interpatagonia.com**   This outstanding site is where you should begin planning your trip to Patagonia. The Argentine-run site covers all of Chilean and Argentine Patagonia, with links to tour outfitters, hotels, and more, as well as suggestions for adventure travel. There is good general coverage of locations and sharp photos. In Spanish and English.

board is open Monday through Friday from 8:30am to 5pm EST. You can download maps of Chile from the Turistel site at **www.turistel.cl**. Maps are often hard to come by in Chile, and it is better to be prepared if you plan to rent a car.

3 Entry Requirements & Customs

ENTRY REQUIREMENTS

Citizens of the United States, Canada, the United Kingdom, and Australia need only a valid passport to enter Chile. Visitors from New Zealand must apply for a tourist visa. Most visitors are unaware that Chile charges a steep **reciprocity fee** for citizens of some countries when they arrive at the Santiago airport before passing through Customs. The U.S. recently upped the fee for Chileans seeking a U.S. tourist visa to $100, so now Chile has responded by charging visitors from the U.S. $100. Visitors from Australia pay $34 and visitors from Canada pay $55. New Zealanders do not pay a fee, nor do visitors from the U.K. The entrance fee must be paid in cash and in U.S. dollars only. The one-time charge is good for the life of your passport; if you are issued a new passport and return to Chile, you will be charged again. Before entering Chile, you'll need to fill out a tourist card that allows visitors to stay for 90 days. You'll need to present this tourist card to Customs when leaving the country, so don't lose it. Also, many hotels waive Chile's 19% sales tax applied to rooms when the guest shows this card and pays with U.S. dollars.

LOST DOCUMENTS

If you lose your tourist card outside Santiago, any police station will direct you to the Extranjería police headquarters for that province (usually the nearest principal city). In Santiago, go to the **Policía Internacional,** Departamento Fronteras, General Borgoña 1052 (© **2/565-7863**), open Monday through Friday from 9am to 5pm. If you lose your passport and are an American, you can get a passport replacement only at the U.S. embassy in Santiago, Av. Andrés Bello 2800 (© **2/232-2600**), open Monday through Friday from 8:30 to 11:30am (telephone business hours are 8:30–11:30am). The fee is $85, and you will need to provide a passport photo. The embassy might require you to file a *constancia* with the police, but without Spanish skills, this can be difficult; call ahead and ask if this document can be waived. It is imperative that you carry a **photocopy of your passport** with you and another form of ID to facilitate the process.

CUSTOMS

Please see "Entry Requirements & Customs" in chapter 2 for information about what you're allowed to take home with you.

4 Money

CASH & CURRENCY

The unit of currency in Chile is the **peso.** The peso strengthened against the dollar during 2003 and 2004, and at press time the value was 600 pesos to the U.S. dollar. While prices for lodging and dining are cheaper than in the U.S., Chile is not as inexpensive as its neighbors Peru and Argentina. Bills come in denominations of 1,000, 2,000, 5,000, 10,000, and 20,000. There are currently six coins in circulation, in denominations of 1, 5, 10, 50, 100, and 500; however, it's rare to be issued 1 peso or 5. In slang, Chileans call 1,000 a *luca,* as in "It cost me *cinco lucas*" (5,000).

Chile levies a steep 19% **sales tax** on all goods and services, called *IVA (Impuesto al Valor Agregado).* Foreigners are exempt from the IVA tax when paying in dollars for hotel rooms; however, you might find this is not the case with inexpensive hotels. Always verify if the price quoted to you is without IVA. The prices given in this book are listed in dollars (adjusted per a 600-pesos-to-the-dollar rate), due to the ambiguous nature of the IVA tax.

EXCHANGING MONEY

Traveler's checks and dollars can be exchanged at a *casa de cambio* (money-exchange house) for a small charge, and they are generally open from 9am to 6pm Monday through Friday (closing 1–3pm for lunch), and Saturday until 1pm. A *casa de cambio* can be found near the center of every major city, but note that they are scarce in small towns. Some banks exchange money for a steep fee, and they are open only until 2pm. Hotels have poor exchange rates, so avoid changing money at one, if possible.

A Chilean ATM is known as a "Redbanc," which is advertised on a maroon-and-white sticker. Redbancs are compatible with a variety of networks, including Cirrus, Plus, Visa, and MasterCard. Chilean banks do not charge a fee to use their ATMs, but your own institution might charge you for foreign purchases or withdrawals, so check before you go. You'll find ATMs in banks, grocery stores, gas stations, and pharmacies.

CREDIT CARDS

Visa, MasterCard, and American Express are widely accepted throughout Chile. In the event of a lost or stolen credit card, call the following numbers (in the U.S.): Visa ℂ **410/581-7931,** MasterCard ℂ **736/722-7111,** and Diner's Club ℂ **210/677-** **0065.** American Express has an English-language number in Santiago: ℂ **800/361002.**

5 When to Go

High season for Chilean, Brazilian, and Argentine vacationers is during the summer from December 15 to the end of February, as well as the two middle weeks of July and Holy Week *(Semana Santa),* the week preceding Easter Sunday. These dates coincide with school vacations. Everybody, it seems, takes their vacation during these dates, and, consequently, the teeming masses seen in popular destinations such as Pucón or Viña del Mar during this time are overwhelming. If that weren't enough, consider that hotels nearly double in price, and some businesses quietly jack up their prices in anticipation of vacationers who come with money to burn. If being in Chile from December to February during the peak of the austral summer is still what you'd prefer, book a room *well* in advance. Or you can do as most North American and Europeans do and come from late September to early December for the spring bloom, or from March to June, when the trees turn color; both seasons have pleasant weather, and everything is less crowded. In fact, it's preferable to be in the extreme regions of Chile during these "off seasons." In northern regions, such as San Pedro de Atacama, the searing heat during the summer is a killer. In Patagonia, the fierce wind blows from October to April but is most consistent in December and January.

CLIMATE

Not only does Chile have a wide degree of climactic differences from the north to south, but its position between the Andes and the Pacific also fosters microclimates, pockets of localized weather that can completely alter the vegetation and landscape of a small area.

The northern region of Chile is home to the driest desert in the world. Summer temperatures from early December to late February in this region can top 100°F (38°C), then drop dramatically at night to 30°F (−1°C). Winter days, from mid-June to late August, are crisp in the sunshine but bitterly cold in the shade and when the sun drops. Along the coast, the weather is mild and dry, ranging from 60°F to 90°F (16°C–32°C).

The central zone that stretches to around Chillán has seasons that are better defined. Temperatures in this region range from 32°F to 55°F (0°C–13°C) in the winter, and 60°F to 95°F (16°C–35°C) during the summer. Santiago and the Central Valley enjoy a Mediterranean climate, whereas the Carretera Austral and the Lake District undergo soaking wet winters, especially in the regions around Valdivia, Puerto Montt, and Chiloé.

The farther south you travel through Patagonia, the more unpredictable the climate becomes, especially during the summer. The Magellanic Region sees extraordinary, knockout windstorms that can reach upward of 120kmph (74 mph), and it's not unusual to experience heavy rain during the summer. The windiest months are from mid-December to early February, but it can blow any time between October and April. Winters are calm, with irregular snowfall and temperatures that can dip to 5°F (−15°C).

HOLIDAYS

Chile's major celebrations are Christmas, New Year's, Easter week, and

Independence and Armed Forces days (Sept 18 and 19, respectively), the latter of which can carry on for days and days of dancing, drinking, and parades. During official holidays, Chilean towns can take on the appearance of a ghost town. Transportation services might be reduced in some areas; government offices, banks, and the majority of stores and markets close.

The following are official holidays: **January 1** (New Year's Day), **Semana Santa** (Holy Week, but just Good Friday is considered a holiday), **May 1** (Labor Day), **May 21** (remembrance of the War of the Pacific victory), **end of May** (Corpus Christi), **August 15** (Asunción de la Virgen), **September 18** and **19** (Independence Day and Armed Forces Day), **October 12** (Día de la Raza), **November 1** (All Saint's Day), **December 8** (Feast of the Immaculate Conception), and **December 25** (Christmas).

CALENDAR OF EVENTS The following are some of Chile's major events and festivals that take place during the year. For 1 week in early **February,** the city of Castro in Chiloé hosts a celebration of the culture, history, and mythical folklore that makes the island unique, including regional cooking, in the **Festival Costumbrista Chilote** (see chapter 16). During late **February,** Viña del Mar hosts its gala **Festival de la Canción,** or the Festival of Song, that showcases Latin American performers during a 5-day festival of concerts held in the city's outdoor amphitheater (see "Viña del Mar" in chapter 13). The spectacle draws thousands of visitors to an already packed Viña del Mar, so plan your hotel reservations accordingly.

In **mid-February,** Valdivia hosts a grand weeklong event called the **Semana Valdiviana.** A variety of maritime-theme activities, contests,

expositions, and more takes place during the week, but the highlight takes place the third Saturday of February, the **Noche Valdiviana,** when the Río Valdivia fills with festively decorated boats and candles, and the skies fill with fireworks. This is a very crowded event, and advance hotel reservations are essential (see chapter 15). The **first Sunday after Easter** is the **Fiesta del Cuasimodo,** an event held mostly in towns in central Chile, in which *huaso* cowboys parade through the streets accompanied by Catholic priests who often pay visits to the infirm and disabled.

On **June 29,** fishermen celebrate the **Fiesta de San Pedro** in towns along the coast of Chile to bring about good fortune, weather, and bountiful catches. Fishermen decorate their boats, light candles, arm themselves with an image of their patron saint, and drift along the coast. A great place to check out this event is Valparaíso.

July 16 sees the celebration of the **Virgen del Carmen,** the patron saint of the armed forces. On this day, military parades take place throughout the country, especially near Maipú, where Chile's liberators O'Higgins and San Martín defeated Spanish forces in the fight for independence.

Chile's rodeo season kicks off on Independence Day, **September 18,** and culminates with a championship in the city Rancagua around late March or early April. There are a variety of rodeo dates throughout the Central Valley, but September 18 and the championships are festivals in their own right, with food stalls, lots of *chicha* (a fermented fruit cider) drinking, and traditional *cueca* dancing. Contact the Federación de Rodeos in Santiago at ©/fax 2/ 420-2553 (**www.huasosyrodeos.cl**) for a schedule of rodeos throughout Chile.

6 Health & Insurance

HEALTH

Chile poses few health risks to travelers. There are no diseases such as malaria or dysentery, so no special vaccinations are required. There are no poisonous plants or animals in Chile to worry about, either. Nevertheless, standard wisdom says that travelers should drop in the doctor's office for tetanus and hepatitis boosters.

DIARRHEA & INTESTINAL PROBLEMS Few visitors to Chile experience anything other than run-of-the-mill traveler's stomach in reaction to unfamiliar foods and any microorganisms in them. Chile's tap water is clean and safe to drink, although not particularly tasty in Santiago. Bottled mineral water is widely available throughout Chile.

Chile's love of shellfish has its consequences, and each year there are a dozen reports of intoxication due to the *marea roja,* or "red tide." This toxic alga poisons shellfish and is due to a rise in the temperature of the sea. Very few, if any, people become intoxicated from bad shellfish in restaurants, but rather, when they have collected shellfish on their own, so don't do it.

ALTITUDE SICKNESS See information on p. 24.

AUSTRAL & ALTIPLANIC SUN See information on p. 24.

WHAT TO DO IF YOU GET SICK AWAY FROM HOME

Medical attention in private hospitals and clinics throughout Chile is up to international standards, but you may find limited or nonexistent service in tiny villages. *Clínicas* are always better than a town's general hospital; in fact, some general hospitals are downright appalling. Most health insurance policies cover incidents that occur in foreign countries; check to see if yours does, and be sure to gather all receipts and information so that you can make a claim back home. The cost of medicine and treatment is expensive, but most hospitals and pharmacies accept credit cards. Many doctors, especially in Santiago, speak basic English; for a list of English-speaking doctors, call your embassy or check out the list available on **www.chip.cl**.

PHARMACIES Chile has more pharmacies than supermarkets, and you'll often find them in odd locations—like the mall and at gas stations. Chilean doctors are notorious for overprescribing drugs, and many pharmacists do the prescribing themselves. Accordingly, pharmacies are nearly always packed, so be sure to take a number when you enter. Many pharmacies are now open 24 hours a day, and a few chains will deliver for a small fee.

INSURANCE

Please see "Health & Insurance," in chapter 2, for information on traveler's insurance.

7 Specialized Travel Resources

For more information on general resources for travelers with special needs, see chapter 2.

FOR TRAVELERS WITH DISABILITIES There are relatively few wheelchair-accessible buildings in Chile, apart from supermarkets and major hotels, which come equipped with ramps and wide doorways. Both the Metro and public buses are not equipped for wheelchair users. It's best to call ahead and inquire about an establishment's facilities, or check out its website, which will often tell you if any of the rooms are accessible.

FOR SENIORS   Seniors traveling in Chile are sometimes offered discounts for attractions and museums (seniors here are called *tercera edad,* or "third age"); however the practice is not as widespread as it is in the U.S. Members of **AARP** (© **800/424-3410;** www.aarp.org) receive discounts on hotels and car rentals (through chains that are represented in Chile). For tours, the most well-respected senior organization is **Elderhostel,** 11 Ave. de Lafayette, Boston, MA 02111 (© **877/426-8056;** www.elderhostel. org), which offers cultural and educational trips to Chile with themes such as "Fjordlands of Chile: People & Nature on Land & Sea" and "The Atacama and Easter Island: Different Worlds."

FOR GAY & LESBIAN TRAVELERS   Gays and lesbians visiting Chile will most likely not encounter any prejudice or outward intolerance. However, public displays of affection between same sexes are rare, even in metropolitan cities such as Santiago. In general, attitudes, especially those of Chilean men, toward gays and lesbians are not very liberal, owing in part to the Catholic, conservative nature of their society. Homosexual relationships have only recently been declared officially legal, and many gays and lesbians are not actively open about their orientation outside their own circles.

The best source for information is the website **www.gaychile.com**, a resource directory that covers gay issues and provides information about travel, gay-oriented businesses and bars, employment, and more. **Gay Adventure Tours, Inc.** (© **888/206-6523;** www.gayadventuretours.com) occasionally offers trips in Chile.

FOR FAMILIES   Chilean tourism enterprises seemingly love children, given the number of family-friendly lodging and kid's specials offered. Many hotels feature playgrounds, swimming pools, child care, and attached rooms or space for additional beds. Some larger resort hotels even arrange activities for kids. Parents might consider renting an apart-hotel or a *cabaña* (found in resort areas), which are self-catering units with living areas and kitchens; they are frequently less expensive. Many hotels offer discounts or grant a free stay for kids traveling with parents, so be sure to inquire when making a reservation.

FOR WOMEN TRAVELERS Underneath their skin, Chilean men are more macho than their Argentine counterparts, however, Chilean men do not whistle and hiss at women the way that Argentines do. They just stare intensely, which can be utterly annoying or make a woman feel uncomfortable. My advice is to just ignore the situation, as any kind of remark just seems to egg them on. Hitchhiking in rural areas by single women is common, but exercise caution. A lift up to a ski resort or into a national park that does not have public transportation is okay, but longer trips up and down the Panamericana Highway are best undertaken aboard one of the country's cheap and plentiful long-distance buses.

8 Getting There

BY PLANE
Several major airlines serve Santiago's Arturo Merino Benítez airport with direct flights from Miami, Atlanta, New York, Dallas–Fort Worth, Los Angeles, and Toronto. Turbulent times in the airline industry mean that fares can vary wildly depending on the time of year, departure location, and price wars that periodically break out. Most flights are red-eyes. For some money-saving tips, see "Flying for Less: Tips

for Getting the Best Airfare" in chapter 2.

THE MAJOR AIRLINES   The following airlines serve Chile from the United States and Canada (where noted). **Lan Airlines** (© **866/435-9526;** www.lan.com), the country's national air carrier, has direct flights to Santiago from New York and Los Angeles, and nonstop from Miami. Lan offers the best service of all carriers, and they offer last-minute deals on their website that are announced every Wednesday, with rock-bottom but heavily restricted fares from Miami to Santiago. **American Airlines** (© **800/433-7300;** www.aa.com) has daily nonstop flights from Miami and Dallas–Fort Worth, with connections from Vancouver, Toronto, and Montreal. **Delta** (© **800/221-1212;** www.delta.com) offers nonstop daily flights from Atlanta. Costa Rica's **Lacsa** airline, of the parent company Taca (© **800/400-8222;** www.taca.com), has flights from San Francisco, Los Angeles, New York, and Miami.

LanChile (© **0800/917-0672** in the U.K.; www.lan.com) serves London to Santiago via Madrid or Brazil, in partnership with Iberia and British Airways, or try booking directly with **Iberia** (© **0845/850-9000** in the U.K.; www.iberia.com). **Air France** (© **0845/0845 111;** www.airfrance.com/uk) has two to five daily flights from London to Santiago via Paris.

Qantas (© **13 13 13** in Australia, or 0800/808767 in New Zealand; www.qantas.com) works in conjunction with LanChile, offering three flights per week from Sydney and Auckland to Santiago. **Aerolíneas Argentinas** (© **2/9234-9000** in Australia, or 9/379-3675 in New Zealand; www.aerolineas.com.ar) has two weekly direct flights from Sydney and Auckland to Buenos Aires, Argentina, with a connecting flight to Santiago aboard Lan.

BY CRUISE SHIP

There are now quite a few 11- to 15-day cruises that sail around Cape Horn, beginning in Buenos Aires and ending in Valparaíso, Chile, or vice versa, and usually with a stop in Montevideo, Uruguay. Ports of call include Chile's Puerto Montt, Puerto Chacabuco, and Punta Arenas; Argentina's Ushuaia and Puerto Madryn; and sometimes the Falkland Islands. Opinions are mixed about cruises because passengers are given too brief a view of each port of call; however, sailing through the fjords is an unforgettable experience. To really see Chile via a cruise ship, consider booking passage on one of the local, smaller cruises, such as Skorpios and Mare Australis (see chapter 18). Several cruise operators with a Chile/Argentina itinerary are **Norwegian Cruises** (© **800/327-7030;** www.ncl.com), **Celebrity Cruises** (© **800/722-4951;** www.celebritycruises.com), **Silverseas Cruises** (© **800/722-9955;** www.silversea.com), and **Princess Cruises** (© **800/ PRINCESS;** www.princesscruises.com). Most offer the Cape Horn trip in both directions, and some add on stops in northern Chile and Brazil.

9 Getting Around

BY PLANE

Chile's enormous length makes flying the most reasonable way to get around. Even flying from Santiago to Punta Arenas takes about 4½ hours. Lan Airlines and the newer, more economical Sky Airlines are the two national carriers with service to major cities. Lan domestically is called LanExpress (© **866/435-9526** in the U.S., or 600/526-2000 in Chile; www.lan.com). Lan has the best coverage of Chile, with flights to Arica, Iquique, Calama, Antofagasta,

Concepción, Temuco, Valdivia, Osorno, Pucón (Dec–Feb only), Puerto Montt, Coyhaique (Balmaceda), and Punta Arenas. Sky Airlines (© 2/353-3169) flies to Arica, Iquique, Calama, Antofagasta, Concepción, Temuco, Pucón (Jan–Feb only), Puerto Montt, Coyhaique (Balmaceda), and Punta Arenas. Some smaller towns can be reached by air taxi; see individual chapters for information.

Lan offers foreigners a **Visit Chile Pass** good for three flights within the country. The price is $311 if flying into Chile on Lan, and $459 if using another carrier. Flights must be used within 14 days of arrival, and travelers have a maximum of 1 month to use the tickets. Lan requires travelers to book their routes when buying, but they allow date and time changes. A pass can be purchased only before arriving to Chile, directly from Lan or a travel agent. *Note:* Though Lan touts this as a substantial savings, the price is sometimes much cheaper if you just book the flights directly through their website.

BY BUS

Traveling by bus is very common in Chile, and there are many companies to meet the demand. Fortunately, most Chilean buses are clean and efficient and a good way to travel shorter distances. Think long and hard before booking a long ride; it can be excruciating.

If you decide to travel for more than a few hours by bus, it helps to know your options. Standard buses go by the name *clásico* or *pullman*. An *ejécutivo* or *semi-cama* is a little like

business class: lots of legroom and seats that recline farther. At the top end of the scale is the *salón cama*, which features seats that fold out into beds. A *salón cama* is an excellent way to get to a region like the Lake District, as riders sleep all night and arrive in the morning. Fares are typically inexpensive, and seats fill up fast, so buy a ticket as far in advance as possible. Ask what is included with your fare, and whether they serve meals or if they plan to stop at a restaurant along the way.

BY CAR

Car rentals for Santiago are totally unnecessary, but they do offer immense freedom if you are in the Lake District or wish to drive along the coast. Weekly rates for a compact vehicle, rented from and returned to the Santiago airport, average about $280 to $375. Prices include basic insurance with no deductible and unlimited mileage, although some companies include full insurance in the price, with the exception of theft of car accessories such as a stereo. Each company sets its own policy, so comb carefully through the contract before signing it.

You may find cheaper rates by booking via an agency's website before you arrive. Most major American rental-car companies have offices in Chile, which are listed under the appropriate chapter for each company's location. To make a reservation from the United States, call **Alamo** (© 800/GO-ALAMO; www.alamo. com), **Avis** (© 800/230-4898; www. avis.com), **Budget** (© 800/472-3325;

Finding an Address

In Argentina and Chile, as in many South American countries, not all addresses have street numbers. This is especially true in rural areas. You'll know there's no number if the address includes the abbreviation "s/n," which stands for *sin número* (without number).

www.budget.com), **Dollar** (© **800/ 800-4000;** www.dollar.com), or **Hertz** (© **800/654-3001;** www.hertz.com). If you haven't made a reservation, you can still rent from an agency kiosk at the airport. Don't overlook a few of the local car rental agencies for cheaper prices; you'll sometimes find better value with the smaller operations. *Note:* If you plan to take the car over the border to Argentina, you'll need to make a request 3 to 4 days ahead of time for the proper paperwork to be set up, and pay $85 to $100 extra for a stay of up to 14 days in Argentina. In this case, you'll need to reserve locally, not through a website or your home country.

You don't need an international driver's license to rent a vehicle—your current driver's license suffices. It's a disappearing practice, but the police, or *carabineros*, are allowed to stop motorists without reason, which they frequently do under the guise of "control." They usually just ask to see your license and then let you pass through their checkpoint.

Driving in Santiago is best compared to driving in New York City, but you'll find more considerate motorists outside of the capital. Drivers use their indicators constantly to signal where they are turning or that they are passing another vehicle—you should, too. On the highway, car and especially truck drivers signal to advise you that it's safe ahead to pass, but don't put your entire faith in the other driver's judgment, and give yourself ample space, as Chilean drivers have a lead foot. Right turns on red are forbidden unless otherwise indicated.

Outside Santiago, especially on roads off the Panamericana Highway, your major concern will be keeping an eye out for bicyclists and farm animals along the road. The Panamericana underwent a huge expansion and modernization program in 2001, and

drivers must now pay for it via **periodic tollbooths** on the highway and at most highway exits. Tolls, or *peajes,* range from 40¢ to $5.50 (tolls are higher on weekends). Most country roads off the Panamericana are dirt, either smoothed with gravel or washboard bumpy and pothole scarred. Gasoline is called *bencina* and comes in three grades: 93, 95, and 97.

Car rental agencies provide emergency road service. Be sure to obtain a 24-hour number before leaving with your rental vehicle.

The **Automóvil Club de Chile** also offers services to its worldwide members, including emergency roadside service. For more information, contact their offices in Santiago at Av. Andrés Bello 1863 (© **2/431-1000,** or toll-free in Chile 600/464-4040; www. automovilclub.cl). **Copec,** the gas station chain, sells Automapa's *Rutas de Chile* road maps at most of their larger stations; however, they often sell out. Hertz offers complete maps to renters, but many rental agencies don't—request one ahead of time and fully expect them to fall through on their promise. If they do, a few shops in the airport sell maps or the excellent **Turistel** guidebooks (also sold at most bookstores and a few kiosks on popular intersections in Santiago). They are in Spanish but provide detailed road maps, city maps, and visitor information—you can even download and print maps from their website **www. turistel.cl** before you leave for your trip.

BY FERRY & LOCAL CRUISES

If you're not packing a lot of action into a short stay, take a slow boat from Puerto Montt (Lake District) to Puerto Natales (Patagonia) instead of flying. To be honest, it is more popular with backpackers with a lot of time to kill, but **Navimag's** exceptional 3-day journey will enrich your Chile experience by introducing you to

A Note on Hitchhiking

Hitchhiking is common in Chile and mostly carried out along country roads with infrequent public transportation. Hitching is never entirely recommended for obvious reasons, but if you feel comfortable with your ride, you might consider it.

remote, virgin fjordland unseen outside of Norway. Also, the camaraderie that often develops among passengers during the journey leaves lasting memories. This is not a luxury liner, but certain berths provide enough standard comfort for finicky travelers.

Transmarchilay has cargo ferries (for vehicles) that link Puerto Montt and Chiloé with the Carretera Austral. **Andina del Sud** and **Cruce de los Lagos** work together to provide countless visitors with a full-day cruise between Argentina and Chile (and vice versa) in a boat-bus-boat combination through Vicente Pérez Rosales National Park near Puerto Varas and Nahuel Huapi Lake at Bariloche, Argentina. The demanding luxury traveler will find ample comfort

aboard the small cruise ships provided by the following companies.

Skorpios has 4- and 7-day cruises from Puerto Montt or Puerto Chacabuco, stopping at Castro and Quellón in Chiloé before or after the Laguna San Rafael Glacier; they also have a new dock in Puerto Natales that takes passengers to Pío XI Glacier (the only advancing glacier off the Southern Ice Field) and the remote village Puerto Eden. The brand-new ship **Mare Australis** offers an unforgettable journey through the untouched wilderness of Tierra del Fuego, either as a round-trip journey from Punta Arenas to Ushuaia and back, or one-way. For more information, see "Ferry Journeys Through the Fjords to Laguna San Rafael," near the end of chapter 17, and chapter 18.

10 Tips on Accommodations

It is imperative that you consider Chile's high season when planning your trip, as prices shoot through the roof and reservations are hard to come by without advance planning. High season runs from December 15 to the end of February, Easter week, and for 2 weeks around the middle of July. Some hotels drop their prices by as much as 50% in the off season. **Price ranges listed in hotel write-ups reflect low to high season.**

The prices listed in this book are **rack rates**—that is, a hotel's standard or advertised rate. *Hotel tip:* Don't be shy about negotiating a **discount** with a hotel. Owners are accustomed to paying a 20% commission to tour operators, so they will often consider dropping the price slightly during the

off season (or for multiple-day stays). As a last resort, check a hotel's website or simply ask if there is a promotion or package deal being offered that you're not aware of.

A sales tactic that is creeping its way into the cheap hotelier's lingo is the "bed-and-breakfast," but don't buy it. The term is redundant because every hotel, with the exception of the dirt-cheap hostal, includes breakfast in its price. Expect a continental breakfast at inexpensive and moderately priced hotels and an "American" or buffet breakfast at larger, four- and five-star hotels.

HOTEL OPTIONS
HOTELS & *HOSTERIAS* An *hostería* is a hotel attended by its

owner, typically found in a country setting.

APART-HOTEL This amalgam is exactly what it implies: an "apartment-hotel," or a hotel room with an additional living area and kitchen. Found primarily in Santiago and other large cities, they offer a wider range of services than a *cabaña*. Some are bargains for their price and come with maid service. However, some are nothing more than a hotel room with a kitchenette tucked into a random corner.

CABAÑAS *Cabañas* are a versatile lodging option. They are commonly found in resort areas and are popular with families and travelers seeking an independent unit. They resemble cabins or chalets and range from bare-bones to deluxe, although all come with fully equipped kitchens, and most have maid service.

RESIDENCIALES & HOSTELS These lodging options are for budget travelers. *Residenciales* are private homes whose owners rent out rooms, and they range from simple, clean rooms with a private or shared bathroom to ugly flats with creepy bathrooms. In towns that see more tourists, a hostel can be a hip and very comfortable place run by foreigners or Chileans, typically from Santiago. Some hostels are private homes that use their living area as a common area, and some of them can be very comfortable.

11 The Active Vacation Planner

Adventurous travelers, get ready. You are about to discover a country that is woefully underrated as an active travel mecca. Here's just a selection of what awaits you in Chile: trekking through primordial rainforests and some of the highest peaks in the world; kayaking pristine lakes; rafting one of the world's top-rated rivers; mountain-biking on hushed country lanes lined with tall poplar trees; skiing powder that lasts for days, not hours; climbing a smoking volcano; or galloping across the Patagonian Pampa with gauchos. Best of all? Even Chileans don't fully appreciate the natural wonders bestowed to them, so national parks and reserves are, for the most part, empty.

Visitors to Chile specifically seeking an adventure travel vacation, whether soft adventure or hard, will do well to book a trip with a tour operator or at an all-inclusive lodge that plans its own activities. If you'd like to just throw a few activities in the mix, local operators can plan day excursions once you arrive.

ORGANIZED ADVENTURE TRIPS

The advantages of traveling with an organized group are plentiful, especially for travelers who have limited time and resources. Be careful of tour operators who try to pack 20 people or more into a trip. The personal attention just isn't there, nor is that bit of breathing room you might find yourself needing after a week on the road. Also, be sure you know what you're getting yourself into. See "Organized Adventure Trips" on p. 31 of chapter 2.

U.S.-BASED ADVENTURE TOUR OPERATORS

These solid companies offer well-organized tours, and they are backed by years of experience. If you have a small group and can afford it, or a larger group that can take over the minimum requirement for a group, I highly recommend crafting your travel itinerary to suit your own tastes. All operators below can custom-design tours. *One caveat:* Though the following operators are highly respected and backed by reams of testimonials, a few of the trips they offer are duplicitous, in that they plan journeys around all-inclusive lodges that already provide guides and transportation. In other words, they are simply booking the reservations for you and providing a minder-guide to solve any glitches from one stop to the next. A few of the operators include luxury accommodations and gourmet dining as part of the travel itinerary and are, therefore, *very* expensive. Remember, the tours shown below do not include airfare!

- **Abercrombie & Kent,** 1520 Kensington Rd., Oak Brook, IL 60521 (© **800/550-7016;** www.abercrombiekent.com), is a luxury-tour operator that organizes packages that include five-star hotel stays. What sets A & K apart is that they have a local office in Santiago to manage trips and solve any problems along the way. A & K offers Chile "highlight" tours, including Patagonia, expedition cruises, Santiago, and the Atacama Desert. Their "Chile, Land of Fire and Ice" tour to Termas de Puyuhuapi and the Atacama Desert for 13 days costs $8,085 per person. Custom tours are available as well.

- **Butterfield and Robinson,** 70 Bond St., Toronto, Canada M5B 1X3 (© **800/678-1147;** www.butterfield.com), was the first tour operator to hit upon the successful combination of active travel and luxury. B & R operates in Patagonia only, with a tour that starts at Estancia Helsingfors in Argentina, continues to Perito Moreno Glacier, then to Torres del Paine and the Explora Lodge, terminating in Punta Arenas. I respect B & R, and their clients leave thrilled with their experience; however, their Patagonia route is easy to organize on your own for drastically less

money. Cost is $5,795 per person ($1,000 single supplement).

- **Mountain-Travel Sobek,** 1266 66th St., El Cerrito, CA 94608 (© **888/MTSOBEK** or 510/594-6000; fax 510/594-6001; www.mtsobek.com), are the pioneers of organized adventure travel, and they offer trips that involve a lot of physical activity that combine camping with hotel stays. Most trips are about 2 weeks long, including rafting the Futaleufú River and trekking in Torres del Paine, the latter of which costs $3,790 (10–19 guests) or $4,190 (7–9 guests). Guides carry the gear and set up camp for guests. Sobek always comes recommended for its knowledgeable guides.

- **Backroads Active Vacations,** 801 Cedar St., Berkeley, CA 94710-1800 (© **800/GO-ACTIVE** or 510/527-1555; www.backroads.com), offers two trips: a biking tour through the lake districts of Chile and Argentina, with stops in Puerto Varas, Bariloche, and Villa la Angostura (with an afternoon of rafting); and hiking in Torres del Paine and Perito Moreno national parks. The 9-day biking trip costs $3,998 per person ($900 extra for single supplement). Their biking tour is an outstanding way to see the Lake District of both countries. Guests lodge in luxury hotels and inns.

- **Wilderness Travel,** 1102 Ninth St., Berkeley, CA 94710 (© **800/368-2794** or 510/558-2488; www.wildernesstravel.com), offers the most complete tour of the Lake District, visiting little-known national parks such as Conguillio and Puyuehue. In addition to hiking in Patagonia, they have a hiking trip in the remote Futaleufú region with lodging in wooden cabins and tree houses, also a pricey cruise to

Easter Island. The cost for the Lake District hiking tour is $3,095 for 12 to 14 guests, and $3,395 for 10 to 11 guests.

- **REI Adventures,** P.O. Box 1938, Sumner, WA 98390 (© **800/622-2236;** www.rei.com/travel), offers multisport and trekking adventures in the Lake District and Patagonia, including a 10-day biking and rafting trip around Puerto Varas and down the Carretera Austral, camping out at the Futaleufú. If you become an REI member for $15, you receive substantial savings on trips. The bike journey down the Carretera Austral is $2,299 per person ($595 for a single supplement). Most of their trips combine camping with lodging in hotels.

- **PowderQuest Tours** (© **888/565-7158** toll-free in the U.S., or 804/285-4961; www.powder quest.com) offers complete ski and snowboard tour packages that take guests on a 9- to 16-day tour of Chilean and Argentine ski resorts, and they offer snowboard and ski camps and heliski camps. Each group has a maximum of eight, and their guides are highly trained and can take skiers and snowboarders farther into the backcountry. I have worked in the ski industry here for years, and I trust this outfit more than any other ski tour company. Prices range from $1,895 to $3,895 per person for 9- to 16-day trips.

TOUR OPERATORS BASED IN CHILE

Tour operators based in Chile (either Chilean-run or foreign-run) typically offer a wider variety of tours in Chile—after all, they operate within their own country. The following active travel operators are good bets.

- **Altué Expediciones,** Encomenderos 83, Las Condes, Santiago (© **2/232-1103;** www.altue.com), is the oldest and most respected tour outfitter in Chile. Their specialties are rafting (rivers Futaleufú, Maipo, and what's left of the Biobío) and horseback riding (Central Andes, La Campana National Park, Patagonia), as well as their terrific kayaking operation/lodge based in Chiloé (with trips around Chiloé and Parque Pumalín). They have exceptionally friendly guides and a solid operation. They can put together any kind of cultural tour or custom tour, including fly-fishing.

- **Cascada Expediciones,** Nueva Las Condes 12265, #10, Las Condes, Santiago (© **2/217-5061;** www.cascada-expediciones.com), offers a ample selection of active trips around Chile but is particularly active in Cajón de Maipo near Santiago, where the company is based. Activities include rafting, kayaking, mountaineering, horseback riding, trekking in Torres del Paine, 1- to multiple-day climbing trips, and more.

- **Latitud 90,** Av. Kennedy 7268, Vitacura, Santiago (© **2/247-9100;** www.latitud90.com), is the most complete tour operator in Chile, offering soft and hard adventure trips and more traditional excursions such as wine tasting and cultural visits to areas outside of Santiago. It's a good outfit for mountaineering, and they also specialize in tailor-made trips.

- **Azimut Expediciones,** Gral. Salvo 159 (© **2/235-1519;** www. azimut.cl). This French and Chilean-run operation is a top choice for adventure travel and traditional tours with an "avant-garde" itinerary—that is, travel that takes you to off-the-beaten-path locations and personally tailored tours. Like Latitud 90, this is a good choice for expeditions in the Atacama Desert.

OTHER GENERAL-INTEREST TOUR AGENCIES & PACKAGE DEALS

- **PanAmerican Travel,** 320 E. 900 S., Salt Lake City, UT 84111 (© **801/364-4359** or 800/364-4300; www.panamtours.com), an excellent company that arranges custom trips for its clients for most destinations in Chile. PanAmerican is the operator for Lan Vacations and can package vacations with usually lower fare deals than normally offered by the airlines directly.
- **Chile Discover,** 1601 NW 97th St., Miami, FL 33102 (© **800/ 169-8163**), not to be confused with Discover Chile below, puts together "Self-Guided" tours, whereby they book the car rental, hotels, and any other reservations; provide you with a map; and send you on your way on an independent tour. Research the hotels that they suggest as part of their itinerary—they may not be the best available.
- **Discover Chile Tours,** 5755 Blue Lagoon Dr., Suite 190, Miami, FL 33126 (© **800/826-4845** or 305/266-5827; www.discoverchile. com), is another excellent resource, offering complete trip planning and set packages, custom tours, and lower-cost deals on flights. Discover Chile is owned by Chile's largest tour operator, Turismo Cocha.
- **Ladatco Tours,** 2200 S. Dixie Highway, Suite 704, Coconut Grove, FL 33133 (© **800/327-6162;** www.ladatco.com), organizes preprogrammed and custom tours in all regions of Chile, including theme-oriented tours such as wine tasting, fly-fishing, glaciers, and more. Ladatco has operated as a Central and South America tour operator for 30 years.
- **Moguls Mountain Vacations** (© **800/666-4857;** www.moguls. com) and **Ski Vacation Planners** (© **800/U-CAN-SKI;** www.ski vacationplanners.com) are specialists in ski and snowboard vacations in Chile and Argentina, and they can put together an entire package, including flights and transfers. These guys offer the best prices and the most knowledgeable information about what resort is right for you.

FAST FACTS: Chile

Business Hours Banks are open Monday through Friday from 9am to 2pm and are closed on Saturday and Sunday. Commercial offices close for a long lunch hour, which can vary from business to business. Generally, hours are Monday through Friday from 10am to 7pm, closing for lunch around 1 or 1:30pm and reopening at 2:30 or 3pm.

Currency Exchange See "Money," earlier in this chapter.

Electricity Chile's electricity standard is 220 volts/50Hz. Electrical sockets have two openings for tubular pins, not flat prongs, so you'll need a plug adapter available from most travel stores.

Embassies & Consulates The only United States representative in Chile is the **U.S. Embassy** in Santiago, located at Av. Andrés Bello 2800 (© 2/ 232-2600; www.usembassy.cl). The **Canadian Embassy** is at Nuevo Tajamar

481, Piso 12 (© 2/362-9660; www.dfait-maeci.gc.ca/chile). The **British Embassy** can be found at El Bosque Norte 0125 (© 2/370-4100; www. britemb.cl). The **Australian Embassy** is at Isidora Goyenechea 3621, 12th and 13th floors; (© 2/550-3600; www.chile.embassy.gov.au). The **New Zealand Embassy** is at Av. El Golf, Office 703 (© 2/290-9802; www.nz embassy.com/chile).

Emergencies Obviously, you'll want to contact the staff if something happens to you in your hotel. Otherwise, for a **police** emergency, call © **133**. For **fire**, call © **132**. To call an **ambulance**, dial © **131**.

Internet Access No matter where you are in Chile, chances are, there is an Internet station, either in a cafe or at the telephone centers CTC or Entel. Most hotels have their own Internet service; if they don't, they'll be able to point out where to find one. Expect to pay $2 to $4 per hour.

Police Police officers wear olive-green uniforms and are referred to as *carabineros* or colloquially as *pacos*. Dial © 133 for an emergency. To file a robbery or crime report, you'll need to file a *constancia* or a *denuncia*.

Safety Santiago is probably the safest major city in South America. Serious violent crime is not unheard of, but it's not common, either. A visitor's principal concern will be pickpockets and car break-ins. Be especially careful in crowded trains on the Metro.

Telephone Each carrier has its own prefix, which you must dial when placing national and international long-distance calls. Telephone centers use their own prefix, and there is a list of prefixes in telephone booths—all offer virtually the same rates. The prefixes are CTC (188), Entel (123), BellSouth (181), and Chilesat (171), among others. To place a collect call, dial a prefix and then 187 for an operator. The country code for Chile is **56**. A local phone call requires 100 pesos; phone cards sold in kiosks and convenience stores offer better rates. Cellular phones are prefixed by 09 and are more expensive to call. To reach an **AT&T** operator while in Chile, dial © **800/800-288**. The access numbers for **MCI** are © **800/207-300** (using CTC) and © **800/360-180** (using Entel). The access number for **Sprint** is © **800/360-777**.

Time Chile is 4 hours behind Greenwich Mean Time from the first Saturday in October until the second Saturday in March; the country is 6 hours behind during the rest of the year.

Tipping Diners leave a 10% tip in restaurants. In hotels, tipping is left to the guest's discretion. Taxi drivers are not tipped.

12

Santiago

Santiago, one of South America's most sophisticated cities, is a thriving metropolis that's home to five million people, or nearly a third of Chile's entire population. Though it ranks third behind Miami and Sao Paulo for Latin American business travel, it is one of Chile's least-popular tourist destinations, given the number of travelers who use Santiago only as a jumping-off point to locations such as Patagonia (see chapter 18) or the Lake District (see chapter 15).

In Santiago, you won't find the rich, vibrant culture that defines cities like Río de Janeiro or Buenos Aires, or a wealth of things to do and see, either. But that said, as the city booms economically and memories of the stifling Pinochet dictatorship fade, Santiago is reinventing itself, and the arts, nightlife, and restaurant scene has improved considerably as of late. Add to that the fact that Santiago is the historical center of the country, and you can see why the capital city deserves at least a 1-day visit. Additionally, no other Latin American city has the proximity that Santiago has to such a diverse array of day attractions, including wineries, ski resorts, and beaches.

Santiago also boasts a one-of-a-kind location sprawled below some of the highest peaks of the Andes range, providing a breathtaking city backdrop when the air is clear and the peaks are

dusted with snow. Visitors are unfortunately not always treated to this view, as smog and dust particles in the air often shroud the view, especially during the winter months. From December to late February, when Santiaguinos abandon the city for summer vacation and the city is blessed with breezier days, the smog abates substantially. These are the most pleasant months to tour Santiago.

Architecturally, Santiago's city planners have shown indifference to continuity of design during the last century. Rather than look within for a style of its own, Chileans have been more inclined to copy blueprints from other continents: first Europe and now the U.S. Earthquakes have flattened many of Santiago's colonial-era buildings, and what remains has been left to decay to the point that tearing down an antique mansion is cheaper than restoring it to its former glory. Thus, it isn't uncommon to see a glitzy skyscraper or cracker-box apartment building towering over a 200-year-old relic, or to see cobblestone streets dead-end at a tacky 1970s shopping gallery. Some neighborhoods look as though they belong to entirely different cities. The residential areas of Providencia and Vitacura are an exception. Here you will find lovely leafy streets, manicured lawns, and attractive single-family homes divided by parks and plazas.

1 Orientation

ESSENTIALS
GETTING THERE
BY PLANE   Santiago's **Comodoro Arturo Merino Benítez Airport** (② 2/ 690-1900) is served by the Chilean national carrier Lan, as well as by most

Santiago at a Glance

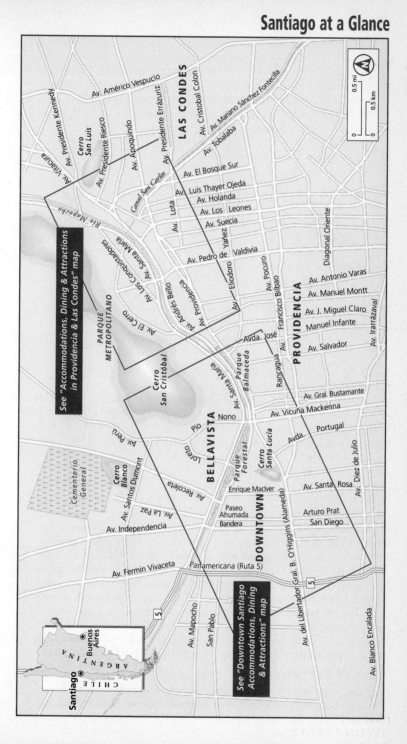

LAS CONDES

Av. Américo Vespucio

Av. Presidente Kennedy

Av. Vitacura

Cerro San Luis

Av. Presidente Riesco

Av. Apoquindo

Av. Presidente Errázuriz

Av. Cristóbal Colón

Av. Mariano Sánchez Fontecilla

Av. Tobalaba

Canal San Carlos

Av. El Bosque Sur

Av. Luis Thayer Ojeda

Av. Lota

Av. Holanda

Av. Los Leones

Av. Suecia

Av. Pedro de Valdivia

Av. Eliodoro Yáñez

Av. Pocuro

Diagonal Oriente

Av. Antonio Varas

Av. Manuel Montt

Av. J. Miguel Claro

Manuel Infante

Av. Salvador

Av. Irarrázaval

Río Mapocho

Av. Los Conquistadores

Av. Santa María

Av. Providencia

Av. Francisco Bilbao

PROVIDENCIA

Av. Andrés Bello

PARQUE METROPOLITANO

Av. El Cerro

Avda. José

Rancagua

Av. Gral. Bustamante

Cerro San Cristóbal

Parque Balmaceda

Av. Santa María

Av. Vicuña Mackenna

Portugal

Av. Diez de Julio

See "Accommodations, Dining & Attractions in Providencia & Las Condes" map

Nono

Pío

Avda.

Av. Perú

Loreto

Parque Forestal

Cerro Santa Lucía

BELLAVISTA

Cerro Blanco

Av. Recoleta

Av. Santos Dumont

Enrique MacIver

Av. Santa Rosa

Cementerio General

Av. La Paz

Paseo Ahumada

Bandera

Arturo Prat

San Diego

Av. Independencia

DOWNTOWN

Gral. B. O'Higgins (Alameda)

Av. del Libertador

Av. Fermín Vivaceta

Panamericana (Ruta 5)

Av. Blanco Encalada

Av. Mapocho

San Pablo

See "Downtown Santiago Accommodations, Dining & Attractions" map

ARGENTINA

Buenos Aires

Santiago

CHILE

0 0.5 mi

0 0.5 km

major international carriers. This relatively new international airport has several restaurants and a number of shops, including a wine shop. Once you pass through Customs, there is a small **currency exchange** kiosk, and just outside the gate there is a cash machine; head right when you exit. Men in khaki jumpsuits at the arrival area and the outdoor departure curb work as airport bellhops, and they will jump in and try to assist you with your luggage for a $1 to $2 tip; if you're okay on your own, just tell them *"No, gracias."*

Depending on traffic, your Santiago destination, and how you get there, the city can be reached in 20 minutes to an hour. When making hotel reservations, ask about transfers because most hotels offer private car or van pickup for around $20; some offer the service for free. A **taxi** to Santiago costs between $16 and $18. Buy a taxi ride at the official counter to the right of the Customs exit door to avoid getting ripped off. The next-cheapest option is the minivan **transfer shuttle** TransVip (© 2/677-3000) that charges, per person, $5.50 for downtown Santiago and $7.50 to Las Condes. When leaving Santiago for the airport, TransVip needs a reservation made 1 day in advance. The transfer shuttle might stop several times for other passengers before arriving at your destination. Cheaper yet are **bus** services that depart from the far ends of the arrival curb and drop passengers downtown, from where they can take the Metro or a taxi. The blue bus Centropuerto leaves every 10 minutes from 6am to 10:30pm and drops passengers at Los Héroes Metro station on the main avenue Alameda. Tur Bus leaves every 30 minutes from 6:30am to 9pm, dropping passengers off at Terminal Alameda at the Univ. de Santiago Metro station. The cost is $2.

BY BUS　There are three principal **bus stations** in Santiago. The station for international arrivals and departures to and from destinations in southern Chile is **Terminal Santiago,** also known as **Terminal Sur,** Alameda 3850 (© 2/376-1755; Metro: Universidad de Santiago). The **Terminal Alameda** next door at Alameda 3712 is the terminal for the Pullman and Tur Bus companies, two well-respected, high-quality services. For departures to northern and central Chile, you'll go to **Terminal San Borja** (also known as Estación Central, though that name is actually for the train station that can also be found there), Alameda 3250 (© 2/776-0645; Metro: Estación Central). The smaller **Terminal Los Héroes,** Tucapel Jiménez 21 (© 2/420-0099; Metro: Los Héroes), has service to a variety of destinations in both northern and southern Chile.

BY TRAIN　Santiago is serviced by the Empresa de los Farrocarriles del Estado (EFE), which provides modern and comfortable service to and from the south (as far as Temuco). Trains leave from the giant Estación Central at Alameda 3170 (© 2/376-8400). Depending on the day, trains leave several times per day to Chillán; the trip takes about 4½ hours. For Temuco, there is one train, which leaves nightly at 10:30pm and arrives at 7:30am. Fares are $16 to $20 one-way for "salon" class and $30 to $35 for "preferred" class, which has seats that recline to 140 degrees. Trains to Chillán cost $12 to $15 for salon seats, and $12 to $14 for preferred. For schedules and train information, check their Spanish-only website (www.efe.cl) or check with your travel agent or hotel for a reservation.

VISITOR INFORMATION

There are several outlets offering information about Santiago and Chile in general, such as the main office of Chile's **National Tourism Service (Sernatur),** which can be found at Av. Providencia 1550 (© 2/731-8300; www.sernatur.cl). Hours are Monday through Friday from 9am to 6:30pm, Saturday from 9am to 2pm, closed Sunday (Metro: Manuel Montt). Sernatur also has an information center at the airport near the duty-free shop that is open daily from 8:30am to 5:30pm, from Monday to Sunday (no phone). Sernatur has a bilingual staff, and though they have improved their quality of service over the past few years, service and the selection of brochures can be inconsistent. Be sure to ask for a brochure if you don't see what you want because they are usually hidden, especially the booklet guides to the wine country, national parks, beaches, and camping. Another option is the **Oficina de Turismo,** located in the Casa Colorada at Merced 860 (Mon–Thurs 10am–6pm, Fri 10am—5pm, closed weekends; ✆ 2/ 632-7783; www.ciudad.cl has city news, but in Spanish). The Oficina de Turismo has a partially bilingual staff; however, all their brochures are in Spanish, and they offer information about the city of Santiago only. The **Yellow Pages** has detailed maps of the entire city of Santiago.

CITY LAYOUT

Santiago incorporates 32 *comunas,* or neighborhoods, although most visitors will find they spend their time in just a few. **Downtown,** or *el centro,* is the thriving financial, political, and historic center of Santiago, although it has been losing clout as more companies opt to locate their offices in burgeoning neighborhoods, such as **Providencia, Las Condes,** and the tiny area that separates the two, **El Golf** (also known as El Bosque). These upscale, modern neighborhoods are residential areas centered on a bustling strip of shopping galleries, restaurants, and office buildings. In comparison, *el centro* is older and scruffier. The residential neighborhood **Vitacura,** next to Las Condes but separated by Avenida Kennedy, is home to Santiago's high-end shopping area and several top restaurants. The middle-class residential communities **Ñuñoa** and **La Reina** offer few attractions and, therefore, little interest to the visitor, with the exception of Plaza Ñuñoa and its booming restaurant scene. Santiago is bisected by the muddy Río Mapocho, a chocolate-brown stream that alternately rushes or trickles down from the Andes and is bordered through downtown and Providencia by the grassy Parque Forestal. On one side of the Mapocho rises the hill Cerro San Cristóbal, a large forested park with lookout points over the city. Below the hill is the bohemian neighborhood **Bellavista,** another restaurant haven and happening night spot.

2 Getting Around

BY METRO   Cheap, clean, and efficient, the Metro is the preferred mode of intercity transportation. There are three Metro lines. Line no. 1 runs from Providencia to west of downtown along the Alameda; this is the most convenient line that will take you to most major attractions. Line no. 2 runs from Cal y Canto (near the Mercado Central) to Lo Ovalle. Line no. 5 runs from La Florida to Baquedano, with a stop in the Plaza de Armas. At print, two new lines had yet to be finished, but the routes are to outlying residential areas that do not benefit travelers. There are two fares, 45¢ and 60¢, depending on the time of day (fares are posted in the ticket window). Visitors can buy a *Multiviaje* card and charge the card with any amount; fares are 20 pesos cheaper, and you won't have to wait in line to buy a ticket each time you travel. The Metro runs from 6am to 10:30pm Monday through Friday, and 8am to 10:30pm Saturday and Sunday. The Metro is safe, but incidents of pickpocket crime are on the rise. For a map, go to www. metrosantiago.cl and click on "Plano Red Metro" at the right of the page.

BY BUS   City buses, or *micros* (or the "yellow sharks") are not worth the headache. There are no posted bus routes, the coaches themselves are old and filthy, and bus conductors are *animales* (and this is what the police call them!) who swerve abruptly in front of passenger vehicles, speed, and then slam on their brakes when they see a fare. Take a taxi or the Metro instead.

BY TAXI Taxis are reasonably priced and plentiful. They are identifiable by their black exterior and yellow roof; there's also a light in the corner of the windshield that displays a taxi's availability. Always check to see that the meter is in plain view, to avoid rip-offs. Drivers do not expect tips. Do not confuse taxis with *colectivos,* which are similar in appearance but without the yellow roof. They are local, shared taxis with fixed routes that are too confusing to visitors to recommend taking one.

BY RENTAL CAR It is unnecessary to rent a car in Santiago unless you plan to drive to any of the peripheral areas, such as Viña del Mar or for an overnight stay in the wine country. Driving on one of the modern highways outside of Santiago is easy, but within the city it can be a hair-raising experience (see "By Bus," above). Also, the city is composed of mostly one-way, narrow streets, and it is absolutely essential that you carry a city map with you. From 5 to 8pm, congested neighborhoods such as Providencia and the downtown area see absolutely phenomenal traffic jams.

Car Rentals At the airport you'll find most international rental agencies, such as **Alamo** (© 2/225-3061; www.alamo.com), **Avis** (© 600/601-9966; www.avis.com), **Budget** (© 2/362-3200; www.budget.com), **Dollar** (© 2/202-5510; www.dollar.com), **Hertz** (© 2/420-5222; www.hertz.com), local agency **Rosselot** (© 800/201 298), and **Thrifty** (© 2/225-6328; www.thrifty.com). All agencies also have downtown or Providencia offices. Generally, Rosselot and Dollar are lower in cost.

Driving Hints Chileans use their horn and their indicators habitually to warn other motorists or advise them of their next move. Right turns on red lights are forbidden unless otherwise indicated. Motorists have the annoying habit of not letting other vehicles merge into their lane, and it can be very frustrating; you'll need to be aggressive to move the car over or wait until all traffic passes by to enter the lane. The two yellow lanes running the length of Avenida Alameda (which changes its name to Apoquindo, Providencia, and 11 de Sept. in other neighborhoods) are bus lanes, and drivers of vehicles may enter only when preparing to make a right turn. Rental agencies can be unhelpful, and they usually do not have maps, especially regional maps. The Turistel website has maps that can be downloaded (**www.turistel.cl**); it is a good idea to arrive prepared, as gas stations are often sold out of maps.

Parking Most hotels offer parking on their own property or in a nearby lot. Parking downtown is difficult during weekdays, although you should be able to find an aboveground or underground lot, called an *estacionamiento,* by driving around. Santiago has begun metering busy streets in Providencia and Bellavista, which is done by an official meter maid who waits on the street and times and charges drivers—he or she will leave a white ticket on your windshield. Chile is also home to a peculiar phenomenon known as parking *cuidador,* where unofficial,

---

Tips **Keep Your Valuables with You**

Do not under any circumstances leave valuable items in your car if you park on the street; break-ins are frequent in all of Chile.

freelance meter maids stake out individual blocks and "watch" your car for you while you go about your business. You're expected to give them whatever change you have (100–300 pesos/15¢–50¢) when you leave your space. *Cuidadores* can be aggressive if you decide not to pay them.

ON FOOT   Visitors to Santiago should always carry a map, as the city streets are not laid out on a perfect grid system and can be confusing. All neighborhoods worth visiting in Santiago (downtown, Providencia, Bellavista, and Las Condes) are located along the shore of the Mapocho River, making the river a good point of reference. Perhaps the most difficult task at hand when wandering through Santiago is putting up with the screeching city buses that careen past, expelling voluminous black plumes of exhaust. Pedestrians should be alert at all times and should not stand on curbs, as buses roar by dangerously close to sidewalks. Also, drivers do not always give the right of way to pedestrians, and, therefore, you should get across the street as quickly as possible. Santiago suffers from a dreadful smog problem, especially during early winter, thanks to a thermal inversion phenomena that occurs around this time. If the smog level is high, especially if it is a "pre-emergency" day, when certain cars are restricted, it can be unbearable to be outdoors. Summer, on the other hand, usually blesses Santiago's residents with cleaner air due to breezy days and the exodus of residents from December 15 to the end of February for summer vacation. Nearly every business is open year-round on Saturdays from 10am to 2pm only, and closed on Sundays; therefore, these are quieter days for exploring the city on foot.

FAST FACTS: Santiago

American Express   The American Express office is at Av. Isidora Goyenechea 3621, Piso 10 (© 2/350-6855); open Monday through Friday from 9am to 2pm and 3:30 to 5pm. Twenty-four-hour customer service in the U.S. is at © 800/545-1171, although you will be charged for the call if you call from outside of the United States.

Banks   Banks are usually open from 9am to 2pm Monday through Friday, closed on Saturday and Sunday. ATMs are referred to as "Redbancs" and can be identified by the maroon-and-white logo sticker. These machines accept Cirrus, PLUS, Visa, and MasterCard. Redbancs can also be found in most gas stations and pharmacies.

Business Hours   Commercial offices close for a long lunch hour, which can vary from business to business. Generally, hours are Monday through Friday from 10am to 7pm, closing for lunch between 1 and 1:30pm and reopening between 2:30 and 3pm. Most stores are open from 10am to 2pm on Saturday and closed on Sunday.

Currency Exchange   All major banks exchange currency, but most charge a commission that is higher than a money-exchange house called a *casa de cambio*. In downtown, there are numerous exchange houses on Agustinas between Ahumada and Bandera. In Providencia, exchange houses are around Avenida Pedro de Valdivia and Avenida Providencia. In Las Condes, there are a couple on El Bosque. Exchange houses are generally open Monday through Friday from 9am to 2pm and 4 to 6pm, Saturday from 9am to 1 or 2pm. Your hotel most likely will exchange dollars for you as well, but not at a good rate.

Emergencies For a **police** emergency, call ⓒ **133.** For **fire,** call ⓒ **132.** To call an **ambulance,** dial ⓒ **131.**

Hospital The American Embassy can provide a list of medical specialists in Santiago. The best hospitals in Santiago are private: **Clínica Las Condes,** Lo Fontecilla 441 (ⓒ **2/210-4000); Clínica Alemana,** Vitacura 5951 (ⓒ **2/212-9700);** and **Clínica Indisa,** Av. Santa María 01810 (ⓒ **2/362-5555).**

Internet Access Virtually every hotel and commercial center in Santiago has Internet access. In Providencia, try **Cyber Café Internet,** Pedro de Valdivia 037 (ⓒ **2/233-3083);** in the downtown area, there are Internet cafes along Merced and Monjitas streets from where they meet to José Miguel de la Barra. Most telephone offices such as **Entel** and **Telefónica** also have Internet access.

Outdoor Equipment Parque Arauco mall has a **North Face** store; Alto los Condes mall, at Av. Kennedy and Padre Hurtado, (ⓒ **2/213-1223),** has a **Doite** camping store (see p. 252 for descriptions of both malls); the **Patagonia** clothing store is at Helvecia 210 (ⓒ **2/335-1796),** and there is a camping store next door. The best outdoor equipment and info can be found at **La Cumbre,** Apoquindo 5258 (ⓒ **2/220-9907;** www.lacumbreonline.cl).

Pharmacies Pharmacies are ubiquitous in Santiago, such as **Farmacias Ahumada, Farmacias Cruz Verde,** and **Farmacias Saldo,** some with branches open 24 hours a day. Look for one around the corner from Ahumada and Huérfanos streets, along Avenida Providencia between Pedro de Valdivia and Suecia, or at El Bosque 164, in Las Condes. For deliveries or information, try Farmacias Ahumada at ⓒ **2/222-4000.**

Police See "Police" under "Fast Facts: Chile" on p. 216.

Post Office The main post office is on Plaza de Armas (Mon–Fri 8:30am–7pm, Sat 8:30am–1pm). There are other branches at Moneda 1155 in downtown and Av. 11 de Septiembre 2239 in Providencia.

Safety See "Safety" under "Fast Facts: Chile" on p. 216.

Taxes See "Cash & Currency" under "Money" on p. 204.

Telephone Santiago's area code is **2;** cellular numbers are prefixed by **09.** The country code for Chile is **56.** Tourists are offered cheaper rates from phone centers than from their hotels. The centers are predominately run by Entel (at Morandé between Huérfanos and Compañia) and Telefónica CTC Chile (found inside the Metro stations Universidad de Chile and Moneda, and in Providencia at the Mall Panorámico at Av. 11 de Septiembre 2155). Most phone centers have fax service and Internet access as well. Alternatively, you can buy a phone card at any telephone center location and at nearly every street kiosk. Also see the "Telephone" section on p. 217.

3 Where To Stay

Where you stay in Santiago will likely shape your opinion of the city. The cheapest accommodations are in the downtown area, *el centro,* and this is the obvious choice if proximity to museums and historical attractions is important to you. However, *el centro* is noisily congested with people and traffic, and more than a few buildings and streets have been neglected and allowed to crumble and decay. The commercial area of Las Condes is upscale and very modern, almost to the point of being antiseptic. Providencia is a happy medium between the two, with leafy streets and plenty of shopping. Don't forget that the quick, efficient Metro links you to downtown attractions if you decide to lodge farther uptown. Most hotels in Santiago are chain hotels; the concept of boutique or independently owned hotels has not taken off here as it has in many major cities, and price is not always the best indicator of quality. Parking at Santiago hotels is free unless otherwise indicated below. A few reviews reflect low- and high-season rates; the low season for Santiago hotels is January through February and June through September.

DOWNTOWN SANTIAGO
VERY EXPENSIVE

Hotel Fundador ★★ Elegant, plushy decorated rooms and a complete range of services define this hotel, located on the edge of the atmospheric Barrio París-Londres. During the summer, the penthouse pool is a welcome respite, and the hotel's location on a quieter yet convenient downtown street is a bonus. Doubles come with two full-size beds instead of twins, which is quite rare in Chile. The suites are on the small side, but they are exceptionally cozy. Adjoining the lobby is a wood-and-leather-walled bar that's a nice place to hole up in for a drink.

Paseo Serrano 34. ① 2/387-1200. Fax 2/387-1300. www.hotelfundador.cl. 150 units. $130 double; $175 junior suite. AE, DC, MC, V. Valet parking. Metro: Univ. de Chile. **Amenities:** 2 restaurants; bar; indoor pool; gym; sauna; business center; conference rooms; gift shop; room service; babysitting; laundry service. *In room:* A/C, TV, minibar, hair dryers, safe.

Hotel Plaza San Francisco ★★ This polished five-star hotel is known for its excellent service and thoughtful details such as fresh flowers in its guest rooms. The decor is traditional and the interior lighting dark, with low wood ceilings, richly colored fabric wallpaper, and Oriental rugs. The style of this hotel makes it popular with business executives, but plenty of tourists lodge here, too. And the Dalai Lama has stayed here twice! The hotel's location on hectic Avenida Alameda is both a plus and minus; it is close to many attractions, but the frenzied pace of traffic outside can be overwhelming—although rooms do have double-paned windows that block the noise. Some of the suites have a kitchenette. The hotel's Bristol Restaurant deserves special mention, as it has been honored with more gastronomic awards than any other Chilean restaurant in the past decade. Live music plays Wednesday through Friday in the lobby bar from 7pm onward, with a happy hour Monday through Friday from 6 to 9pm.

Alameda 816. ① 2/639-3832. Fax 2/639-7826. www.plazasanfrancisco.cl. 155 units. $129–$139 double; $159–$190 junior suite; $159–$245 executive suite. AE, DC, MC, V. Metro: Univ. de Chile. **Amenities:** Restaurant; bar; indoor pool; gym; whirlpool; concierge; LanChile office; business center; room service; massage; laundry service; wine shop; art gallery. *In room:* A/C, TV, stereo, minibar, safe.

MODERATE

Hotel Foresta ★★ If you can get past the dungeonlike lobby, the Hotel Foresta offers comfortable, spacious rooms (except the single rooms), a rooftop restaurant with panoramic windows, and leafy views of Cerro Santa Lucía. It is an excellent location for both the neighborhood's antique, cafe-filled charm and its proximity to downtown. This is where I send friends and family looking for moderate accommodations in Santiago. The Foresta is also around the corner from some of the only restaurants open at night in downtown. Doubles, specifically a "matrimonial," that face Calle Subercaseaux are large enough to be junior suites, and each room is decorated differently with an eclectic mix of furniture—as if they furnished the hotel with purchases from a day at the flea market. It's an older hotel, and its funkiness makes for a fun place to stay.

Downtown Santiago Accommodations, Dining & Attractions

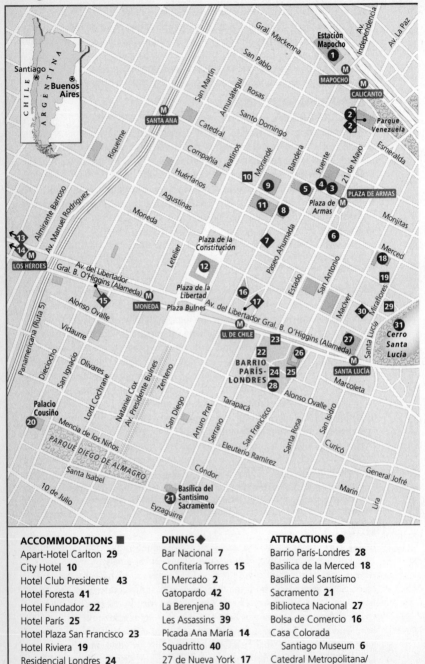

ACCOMMODATIONS ■

Apart-Hotel Carlton **29**
City Hotel **10**
Hotel Club Presidente **43**
Hotel Foresta **41**
Hotel Fundador **22**
Hotel París **25**
Hotel Plaza San Francisco **23**
Hotel Riviera **19**
Residencial Londres **24**

DINING ◆

Bar Nacional **7**
Confitería Torres **15**
El Mercado **2**
Gatopardo **42**
La Berenjena **30**
Les Assassins **39**
Picada Ana María **14**
Squadritto **40**
27 de Nueva York **17**
Zully **13**

ATTRACTIONS ●

Barrio París-Londres **28**
Basílica de la Merced **18**
Basílica del Santísimo
  Sacramento **21**
Biblioteca Nacional **27**
Bolsa de Comercio **16**
Casa Colorada
  Santiago Museum **6**
Catedral Metropolitana/
  Museo de Arte Sagrado **5**

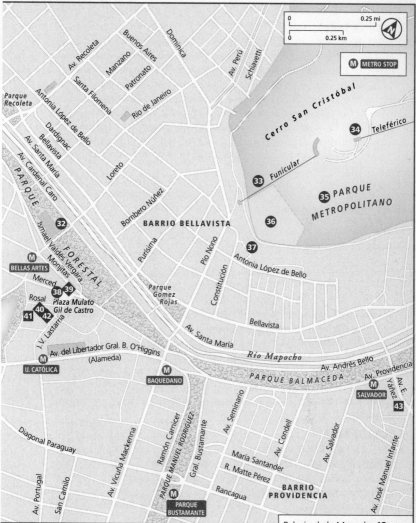

Victoria Subercaseaux 353. © **2/639-6261** or 2/639-4862. Fax 2/632-2996. 35 units. $36 for 2 twins; $48 matrimonial with queen-size bed. AE, DC, MC, V. Metro: Santa Lucía. **Amenities:** Restaurant; bar. *In room:* A/C, TV, minibar.

INEXPENSIVE

Hotel París ☆ *(Value)*   This is a good budget hotel, a step above most, located in the picturesque Barrio París-Londres neighborhood. Its newer annex has a better quality of rooms and more charming interiors than most budget hotels. Budget backpackers from all over the world bunk in the older annex, but you really need to be a backpacker to not mind the simplicity and worn-out look of the rooms. Pay a little extra here and opt for a room in what's referred to as the Hotel Nuevo París, where rooms are quieter and include Oriental rugs and mahogany molding. A few of these rooms even come with a glass-enclosed alcove or tiny outdoor terrace; they are the same price and worth asking for. Continental breakfast costs $2.

París 813. © **2/664-0921.** Fax 2/639-4037. carbott@latinmail.com. 40 units. $30 double new wing; $23 double. AE, DC, MC, V. Parking across the street $3–$5 per day. Metro: Univ. de Chile. **Amenities:** Cafe; laundry service. *In room:* TV (not all rooms).

Residencial Londres ☆   Residencial Londres is one of the best choices for travelers on the cheap in Santiago and is, accordingly, wildly popular in the summer—make reservations well in advance. There are four floors of basic rooms that wrap around an interior patio here; some rooms have French doors that open onto Calle París. Residencial Londres is stuffed with antiques; some rooms come with armoires, tables, and chairs. However, the mattresses are thinnish foam, and lighting can be a bare bulb hanging from the ceiling. Bring your down parka during the winter because there is no heating. Rooms do not have televisions, but there is a TV lounge. The hotel is frequented more by backpackers and younger travelers, and many use the interior terrace to dry tents and store bicycles. Breakfast is an additional $1.50. Don't confuse this hotel with the copycat across the street that uses the same name; it's not of the same quality.

Londres 54. ©/fax **2/638-2215.** 25 units. $26 double with private bathroom; $23 double with shared bathroom. No credit cards. Metro: Univ. de Chile. *In room:* No phone.

PROVIDENCIA
VERY EXPENSIVE

The Park Plaza ☆☆   The Park Plaza is easily confused with the Plaza Hotel downtown, and indeed their styles are quite similar. This exclusive hotel also caters predominately to traveling executives and diplomats, although its discreet location, tucked away on Avenida Lyon in Providencia, is more tranquil. The Park Plaza is a boutique hotel without any trendiness. Rooms here are elegant and refined with a decor using brocade and other rich fabrics. All rooms have plenty of space and good light. The hotel is conveniently located near shops and a block from the Metro, but what really stands out is the Park Plaza's attentive service. I recommend the Park Plaza's **Park Suite Apartments** around the corner (Lota 2233), which, at $100 for a one-bedroom, are a deal because they come with fully furnished kitchenettes and seating areas. Prices for these apartments are reduced for multiple-day stays.

Ricardo Lyon 207. © **2/372-4000.** Fax 2/233-6668. www.parkplaza.cl. 104 units. $125–$220 standard double; $215–$310 suite. Parking available. Metro: Los Leones. **Amenities:** Restaurant; bar; indoor pool; city tours and transfers to tennis and golf courts; gym; sauna; business center; room service; babysitting; laundry service; Internet. *In room:* A/C, TV, minibar, hair dryer, safe.

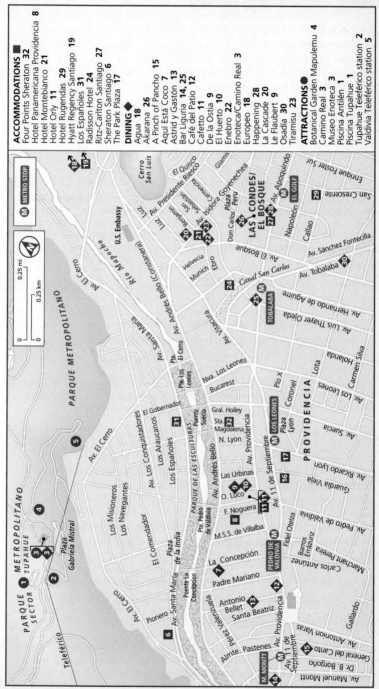

Accommodations, Dining & Attractions in Providencia & Las Condes

ACCOMMODATIONS ■
Four Points Sheraton **32**
Hotel Panamericana Providencia **8**
Hotel Montebianco **21**
Hotel Orly **11**
Hotel Rugendas **29**
Hyatt Regency Santiago **19**
Los Españoles **31**
Radisson Hotel **24**
Ritz-Carlton Santiago **27**
Sheraton Santiago **6**
The Park Plaza **17**

DINING ◆
Agua **18**
Akarana **26**
A Pinch of Pancho **15**
Aquí Está Coco **7**
Astrid y Gastón **13**
Bar Liguria **14, 25**
Café del Patio **12**
Cafetto **11**
De la Ostia **9**
El Huerto **10**
Enebro **22**
Enoteca/Camino Real **3**
Europeo **18**
Happening **28**
La Cascade **20**
Le Flaubert **9**
Osadía **30**
Tiramisu **23**

ATTRACTIONS ●
Botanical Garden Mapulemu **4**
Camino Real **3**
Museo Enoteca **3**
Piscina Antilén **1**
Piscina Tupahue **1**
Tupahue Teleférico station **2**
Valdivia Teleférico station **5**

229

Sheraton Santiago ★★ With its crystal chandeliers and marble floors, the Sheraton Santiago is all about glamour, whereas the Park Plaza is low-key elegance. The Sheraton complex offers more room sizes and amenities than are possible to list in this description, especially since the relatively new addition of the luxurious executive rooms in the **San Cristóbal Tower** ★★★. The regular Sheraton Hotel has standard doubles and suites. The upside of the Sheraton's location is that you are close to shops and dining; the downside is that the hotel sits on the other side of the Río Mapocho—psychologically, you're cut off from the city, even though it's just 5 blocks from downtown Providencia. Also, the entire Sheraton can be sold out for a week at a time due to visiting conventioneers, although this is not very common. Anything over the 10th floor offers spectacular views of Santiago and the Andes beyond. All rooms are well appointed with the same high-quality linens and contemporary furnishings. The Neptune Pool & Fitness Center competes only with the Hyatt and the Ritz's centers, and there is also an outdoor pool. Call or check their website for promotions.

Av. Santa María 1742. ✆ **800/335-3535** in the U.S., or 2/233-5000. Fax 2/234-1066. www.sheraton.cl. 379 units. $90 double standard, $215 executive suite; San Cristóbal Tower $150 executive double, $450 suite. AE, DC, MC, V. Metro: Pedro de Valdivia. **Amenities:** 3 restaurants; bar; outdoor and indoor pools; tennis courts; whirlpool; sauna; concierge; travel agency; rental car agency; business center; shopping gallery; salon and barber; massage; babysitting; laundry service. *In room:* A/C, TV, stereo, minibar, hair dryer, safe.

EXPENSIVE

Four Points Sheraton ★ The Four Points has rooms that cost far less than the Santiago Sheraton (see above) but offer the same standard amenities. A bland exterior is virtually indistinguishable from the office buildings that surround it, but the location ensures quiet evenings. The hotel is a safe bet for anyone used to American chains: prompt, professional service and standard rooms. The rooms are saturated in rose and cream, lending warmth, and the beds are comfortable. A great detail here is the rooftop pool and solarium.

Santa Magdalena 111. ✆ **2/750-0300.** Fax 2/750-0350. www.starwood.com/fourpoints. 128 units. $129 double. AE, DC, MC, V. Metro: Los Leones. **Amenities:** Restaurant; bar; outdoor pool; gym; whirlpool; sauna; business center; 24-hr. room service; laundry service. *In room:* A/C, TV, minibar, coffeemaker.

Hotel Orly ★★★ *Finds* This irresistible boutique hotel is one of my favorites in Santiago, and it is close to absolutely everything. The Orly is housed in a renovated mansion with French-influenced architecture. The lobby has a few cozy nooks with reading lights for relaxing and a small, glass-roofed patio; there's also a bar and a dining area for breakfast. The interiors are a restful white and accented with contemporary art and ambient light. Room sizes vary; doubles come with two twins or a full-size bed and are of average size; singles can be claustrophobic. All rooms have desks, and junior suites have a sitting area within the same room; however, I recommend the Queen Room for its spaciousness. What makes this hotel shine is its combination of everything a traveler looks for: a conscientious, friendly staff, unbeatable location, reasonable price, and an eye-catching decor. For those who need peace and quiet, request a room in the back.

Av. Pedro de Valdivia 027. ✆ **2/231-8947.** Fax 2/334-3304. www.orlyhotel.com. 28 units, 2 suites. $66–$98 double; $100–$124 junior suite. AE, DC, MC, V. Metro: Pedro de Valdivia. **Amenities:** Cafe; bar; room service; laundry service. *In room:* A/C, TV, minibar, hair dryer, safe.

Radisson Hotel ★★ *Value* I have always thought the Radisson chain provides a lot of value; I've never stayed in one that didn't offer attentive service and attractive accommodations for a reasonable price, and this Radisson is no different. The hotel is housed within the glitzy World Trade Center building, one of the more interesting, avant-garde skyscrapers in Santiago. The location is very convenient for tourists and business travelers alike because it is close to Las Condes–district businesses and the El Bosque eatery row, as well as a few good bars. The guest rooms are nicely appointed; try to get a room that faces the Andes (fifth floor and up). At night, the towering ultramodern buildings that surround the hotel provide glittering nighttime views. Business travelers will especially love the hotel's extensive business center, with two bilingual secretaries for hire. The health club and pool on the rooftop have panoramic views.

Av. Vitacura 2610. © 800/333-3333 in the U.S., or 2/203-6000 in Santiago. www.radisson.cl. 159 units. $120 double; $160 junior suite. AE, DC, MC, V. Metro: Tobalaba. **Amenities:** Restaurant; 2 bars; indoor pool; whirlpool; sauna; concierge; travel agency; business center; salon; babysitting; laundry service; wine shop. *In room:* A/C, TV, minibar, hair dryer, safe.

MODERATE

Hotel Club Presidente 🟊 (Value) The Hotel Club Presidente is one of the best values in this category. The rooms here are fresh, tidy, and comfortable, although a little on the small side and slightly dark. The Presidente is a small hotel but doesn't skimp on friendly, professional service. The compact foyer leads to a restaurant and a high-walled patio draped in foliage and serenaded by a bubbling fountain. The hotel is located on a residential street just a 3-minute walk away from the Metro, about halfway between Providencia and downtown. The price here is just unbeatable. The Club Presidente also owns the **Apart-Hotel Club Presidente** in Las Condes at Luis Thayer Ojeda 558 (© **2/233-5652**), with double rooms of the same quality as this hotel, plus a full kitchen—a solid deal for extended stays in Santiago. Rates for a two-bedroom apartment run from $72 to $83.

Av. Eliodoro Yañez 867. © 2/235-8015. Fax 2/235-9148. www.presidente.cl. 50 units. $55 double. Metro: Salvador. **Amenities:** Restaurant; bar; room service; laundry service. *In room:* A/C, TV, minibar.

Los Españoles 🟊 This is a good hotel for travelers seeking dependable, familiar comfort, and for that reason, it is popular with Americans. Los Españoles is part of the Best Western chain, although it has been run by the same family for 26 years—in fact, the hotel is their old family home, and they do a decent job making you feel at home yourself. The rooms are sized differently and laid out in a maze. Top-floor suites have attached terrace patios, and all rooms are comfortable, modern, and neat. This hotel sits beside the Mapocho River in a quiet residential area and is a 10-minute walk to the commercial center of Providencia and the closest Metro station.

Los Españoles 2539. © 800/332-7836 in the U.S., or 2/232-1824. Fax 2/233-1048. www.bestwestern.com. 48 units, 2 suites. $65 double; $75 suite. AE, DC, MC, V. Metro: Pedro de Valdivia. **Amenities:** Restaurant; bar; whirlpool; sauna; business center; room service; babysitting; laundry service. *In room:* A/C, TV, minibar, hair dryer, safe.

LAS CONDES & EL GOLF
VERY EXPENSIVE

Hyatt Regency Santiago 🟊🟊🟊 A decade ago, the Hyatt brought a whole new concept in five-star luxury to Santiago: 310 spacious, opulent rooms; hip restaurants; a plethora of services; and sky-high prices. The Hyatt is a 24-story atrium tower with two adjacent wings and four glass elevators that whisk guests up to their split-level rooms and terraced suites. Inside it feels as spacious as an airport hanger. Unfortunately, for this reason, the Hyatt can't help feeling somewhat antiseptic, a fact exacerbated by bland, uniform brownstone interiors. Nevertheless, guests are usually wowed by this behemoth and always rave about the flawless service provided by the staff. The palm-and-fern-fringed pool and fully staffed gym are superb. The Hyatt's standard rooms are as large as average suites, meaning the executive suites are enormous. Guests in suites enjoy their own 16th-floor private lounge for lingering over breakfast and soaking up the spectacular view. A complete business center rents out computers and cellphones. The Hyatt hosts daily tea in their lobby lounge, which is open to the public, as are their top-notch restaurants. It's close to a shopping mall and Chile's version of Rodeo Drive, but otherwise you'll always need to take a taxi because the location at the head of a crazy traffic loop makes it difficult and too far away to walk anywhere from here. Cheaper deals can be found when booking on their Internet site.

Av. Kennedy 4601. ⓒ 2/218-1234. Fax 2/218-3155. www.santiago.hyatt.com. 310 units, 26 suites. $145–$165 double; $265 Regency Suite; $365 Regency Terrace Suite. AE, DC, MC, V. **Amenities:** 3 restaurants; bar; outdoor pool; tennis courts; gym; whirlpool; sauna; concierge; American Airlines office; Hertz car-rental office; business center; shopping arcade; salon; room service; massage; babysitting; laundry service; solarium; valet service; billiards room (suites only). *In room:* A/C, TV, minibar, hair dryer, safe.

Ritz-Carlton Santiago 🏶🏶🏶   Expect to be pampered here. While the exterior of the new Ritz-Carlton is remarkably plain when compared to other hotels in the city, this is undoubtedly Santiago's finest hotel. Not only are the interiors luxurious in the Ritz-Carlton fashion, but the hotel has a fabulous rooftop health center under a glass dome that offers a sweeping view of the city and the Andes. The Ritz is conveniently located near restaurants and a thriving economic hub of Santiago. But what really stands out here is the gracious, attentive service. The hotel's lobby, which has a two-story rotunda and floors made of imported marble with a Mediterranean-style black-and-gold inlay, leads to the hotel lounge and a plush wine bar. In the spotless guest rooms, the beds are heavenly comfortable. Indulge in their "bath butler" service, with a nightly package of soaps and bubbles, and brandy and a cigar to be enjoyed "at the end of another successful day," as the accompanying note confidently states. I recommend that guests head to the hotel's high patio at sunset to soak in the breathtaking view of the Andes. Later, head to the bar/restaurant 345, where, for $12, guests may sample a hefty pouring of four different Chilean wines and a range of appetizers. The Ritz here is more economically priced than many of their other hotels, and they offer special packages on their website.

El Alcalde 15. ⓒ 800/241-3333 from the U.S., or 2/470-8500. Fax 2/470-8501. www.ritzcarlton.com. 205 units. $185 Deluxe Room; $245 Club Room; $285 Club Executive Suite. AE, DC, MC, V. Metro: El Golf. **Amenities:** 3 restaurants; bar; indoor rooftop pool; gym; whirlpool; sauna; concierge; car rental; business center; salon; room service; massage; babysitting; laundry service; valet service. *In room:* A/C, TV, minibar, hair dryer, safe.

EXPENSIVE

Hotel Montebianco 🏶   This small hotel is an excellent choice for travelers seeking a Las Condes/El Golf address with cheaper prices than the Hyatt or the Ritz-Carlton. Located in the middle of the El Bosque restaurant alley, the white stucco and Mediterranean influence of its interior design are attractive and upscale enough for discriminating travelers. The rooms are average size with large bathrooms, and the Montebianco Pieza suites are larger and come with an attached patio, for an additional $25. One of the perks here is the Montebianco's private minibus, which it uses for city tours, tours to outlying destinations, and airport pickup, all at an extra charge.

Av. Isidora Goyenechea 2911. ⓒ 2/233-0427. Fax 2/233-0420. www.hotelmontebianco.cl. 33 units. $88 double; $113 suite with patio. AE, DC, MC, V. Metro: El Golf. **Amenities:** Restaurant; business center; room service; laundry; city tours. *In room:* A/C, TV, safe.

Hotel Rugendas ★★ The Hotel Rugendas is a high-quality choice in Las Condes for its location close to El Bosque, but unlike the Montebianco, the Rugendas is located on a leafy residential street several blocks from busy Avenida Apoquindo. During the week, businessmen are the hotel's primary clients, meaning the price drops on weekends, so ask for promotions when booking a Friday or Saturday. The hotel is housed in a tall brick building whose top floor is encased with glass; here you'll find a game room with card tables and a billiards table, not to mention a breathtaking view. For a room with a view, book anything on the fifth floor and up, but ask for a room orientated toward the Andes for the best view. The Rugendas's state-of-the-art gym is open 24 hours a day.

Callao 3121. ℂ 2/370-5716. Fax 2/372-0247. www.rugendas.cl. 48 units. $80–$100 double. AE, DC, MC, V. Metro: El Golf. **Amenities:** Restaurant; bar; gym; sauna; game room; business center; laundry. *In room:* A/C, TV, minibar, hair dryer, safe.

4 Where to Dine

Santiago's gastronomic scene has undergone a culinary revolution, and hungry diners can expect to find dozens upon dozens of restaurants that serve innovative Chilean cuisine. Ethnic restaurants, led by a sushi craze, have slowly made their way into the market. Really, apart from Thai food, there isn't any kind of cuisine that can't be found in Santiago. Downtown eateries cater to office workers, and, therefore, most are open for lunch only and closed on weekends. It is possible to eat quite cheaply in the downtown area; most restaurants have a *menú del día, menú ejecutivo,* or *coloación,* a fixed-price lunch for about $4 to $7 that includes an appetizer, main course, beverage or wine, coffee, and dessert. *Autoservicios,* or self-service restaurants, abound, and most restaurants advertise their prices on sandwich boards or on signs posted near the front door. These restaurants are a dime a dozen, and quality is about the same. Look for many along the pedestrian walkways on Huérfanos and Ahumada streets.

In the peculiar Chilean fashion of concentrating similar businesses in one neighborhood (Av. 10 de Julio, for example, is lined for blocks with just auto mechanics), restaurant "clusters" have been popping up like mushrooms around the city. Bellavista is perhaps the best neighborhood to see this phenomenon, with its mind-boggling number of hip restaurants, from Chilean to Cuban to Mediterranean. Both El Bosque and its parallel street Avenida Isidora Goyenechea are lined nearly door to door with a wide variety of flavorful offerings, and now Avenida Italia in Providencia looks to be the new dining hot spot. A few of the local favorites from these neighborhoods are listed below, but you could really just stroll the streets until something strikes your fancy. All major hotels have outstanding restaurants open to the public. Highlights are the Hyatt's **Anakena** and **Matsuri** restaurants, the Ritz-Carlton's **Adra** restaurant, and the Plaza San Francisco's acclaimed **Bristol** restaurant. Chile is to seafood what Argentina is to beef; don't miss out on the wonderful varieties it has to offer.

Santiago is not the cafe society that Buenos Aires is; however, here are a few recommendations. **Café Tavelli** (ℂ 2/333-8481) has two branches, and both are plum spots for people-watching. The branch at the corner of Tenderini and Agustinas in downtown occupies the northeastern corner of the Municipal Theater building; this is where you come to see executives, politicians, and society ladies. Lofty ceilings give the cafe a sense of grandeur, but the outdoor tables are where to watch the city street action. There is another bustling Café Tavelli on Andres de Fuenzalida 36 in Providencia, with a more artsy and middle-class crowd. For rich desserts, ice cream, and other sweet delights, try the chain

Coppelia (© 2/232-1090) in Providencia, with locations at Manuel Montt 2517, Av. Providencia 2211, and Av. Ricardo Lyon 161.

DOWNTOWN

Nearly every restaurant in the downtown area is closed on Sunday, and many are open only for lunch. However, restaurants in the Lastarria St./Plaza Mulato Gil de Castro micro-neighborhood offer evening dining if you are staying downtown and would rather not wander too far (located on the other side of Cerro St. Lucia). Two to check out here are **La Pérgola de la Plaza** (© 2/639-3604; open Mon–Fri 11am–midnight, Sat 11am–2am, Sun 11am–4pm), a pretty little cafe with a good fixed-price lunch menu and outdoor seating, and **"R"** (© 2/664-9844; open Mon–Sat 12:30–4:30pm and 7:30pm–1:30am), a cozy spot for wine and conversation, although the ambience is better than the food: "R" is one of the best places in Santiago to enjoy an afternoon pisco sour and watch an eclectic group of locals meander by. The only parking available in this area is at Merced 317.

EXPENSIVE

Squadritto 🏔🏔 ITALIAN   Squadritto is on a charming, tree-filled street, near the Plaza Mulato Gil de Castro, and its Tuscan-style dining room is a preferred setting for executives and a sophisticated crowd. The warm, semiformal interior is filled with plants and twinkling lights—ideal for a romantic dinner. Squadritto serves arguably the best food in the neighborhood. The fresh pastas are rich and pleasing, and though the menu changes seasonally, examples of entrees are a salmon ravioli in a bay shrimp sauce and a vegetable lasagna, although the fish and meat dishes are similarly appetizing. There is an extensive wine list, too.

Rosal 332. © 2/632-2121. Reservations recommended. Main courses $7–$12. AE, DC, MC, V. Mon–Fri 12:30–4pm and 7:30pm–midnight. Metro: Universidad Católica.

Zully 🏔🏔🏔 *Finds* GLOBAL   Chic yet true to the utterly charming historical neighborhood in which it is located, Zully is the new restaurant of the moment—and a fun place to dine. To get here, you'll have to head west of downtown to Barrio Brasil and its "Concha y Toro" micro-neighborhood. The American-owned restaurant covers four floors of a lovingly restored old home and boasts a wine-tasting cellar, an interior patio, and trendily decorated dining rooms, some small enough for a private party of six. The house-proud staff deliver attentive, friendly service. The menu spans the globe, and though normally this tells me the food will not be up to par because a kitchen staff is trying too hard, the cuisine here is quite good. There's African-style ostrich carpaccio with almonds, and the familiar American-style prime rib, for example, and a sushi bar, too. Zully is packed on weekends with young, hip professionals, who head up to the restaurant's nightclub after eating (the nightclub closes when the last guest leaves). Take a cab here at night, as the outlying area is a little rough.

Concha y Toro 34. © 2/696-1378. www.zully.net. Reservations recommended on weekends. Main courses $8–$15. AE, DC, MC, V. Mon–Fri 11am–midnight or later; Sat 7pm–3am or later; Sun for brunch 11am–3pm Nov–Mar only.

MODERATE

Bar Nacional 🏔 CHILEAN   These traditional restaurants have been a hit with downtown workers for more than 50 years, serving honest Chilean food in a dinerlike atmosphere. There are two, on Calle Bandera and Paseo Huérfanos, both relatively identical. This is where you can try Chilean favorites such as empanadas, *cazuela* (a hearty chicken soup), and the cholesterol-boosting *lomo a lo pobre,* steak and fries topped with sautéed onions and a fried egg. There is a fixed-price lunch, which is typically gone by 3:30pm. The dated interior is a fitting backdrop for the characters that come here to eat, gossip, and smoke.

Bar Nacional 1 at Huérfanos 1151. © 2/696-5986. Bar Nacional 2 at Bandera 371. © 2/695-3368. Reservations not necessary. Main courses $7–$10; sandwiches $3–$4. AE, DC, MC, V. Mon–Sat 7am–11pm. Metro: Plaza de Armas.

Confitería Torres 🏆🏆 *Moments* CHILEAN

Saved from developers who wanted to tear down this restaurant and build a parking garage, the Confitería Torres, Santiago's oldest restaurant, with 120 years under its belt, has been splendidly renovated and reborn as a chic eatery serving a sophisticated crowd. This restaurant was the haunt of intellectuals, writers, and poets for decades, including Rubén Darío and Vincente Huidrobo, who often met with high society when the area was still fashionable. The Chilean couple who invested in this project rescued the original Art Deco–style oak bar, reset the great clock that had stopped years ago, and refurbished the original Queen Anne chairs and tables. Trendy cherry-red booths and smart white tablecloths have replaced the restaurant's fatigued ambience, and, thankfully, the menu has been updated. Rescuing traditional recipes from high society during the late 1800s and giving them a modern flair, the chef here turns out tasty dishes such as beef marinated in cilantro, and conger eel with a barnacle sauce. On weekends, the restaurant has live jazz, bolero, and tango music. If you are downtown, especially if visiting the Palacio Cousiño museum nearby, don't miss this historical landmark. At night, take a cab.

Alameda 1570. © 2/688-0751. Reservations accepted (ask for a table on the main floor). Main courses $6–$10. AE, DC, MC, V. Mon–Sat 8am–1am or later on weekends. Metro: Universidad de Chile.

Gatopardo 🏆 MEDITERRANEAN/CHILEAN

Tasty nouvelle cuisine has made this restaurant a local favorite—especially for lunch. Their fixed-price lunch menu can include stuffed calamari or lamb chops with rosemary and a run through the enticing and varied salad bar, which, with the wine and dessert included, makes $8 seem like a steal. Gatopardo specializes in Chilean and Mediterranean cuisine, though other influences, such as tacos and steamed mussels, have made their way onto the menu. The airy interior is lit by a glass atrium supported by giant oak trunks felled by an earthquake in the south of Chile.

Lastarria 192. © 2/633-6420. Reservations not necessary. Main courses $8–$15. AE, DC, MC, V. Mon–Fri 12:30–3:30pm and 7:30pm–midnight; Sat 7:30pm–1am. Metro: Universidad Católica.

Les Assassins 🏆 FRENCH

One of the tiniest restaurants in Santiago, Les Assassins is a romantic hole-in-the-wall—on nights when they have turned the fluorescent light down, that is. This French bistro, located across from the Mulato Gil de Castro plaza, is a downtown classic that once hosted government leaders and socialites, though new restaurants have won their patronage more recently. There are two floors; the downstairs "cave" is a cozy little spot to enjoy coq au vin and a cold bottle of Chilean chardonnay. There's also rabbit stew, a delicious sole in snow crab sauce, and crème brûlée for dessert.

Merced 297. © 2/638-4280. Reservations recommended for parties of more than 2. Main courses $6–$8. DC, MC, V. Mon–Fri 12:30–3:30pm and 7pm–11am; Sat 7pm–midnight. Metro: Universidad Católica.

Picada Ana María 🏆 *Finds* TRADITIONAL CHILEAN

This little-known, old-fashioned restaurant is quintessentially Chilean, and they specialize in wild game entrees such as boar, venison, and quail. The Picada started out as that, a *picada,* or restaurant that serves inexpensive Chilean snacks, but its popularity prompted the owners to break out the tablecloths and open a full-service restaurant. Located within a handsome antique home with just a little sign by the door to orient you, the uniqueness of this establishment draws politicians and businessmen at lunch and families on weekends, making it a good place to people-watch. The restaurant is located on the other side of the Panamericana Highway and hard to get to by Metro or foot, so take a cab.

Club Hípico 476. © 2/698-4064. Reservations recommended at night. Main courses $7–$12. AE, DC, MC, V. Mon–Sat noon–5pm and 7pm–midnight.

27 de Nueva York *&* INTERNATIONAL/CHILEAN   Located in the heart of the financial district, 27 de Nueva York is one of the more upscale restaurants to stop in for lunch if you are around the Bolsa de Comercio or Plaza de Armas. Its warm, attractive dining area is a favorite with businesspeople. The restaurant serves grilled meats, fish, and salads, and it also owns an *autoservicio,* or self-serve, restaurant next door, which is recommended if you're in a hurry.

Nueva York 27. © 2/699-1555. Reservations recommended at night. Main courses $5–$9. AE, DC, MC, V. Mon–Fri 8am–10pm. Metro: La Moneda.

INEXPENSIVE
El Mercado *&& Moments* SEAFOOD   You'll see a lot of tourists here, but the lively, colorful atmosphere isn't an overrated experience. This lofty, steel barn of a building is home to the central fish and vegetable market (see "Seeing the Sights," later in this chapter), as well as simple seafood restaurants that serve Chilean traditional dishes such as *paila marina,* a seafood stew cooked with cilantro; *ceviche,* fish cooked in lemon juice; and the much-adored *loco* (abalone). Strolling musicians and garrulous vendors provide the soundtrack noise while waiters in bow ties bustle about. The best and easiest-to-find restaurant here is Donde Augusto.

Enter on Ismael Valdés Vergara between 21 de Mayo and Puente. No phone. Main-course prices vary. AE, DC, MC, V. Sun–Thurs 6am–4pm; Fri 6am–8pm; Sat 6am–6pm. Metro: Cal y Canto.

BELLAVISTA
MODERATE
Azul Profundo *&& Kids* SEAFOOD   If you love seafood, the "Deep Blue" is the place to come. Salmon, conger eel, swordfish, sea bass, and more come grilled, or *a la plancha* (it comes sizzling out of the kitchen on a cast-iron plate), and are served alone or with tantalizing sauces. Everything on the menu is appealing; therefore, decisions are not easily made, so try getting started with an appetizer of one of eight different kinds of *ceviche.* The cozy, nautical-themed ambience includes a wooden siren hanging from a mock ship's bow, as well as bathroom doors that look like they lead to a sailor's bunk. Due to the whimsical decor, this is a good place for kids.

Constitución 111. © 2/738-0288. Main courses $7–$13. AE, DC, MC, V. Daily 1–4pm and 8:30pm–midnight. Metro: Baquedano.

Etniko *&&* ASIAN   Etniko is one of Santiago's hippest restaurants, serving Asian-influenced cuisine to the modern beat of house music played by resident DJs. The place is trendy and sophisticated, and frequented by Santiago's stylish yuppies and expats. The menu offers a diverse selection, but the mainstay is its 16 varieties of sushi. Also on offer are Japanese tempura and Chinese and Vietnamese stir-fries. The bar is a lively, fun place for a cocktail, and there is an extensive wine and champagne menu. Don't expect the place to fill until 9 or 10pm.

Constitución 172. ℂ 2/732-0119. Reservations recommended. Main courses $7–$14. AE, DC, MC, V. Daily noon–4pm and 8pm–midnight (until 2am Fri–Sat). Metro: Baquedano.

INEXPENSIVE

Caramaño ℛ CHILEAN   They call themselves the "anti-restaurant," and they're probably right. The Caramaño is totally anonymous from the street, and diners used to miss it until they put a sign up this year. Just ring the front bell to enter. Inside, graffiti-scrawled walls are something of a contrast to the tables filled with men and women in suits. Service is casual, and the food classic Chilean: inexpensive and good.

Purísima 257. ℂ 2/737-7043. Main courses $3–$9. AE, DC, MC, V. Daily 1–4pm and 7pm–12:30am. Metro: Baquedano.

Galindo CHILEAN   This local favorite is a hit for its cheap prices and its *comida casera:* simple, hearty dishes like your mother used to make—if your mother were Chilean, that is. Virtually any kind of typical meal served in Chilean homes can be found here, including *pastel de choclo* (a ground beef and chicken casserole) and *cazuela* (chicken soup with vegetables). The atmosphere is very casual; in the evening, the restaurant serves as a meeting place for writers, artists, and other local folk to share a bottle of wine and good conversation. There's additional seating outside on the sidewalk, and it's open late into the evening.

Dardignac 098. ℂ 2/777-0116. Main courses $3.50–$9; fixed lunch $5. AE, DC, MC, V. Mon–Sat noon–3am. Metro: Baquedano.

Off the Record ℛℛ *Finds* CHILEAN   Part old-fashioned cafe, part writer's haunt, this is a good place for a casual meal and a pisco sour. The cafe pays tribute to local writers and poets, giving them mike time every Monday evening at 8pm for readings and talks; and accordingly, the walls are covered with photos of famous artists, past and present. Even the placemat has the Last Supper retouched to figure Chilean artists in place of the disciples. Crepes, sandwiches, salads, and a few meat dishes—nothing fancy, but all good—can be found here. Try to grab one of the cozy booths up front.

Antonia Lopez de Bello 0155. ℂ 2/777-7710. Main courses $3.50–$8. AE, MC, V, D. Mon–Fri 9am–2pm; Sat 10am–2am; Sun 10am–1am. Metro: Baquedano.

PROVIDENCIA

Ask a cab driver or hotel clerk where to dine or drink in Providencia, and their knee-jerk reaction will be Avenida Suecia (at Av. Providencia). Don't listen to them. Apart from a few reasonably quiet bars, the three-block radius is like a frat house gone wild on weekends. Some here call it *gringolandia,* for its resemblance to the United States; happy hours and a couple of restaurants serving typical American food, including Cajun, can be found here.

For lunch or a casual dinner in Providencia, try **Los Insaciables,** Andres de Fuenzalida 40 (ℂ 2/232-3668), open Monday to Saturday 10am to 1am and Sunday noon to midnight. From 1 to 3:30pm and 8 to 11:30pm, the Italian restaurant serves slices of all-you-can-eat thin-crust pizza that you choose from passing waiters who tempt you with a dozen or so different varieties. All-you-can-eat pizza costs about $5.50. There are pastas and salads, too, and a pleasant, lively outdoor seating area.

EXPENSIVE

Aquí Está Coco ℛℛℛ SEAFOOD   This eclectic restaurant not only serves the freshest seafood, it's also a fun place to dine. Housed in a 140-year-old home, the restaurant is owned by one charismatic Jorge "Coco" Pacheco, who gave the place its name: "Here's Coco." Jorge traveled the world for 3 years and brought back boxes of crazy knickknacks and a wealth of tantalizing recipes, both of which give Aquí Está Coco its unique flavor. Nearly every kind of seafood is offered, including hake, swordfish, cod, sea bass, and more, served with sauces such as caper, black butter, or tomato-wine. I recommend the trout stuffed with king crab and a "thermidor" sauce—I order it every time I'm here. The appetizers are mouthwatering, such as crab cakes or broiled scallops in a barnacle sauce. Attentive service and a menu in English are reasons you'll see many gringos here, but it is just as popular with Chileans.

La Concepción 236. © 2/235-8649. www.aquiestacoco.cl. Main courses $9–$16. AE, DC, MC, V. Mon–Sat 1–3pm and 8–11pm. Metro: Pedro de Valdivia.

Astrid y Gastón ★★★ INTERNATIONAL   Frequently hailed by critics as the best new restaurant on the scene, Astrid y Gaston is also one of the most expensive. This is where you come to blow your budget on gourmet cuisine and wine. There is an on-site sommelier to help you select your cabernet, and the lengthy wine list stands out for the variety it offers. Astrid y Gastón is named for the Peruvian and German couple who own and run this restaurant (in Peru, where they launched their first restaurant, Gaston is considered a food god, and he has his own TV cooking show). The menu is eclectic, with Peruvian, Spanish, French, and Japanese influences, and the chef uses only the finest ingredients, combined so that each plate bursts with flavor and personality. Try the duck salad, the glazed pork, or the tuna filet bathed in a honey sauce. Dessert orders are usually placed early so they can make each one specially.

Antonio Bellet 201. © 2/650-9125. Reservations required. Main courses $10–$15. AE, DC, MC, V. Mon–Sat 1–3:30pm and 8pm–midnight. Metro: Pedro de Valdivia.

Enoteca/Camino Real ★★ *Moments* INTERNATIONAL/CHILEAN   There's nothing quite like dining in Santiago with the city lights twinkling at your feet. This restaurant/wine bar and museum is located atop Cerro San Cristóbal, affording sweeping views across the valley and up to the Andes. Smog is an issue if you come for lunch, but even bad air can't mask the thousands of lights at night. The menu is imaginative but expensive, with dishes such as lamb chops with lentils and bacon, grilled sole with barnacle raviolis, and chestnut pudding with cream. What you're really here for, ultimately, is the view, and it's worth the splurge.

Parque Metropolitano, Cerro San Cristóbal. © 2/232-1758. Reservations required. Main courses $15–$25; fixed-price lunches/dinners $20. AE, DC, MC, V. Daily 12:30–4pm and 8–11pm.

MODERATE

De la Ostia ★★ SPANISH   This brand-new tapas restaurant is perfect if you're just looking to order a few snacks rather than an entire meal. The young Spanish chef here stays true to his roots with tapas and *bocatas,* Spanish sandwiches, many of the ingredients imported directly from Spain and blended with fresh Chilean products. Try the octopus Gallego-style; the "Bomba," or potato balls with beef, onion, and chile; stuffed mushrooms; or the classic Spanish *tortilla.* The food here is of excellent quality, and the service is attentive, too.

Orrego Luco 065. © 2/335-1422. Reservations not accepted. Tapas $2–$7. AE, DC, MC, V. Mon–Fri 12:30–11pm; Sat 7pm–midnight. Metro: Pedro de Valdivia.

El Huerto ★★ VEGETARIAN   The popular El Huerto is the best vegetarian restaurant in Santiago, whipping up creative, appetizing dishes, from burritos to pasta to Chinese stir-fries. Add one of their fresh apple, raspberry, or peach juices, and it makes for a very healthful meal. Prices have risen slightly recently, but the owners have opened up a more economical cafe, La Huerta, next door, with a limited but good fixed-price menu for lunch only. The softly lit, mellow dining room of El Huerto has a restful atmosphere, and there is an on-site store selling mostly ecologically oriented books, calendars, posters, and more.

Orrego Luco 054. © 2/233-2690. Main courses $4–$10. AE, DC, MC, V. Mon–Thurs 12:30pm–midnight; Fri–Sat 12:30pm–1am. Cafe 9am–1pm.

Le Flaubert ★★ *(Finds* FRENCH/CHILEAN   Have you ever had a favorite restaurant that you felt inclined not to promote in fear of letting the secret out? This is mine. It's a little French/Chilean bistro whose understated elegance and romantic atmosphere is the ideal spot for a date or intimate meal among friends. If you are familiar with Chilean arts or television, you'll always spot a writer or actor here. The plant-filled outdoor dining area in the back patio is soothing and cool on a hot day, and service is attentive—something that is difficult to find in Chile. Le Flaubert offers an abbreviated menu presented on a chalkboard, with a delicious fare such as duck confit, crab casserole, and a recommended *corvina* (sea bass) with a shrimp and avocado sauce. Also, this is one of the only restaurants in Providencia that is open on Sunday.

Orrego Luco 125. © 2/231-9424. Main courses $9–$15. AE, DC, MC, V. Mon–Fri 12:30–11:30pm; Sat noon–11:30pm; Sun 12:30–9pm. Metro: Pedro de Valdivia.

A Pinch of Pancho ★★ NORTH AMERICAN   This restaurant serves American-style fare, such as barbecue ribs, Cajun chicken, and Caesar salads in a rather odd crossover atmosphere between comfortable elegance and American kitsch. The entrance is hidden behind a plant-covered metal fence; you'll see a *Miami Herald* newsstand by the door. Impeccable service and a menu that is 100% recognizable by Americans are the reasons you usually see a few U.S. businessmen having lunch here on weekdays. Don't miss the mouthwatering desserts, even apple pie a la mode.

General de Canto 45. © 2/235-1700. Reservations recommended. Main courses $7–$15. AE, DC, MC, V. Daily 1–3:30pm and 8–11:30pm. Metro: Pedro de Valdivia.

INEXPENSIVE

Bar Liguria ★★★ *(Moments* CHILEAN BISTRO   This bistro/bar is one of my favorites in Santiago. Bar Liguria (there are three locations in Santiago, but stick to the two mentioned here) is vibrant, warm, and the "in" spot in Providencia for actors, writers, businesspeople, and just about everyone else who comes to soak up the kitschy, bohemian atmosphere. The newest Liguria at Luis Thayer Ojeda Street has been a phenomenal success since opening day, due to its large and lofty upstairs dining room that allows energy to simply radiate through the place (the location at Manuel Montt is very lively, too, and it's the flagship restaurant that has been around for decades). The Liguria serves ample portions of emblematic Chilean dishes (and a few Italian dishes), as well as hefty sandwiches and salads that are reasonably priced. In the evening, the Bar Liguria is absolutely packed, and you might have to wait 10 to 15 minutes at the bar before you get a table.

Luis Thayer Ojeda 019: © 2/231-1393. Av. Providencia 1373: © 2/235-7914. Reservations not accepted. Main courses $4–$9. AE, DC, MC, V. Mon–Sat noon–3am. Metro: Los Leones (Ojeda branch), and Manuel Montt (Providencia branch).

Cafetto ★ CAFE   Cafetto is a pleasant little cafe where you can grab a snack or meal at any time of the day. It's popular for its creative fixed lunches, which usually sell out before 3pm, and for staying open all day long. The menu offers soups, sandwiches, pizzas, pastas, and more. There is a bright, glass-enclosed dining area. There's also an Internet cafe and English-language magazine store next door.

Av. Pedro de Valdivia 23 ✆ 2/252-0053. Main courses $4–$7. AE, DC, MC, V. Mon–Sat 7am–1am. Metro: Pedro de Valdivia.

LAS CONDES/EL BOSQUE/VITACURA

Around El Bosque and Goyenechea streets, you'll find everything and anything, from upscale French cuisine to a fast-food court. You'll spot gringos who live in Santiago at **New York Bagel,** Roger de Flor 2894 (✆ **2/246-3060**), or **Cafe Melba,** Don Carlos 2898 (✆ **2/232-4546**). Cafe Melba is a bustling, friendly restaurant and the best spot in El Bosque for lunch—and it serves American-style breakfasts such as eggs Benedict. It is even open early (from 7:30am on weekdays, 8:30am weekends). More thought is put into the lunch menu here than at nearby competing restaurants, with a seasonally changing menu that features pastas, salads, meats, and seafood, and there's an Internet cafe and an outdoor seating area on the premises.

You'll need a cab to reach restaurants in Vitacura, as there is no public transportation to that neighborhood.

EXPENSIVE

Agua ★★★ FUSION   This is Santiago's trendiest restaurant and the chic place to see and be seen. The minimalist design of concrete and glass can feel a bit cold, but it is as tasteful as the fusion cuisine the restaurant specializes in. The young chef at Agua has catapulted to culinary fame in Santiago for his creations that combine Chilean specialties such as Patagonian lamb with international recipes. Try the tuna, either tartar or rolled with king crab and served over an avocado and shrimp relish, or the shrimp bisque. Unlike many Chilean restaurants, the chefs here prepare food from behind an open window; it's an ego thing but enjoyable to watch nevertheless. The wine list is lengthy and well chosen, and there is outdoor seating during the summer.

Nueva Costanera 3467. ✆ 2/263-0008. Reservations recommended. Main courses $8–$15. AE, DC, MC, V. Mon–Sat 1–3:30pm and 8:30pm–midnight.

Enebro ★★ CHILEAN   This is an excellent spot for delicious high-end Chilean cuisine created by the now-defunct Hotel Carrera's (Chile's oldest five-star hotel, which closed in 2004) ex-chef. The dining area is formal; however, there is more informal seating outside on the sidewalk. Dishes such as beef with a king crab sauce and Chilote garlic vegetables, and a tuna carpaccio with an oyster vichyssoise are just two of the restaurant's offerings. There is a buffet lunch for about $10 and a daily executive menu. There are also excellent desserts, including homemade ice cream, and a menu in English, too.

El Bosque Norte 0210. ✆ 2/498-1890. Reservations recommended for dinner. Main courses $10–$15. AE, DC, MC, V. Mon–Sun 12:30–4pm and 7pm–1am. Metro: El Golf.

Europeo ★★★ CENTRAL EUROPEAN   Europeo, which many food critics consider the best restaurant in Santiago, is named for its cuisine: central European–based cuisine expertly prepared by the restaurant's Swiss-born and -trained chef. In a word, the food is heavenly, and the option of a more upscale main dining area and a more economical adjoining bistro makes Europeo suitable for any budget. Foie gras sautéed in a reduction of white wine, leg of lamb in a merlot sauce and served over polenta, and king crab ravioli stand out on the menu, as do the Austrian-style desserts. The bistro, La Brasserie, offers a less formal ambience and a menu that is not as elaborate as the restaurant's, but of excellent quality nonetheless.

Alonso de Córdova 2417. © 2/208-3603. Reservations recommended for the restaurant. Main courses $10–$15. AE, DC, MC, V. Mon–Sat 12:30–4:30pm and 7–11pm.

Happening 🎯🎯 ARGENTINE/CHILEAN   If you're in the mood for steak, this Argentine-owned restaurant (there's another Happening in Buenos Aires) is your place. The grilled meat selection is endless, cooked on an enormous indoor barbecue and served in a refined, semiformal ambience. There's also a variety of salads, fish, and pastas to choose from. It's housed on a busy corner in a handsome chocolate-brown building and is a good place to bring clients for lunch or to have a candlelit dinner in the evening.

Av. Apoquindo 3090. © 2/233-2301. Reservations recommended. Main courses $7–$13. AE, DC, MC, V. Mon–Sat noon–4pm and 8pm–midnight. Metro: El Golf.

La Cascade 🎯🎯 FRENCH   This traditional French restaurant has been on the scene since 1962, drawing Santiago's elite to savor traditional dishes such as coq au vin, duck à l'orange, escargot, and goose liver pâté. The executives who dine here are such frequent guests that they are welcomed by name. The menu is varied and includes meat, fowl, and seafood entrees, as well as an extensive wine list. Waiters deliver outstanding personal attention, and the atmosphere is elegant and stylish; in the evening, this candlelit restaurant is a good choice for a romantic dinner.

Av. Isidora Goyenechea 2930. © 2/232-2798. Reservations recommended. Main courses $10–$15. AE, DC, MC, V. Mon–Sat noon–4pm and 8pm–midnight. Metro: El Golf.

Osadía 🎯🎯🎯 FUSION   One of Santiago's newer restaurants boasts a fantastical design of semidemolished brick walls painted white and dripping with candles and spidery lamps that dangle above each white linen table. The food is as out there as the restaurant's decor, with high-concept blends of flavors and complicated presentations that can often be difficult to figure out how to eat. It's an offbeat place to dine, elegant yet fun, and they serve exquisite dishes such as rabbit cooked with tarragon and beer and served with spaetzle, crab ravioli with mushroom sauce, and smoked mussels in a cilantro vinaigrette. Instead of coffee, order an *aguita* (tea), which comes with a bushel of fresh herbs to choose from.

Tobalaba 477. © 2/232-2732. Reservations recommended. Main courses $9–$15. AE, DC, MC, V. Mon–Fri 1–4pm and 8pm–midnight; Sat 8pm–midnight.

MODERATE

Akarana 🎯🎯🎯 *(Finds* FUSION   Akarana is a welcome new addition to the El Bosque area, opened recently by the owner of the Cafe Melba, who is from New Zealand. She has created a menu that reflects the tastes from her home country, fusing Asian cuisine with New Zealand specialties to create a wonderful feast for the palate. Appetizers include gingery egg rolls and tempura, or try a plate of fresh oysters, served with one of three recipes. Move on to grilled, herbed sea bass with radish puree and aioli, one of their unconventional pizzas, or a steak with portobello mushrooms and Parmesan mashed potatoes. The all-white interiors are fresh and airy, and the wraparound patio dining area offers undoubtedly the most pleasant outdoor seating in the area.

Reyes Lavalle 3310. © 2/231-9667. Reservations recommended. Main courses $6–$10. AE, DC, MC, V. Daily noon–midnight. Metro: El Golf.

INEXPENSIVE

Tiramisu ✿✿ PIZZA/SALADS   This is a very popular lunch spot during the weekdays, so come early or make a reservation. Tiramisu serves thin-crust pizzas baked in a stone oven (which are large enough for two with a salad) and served in a delightful wood-and-checkered-tablecloth atmosphere. With dozens and dozens of combinations, from traditional to arugula with shaved Parmesan and artichokes, you'll have a hard time choosing your pie. There are fresh, delicious salads, too, and desserts that, of course, include tiramisu. The dining area is mostly outdoor covered seating.

Av. Isidora Goyenechea 3141. ✆ 2/335-5135. Reservations accepted. Main courses $4–$7. AE, DC, MC, V. Daily 1–4pm and 7pm–midnight. Metro: El Golf.

5 Seeing the Sights

Visitors with little time can pack in a lot of attractions in just 1 day, and, really, few spend more than 2 or 3 days here. Fortunately, the city's highlights are found in a localized area that runs along the length of the Mapocho River.

I recommend that visitors begin in *el centro*, the city's historic downtown and home to museums, cathedrals, cultural centers, and civic institutions. Read the descriptions below and choose a few attractions that pique your interest; then walk over to Cerro Santa Lucia. From this hilltop park, cross Avenida Alameda to see the Barrio Londres/Paris neighborhood, then backtrack to Lastarria Street and Santiago's burgeoning art-and-cafe neighborhood, Parque Forestal (and the Plaza Mulatto Gil de Castro). From here, it is just a short walk across the Mapocho River to the Bellavista neighborhood and Cerro San Cristóbal. If you still have time, wander around the shopping district of Providencia by crossing back over the river. If you have more than a day, you can take this tour at a more leisurely pace, or check out areas such as the Quinta Normal park.

There are public restrooms downtown at Ahumada 80 and 360, Estado 164, and Huerfanos 1216.

DOWNTOWN HISTORIC & CIVIC ATTRACTIONS
PLAZA DE ARMAS

Begin your tour of Santiago at the **Plaza de Armas** ✿✿✿ (Metro: Estación Plaza de Armas). Pedro de Valdivia, who conquered Chile for the Spanish crown, founded this plaza in 1541 as the civic nucleus of the country and populated it with the Royal Court of Justice (now the Natural History Museum), the Governor's Palace (now the Central Post Office), the Metropolitan Cathedral, and the grand residences of principal conquistadors, including Valdivia himself. In the mid-1800s, the somber plaza was spruced up with gardens and trees, creating a promenade that became a social center for fashionable society. Though fashionable society has since moved uptown, the plaza still ranks as one of Santiago's most dynamic areas to sit and watch the world go by. Between the hustle and bustle of city workers, there is an eclectic mix of characters who spend a portion of their day here: soap-box speakers and shoe shiners, charlatans and religious fanatics, garrulous old men playing chess and young couples embracing on park benches, street photographers and artists hawking paintings.

As for Pedro de Valdivia, there is an equestrian statue commemorating his conquest of Santiago, and a giant chiseled-stone sculpture dedicated to the indigenous people who lived here when he did. There is also *A la Libertad de América*, a marble statue commemorating independence from Spain.

Catedral Metropolitana and Museo de Arte Sagrado ⭐⭐   The newly renovated Metropolitan Cathedral stretches almost an entire city block, and its intricate interior handiwork warrants a quick duck inside. This is the fifth cathedral to have been erected at this site because of seismic damage. The cathedral began construction in 1748 but was completed in 1780 by the Italian architect Joaquín Toesca, who designed the building's neoclassical-baroque facade. Toesca virtually launched his career with this cathedral, and he went on to design many important buildings in colonial Chile, including La Moneda and the Governor's Palace. The tremendous cypress doors were carved by Jesuits; these open into three interior naves, the central of which holds the cathedral's ornate altar, brought from Munich in 1912 and made of marble, bronze, and lapis lazuli. Just off the main body of the church is the cathedral's religious museum, the Museo de Arte Sagrado, where you'll find a collection of paintings, furniture, antique manuscripts, and silverwork handcrafted by Jesuits.

Paseo Ahumada, on the west side of the plaza. No phone. Free admission. Mon–Sat 9am–7pm; Sun 9am–noon. Metro: Plaza de Armas.

Correo Central and Museo Postal   The pink, Renaissance-style Central Post Office was built in 1882 on the remains of what was once the colonial Governor's Palace and the post-independence Presidential Palace. After the building succumbed to fire in 1881, workers rebuilt, incorporating several of the old building's walls. In 1908, architect Ramón Feherman added a third floor and a glittering metal-framed glass cupola. Unless you have postcards to mail, there isn't much to see here.

Calle Puente, north side of the plaza. ℂ 2/601-0141. Free admission. Mon–Fri 9am–5pm. Metro: Plaza de Armas.

Palacio de la Real Audiencia/Museo Histórico Nacional ⭐⭐⭐   The handsome, neoclassical Palacio de la Real was completed in 1807, and in spite of the fact that the building has undergone several transformations, the original facade is still intact. The Palacio housed the Supreme Court for 2 years while under Spanish rule and then became the site of the first Chilean congressional session following independence. It is a fascinating stop here in the Plaza because today the Palacio is home to the National History Museum, with more than 70,000 artifacts and collectibles from the colonial period, including antiques, clothing, suits of armor, weapons, home appliances, industrial gadgets, flags— you name it. There is also a collection of money and medallions, including tokens used at salt mines. Perhaps the most insightful exhibition here is the interpretive timeline and photomontage of the history and social issues that have shaped modern Chile.

Plaza de Armas 951. ℂ 2/638-1411. Admission 80¢ adults, 50¢ children under 18; free Sun and holidays. Tues–Sun 10am–5:30pm. Metro: Plaza de Armas.

NEAR THE PLAZA DE ARMAS

At the southwest corner of the plaza is **Paseo Ahumada,** which bisects **Paseo Huérfanos** a block away. Like Plaza de Armas, these lively pedestrian walkways are a good place to get a feel for downtown Santiago and the people who work here. Both walkways are lined continuously with shops and restaurants, and they can get frenzied during the lunch hour. This is also where you'll find a few of the city's renowned cafes that serve "coffee with legs," meaning waitresses in skimpy ensembles serving ogling businessmen from behind a stand-up bar. **Café Haiti** (ℂ 2/737-4323; locations at Ahumada 140 and 336, Huérfanos 1194, and Bandera 335) and **Café Caribe** (ℂ 2/695-7081; locations at Ahumada 120 and

Huérfanos 796, 945, and 1164) are two of the better-known cafes, and because both are tame compared to the raunchier versions with darkened windows, these two cafes are patronized by women as well as men.

Basílica de la Merced ⭐   One block from the Casa Colorada on Merced at the corner of MacIver sits this intriguing neo-Renaissance-style church and museum. Built in 1735, the church boasts a magnificent Bavarian baroque pulpit and arched naves. What makes this church stand out from the others is its collection of Easter Island art, including wooden Moai sculptures. There are also 78 wood and ivory Christ Child figures, among other religious artifacts.

MacIver 341, corner of Merced. No phone. Admission 75¢ adults, 25¢ students. Tues–Fri 10am–1pm and 3–6pm; Sat 10am–1pm. Metro: Plaza de Armas.

Casa Colorada Santiago Museum ⭐ *Overrated*   The Casa Colorada is a half-block from the Plaza de Armas, and it is widely regarded as the best-preserved colonial structure in Santiago, built between 1769 and 1779 as a residence for the first president of Chile, Mateo de Toro y Zambrano. Today it houses the Santiago Museum, depicting the urban history of the city until the 19th century. This museum always comes recommended, but I find the whole production somewhat amateurish and small. Kids will like it here more than adults. There is also a **visitor center** with information about Santiago here.

Merced 860. ☎ 2/633-0723. Admission 70¢. Tues–Fri 10am–6pm; Sat 10am–5pm; Sun 11am–2pm. Metro: Plaza de Armas.

Ex-Congreso Nacional and Palacio de los Tribunales ⭐   Two blocks from Plaza de Armas you'll find these two grand civic buildings across the street from each other on Compañía. The ex–Congress Building, with its French neo-classical design and Corinthian pillars, is a handsome edifice inaugurated in 1901. The National Congress convened here until the coup d'état on September 11, 1973, which dissolved the congress; Pinochet eventually moved the congress to Valparaíso. The dove-white building is surrounded by lush gardens and is now occupied by a branch of the Ministry of Foreign Affairs. Across the street, the Palace of the Courts of Justice stretches the entire block. The palace is home to the Supreme Court, the Appeals Court, and the Military Court, and it was the site of the birth of the First National Government Assembly. The building's stern exterior belies the beauty found once you step inside. Leave your ID at the front, and take a stroll through the exquisite hallway whose vaulted metal and glass ceiling runs the length of the building, dappling the walls with light.

Morandé and Compañía. No phone. Palacio Mon–Fri 1–7pm.

Museo Chileno de Arte Precolombino ⭐⭐⭐   Heading back on Merced and past the plaza to Bandera, you'll find the highly regarded Chilean Museum of Pre-Columbian Art, housed in the old Royal Customs House that was built in neoclassical design in 1807. This is one of the better museums in Chile, for both its collection of pre-Columbian artifacts and its inviting design. You can spend up to an hour here, no more, as the collection is encompassing but not as extensive as, say, the Anthropological Museum of Mexico. That said, there still are more than 1,500 objects on display here, including textiles, metals, paintings, figurines, and ceramics spread through seven exhibition rooms. It's not a stuffy old museum, but a vivid exhibition of indigenous life and culture before the arrival of the Spanish. The material spans from Mexico to Chile, incorporating all regions of Latin America divided into four areas: Mesoamérica, Intermedia, Andina, and Surandina. Downstairs there's a patio cafe and a well-stocked bookstore that also sells music, videos, and reproductions of Indian art, textiles, and jewelry.

Bandera 361. © 2/688-7348. www.precolombino.cl. Admission $3.25 adults, free for students and children, free Sun and holidays for everyone. Tues–Sun 10am–6pm. Closed Mon.

PLAZA CONSTITUCION & THE COMMERCE CENTER

The Plaza Constitución, located between streets Agustinas, Morandé, Moneda, and Teatinos, is an expansive plaza used primarily as a pedestrian crossway. It's also the site of the famous **Palacio de la Moneda** ⟨★★⟩, the Government Palace that was first built as headquarters of the Royal Mint (hence its name). The largest building erected by the Spanish government during the 18th century, the palace was criticized for being too ostentatious, but today it's considered one of the finest examples of neoclassical architecture in Latin America. The president does not reside here; instead, the building houses presidential offices. You cannot enter the building, though you may walk through its central plaza.

Joaquín Toesca, the Italian architect responsible for setting the neoclassical tone of civic buildings in Santiago, directed the design of the palace until his death in 1799. From 1846 to 1958, it was the official presidential residence, and it continued as presidential headquarters until the infamous coup d'état on September 11, 1973, when Pinochet's troops shelled and bombed the building. During the event, ex-President Allende killed himself, and Pinochet stepped in as a dictator who would run the country for the next 17 years.

Try to visit to the palace at 10am during the **changing of the guard** ⟨★★⟩, when soldiers march in step in front of the palace—though they do so every other day, so there's no guarantee you'll witness it. Across Alameda is the **Plaza Bernardo O'Higgins,** named for Chile's liberator and first president. His remains are buried under the monument dedicated to him in the center of the plaza.

One block from the plaza at Moneda and Bandera is the **Bolsa de Comercio** ⟨★★⟩ (© 2/399-3000; www.bolsadesantiago.cl), Santiago's stock market exchange, housed in a 1917 building that is topped with an elegant metal dome roof. Inside the Bolsa, traders group around La Rueda (The Wheel), a circular railing where they conduct hectic transactions—few people know that you can observe the action Monday to Friday 10:30 to 11:20am, 12:30 to 1:20pm, and 4 to 4:30pm. The Bolsa is a triangular building set among several picturesque cobblestone streets that boast some of the most intriguing architectural styles in Santiago (New York, La Bolsa, and Club de la Unión streets).

ATTRACTIONS OFF THE ALAMEDA

Hectic, heavily trafficked Avenida Bernardo O'Higgins is commonly referred to as *la Alameda,* and it's the main artery that runs through downtown Santiago. You'll find some of the city's interesting attractions along this avenue, but the ear-splitting noise can give you a headache if you're walking along it for too long.

Barrio París-Londres ⟨★★⟩ This incongruous neighborhood is just a few blocks in diameter and was built between the 1920s and 1930s on the old gardens of the Monastery of San Francisco. The neighborhood oozes charm—it looks as if a chunk of Paris's Latin Quarter was airlifted and dropped down in the middle of downtown Santiago because the cobblestone streets of this neighborhood end at tacky '70s-style *gallerias* and other mismatched buildings on the neighborhood's outskirts.

The streets between Prat and Santa Rosa, walking south of Alameda.

Biblioteca Nacional ⭐ The country's National Library is housed in a French neoclassical stone building that occupies an entire city block. Inside its handsomely painted interiors are over six million works, as well as historical archives and a map room, although the only really accessible attraction here is the Jose Medina reading room, offering a glimpse into an early-21st-century library with antique books stacked in tiers, leather-topped reading desks, and a giant spinning globe.

Av. Bernardo O'Higgins 651. © 2/360-5259. Mon–Fri 9am–6:30pm.

Calle Dieciocho and Palacio Cousiño Macul Heading west on Avenida Alameda, past the giant Entel tower and across the street, is the street **Calle Dieciocho,** where Santiago's elite lived during the turn of the 20th century. The tourism brochures tout this street as an opportunity to step back in time and marvel at the elegant barrio that once defined downtown Santiago, but I find the architecture far more interesting in Barrio Brasil across the Panamericana Highway. There is one attraction that merits mention, however: the **Palacio Cousino Macul** ⭐⭐, located at Calle Dieciocho 438, once the residence of Chile's most successful entrepreneurial dynasty, the Goyenechea-Cousiño family. Apart from their well-known wine business and ownership of the Lota coal mines, the family also had interests in copper, thoroughbred horses, shipping, and railways. When construction was completed in 1878, the palace dazzled society with its opulence: lavish parquet floors, Bohemian crystal chandeliers, Italian hand-painted ceramics, and French tapestries—nearly everything in the home was imported from Europe. If anything, the museum offers a chance to view the most exquisite European craftsmanship available during the late 1800s.

It is a 10-minute walk south down Dieciocho to the palace, or you can take the Metro to Estación Toesca (turn left when you walk out). Probably the best way to get here is to take a cab from downtown. If you visit the Palacio, take a 10-minute detour around the corner (east on San Ignacio) to Parque Almagro, a scruffy park that nevertheless affords a view of the little-known, almost Gaudiesque **Basílica del Santísimo Sacramento,** constructed between 1919 and 1931, which was modeled after the Sacre Coeur church in Montmartre, Paris.

Dieciocho 438. © 2/698-5063. Admission $2 adults, $1 children under 12. Bilingual tours given Tues–Fri 9:30am–11:30pm and 2:30–4pm; Sat–Sun 9:30am–12:30pm.

Iglesia, Convento y Museo de San Francisco ⭐⭐⭐ The Church of San Francisco, built between 1586 and 1628, is the oldest standing building in Santiago, having miraculously survived three devastating earthquakes. At the altar sits the famous *Virgen del Socorro,* the first Virgin Mary icon in Chile brought here to Santiago by Pedro de Valdivia, the conquistador of Chile. Valdivia claimed the icon had warded off Indian attacks. The highlights, however, are the museum and the convent, the latter with its idyllic patio planted with flora brought from destinations as near as the south of Chile and as far away as the Canary Islands. The garden, with its bubbling fountain and cooing white doves, is so serene you'll find it hard to believe you're in downtown Santiago. The museum is small, but it houses a venerable collection of one of the largest and best-conserved examples of 17th-century art in South America, 54 paintings depicting the life and miracles of San Francisco de Assisi. A sizeable portion of colonial-period furniture, keys, paintings, and other items were crafted in Peru when it still was the seat of the Spanish government in Latin America.

Av. Bernardo O'Higgins. © 2/638-3238. Admission to convent and museum $1. Tues–Sat 10am–1pm and 3–6pm; Sun and holidays 10am–2pm.

CERRO SANTA LUCIA & PLAZA MULATO GIL DE CASTRO

Materializing as if out of nowhere on the edge of the city's downtown limits, the lavishly landscaped and historically significant **Cerro Santa Lucía** 🏛🏛🏛 is a triangular-shape hilltop park, one of the more delightful attractions in Santiago. This is where Pedro de Valdivia, the conqueror of Chile, founded Santiago in 1540 for the crown of Spain. For centuries, the rocky outcrop was seen as more of an eyesore than a recreational area (the Mapuche Indians called it *Huelén,* or "curse"), until 1872, when 150 prisoners were put to work landscaping the hill and carving out walkways and small squares for the public to enjoy. Today office workers, tourists, couples, schoolchildren, and solitary thinkers can be seen strolling along leafy terraces to the Caupolicán Plaza for a sweeping view of Santiago. It's open daily from 9am to 8pm from September to March, 9am to 7pm from April to August; admission is free, though you'll be asked to sign a guest registry when entering. Enter at Avenida Alameda and St. Lucia, or St. Lucia and Merced; alternatively, you could take the elevator to the top on St. Lucia Street at Agustinas. At the top of the hill is the Castle Hidalgo, which operates as an event center. For information about the park or for maps of Santiago, visit the **Tourism Office** at the entrance on Avenida Alameda (✆ **2/632-7783;** open daily 9am–1:30pm and 3–6pm). The tourism office has bilingual tours of the hill on Thursday only, at 11am. The **Centro de Exposición de Arte** is also here, offering a variety of indigenous crafts, clothing, and jewelry from all over Chile. Across the street is a bustling crafts and junk market, the **Centro Artesanal de Santa Lucía,** with handicrafts, T-shirts, and more.

Behind the park, at José Victorino Lastarria 307, you'll find the **Plaza Mulato Gil de Castro** 🏛🏛🏛 (closed Sun). This tiny plaza sits amid Santiago's up-and-coming, artsy neighborhood Lastarria, and I highly recommend stopping here even if for a few minutes to check out the antique and book vendors who sell from Thursday to Sunday (sometimes other days, too, when they feel like it). The plaza is named for the 18th-century Peruvian army captain and portrait painter José Gil. Today the plaza is home to two of the prettiest cafes in Santiago, the newish arts museum, **Museo de Artes Visuales,** and the **Museo Anthropología** 🏛🏛🏛 (no phone; both are open Mon–Sun 10:30am–6:30pm, $3 admission price covers admission to both museums). The split-level, quiet interiors of the museum are a restful place to view paintings and sculptures by some of Chile's most promising young and contemporary artists. There is a good shop here that sells art, posters, and books, too. Next door, the newly renovated cultural anthropology museum displays 3,300 pieces of ceramics, textiles, and other artifacts produced by indigenous peoples from all over Chile. During the afternoon, the restaurant "**R**" has a few tables outside that are good spots for watching an eclectic group of students, hipsters, and businessmen walk by.

PARQUE FORESTAL

This slender, manicured park, landscaped in 1900 with rows of native and imported trees, skirts the perimeter of the Río Mapocho from Vicuña Mackenna at the Metro station Baquedano to its terminus at the Mapocho station. The winding path takes walkers past several great attractions and makes for a pleasant half-hour to 1-hour stroll, especially on a sunny afternoon when the air is clear. If you plan to walk the entire park, try to finish at the Mercado Central (see below) for lunch.

Estación Mapocho 🏛   Built in 1912 on reclaimed land formed by the canalization of the Río Mapocho, this behemoth of a building served as the train station for the Santiago-Valparaíso railway. In 1976 it was abandoned, and 15 years later repaired and converted into a cultural center that hosts events such as rock concerts and the International Book Fair, which takes place the last week of November. If you're already at the Mercado Central, walk across the street for a look inside (the center has a bookstore, restaurant, and crafts store). Architecturally, the only thing worth viewing is the 40-ton copper, marble, and glass roof.

Bandera and Río Mapocho. © 2/361-1761. www.estacionmapocho.cl. Daily 9am–5pm; other hours according to events.

Mercado Central ★★★ It's the quintessential tourist stop, but the colorful, chaotic Mercado Central is nevertheless a highlight for visitors to Santiago. Chile's economy depends on the exportation of natural products such as fruits, vegetables, and seafood, and the market here displays everything the country has on offer. Lively and staffed by pushy fishmongers who artistically gut and fillet while you watch, the market displays every kind of fish and shellfish available along the Chilean coast. The market's lofty steel structure was fabricated in England and assembled here; it is a beautiful structure especially for its high windows that allow light to softly cascade in. In the center of the market, baskets overflow with fresh produce, and there are a few handicraft stalls. Depending on your perspective, the barking fishmongers and waiters who harangue you to choose *their* sea bass or *their* restaurant can be entertaining or somewhat annoying. Try to plan your visit during the lunch hour, for a rich bowl of *caldillo de congrio* (a thick conger eel soup) or a tangy *ceviche* at one of the many typical restaurants (see "Where to Dine," earlier in this chapter).

Vergara and Av. 21 de Mayo. No phone. Daily 7am–3pm. Metro: Cal y Canto.

Palacio de Bellas Artes ★★ The Palacio de Bellas Artes houses both the Fine Arts and Contemporary Art museums in a regal neoclassical building inaugurated on the eve of Chile's centennial independence day in 1910. The palace has a noteworthy glass cupola that softly lights the vast lobby. The importance of the permanent installations in the Fine Arts museum may be debatable (an uneven mix of Chilean and international artists' works since the colonial period), but lately they've been hosting temporary exhibitions of international artists such as Damian Hirst, Henri-Cartier Bresson, and David Hockney, to name a few, so it's worth stopping by to see what is on offer. The Contemporary Museum features more than 2,000 paintings, sculptures, and other works by well-known Latin American artists.

Parque Forestal, by way of Jose Miguel de la Barra. © 2/632-7760. www.mnba.cl. Admission Museum of Fine Arts 75¢ adults, 35¢ students; Museum of Contemporary Art 55¢ adults, 30¢ students. Museum of Fine Arts Tues–Sun 10am–7pm. Museum of Contemporary Art Tues–Fri 11am–7pm; Sat–Sun 11am–2pm. Guided tours Tues–Fri 10am–6pm; Sat–Sun noon–4:30pm.

BARRIO BELLAVISTA & PARQUE METROPOLITANO

These two attractions are next to each other, so it makes sense to see both in one visit. But here's a word of caution: The sweeping views at the top of Cerro San Cristóbal can be ruined if it is a particularly smoggy day. But if the air is clear, this attraction rates as one of the best in the city, offering a breathtaking panorama of sprawling Santiago and its city limits that stop just short of the craggy Andes.

The Cerro San Cristóbal and its Metropolitan Park rise high above Santiago's bohemian quarter, **Bellavista** ★★. One of the more interesting neighborhoods in the city, its streets are lined with trees and colorful antique homes, many of which have been converted into restaurants and studios for artists and musicians.

It's a pleasant place for an afternoon stroll; in the evening, Bellavista pulses to the beat of music pouring from its many discos and bars.

You might begin your visit with a trip to Bellavista's prime attraction, **La Chascona** ★★★, Fernando Márquez de la Plata 0192 (📞 2/777-8741). Located a block east of the Plaza Caupolican (entrance point to the Parque Metropolitano), this is one of three homes once owned by Chile's most famous literary artist, the Nobel Prize–winning poet Pablo Neruda. As with Neruda's other two homes, La Chascona was built to resemble a ship, with oddly shaped rooms that wind around a compact courtyard. It's fascinating to wander through Neruda's quirky home and observe his collection of precious antiques and whimsical curios collected during his travels. Neruda's library is especially interesting, and it holds the antique encyclopedia set he purchased with a portion of his earnings from the Nobel Prize. The home is headquarters for the Fundación Pablo Neruda, which provides guided tours. Admission is $3.25 for adults on a Spanish tour and $5 for the English tour, and it's open Tuesday through Sunday from 10am to 1pm and 3 to 6pm. Call to make a reservation; otherwise, if you just show up, you may need to wait in the cafe until a guide frees up.

The **Parque Metropolitano** ★★★, atop Cerro San Cristóbal, is a 730-hectare (1,803-acre) park and recreation area with swimming pools, walking trails, a botanical garden, a zoo, picnic grounds, restaurants, and children's play areas. It's the lungs of Santiago, and city dwellers use the hill's roads and trails for jogging, biking, or just taking a stroll. The park is divided into two sectors, Cumbre and Tupahue, both of which can be accessed by car, cable car, funicular, or foot. In Bellavista, head to the end of Calle Pío Nono to Plaza Caupolicán, where you'll encounter a 1925 **funicular** that lifts visitors up to a lookout point, open Monday 1 to 6pm and Tuesday through Sunday 10am to 6:30pm; tickets cost $2 adults, $1 children.

Along the way, the funicular stops at the **Jardín Zoológico** (📞 2/777-6666) ★★, open Tuesday through Sunday from 10am to 6pm; tickets cost $2.50 adults, $1.25 children ages 3 to 13. This surprisingly diverse zoo features more than 200 species of mammals, reptiles, and birds—it's a rather outmoded, sad affair, but fascinating just the same for how close you're allowed to get to some of the animals' cages compared to zoos in the U.S. Unfortunately, this closeness compels kids to feed monkeys cotton candy and Fanta.

At the top where the funicular ends, a lookout point is watched over by a 22m-high (72-ft.) statue of the **Virgen de la Inmaculada Concepción,** which can be seen from all over the city. Below the statue is the *teleférico* **(aerial tram)** that connects the two sections of the park, open Monday 1:30 to 5:30pm and Tuesday to Sunday from 11:30am to 5:30pm; tickets cost $2.25 adults, $1 children. A round-trip ticket combo with the funicular costs $4 adults, $2 children. The teleférico is a lot of fun, especially for kids, but it can be a roasting oven in the summertime heat.

Arriving at Tupahue, the Mapuche name for this hill that means "place of God," you'll find the **Piscina Tupahue** and **Piscina Antilén.** These are not your run-of-the-mill YMCA pools; in fact, I quite recommend them for a hot summer day because they are clean and attractively landscaped and, in the case of **Piscina Antilén,** offer sweeping views of the city (no phone; both open Nov 15–Mar 15 Tues–Sun 10am–7pm; $7 adults, $5 children). You'll need a cab to Antilén, or you can walk northeast past the Camino Real to get here, about a 10-minute walk.

The **Camino Real** and its wine museum **Museo Enoteca** (📞 2/232-1758) are on the left side of the road when walking down from the tram stop. The museum is disappointing, but the restaurant is worth the visit for the marvelous views from the dining area and patio (p. 238). The museum offers a basic wine tasting for $2 per glass. Nearby is the **Botanical Garden Mapulemu** (no phone). It's open daily from 9am to 6pm; admission is free weekdays, 25¢ weekends. From Tupahue, you can either head back on the tram to Cumbre and the funicular or take the Valdivia *teleférico* down, which will drop you off at the end of Avenida Pedro de Valdivia. It's about an 8-block walk down to Avenida Providencia. Of course, this trip can be done in the reverse direction, which might be more convenient if you're starting from Providencia or Las Condes.

Note: If you drive up to the Camino Real, enter and leave via Avenida Pedro de Valdivia because the restaurant/museum will give you a free entrance voucher. The Parque Metropolitano's hours are daily from 8:30am to 9pm.

PARQUE QUINTA NORMAL

One of Santiago's loveliest parks, the Quinta Normal commenced in 1841 as a plant-acclimatization nursery for imported species, when the area was still outside the boundaries of Santiago. The park grew to include 38 hectares (96 acres) of grassy lawns, dozens of varieties of trees (splendid mature examples of Monterey pine, Douglas firs, Sequoias, Babylonian willows, and more), sporting facilities, and a lagoon with paddle boat rental. There are also four museums here, including the **Natural History Museum** (© 2/680-4600; www.mnhn.cl), open Tuesday through Saturday from 10am to 5:30pm, Sunday from noon to 5:30pm; admission is 75¢ adults, 35¢ children under 18. The museum occupies a handsome neoclassical building; however, the museum is underfunded and many of the displays are in need of renovation. More worthwhile is the **Artequín Museum**, Av. Portales 3530 (© 2/681-8656), open Tuesday through Friday from 11am to 1:30pm (doors shut at 1:30pm, but if inside already, you may stay until 3pm); Saturday and Sunday 10am to 5pm; admission is $1 adults, 50¢ students; Sunday free.

The museum is housed in a cast-iron building accented with a kaleidoscope of colorful glass; it was first used as the Chilean exhibition hall at the 1889 Parisian centenary of the French Revolution. Workers took the building apart, shipped it to Santiago, and reassembled it here. The museum displays only reproductions of famous paintings by artists from Picasso to Monet, the idea being to introduce visitors to important works of art. A very popular museum with kids here is the **Museo de Ciencia y Tecnología (Museum of Science and Technology)** (© 2/681-6022) for its engaging, hands-on displays. It is open Tuesday through Friday from 10am to 5pm, Saturday and Sunday from 11am to 6pm; admission is $1 adults, 50¢ students. At the southern end of the park, on Avenida Portales, is the fourth museum here in the park, the **Museo Ferroviario (Railway Museum)** (© 2/681-4627), with railway exhibits that include 14 steam engines and railway carriages, including the train that once connected Santiago with Mendoza, until 1971. It's open Tuesday through Friday from 10am to 5:30pm, Saturday and Sunday from 11am to 5:30pm; admission is $1 adults, 50¢ students.

ESPECIALLY FOR KIDS

The Parque Metropolitano Zoo, the aerial tram at Cerro San Cristóbal, the Museum of Science and Technology, and the Railway Museum described above are all kid-friendly. The spacious **Parque Bernardo O'Higgins** is a tired, worn-down park frequented by blue-collar Santiaguinos who come to fly kites and barbecue on the weekends; nothing worth seeing here except **Fantasilandia,** a modern amusement park (℃ **2/476-8600**); admission is $5.50 adults, $4 children. It's open April through November on Saturday, Sunday, and holidays only from 11am to 8:30pm; December through March Tuesday through Friday from 2 to 8pm, Saturday and Sunday from 11am to 8pm. It's the largest amusement park in Chile, with four stomach-churning roller coasters, a toboggan ride, and a haunted house. The **Museo Interactivo Mirador (MIM)** 𝔸𝔸𝔸 and the **Santiago Aquarium** 𝔸𝔸 are neighbors within an 11-hectare (27-acre) park in the La Granja barrio. Inaugurated in 2000, MIM dedicates itself to providing children with an introduction to the world of science and technology. Adults will be fascinated by MIM, too. The ultramodern museum has more than 300 exhibits, mostly interactive displays that cover the range of paleontology, computer animation, robotics, and 3-D cinema. You could spend nearly a full day here if you choose to check out the aquarium and its frolicking sea lion show. Buy a combo ticket for both if you have enough time. To get here, take Metro Line 5 to the Mirador stop (two entrances: Sebastopol 90 and Punta Arenas 6711; ℃ **2/280-7800;** www.mim.cl; $5 adults, $3.25 children; combo ticket with aquarium $8 adults, $6 children).

ORGANIZED TOURS

Major hotels work with quality tour operators and can recommend a tour even at the last minute; however, you'd be better off planning ahead and reserving a tour with an operator who can show you the more interesting side of Santiago or who is more attuned to foreign guests' desires or needs (that is, a guide who is truly bilingual). Last-minute city group tours are available daily from travel agencies such as **ADS Mundo** (℃ **2/387-7069;** www.adsmundo.com) and **CTS Tours** ℃ **2/251-0400;** www.ctsturismo.cl). These city tours might include a visit to Cerro St. Lucía, the Plaza de Armas, Club Hípico, the Estación Mapocho, and the Fine Arts Museum, among other attractions. The average price per person is $30.

The following tour operators are my picks. All three are operated by Chilean-American outfits.

- **Santiago Culinary Tours**, operated by American expat Liz Caskey, presents a unique way to see, and taste, a different side of Santiago. The tour kicks off with a walking tour through Barrio Brasil, the oldest neighborhood in Santiago, to view historic plazas and turn-of-the-20th-century architecture, followed by a visit to a typical farmer's market to purchase ingredients for lunch. Lunch and cocktails are served at Liz's 1920s restored loft in Barrio Brasil, and guests are welcome to join in on the cooking if they wish. Tours are available Tuesday through Sunday and depart at 10:30am. The tour lasts about 4 to 5 hours. For more information and a price quote, contact ℃ **2/681-6939** or 9/821-9230; www.lizcaskey.com.
- **Chip Tours** is the only agency to offer a deeper understanding of the Pinochet era with its "Human Rights Legacy" tour. The tour visits the landmarks that were central to the 17-year military dictatorship of Augusto Pinochet, such as La Moneda, the Grimaldi Peace Park, the General Cemetery, the Military Academy, and the Pinochet Foundation. A half-day tour visits two sites; a full-day tour visits four to five sites and includes a typical Chilean lunch. Prices depend on how many people are in your group. They are, per person, half-day: $60 (two guests), $30 (four guests); full day $100 (two guests), $70 (four guests). Prices drop more if there are more than four

guests. Book at least 24 hours in advance. Chip Travel can be reached at ⓒ 2/777-5376 or www.chip.cl.

- **Santiago Adventures** offers a half-day historical and cultural tour of the city, beginning in the Plaza de Armas and visiting La Moneda, the Paris-Londres neighborhood, the San Francisco colonial church, the Bellavista neighborhood, and the Cerro San Cristóbal. Daily tours are half-day (4 hours) or full day (8 hours), and visitors may choose one museum for a half-day tour or two for a full-day tour: Cousiño Macul museum, the pre-Columbian Museum, or Pablo Neruda's house. Tours cost, per person, half-day: $70 (two or three guests), $65 (four or five guests); full day, including lunch: $135 (two or three guests), $125 (four or five guests). Santiago Adventures can be reached at ⓒ 2/334-6989; www.santiagoadventures.com.

SPECTATOR SPORTS & RECREATION

GYMS   Try **Fisic,** Tobalaba 607 in Providencia (ⓒ 2/232-6641), or **Sportlife,** Bandera 101 downtown and Helvecia 280 in Vitacura (ⓒ 2/236-5080). Both charge about $8 per visit.

HORSE RACING   Two racetracks hold events on either Saturday or Sunday throughout the year: the recommended **Club Hípico,** Blanco Encalada 2540 (ⓒ 2/683-9600), and the **Hipódromo Chile,** Avenida Vivaceta in Independencia (ⓒ 2/270-9200). The Hípico's classic event, El Ensayo, takes place the first Sunday in November and always provides a colorful Chilean spectacle as attendees arm themselves with grills and barbecue meat in the middle of the racetrack oval. The Hipódromo's classic St. Leger is the second week in December, but it is farther to get to than the Club Hípico.

POOLS   Your best bet are the public pools **Tupahue** and **Antilén,** atop Cerro San Cristóbal; see "Barrio Bellavista & Parque Metropolitano" above for details.

SKIING   For information about skiing in the area, see chapter 13.

SOCCER (FOOTBALL)   Top football (as soccer is called here) games are held at three stadiums: **Estadio Monumental,** Avenida Grecia and Marathon; **Universidad de Chile,** Camp de Deportes 565 (both are in the Ñuñoa neighborhood); and **Universidad Católica,** Andrés Bello 2782, in Providencia. Check the sports pages of any local newspaper for game scheduling. Though *fútbol* is popular in Chile, fans aren't quite as maniacal as they are in Argentina and Brazil.

TENNIS   Try one of the 22 courts at **Parque Tenis,** Cerro Colorado 4661, near the Parque Arauco mall in Las Condes (ⓒ 2/208-6589).

6 Shopping

SHOPPING CENTERS

Santiago is home to two American-style megamalls: **Parque Arauco,** Av. Kennedy 5413, open Monday through Saturday from 10am to 9pm, Sunday and holidays from 11am to 9pm; and **Alto Las Condes,** Av. Kennedy 9001, open Monday through Sunday from 10am to 10pm. Both offer a hundred or so national brands and well-known international chains, junk-food courts, and multiscreen theaters (Parque Arauco is closer to Providencia). The best way to get to Parque Arauco is by cab (about $4–$5 from Providencia), or take the Metro to Escuela Militar and take a blue "Metro Bus" that will drop you off at the door. Note that weekends are hectic and jam-packed with shoppers. There are no metro stops near Alto Las Condes.

Like most Latin American nations, many Chileans sell out of shopping *galerías,* labyrinthine minimalls with dozens of compact shops that independent vendors can rent for considerably less money than a regular storefront. Most are cheap to midrange clothing stores, upstart designers with fun styles but so-so fabrics, or importers of crafts, antiques dealers, tailors, and so on. A vibrant, bustling example is the **Mall Panorámico,** Avenida Ricardo Lyon and Avenida 11 de Septiembre (Metro: Pedro de Valdivia), with 130 shops and a department store across the street. For funky boutiques, try the "Drugstore," on Avenida Providencia between Las Urbinas and Avenida de Fuenzalida (walk back to where the café seating is and go left). Several blocks away on General Holley, Suecia, and Bucarest streets, you'll find more expensive, upscale clothing boutiques. Chile's version of Rodeo Drive is Alonso de Córdova in the Vitacura neighborhood—there are also good-quality boutiques here, including furniture, household goods, and jewelry.

CRAFTS MARKETS

Crafts markets can be found around Santiago, as either permanent installations or weekly events; however, I recommend **Los Domínicos** above all other markets for selection and quality (Av. Apoquindo 9085; no phone), open Tuesday through Sunday and holidays from 10:30am to 7pm. The permanent shopping area, designed like a mock colonial village, is a one-stop shopping arcade for those who want to buy gifts all in one fell swoop. There are hand-knit sweaters, lapis lazuli, arts and crafts, antiques (expensive), and Chilean traditional wear such as ponchos. It sits next to the (usually closed) **San Vicente Ferrer de Los Domínicos Church,** built in the 18th century. To get here, you'll need a taxi because the market is high in Las Condes. The cost to get here is $3 to $5 one-way if coming from Providencia.

If you are short on time, then try the largest market in Santiago, the **Feria Santa Lucía,** at Cerro Santa Lucía (on the other side of Alameda; Metro: Santa Lucía). The outdoor market is hard to miss, with its soaring billboards and sprawl of stalls hawking clothing, jewelry, and arts and crafts—even some antiques and collectibles. Hours vary, but it's generally open Monday through Saturday (sometimes Sun) from 10am to 7pm. In **Bellavista** on weekends, a crafts fair runs along Calle Pío Nono (Metro: Salvador), where you'll find dozens of booths selling a variety of goods such as jewelry and old records, but it's pretty scrappy and most vendors are do-it-yourselfers with trinkets displayed on fabric laid out on the sidewalk. For antiques fairs, see below.

SHOPPING FROM A TO Z
ANTIQUES

The best and most inexpensive collection of antiques can be found at the **Anticuarios Mapocho,** located at Mapocho and Brasil streets (open Sat–Sun 9am–late afternoon). The prices here are more expensive than at the Bío Bío Market, but, then, the quality is often better (the vendors here refinish their antiques before selling them) and the market is within the confines of one huge red warehouse. This market is on the other side of the Panamericana, so a taxi here is about $3 from the Plaza de Armas, or take the Metro to Santa Ana station, head west on Catedral Street for 3 blocks to Avenida Brasil, turn right, and walk north 8 blocks until you reach Mapocho Street.

A collection of antique stores can be found clustered around Malaquias Concha and Caupolican streets, between Condell and Italia avenues. The bonus here is that the area is home to several fashionable restaurants as well. The priciest collection of shops is at Calle Bucarest and Avenida Providencia, where a collection of galleries offers paintings, china, furniture, and nearly every knickknack imaginable. Lastly, the Plaza Mulato Gil de Castro, on Lastarria Street at Rosal, has a small antiques fair (mostly china, purses, and jewelry) on Saturday and Sunday from about 9am to 5pm.

ARTESANIA

In addition to the markets listed above, arts and crafts can be found at **Artesanías de Chile** at the Mapocho Station Cultural Central, open Monday through Friday from 10am to 8pm, Saturday from 10:30am to 1:30pm. This is a good place for ceramics, lapis lazuli, textiles, baskets, woodwork, and more. **Chile Típico,** Moneda 1025, Local 149 (© 2/696-5504), open Monday through Friday from 9:30am to 7:30pm and Saturday from 10am to 2pm, sells everything from ceramics to those great wooden stirrups and pinwheel spurs that *huaso* cowboys use. An excellent selection of arts and crafts can be found at the **Apumanque market** behind the Apumanque shopping center, at Manquehue 31 at Avenida Apoquindo. Many museums have small shops that sell a variety of photo books and arts and crafts, such as the **Museo Chileno de Arte Precolombino** (p. 244).

BOOKS

Libro's sells a diverse, but very expensive, array of English-language magazines and a smaller assortment of paperbacks at the Parque Arauco Mall, and at Av. Pedro de Valdivia 039 in Providencia (© 2/232-8839; Metro: Pedro de Valdivia), open Monday through Friday from 10am to 8pm, Saturday from 10am to 2pm. **Librería Inglesa,** with shops at Av. Pedro de Valdivia 47 (© 2/231-6270); Paseo Huérfanos 669, Local 11 (© 2/632-5153); and Vitacura 5950 (© 2/219-2735), sells English-language literature, nonfiction, and children's books. For the largest selection of books in Spanish, the **Feria Chilena del Libro,** Paseo Huérfanos 623 (© 2/639-6758), is your best bet, and it sells local and national maps. It has a smaller branch in Providencia at Santa Magdalena 50 (© 2/232-1422).

WINE

There are a few full-service wine stores in Santiago, but don't forget that there is a Vinopolis wine shop in the airport if you want to put off wine shopping until the very end of your trip. The huge **El Mundo de Vino** at Av. Isidora Goyenechea 2931 (© 2/244-8888), open Monday through Saturday from 10:30am to 8:30pm, Sunday from 10:30am to 8pm, has a wide selection and a very knowledgeable staff. Also on Avenida Isidora Goyenechea at 3520 is **La Vinoteca** (© 2/334-1987), open Monday to Friday from 9:30am to 8pm, Saturday 11am to 3pm. In the Vitacura neighborhood, try **Vinoscyt,** Alonso de Cordova 23911 (© 2/476-5486), open 10am to 8pm Monday to Friday, and Saturday 10am to 2pm. Most shops will ship wine for you, but it is expensive. Wine shops promote boutique vineyards and up-and-coming vineyards, whereas supermarkets offer a wide selection of more traditional wines, but at cheaper prices.

7 Santiago After Dark

Residents of Santiago adhere to a vampire's schedule, dining as late as 11pm, arriving at a nightclub past 1am, and diving into bed before the sun rises. But there are many early-hour nighttime attractions if you can't bear late nights. Several newspapers publish daily movie listings and Friday weekend-guide supplements, such as *El Mercurio*'s "Wiken" or, even better, *La Tercera*'s "Guía Fin de Semana." Both contain movie, theater, and live music listings and special events.

THE PERFORMING ARTS

Santiago is known for its theater, from large-scale productions to one-person monologues put on at a local cafe. However, it might be difficult to find a production that interests you because newspaper listings typically advertise the title, address, and telephone number, nothing else. Ask around for recommendations, or ask the staff at your hotel.

The following are some of the more well-established theaters in Santiago. I recommend two theaters in Bellavista that offer contemporary productions and comedies in an intimate setting: **Teatro Bellavista,** Dardignac 0110 (© 2/735-2395; Metro: Salvador), and **Teatro San Ginés,** Mallinkrodt 76 (© 2/738-2159; Metro: Salvador). As the name implies, the nearby **Teatro La Comedia,** Merced 349 (© 2/639-1523; Metro: Baquedano), hosts comedy, but it is better known for cutting-edge productions. The cultural center **Estación Mapocho,** at the Plaza de la Cultura s/n (© 2/787-0000; Metro Cal y Canto), hosts a large variety of theater acts, often concurrently.

But let's be realistic. If you do not speak Spanish, even the city's hit production of the moment is going to be a waste of your time and money. Stick to something more accessible, such as a symphony, ballet, or opera at the city's gorgeous, historic **Teatro Municipal,** located downtown at Agustinas 749 (© 2/639-0282; www.municipal.cl; Metro: Universidad de Chile). The National Chilean Ballet and invited guests hold productions from April to December, with contemporary and classic productions such as *The Nutcracker.* There are musical events and special productions throughout the year; the best way to find out what's on is to check the theater's website. You can even **reserve and buy tickets** by clicking on the event on the corresponding date in the "Calendario Anual" and following the prompts, or by e-mailing the director of sales Luciano Lago at ventas@municipal.cl. The website allows you to select a seat from a diagram and find out which seats have only a partial view. Tickets are also sold over the phone at © 2/463-8888 from Monday to Friday 10am to 6pm, or bought in person at the theater itself from Monday to Friday 10am to 7pm and Saturday and Sunday from 10am to 2pm. Tickets are sold beginning 1 month before the starting date.

Visiting orchestras, the Fundación Beethoven, and contemporary acts play at the **Teatro Oriente,** Av. Pedro de Valdivia 099 (© 2/334-2234); buy tickets at the theater or by Ticketmaster (see below). **Teatro Universidad de Chile,** Av. Providencia 043 (© 2/634-5295; http://teatro.uchile.cl), hosts ballet and symphony productions, both national and international, throughout the year. You may buy tickets at the theater near Plaza Italia or by phone. **Ticketmaster** sells tickets for nearly every act in Santiago at CineHoyts cinemas, at Falabella department stores, or by calling © 2/690-2000 from 10am to 7pm.

THE CLUB, MUSIC & DANCE SCENE

Crowd-pulling national and international megabands typically play in the **Estado Nacional** or the **Estación Mapocho.** You'll find listings for these shows in the daily newspaper or the *El Mercurio*'s website, **www.emol.com.** If you're looking for something more mellow, **Bellavista** is a good bet for jazz, bolero, and folk music that is often performed Thursday through Saturday in several restaurants/cafes. **La Tasca Mediterráneo**'s next-door cafe at Purísima 161 (© 2/735-3901) hosts mostly jazz acts from Thursday to Saturday in a cozy atmosphere, but it can get crowded as the night wears on.

Also in Bellavista, there are four small, informal cafe/bars at Antonio López and Mallinkrodt; try **La Casa en el Aire,** Antonia López de Bello 0125 (✆ 2/735-6680), with a cozy, candlelit ambience and frequent live folk music. Across the street, at López de Bello 0126, is **El Perseguidor** (✆ 2/777-6763), a jazz club that I highly recommend, with performances Thursday through Sunday evenings. For salsa dancing, try **Habana Salsa,** Dominica 142 (✆ 2/737-1737). Despite the hokey exterior of faux building facades, it's where many salsa fanatics spend their weekend nights. For a trendier scene, try **Heaven,** Recoleta 345, with its scaffolding-like stairs and balconies, good sound system, and smallish dance floor.

There are dozens of music venues spread across the city, but the one that attracts the best bands and has the most variety is **La Batuta,** Jorge Washington 52 (✆ 2/274-7096), located in the Ñuñoa neighborhood, about a 10- to 15-minute taxi ride from downtown and Providencia. The atmosphere is underground, but the crowd profile depends on who's playing.

The **Club de Jazz,** José Pedro Alessandri 85 (✆ 2/274-1937), is one of the city's most traditional night spots (Louis Armstrong once played here). Bands jam every Thursday, Friday, and Saturday beginning at 11pm.

Santiago's club scene caters to an 18- to 35-year-old crowd, and it all gets going pretty late, from midnight to 6am, on the average. If you like electronica music, you might check out "fiestas" publicized in the weekend entertainment sections of newspapers that list 1-night-only raves and live music, or, in Bellavista, try **La Feria,** Constitución 275, a smallish nightclub located in an old theater. **Blondie,** Alameda 2879 (✆ 2/681-7793), is like spending a night in 1985, with an '80s revival scene and music to match. **Laberinto** operates as a club and a music venue; check their website for upcoming events (Vicuña Mackenna 915; ✆ 2/635-5368; www.laberinto.cl).

THE BAR SCENE

For the amount of pisco and wine that Chileans drink, bars have strangely never caught on; most bars are also restaurants or cafes by day. Bars that also feature live music can be found in "The Club, Music & Dance Scene," above. Hotel bars, such as the Hyatt's Duke's Bar or the Ritz's Lobby Bar, offer a more refined cocktail service. Most bars have happy hours from 5 to 7pm.

DOWNTOWN

There are several bars near the Plaza Mulato Gil de Castro, such as **Bar Berri,** Rosal 321, a pub-style watering hole frequented by locals and college students; it's a little on the mellow side, however. The **Confitería Torres,** Av. Alameda 1570 (✆ 2/698-6220), is a renovated turn-of-the-20th-century restaurant/cafe that has live music on weekends.

PROVIDENCIA

The **Bar Liguria,** Luis Thayer Ojeda 019 (✆ 2/231-1393) and Av. Providencia 1373 (✆ 2/235-7914), is highly recommended for any age; in fact, both restaurant/bars are the most happening spots in Santiago. The Ligurias are open until 2am on weeknights, until 5am on weekends, and are closed Sunday; they serve food practically until closing time. The **Phone Box Pub,** Av. Providencia 1670 (✆ 2/235-9972), open Monday through Thursday until 1am, weekends until 3am, closed Sunday, is good for a pint of brew and a snack. The pub is inside a small plaza off the main drag, and there's outside seating under a trellised roof. In the same plaza is **Café del Patio** (✆ 2/236-1251), open Monday to Thursday until midnight, Friday and Saturday until 1:30am, a stylish vegetarian restaurant with a bar, outside seating, and DJ music on weekends. Low-light and live cover bands set the tone at **Clandestino,** Guarda Vieja 35 (© **2/335-5293**).

Santo Remedio, Roman Díaz 152, provides one of the funkier atmospheres in Santiago, plus outside seating is available. **The Barcelona** restaurant/bar, Santa Beatriz 40 (© **2/235-6292**), serves drinks and tapas—-and nothing else—in a warm, low-lit atmosphere. The new hip spot in Providencia is **Casino Royale,** Manual Montt 1684 (© **2/269-5942**), which specializes in performances (music, comedy, theater) on Thursday, Saturday, and Sunday. As the name states, **El Sofa,** Santa Isabel 0151 (© **09/663-0163**), takes comfort to a new level with lots of couches to lounge in (in addition to a good wine selection).

Mister Ed, Av. Suecia 152 (© **2/231-2624**), open Monday through Saturday from 6pm to 5am (open Sun during the summer), is a bar that transforms into a dance hall at 2am with live music and is frequented by many young gringos. **Brannigan's** is a little more low-key than Mister Ed, and it can be found on the same street at 035 (© **2/232-7869**). And, also in the same neighborhood, the popular bar **Boomerang,** Holley 2285, has loud music, lots of gringos, and expensive drinks, but remains fashionable nevertheless. The Suecia micro-neighborhood is not recommended for dining, and the atmosphere on weekends often fills with college-age party animals, but there are a few places (like Brannigan's above) that are more on the mellow side. Happy hours are a standby in nearly every bar here.

LAS CONDES

Several restaurants convert into pubs or cocktail lounges in the evening. One of them is **Flannigans's Geo Pub,** Encomenderos 83 (© **2/233-6675**), open until midnight on weeknights, 2am on weekends. It's a cozy, contemporary Irish pub (with the usual pints on draft) that's very popular with an international crowd. **PubLicity,** El Bosque Norte 0155 (© **2/246-6414**), open until 1am on weeknights and 3am on weekends, is almost too much of a sensory overload, combining English architecture with urban "publicity," or advertisements. It's very popular with young adults and yuppies, and there is often live music. At **Agua** (© **2/263-0008**), the trendy, minimalist-style restaurant (p. 240), there is a bar called "Fuego" on the second floor with live DJ music, which is open until 2am. If it's a summer evening and you're looking for a relaxing place to have a cocktail with a crowd in their 30s and up, try **Zanzíbar,** in the multi-restaurant complex BordeRío at Av. Escrivá de Balaguer (about a $4 taxi ride from Las Condes; © **2/218-0120**). This Mediterranean/Moroccan restaurant and bar has an outdoor, candlelit terrace on the second floor furnished with pillows and comfy chairs to kick back in and take a look at the stars. Excellent snacks and food are available, too. The restaurant is open for lunch Monday to Thursday from noon to 5pm, and dinner from 6:30pm to 1am Monday to Thursday and until 2am Friday and Saturday, Sunday open from 10am to 6pm. Their outdoor terrace opens at 6pm. Also at the BordeRío is the **Lamu Lounge** (#11; © **2/218-0116**), which has cocktails and tapas served in an African-style atmosphere. Lamu Lounge is open from 7pm to 2am Monday through Saturday.

CINEMAS

Megaplexes such as CineHoyts and Cinemark, with their multiscreened theaters, feature the widest variety of movies and a popular Monday-to-Wednesday discount price. More avant-garde and independent films can be found in "Cine Arte" theaters, such as **Cine Alameda,** Alameda 139 (© **2/664-8842**), and **El Biógrafo,** Lastarria 181 (© **2/633-4435**). The entertainment sections of *El Mercurio, La Tercera,* and *La Segunda* list titles, times, and locations.

13

Around Santiago & the Central Valley

Santiago is an excellent jumping-off point for a wealth of distinctive attractions and destinations: Fine beaches, an eccentric port town, nature preserves, hot springs, and wineries are just a few examples of what's nearby. You'll also find a multitude of outdoor activities, including skiing at world-renowned resorts, hiking, rafting, biking, horseback riding, and more. Although some of the destinations listed in this chapter require an overnight stay, most attractions are within a half-hour to 2-hour drive from Santiago, meaning it is possible to pack a lot of action into just a few days.

EXPLORING THE REGION

Wineries, ski resorts, and coastal communities around Santiago can all be explored on day trips. Nevertheless, I strongly recommend that you stay the night at one of these destinations (longer if you plan to ski at one of the four local resorts). A rental car provides a lot of freedom to explore at your own pace, especially if you are heading to the coast. If you can afford a rental, get one, but it's a waste of money to rent a vehicle to get to a ski resort; resorts near Santiago are all-inclusive hotels with no town to navigate. Organize a shuttle instead.

I've known more than a few travelers who, upon arrival or departure from Santiago, rent a vehicle at the airport, drive to the coast or the wine country, return the rental at the airport, and then taxi into Santiago (or vice versa).

Taking the bus is not a bad option, either—in fact, Santiago's national coach system is better than that of the U.S. Buses are modern and clean, and there are usually a dozen or so daily departures to most major destinations. Bus terminals are all located downtown but are easily reached by the Metro.

This chapter proposes ideas for 1-day or multiple-day adventures outside of Santiago. You'll find information about where to find the best ski resorts, where to go wine-tasting, where to see Chile's rural traditions and old-world haciendas, where to take a soak in a hot spring, and where to take a hike and stretch your legs a bit.

Beach retreats are the Chilean's favorite weekend getaway, and this chapter covers, in depth, Chile's better-known and most intriguing coastal cities, **Viña del Mar** and **Valparaíso.** Other, smaller villages that dot the coast have their own strongly defined characteristics (and clear-cut socioeconomic levels), and visitors with a rental car will take pleasure in discovering each new village around the bend. You can also arrange a tour to coastal destinations that are not part of the "usual" itinerary. **Zapallar** is home to Chile's moneyed elite, and it's the prettiest cove in the region (Margaret Thatcher's favorite restaurant, and mine, is here, too). **Cachagua** and **Maitencillo** are where the upper-middle and middle classes own their second homes. **Con Con** is where you'll find the cheapest— and the freshest—seafood restaurants; **Reñaca** is where the "beautiful people"

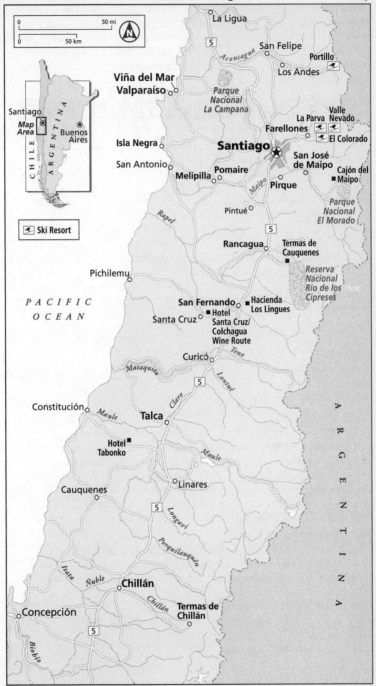

Around Santiago & the Central Valley

loll in the sun. Farther south is another middle-class hub, **Algarrobo** (nothing much to see here), and **Cartegena,** the oldest seaside resort in Chile, which has now fallen out of favor (Chileans commonly use the phrase "tackier than a honeymoon in Cartegena"). Lastly, I highly recommend the tiny town **Isla Negra,** where Pablo Neruda spent most of his time in one of his three homes, which is now a museum (p. 278).

1 Viña del Mar

120km (74 miles) northwest of Santiago; 8km (5 miles) north of Valparaíso

Viña del Mar is one of Chile's most fashionable beach resorts. The city was founded in 1874 as a weekend retreat and garden residence for the wealthy elite from Valparaíso and Santiago, and it has remained a top beach destination for Santiaguinos ever since. Most simply call the city "Viña"—you'll call it "chaos" if you come any time between December and late February, when thousands of vacationers arrive, crowding beaches and creating traffic. There is, however, a heightened sense of excitement during these months when so much activity is happening in the area.

Viña's attractive homes, manicured lawns, towering apartment buildings, and golden beaches filled with sunbathers are quite a contrast to the ramshackle streets of Valparaíso. The area has plenty of fine beaches, but the beach to see and be seen is in Reñaca, about 6km (3¾ miles) north of Viña (see "What to See & Do," later in this chapter). Unfortunately, the Humboldt Current that runs the length of Chile to Antofagasta makes for cold swimming conditions, even during the summer. Regardless of the season, Viña is a wonderfully relaxing place to spend 1 or 2 days.

The city is divided into two sectors: downtown and the beachfront. Several downtown locations are desirable for their proximity to the lush Quinta Vergara Park and shops, but you'll be a 15-minute walk away from the beach. The beachfront is better suited for tourism, with many hotels and restaurants.

ESSENTIALS

GETTING THERE Frequent, comfortable buses leave the Terminal Alameda in Santiago at Alameda O'Higgins 3712 (1 block from Terminal Santiago; Metro: Universidad de Santiago), about every 15 minutes. Tur Bus and Pullman both offer service to and from Viña del Mar, for about $2.60 each way. The trip takes about 1 hour and 15 minutes, depending on traffic. In Viña, you'll disembark at the terminal located at Avenida Valparaíso and Quilpué; it's close to the main plaza, and taxis are available.

VISITOR INFORMATION The **Oficina de Turismo de Viña** is located on Plaza Vergara, next to the post office near avenidas Libertad and Arlegui (© **800-800-830,** toll-free in Chile). Summer hours are Monday through Saturday from 9am to 9pm; off-season hours are Monday through Friday from 10am to 7pm (closed 2–3pm), and Saturday from 10am to 7pm. A helpful staff (a few speak basic English) can provide visitors with maps and events details. The center provides accommodations information (without ratings), plus information about temporary apartment rentals.

GETTING AROUND Nearly everything worth seeing in Viña can be done on foot, and Viña's beachfront promenade and the lush Quinta Vergara Park are ideal places for getting out and stretching your legs. Those with a rental vehicle are recommended to take a short drive north toward Concón, for splendid coastal views and a chance to see fat sea lions sunning themselves on the rocky shore (follow the coastal road Av. San Martín, which becomes Av. Jorge Montt, out of town, and when you tire of the drive, simply turn around and head back the same way). **Parking** in Viña can be difficult in January and February (when the streets and hotel garages really fill up). **Taxis** can be hailed in the street, or your hotel can call one.

SPECIAL EVENTS   During the second or third week of February, Viña plays host to the **Festival de la Canción** (www.vinadelmar.cl), a week-long event that draws national and international musicians to perform in the outdoor amphitheater in Quinta Vergara Park. It's the largest music festival in Chile, with almost 30,000 spectators nightly. The city bursts at the seams during this event, and hotel reservations are imperative. Viña also hosts an excellent **Film Festival** during the second or third week of October (www.munivina.cl). The Festival highlights Latin American productions, and all films shown are in Spanish and Portuguese only. Inquire at the visitor center for more information.

FAST FACTS: Viña del Mar

Banks Most major banks can be found on Avenida Arlegui, and although they're open Monday through Friday from 9am to 2pm only, nearly all have ATMs (Redbancs).

Car Rentals Try **Rosselot,** Av. Libertad 892 (© **32/382373;** www.rosselot.cl) and Av. Alvares 762 (© 32/382888); **Hertz Rent-A-Car,** Av. Quillota 766 (© **32/381025;** www.hertz.com); or **Verschae Rent-A-Car,** Av. Libertad 1045 (© **32/267300;** www.verschae.cl). Daily rental prices range from $30 for a compact car to $45 for a midrange vehicle.

Currency Exchange Cambios (money-exchange houses) are open in the summer Monday through Friday from 9am to 2pm and 3 to 8pm, and Saturday from 9am to 2pm; and in winter Monday through Saturday 9am to 2pm and 4 to 7pm, and Saturday from 9am to 2pm. Several cambios can be found along Avenida Arlegui.

Emergencies For **police,** dial © **133;** for **fire,** dial © **132;** and for an **ambulance,** dial © **131.**

Hospital For medical attention, go to **Hospital Gustavo Fricke** on calles Alvarez and Simón Bolívar (© **32/675067,** or for emergencies 32/652328).

WHERE TO STAY
EXPENSIVE

Hotel del Mar ⭐⭐⭐ *Moments*   This five-star hotel is Viña's first and only luxury lodging option in town—that is, until the opening of the Sheraton's Miramar Hotel scheduled for late 2005. The Hotel del Mar was built only recently, in 2003, but it carefully adapted its architecture to match the handsome eggshell-colored casino building that it fronts, with beautiful results. The guest rooms are contemporary and spacious, and most come with balconies; this hotel offers the best sea views of any hotel in the area. It's also centrally located and close to everything. The Salute Health Center and its infinity pool deserve special mention for their panoramic views, too. After a rough beginning, the hotel staff has streamlined its service and guests can now expect prompt, friendly assistance with whatever needs they may have. The hotel also features some of the best restaurants in the area, and rooms include free entrance to the casino and shows.

Av. San Martín 199. ⓒ 600/700-6000. Fax 32/500601. www.hoteldelmar.cl. 60 units. $200–$250 double standard; $330–$390 suite. AE, DC, MC, V. Valet parking. **Amenities:** 4 restaurants; bar; indoor pool; gym; sauna; children's game room; business center; room service; massage; babysitting; laundry service; solarium; art gallery. *In room:* A/C, cable TV, DVD and CD player, safe.

Hotel Monterilla ★★ *Finds* This appealing family-run boutique hotel, located near the beach and casino, is an excellent value and one of the best places to stay in Viña del Mar. Warm, personal service and a central location are definite draws, but the chic, contemporary design is what really makes the Monterilla special. Chromatic furniture contrasted against white carpet, and walls adorned with colorful postmodern art create crisp, attractive surroundings, and though rooms are not large, they're very comfortable. Some rooms for two to five people have kitchenettes, a great deal for families or those staying longer than a few days. A small common area has several sofas for reading or relaxing. Off season the hotel offers "kids free" and other discounts.

Dos Norte 65, Plaza México, Viña del Mar. ⓒ 32/976950. Fax 32/683576. www.monterilla.cl. 20 units. $72 junior single; $131 superior double; $158 apt for 2. AE, DC, MC, V. **Amenities:** Cafeteria; bar; office services; laundry service. *In room:* Cable TV, minibar.

Hotel O'Higgins ★ This traditional hotel, a stone landmark constructed in the heart of Viña in 1934, attracts dignitaries and a few celebrities because of its historic appeal, downtown location (close to shops and the Quinta Vergara park), and outdoor pool. However, the hotel stubbornly refuses to update itself and, for that reason, is not as much of a value as the Hotel Monterilla (below). The staff is friendly and helpful and offer complete services, but the stale lobby, dark hallways, and worn furniture reveal that the glory days of the O'Higgins are over. Ask to see the accommodations, if at all possible, as quality varies from room to room, and those facing the main plaza are in better shape than side rooms. Ask for price specials when booking.

Plaza Vergara, Viña del Mar. ⓒ 32/882016. Fax 32/883537. www.panamericanahoteles.cl. 265 units. $70–$80 double; $130 suite. AE, DC, MC, V. **Amenities:** 2 restaurants; bar; disco (Jan–Feb only); outdoor pool; children's activities and disco (Jan–Feb only); car-rental agency; business center; room service; babysitting; laundry service. *In room:* A/C, cable TV, minibar, safe.

The Oceanic ★★ If you're looking for a quiet hotel outside of town, this is your place. The Oceanic boasts a privileged location on a rocky promontory with dramatic coastal views of the ocean crashing against the shore. The hotel is warm and friendly and full of places to sit and relax to the soothing sound of the sea. During the summer, the pebbled terrace with its ocean-side pool and lounge chairs is the best around. Four rooms facing the road are $45 cheaper, but the beachfront rooms are worth the extra money. A "suite," spacious rooms with a breakfast nook and great views, is only $10 more than a standard double. The hotel has a decent French-influenced restaurant, if you prefer to stay in and not take the 15-minute walk or 5-minute taxi ride to Viña.

Av. Borgoño 12925, Viña del Mar. ⓒ 32/830006. Fax 32/830390. www.hoteloceanic.cl. 28 units. $120 standard double; $130 suite. AE, DC, MC, V. **Amenities:** Restaurant; bar; outdoor pool; sauna; souvenir shop; salon; babysitting; laundry service. *In room:* Cable TV, minibar.

MODERATE

Cap Ducal ★ Designed to look like a ship moored to the shore, this offbeat hotel has been a Viña institution since 1936. The hotel's location at the coastal entrance to the city affords views of the crashing surf from all of its 25 rooms. Inside, the nautical theme continues, with compact halls made of wood-paneled walls with brass handrails, and the low-ceilinged rooms look and feel much like a ship's compartment. An altogether cozy, if not wacky, place to bunk for the night, and about a 2-block walk to the casino area. Ask for a nonsmoking room, as the smell in smoking rooms will bother even a smoker. Also, consider paying the extra $20 for a junior suite with a little more room.

Av. Marina 51, Viña del Mar. ℂ **32/626655.** Fax 32/665471. www.capducal.cl. 25 units. $100–$110 standard double; $110–$130 junior suite; $150 (year-round) suite. AE, DC, MC, V. **Amenities:** Restaurant; cafe; laundry service. *In room:* Cable TV, minibar.

Hotel Albamar ★ The Hotel Albamar offers good value for the price because of its location—near restaurants and a block from the casino and the beach—and its comfortable rooms, despite the slightly frilly, romantic decor. A separate building in the back is recommended for its ample "superior" rooms and newer furnishings, but rooms in the main building are also decent, apart from a few that are quite dark. The "double special" has space for a table and chairs.

Av. San Martín 419, Viña del Mar. ℂ **32/975274.** Fax 32/970720. www.hotelalbamar.cl. 30 units. $40 double; $50 suite. AC, DC, MC, V. **Amenities:** Cafe; office services; babysitting; laundry service. *In room:* A/C, cable TV, minibar.

Offenbacher-hof Residencial ★★ Housed in a lovely Victorian building perched high atop Cerro Castillo, the Offenbacher has sweeping views of Viña del Mar (the city and hills, not the beach) and a sunny patio with an adjoining roofed cafe. Still, it is the friendly German-Chilean owners of the Offenbacher that make this bed-and-breakfast really special. The interiors could use an update—each room is decorated differently with what looks like flea market purchases—but most rooms are spacious. Attic rooms are smaller but well lit, with access to a tiny deck. You'll be wowed by the view, so be sure to get a room that has one. At night, the patio cafe is open to the public from 6pm to midnight, often with live music.

Balmaceda 102, Cerro Castillo, Viña del Mar. ℂ **32/621483.** Fax 32/662432. www.offenbacher-hof.cl. 15 units. $39–$47 standard double; $45–$58 superior double. AE, DC, MC, V. **Amenities:** Cafe; bar; sauna; gym; laundry service; sightseeing tours. *In room:* Cable TV.

WHERE TO DINE

There are surprisingly few seafood restaurants in Viña, given its coastal location, and here's why: Seafood wholesalers buy fish and shellfish in bulk and then, inconceivably, send the goods to Santiago, where they are distributed and then sent back to Viña. In other words, you have a better chance of dining on fresh fish in Santiago than in Viña. For the freshest fish around, take a taxi or drive your rental vehicle north along the coast to Concón (16km/10 miles from Viña), where you will find dozens of "picadas" (something like a dive—cheap but hearty and delicious) lining the road. The best picada in Concón is **La Gatita,** Avenida Borgoño (ℂ **32/814235**). It's a local favorite, so get there early or prepare to wait. There is no street number, so look for a small fish market on the left (when driving north) that sits next to the restaurant. Try Chile's famous Caldillo de Congrio (Conger eel soup) here. There are dozens of restaurants lining Avenida San Martín, including fast food joints Pizza Hut and McDonald's, and visitors will find cheap eateries and sandwich shops in downtown Viña along Avenida Valparaíso and around the plaza. For afternoon tea, try **The Tea Pot,** 5 Norte 475 (ℂ **32/687671**), which offers more than 60 kinds of tea and delicious pastries. Along the beach you'll find several wood-and-glass concessions that serve sandwiches, drinks, coffee, and pastries.

Barlovento ✿ INTERNATIONAL   Chic with its minimalist design of cement, steel, and glass, Barlovento is one of the trendier establishments in Viña. Most dishes on the menu are good; however, Barlovento's strength is its appetizers and lengthy list of cocktails—which are excellent. This is the only place in the region where you'll find a proper cosmopolitan or a well-made Bloody Mary. Barlovento is a good choice for relaxed nightlife, especially for their relaxed second-floor lounge with a glass cupola that offers a panoramic view. Barlovento is not open for lunch.

2 Norte 195. ✆ 32/977472. Main courses $5–$10 per person. AE, DC, MC, V. Daily 6pm–2am.

Cap Ducal ✿ SEAFOOD   This restaurant hangs from the shore and is built to resemble a ship moored against the cliff. If you're looking for an intimate, candlelit setting to dine with a view of the sparkling coastline, this is your place. However, the ambience outshines decent food that often lacks creativity. The focus here is Chilean and international-style seafood, and dishes tend to float a bit in too much sauce, so you might want to order it on the side. One exception is their Congrio Oriental, with soy-flavored vegetables.

Av. Marina 51. ✆ 32/626655. Main dishes $6–$9. AE, DC, MC, V. Daily 1pm–midnight.

Divino Pecado ✿✿ ITALIAN   Cozy and centrally located, this newer chef-owned restaurant boasts delectable fresh pastas and other Italian dishes, with sharp service, to boot. For an aperitif, order a pisco sour—this restaurant is known for their delicious Peruvian variety. The menu allows you to concoct a pasta dish from a build-your-own section, or you can pick from their specialties, including the knockout "black" raviolis made with calamari ink and stuffed with curried shrimp. Excellent meat options include filet mignon with a mushroom and sweet-wine sauce. Pastas here are served very al dente; let your waiter know how you would like your noodles cooked.

Av. San Martín 180 (in front of casino). ✆ 32/975790. divinopecado@terra.cl. Reservations recommended. Main courses $6.50–$11. AE, DC, MC, V. Daily 12:30–3:30pm and 8–11pm; Sat–Sun. until 1am.

El Gaucho ✿ STEAKHOUSE/ARGENTINE   Carnivores should head to El Gaucho for ample servings of just about any kind of meat, served sizzling off the *parrilla* (grill). The Argentine-style "interiors" appetizers include blood sausage, sweetbreads, and crispy intestines. If that doesn't make your mouth water, try starting with grilled provolone cheese with oregano. Entrees include beef loin, ribs, chicken, sausages, and other grilled items and salads. Wood floors and brick walls create a warm, comfortable ambience.

Av. San Martín 435. ✆ 32/693502. Main courses $6–$14. AE, DC, MC, V. Daily 12:30–3:30pm and 7:30–11pm.

Enjoy del Mar ✿✿ INTERNATIONAL   Another restaurant owned and run by the Hotel del Mar, but located across the street, the informal Enjoy del Mar offers the best outdoor dining in Viña—though, really, this restaurant is better for a snack and a cocktail, as the majority of the menu revolves around "tablas," or assorted finger foods and cheese platters, and desserts. If you are hungrier, order one of their brochettes from the outdoor barbecue that comes with a salad bar. The menu has salads and sandwiches as well, and it is open all day, early until well into the after-hours. The outdoor deck is encircled by glass, and there is indoor seating as well inside a light, airy, glass-and-steel structure. The restaurant hosts live music on weekends.

Av. Peru 100. ℭ **32/687755**. Reservations not necessary. Main courses $5–$10. AE, DC, MC, V. Sun–Wed 7:30am-2am; Thurs–Sat 7:30am–4am.

Haiku ℛ JAPANESE   The Hotel del Mar has an excellent Sushihana restaurant, but this is where locals go for sushi and other Japanese delights, given the intimate ambience and generous praise the restaurant has received from food critics. It's a tiny hole-in-the-wall, with only 10 tables on the first floor and floor seating on woven straw tatami mats on the second, and the owner personally waits on each table. Beyond traditional sushi, Haiku offers dishes such as salted tofu, soy-marinated grouper fish, and tuna tempura. On Sunday from 7pm to 11pm, sushi rolls are 30% off, and from Tuesday to Saturday, 7pm to 9pm, 14 pieces of sushi and two pisco sours go for $7.

6 Norte 96. ℭ **32/993438**. Average $5–$10. AE, DC, MC, V. Tues–Sun 1–4pm and 7pm–midnight.

La Ciboulette ℛℛ *Finds* BELGIAN/CHILEAN   The unwelcoming facade of this tiny restaurant keeps tourists away, but La Ciboulette is a local favorite and has won various culinary awards for its inventive Belgian/Chilean cuisine. The nightly menu changes are chalked on a board and might include country duck with a blackberry and pepper sauce; beef stewed in beer, onion, cinnamon and ginger; or a cassoulet of scallops and shrimp, with chives and Noilly Prat, accompanied by a well-chosen wine list.

1 Norte 191-A. ℭ **32/690084**. Main courses $8–$11. Tues–Sat 1–4pm and 8pm–midnight; Sun 1:30–4pm.

Las Delicias del Mar ℛ SEAFOOD   Las Delicias serves sumptuous seafood dishes that are matched by attentive service. This Basque-influenced restaurant is known for its paella, but it's the fish dishes that shine. Creative recipes give new life to sea bass, salmon, or conger eel—served with a rich cream, mushroom, and shrimp sauce and topped with Parmesan, for example, or stuffed with cheese and prawns. Tangerine-colored walls, leafy plants, and colorful linens make for a warm, comfortable atmosphere.

Av. San Martín 459. ℭ **32/901837**. Main courses $10–$12. AE, DC, MC, V. Daily 12:30–4pm and 7:30pm–midnight.

Savinya ℛℛℛ INTERNATIONAL   Viña's most refined (and expensive) restaurant serves mouthwatering, seasonally changing cuisine that should not be missed. Located within the Hotel del Mar, and affording sweeping views of the ocean, Savinya's fusion-style cuisine pairs common and uncommon ingredients that work surprisingly well together, complemented by a list of palate-pleasing wines. The menu changes often, but I enjoyed an appetizer of king crab, pistachio and sweet pea mold, served with quail eggs and black caviar; an entree of rich, creamy asparagus-and-scallop risotto; and a dessert of green apple sorbet with a muscatel sauce. Attentive, agreeable service comes with the price. The gorgeous daytime view of the ocean makes this a special place for lunch.

Av. Perú and Los Héroes. ℭ **32/500800**. www.hoteldelmar.com. Reservations on weekends recommended. Main courses $10–$17. AE, DC, MC, V. Daily noon–4pm and 8pm–1am.

WHAT TO SEE & DO
BEACHES
The **Playa Caleta Abarca** beach is located in a protected bay near the entrance to Viña del Mar, next to the oft-photographed "flower clock" and the Cerro Castillo. In the northeast, fronting rows of terraced high-rise apartment buildings, you'll find **Playa Acapulco, Playa Mirasol,** and **Playa Las Salinas** (near the naval base). These beaches all see throngs of vacationers and families in the

summer, but **Reñaca,** just up the coast, is *the* hot spot for beaches, and visitors to Viña might consider grabbing a taxi (about $5 one-way) or a bus (nos. 1, 10, or 111 at avenidas Libertad and 15 Norte) to get there. The first stretch of the beach at Reñaca is popular with families, while the end is the "cool" spot for young adults and teens. Because Chileans party late into the night, you probably won't see many people on any beach until about noon.

THE TOP ATTRACTIONS

Casino Municipal ✦✦✦   Built in 1930, the Casino Municipal was the most luxurious building in its day and is worth a visit even if you're not a gambler. The interior has been remodeled over time, but the facade has withstood the caprices of many a developer and is still as handsome as the day it opened. Semiformal attire is required to enter the gaming room: no T-shirts, jeans, or sneakers. Minimum bets of 5,000 pesos ($8) may deter some budget travelers, although there are slot machines and video poker. The casino holds periodic art exhibits on its second floor, and there are three bars if you're looking for nightlife that's a step up from the teen clubs in Viña.

Plaza Colombia between Av. San Martín and Av. Perú. ⒞ 32/500600. www.hoteldelmar.cl. Hours vary, but generally in winter game room Mon–Thurs noon–4am, Fri–Sun 24 hr.; in summer daily 24 hr.

Museo de Arqueología e Historia Francisco Fonck ✦✦   This museum boasts a large collection of indigenous art and archaeological items from Easter Island, with more than 1,400 pieces and one of the six Moai sculptures outside Easter Island (the others are in England, the U.S., Paris, Brussels, and La Serena in Chile). There is also a decent archaeological exhibition of Mapuche pieces and other items from the north and central zones of Chile. The Museum of Natural History on the second floor features birds, mammals, insects, and fossils.

Av. 4 Norte 784. ⒞ 32/686753. Admission $2 adults, 50¢ children. Tues–Sat 10am–6pm; Sun 10am–2pm.

Museo Palacio Rioja ✦✦   This grand 1906 Belle Epoque stone mansion is worth a visit for a peek into the lives of the early-20th-century elite in Viña del Mar. Built by Spaniard Fernando Rioja, a banker, and originally spanning 4 blocks, the palace took opulence to a new level, with a stone facade featuring Corinthian columns and a split double staircase. Interiors are made of oak and stone, with enough salons to fit a family of 10. The palm-fringed garden surrounding the house is just a fraction of the original but is still an idyllic place for a quick stroll. Unfortunately, no tours are available in English, and informational material is weak, but the museum is still worth a visit.

Quillota 214. ⒞ 32/483664. Admission 60¢ adults, 20¢ children. Tues–Sun 10am–1:30pm and 3–5:30pm.

Quinta Vergara Park/Museum of Fine Art ✦✦✦   One of the loveliest parks in central Chile, the Quinta Vergara is also home to a large amphitheater that holds Viña's yearly Song Festival as well as the Museum of Fine Art. The Quinta, whose area is naturally fenced in by several steep hills, was once the residence of Portuguese shipping magnate Francisco Alvarez and his wife, Dolores, who created the park, planting a multitude of native and other exotic species. The museum is housed in the ornate **Palacio Vergara,** which was built by Francisco's great-granddaughter, and the collection includes art from the family collection and other works from collectors in Viña. If you have the time, don't miss a visit here.

Near Plaza Parroquia. Museum ⒞ 32/252481. Park: Free admission. Daily 7am–6pm (until 7pm in summer). Museum: Admission 60¢ adults, 30¢ children. Tues–Sun 10am–2pm and 3–6pm.

2 Valparaíso

115km (71 miles) northwest of Santiago; 8km (5 miles) south of Viña del Mar

Valparaíso is Chile's most captivating city, and, accordingly, it is the most popular coastal destination and an obligatory cruise ship port of call. But like a penniless aristocrat, this port town has retained only traces of the architectural splendor that once set it apart from the others. This is Viña's blue-collar sister, yet the historical importance of this city paired with the vibrant culture of local *porteños* is far more fascinating. In 2002, UNESCO designated Valparaíso a World Heritage Site.

Much like San Francisco, the city is made of a flat downtown surrounded by steep hills, but unlike that city, the irregular terrain in Valparaíso presented far more challenges for development. The jumble of multicolored clapboard homes and weathered Victorian mansions that cling to sheer cliffs and other unusual spaces are testament to this, and you could spend days exploring the maze of narrow passageways and sinuous streets that snake down ravines and around hillsides.

Because of the run-down buildings and the rollicking seafront bars, Valparaíso is a little rough on the edges—but the city has a characteristic bohemian flair so lacking in overdeveloped coastal towns. In fact, this may change somewhat with UNESCO designation, which has set off a property value boom and a frenzy of redevelopment, especially on popular hills such as Cerros Alegre and Constitución.

Valparaíso has spawned generations of international poets, writers, and artists who have found inspiration in the city, including the Nobel prize–winning poet Pablo Neruda, who owned a home here. The city is known for its eccentric and antiquated bars that stay open into the wee hours of the morning, and its restaurants, some of which have the most dramatic sea views found anywhere in Chile.

But the real attractions here are losing yourself in the city's streets, admiring the angular architecture that makes this city unique, and especially riding the century-old, clickety-clack *ascensores,* or funiculars, that lift riders to the tops of hills. If you're the type who craves character and culturally distinctive surroundings, this is your place.

ESSENTIALS

GETTING THERE   By Bus   Frequent, comfortable buses leave the Terminal Alameda in Santiago at Alameda O'Higgins 3712 (1 block from Terminal Santiago; Metro: University de Santiago), about every 15 minutes. Tur Bus and Pullman offer service to and from Valparaíso, with fares running an average of $4.25 one-way. The trip takes about 1 hour and 15 minutes, depending on traffic. In Valparaíso, you'll disembark at the terminal at Avenida Pedro Montt; taxis are available and a good idea at night. Consider buying a round-trip ticket if you plan to travel on weekends or holidays.

By Car   To get to Valparaíso from Santiago, take Avenida Alameda (Av. Bernardo O'Higgins) and follow the signs for Valparaíso west until it changes into RN 68. Ten kilometers (6¼ miles) from the coast, follow the signs to Valparaíso. There are two tollbooths along the way; the toll varies between 1,000 and 3,300 pesos ($1.40–$4.50), depending on the time and day. Valparaíso is 115km (71 miles) northwest of Santiago. No hotels have their own parking, but street parking is usually available. The safest place to park is the underground garage on Calle Errázuriz, across from the Plaza Sotomayor. Do not park your car full of belongings on the city street at night, as break-ins are common.

By Train To get to Valparaíso from Viña del Mar, take a taxi (about $5) or the commuter train Merval at Francisco Vergara between Bohn and Alvarez streets—this is highly recommended even for those with a vehicle, as Valparaíso is difficult to navigate and the city is compact enough to see everything on foot. The Merval train runs every 20 minutes from about 6am to 10pm and costs 35¢. In Valparaíso, get off at the final stop, Estación Puerto (at the pier next to the visitor center).

VISITOR INFORMATION/CITY TOURS There are several **tourist offices** in Valparaíso; the best is at Muelle Prat (*©* **32/939489**), open daily from 10am to 6pm (closed 2pm–3pm). There's also an information kiosk at the bus station open daily from 8:30am to 5:30pm. The Municipality offers free 1½- to 2-hour walking tours of the city in English if you book in advance by e-mail at turismo@municipalidadvalparaiso.cl. Be sure to list the number of people, the day and time, and the fact that you need an English guide. Another excellent option is a day or night city tour with the company **Ruta Valparaíso** (*©* **32/911972;** www.rutavalparaiso.cl), although they offer tours Tuesday through Sunday only, and reservations must be made at least 24 hours in advance. Ruta's Valparaíso and Lonely Tours, which take visitors to Cerros Alegre and Concepción, the Pablo Neruda Museum, and a boat trip in the bay, can be taken from 9:30am to 2:30pm or 3:30pm to 7:30pm, and there is a Sleepwalkers Tour that takes visitors to bohemian bars and vista points for sparkling night views. The cost is from $20 to $42, and does not include extras.

GETTING AROUND Walking is the only way to see Valparaíso; parking is limited, and most attractions are within a compact area. To get to and from Viña del Mar, take a taxi or ride the Merval, a commuter train that runs every 20 minutes from the Estación Puerto (next to Valparaíso's visitor center) and costs about 35¢ to 75¢.

SPECIAL EVENTS Valparaíso's famed **New Year's Pyrotechnic Festival** is an event so spectacular even Chileans consider it something they must see at least once in their lives. Thousands of partiers crowd the streets and hilltops to take in the radiant lights that explode over the shimmering bay. You'll want to stake out your "corner" early atop one of the hills—savvy Chileans arrive in the early afternoon and bring chairs, barbecues, and a day's ration of food and drink to save their viewing platform for the nighttime fireworks display. Another highlight, during late October, is **Regatta Off Valparaíso,** a traditional Chilean regatta organized by the Arturo Prat Naval Academy, featuring more than 50 competing yachts. Call the tourism office for dates, or check the Valparaíso naval website at www.armada.cl.

WHERE TO STAY

Just a few years ago, decent lodging was so scarce in Valparaíso that even the city's own tourism board recommended travelers lodge in Viña. It took the UNESCO World Heritage designation and the vision of the new Fundación Valparaíso to give budding entrepreneurs the push they needed to open a couple of petite, boutique-style hotels here. Yes, there still are a few *hostales* whose pretty, flower-boxed facades belie the horror within. But to set some kind of guidelines for these *hostales,* the foundation recently created a Bed and Breakfast association that some have chosen to join, but I've found that only a few really meet all my Valpo-lodging criteria: that is, a central location, tasteful decoration, and cleanliness. You can check out the Bed and Breakfast website at www.bbvalparaiso.cl.

Valparaíso

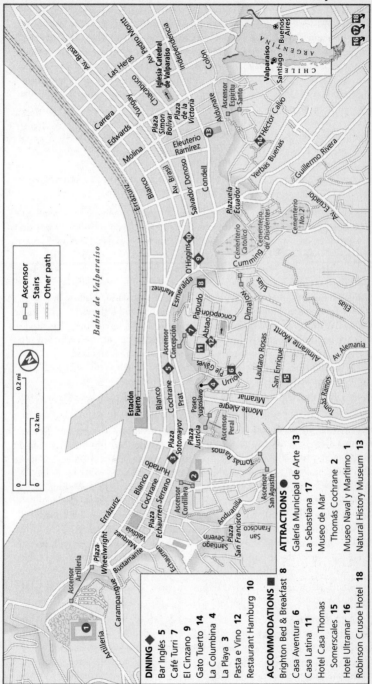

Bahía de Valparaíso

Ascensor
Stairs
Other path

Estación Puerto

DINING ◆
Bar Inglés **5**
Café Turri **7**
El Cinzano **9**
Gato Tuerto **14**
La Columbina **4**
La Playa **3**
Pasta e Vino **12**
Restaurant Hamburg **10**

ACCOMMODATIONS ■
Brighton Bed & Breakfast **8**
Casa Aventura **6**
Casa Latina **11**
Hotel Casa Thomas
  Somerscales **15**
Hotel Ultramar **16**
Robinson Crusoe Hotel **18**

ATTRACTIONS ●
Galería Municipal de Arte **13**
La Sebastiana **17**
Museo de Mar
  Thomás Cochrane **2**
Museo Naval y Marítimo **1**
Natural History Museum **13**

EXPENSIVE

Hotel Casa Thomas Somerscales ★★★ *(Moments)*   This exquisite hotel is the most luxurious in Valparaíso, and it is located reasonably close to attractions and restaurants. The hotel is actually the former home of Valparaíso's most famous painter, Thomas Somerscales, renowned for his portraits of the city and the War of the Pacific. The new patrons have shown superb taste during the restoration of the property, dressing the rooms with fresh white linens and curtains, and embellishing rooms and the lobby with fine 19th-century antiques and ornaments. The stairwell is cheerfully lit by a two-floor stained-glass window, and the front patio still has its lovely black-and-white checkered tiles. Breakfast is served in their dining area or, better yet, to you in bed. For most Americans, the price makes this hotel an excellent value.

San Enrique 446, Cerro Alegre. ✆ 32/331006. www.hotelsomerscales.cl. 8 units. $66 double; $110 double with terrace and bay view; $100 triple. AE, DC, MC, V. **Amenities:** Cafeteria. *In room:* TV, minibar, safe.

Hotel Ultramar ★★★ *(Moments)*   Valparaíso's newest hotel is also the trendiest. The hotel sits up high and affords dynamite views of the entire city from the guest rooms (probably the best views of any hotel here), and its location at about the same height as Cerro Concepción means you can walk there on a flat road in about 10 minutes (not the most attractive walk, however). This is Chile's first hip boutique-style hotel, and it really shows what can be accomplished when an architect puts imagination into the renovation of Valparaíso's historic buildings. The hotel is housed within a brick 1907-era building and features 17 eclectically decorated rooms in a vibrant, postmodern decor. The lovely lobby has black-and-white checkerboard tile floors with tall windows that let the afternoon sun stream in. The restaurant is made of glass, steel, and wood, and is light and airy; there is also a terrace for soaking in the view. The owners seem eager to negotiate lower prices during the off season, so ask before booking.

Calle Pérez 173, Cerro Cárcel. ✆ 32/210000. www.hotelultramar.cl. 17 units. $73 double; $83 double with bay view; $150 suite. AE, DC, MC, V. **Amenities:** Restaurant. *In room:* TV.

Robinson Crusoe Hotel ★★ *(Finds)*   They don't have a website, nor do they seem to want much publicity, which makes this little bed-and-breakfast a find in Valparaíso. The Robinson Crusoe is a stylish inn topped with a terrace lounge that offers a knockout view of the city; unfortunately, however, none of the rooms has a view. The inn was once a collection of several run-down homes that were enclosed to form one unit, retaining the antique charm of the building's stained glass, high windows, and towering doors. The interiors are a soothing, rich plum and ornamented with arts and crafts and nautical decor. The hotel is about a 15-minute walk to downtown Valparaíso, and you must walk several blocks up from the Espíritu Santo funicular to get back. Close to the Pablo Neruda museum and the Gato Tuerto restaurant and bookstore.

Héctor Calvo 389, Valparaíso. ✆ 32/495499. robinsoncrusoeinn@hotmail.com. 14 units. $75 double. AE, DC, MC, V. **Amenities:** Restaurant. *In room:* TV.

INEXPENSIVE

Brighton Bed & Breakfast ★★ *(Moments)*   Location, location, location—wow, does this little hotel have it. Perched vertiginously high atop a cliff on Cerro Concepción, this canary-yellow Victoria provides sweeping views of the harbor and the city center below (although only the suite and three doubles have the view). Because this is a converted home, room sizes vary, and most rooms are unremarkable, but the location more than makes up for it. There's a popular cafe on the first floor with two terrace patios that seem to hang over the city—it's

mesmerizing and encourages you to linger long after you've finished breakfast. On weekends, the cafe has live bolero and tango music, and it stays open until 4am. To get here, take the Concepción *ascensor* and go left.

Paseo Atkinson 151–153, Cerro Concepción, Valparaíso. ℂ/fax **32/223513**. www.brighton.cl. 6 units. $28 double without bathroom; $34 double with bathroom; $35 double with bathroom and sea view. AE, DC, MC, V. **Amenities:** Cafe.

Casa Aventura ⭐ *(Value)* This gem of a *hostal* is a good bet for budget travelers: a central location, clean interiors, on-site laundry, and kitchen privileges. There are five rooms (two triples, two doubles, and one quad); the atmosphere is quiet and intimate, with a sunny living area and couches for hanging out. The interiors have a folksy decor that you see in a lot of backpacker hostels. The German-Chilean couple who run the hostel offer on-site optional Spanish courses, too. The con: If your room isn't full, you might end up sharing with a stranger, and the double rooms are windowless. Beds have down comforters. Casa Aventura also arranges tours in and around Valparaíso.

Pasaje Gálvez 11, Cerro Alegre, Valparaíso. ℂ/fax **32/755963**. www.casaventura.cl. 5 units. $9 per person. No credit cards. **Amenities:** Self-service laundry; kitchen facilities; tours; Spanish lessons.

Casa Latina ⭐ These are spartan accommodations (a bed, night table, and lamp—no adornments), but the location on Cerro Concepción next to several excellent restaurants and a funicular make the Casa Latina a steal at just $15 per person. There are just three guest rooms: one triple, one double with twins, and one double with a full-size bed, and just one communal bathroom that you'll have to share. A kitchenette is available for cooking, although breakfast is included. The friendly couple who run the Casa live on the first floor, and they don't seem to answer their e-mails often, so try calling if no one gets back to you.

Papudo 462, Valparaíso. ℂ/fax **32/494622**. casalatina@bbvalparaiso.cl. 3 units. $15 per person. No credit cards. **Amenities:** Kitchen facilities.

WHERE TO DINE
MODERATE

In addition to the restaurants listed below, there are two cafes in the Plaza Aníbal Pinto. One, the **Café Riquet,** located at no. 1199, is an old standby in Valparaíso and a popular point of reunion for writers and artists and a host of characters (with good fixed-price lunches). Nearly next door, the more modern **Café del Poeta,** no. 1181, is the place for coffee and pastries; try Chile's famous *onces* (afternoon tea).

Bar Inglés CHILEAN So-so food and a slightly overpriced menu do not make the Bar Inglés a great value, but the old-world atmosphere merits a visit. The interiors haven't changed much since the early 1900s, and the long oak bar, wooden pillars, and walls are the original deal. Smaller items such as sandwiches are usually good, but main courses are too simple for the price. Still, the Bar Inglés remains a local favorite among businessmen, who spend long lunches pounding out deals.

Entrance on Cochrane 851 or Blanco 870. ℂ **32/214625**. Main courses $7–$11. AE, MC, V. Mon–Fri 9am–midnight.

Café Turri ⭐ *(Overrated)* INTERNATIONAL/CHILEAN Regionally famous, the Café Turri is down to one star for increasingly poor food and service. The views from their terrace are gorgeous, and considering this, it does make for a good place to stop off for a cup of coffee or a snack. But once the sun goes down and the fluorescent lights come on, the ambience is glum, and the can't-be-bothered waiters make you feel like you're wasting their time. The specialty here is seafood (bass, salmon, congrio, swordfish, and more, cooked 24 different ways), but for the money, you'd be better off eating at Pasta e Vino or La Columbina.

Calle Templeman 147 (Cerro Concepción; take the Concepción lift). ⓒ **32/259198**. Dinner reservations recommended for outdoor seating. Main courses $5–$15. AE, DC, MC, V. Daily 10am–11pm.

Gato Tuerto 🐱🐱 INTERNATIONAL   The Gato Tuerto shares its space with the Fundación Valparaíso in a sunflower- and cobalt-colored Victorian that hovers over Plaza Victoria. You can't miss it, and let's hope you don't—this restaurant serves good fare from all over the world, and they have an excellent bookstore and Internet cafe. There are about 20 dishes from a dozen different countries, ranging from Moroccan to Thai to Indonesian, such as Nasi Goreng, a dish with shrimp, red pepper, squash, and almonds, or good old lasagna. Come here if you have a group that can't decide what kind of food to eat. Attentive service, and a wine list featuring up-and-comers, too.

Héctor Calvo 205 (Espíritu Santo Funicular). ⓒ **32/593156**. Main courses $6–$10. AE, DC, MC, V. Daily 1–11pm.

La Columbina 🐱🐱 *(Moments)* INTERNATIONAL/CHILEAN   This terrific restaurant occupies a beautiful Victorian building and includes a tearoom with stained-glass windows and a panoramic view and a restaurant/pub with parquet floors and a pretty terrace shaded by striped awnings. The antique building is an old servants' quarters for the nearby Palacio Baburizza, and at press time, the owners were busy expanding the restaurant by adding to the top floor in order to expand the view. In the evening, there is an additional menu of appetizers, including Mexican and Thai platters, as well as very tasty entrees such as filet mignon marinated in dark beer and fresh herbs. Wood-burning stoves, sumptuous views, an amicable staff, and live jazz, tango, and bolero music on Friday and Saturday make for a great atmosphere.

Pasaje Apolo 91–77. ⓒ **32/236254**. Reservations recommended for dinner. Main courses $5–$10. AE, DC, MC, V. Tues–Sat 9am–4pm, 4–8pm (tearoom only), and 8pm–midnight (Fri–Sat until 2am); Sun–Mon 9am–4pm.

Pasta e Vino 🐱🐱🐱 INTERNATIONAL/ITALIAN   I wish more Chilean restaurants were like this delightful little eatery: intimate, inventive, and owner-attended. The young chef at Pasta e Vino takes Chilean products and really puts them to work, creating absolutely delicious cuisine. The last time I was here, we ordered ginger-lime clams, squid risotto, salmon ravioli, and a fresh green salad. I can't remember the last time I enjoyed a meal so much. The ambience is chic and cozy, with brick walls and just six wooden tables. Reservations are imperative—however, show up early on a weeknight, and they might be able to fit you in.

Templeman 352. ⓒ **32/496187**. Reservations recommended. Main courses $6–$9. AE, DC, MC, V. Wed–Sat 8pm–midnight; Sunday 1–5pm.

Restaurant Hamburg 🐱 *(Kids)* GERMAN/CHILEAN   I recommend this restaurant if you have a hearty appetite because the portions here are generous. The kitschy interiors are a lot of fun, too, especially for kids. The German owner was a merchant sailor who dropped anchor in Valparaíso 20 years ago; he launched Hamburg so that he could have the dishes he so loved from back home: pickled herring, pork chops and sauerkraut, goulash, and more. But most of the menu is Chilean, with standard fare such as steak *a lo pobre,* and grilled fish with mashed potatoes. The restaurant is jammed-packed with memorabilia the owner had collected from around the world. Local politicians often dine here.

Calle O'Higgins 1274. ⓒ **32/413144**. Main courses $6–$9. AE, DC, MC, V. Mon–Sat 10am–11:30pm.

INEXPENSIVE

El Cinzano ☆ *Moments* CHILEAN   Since 1896, this restaurant has been the popular hangout for poets, intellectuals, and musicians, who come for late-night *chorrillanas,* a Valparaíso specialty of steak, eggs, onions, and french fries tossed together and heaped on a platter. Waiters in smart black jackets and bow ties serve typical Chilean seafood fare and grilled meats, as well as their other specialty: *vino arreglado,* or "fixed" wine with strawberry, peach, or *chirimoya* (custard apple). Really, you're here for the atmosphere, not the quality of the food. On weekends, tango singers serenade diners (see "Valparaíso After Dark," below).

Aníbal Pinto 1182. ℰ **32/213043.** Main courses $3.50–$8. AE, DC, MC, V. Daily 10am–1am (until 4:30am Thurs–Sat).

WHAT TO SEE & DO

The **Natural History Museum** will undergo a desperately needed renovation in late July 2005. The project is slated for completion in early 2007. If you are in the area, you might check on the off chance that it is open (Av. Condell 1546). The **Galería Municipal de Arte,** located in the basement level of the building (Av. Condell 1550; open Tues–Sun; erratic hours dependent on current exhibition), featuring paintings and sculptures by regional artists, usually thematic and related to the Valparaiso area.

La Sebastiana ☆☆☆   La Sebastiana is one of poet Pablo Neruda's three quirky homes that have been converted into museums honoring the distinguished Nobel Laureate's work and life. What makes La Sebastiana special is that the staff allows visitors to wander about freely without an accompanying guide, unlike the Neruda museums in Santiago and Isla Negra.

Even if you haven't familiarized yourself with Neruda's work, this museum is worth the visit to explore this eccentric home, with its whimsical collection of knickknacks Neruda liked to collect during his journeys through the Americas and abroad. There are self-guiding information sheets in a variety of languages that explain the significance of important documents and items on display. You can't help becoming captivated by the charisma the artist lavished throughout this home. Below the museum is a gallery and gift shop.

The walk from Plaza Victoria is a hike, so you might want to take a taxi. From Plaza Ecuador, there's a bus, Verde D, or the *colectivo* no. 39. Or you might opt to take *La Cintura* **(The Waist),** a bus route that takes riders up and down and around the snaking streets of Valparaíso and eventually stops a block or so from Neruda's house (be sure to tell the driver that's your final destination because the bus continues on). To take this route, board Bus Verde O at Plaza Echaurren near the Customs House (La Aduana).

Calle Ferrari 692. ℰ **32/256606.** Admission $3.25 adults, $1.50 students. Tues–Sun 10am–6pm.

Museo de Mar Thomás Cochrane ☆   High atop Cerro Cordillera sits Lord Cochrane's Museum of the Sea inside the old residence of one Juan Mouat, an English immigrant. Mouat built the house in 1841 in colonial style with all the trimmings, including its own observatory—the first in Chile. The museum houses an impressive display of model ships that belonged to Cochrane, and the museum affords one of the best panoramic views in the city.

Calle Merlet 195 (via the Ascensor Cordillera). ℰ **32/939486.** Free admission. Tues–Sun 10am–6pm.

Museo Naval y Marítimo ☆☆   This fascinating museum merits a visit even if you do not particularly fancy naval and maritime-related artifacts and memorabilia. The museum is smartly designed and divided into salons: the War of

Independence, the War against the Peru-Bolivia Confederation, and the War against Spain. Each salon holds artifacts such as antique documents and correspondence, ship accessories, uniforms, and war trophies. Of special note is the Arturo Prat room, with artifacts salvaged from the *Esmeralda,* a wooden ship that sunk while valiantly defending Valparaíso against the Peruvian iron ship *Huascar* during the War of the Pacific.

Paseo 21 de Mayo, Cerro Artillería. ℭ **32/283749.** Admission 90¢ adults, 35¢ kids under 12. Tues–Sun 10am–5:30pm.

WALKING TOUR	FROM THE PORT TO THE HEIGHTS OF VALPARAISO

Start: Muelle Prat, Visitor Center.
Finish: Ascensor Concepción or Calle Esmeralda.
Time: 1 to 3 hours.
Best Times: Any day except Monday, when most museums and restaurants are closed.

The Fundación Valparaíso has done an exceptional job of mapping out a new "Bicentennial Heritage Trail," a looping 30km (19-mile) walking tour divided into 15 thematic stages. I urge visitors to pick up a copy of the trail guide to supplement the walking tour described below; the guide can be found at the Gato Tuerto bookstore, located at Héctor Calvo 205 (Espíritu Santo Funicular), or bookstores (if you are cruising, you may find the book at the Baron's Pier shopping gallery). Each stage takes approximately 90 minutes to 3 hours to walk, and the guide provides fascinating historical data, literary gossip, architectural information, and fun anecdotes about the city. To help navigate you, the fundación has placed arrows on the street at various stages of the trail. For visitors with limited time in the city, the walking tour outlined below will take you to the city's finest viewpoints and top attractions.

❶ Muelle Prat/Visitor Center
Begin at the visitor center at Prat Pier. There is quite a bit of hullabaloo at the dock here, with skippers pitching 20-minute boat rides around the bay to tourists aboard one of their rustic fishing skiffs. It's not a very professional operation, but for $1, what do you have to lose? There are few places in the world where you can get so close to commercial ships (docked here in the harbor). Valparaíso has changed little in the past century, and to view the city from this perspective is to see the city as many a sailor did when arriving here for the first time after a long journey around Cape Horn. There is a row of curio shops by the dock, which are packed with tourists when a cruise ship docks here.

Head away from the pier and cross Errázuriz to reach:

❷ Plaza Sotomayor
Until the late 1800s, the sea arrived just a few feet from the edge of this plaza, lapping at the gates of the Naval Command Headquarters on the west side of the plaza. Built in 1910, the grand neoclassical building was once the summer residence for several of Chile's past presidents. At the plaza's entrance you'll encounter the **Monument to the Heroes of Iquique.** The heroes of the War of the Pacific, Prat, Condell, and Serrano, are buried underneath this monument. This tremendous battle in 1879 pitted Chile against a Peru-Bolivia confederation, and Chile's victory against the two resulted in the capture of the mineral-rich northern territory, cutting

Walking Tour: From the Port to the Heights of Valparaíso

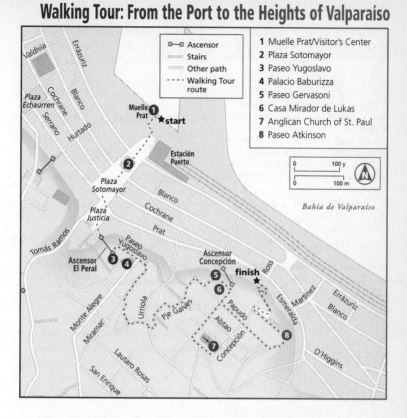

Legend:
- ▢—▢ Ascensor
- Stairs
- Other path
- - - - Walking Tour route

1 Muelle Prat/Visitor's Center
2 Plaza Sotomayor
3 Paseo Yugoslavo
4 Palacio Baburizza
5 Paseo Gervasoni
6 Casa Mirador de Lukas
7 Anglican Church of St. Paul
8 Paseo Atkinson

Bahía de Valparaíso

Bolivia off from the sea and extending Chile's size by nearly a third (to learn more about the war, visit the Naval Museum). Underneath the plaza, where you now stand, are shipwrecks and remains of the old pier, which you can view at the tiny underground museum (at the plaza's center, open daily 10am–6pm). The pier and artifacts such as anchors, ballast, and cannons were discovered while excavating land to build the parking garage at the northeast edge of the plaza. Next to the old post office is the "American Fire House," the first volunteer fire station in Latin America. Cross the plaza toward the Justice Palace.

To the left of the plaza, next to the Palacio de Justicia, ride the Ascensor Peral (ca. 1902) for 10¢ to the top of Cerro Alegre and there you'll find:

❸ Paseo Yugoslavo

Nitrate baron Pascual Baburizza built this pretty terrace walkway and dubbed it Yugoslavian Promenade in honor of his heritage.

Continue along the terrace until you pass:

❹ Palacio Baburizza

This Arte Noveau palace was built in 1916 for Ottorino Zanelli and later sold to Baburizza, who lived here until his death in 1941. The palace is a fine display of the best European handiwork available during the early 1900s; however, today it is the city's Fine Arts Museum, housing a collection of 19th- and 20th-century Chilean and European paintings. The museum is most interesting for its paintings of early Valparaíso by local artists Juan Mauricio Rugendas and Thomas Somerscales. Occasionally, the museum hosts temporary exhibitions (open Tues–Sun 10am–6pm; free admission).

Continue along Paseo Yugoslavo, past the La Columbina restaurant. The road curves to the right around a tiny plaza; follow it until you reach Calle Alvaro Besa. Take Alvaro Besa as it winds down the hill, or take the shortcut down Pasaje Bavestrello, a cement stairway at the left. Continue until you reach Calle Urriola, which you'll cross, then walk up 20m (66 ft.) and turn left into another stairway, Pasaje Gálvez. The narrow walkway twists and turns, passing the colorful facades of some of the most striking homes in Valparaíso. At Calle Papudo, climb the stairway and turn left into:

❺ Paseo Gervasoni

Another of Valparaíso's characteristic promenades, this *paseo* fronts a row of stately 19th-century mansions.

At the end of the walkway, you'll find Café Turri, a popular Valparaíso restaurant and a good spot for a snack or coffee (but please see the review on p. 271 first). Before the cafe, to the right, is the:

❻ Casa Mirador de Lukas

This museum is dedicated to the much-loved "Lukas," aka Renzo Pecchenino, a brilliant cartoonist and satirist who worked for years for the newspaper *El Mercurio* (open Tues–Sun 11am–8pm; admission is 70¢). Lukas dedicated his career to drawing Valparaíso and the eccentric characters found here; a collection of his drawings is available for sale, *Apuntes Porteños,* which makes an excellent Valparaíso souvenir. It is possible to terminate the walking tour

here and descend via Ascensor Concepción, but I recommend that you keep walking.

Continue around Gervasoni until you reach Papudo. You take a detour here 2 blocks up Calle Templeman to visit the:

❼ Anglican Church of St. Paul

Built in 1858, this Anglican church was not officially recognized until 1869, when the Chilean government repealed a law banning religions other than Catholicism. The church houses a grand organ donated by the British in 1901 in honor of Queen Victoria. You can hear this magnificent instrument at work at 12:30pm every Sunday.

Double back to Calle Papudo, head southeast (turning right if returning from the church) until reaching:

❽ Paseo Atkinson

At the entrance to Paseo Atkinson, you'll pass the city's Lutheran church, built in 1897 for the large German population here in the early 19th century. Paseo Atkinson is another breathtaking pedestrian walkway, bordered by antique homes with zinc facades and guillotine windows popular with the British in the early 20th century. Continue down the pedestrian stairway until you reach Calle Esmeralda and the end of the walk. You can also descend by doubling back and riding the Ascensor Concepción to Calle Prat.

OTHER SHORT WALKS

At the southwest corner of the Anglican church, walk up Templeman and left on Urriola. Just past the El Desayunador cafe on the left is a barely perceptible promenade, called Dimalow. Halfway down the esplanade, you will encounter the **best viewpoint** in Valparaíso here, a truly spectacular vista of the bay, the tall steeple of the Lutheran church and the colorful, tumbledown homes clinging to the hills. This is your best photo opportunity. The Queen Victoria Funicular is here, and you can ride it down to Cumming Street, head left 1 block to the Plaza Aníbal Pinto, then down Esmeralda until reaching the Plaza Sotomayer.

THE PORT NEIGHBORHOOD   Begin at the **Customs House (Aduana),** the grand, colonial American–style building built in 1854 and located at the north of town at Plaza Wheelwright at the end of Cochrane and Calle Carampangue. To the right you'll find the **Ascensor Artillería,** built in 1893; it costs 10¢. The wobbly contraption takes visitors to the most panoramic pedestrian walkway in Valparaíso, **Paseo 21 de Mayo.** Don't miss the view of the port from the gazebo. Follow the walkway until reaching the **Museo Naval y Marítimo** (described in "What to See & Do," above). To return, double back and descend via the *ascensor,* or head down the walkway that begins at the cafe, and take a left at Calle Carampangue.

FROM PLAZA VICTORIA TO LA SEBASTIANA (PABLO NERUDA'S HOUSE)

Plaza Victoria is the most attractive plaza in Valparaíso. In the late 1880s, it was the elegant center of society; the grand trees, trickling fountain, and sculptures imported from Lima recall that era's heyday.

From the plaza, head south on Calle Molina to Alduante for the **Open Air Museum,** which features more than 20 murals painted on cement retainer and building walls along winding streets. Begin at the steep stairway at Calle Alduante and turn left at Pasaje Guimera, and left again at the balcony walkway that leads to **Ascensor Espíritu Santo;** you can ride the funicular up and backtrack this route, walking down. Continue along Calle Rudolph until reaching Calle Ferrari. (Alternatively, follow Calle Rudolph to Guimera and Hector Calvo, where you'll find the Gato Tuerto bookstore/restaurant.) Walking up Ferrari to no. 692, you'll find the must-see **La Sebastiana,** Pablo Neruda's old house (described in "What to See & Do," above). *Note:* Calle Ferrari is Valparaíso's steepest street, so walking the several blocks to the museum is quite a hike.

VALPARAISO AFTER DARK

Valparaíso is famous for its nightlife, especially its bohemian pubs and bars where poets, writers, tango aficionados, sailors, university students, and just about everyone else spend hours drinking, dancing, and socializing well into the early morning hours. In fact, most restaurants and bars do not adhere to a set closing hour, but instead close "when the candles burn down."

Most places serve snacks, especially bars and pubs that operate as restaurants by day. The **Cinzano,** facing Plaza Aníbal Pinto on Calle Esmeralda (© 32/213043), is a traditional yet kitschy watering hole (and restaurant) known for its kooky tango singers who break out the mike Thursday through Saturday after 10pm. But you need to get here earlier, or you'll end up waiting for a table. **La Columbina** (© 32/236254) is frequented by an adult crowd for its comfortable ambience, live jazz and bolero music, and view of the glittering lights of Valparaíso that spread out below; take a cab or the funicular Ascensor Peral and walk down Paseo Yugoslavo. **La Playa,** Serrano 568 (© 32/594262), is one of Valparaíso's oldest restaurants, and its bohemian ambience on weekends draws an eclectic mix of characters who come to eat, drink, and listen to live music or poetry readings well into the early morning. This is the epicenter of late-night life and can get packed after midnight.

The Almirante Montt and Cumming street areas are home to several bohemian, funky bars such as **Charles Baudelaire,** Almirante Montt 42 (© 32/968357), decorated in red and black, with electronic music and periodic expositions. Between both streets, at Wagner 129, is the artsy bar **Fetiche** (© 32/493909), located in an old iron storage building. **Bitácora,** Cumming 68 (© 32/226412), is a popular cultural center featuring local artists; there's a bar on the first floor and a second-floor salon dedicated to theater and music.

Bars and nightspots keep popping up on Calle Errázuriz and include **La Piedra Feliz,** Errázuriz 1054 (© 32/256788), built within the old storehouse of a shipping company. This modern, trendy bar has a subterranean lounge and club with DJs (lounge open Thurs–Sat). They also have two salons with salsa and tango lessons. **La Cueva del Chivato,** Errázuriz 1152 (© 32/758160), plays live music amid a chaotic ambience, and there is a disco here. This bar/club caters to the 30s-and-up crowd.

On Cerro Concepción, a trendy hole-in-the-wall is the bar **Gremio,** Pasaje Gálvez 173 (© **32/228394**), with periodic arts exhibitions and snacks.

3 Excursions Outside Valparaíso & Viña del Mar

ISLA NEGRA
125km (78 miles) west of Santiago

Isla Negra is mostly known as "the place where Pablo lived"—Pablo Neruda, that is. His third—and favorite—home is here, perched high above the sand and sea that inspired him, and it is now a museum. The endearing little town is about 1½ hours south of Valparaíso, and anyone planning to spend the night in that city might consider this recommended destination as a first stop. After lunch here at one of two excellent restaurants, you can head north for a beautiful coastal drive to Valparaíso. The **Casa Museo Pablo Neruda** ⟨⟨⟨, at Calle Poeta Neruda s/n (© **32/461284;** open March–Dec 10am–2pm and 3–6:30pm; Jan–Feb 10am–8:30pm; closed on Mon), is larger than Neruda's other two homes, and his collections of knickknacks here are extraordinary: glass bottles, wooden sirens salvaged from ships' bows, butterflies, shells, African masks, ships-in-bottles, and more. Neruda, it seems, when not penning verse, liked to travel, hunt out treasures, and spend a lot of cash. The museum is a wonderful place to visit, and kids love it, too. The tomb of Neruda and his wife is also on view here.

At the back of the museum is **Café del Poeta** (© **32/461774**), with pleasant outdoor seating and a direct view of the rocky beach and crashing waves below. You'll find good pisco sours and seafood dishes here. **Hostería La Candela,** Calle de la Hostería 67 (© **32/461254;** www.candela.cl), has Isla Negra's other good seafood restaurant, in addition to a little hotel, if you decide to spend the evening.

The coastal strip of Isla Negra has been declared a *Zona Típica* (Heritage Zone) to preserve the area from becoming overrun by multistoried apartment buildings. You can get here from Valparaíso **by bus** with the **Pullman** company (© **32/224025**), which leaves every 30 minutes until 10pm from Santiago's Universidad de Chile Terminal (Metro: Univ. de Chile). A bus leaves two or three times per hour on **Tur Bus** (© **2/270-7500**) from the same terminal. To get here **by car,** from Valparaíso, drive back out toward Santiago on Ruta 68 and follow the sign to Algarrobo (Isla Negra is south of Algarrobo).

ZAPALLAR, MAITENCILLO & COLCHAGUA

Zapallar is the refuge of Chile's moneyed elite, and the stalwart residents who have lived here over the past century have lobbied successfully to keep the riffraff out and construction to a minimum. Accordingly, it is the loveliest residential cove along the shore of the Central Coast. Each home flourishes with exotic landscaping, and the beach is so pristine, it looks as though it has been raked with the meticulousness of a Zen master.

All this aside, Zapallar is also where you'll find one of the best restaurants around: **El Chiringuito** (© **33/741024;** no credit cards accepted), which has no address, so look for it on the south end of town. The restaurant's pleasant outdoor seating encourages you to linger for a long lunch. Try the seafood, especially the Parmesan razor clams. If you'd like to spend the night, try a comfortable bed-and-breakfast, the **Hotel Isla Seca,** Ruta F-30 E, #31 (© **33/741224;** www.hotelislaseca.cl; 38 units; $130–$160 double with terrace and ocean view).

Neighboring Zapallar is Colchagua and farther south, Maintencillo, two middle-class weekend retreats for Santiaguinos. There isn't really any lodging here apart from the ubiquitous *cabañas;* however, a few attractions stand out. At the northern end of the beach in Cachagua, there is a rocky pathway that takes visitors past the **Island of Cachagua Nature Sanctuary,** where you can view Humboldt penguins and sea otters (good idea to bring binoculars). In Maitencillo, at Playa Caleta, there is a **fisherman's market** with stands selling shellfish and fish just pulled from the sea. This is as fresh as it gets: Order a plate of raw clams or live scallops, and watch the fishmongers expertly fillet the catch of the day. Also in Maitencillo is the opportunity to **tandem paraglide** with a certified pro (© 09/233-0349; www.parapente.cl; 20–30 min. $70; 40 min. $100).

PARQUE NACIONAL LA CAMPANA

La Campana National Park as an "outdoor" destination doesn't offer the diverse array of activities or infrastructure that you find in Cajón de Maipo, but it has two main highlights: its dense concentration of the southernmost species of palm tree in the world, the Palma Chilena *(Jubaea chilensis),* and the Cerro La Campana, the best 360-degree summit lookout point in the central region (but it's a *strenuous* hike to get to it). Charles Darwin immortalized this 1,800m-high (5,904 ft.) lookout point in his book *Voyage of the Beagle,* stating he never so thoroughly enjoyed a day as the one he spent atop this summit. Nevertheless, it is one of the most overlooked national parks in Chile.

Parque Nacional La Campana is located in the dry coastal mountains, 110km (68 miles) from Santiago, close enough for a day visit or as a stop on the way to or from Valparaíso. There are three sectors with separate entrances. **Sector Ocoa** has the concentration of palms and is a lovely day hike winding through palm groves and ending at a waterfall. The trail is mostly flat and about 6km (3¾ miles) long. The stout-trunk palms that you see here grow very slowly and live as long as 800 years. Hundreds of thousands once blanketed the central region, but they were nearly harvested to extinction for their sap, which was used to make *miel de palma,* something like a pancake syrup. Reach this sector from the Panamericana Highway; the signs for the park exit are very visible.

The Sector **Cajón Grande** has a 7km (4¼-mile) trail through oak groves (best to view in the autumn) that is easy to moderate. By far the most popular is the **Sector Granizo,** where you'll find the trail head for Darwin's climb to Cerro La Campana. The trail is very steep in parts, especially the last 90 minutes, but if you can hack it, the breathtaking view at the end sweeps from the Andes mountain range to the coast, allowing you to see Chile "as in a map," said Darwin. The trail is 7km (4 ¼ miles) and takes approximately 7 to 8 hours to complete. Both sectors Grande and Granizo are in the park's southern region, with both entrances close to the town Olmué. The materials and information offered by the park rangers at Conaf are well designed and very informative. There are campsites in all three sectors, which cost $10 per night for one to six people; admission to the park is $2 adults and $1 children; open year-round from 9am to 6pm (© 33/442922; www.parquelacampana.cl). Bus service here is spotty; better to rent a car, or Santiago Adventures arranges tours here.

4 Cajón de Maipo

San Alfonso is 65km (40 miles) east of Santiago

Cajón de Maipo is part *huaso* (a cowboy from the central valley), part artist's colony, part small-town charm tucked into a valley in the foothills of the Andes.

From Santiago it's less than 1 hour to the heart of the Cajón, the reason so many city denizens come to exchange the city smog and cement for the area's rugged, pastoral setting of towering peaks, freshly scented forest slopes, and the roar of the Maipo River as it descends along its route to the sea. If you have a day and would like to get a feel for the Andes and its rugged beauty, I highly recommend a visit here.

The highlight of this area is **El Morado National Park** (see "Attractions & Activities," below), but it is certainly not a requisite destination. Cajón de Maipo offers a wide array of outdoor activities, such as rafting, horseback riding, hiking, climbing, and more, but it also offers a chance to linger over a good lunch or picnic, stroll around the area, and maybe even lay your head down for the night in one of the charming little *cabañas* that line the valley.

The well-paved road through this valley follows the path of the Maipo River. Along the way you'll pass dozens of stalls set up by locals who sell fresh bread, honey, *kuchen* (a dense cake), empanadas, and chocolate to passersby.

Then you'll pass the tiny hamlets of Vertientes and San José de Maipo, the principal city of the area, founded in 1792 when silver was discovered in the foothills. The colonial adobe homes and 18th-century church still surround the traditional plaza in the center of town. Continuing southeast, the road curves past San Alfonso and eventually reaches a police checkpoint where drivers register before continuing on the dirt road to El Morado. About a half-hour farther (due to the condition of the road), there are fabulous clay hot springs surrounded by soaring alpine peaks. *A word of caution:* The weekends are packed with day-trippers, the hot springs are overflowing with people, and traffic on the way back is horrible. Plan to come on a weekday, if you can.

ESSENTIALS
GETTING THERE   By Bus   Blue-and-white buses leave daily from the Metro station at Parque O'Higgins in Santiago (line no. 2) to San José de Maipo about every 15 minutes from 6am to 11:30pm, and every half-hour for San Alfonso. The company **Tursmontaña** (© 2/850-0555) leaves Saturday, Sunday, and holidays from the bus stop next to the huge CTC building on Avenida Bustamante at Avenida Providencia. The transfer leaves at 7:30am and goes as far as Baños Morales, leaving for the return ride from Baños Morales at 6pm; cost is $9 round-trip and a reservation is required. Rental vehicles offer the most freedom to explore, or you can organize a tour with Latitud 90 or Santiago Adventures. The Refugío Aleman and Cascade activity complexes can be reached by bus; from there they arrange transportation within the Cajón.

By Car   The route to Cajón de Maipo is fairly straightforward, but it's possible to miss the turnoff if you're not paying attention. Head south on Avenida Los Leones in Providencia. The road will change its name to España, then Macul. Continue through the neighborhood of La Florida, and take a left at the fork at Puente Alto. If you are downtown, following Vicuña Mackenna street will take you directly there. Take a map and count on snarling weekend traffic. If you plan to go to El Morado, note that there is a police checkpoint where drivers are sometimes asked to show their documents, including a passport.

WHERE TO STAY
Cascada de las Animas *★★ (Kids)*   This tourism center is run by the bohemian Astorga-Moreno family, long-time residents who own a tremendous amount of acreage outside San Alfonso (part of which is used for horseback riding excursions), and 80 campground and picnic sites scattered about a lovely

wooded hillside. What is really special here, however, are their log cabins, set amid sylvan, leafy surroundings and uniquely built with carved wood details. For the price, you're better off here than La Bella; however, there is a lot more activity going on around here, especially weekends and during the summer. The cabins are rustic but snug and comfortable, with fully equipped kitchens and wood-burning stoves. Apart from horseback riding, Cascada offers rafting the Maipo River, kayaking, and hiking; there are also meditation sessions, healing programs, and a women's spiritual retreat. The staff here, unfortunately, can often be aloof, but as an independent lodging operation, you don't interact often with employees here. Guests lodging in cabins receive a discount on excursion prices.

San Alfonso s/n, San Alfonso. © 2/861-1303. www.cascadadelasanimas.cl. 8 units. $67 *cabaña* for 1–4 people. AE, DC, MC, V. **Amenities:** Restaurant; outdoor pool; guided activities.

La Bella Durmiente ★ *(Kids)* Located at the end of a steep dirt road, these *cabañas* seem as if they've jumped out of the tale *Sleeping Beauty,* which is what the name means—but the word *durmiente* also refers to the thick wooden railroad planks used in the cabins' construction. Each *cabaña* is distinct, but all are handcrafted from wood and stucco and set among a grove of trees; for this reason, they are on the dark side. The price is pretty steep for what you get here, except during the summer because of their grass-fringed pool. Try to get the "honeymoon" cabin—it's the best here. Each *cabaña* has a kitchen and barbecue.

Calle Los Maitenes 115, San Alfonso. © 2/861-1525. www.labelladurmiente.cl. 5 units. $55 cabin for 2; $70 cabin for 4. AE, MC, V. **Amenities:** Restaurant; outdoor pool (summer only); organized excursions. *In room:* TV.

Piedra Luna ★ Piedra Luna offers *cabañas* within one large building, somewhat like a rustic, wood-and-stone condominium. It's just across the road from La Bella, and the couple who own and run the establishment strive to help you de-stress; they offer relaxation courses, if you are so interested. The *cabañas* have comfy beds and large windows; two have mountain views, but the kitchens are pretty basic. Make sure your *cabaña* for four has two bedrooms and not one room with a bed in the living room (their website has photos). In the main house, there is a lounge for guests' use and a large-screen TV; the English- and German-speaking owners can often be found here.

Calle Los Maitenes 100, San Alfonso. ©/fax 2/861-1542. www.piedraluna.cl. 5 units. *Cabañas* $43–$57 for 2; $65 for 4. No credit cards. **Amenities:** Organized excursions.

WHERE TO DINE

Casa Bosque ★★★ *(Kids)* STEAKHOUSE If you don't eat at Casa Bosque, stop here anyway to check out the restaurant's fabulously outlandish architecture. The local artist who designed Casa Bosque has left his mark on many buildings in Cajón de Maipo, but none as dramatically as here: Polished, raw tree trunks are kept in their natural shape, forming madcap door frames, ceiling beams, and pillars; oddly shaped windows and stucco fill in the gaps. It's pure fantasy, and adults will love it as much as kids. Casa Bosque is a *parrilla,* and it serves delicious grilled beef, chicken, and sausages from a giant indoor barbecue, which you can pair with fresh salads, creamy potatoes, or a grilled provolone cheese, along with a few vegetarian dishes. During the weekend lunch hour, this restaurant can get packed, mostly with families with lots of kids.

Camino el Volcán 16829. © 2/871-1570. Main courses $5.50–$12. AE, DC, MC, V. Mon–Thurs 12:30–6pm; Fri–Sat 12:30pm–midnight; Sun 12:30–7pm.

La Petite France ★★ *(Finds)* FRENCH BISTRO The walls of La Petite France, with its Edith Piaf posters and ads for French products, are pure French kitsch. The locals love it, and you will, too. Since opening 2 years ago, La Petite's cuisine has drawn in diners with a menu that successfully blends French bistro fare with flavorful Chilean and international dishes. On offer are dishes such as filet mignon in a puff pastry with Roquefort sauce, and turkey breast stuffed with almonds, plums, and apples in a cactus sauce. Of course, there's also pâté, escargot, and Croque Monsieur. During tea time on weekends, mouthwatering desserts are laid out enticingly across a long table: tarte tatin, crème brûlée, and chocolate layer cake are just a few choices. It's a pretty spot for outdoor dining.

Camino el Volcán 16096. ℂ 2/861-1967. Main courses $5–$8. AE, DC, MC, V. Tues–Sun noon–6pm and 8pm–midnight.

Trattoria Calypso ⭐⭐ ITALIAN   Owned and operated by a Genovese family who immigrated to this region little more than a decade ago, Trattoria Calypso serves delicious homemade pastas and stone oven–baked pizzas (pizzas are served Sat only). Everything is made using organic and local farm ingredients, such as the mozzarella bought from a family in Cajón de Maipo and smoked here at the restaurant. Pastas include raviolis, cannelloni, fungi fettuccine, and pesto lasagna, but you might want to nibble an antipasti platter with fresh focaccia bread. The cozy restaurant has indoor and outdoor seating at wooden tables; the staff gives a warm welcome to all who pass through the doors. It's open Friday through Sunday only, but if you're in the area during one of these days, don't miss a stop here.

Camino el Volcán 9831. ℂ 2/871-1498. Main courses $7.50–$9. AE, DC, MC, V. Fri–Sat 12:30–10pm; Sun 12:30–6pm. Closed Mon–Thurs.

ATTRACTIONS & ACTIVITIES

EL MORADO NATIONAL PARK   This 3,000-hectare (7,410-acre) park is 90km (56 miles) from Santiago. It takes its name from the sooty-colored rock of the Morado mountain (*morado* means "purple" or "bruised"). The views at El Morado are impressive, and a relaxing spot to take in all this beauty is the Tyrolean mountain lodge **Refugio Lo Valdés** ⭐⭐, San José de Maipo (ℂ 09/ 220-8525; www.refugiolovaldes.com). The *refugio* (meaning "refuge," but really a rustic lodge made of stone) serves excellent food and a fixed-price lunch and dinner, and you can eat out on the deck while gazing out at the snowcapped peaks. The *refugio* is owned by the same people at La Cumbre mountain store in Las Condes (see "Fast Facts: Santiago" in chapter 12), and they offer outdoors activities such as day hiking or overnight climbing trips, horseback riding, visits to the hot springs, and nature tours. There are clean, bunk bed–style accommodations, should you decide to spend the night (there is just one double), and a cozy dining area warmed by a wood stove that nearly takes up the whole room. Rates are $27 per adult, $20 children 6 to 12, and $10 kids 1 to 5; breakfast is included.

You'll find the Conaf park ranger hut at **Baños Morales.** The park is open daily October through April from 8:30am to 6pm, and costs $2 to enter. There is an 8km (5-mile) trail that varies between easy and intermediate terrain, eventually passing by an alpine lake and a glacier with a profile view of the El Morado mountain. This is a first-rate day hike (about 6 hr. average round-trip), and there is a place to camp near the lake. The raggedy little village of Baños Morales has several very hot spring pools open daily from 8:30am to 8pm during the summer and from 10am to 4pm April through September, but they are not particularly inviting, and they're crammed with Santiaguinos during the peak of summer. There are better natural hot springs at **Termas de Colina,** in the form of clay pools descending a slope. The expansive alpine setting adds a sense of grandeur to the experience. It takes time to get here due to the condition of the road; continue past Lo Valdés for 12km (7½ miles). If you don't have a car, try **Manzur Expediciones** (© 2/777-4284; reservations necessary; $14 adults, $11 children), although they go only on weekends, and that is when the hot springs are at maximum capacity. Too many people ruins the experience of getting away from it all. The entrance fee is $6.

RAFTING   Rafting the Maipo River is very popular among Santiaguinos and foreigners alike—it is just amazing that this activity exists so close to a major metropolitan city. Although the season runs from September to April, the river really gets going from November to February, when rafters can expect to ride Class III and IV rapids. Two reliable companies offer half-day rafting excursions: **Cascada de las Animas** (© 2/861-1303; www.cascadadelasanimas.cl) is based in the Cajón, and they arrange rafting trips from its tourism complex (see "Where to Stay," above) in San Alfonso, but it's best to reserve beforehand. Another highly respected, and friendlier, outfitter is **Altué Expediciones,** in Santiago, Encomenderos 83 (© 2/232-1103; www.altue.com). They are based in Santiago and can arrange transportation for you to the Cajón de Maipo.

HORSEBACK RIDING   The same two companies above offer horseback riding in the Cajón de Maipo, either for the day or for multiple-day riding (with themes such as "Following Darwin's Footsteps"). I can't express enough how enjoyable a horseback ride in the Andes is: the sweeping views from high, the grassy meadows, galloping home. . . . There is an indefinable magic about crossing the Andean peaks the way Butch Cassidy and the Sundance Kid did. Cascada de las Animas has tours through its own private chunk of the Andes (see above). Horseback rides are suitable for families and even those with little experience.

5 The Central Valley

The minute you drive out of Santiago, the scenery changes dramatically to wide fields of grapevines, a testament to the nation's thriving wine industry. As you head farther south, the smog begins to thin and more fields unfold until you enter what's known as the Central Valley. The region has both rich soil and a Mediterranean climate conducive to agriculture, and the fresh fruits and vegetables grown here can be bought from one of the many food stands that dot the Panamericana Highway. The region is indeed a food-lover's delight—with so many savory country restaurants along the Panamericana outside Santiago, many call it the gastronomic axis.

The Central Valley is both urban and rural: Semis and cars race along the Panamericana from Santiago to flourishing cities such as Rancagua and Talca, but outside those cities, a quick detour off the interstate puts you between poplar-lined, patchwork fields on dirt roads that see more hooves than wheels. Below are a few of this region's highlights, plus a section on the booming wine-tasting regions and the many opportunities to day tour or spend the night here.

A THERMAL SPA

Termas de Cauquenes   ✸✸   This out-of-the-way thermal spa (about 115km/71 miles from Santiago) is a tremendously relaxing sanctuary tucked away in the Cachapoal Valley, and it can be combined with a visit to the El Teniente Mine or a visit to a winery (see "The Wineries of the Central Valley," p. 288). The highlights here are the gorgeous antique spa facilities inspired by Vichy in France, the spa's regionally renowned restaurant, and the historical appeal of enjoying Chile's oldest publicly used hot springs. Charles Darwin even paid a visit in 1834.

The "Wild West" of South America

During the colonial period, the Central Valley was fundamentally agrarian and largely dependent on cattle production. Wealthy families, who owned the bulk of land, developed their property into ranches called *haciendas* or *estancias*. To tend their giant herds of cattle, hacienda owners hired Chilean "cowboys" called *huasos*.

You'll recognize a *huaso* by his wide-brimmed hat, a poncho that is either colorful and short-waisted or long and earth-toned, and metal spurs the size of a pinwheel. Often, especially when attending a special event, the *huaso* wears black leather chaps that cover the leg from ankle to knee and are adorned with tassels.

The *huaso* struts his stuff in one of the occasional **rodeos** that are popular in the Central Valley. The rodeos take place in a half-moon arena called a *medialuna*. Here *huasos* begin the match by demonstrating their agility atop their mounts, followed by the main event in which a *huaso* attempts to pin a young bull against a wall while on horseback.

Rodeos are held from September to May, especially during the Independence holiday on September 18 and 19. The city of Rancagua hosts the rodeo championships in September. For more information, call the Federación del Rodeo Chileno at ℂ **2/699-0115; www.caballoyrodeo.cl.**

There is a tiny chapel and a beautiful Gothic-style thermal pavilion fitted with colorful stained glass, marble floors, and two facing rows of cubicles with marble bathtubs. I'll be honest, the turn-of-the-20th-century tubs really look their age, but the spa has added a couple of modern whirlpools.

Termas de Cauquenes is now owned by a Swiss chef and his daughter, both of whom are hailed by critics for their fine cuisine. Really, this is the real reason to visit this landmark. The changing menu features fresh seafood and meats that embrace regional recipes. The dining area is sunny and spacious, with leather chairs and a long oak bar. A fixed lunch here costs $14 per person, and many visitors are day-trippers from Santiago. There is a weekend "tasting" menu for $25 on Friday, and a full-dress dinner on Saturday for $29. The hotel rooms are nothing to write home about, yet the tranquillity that the tree-shrouded premises exude keeps you from noticing. The swimming pool is for hotel guests only. Massages, manicures, and pedicures are also offered. To get here, you'll need to drive or take a bus to Rancagua, where the hotel can arrange transportation for you.

Road to Cauquenes, near Rancagua. ℂ/fax 72/899010. www.termasdecauquenes.cl. 50 units. $91 per person double for full pension and use of spa baths; $63 per person double for breakfast only and spa baths. AE, DC, MC, V. **Amenities:** Restaurant; bar; outdoor pool (guests only); massage; thermal baths. *In room:* TV, minibar.

A HACIENDA

Hacienda Los Lingues ✪✪✪ *(Moments* About 125km (78 miles) south of Santiago and nestled among poplar-lined country fields and rolling hills is the Hacienda Los Lingues, one of the oldest and best-preserved haciendas in Chile. The hacienda is now run as a splendid full-service hotel and is a member of the exclusive Relais & Châteaux group. If you can't stay overnight, consider a day tour ($46 per person) that includes a welcome cocktail, tour of the hacienda, lunch in the cavernous wine *bodega*, horse demonstration, and optional use of a swimming pool. There's also horseback riding at an additional cost.

King Phillip III bestowed this lovely estate to the first mayor of Santiago in 1599, and it has remained in the same family for 400 years. The center of the estate features portions of the structures that were built here in the early 17th century, but most of the buildings were built around 250 years ago and have been superbly maintained.

Every room is accented with crystal chandeliers, Oriental rugs, and antique furniture, and literally brimming with decorative pieces, family photos, collector's items, and fascinating odds and ends. The guest rooms are decorated individually with antique armoires and tables, iron bed frames and crocheted bedspreads, ancestral family photos, fresh flowers, and a bucket of champagne. The bathrooms have recently been upgraded, which they needed. Breakfast is not included, but it is served to you in bed. Dinner is served family style at a long table and is very good but overpriced.

For day tours, rent a car or have the hotel arrange a shuttle (two–six people, $200 round-trip), or take the Metro to Estación Central and take a "Metro Train" toward San Fernando (get off at Pelequén). The hotel will send a taxi (arrange this first, for about $10 one-way).

I recommend visiting this venerable old hacienda, and, if you can, combine the visit with a stop at the old Teniente Mine, a winery in the Cachapoal Valley, or the Río Cypress Natural Reserve. If you have a rental vehicle, you can stop for lunch at the Termas de Cauquenes.

Reservations in Santiago: Av. Providencia 1100, #205. 🕾 2/235-5446. Fax 2/235-7604. www.loslingues. com. 19 units, 2 suites. $100 double May–Aug; $150 Sept–Oct; $190 Oct–Apr. Breakfast $19 per person, dinner $62 per person. Day tours $46 per person. AE, DC, MC, V. **Amenities:** Outdoor pool; 2 clay tennis courts; game room; room service; horseback riding; fly-fishing.

Pomaire Pottery

Every region in the central valley has a specialty good that they produce with pride, and Pomaire's is ceramic pottery. Pomaire is a small, dusty village 65km (40 miles) west of Santiago that was known as a *pueblo de indios,* a settlement the Spanish created for Indians. The area is rich in brown clay, and the main street (almost the only street here) overflows with shops hawking vases, funny little figurines, decorative pieces, and pots, plates, and other kitchen crockery—all at reasonable prices. This is also the place to sample homespun, country cooking (try San Antonio or Los Naranjos restaurants) such as the stews *cazuela* and *charquicán,* and Pomaire's famous half-kilo empanada; some restaurants even have *cueca* shows, the national dance of Chile.

Most tour companies offer this excursion, or you can rent a car or take **Buses Melipilla,** which has several daily trips from the San Borja Terminal in Santiago at Alameda O'Higgins 3250. The bus will leave you at the end of the road to Pomaire, where you'll have to take a *colectivo,* or shared taxi, into town. To get here by car, take the Panamericana Highway to the turnoff for Ruta 78 to San Antonio; follow the highway until you see the sign for Pomaire 3km (1¾ miles) before Melipilla. Note that Pomaire is shut down on Monday, and weekends are crowded.

A Select Tour of Chile's Vineyards

The practice of "tasting" Chilean wine has been slow to catch on, but each year more and more wineries open their doors to the public for tours. A few of the wineries listed here are close enough to visit in a half-day; others require a full-day or overnight excursion, meaning you must join a tour or rent a car. For complete "Wine Routes," lodging, tours, and dining information, see the section "The Wineries of the Central Valley," below. It is imperative that you make reservations. Most require 24 hours, but some, such as Concha y Toro, require 4 days notice. The first three wineries have regular scheduled tours; contact the others directly for private reservations or for tour times.

- **Cousiño-Macul,** Av. Quilin 7100 in Peñalolen, near Santiago (© 2/ 351-4175; www.cousinomacul.cl). If you have time to visit just one winery while in Chile, make it the Cousiño-Macul. The first vines in Chile were planted here in 1546. The beautiful estate and its lush, French-designed gardens are as impressive as the winery's Antiguas Reservas traditional red, and it's just a cab ride away ($10–$15 one-way) from Santiago. Bilingual tours are Monday to Friday 11am and 4pm, and Saturday 11am (Saturday Spanish only; reserve an English guide if you have a group). Cost: $6, includes souvenir wine glass.

- **Concha y Toro,** Virginia Subercaseux 210 in Pirque, near Santiago (© 2/476-5269; www.conchaytoro.com). Chile's most popular winery produces the lion's share of wines, from inexpensive table reds to some of Chile's priciest cabernet sauvignons, as well as Chile's top traditional red, Don Melchor. Like Cousiño Macul, the winery itself is part of the attraction, with gardens large enough to require eight full-time gardeners, and antique *bodegas* whose interiors are part of your tour. Concha y Toro is also close enough to Santiago to get there by cab, but ask your hotel to book a tour van, as it will most likely be cheaper. Tours in English Monday to Friday 11:30am and 3pm; Saturday 10am and noon. Closed holidays. Cost: $6, includes souvenir wine glass.

- **Viña Santa Rita** in Buin, near Santiago (© 2/362-2594, or 2/362-2590 on weekends; www.santarita.cl). Santa Rita is a traditional winery that stands out for its restaurant, Doña Paula, and its lovingly maintained estate. Also, should you decide to spend the night, their former estate house has been converted into an elegant but very expensive inn, and it is a good lodging option for those who want to be close to Santiago without being in it. About a 1-hour drive from Santiago or the airport, it makes for a pleasant day trip and a good base for exploring the Central Valley. Tours are Tuesday to Friday at 10am, 11:30am, and 4pm (tasting only, $11, including souvenir wine glass); the 12:15pm and 3pm tours, and the Saturday and Sunday tours at noon and 3:30pm are wine tastings and lunch, for a minimum of $16 per person.

- **Veramonte** in the Casablanca Valley, near Valparaíso (© 3/274-2421; www.veramonte.com). The Casablanca region is relatively new to winemaking, yet it is an ideal location for growing chardonnay and sauvignon blanc grapes. This modern winery has invested heavily in Casablanca's potential with a state-of-the-art facility capable of crushing 75 tons of grapes per day. The winery prides itself on its

"Napa Valley–style" wine-tasting facilities, with a service-oriented staff and an attractive tasting room with a soaring rotunda and glass walls that let you peek into the barrel caves below. The winery makes for a perfect stop on the road from Santiago to Valparaíso.

- **Viña Aquitania** in Peñalolén, in Santiago (𝄐 2/284-5470; www.aquitania.cl). This relatively new boutique, Bordeaux-style winery is a good alternative for a more intimate visit and a chance to taste excellent premium wines. It is a low-yield winery focusing on top quality, and they employ the *terroir* concept. Tastings allow visitors to choose which wines they would like to try (prices vary), and the best part is that it is only 20 minutes from Providencia and Las Condes.

- **Viña Almaviva,** Santiago (𝄐 2/852-9300; www.conchaytoro.com). Almaviva is Chile's top winery, a world-class joint venture between Baron Philippe de Rothschild S. A. and Viña Concha y Toro. The winery's slick design for its cellars and tank areas reminds one vaguely of Opus One in Napa. The wine itself is phenomenal; their 2001 cabernet was awarded 95 points by *Wine Spectator.* It is worth the visit just to try a glass of this nectar, (a bottle of Almaviva costs around $100). Reservations are required; the winery can be visited in tandem with Concha y Toro and is close enough for a taxi.

- **Odfjell Vineyards,** Camino a Valparaíso viejo 7000, in the Isla de Maipo, near Santiago (www.odfjellvineyards.cl). A recent newcomer to the Isla de Maipo scene (located west of Santiago), this unique, nontraditional boutique winery is the creation of Norwegian shipping magnate Dan Odfjell, in partnership with his son Laurence. It looks every bit the fancy winery and is no small operation. The wines routinely score high (85–89 on the *Wine Spectator* scale), but perhaps the setting and design of the winery really make the visit worth the trip—its stylish new gravity-flow facility is built into the hillside overlooking the estate.

- **Matetic Vineyards,** Fundo Rosario, Lagunillas in the Casablanca Valley (𝄐 2/232-3134 or 32/741500; www.mateticvineyards.cl). Proud producers of one of Chile's most interesting Syrahs (the EQ), this beautiful winery is in the up-and-coming valley of San Antonio. The cool coastal climate here allows the winery to produce Syrah, pinot noir, and sauvignon blanc (the only three varieties they currently produce). You can stop here on the way to Isla Negra, or if you prefer, overnight in the winery's small guesthouse.

- **Montes,** Av. Del Valle 945, Of. 2611 (𝄐 2/248-4805; www.monteswines.com). If you have time for only one tour while in the Santa Cruz area, this is the winery to visit. Located in the microvalley of Apalta in Colchagua, Montes has found the perfect *terroir* and the right climate to produce spectacular reds—particularly their Montes "M" and Folley. The tour itself is an adventure. Visitors are taken on a tractor ride through the slope vineyards (climbing a steep hill). Guests begin with a tour of the brand-new, first-class facilities and end sipping a glass of Montes Alpha Syrah from an observation deck above the vineyards, with a panoramic view of the Colchagua valley with the Andes.

OTHER ATTRACTIONS IN THE AREA

Close to Rancagua, **El Teniente** is the world's largest underground copper mine and an utterly fascinating trip into the bowels of the earth. El Teniente began in 1905 and once employed 15,000 workers, who, at the time, lived at the mine in the town **Sewell** (www.sewell.cl). Dubbed the "city of stairs" for its location on a mountain slope, it is now a ghost town and national monument, and many of the old homes have been restored as interpretive museums. About 3,000 Chileans still work here in shifts, 24 hours a day, and a tour here puts you in safety gear and shows you how they do their job. You will be blown away at the immense size of this mine; however, claustrophobia suffers should think twice about this tour. Vip Transport Service offers this trip (© **72/ 210290;** www.vts.cl), but make sure they provide you with a guide with good English skills. Also, if you are planning to combine this tour with another attraction in the area, see if they can arrange a half-day tour.

While in the area, you'll want to pay a visit to the underrated **Reserva Nacional Rio Los Cipreses,** a little-known nature reserve 14km (8¾ miles) from Cauquenes; it's open daily from 8:30am to 6pm (8pm Dec–Feb); admission is $3. There is a park administration center with information, including trails and a guide to the flora and fauna of the reserve. Here it is possible to watch wild parrots swoop from trees and tiny caves high on cliffs; there are also rabbitlike *vizcachas* and red foxes, and, of course, a blanket of cypress trees.

You'll need your own car to get here. If you plan to stay at Termas Cauquenes (or Hacienda los Lingues), have them plan a visit for you.

6 The Wineries of the Central Valley

The international popularity of Chilean wine has soared over the past decade, primarily because Chilean wines offer high quality for a lower cost than their California and French counterparts. Chileans often brag about their industry, claiming a wine tradition that stretches back to the days of the Spanish conquest. But wine production didn't really take off until the late '70s, when Spaniard Miguel Torres introduced modern techniques that revolutionized the industry. Chileans themselves have been slow to appreciate finer wines, and, consequently, many winegrowers export the bulk of their product to Europe and the United States. French and American companies such as Châteaux Lafite and Robert Mondavi have formed partnerships with vineyards in Chile, taking advantage of cheaper land prices and ideal growing conditions to produce wine that now competes in—and often wins—international competitions.

What is unique about Chilean wine is that vintners imported their rootstock from Europe more than a century ago, long before European roots were affected with *phylloxera,* a pest that nearly wiped out the whole of the European wine industry. Chilean rootstock, having not been affected by this plague, is therefore the oldest original European rootstock in the world. Chileans only recently discovered the **Carmenere** grape growing among its merlot vines, a grape rarely seen any longer in France due to the difficulty in growing the grape and its late harvest. It is superior to a merlot, and it is now Chile's trademark wine.

The traditional wineries of Chile (Cousiño Macul, Concha y Toro, and Santa Rita) are located within 35km (22 miles) of Santiago, as well as a few up-and-coming boutique wineries—meaning it is possible to spend a day wine tasting without having to travel very far. Prominent wine-growing valleys outside Santiago limits that you will hear of are Casablanca, San Antonio, Aconcagua, Maule, Curicó, and, most important, the Colchagua Valley, which is centered on the town Santa Cruz, about a 2½-hour drive from Santiago.

WINE ROUTES

There are six formally established wine routes in central Chile: Aconcagua, Cachapoal, Casablanca, Curicó, Colchagua, and Maule. However, the concept is so new that only two—**Colchagua** and **Maule**—have worked the bugs out and are now efficiently run (that is, with bilingual guides who know about wine and attentive service, wineries with modern tasting facilities, and clearly marked signs and maps for those on their own). I recommend the Colchagua wine route above all others. However, you might find it more convenient to visit a route that is closer to Santiago or one between the city and the Argentine border (Aconcagua), if you are headed for Mendoza.

TOURING THE WINE ROUTES

There are three ways to follow a wine route:

1. **Join the scheduled tour** run by the wine route's association. For this option, you'll have to provide your own transportation to the meeting point (in the case of Colchagua and Maule, the towns Santa Cruz and Talca, respectively).

2. **Book a customized tour** that will provide local insight through wine tastings with winery owners, cultural and historical information, and stops for hearty country fare or gourmet cuisine.

3. **Rent a car and follow a wine route at your leisure,** visiting only the attractions that interest you most. Before you set out, make a reservation at a winery, as most do not hold regular business hours. Visit each valley's wine route website for maps, directions, and the wineries' e-mail reservation addresses.

Be sure to pick up Turiscom's excellent *Guía de Vinos* wine guide series sold at bookstores and wine shops (check out the wine store at the airport, as they usually have copies), which comes with a detailed map of the entire Chilean wine region. You can also purchase a copy online at www.turistel.com. Many of these routes combine nature, culture, and historical attractions as part of the tour.

GUIDED TOURS OF THE WINE ROUTES

A lot of tour companies can take you to wine country, but only a few do it well. Also, wine tour companies outside of Chile subcontract local operators and really sock you with an inflated price—so go directly to the local source. **Liz Caskey, Inc.** (© 2/681-1799 or 9/821-9230; www.lizcaskey.com) specializes in custom-made wine and food (gourmet picnics, snacks, and lunches) tours to all the valleys, particularly focusing on many boutique wineries where guests can meet the winemakers or visit a winery in an intimate group setting. Caskey, an American expat, can combine stops to organic olive oil plants, artesian cheese factories, and, in the case of the San Antonio valley, a visit to Isla Negra, Pablo Neruda's coastal home.

For more traditional tours, try **Latitud 90,** Av. Kennedy 7268 (© 2/2479100; www.latitud90.com), which has more than a dozen structured day and overnight tours with titles such as "The Modern and Romantic Wineries" and "Premium Wines and Spas." The websites www.winesofchile.org and www.sommeliersde chile.cl can be helpful when planning your journey.

THE WINE ROUTES

Ruta del Vino, Colchagua Valley, Plaza de Armas 298, Santa Cruz (© 72/ 823199; www.colchaguavalley.cl; reservations required 24 hr. in advance), incorporates some of the most important wineries in Chile, including **Viña Montes, Viña Bisquertt, Viña Los Vascos,** and **Casa Lapostolle** (whose Clos de Apalta cabernet sauvignon was chosen by *Wine Spectator* as the second-best wine in the world in 2004). The valley is an appellation of the larger Rapel Valley, and the region is famous for its big, bold reds such as cabernet sauvignons. The half-day tour visits two wineries; the full-day visits three wineries, or two wineries and the **Museo de Colchagua** (see below). You may use your own rental vehicle and hire a Ruta del Vino guide to accompany your group (although each winery has its own guide), or you can join their shuttle van, which leaves from the Hotel Santa Cruz Plaza. The included lunch for the full-day tour is at the Hotel Santa Cruz, La Hacienda, or Panpan Vinovino. Based on the number of participants, prices for a full-day tour, per person (including lunch), are $150 (one person), $95 (two people), $73 (three–five people), $55 (six or more); half-day tours without lunch cost $95, $73, $42, and $30. If you have your own vehicle, subtract $5 off the per-person rate.

Ruta del Vino Valle Maule, Km 7 Camino San Clemente, Talca (© 71/ 246460; www.valledelmaule.cl; reservations required 24 hr. in advance), offers half-day visits to two wineries and full-day visits to four wineries for $22 (half-day) or $44 (full-day). The cost of lunch at the Hotel Tabonkö (see below) is not included. This is the southernmost wine route, known for its cooler climate that is more suitable for aromatic, less full-bodied reds like pinot noir. Most visitors here spend the night at the Tabonkö or the Hotel Santa Cruz; if staying in the region, you'll want to combine this tour with Colchagua. You won't make it from Santiago for the early half-day tour that starts at 9am because it is a 3½-hour drive here. The Wine Route office in Talca has a wine-tasting center where you can sample wines from all 18 wineries in the area. Wineries to visit here are Viñas J. Bouchon, Cremaschi, Terranoble, Gilmore (also known as Tabontinaja, and where you'll find the Hotel Tabonkö), and Viña Calina, the winery that is co-owned by California's Kendall Jackson.

Ruta del Vino Valle Cachapoal, Calle Comercio 435 (© 72/553684; www. cachapoalwineroute.cl), in spite of their spiffy website, follows a difficult route along (largely unmarked) country dirt roads, so arm yourself with a good map and find your adventurous side. This valley is close to Santiago and is a subappellation of the Rapel valley, and home to midrange wineries such as Misiones del Rengo, Porta, and Anakena. This region specializes in merlot, especially Carmenere. The bonus with this route is that you can tour it in conjunction with a stop at the **Hacienda Los Lingues,** the **Termas de Cauquenes,** or **El Teniente Mine** (p. 288). This route is suited for independent travelers with a rental vehicle, or with an organized tour from Santiago.

Ruta del Vino Curicó, Merced 341, Curicó (© 75/328972; www.rvvc.cl), covers the Curicó Valley, home to some of the oldest—and newest—wineries, and their tours are centered on themes such as "The Secret of Wine," a half-day visit to the town square, and two wineries; and "The Charm of Wineries," a 1-day program with a visit to three wineries, including lunch. This is probably the least popular route with foreign travelers, mainly because they are so unfamiliar with many of the wineries in the region, with the exception of Miguel Torres. The Curicó region is south of Santa Cruz, and it can be combined with that tour if you have enough time.

Ruta del Vino Casablanca, Constitución 252, #A, Casablanca (℃ **32/ 743933;** www.casablancavalley.cl), covers a young wine region has a cooler climate due to its proximity to the coast, and it produces most of Chile's white wines and some pinot noirs. The region strives to be the Napa Valley of Chile, with slick wine-tasting facilities, high-volume visitor capacities, and a couple of stylish restaurants. For this reason, it is very easy to rent a car and visit this region on your own, and, this is a perfect half-day stop for travelers on their way out to Viña del Mar and Valparaíso. See the Veramonte and Matetic wineries above. I recommend that you visit one or both of these wineries and forget the formal tour as of now, until it is better organized (check their website for updates on tours).

Ruta del Vino Aconcagua, Pascual Baburizza 786, #17, Los Andes (℃ **09/ 479-0278;** www.aconcaguavinos.cl), is the new kid on the block in terms of wine routes, and the only two wineries worth visiting here are Viñas Errázuriz and Von Siebenthal—and I recommend you visit the two on your own because the "official" wine route tour requires a minimum of eight guests. Errázuriz is a lovely place to visit, the staff are very welcoming, and their Don Maximiano is one of the best cabernets available in Chile. I suggest you visit this region when on your way to Argentina. Try to plan lunch at the Hotel Portillo high in the Andes (whether or not you're heading to Argentina)—it's another 45 minutes to get there, but the majestic Alpine views are worth the extra drive.

WHERE TO STAY

In the "Central Valley" section, I've listed the Hacienda los Lingues (p. 284) and the Termas de Cauquenes (p. 283) as options for spending the night in this region. Here are a few more.

Hotel Santa Cruz Plaza ⭐⭐ This hotel has turned the town of Santa Cruz into a destination in its own right, although visitors come to wine-taste and visit the town's outstanding museum more than the town itself. The hotel sits on the main plaza yet is relatively inconspicuous, with its mellow mustard wash and ironwork window terraces, a style reminiscent of colonial Mexico. The guest rooms and bathrooms are not huge, but they offer enough space for comfort and are decorated in a terra cotta–colored country style featuring antiques and decorations found throughout the Santa Cruz area.

Service is this hotel's weakness, but the staff is friendly enough and will assist you with your day plans. Once at the hotel, dining in their restaurant is really the only option in town unless you are adventurous and cross the plaza and pick one of the handful of local restaurants (all fairly good). Their buffet breakfast is terrific. The hotel offers a deal for 1 night/2 days that includes accommodations, full board, and visits to Colchagua's vineyards and the Colchagua Museum, for $145 per person. They can arrange a transfer for you from Santiago for an additional charge.

Plaza de Armas 286, Santa Cruz. ℃/fax **72/821010.** www.hotelsantacruzplaza.cl. 41 doubles, 3 suites. Double $105–$115, breakfast included. AE, DC, MC, V. **Amenities:** Restaurant; outdoor pool; sauna; babysitting; laundry service. *In room:* A/C, TV.

Hotel Tabonkö ⭐⭐ This newer hotel is the farthest away from Santiago, but it has a spa that employs "wine therapy," or rubdowns using cabernet sauvignon exfoliation, among other treatments. The hotel is whimsically designed, with odd angles, minimalist interiors, and one huge wine barrel that forms the corner of the building's facade. The rooms are light and airy, with white down comforters and tile floors, but for all its sophistication, the rooms can feel a bit cold. Their excellent restaurant, La Cava de Francisco, is the only dining option, really, and they put together all-inclusive packages with full board. The guest room Jacuzzis feature mineralized water for a relaxing soak.

Valle de Loncomilla, Maule Valley. ℂ 73/197-5539. www.tabonko.cl. 14 units. $330 all-inclusive for 2. AE, DC, MC, V. **Amenities:** Restaurant; spa; wine tour.

Hotel Viña Santa Rita ✮✮✮ *(Finds)*   One of the loveliest places to spend the night near Santiago is Santa Rita winery's picturesque 19th-century hotel. Built in 1885 and refurbished in 1996, this wonderful bed-and-breakfast is surrounded by lush gardens and mixes contemporary decor with antique lamps, rugs, and furniture. It's a very exclusive place, and the price certainly reflects that. A stunning neo-Gothic chapel on the property offers a quiet place for reflection, as does the pretty patio with its bubbling fountain. There's also an old-fashioned game parlor with a piano and a pool table imported from England. Two outstanding restaurants can be found on-site, one at the winery and one within the hotel itself. Rates include breakfast only; lunch and dinner rates run from $10 to $20 per person for a set menu.

Camino Padre Hurtado 0695, Alto Jahuel. ℂ 2/821-9966. www.santarita.cl. 16 units. $220 double. AE, DC, MC, V. **Amenities:** 2 restaurants; game room.

WHERE TO DINE

The Central Valley region abounds with simple country restaurants that serve delicious, typical Chilean fare. A new trend finds chic eateries opening in winegrowing regions, several of which are quite good.

NEAR SANTIAGO   **Doña Paula** at the Hotel Santa Rita (see above) bills itself as an elegant, top-notch restaurant, and though it comes close, it is a bit overpriced for what you get. Nevertheless, this is an ideal all-in-one wine destination (tastings, hotel, and restaurant), and it's close to Santiago.

CASABLANCA VALLEY   There are two options here. The **House of Morandé,** part of the Morandé vineyard and located just off Highway 68, Km 61 (ℂ 2/270-8900; www.morande.cl), is a stylish eatery with reinvented Chilean dishes. It is hard to tell which direction their new chef will take the restaurant, but regardless, the ambience remains enjoyable. The restaurant that really shines in this region is **Restaurante Indómita,** Ruta 68, Km 63 (ℂ 32/743869; www.indomita.cl), part of the newer Viña Indómita and a sophisticated eatery with a top chef who lends a modern flair to Chilean dishes.

CENTRAL VALLEY SOUTH OF SANTIAGO   **Juan y Medio,** Ruta 5 Sur, Km 108, near Rosario (ℂ 72/521726; open daily 7:30am–1am), is undoubtedly the best locale for traditional country cooking such as porotos gratinados, pastel de choclo, and cazuela. The restaurant (which means "Juan and a half," due to the founder Juan's bulky physique) opened in 1947 and has a reputation for high quality and low price. The **Hotel Santa Cruz** (p. 291) offers good Chilean country cooking in a pleasant ambience, with available outdoor seating. However this restaurant's kitchen is inconsistent, and the food here can be good or just so-so.

A MUSEUM

Museo de Colchagua ✮✮✮ *(Kids)*   One of Chile's best museums, the diverse collection here displays pre-Columbian archaeological artifacts from throughout the Americas, plus local Indian artifacts, Spanish conquest–era helmets and artillery, immigrant household items, farm machinery, and more. There are so many artifacts on display here that it is difficult to believe it all belongs to the private collection of Carlos Cardoen, who also owns the Hotel Santa Cruz.

Av. Errazuriz 145. ℂ 72/821050. www.museocolchagua.cl. Admission $4. Mon–Sun 10am–6pm.

7 The Nearby Ski Resorts

The word's out about skiing and snowboarding in Chile, and with so many North Americans heading south from June to October for a ski vacation, they are now the number one client in terms of guest visits. The lure? Admittedly, the idea of skiing during the summer is alluring for the novelty alone, but skiers have discovered that the Andean terrain is awesome, with everything from easy groomers to frightening steeps, and with so few people on the slopes here, powder lasts for days, not hours. There are few lift lines, and the ambience is relaxed and conducive to making friends and waking up late. For families, the kids are on vacation, and most resorts offer reduced rates or even free stays for kids under 12. Before you consider skiing in Argentina because of the low cost brought on by the economic crisis, consider that the snow is lighter, drier, and more consistent in Chile.

The major resorts in Chile are top-notch operations with modern equipment and facilities. Resorts centered on the Farallones area, such as Valle Nevado, La Parva, and El Colorado, can be reached in a 1- to 1½-hour drive from Santiago or the airport. At a little over 2 hours from Santiago, world-renowned Portillo is the most popular destination for international skiers, and anyone thinking of skiing for several days or a week might consider bunking in its all-inclusive hotel. Termas de Chillán is a short flight and 1-hour transfer shuttle from Santiago, or a 5-hour train ride, offering more tree skiing and an extensive spa.

GETTING TO THE RESORTS   Portillo organizes transfers through its own company, Portillo Tours & Travel, when you reserve. For day trips to Portillo or to Farallones, contact **Ski Total** (© 2/246-0156; www.skitotal.cl), which offers minivan transfers for $12 per person to Farallones, or $22 per person (minimum three people) to Portillo. You must come to their offices at Av. Apoquindo 4900, #42 (in the Omnium shopping mall in Las Condes—the best way to get there is by taxi) for one of their 8:30am shuttles; if your hotel is reasonably close, they'll pick you up. They also have pick-up at the Esso station at Av. Las Condes 12373. It is best to send an e-mail or call to confirm a transfer.

PORTILLO

Internationally famous, Portillo is South America's premiere ski resort and a destination so unique that most international skiers make this their only destination in Chile. Portillo is set high in the Andes on the shore of beautiful Lake Inca, a little more than 2 hours from Santiago, near the Argentine border. Unlike most resorts, Portillo is just one hotel, a grand, sunflower-yellow lodge (and two small, more economical annexes), and there is no town. Although open to the public for day skiing, Portillo really operates as a weeklong, package-driven resort that includes lodging, ski tickets, all meals, and use of their plentiful amenities. The ski area is smaller than Valle Nevado or Termas de Chillán; however, Portillo is much like a private ski club with uncrowded runs and no lift lines. The terrain is steeper and more varied here than at the other two resorts, so advanced skiers and snowboarders will find more to satisfy themselves here. Perhaps the most identifying characteristic here is the camaraderie that develops between guests, and the personalized service that the staff provides (with one employee per guest). The setting is simply magnificent, surrounded by an amphitheater of 5,400m (18,000-ft.) peaks and fronted by the emerald-hued Lake Inca.

Portillo is not for everyone, specifically for groups with a member who does not ski. There are no TVs in the rooms, which most guests say they appreciate. Intermediate skiers are strongly urged to take advantage of Portillo's top-rated ski school (the best in South America) and use the week as a summer "training camp." Otherwise, consider another resort that offers more intermediate runs. The grand, yet rustic lodge (lots of leather, stone, and wood) forgoes glitz for a more relaxed atmosphere encouraged by its American owners. The Octagon annex is a good bet for a group of friends seeking cheaper accommodations, and the Inca annex is for backpackers. Dining takes place in the hotel's main restaurant, the cafeteria, or their mountainside restaurant, the latter of which provides skiers with a barbecue lunch surrounded with one of the most dramatic views of any ski resort in the world. On certain nights, the party can really ignite with live music in the hotel bar, a disco, and an off-premise cantina-style bar.

There are 12 lifts, the most modern in Chile: five chairs, five T-bars, and two Va et Vient "slingshot" lifts that tow you up the hill faster than you can ski it going down. The terrain is 43% beginner and intermediate, 57% advanced/expert. The helicopter skiing here is outstanding and costs an average of $150 to $180 for the first run, $100 thereafter. Lift tickets are $30 adults, $20 kids 12 and under. The first and last 3 weeks of the season are Kids Ski Free weeks, when two children under 12 per family ski free. Daycare is free from 9am to 8pm.

WHERE TO STAY   **Hotel Portillo**'s 7-day packages include lodging, lift tickets, four meals per day, and use of all facilities. Per-person rates are: double with lake view $1,050 to $2,100, with valley view $1,000 to $1,920; suites $1,500 to $3,350; family apartments (minimum four people) $89 to $1,850. Children under 4 stay free, kids 4 to 11 pay half-price, and kids 12 to 17 pay about 25% less than adults. The **Octagon Lodge** features four bunks to a room (you may have to share with strangers) and includes the same amenities as above for $650 to $1,100. The **Inca Lodge** is cheap, but rooms are tiny, the bathrooms are communal, and guests eat in the cafeteria ($420–$490). The first and last 3 weeks of the season, two kids under 12 per family ski free.

For more information or to make reservations at any of the lodges mentioned, contact the resort at ⓒ **800/829-5325** in the U.S., or 2/263-0606; fax 2/263-0595; www.skiportillo.com. Resort amenities (available to guests at any of the lodges) include an outdoor heated pool, Jacuzzi, fitness center, sauna, massage, full-court gymnasium, disco, cybercafe, and cinema.

VALLE NEVADO

Valle Nevado sits high above Santiago, in the Three Valleys (Farallones) area, and it is the only hotel that offers a full-service tourism infrastructure out of the three resorts located here. The ski resort complex is not a town, but there are shops, seven restaurants, three hotels, and two condominium buildings, and, therefore, Valle is better suited for nonskiing guests accompanying their family or friends. Valle is French designed, somewhat like the Les Arcs of Chile, and it offers plenty of long, groomed intermediate runs. The resort connects with neighboring La Parva and El Colorado resorts, offering an enormous amount of terrain (though their claim of 8,892 hectares/22,230 acres is an exaggeration). Snowboarders will feel at home here with the resort's world-class half-pipe and terrain park; Valle also hosts the Nokia Snowboarding World Cup every year.

Valle Nevado can get *very* busy on weekends but the slopes are often uncrowded on weekends. The best nightlife is in Farallones, a 10-minute drive away. Valle Nevado offers lodging in three modern, attractive hotels for different budgets; the Tres Puntas Hotel, the cheapest, has regular guest rooms and bunk arrangements. If you come during the off season, check to see what is open because two of the three hotels close and only one restaurant (an Italian pasta restaurant) remains open. Valle Nevado recently closed their disco and reopened it as a spa, with facial treatments, sauna, massage, and special wellness programs.

The ski resort has 27 runs serviced by three chair lifts and six T-bars, as well as a helicopter service for those who want to ski steep powder. There's also hang gliding, paragliding, and organized ski safaris. The terrain is 15% expert, 30% advanced, 40% intermediate, and 15% beginner.

WHERE TO STAY   Prices include lodging, ski tickets, breakfast, après-ski, and dinner (which can be taken in any one of the resort's restaurants), and are per person, based on double occupancy. Guests who stay 5 nights or more receive one free group ski or snowboard lesson daily. The upscale option is the **Hotel Valle Nevado,** with full amenities and a ski-in, ski-out location for $180 to $320 per night. There's also a piano bar, glass-enclosed gym, sauna, lounge, and more.

The four-star **Hotel Puerta del Sol,** which is the most popular among North Americans and Europeans, consists mostly of suites that go for $145 to $375 a night, which isn't that much more than a double. North-facing rooms with balconies and views of the mountain are $147 to $293 per night; south-facing rooms that overlook the parking lot and do not have balconies are $136 to $262 per night. Amenities at the Puerta del Sol include cable TV, sauna, game room, piano bar, Internet cafe, and gym.

Hotel Tres Puntas has many bunk-bed rooms; each features a minibar, cable TV, and a full bathroom. This hotel is frequented by a younger crowd and has the liveliest bar; room prices range from $100 to $200 per night.

The Edificio de Sol building has condos for up to six guests, for $300 to $618 per night, not including meals or lift tickets.

Valle Nevado has many good, even excellent restaurants that serve international, French, Italian, and Chilean cuisine—and there is sushi in the lounge bar. There is a second bar in the Hotel Tres Puntas.

Lift tickets are $30 adults, $20 kids 12 and under. For more information or to make reservations at any of the hotels mentioned, contact the resort at ℂ 2/ 477-7700; fax 2/477-7736; www.vallenevado.com.

In addition to the amenities mentioned for each specific hotel, the following amenities are offered for all hotels: outdoor heated pool, fitness gym, spa, game room, and cinema. For the public, there's a bank, boutiques, and a minimarket.

LA PARVA

La Parva caters to Santiago's well-heeled skiers and snowboarders, many of whom have condos or chalets here. Apart from a condominium complex with independent units, there are few services for the ordinary tourist. However, I enjoy La Parva's ambience, as it seems more like a tiny village, and the bars in Farallones are closer than in Valle Nevado. La Parva offers good off-piste skiing conditions and the steepest inbounds terrain of the resorts in the area (but an interconnect ticket means you can traverse over to La Parva from Valle Nevado).

The resort's terrain breaks down into 15% expert, 30% advanced, 40% intermediate, and 15% beginner. There are four chairs and 10 surface lift runs, such as T-bars. There are several on-slope cafes for lunch and a few at the base of the resort, including the yodely, fondue-style restaurant **La Marmita de Pericles, El Piuquen Pub** for pizzas, and the **St. Tropez** for breakfast, fine dining, and a bar with excellent pisco sours.

Lodging is available in smart condos for eight or six guests, and during the high season (July), they may be rented only for 7 nights from Friday to Friday (last -minute inquiries might net you a shorter stay, and shorter stays are usually available during the low season). Condos have kitchens, living areas, and TV; the cost is $1,600 to $2,600 for six people, $2,600 to $3,400 for eight people; maid service is an additional $20 per day. Buy groceries in Santiago. Lift tickets are $25 to $33 adults, $20 to $23 teens and seniors, and $7 to $9 children. For more information, contact the resort (© **2/431-0420** in Santiago, or 2/220-9530 direct; fax 2/264-1575; www.laparva.cl).

EL COLORADO & FARELLONES

Farellones is a sprawl of chalets and small businesses spread across a ridge below the ski area El Colorado. This ski area is La Parva's blue-collar brother, an older, more economical option that is popular with beginning skiers, tubing aficionados, snowman builders, and the like. There is a wide variety of terrain, and fewer skiers and snowboarders on the slopes than the neighboring resorts, but the lift system is dated. If you are looking for cheaper lodging at the Three Valleys area, this is where you'll find it. There is even a backpacker's lodge.

The resort has plenty of beginner and intermediate terrain, and the best advanced terrain can be found on the east side, known as the Cono Este. Be sure not to ski beyond the Cono Este T-bar, or you will be in Valle Nevado, where your ticket is not honored, unless you've purchased an interconnect ticket.

The resort has five chair lifts and 17 surface lifts, such as T-bars. There's a bit of off-piste skiing, and there are 22 runs: 4 for experts, 3 advanced, 4 intermediate, and 11 beginner. Lift tickets $25 adults and $16 kids on weekdays, and $33 adults and $20 kids on weekends. For more information, contact the resort at © **2/246-3344;** fax 2/206-4078; www.elcolorado.cl.

The best **lodging** here is the **Aspen Apart-Hotel** (© **2/321-1006;** reservas@elcolorado.cl), with prices at $190 to $250 for two to four people, and $250 to $310 for six. A backpacker's lodge with very basic accommodations is the **Refugio Alemán,** Cóndores 1451 (© **2/264-9899;** http://refugioaleman.tripod.cl), with shared accommodations in rooms with four, five, and six beds, and full-board stay for $30 per person per night. Prices include transportation to the ski resort.

8 Chillán & Termas de Chillán Resort

407km (252 miles) south of Santiago

Chillán is a midsize city known for three things: Chilean liberator Bernardo O'Higgins, who was born here; **Termas de Chillán,** one of South America's largest and most complete ski and summer resorts; and the **Feria de Chillán,** one of the largest crafts and food markets in the country. If you aren't planning to visit any other markets during your stay in Chile, stop here.

A tidy city of 145,000, Chillán is resembles many of Chile's Central Valley towns: spruce plazas and tree-lined streets; flat-fronted, porchless homes; and a busy little pedestrian shopping area. It's not a very attractive place, but to be fair, the city's history is one of relocations and disasters. Founded as a fort in 1565, Chillán was attacked, abandoned, and rebuilt several times until the government moved the whole settlement to what is now Chillán Viejo, or Old Chillán. Probably the worst tragedy to hit the town happened in 1939, when an earthquake destroyed 90% of the city and killed 15,000 of its residents.

From the plaza, walk 1 block southeast on Constitución and right on Avenida 5 de Abril for 2 blocks until you reach the **Fería de Chillán** ★★ (open daily). If you like to shop, you'll spend an easy hour here browsing through stalls selling baskets, *huaso* clothing and saddles, chaps and spurs, pottery, knitwear, jewelry, and more. There's a colorful fish and vegetable market here, too, where locals do their grocery shopping. The market is generally safe, but beware of pickpockets.

ESSENTIALS

GETTING THERE   By Air   Chillán is served by the Aeropuerto Carriel Sur in Concepción, about an hour away. **Lan** offers direct flights from Santiago several times daily. If you've made hotel reservations in town or in Termas de Chillán, their transfer service will pick you up. If not, you must take a taxi to the bus terminal, where buses for Chillán leave every 20 minutes.

By Bus   Línea Sur and **Tur Bus** offer daily service from most major cities, including Santiago. The trip from Santiago takes about 5 to 6 hours and costs $11 one-way. The bus terminal in Chillán is located at Av. O'Higgins 010, and from there you can grab a bus for the Termas.

By Train   Ferrocarriles del Sur offers a scenic 5-hour train trip from Santiago, leaving from the Estación Central and arriving in Chillán at the station at Calle Brasil. Along the way, the train passes through orchards and farmland, much of it still tilled by horse. The cost is about $14 per person, and there are three trips daily. The dining car has snacks, sandwiches, wine, even real coffee (not Nescafé). Splurge on a hot lunch for $8.50 that is served at your seat, and just enjoy the scenery passing by.

VISITOR INFORMATION   Sernatur can be found at 18 de Septiembre 455 (© 42/223272); it's open Monday through Friday from 8:30am to 1:30pm and 3 to 6pm, and closed on weekends. It has a large amount of published material.

WHERE TO STAY & DINE

If you're looking for local color and cheap prices, go to the **Municipal Market** across the street from the Feria de Chillán, where simple restaurants prepare seafood and local dishes, some featuring Chillán's famous sausages (though I've never figured out what the fuss is about—they're merely okay). Pushy waitresses will battle for your business, so come prepared. Also, across the street from the Café París is the **Fuente Alemán** (© 42/212720), with the chain's trademark sandwiches, quick meals, and food to go.

Café París CAFE/CHILEAN   The París has a cafe on its bottom floor and a smaller restaurant upstairs, both offering the same menu, but diners usually order full meals upstairs and sandwiches below. The upstairs is tacky but comfortable, and the staff is friendly. The menu is exhaustive, with sandwiches, soups (and a very good *cazuela,* a chicken soup), quick dishes, meats, seafood, empanadas, even a mini ice-cream parlor. Open late if you're stopping to eat while driving south.

Arauco 666. © 42/223881. Main courses $3–$8. AE, DC, MC, V. Daily 9am–3am.

Gran Hotel Isabel Riquelme ⭑⭑⭑   The Gran Hotel recently completed an exhaustive renovation. Everything has been overhauled, and the results are stunning, from the shiny new lobby to the sophisticated bar, to the sumptuous bedrooms. Boy, what an improvement. Chillán's first hotel can now reclaim its status as the best hotel in town. The guest rooms are very spacious, almost twice the size of the rooms at Las Terrazas, and are flooded with natural light. There is a large restaurant just past the lobby, which serves Chilean and international fare, really the best place to eat in town.

Arauco 600, Chillán. © 42/213663. Fax 42/211541. 75 units. $70 double. AE, DC, MC, V. **Amenities:** Restaurant; bar; room service; laundry. *In room:* TV.

TERMAS DE CHILLAN

The region's premier attraction, **Termas de Chillán** (80km/50 miles from the city Chillán) is a full-season resort principally known for skiing, but the resort draws in visitors for the great hiking, biking, and horseback riding opportunities available here outside of winter. Most visitors to Chile head to Pucón, Puerto Varas, or even Patagonia for those kinds of summer-season activities because the locations are more uniquely beautiful than Chillán. However, you can't deny the appeal of a hot springs spa and a 5-hour distance from Santiago.

The resort base is nestled in a forested valley, but the ski runs rise high above tree level, under the shadow of the 3,212m (10,535-ft.) Chillán Volcano. Skiers heading to Chile often find difficulty in choosing a ski resort. The pros here are the vast amount of terrain, especially long, groomed intermediate runs. When the snow is in good shape, especially powder days, this resort is a ton of fun, with lots of off-piste skiing. The downside here are the lifts, which are either archaic chairlifts or long T-bar tows. The cafeteria food on the mountain is bad, too, so eat in one of the hotels or bring your own lunch. The resort has 28 runs, three chair lifts, and five T-bars, as well as heli-skiing, dog-sledding, an international ski school, equipment rental, and restaurants.

But Termas is known for its spa facilities and hot springs, produced by the natural geothermal fissures in the area. The Gran Hotel is spa central; you'll find hydrotherapy, aromatherapy, mud baths, and massages, not to mention a space-age "Sensory Capsule." Guests who are not lodging here at the Termas de Chillán resort can use the spa facilities and hot springs only until around 1pm, which is usually when you want to be out on the slopes.

There are two hotels at the base of the lifts, the five-star **Gran Hotel Termas de Chillán,** with 120 rooms, and the three-star **Hotel Pirigallo,** with 48 rooms; there is also one hotel closer to Las Trancas, the **Hotel Pirmahuida** (transportation available to and from the resort). The Gran Hotel is really where you'll find the only appetizing food in the entire Chillán area, and I recommend you dine here even for lunch, if you can afford it. The Hotel Pirigallo, however, is another secret lunch spot during the day—hardly anyone is there, and the food is decidedly better than anything on the slopes. You won't find the party here at the resort; you'll find it down at Las Trancas.

Rooms are very comfortable, but the Gran Hotel's are not as luxurious as you'd expect from a five-star resort—but you'll spend little time in your room anyway. Rates include breakfast and dinner, ski tickets, and spa facilities. The Pirigallo has an outdoor thermal pool; otherwise, guests must pay extra to use the Gran Hotel's facilities. Seven-night stays receive 6 hours of free group ski or snowboard instruction.

Prices are per person, based on double occupancy: Gran Hotel $1,100 to $2,000; Hotel Pirigallo $730 to $1,280. The Hotel Pirmahuida is the real deal, at $550 to $700; sure, you're not at the resort, but you are close to restaurants and pubs in Las Trancas. There are also condominium units at the resort for four to six guests, and they run $1,050 to $1,860. Hotel lift tickets are about $30 adults, $20 children, but prices fluctuate throughout the season. For more information, contact the resort at ⓒ **42/434200** (in Chillán) or 2/233-1313 (in Santiago).

LODGING OUTSIDE THE RESORT

Before reaching the resort, you'll pass through Las Trancas, a scattering of hotels, *cabañas,* restaurants, gear-rental shops, and other small businesses dependent on tourism. The party is rowdier here than the relatively tame nightlife at the resort,

Tips **Get Your Funds in Order Before You Arrive**

Note that there are no ATMs anywhere in Termas de Chillán or Las Trancas, so do your banking beforehand.

and prices here are cheaper than at the resort. In spite of the 10 or so restaurants here, none of them is particularly memorable. With this in mind, you might find renting a cabin with a kitchen a better proposition, but double-check that there is a dining area and especially a living area, or otherwise you'll have only a bed to kick back on. Also, hardly any property in Las Trancas has transportation to the resort, so verify this or else you'll be taking the once-a-day bus or be forced to rent a car.

Cabañas and Restaurant Rucahue *Kids*   Here you'll find comfortable cabins for 2 to 10 people, with kitchens and living areas. The best thing about these cabins is that they are part of a complete service complex, including a game room with video games and pool tables, a cybercafe, and a general store, and they also have the best restaurant in town, the **Restaurant Rucahue,** serving international and vegetarian dishes.

Km 72, Las Trancas. *©* **42/236162.** www.rucahueescalador.cl. 6 units. $75 cabin for 4. AE, DC, MC, V. **Amenities:** Restaurant; game room; cybercafe. *In room:* TV.

Hotel Robledal   This newer hotel, surrounded by oak and beech trees and serenaded by a babbling creek, is an excellent choice for lodging outside the Termas de Chillán ski resort. The entrance is flanked on one side by an airy, comfortable lobby with a copper fireplace and bar, and on the other by a restaurant. Guest rooms feel like condominiums, starkly decorated but brightly lit by an abundance of windows; some have terraces. A solid option for skiers seeking hotel accommodations. The outdoor heated pool is, unfortunately, covered by a plastic bubble, making it one hot, stuffy swim.

8km (5 miles) from Termas de Chillán. *©*/fax **42/214407.** www.hotelrobledal.cl. 22 units. $35–$48 per person, including breakfast and dinner. AE, DC, MC, V. **Amenities:** Restaurant; bar; outdoor pool; gym; Jacuzzi; sauna; babysitting. *In room:* Cable TV, minibar.

Mission Impossible Lodge   After stints in Puerto Octay and Pucón, the owners of MI Lodge, a French trio, found their home here in Las Trancas and built a lofty and bright lodge for snowboarders and skiers (heavy on snowboarding here). The 360-degree views from here are the best in Las Trancas; however, it is a long walk to the road, and you'll need to either have a car or ask the owners to transport you to the resort or Las Trancas. This is also not an ideal place for solo travelers, as you might feel lonely here. The lodge runs packages that include meals, and they have an excellent snowboard shop with demo boards they'll let you try out. Friendly, knowledgeable staff are the best in the area for tips on secret powder stashes and backcountry terrain. There's a fire-powered hot tub and snowmobile backcountry trips, too.

Fundo Los Pretiles, Parcela 83, Sector C, Las Trancas. *©* **09/623-0412.** www.misnowchile.com. 6 units. $46–$79 per person, double occupancy, full board. AE, DC, MC, V. **Amenities:** Restaurant; snowmobiles.

14

The Desert North &
San Pedro de Atacama

Northern Chile is home to the driest desert in the world and the idyllic, dusty little adobe village San Pedro de Atacama. With a bounty of archaeological ruins, activities for every kind of sports enthusiast, an outstanding tourism infrastructure, and one of the funkiest, Taos-style village ambiences in Chile, it is difficult to understand why this region hasn't caught on with North American travelers. Though little more than a decade ago, few besides copper miners came to this region (and San Pedro never even made it onto maps of the country), it is now it is one of the most popular destinations in the country for Chileans on holiday. Get here before the rest of the world discovers this wonderful destination.

EXPLORING THE REGION

Calama, a scrappy boomtown, is the gateway to the Atacama Desert. Calama's airport is the closest to San Pedro, and the city is a convenient jumping-off point to the outdoor attractions and colonial villages that lie in the Atacama Desert region. Plan for at least 4 days to visit this region's highlights, or 6 to 7 days to really explore the region thoroughly, especially if you're a fan of active travel. The best—and really only—place to base yourself in this area is San Pedro; from here you can take part in a multitude of day trips. Spend the night in Calama only if you want to visit the Chuquicamata mine.

Immense distances between sites of interest means that travelers do best when focusing on one area of Chile's northern desert rather than trying to pack in too many stops. We've covered Chile's "hot spot" in the northern desert, the Atacama Desert and the village of San Pedro, but many tour operators offer multiple-day excursions to a variety of locations in this otherworldly environment, some of which may not be highlighted in this book. If you've rented a car or have signed on with a tour agency, it is imperative that you consider safety first. **Bring plenty of water**—a gallon per person per day—and extra food, as well as sunscreen, a hat, sunglasses, warm clothing, and even a blanket (in the event you have to spend a chilly night on the road). Your rental agency will provide you with a phone number for breakdowns and emergencies; however, even if you are carrying a cellphone, the signal will not be in range while on the road. *Always* double-check the state of any spare tires. Be certain to give at least one person your planned itinerary, even if it's the car-rental agency. For obvious reasons, solo travel is *not* the ideal way to explore this region, and really, rental vehicles are not necessary, considering the compact size of the village and the plentiful guided tours available to all destinations.

Another serious consideration is flash floods. Though the region receives only a few days of rainfall each year, it can come in a torrential downpour known as the "Bolivian Winter," which impedes travel and drowns the region in flash

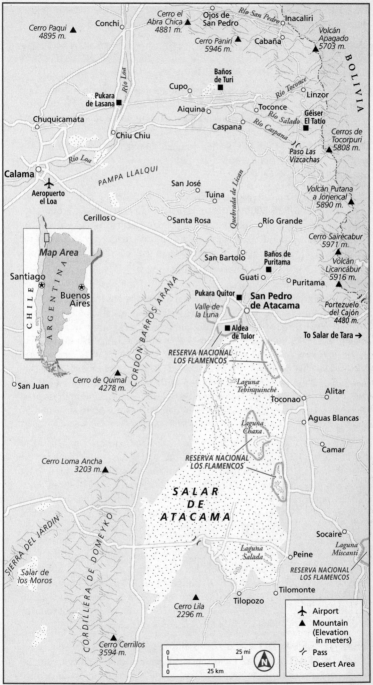

Cerro Paqui 4895 m.
Conchi
Cerro el Abra Chica 4881 m.
Ojos de San Pedro
Río San Pedro
Inacaliri
Volcán Apagado 5703 m.
Cerro Paniri 5946 m.
Cabaña
BOLIVIA
Baños de Turi
Cupo
Río Toconce
Linzor
Pukara de Lasana
Aiquina
Toconce
Géiser El Tatio
Chuquicamata
Caspana
Río Salado
Río Caspana
Cerros de Tocorpuri 5808 m.
Chiu Chiu
Paso Las Vizcachas
Río Loa
Calama
PAMPA LLALQUI
Aeropuerto el Loa
San José
Tuina
Quebrada de Lican
Volcán Putana a Jorjencal 5890 m.
Cerillos
Santa Rosa
Río Grande
Cerro Sairécabur 5971 m.
Map Area
San Bartolo
Baños de Puritama
Volcán Licancábur 5916 m.
Santiago
Guati
Puritama
CHILE
ARGENTINA
Buenos Aires
Pukara Quitor
San Pedro de Atacama
Portezuelo del Cajón 4480 m.
Valle de la Luna
CORDON BARROS ARANA
Aldea de Tulor
To Salar de Tara →
San Juan
Cerro de Quimal 4278 m.
RESERVA NACIONAL LOS FLAMENCOS
Laguna Tebinquinché
Toconao
Alitar
Laguna Chaxa
Aguas Blancas
Camar
Cerro Loma Ancha 3203 m.
RESERVA NACIONAL LOS FLAMENCOS
SALAR DE ATACAMA
SIERRA DEL JARDIN
Socaire
Laguna Miscanti
Laguna Salada
Peine
RESERVA NACIONAL LOS FLAMENCOS
Salar de los Moros
CORDILLERA DE DOMEYKO
Tilomonte
Cerro Lila 2296 m.
Tilopozo
Cerro Cerrillos 3594 m.
0   25 mi
0   25 km

✈ Airport
▲ Mountain (Elevation in meters)
⌇ Pass
⠐ Desert Area

floods and causes substantial damage to roads and bridges. The Bolivian Winter can strike anywhere during the summer between December and early March.

1 Calama & the Chuquicamata Copper Mine

1,574km (976 miles) north of Santiago; 98km (61 miles) northwest of San Pedro de Atacama

Calama, a city of 120,000, is alive due to the mining interests in the area. Like most boomtowns, it is ugly and hodgepodge, and recent reports of petty crime have soared here. Most travelers spend the night only to see the Chuquicamata Copper Mine. The Indian ruins **Pukará de Lasana** and the colonial village **Chiu Chiu** are also close to Calama, although they can be visited on the way back to Calama from San Pedro via the Tatio Geysers.

GETTING THERE

BY PLANE   Calama's **Aeropuerto El Loa** (© 55/361956) is served by **Lan-Express** (© 600/526-2000; www.lan.com) and **Sky Airlines** (© 600/600-2828). Lan has three daily flights from Santiago to Calama; Sky has two. A taxi to Calama costs around $7. To get to San Pedro de Atacama, hire one of the transfer services that wait for each flight to land; they cost around $10 per person. Or take a taxi, which will cost about $30 to $35—be sure to fix a price before leaving the airport.

BY BUS   It takes around 21 hours to reach Calama by bus from Santiago, and another 1 hour to get to San Pedro. Buses are an economical choice, but even a *cama salon,* with reclining seats, hardly mitigates a torturously long ride. **Tur Bus** (© 2/270-7500; www.turbus.com) has service to Calama that carries on to San Pedro, leaving from Santiago's Terminal Alameda at Av. Alameda 3750 (Metro: Univ. de Santiago); **Pullman Bus** (© 2/560-3799 or 600/320-3200; www.pullman.cl) leaves from Estación San Borja (Metro: Estación Central) but does not go on to San Pedro, so you'll need to transfer at the station in Calama. Buses to Calama leave about six times per day. Prices for a *cama salón* are $50 one-way.

BY CAR   Few visitors with little time in Chile choose to drive to Calama or San Pedro from Santiago (a 20-hr. trip), but rental cars are available at the Calama airport. A word of caution, however, if you choose to rent: This is a vast desert and most areas are fairly isolated; roadside service is available from rental agencies, but without any services or phones on most roads, you will have to flag someone down for help—if someone comes along, that is. If you stay to main routes, you should have no problem, but outside of that, travel prepared for the worst, and bring extra water and food and warm clothes in case you must spend the night on the road. A 4×4 is unnecessary unless you plan an expedition along poorly maintained roads. The airport has rental kiosks for **Avis** (© 600/601-9966 or 55/363325; www.avischile.cl), **Budget** (© 2/362-3200; www.budget.cl), and **Hertz** (© 2/420-5222 or 55/341380; www.hertz.cl). Rates include insurance. Alamo (© 2/225-3061; www.alamochile.com) is the cheapest, but you may want to check with a local agency when you arrive at the airport for deals.

WHAT TO SEE & DO

TOUR OPERATORS   The following tour operators offer excursions around the Calama area and trips to the Tatio Geysers and San Pedro de Atacama: **Tungra Expediciones,** Turi 2098 (© 55/363010), and **Atacama Explorer,** Lascar 4182, Villa Ayquina (© 55/335527). Your hotel in Calama can put you in touch with a reputable tour operator.

SHOPPING   The new shopping mall in Calama, Av. Balmaceda 3242 (no phone; open daily 11am–9pm), brandishes all the usual chain stores and a cinema with mostly North American films.

CHUQUICAMATA COPPER MINE

Ghost towns throughout the northern desert bear traces of Chile's nitrate-mining glory days, but the copper-mining industry here is alive and well, as is evident by Calama's Chuquicamata mine, the largest open-pit mine in the world. Few wonders generate the visual awe a visitor experiences when gazing into this gigantic hole in the ground; in fact, the mine is so expansive that it can be seen from space. That said, with so much to see in San Pedro and around, a tour here may appeal more to those with an interest in mining and engineering. The principal pit measures 4km (2½ miles) across and more than half a kilometer deep—everything at its bottom looks Lilliputian. The North American Guggenheim brothers initiated construction of the mine in 1911, but today the mine is owned by the government-controlled company Codelco, yielding more than 600,000 tons of copper per year, translating into 25% of Chile's export income. Codelco is currently uprooting all 13,000 residents at the mine's company town and transferring them to Calama, due to environmental health concerns.

Tours run every weekday, except holidays, from 2pm to 3:30pm; however, you must present yourself at the Chuquicamata office at the mine (Av. Tocopilla and José Miguel Carrera) at 1:30pm. For reservations, call © **55/327469** from 8:30am to 11:30am or 3 to 4pm, or e-mail cescalan@codelco.cl. To get to the office, take an all-yellow *colectivo* taxi signed CALAMA CHUQUI from the corner of Ramirez and Aboroa in the plaza, or hire a regular taxi for about $7 one-way. There is no charge for the tour, but they do encourage you to make a donation to a foundation for underprivileged kids. For safety reasons, it is recommended that visitors wear pants, long-sleeved shirts, and closed shoes.

OTHER ATTRACTIONS

Museo Arqueológico y Etnográfico ⚐   If you've got time to kill in Calama, take a taxi or *colectivo* no. 5 or 18 at the corner of Vicuña Mackenna and Latorre to Parque el Loa, to view this museum's interesting collection of artifacts from the Atacama region and displays interpreting pre-Columbian history and civilization. The surrounding park offers some of the only greenery in town, with terraces and lookout points, a pool, and a few stands selling arts and crafts.

Parque El Loa. No phone. Admission $1, free for seniors. Tues–Fri 10am–1:30pm and 2:30–6pm; Sat–Sun 11am–6:30pm.

WHERE TO STAY

Hotel Claris Loa   Budget travelers will find the Loa a very simple but decent option in Calama. It's a little low on style, but it's very clean, and there's a kitchen that can be used by guests. Bathrooms are communal. The hotel has a fair number of singles, so if you're traveling alone and looking for cheap digs, this is your place. It can get crowded in the summer, especially singles, so reserve in advance.

Av. Granaderos 1631. © 55/311939. 30 units. $13 per person. No credit cards. *In room:* No phone.

Hotel El Mirador ⚐⚐   If you choose to spend a night in Calama, I recommend this hotel over all others. Housed in a late-19th-century English home built by a cattle baron of that era, the hotel exudes charm with its elegant antique-filled living area. Spotless, comfortable rooms come with bathrooms with claw-foot tubs; there's a pleasant patio out back. The hotel offers several tours around the area, including Chuquicamata, and is close to shops, banks, and other services.

Sotomayor 2064. ©/fax 55/340329. www.hotelmirador.cl. 15 units. $55 double. AE, MC, V. **Amenities:** Restaurant; tours; laundry. *In room:* TV.

Park Hotel ★★ ⟨Value⟩ On the deluxe end, Calama's Park Hotel has dropped its prices, making this a deal for travelers seeking dependable, high-quality accommodations—and free airport pick-up. The hotel interiors are a soothing mix of pastels and understated desert style, but the outdoor pool makes for the most refreshing respite from the heat. Rooms are spacious and comfortable, and though the hotel is located on the road to the airport, the restaurant is the best around, so there is no need to venture into town if you don't feel up to it. The hotel arranges tours to the Chuquicamata mine and nearby destinations such as the Pukará de Lasana.

Camino Aeropuerto 1392. © **55/319900.** Fax 55/319901. www.parkplaza.cl. 102 units. $65 double standard; $95 double superior. AE, DC, MC, V. **Amenities:** Restaurant; bar; outdoor pool; tennis court; gym; sauna; car rental; tours; 24-hr. room service; laundry service. *In room:* A/C, TV, minibar, safe.

WHERE TO DINE

For hearty dishes and barbecued meat, try the popular **Adobes de Balmaceda,** Av. Balmaceda 1504 (© **55/313195**). Found on the outskirts of town in a converted old home, this restaurant is a good value. The **Club de Croata,** Abaroa 1869 (© **55/342126**), is midrange in terms of price and culinary inspiration. On the higher end, there's fine international cuisine at the **Park Hotel,** Camino Aeropuerto 1392 (© **55/319990**), but if you are in town, you will need to take a taxi to get there.

NEARBY EXCURSIONS TO COLONIAL VILLAGES & PUKARAS

These agricultural, colonial-era villages and 12th-century Atacama Indian ruins merit a stop on the return trip to the airport, after an early morning visit to the Tatio Geysers. That said, this can be an exhausting journey, considering the 4am wakeup call and the long drive thereafter. If you can't muster the stamina, try a day visit from Calama.

Chiu Chiu is a tiny village founded by the Spanish in the early 17th century, and it boasts the most picturesque church in the north, the **Iglesia San Francisco.** The whitewashed adobe walls of this weather-beaten beauty are 120 centimeters (47 in.) thick, and its doors are made of cedar and bordered with cactus, displaying a singular Atacamanian style. Chiu Chiu saw its first Indian inhabitant around 1000 B.C., and it was part of an extensive trading route that included Brazil; it continued as such until the railway began service in 1890.

But it is perhaps more fascinating to explore the ruins of the **Pukará de Lasana,** a 12th-century Indian fort abandoned after the Spanish occupation and restored in 1951. You'll want to spend some time wandering the labyrinthine streets that wind around the remains of 110 two- to five-story buildings.

North of Chiu Chiu is the engaging village of **Caspana,** surrounded by a fertile valley cultivated in a terraced formation like a sunken amphitheater. The village is characterized by its rock-wall and thatched-roof architecture. In the center, there is a tiny museum dedicated to the culture of the area and an artisan shop selling textiles made from alpaca. Cactus lampshades sold here do indeed give off a pretty flickering light, but pass them up because the species is closing in on extinction. Caspana also boasts a colonial-era church, the **Iglesia de San Lucas,** built in 1641 of stone, cactus, and mortar and covered in adobe.

North of Caspana, the 12th-century **Pukará de Turi** was the largest fortified city built in the area; the Incas used the city as an administrative center until the late 1400s. The size of these ruins, with their circular towers and wide streets, is impressive, and you'll need a good half-hour to soak it all in.

2 San Pedro de Atacama

98km (61 miles) southeast of Calama; 1,674km (1,038 miles) north of Santiago

Quaint, unhurried, and built of adobe brick, San Pedro de Atacama sits in the driest desert in the world, a region replete with bizarre land formations, giant sand dunes, jagged canyons, salt pillars, boiling geysers, and one smoking volcano. It seems better to call it a moonscape rather than a landscape. For adventure seekers, there is a wealth of activities to participate in, including hiking, mountain biking, and horseback riding—or you can just sightsee with a tour van. This region was the principal center of the Atacamanian Indian culture, and relics such as Tulor, an ancient village estimated to have been built in 800 B.C., still survive. There's also a superb archaeology museum that boasts hundreds of artifacts that have been well preserved by the desert's arid climate.

But it is perhaps San Pedro's intangible magic that captivates its visitors in the end. Many will tell you it is as much of a place for one's "inside" as it is for one's "outside," meaning a spiritual sense of peace San Pedro puts forth, with its soundless streets and rarefied air. This is one of the top stargazing areas in the world; once you leave the village and are enveloped by a thick blanket of twinkling lights, you'd be forgiven for feeling that the galaxy was not so far, far away after all. Additionally, San Pedro's streets have a pleasant, artistic, bohemian vibe. For the burgeoning amount of visitors, the town has grown at a very prudent rate, while being able to maintain its mellow charm.

Proximity to the equator (no drastic changes in the length of daylight hours) and a stable climate make any time of the year a good time to visit here. However, some factors to consider are: If you dislike the cold, June through September can be uncomfortable when temperatures drop at night. Also, if you want to avoid the crowds, you should know that tourism has recently exploded during the summer months here, so you might feel overwhelmed by the number of tourists if you come from December through February, mid-July, or the Independence Days of September 18 and 19.

ESSENTIALS

GETTING THERE   By Car   From Calama, head southeast on the route marked "San Pedro de Atacama" and continue for 98km (61 miles).

By Bus   For buses to San Pedro, see "Getting There" in the Calama section. Several bus companies provide service to San Pedro from Calama: **Buses Frontera,** Antofagasta 2041 (© **55/318543**), has eight trips per day for $2.25; and **Tur Bus,** Av. Balmaceda 1852 (© **55/220240**), has five trips to San Pedro daily for $2.

VISITOR INFORMATION   Sernatur operates a small visitor center at the plaza on the corner of Antofagasta and Toconao (no phone). Hours are Saturday through Thursday from 9:30am to 1:30pm and 3 to 7pm. The best site for information is **www.sanpedroatacama.com**, in English and Spanish.

ORIENTATION   San Pedro de Atacama is divided into several *ayllus,* or neighborhoods; however, the principal area of the town can be walked in about 10 minutes or less. As more businesses pop up, residents are beginning to use

Important Info to Know Before Arriving in San Pedro

The altitude here will slow you down at first, though few are gravely affected by it. Don't plan on undertaking any grand expeditions to extreme altitudes during your first two days in San Pedro. Instead, allow yourself to acclimatize slowly. See "Health & Insurance" in chapter 11 for more information. There is just one small medical clinic in town, no hospital. Do not drink tap water here, as the local supply contains trace amounts of arsenic. Bring a flashlight—the streets off the main drag are not lit at night, and even a 2-block walk can be difficult to negotiate.

street numbers, but many cling to "s/n" for *sin número*, or without number. Several sights are within walking or biking distance, such as Quitor and Tulor, and it is possible to bike to the Valley of the Moon and through Devil's Canyon. But you'll need a tour to get to the Tatio Geysers.

WHAT TO SEE AND DO

SHOPPING   San Pedro is chock-full of handicraft boutiques, and there is an artisan fair that begins at the plaza, between the Municipal Building and the museum. For more modern, sophisticated works of art influenced by the Atacaman culture, try **La Mano de Arte,** Caracoles 101-B (© **55/851312;** open daily 10am–1pm and 3–8pm), which stocks pottery, jewelry, and sculptures.

TOUR OPERATORS   The boom in tourism has given birth to dozens of tour operators that line the streets of San Pedro, which can be classified into two divisions: traditional tours and active expeditions (although a few offer both). Always try to book a reservation ahead of time, especially during the summer. Tour operators have minimum group sizes, but if you've made a reservation, they will take you regardless of the group size being under the minimum.

If you can afford it, I strongly recommend hiring a private guide. A private guide will take you on uncommon tours, such as the remote salt flat Salar de Tara, and can adapt to your whims. Many are ex-guides from luxury hotels, with years of experience and insider contacts around town. **Nativa Expeditions** can put together any kind of tour, whether soft or hard adventure, with some of the most experienced guides in the area (contact Camilo Beeche at © **09/413-4852;** cbeeche@yahoo.com or nativaexp@yahoo.com for more information). Another respected company, **Azimut 360** (© **2/235-1519;** www.azimut.cl), offers adventure trips and classic day trips around San Pedro. Both Nativa and Azimut 360 can guide climbers up one of the four volcano routes in Chile and Bolivia. Costs vary; normally, a private guide charges one fee, around $65 to $80 per day for two to four people, and $100 for six. Extras, including lunch, a car and driver, and entrance fees, can push the daily cost up to around $250 for a group of two to four people.

For traditional tours (Valle de la Luna, the Salar de Atacama, Tatio Geysers, and archaeological tours), the following are tried and true: **Desert Adventure,** corner of Tocopilla and Caracoles (©/fax **55/851067;** www.desertadventure.cl); **Cosmo Andino Expediciones,** Caracoles s/n (© **55/851069**); or **Atacama Connection,** Caracoles and Toconao (©/fax **55/851421;** www.atacama connection.com). For traditional tours with an ecological or nature theme (such as bird-watching), try **Cuna Expeditions** (Domingo Atienza 388; © **09/939-2460;** www.cuna.cl). For mountain biking and sandboarding, try Vulcano Expeditions (© **55/8511373;** www.vulcanochile.cl).

Average prices are: Valle de la Luna, $10; Tatio Geysers, $40; Salt Flat and altiplanic lakes, $45.

The Atacama Desert is the apex of **stargazing** in the world, due to a lack of moisture in the air, low light pollution, and the high altitude. The Hotel Explora offers stargazing as part of their guest packages, but for the rest of us, a new operation called **Celestial Explorations** gives amateur astronomers an opportunity to view the galaxy's most stunning constellations that are visible only in the Southern Hemisphere. The 2½-hour tour leaves nightly except for evenings around a full moon, and costs $12, which includes transportation, use of powerful telescopes, and an easy-to-understand interpretation of the stars by a trilingual astronomer (Caracoles 166; ℂ 55/851935; www.spaceobs.com).

A CAN'T-MISS ATTRACTION IN TOWN

Museo Arqueológico Padre le Paige ᐱᐱᐱ   This tiny museum near the plaza displays one of South America's most fascinating collection of pre-Columbian artifacts, gathered by Padre le Paige, a Belgian missionary. The Atacaman Desert is so arid that most artifacts are notably well preserved, including hundreds of ceramics, textiles, tablets used for the inhalation of hallucinogens, tools, and more, all displayed according to time period. However, the unquestionable highlights here are the well-preserved mummies, including "Miss Chile," a female mummy that still has bits of skin and hair intact, and the creepy display of skulls that shows how the elite once used cranial deformation as a show of wealth. The museum recently opened an Atacaman art exhibition hall. Not much to buy here at the gift shop.

Toconao and Padre le Paige. ℂ 55/851002. Admission $3 adults, $1.50 children. Jan–Feb daily 10am–1pm and 3–7pm; rest of the year Mon–Fri 9am–noon and 2–6pm, Sat–Sun 10am–noon and 2–6pm.

NATIONAL FLAMINGO RESERVE: THE SALAR DE ATACAMA, VALLE DE LA LUNA & THE SOUTHERN ALTIPLANIC LAKES

The **National Flamingo Reserve** is divided into seven sectors and distributed over a vast area of land, including portions of the **Salar de Atacama (Atacama Salt Flat)** ᐱ. When San Pedro tourism was in its infancy, a trip to the Salar bordered on a major expedition trip; now it is among the most accessible destinations (as is Valle de la Luna). The Salar is a tremendous 100km-long (62-mile) mineralized lake with no outlet, and it is covered nearly completely by saline minerals and dust that combine to create a weird putty-colored crust. The salt flat is the largest in Chile, and it is home to 40% of the world's lithium reserves. In some areas, lagoons peek out from under the crust, such as at Laguna Chaxa, the traditional stop at the Salar due to the Conaf interpretative center here (open daily Sept–May 8:30am–8pm and June–Aug 8:30am–7pm). But it is difficult to see flamingoes at Chaxa, and as destinations go, it is a fairly boring stop. Head instead to the little-known **Laguna Sejar** ᐱ, where the locals go, 19km (12 miles) from San Pedro. This emerald lagoon is encircled by white salt encrustations that resemble, and feel, like coral reef—so bring flip-flops. Sejar affords an almost bizarre swimming experience, floating in water so saline it renders you virtually unsinkable. Bring a large bottle of fresh water to rinse yourself off with afterward. Check with a tour operator for a half-day trip, or rent a bike (**Warning:** some areas of the road are very sandy). The way here can be a little tricky, so ask someone at your hotel to explain the route to you carefully. Early is best to visit, when there is no wind.

The **Valle de la Luna (Valley of the Moon)** ⟨★★⟩ still ranks as one of the best attractions here, but you'll share the lookout point during the sunset hour with a hundred or more tourists, especially during the summer. The valley is a depression surrounded by jagged spines of salt-encrusted hills, with an immense sand dune running between two ridges. Try to organize a tour for an afternoon hike through the Cordillera de Sal (Salt Hill Range), ending at the lookout point at sunset. This is the best site to enjoy Atacama Desert's colors as they melt from pink to gold. For an unforgettable night, come on the eve of a full moon, when ghostly light casts shadows on an already eerie landscape. The Valle is 15km (9¼ miles) from San Pedro and can be reached by bicycle or vehicle. To get here, head west on the street Licancabúr toward Calama, and follow the left-turn sign for Valle de la Luna.

Heading south 38km (24 miles) from San Pedro, you will reach the oasis towns Toconao, Camar, and Socaire. These three towns are not as picturesque as their counterparts in the Atacama Desert, so you might want to just continue on. What you are headed for are the high altiplanic lakes, **Laguna Miscanti** and **Laguna Miñeques,** two stunning cobalt-blue lakes at the foot of their respectively named peaks, and the **Salar de Talar** and the **Laguna de Tuyajto,** where it is easier to spot flamingos than at the Salar de Atacama. This journey is recommended in order to view high-altitude lakes on a less strenuous trip than the **Salar de Tara** ⟨★★★⟩, near the Argentina/Bolivia/Chile border. More adventurous types are better off visiting Tara because the reserve is larger, the salt flat's colors are more intense, and there are no other tourists. The Salar de Tara (also part of the Flamingo Reserve) rates as one of the most memorable journeys in the Atacama area, but few visitors are aware of this. The trip requires a round-trip 200km (124-mile) drive mostly along bumpy roads in a 4×4, with a moderate hike.

GEYSERS DEL TATIO/BAÑOS DE PURITAMA ⟨★★★⟩

Without a doubt a highlight in the Atacama Desert, the **Geysers del Tatio (Tatio Geysers)** are nonetheless not the easiest excursion—there's not a lot of physical activity required, but tours leave at 4am or 5am (the geysers are most active around 6–8am). At 4,321m (14,173 ft.), these are the highest geysers in the world, and it is a marvelous spectacle to watch thick plumes of steam blow from holes in such a windswept, arid land. Interspersed between the geysers, bubbling pools encrusted with colorful minerals splash and splutter—but exercise extreme caution when walking near thin crust; careless visitors burn themselves here frequently. Herds of *vicuñas,* the llama's wild cousin, graze in this area, so keep your eyes open for these delicate creatures. There is a hot springs pool at the geyser site that most tours stop at, but I urge you to find a tour company that includes Baños de Puritama (see below) as part of its itinerary. The geysers are 95km (59 miles) north of San Pedro. I strongly recommend travelers with their own vehicle not drive here—even habitual drivers to the geysers can get lost in the dark morning. If you insist, buy a map in San Pedro, or download a detailed map from **www.turistel.cl** and get an experienced driver to run you through details of the route, or hire a day guide.

Due to the high altitude, this journey is not recommended on the first or second day of your stay in San Pedro. Some travelers save this trip for the last day, returning directly to Calama with stops at colonial villages and ruin sites (see the "Nearby Excursions to Colonial Villages & Pukaras" section under "Calama & the Chuquicamata Copper Mine" above). But it is a long journey, and a far better option is to head back to San Pedro and stop at the **Baños de Puritama** ⟨★★⟩, a sybaritic hot springs oasis composed of well-built rock pools that descend down a gorge, about 60km (37 miles) from the geysers (or 28km/17 miles from San Pedro, heading out on the road that borders the cemetery). They are run by the luxury Hotel Explora (see "Where to Stay," below) and cost a steep $16 to enter, but it is worth it. You may want to tote a snack and a bottle of wine to enjoy while there. There are changing rooms and bathrooms on the premises.

PUKARA DE QUITOR ★★

The Pukará is a 12th-century, pre-Inca defensive fort that clings to a steep hill-side some 3km (1¾ miles) outside San Pedro. Although formidable, the fort was no match for the Spanish, with their horses and arms made of metal, and it was conquered in 1540 by Francisco de Aguirre and 30 men. This is an ideal bike ride from San Pedro but a searing, hot walk during the middle of the day. On bike, you may want to continue north from the Pukará up through the valley along the dirt road for a few kilometers. Go west out of San Pedro on Tocopilla Street and continue along the river until you see Quitor at your left.

ALDEA DE TULOR ★★

Tulor, Atacama's oldest pueblo, is a fascinating attraction, if only because of its age, estimated to have been built around 800 B.C. The site remained intact in part because it had been covered with sand for hundreds of years, and today it is possible to see the walls that once formed the structures of this town. There are a few reconstructed homes on view as well. Tulor is 9km (5½ miles) south-west of San Pedro.

BOLIVIA'S LAGUNA VERDE ★★★

Why not visit Bolivia for the day? Early-afternoon journeys to the shimmering turquoise lakes on the back side of Volcano Lincancabur put travelers in a high-altitude wonderland, and there's a hot springs pool here, too. This is an easy journey, but perhaps not as grand as the Salar de Tara. Rental vehicles may not cross the border; if you have your own vehicle, you'll need to register at Customs on the road out to Bolivia and pay an entrance fee at the Bolivian border. Better still, go with a Bolivian tour operator out of San Pedro. Try **Colque Tours** (at the corner of Caracoles and Calama sts.; ℂ **55/851109;** www.colquetours.com).

OUTDOOR ACTIVITIES

BIKING The Atacama region offers excellent terrain for mountain-bike riding, including the Quebrada del Diablo (Devil's Gorge) and Valle de la Muerte (Death Valley); however, it is also enjoyable to ride across the flat desert to visit sites such as Tulor. Bike rental shops can be found along Caracoles, and they all are the same in terms of quality and charge about $7 per day.

HORSEBACK RIDING Horseback riding is a quiet, relaxing way to experience the Atacama and view Indian ruins that are inaccessible by bike. If you are adept at galloping, fulfill your Lawrence of Arabia fantasies and race across a sand dune. **Rancho Cactus,** Toconao 568 (ℂ **55/851506;** www.rancho_cactus.cl), and **La Herradura,** Tocopilla s/n (ℂ **55/851087;** laherraduraatacama@hotmail.com), offer short and full-day rides to a variety of destinations for an average of $7 per hour. They also plan overnight trips; consult each agency for details and prices. La Herradura has the slight edge with quality of horses; however, Farolo and Valérie at Cactus are more fun to amble down the trail with.

VOLCANO ASCENTS Climbing one of the four volcanoes in the area requires total altitude acclimatization and a good physical state. It is a heart-pounding hike up, but if you can hack it, the sweeping views and the experience in itself are exhilarating. The most popular ascent is up the active Volcano Láscar to 5,400m (17,712 ft.), about a 4-hour climb, and leaves San Pedro before sun-up. Volcano Lincancabúr is also popular, but it requires an overnight stay at a rustic refugio just across the border and a Bolivian guide. Many tour companies offer these excursions; try **Nativa Expediciones,** Domingo Atienza s/n (© **55/851095;** nativaexp@yahoo.com), or **Azimut 360,** Caracoles s/n (© **2/235-1519;** www. azimut.cl).

WHERE TO STAY

You'll find dozens of options here, but midrange hotels seem to be lacking the most. Lodging in San Pedro (even at the top of the range) does not come with televisions, and many rooms do not have phones. This is where you come to disconnect. Do not underestimate the luxury of a swimming pool, especially during the summer; these places do not have air-conditioning, though their style of architecture is dark and cool to keep heat out—plus, there are usually ceiling fans. For camping, the only shady, central spot is **Hostal Takha Takha,** Caracoles 101-A (© **55/851038**), which has a few simple rooms as well. There are two private homes for rent; one small but recommended home is on the corner of Caracoles and Domingo Atienza (© **55/851095;** nativaexp@yahoo.com; $65–$80 per night); or for a group of 4, the **Casa Grande** (© **55/851032;** casagrande@sanpedroatacama.com; $130–$150 per night).

VERY EXPENSIVE

Hotel Explora ★★★ *Moments* The internationally acclaimed Hotel Explora is San Pedro's five-star lodging option—very expensive, but worth every peso if you can afford it. The hotel operates as a package-inclusive hotel, and due to its 3-block walk from town and amenities galore, guests often spend little time in San Pedro itself. Like its counterpart in Patagonia, the Explora in Atacama is elegant yet unpretentious. The exteriors are plain, yet the lounge and guest rooms are tastefully appointed, decorated with local art and painted in quiet, primary tones. The lounge, with soaring ceilings, is enormous, stretching the length of the building and scattered with plush, multicolor couches for sinking into and cooling off with a pisco sour. Guest rooms have ultracomfortable beds with crisp linens and fluffy down comforters; each bathroom comes with a Jacuzzi tub. A wall-to-wall cutout window affords a panoramic view; try to get a room facing the Volcano Licancabúr. Slatted boardwalks lead guests around the property to a sybaritic, adobe-walled massage salon; a star-gazing platform (with state-of-the-art telescopes); a barbecue *quincho;* and their four irrigation-style pools, whose chic design and quenching allure beckon you to dive in. The cuisine, a daily set menu, is superb.

Explora's excursions seek to introduce guests to the unknown, those off-the-beaten places where few others go. If a destination is popular, Explora guides show guests the other side or encompass the destination into part of a more thorough expedition. The hotel has recently refocused its excursions to prioritize full-day trips, which involve some kind of physical exertion. There are few excursions for inactive guests, however, if the price fits your budget, this is the best hotel in town. One wing of the hotel is an "Explorer's Room," with an extensive library and large-scale maps to help plan your daily journeys with your guide. Packages include lodging, all excursions, meals, airport transfers, and an open bar.

Domingo Atienza s/n (main office: Américo Vespucio Sur 80, Piso 5, Santiago). © **55/851110** (local), or 2/395-2533 in Santiago (reservations). Fax 2/228-4655; toll-free fax 800/858-0855 (U.S.), 800/275-1129

(Canada). www.explora.com. 52 units. All-inclusive rates, double occupancy, per person: 3 nights $1,546; 4 nights $2,060; 7 nights $3,250. Reduced rates available for children and teens. AE, DC, MC, V. **Amenities:** Restaurant; bar; 4 outdoor pools; sauna; mountain bikes; massage; babysitting; laundry service; TV room; library; horseback riding.

EXPENSIVE

Hotel Altiplánico ★★★   The newest addition to lodging options in San Pedro sits just outside of town, on the road to the Pukará de Quitor. Like that of its predecessors, the striking architecture stays true to the style of the zone: river rock patios, adobe walls, peaked straw roofs, and tree trunks left in their spindly, natural state. It is quite an attractive hotel and a lower-cost option than Explora (see above), and it is located on a spacious property with open views. Rooms are simple but for a few tasteful adornments, with soothing dark walls and cutout windows that let in streams of soft light, and rooms all have a small patio. The friendly staff arranges excursions at an additional price. This is a good hotel for a group, as it has a barbecue area near the pool for private parties.

Domingo Atienza 282. ℂ 55/851212. Fax 55/851238. 16 units. $140 double; $280 family apt for 5. AE, DC, MC, V. **Amenities:** Cafeteria; large outdoor pool; bicycles. *In room:* No phone.

Hotel Tulor ★   This hotel is owned by the person who discovered the Tulor ruin site, hence the name. The Tulor is on a quiet street just down from the Hotel Kimal (see below) and behind an adobe wall. The circular buildings are made of adobe and thatched roofs. The rooms are unremarkable, with nondescript beige walls, thin carpet, and a tiny table and chair; some seem crammed with too many beds. The hotel is overpriced, and you'd do better at the Kimal. However, the Tulor does have an outdoor swimming pool, and its standalone restaurant is very appealing. The owner will gladly share information about the Tulor site and arrange excursions there and to other attractions in the area.

Domingo Atienza s/n. ℂ/fax 55/851027. www.hoteltulor.cl. 9 units. $120 double. AE, DC, MC, V. **Amenities:** Restaurant; bar (high season only; cafeteria rest of year); outdoor pool.

La Aldea ★★   This chic adobe hotel is owned by two architects, who have bestowed great taste to its interiors, all of which have been remodeled recently. The principal drawback here is the 10-minute dusty walk to the center of town, which is a bother during the day and a pitch-dark ramble at night. The welcoming lobby, lounge, and restaurant are built of stone, adobe walls, cinnamon-colored wood, ironwork, and thatched roofs. The guest rooms are dark, but they have a cooling effect on a hot day. They are also spacious enough to give some breathing room. Perhaps the best rooms are in the separate *cabañas,* which are a cylindrical two stories with fresh white walls and lots and lots of light.

Solcor s/n. ℂ/fax 55/851149 or 55/851247. www.hotelaldea.cl. 9 units, 3 *cabañas.* $90 double; $200 4-person *cabaña.* AE, MC, V. **Amenities:** Restaurant; outdoor pool; bicycles; room service; laundry service; TV room; horseback riding.

Lodge Terrantai ★★   If the prices at the Explora (see above) are a little beyond your budget but you're looking for an all-inclusive package, you might try this exclusive little hotel near the main street. The Terrantai is in a 100-year-old home that was renovated by a well-known Chilean architect, who preserved the building's flat-fronted facade, adobe walls, and thatched roof. The style is pure minimalism, and every inch of the interior hallways and the rooms is made of stacked river rock. The rooms are very comfortable, with down comforters, linen curtains, soft reading lights, and local art. Most rooms have large floor-to-ceiling windows that look out onto a pleasant garden patio. The Terrantai has a small restaurant for its inclusive meals, and there is outdoor dining. It's in a good central location. Packages include meals, airport transfers, and daily excursions with guides—the hotel does not book hotel-only stays.

Tocopilla 411. ℭ 55/851045. Fax 55/851037. www.terrantai.com. 14 units. Packages per person based on double occupancy: 2 nights/3 days $542; 4 nights/5 days $870. Spanish-guided packages slightly cheaper. AE, MC, V. **Amenities:** Restaurant; outdoor pool (more like a soak tub); laundry service; daily excursions with bilingual guides.

MODERATE

Hostería San Pedro ⍟ *Kids*   Hostería San Pedro was the first hotel in the area, and it is a block or so from the busy downtown. Laid out like an adobe motel, the rooms are comfortable, though slightly overpriced and not as artistically decorated as its counterparts. It does have a very quiet location, however. Across from the main building are seven *cabañas*—each with two bedrooms and spacious bathrooms, but no living area—that sleep a total of four to five people. All are carpeted and clean. The outdoor pool is huge, and this, plus the spaciousness of the hotel's property, makes the hotel a good place for kids.

Toconao 460. ℭ 55/851011. Fax 55/851048. www.diegodealmagrohoteles.cl. 25 units. $100 double; $140 *cabaña* for 4. AE, DC, MC, V. **Amenities:** Restaurant; bar; outdoor pool; shop; gas station. *In room:* No phone.

Hotel Kimal ⍟⍟ *Finds*   The Hotel Kimal is one of my favorites here in San Pedro. It doesn't have the bang and prestige of Explora (see above), but it does offer a little slice of tranquillity for the traveler. The location is central but not in the thick of it, the guest rooms are handsome, and the beds are heavenly soft. The hotel feels more intimate than most in San Pedro, in a way that makes you want to strike up a conversation with a guest at the table next to you. The rooms are softly lit by skylights and are fringed outside by pimiento trees and stone walkways, and most rooms have a little seating area outside. The restaurant is principally outdoors, and its proximity to the circular pool makes it a refreshing place to sit on a hot day. There is friendly service, too. Consult their website for adventure-travel and relaxation-oriented packages.

Domingo Atienza 452 (at Caracoles). ℭ 55/851152. Fax 55/851030. www.kimal.cl. 19 units. $83 single; $115 double; $150 double suite. AE, DC, MC, V. **Amenities:** Restaurant; laundry. *In room:* Minibar.

La Casa de Don Tomás ⍟   The Don Tomás seems a bit expensive for what it has to offer. The hotel is made of adobe brick centered on a gravel courtyard/parking lot, and there are a few large *cabañas* behind the main unit. The main building has a dining area and a minilounge; a dozen rooms branch off from this central area, but the majority have separate entrances, much like a motel. The rooms are average size, with white ceramic floors that are a little on the cold side. The service is friendly and, on the average, it's a decent place, but you might want to check out other hotels before booking here.

Tocopilla s/n. ℭ 55/851055. Fax 55/851175. www.dontomas.cl. 38 units. $85 double; $207 cabin for 4–7. AE, DC, MC, V. **Amenities:** Restaurant; outdoor pool. *In room:* No phone.

INEXPENSIVE

Hostal Katarpe ⍟   The Tambillo has an edge on this hostal, but room nos. 10 through 14 are tucked away in a quiet spot with a little greenery, and the sparse, smallish rooms are clean and neat. This is a good-value hotel, and the owners/hosts are very friendly. There is a seating area outside and a cafe, and the location is central.

Domingo Atienza 441. ℭ 55/851033. katarpe@sanpedroatacama.com. 14 units. $50 double. AE, DC, MC, V. *In room:* No phone.

Hotel Tambillo ℛ   The Tambillo is the best option in this price range. The 12 rooms here are lined along both sides of a narrow, attractive pathway inlaid with stone. Rooms have arched windows and doors, and no decoration other than a light, but it's not unappealing—on the contrary, the atmosphere is fresh and clean. There's also a large restaurant and a tiny sheltered patio. It's a 4-block walk to the main street.

Gustavo Le Paige 159. ℂ/fax 55/851078. www.hoteltambillo.cl. 15 units. $50 double. No credit cards. **Amenities:** Cafeteria. *In room:* No phone.

WHERE TO DINE

Many restaurants fill up quickly after 9pm, especially during the summer, so arrive early or consider making a reservation if the restaurant accepts them. Most restaurants offer both a day and an evening fixed-price menu that is a good value. Competition has drawn waiters onto the street to harangue for business, but it isn't too overwhelming. If you're looking for a quick, light lunch, try **Petro Pizza,** Toconao 447 (ℂ **09/2916347;** pizzas $1–$4), which serves a variety of stone oven–baked pizzas with toppings for vegetarians and meat eaters. They also offer tacos and empanadas. For a splurge, dine at the **Hotel Explora** (see above), which serves incontestably the best fusion cuisine in northern Chile. Reservations must be made 24 hours in advance, and the cost is $50 per person (both for dinner and for lunch) for a set menu that includes drinks.

MODERATE

Adobe ℛℛ CHILEAN   This is the best choice in San Pedro, for both the food and the cozy ambience. Though nothing on the menu deviates much from a typical Chilean menu, everything is delicious and nicely presented. The stone oven–baked pizzas are a standout, and the nightly fixed menu is always tasty and filling for about $7 to $9; the Adobe is also recommended for its appetizing breakfasts. What sets the mood here, though, is the blazing bonfire, around which diners sit at wooden tables under a semienclosed thatched roof. Good-looking waiters dressed in black provide attentive service. Live music often begins at 9pm, and although the Adobe serves dinner only until 10:30pm, the restaurant converts into a bar with light snacks thereafter.

Caracoles 211. ℂ 55/851132. www.cafeadobe.cl. Reservations accepted. Main courses $5–$10. AE. Daily 8am–1am.

Cafe Export ℛ CHILEAN/INTERNATIONAL   Cafe Export is very popular with the local scene, though, unlike the Adobe, it lacks a touch of sophistication. That said, the ambience can be amusing in the evening, when a battery of eccentric characters and local folk bands drop in and out through the night. The food is surprisingly good and the plates are heaping, and service, for the most part, is okay. Try their fresh pastas, abundant salads, or any of their specials of the day (pork loin with an herbed cream sauce and roasted potatoes, for example). Though they make a good cup of coffee, the interiors are too dark and slightly grungy during the morning and lunchtime to recommend dining here during the day.

Caracoles at the corner of Toconao. No phone. Reservations not accepted. Main courses $5–$9; sandwiches $2.50–$4. No credit cards. Daily 9am–10:30pm.

Encanto ℛℛ CHILEAN   Encanto is the newest eatery on the scene, with a menu that highlights local Atacaman dishes and products such as *sopa de gigote,* or "poor-man's stew," and dishes with the local grain quinoa. The ambience is fresh and clean, with molded adobe booths and soft light, and there's a very pleasant outdoor seating area with a fire pit. This is a good choice if you'd like to taste a few local items. It also has a solid wine list.

Caracoles 195. ℂ 55/851939. Reservations not accepted. Main courses $6–$10. No credit cards. Daily 9am–1am.

La Casona 🏶🏶 CHILEAN   La Casona is a newly renovated restaurant/bar housed in an old colonial building with soaring ceilings. Candlelit wooden tables adorned with a few sprigs of flowers and a crackling fireplace set a quieter ambience. There's also daytime outdoor seating, a pub, and an outdoor bar in the back warmed by a blazing fire, and though it isn't the hot spot it once was with locals, it can get lively at night nevertheless. La Casona serves predominately Chilean specialties but in a slightly updated style, and delicious breakfasts. Don't miss their new wine shop with an outstanding selection; it is really the only place to buy a decent bottle of wine in town.

Caracoles 195. ℂ 55/851004. Reservations accepted. Main courses $6–$10. AE, DC, MC, V. Daily 8am–11pm.

La Estaka 🏶 INTERNATIONAL/CHILEAN   La Estaka has been on the local scene for years. Owned by the same people who own the Adobe, this is their hippie version, with a funkier interior and a staff that is so laid-back they can often be inattentive. The menu leans toward more casual fare, serving crepes, pasta, and salads, in a semioutdoor seating area with a thatched roof, dirt floor, and molded banquettes.

Caracoles 259. ℂ 55/851201. www.laestaka.cl. Reservations not accepted. Main courses $5–$10; sandwiches $2–$4.50. AE, DC, MC, V. Daily 8:30am–1:30am.

INEXPENSIVE

Cafe Tierra 🏶 NATURAL FOODS   This predominately vegetarian restaurant is known for its whole-grain empanadas and sandwiches made from scratch while you wait. Of course, the wait can be long, but it's worth it. This is an excellent spot for a continental-style breakfast, with fresh bread and juice, and strong coffee. They've expanded, so there is plenty of room now, all outdoor seating. Tierra also serves crepes, pastas, and a few meat dishes; however, I don't recommend the pizzas.

Caracoles 271. ℂ 55/851585. Reservations not accepted. Empanadas and sandwiches $2.50–$4; main courses $5–$7.50. No credit cards. Daily 9am–12:30am.

15

The Chilean Lake District

The region south of the Biobío River to Puerto Montt is collectively known as the Lake District, a fairy-tale land of emerald forests, white-capped volcanoes, frothing waterfalls, and plump, rolling hills dotted with hundreds of lakes and lagoons that give the region its name. It is one of the most popular destinations in Chile, not only for its beauty, but also for the diverse outdoor and city-themed activities available and its well-organized tourism structure.

The Lake District is home to the Mapuche Indians, who fiercely defended this land against the Spanish for 300 years. German settlers came next, clearing land and felling timber for their characteristic shingled homes. Both ethnic groups have left their mark on the region through architecture, art, and food.

The region is dependent on fishing, tourism, and, unfortunately, the timber industry, which has done much to destroy the Lake District's once nearly impenetrable forests. However, the many national parks and reserves give visitors a chance to surround themselves in virgin forest that is unique for its stands of umbrella-shaped *araucaria* and 1,000-year-old *alerce* trees (see "The *Alerce* & the *Araucaria:* Living National Monuments," on p. 320).

EXPLORING THE REGION

The Lake District is composed of the **Región de la Araucanía,** which includes the city **Temuco** and the resort area **Pucón,** and the **Región de los Lagos,** where you'll find the port cities **Valdivia** and **Puerto Montt;** charming villages such as **Puerto Varas** and **Frutillar;** and the island **Chiloé** (see chapter 16). There's plenty more to see and do outside these principal destinations, including hot springs, boat rides, adventure sports, beaches, and kilometer after kilometer of bumpy dirt roads that make for picturesque drives. Towns such as Puerto Varas and Pucón make for excellent bases to take part in all of these activities. Another great attraction here is Chile's proximity to the **Argentine Lake District** (see chapter 9), where you'll find the equally beautiful cities of **Bariloche** and **San Martín de los Andes.** If you're planning on visiting both countries, it makes sense to cross the border in the Lake District, where Chile and Argentina are separated by a 1- to 2-day boat ride or several hours by road. It is entirely feasible to loop through both countries' lake districts; most visitors find they need just 2 to 4 full days to explore any of the aforementioned destinations.

1 Temuco

677km (420 miles) south of Santiago; 112km (69 miles) northwest of Pucón

Temuco is Chile's sixth-largest city and the jumping-off point for popular destinations such as Pucón and Conguillío National Park. Unless you've got an early flight or you are driving a long distance down the Panamericana Highway and need a rest, I do not recommend an overnight stay here. You'll need to fly here and transfer to Pucón during the winter; there is direct service to Pucón during the summer.

Historically known as La Frontera (The Frontier), this is where the Mapuche Indians kept Spanish conquistadors at bay for 300 years until Chile's Frontier Army founded a fort on the shore of the River Cautín in 1881. The city grew like a boomtown as Spanish, German, French, Swiss, and English immigrants poured into the region. Only traces of the architectural influence left by these European immigrants still exist as rampant development has converted Temuco into yet another hodgepodge Chilean city with wildly divergent architectural styles. Temuco is still one of the country's fastest-growing cities, as is evident by the thundering buses, bustling downtown crowds, and increasingly poor air quality that threaten to absorb whatever charm remains in this historic town.

Temuco is near a handful of national parks, such as **Conguillío, Villarrica,** and **Huerquehue.** It is also the gateway to the wildly popular **Pucón.** If you plan to use Temuco solely as a transfer point for outlying regions, you might consider visiting the Mercado Municipal (Municipal Market), described on p. 318.

ESSENTIALS
GETTING THERE
BY PLANE The **Maquehue Airport** (© 45/554807) is about 8km (5 miles) from the city center. To get to Temuco, hire a cab (about $8) outside or arrange transportation with Transfer & Turismo de la Araucanía, a minivan service at the airport that charges $6 for door-to-door service (© 45/339900). This transfer service has service to Pucón for $12 per person, but it might cost more if they are unable to arrange a group. LanExpress (© 45/740375, or toll-free **600/526-2000;** www.lan.com) serves Temuco with an average of four daily flights from Santiago and one daily flight to Puerto Montt. Sky Airlines (© 45/747300, or toll-free **600/600-2828;** www.skyairline.cl) serves Temuco with one daily flight from Santiago and two weekly flights to and from Puerto Montt.

BY BUS To get to Temuco from Santiago by bus, try **Tur Bus** (© 2/270-7500; www.turbus.com), which leaves from the Terminal Alameda at Av. Bernardo O'Higgins 3786; or **Cruz del Sur** (© 2/770-0607), which leaves from the Terminal Santiago at Av. Bernardo O'Higgins 3848. The trip takes about 8 hours, and a one-way economy ticket costs about $9; a seat in executive class costs $25. Most buses arrive at Temuco's **Terminal Rodoviario** at Vicente Pérez Rosales 01609 (© 45/225005). From here you can take a taxi to your hotel.

BY TRAIN EFE (© 2/376-8500 in Santiago, or 45/233416 in Temuco; www.efe.cl) offers one of the few train services in Chile, with salon and sleeper coaches. The general opinion of the train is very good; in fact, it is quite an enjoyable experience now that service is faster and the company has installed new train cars. Their Terrasur train has daily service to Santiago, leaving at 10pm and arriving at 7am; from Santiago to Temuco, the departure time is 10:30pm, with an arrival at 7:30am. The train station in Temuco is at Barros Arana and Lautaro; in Santiago, the station is at Alameda 3170. Tickets are $32 sleeper, $20 salon.

BY CAR The Panamericana Highway takes motorists to Temuco.

VISITOR INFORMATION
Sernatur operates a well-stocked tourism office at the corner of Claro Solar and Bulnes streets at Plaza Aníbal Pinto (© 45/211969). Hours from December to February are Monday through Saturday from 8:30am to 8:30pm, Sunday 10am

Chile's Lake District

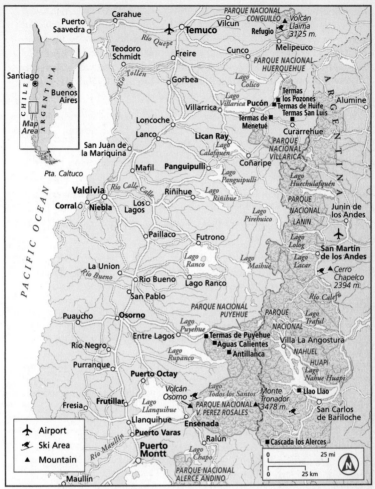

Airport
Ski Area
Mountain

to 2pm. The rest of the year, the office is open Monday through Friday from 9am to 2pm and 3 to 5pm.

GUIDED TOURS IN THE CITY & BEYOND

Sur Expediciones, Arturo Prat 712, local 6 (© 45/230291 or 09/452-4180; www.surexpediciones.com) offers a wide variety of bilingual excursions, including city tours, day trips to Conguillío National Park, and cultural trips to Mapuche communities. These cultural trips include visits to a *ruca*, a typical Mapuche Indian home, and the opportunity to visit with Mapuches.

GETTING AROUND

Getting around Temuco is easy by foot. To get to outlying areas such as national parks, it's best to rent a car or go with a tour. To get to Pucón (see "Villarrica & Pucón," later in this chapter), try **Buses JAC,** corner of Balmaceda and Aldunate (© 45/231340), which operates from its own terminal, leaving every half-hour on weekdays and every hour on weekends and holidays.

If you want to rent a car to see the outlying sights, Hertz, Avis, First, and Econorent all have kiosks at the airport. Outside of summer, it is possible for walk-ins to get a car easily. During the summer, it is important to reserve in advance. In downtown Temuco, **Hertz** can be found at Las Heras 999 (© **45/ 318585**), **Avis** at Vicuña Mackenna 448 (© **45/238013**), and the cheapest cars at **Econo Rentacar,** Patricio Lynch 471 (© **45/215997;** fax 45/214911).

FAST FACTS: TEMUCO

Currency Exchange   There are a few casas de cambio and banks with 24-hour cash machines along Calle Bulnes at the main plaza. Try **Intercam,** Casa de Cambios, Claro Solar 780, Local 5; or **Comex,** A Prat 427.

Hospital   Temuco's highest-quality hospital is the **Clínica Alemana,** located at Senador Estébanez 645 (© **45/244244**).

Laundry   Marva laundromat has two locations: 415 and 1099 Manuel Montt (© **45/952200**).

Travel Agency   Try **Agencia de Viajes y Cambios Christopher,** Bulnes 667 (© **45/211680**).

Internet   Try the Internet cafe **Kafé.com,** Bulnes 314 loc. 8 (Mon–Sat 9am–10pm, Sun 10am–8pm); or the **Entel** office, Prat 505 (Mon–Fri 10am–8pm, Sat 10am–2pm; closed Sun).

WHAT TO SEE & DO

In spite of Temuco's general ugliness, there are a few worthwhile attractions here. Of course, those pressed for time would do well to cross Temuco off their attractions list. For a sweeping view of Temuco, take a taxi or hike up the heavily forested **Cerro Ñielol,** which also features four trails and a restaurant near the summit. It's open daily from 8am to 10pm; admission is $1 adults, 50¢ children (© **45/298222**). At the site marked LA PATAGUA, you'll find a plaque commemorating the agreement signed here in 1881 between the Mapuche Indians and the Chilean Army for peaceful settlement of Temuco.

The manicured grounds of **Plaza Aníbal Pinto** in the city center are a relaxing break from the commercial bustle surrounding it. Within the plaza you'll find the sizeable *La Araucanía* monument depicting the clash between the Mapuche and the Spanish. There's also a gallery here with temporary exhibits.

Walk up Calle Bulnes to Portales to enter one of Chile's best markets, the **Mercado Municipal** 🅐🅐, open Monday through Saturday from 8am to 6pm (8pm in summer), Sunday and holidays from 8am to 3pm; from April to September the market closes at 5pm. Rows of stalls sell high-quality woven ponchos, knitwear, textiles, woodwork, hats, *mate* gourds, and assorted arts and crafts, but what's really special here is the abundance of silver Mapuche jewelry. Around the perimeter, fishermen and food stalls aggressively vie for business while butchers in white aprons hawk their meats from behind dangling sausages and fluorescent-lit display cases. Another market, the **Feria Libre** at Aníbal Pinto, offers a colorful chaos of fruit and vegetable stands as well—the highlight here is the traditional Mapuche Indian vendors who come in from *reducciones* to sell their goods. The market is open Monday through Sunday from 8:30am to 6pm; from March to December, it closes at 5pm.

Temuco also has the free **Museo Regional de La Araucanía,** Alemania 084 (© **45/730062**), open Monday through Friday from 10am to 5:30pm, Saturday from 11am to 5pm, Sunday from 11am to 2pm. The museum features exhibits charting Indian migration and history, along with displays of Mapuche jewelry and weapons, and an antique photo collection. There's really not a lot to see, so you should consider visiting this museum only if you've run out of things to do.

WHERE TO STAY

Holiday Inn Express *(Kids)*   Predictable the way a Holiday Inn always is, this hotel is best used as an overnighter for those on their way out of Temuco. With clean rooms, comfortable beds, cable TV, and a location a half-block from an American-style shopping mall with the usual fast-food joints, you might feel like you never left the States. The principal drawback of this hotel is its distance from downtown; however, it is close to the highway. Kids under 18 can room with their parents for free.

Ortega 1800, Temuco. ⓒ **800/36666** or 45/223300. Fax 45/224100. www.holidayinn.cl. 62 units. $77 double. Rates include buffet breakfast. AE, DC, MC, V. **Amenities:** Small outdoor pool; exercise room; Jacuzzi; business center. In room: A/C, TV, coffeemaker, safe.

Hotel Aitué   This family-owned and -operated hotel offers good value for the price, including a business center with an Internet connection and free airport pickup. Double rooms are average size; junior suites are substantially larger. Each well-lit room comes with mahogany furniture and fairly comfortable beds. The staff is knowledgeable and friendly, and strives to make guests feel at home. The hotel has a popular convention salon downstairs, and it also offers a small bar and lounge, as well as a fireside dining area serving breakfast and snacks.

Antonio Varas 1048, Temuco. ⓒ 45/211917. Fax 45/212608. www.hotelaitue.cl. 35 units. $52 double; $60 junior suite. AE, DC, MC, V. **Amenities:** Restaurant; bar; lounge. *In room:* TV, minibar.

Hotel Continental *(R) (Moments)*   Inaugurated in 1888, the Continental is the oldest hotel in Chile, with a rich local history and a guest book that has registered names such as Gabriela Mistral and Pablo Neruda. Virtually nothing has changed at the Continental, certainly not the wooden bar where locals still meet for the dice game *cacho,* nor the elegant dining room with period bronze chandeliers and mounted deer antlers. The stark rooms come with high ceilings, antique furniture, and a sink; most have tiny windows. Room no. 9 is the only one with a TV. This hotel, though worth a visit for historical reasons, isn't for anyone who isn't budget- or bohemian-minded because nothing has changed, really, since 1888: There are cotlike beds and squeaky floors, all very spartan. On the other hand, where else can you spend the night in the same room as ex-presidents Aguirre and Salvador Allende (room no. 11)? See below for a review of the restaurant.

Antonio Varas 708, Temuco. ⓒ 45/238973. Fax 45/233830. www.turismochile.cl/continental. 40 units. $46 double with bathroom; $31 double with shared bathroom. Rates include continental breakfast. AE, DC, MC, V. **Amenities:** Restaurant; bar.

WHERE TO DINE

Head to the **Mercado Municipal,** open Monday through Saturday from 8am to 8pm and Sunday from 8:30am to 3pm, for a quick, inexpensive lunch at one of the market's dozen or so restaurants. To get there, enter at Portales at Bulnes or Aldunate streets. Waiters will harangue you until you're suckered into choosing their establishment, but the best bet is at **La Caleta** (local 27). For sandwiches and other quick meals, try **Dino's,** at Montt 756 inside Almacenes París-Patio de Comidas (ⓒ **45/403306**), or **Ñam Ñam,** at the corner of Portales and Prat (no phone).

The Continental Hotel *(R) (Finds)* CHILEAN   Located in an antique hotel of the same name (see above), The Continental is still the traditional favorite in

The *Alerce* & the *Araucaria:* Living National Monuments

The Lake District and its neighboring forests in Argentina are home to two of the oldest trees on the planet: the *alerce* and the *araucaria,* otherwise known as larch and monkeypuzzle trees, respectively. The *alerce* is a sequoia-like giant that grows less than 1 millimeter each year and can live for more than 3,000 years, making it the world's second-oldest tree after the California bristlecone pine. They are best viewed in the Alerce Andino National Park and Pumalín Park.

The *araucaria,* called *pehuén* by the Mapuche, is unmistakable for its gangly branches and thick, thorny leaves that feel waxy to the touch. Mature trees can grow as high as 50m (164 ft.) and take on the appearance of an umbrella, which is why they're often called Los Paraguas (The Umbrellas). They do not reach reproductive maturity until they are about 200 years old, and they can live as long as 1,250 years. They are best seen in Tolhuaca, Villarrica, and Conguillío national parks, but they're virtually everywhere around the Lake District. The *araucaria* seed (piñón), an edible nut, was the principal source of food for the Mapuche Indians; later the tree was coveted for its quality wood, and, as with the *alerce,* aggressive harvesting destroyed the majority of its forests. Today both the *alerce* and the *araucaria* have been declared protected national monuments.

town. The food is prepared simply, with many dishes following the standard fried-entree-with-mashed-potatoes format. Several highlights are cheese soufflé, crab stew, and Parmesan scallops. One of the best reasons to dine at the Continental is for the old-world ambience. Inside the century-old, barn-size dining area, giant bronze chandeliers hang from a soaring ceiling; the room is so spacious that conversation echoes when there are only a few diners. The restaurant offers a set menu for lunch Monday through Friday for $6.

Antonio Varas 708. © 45/238973. Main courses $4–$10. AE, DC, MC, V. Daily noon–3pm and 8–11pm.

La Pampa ⋒ STEAKHOUSE/ARGENTINE   Excellent grilled meats, fresh salads, seafood, and an extensive wine list that includes export-only varieties make La Pampa a good place to dine. It was opened years ago by two Argentine transplants who came for a visit and never went home. Try the trout with Roquefort sauce or one of the Argentine specialties such as *matambrito alla pizza,* thin meat rolled with spinach and egg. On weekends there is an excellent *asado criollo,* thick ribs slowly grilled for 3 hours.

Caupolicán 0155. © 45/329999. Main courses $6–$16. AE, DC, MC, V. Mon–Sat noon–4pm and 7:30pm–midnight; Sun noon–4pm.

Quick Biss *Value* *Kids* CAFETERIA   This modern cafeteria, with wooden booths and zebra-striped walls, is very popular with downtown workers for its reasonable prices. Diners fill their trays with items such as salads, hot dishes, sandwiches, soups, and desserts, or a simple empanada. Solo diners often sit at a large bar near the entrance where they watch the news or a soccer game while eating. The *autoservicio,* or self-service, lunch runs from 12:30 to 4pm, dinner from 6 to 9pm, and there is also a simple menu offered all day.

Antonio Varas 755. © **45/211219**. Main courses $4–$6. AE, DC, MC, V. Daily 11am–11pm.

EXCURSIONS FROM TEMUCO
CONGUILLIO NATIONAL PARK ⭑⭑

Ranked as one of Chile's finest national parks, Parque Nacional Conguillío surrounds the spectacular smoking cone of Volcán Llaima and features a dense forest of spindly *araucaria* trees, which the park was created to protect. It's a lovely park and a great attraction year-round due to several splendid hiking trails, a ski resort, and an outstanding park information center. Volcán Llaima is one of the most active volcanoes on Earth and has registered 40 eruptions since 1640, most recently in 1994. In the southern section of the park, it is possible to witness the tremendous destruction lava has wreaked on the surrounding forest. Conguillío is divided into three separate sectors with as many access points. The western side of the park is commonly known as Los Paraguas (The Umbrellas); the eastern side is accessed from the north in sector Laguna Captrén, and the south at Sector Truful-Truful. Visitors will find the park's administration center, campgrounds, and most hiking trails here in the eastern sector.

The eastern access point is at the village **Cherquenco;** from here a 21km (13-mile) rutted road ends at the **Centro de Esquí Las Araucarias** (© **45/274141;** www.skiaraucarias.cl) in Los Paraguas. This ski center has four T-bars, a ski school, equipment rental, and a restaurant and bar. Ticket prices are $19 Monday through Friday and $25 on weekends. The center offers dormitory-style lodging in two single-sex rooms with about 10 to 15 bunk beds without bedding for $11 per person (and two dormitories for 10–11 people for $13 per person). Other lodging options are the **Apart Hotel Llaima** (five apartments with four beds each; $100 a night), **Refugio Pehuén** (three units; $30–$40 double), and the **Refugio Los Paraguas** (one unit, six beds; $80). Check www.skiaraucarias.cl for reservations. Las Araucarias is not a well-known ski resort, and its T-bars are tiresome, but if you are a ski buff and are in the area, this little resort is worth the visit for its surrounding forest of *araucaria* and simply breathtaking views. The road here is in bad shape, so bring a vehicle with high clearance and a pair of chains.

An unpaved and poorly maintained road connects a Conaf (park service) **visitor center,** which is open daily from 9am to 1pm and 3 to 7pm (© **45/298213;** www.parquenacionalconguillio.cl), with the towns **Curacautín** in the north and **Melipeuco** in the south. The information center has interpretive displays highlighting the park's flora, fauna, and physical geology, including an interesting section devoted to volcanism. During the summer, park rangers offer informative talks and walks and a host of educational activities, which they post in the visitor center. (English-language talks can be sometimes be arranged; send an e-mail to info@parquenacionalconguillio.cl, or check directly at the center.)

There's an easy, hour-long, self-guided trail that leaves from the Conaf center, but if you really want to get out and walk, you'll want to take the **Sierra Nevada trail.** This moderate 5-hour hike is the best in the park, taking visitors through thick forest and rising to two lookout points that offer sensational volcano and lake views before dropping back down to the Captrén Lagoon near the Conaf center. The trail head is on the western shore of Lake Conguillío, at the Conaf center. A second 5-hour hike along moderate terrain, **Los Carpinteros,** weaves its way through stands of *araucaria* trees that are several hundred, some more than 1,000, years old. This trail leaves from Laguna Captrén at the Conaf center.

GETTING THERE & BASICS   If you plan to rent a vehicle, try to get one with a high clearance—it's not essential, but it helps. Most tour companies in Temuco plan excursions to this park. Bus service from Temuco's main terminal is available only to Curacautín and Melipeuco; from here you'll need to take a taxi or hitch a ride. The road is paved only to the park entrance, so during the winter, you'll usually need a 4×4 or tire chains to get to the ski center.

The park is officially open daily April through November from 8am to 11pm, and May through October 8:30am to 5pm—but you can really enter at any time of the day. The park entrance fee is $4.50 for adults and $1.50 for children (free for those under 12 years). There is a cafeteria and a store at Conaf's park information center in front of the lake.

WHERE TO STAY   There are seven campsites along the shore of Lago Conguillío; backcountry camping is not permitted. Campsites cost about $15. From October to April, the park service has cabins that go for an average of $50 per night; information about rentals can be found inside the store next to the visitor center in Sector Truful-Truful. A great option is one of the wooden cabins at **La Baita** (✆ **45/416410** or 09/733-2442; fax 45/415462; www.labaita conguillio.cl) for $85 per night, located midway between Conaf and the town Melipeuco. Here you'll find a restaurant, a store, park information, and guided excursions such as hiking, randonee skiing, and snowshoeing.

2 Villarrica & Pucón ★★

Villarrica is 25km (16 miles) west of Pucón and 764km (474 miles) south of Santiago; Pucón is 112km (69 miles) east of Temuco and 789km (489 miles) south of Santiago

Pucón is where the tourists head, but Villarrica is where the locals live. It's a quiet town that never really took off as a vacation resort, in spite of the fact that the view is so much better here, with the volcano rising majestically beyond the lake. There are a few good and inexpensive lodging options here, if you decide to leave the tourism hubbub Pucón. But it's farther away from Villarrica and Huerquehue national parks and the ski resort.

Nationally and internationally known as the "Adventure Capital of Chile," Pucón offers a multitude of outdoor activities, including rafting, hiking, skiing, canyoning, kayaking, and fly-fishing. Yet what makes Pucón a great all-around destination is its flexibility. There's also an abundance of low-key activities, such as hot spring spas and scenic drives through gorgeous landscapes. Or you can just relax with a good book on the porch of a cabin or throw a towel on the beach and sun yourself, as hundreds do during the summer.

VILLARRICA

Villarrica does have a charm of its own; it's a more authentic Lake District pueblo, and some travelers find that aspect more appealing, especially in the summer. The center of town here hums with activity as regular townsfolk go about their daily business. The town is also closer to Temuco and attractions such as Lican Ray on Lake Calafquén, Panguipulli, and the Coñaripe and Geometric hot springs.

GETTING THERE   Buses JAC (✆ **45/443693**) leave Villarrica every half-hour for Pucón from its location at Bilbao 610, near Pedro de Valdivia. In Pucón, JAC's location is Uruguay 505 near the hospital. The fare is under a dollar. A taxi to or from Pucón costs about $10. For more information on getting to the region, see "Getting There" for Pucón, below.

VISITOR INFORMATION   A good **tourism office** can be found at Av. Pedro de Valdivia 1070 (© **45/206619**). It's open daily from 8:30am to 11pm from December 15 to March 15, and daily from 8:30am to 6:30pm the rest of the year; it often closes on winter afternoons when the weather is rotten. You can also visit www.villarrica.com for more information.

WHAT TO SEE & DO

You might consider a 2-hour trip to Villarrica to stroll the streets, have lunch, and drop in to visit the **Museo Histórico y Arqueológico** (Pedro de Valdivia 1050; no phone), with displays of Mapuche items and trademark silver pieces and jewelry. Outside you'll find an authentically thatched *ruca*, a traditional Mapuche home. The museum is open Monday through Friday from 9am to 1pm and 3 to 7:30pm. The festival **Muestra Cultural Mapuche** takes place here in Villarrica from January to late February, with music, handicrafts, dancing, and other activities (for more information, call the visitor center at © **45/206618**).

HUIFQUENCO FUNDO 🌟🌟🌟 *(Moments) (Kids)*   Whether you are staying in Villarrica or Pucón, a trip to the Huifquenco Farm is a must. Opened for tourism in 2002, this 862-hectare (2,129-acre) estate is the third largest in the region and boasts over 5,000 head of cattle, bulls, wild boar, llamas, and sheep, among other animals. Choose to tour the farm on your own horse or relax and enjoy the view in one of their antique carriages. A real-life *huaso* leads you along a magnificent tree-lined road, past lagoons and along rolling meadows with fantastic volcano and lake views. Get a feel for farm life in the region; go fishing, cycling, or canoeing; or take in a rodeo show at the *media luna*. Finish off your tour with a Chilean-style barbecue. If you are lucky, you can personally meet the farm's owner, Don Mario Cortes Vornand, a true character and generous host. Full- and half-day tours are available, and special programs are available upon request. (Camino Villarrica, Huifquenco at Km 0.5; ©/fax **45/415040;** www.fundo huifquenco.cl.) For transportation to Huifquenco and a bilingual guide, contact Enjoy Tour (Miguel Ansorena 123; © **45/442313;** www.enjoytour.cl).

WHERE TO STAY

Hostería de la Colina 🌟, Las Colinas 115 (©/fax **45/411503;** aldrich@entel chile.net), is owned and managed by an American couple, Glen and Beverly Aldrich, who have lived in Chile for 14 years. The inn is located on a hill with a panoramic view of the lake and volcanoes and offers seven comfortable rooms in the main house and two cottages located in the peaceful gardens, as well as a Jacuzzi. The owners will help you plan your stay, and they serve hearty Chilean meals in the pleasant dining room. Doubles run from $60 to $85; cottages start at $98. Rates include full breakfast.

    Hostería Kiel, General Korner 153 (© 45/411631; fax 45/410925), has comfortable rooms ($35–$55 double) and a direct view of Volcán and Lake Villarrica that you can enjoy from your very own porch. Or try **Cabañas Monte Negro,** at Pratt and Montt streets (© 45/411371); it charges $110 for two to six people (no credit cards), and has eight newer cabins near the lake with a direct view of the volcano. Private parking or ample street parking is available and free.

A New Luxury Hotel

Villarrica Park Lake 🌟🌟 *(Finds)*   Inaugurated by the president of Chile in November 2002, this is the region's top new hotel. Luxurious and expansive, this property is striving to be the best in Southern Chile. It has only 69 rooms, but it feels like a big corporate hotel, with its large lobby and aloof but polite staff. Extra-wide doors made of local wood lead into comfortable and spacious modern rooms, all with sliding French doors that open up onto a balcony with a view of the lake. The marble bathrooms come with a tub/shower and heated towel racks. The spa has an exquisite selection of facials and bodywork offerings. This is an excellent base for travelers who prefer large, full-service hotels, although you'd be well advised to book way in advance, as it occasionally fills up with corporate retreat groups for days at a time. Always request promotional rates when making your reservations.

Camino Pucón–Villarrica Km 13. ℂ **45/450000.** Fax 45/450202. www.villarricaparklakehotel.cl. 69 units. $180–$255 double; from $220 suite. AE, DC, MC, V. **Amenities:** Restaurant; bar; lounge; heated indoor pool; health club and spa; limited watersports equipment; concierge; business center; salon; room service; massage; laundry service; dry cleaning. *In room:* TV, minibar, hair dryer, safe.

WHERE TO DINE

For excellent seafood dishes, try **El Rey de Marisco,** on the coast at Valentín Letelier 1030 (ℂ **45/412093**), or **Hostería Kiel,** General Korner 153 (ℂ **45/411631**), for simple Chilean fare and a superb view of Volcán Villarrica. **The Travellers,** Valentín Letelier 753 (ℂ **45/413617**), has that international traveler's hostel vibe, and a menu to match, with Chinese, Indian, Mexican, Thai, and Chilean dishes, plus the ever-popular happy hour from 6 to 9:30pm.

PUCON ★★

Pucón is a picturesque little town almost entirely dependent on tourism, but, thankfully, it has not embellished its streets with gaudy tourist traps. Instead, a creative use of timber creates the architectural tone. During the early 1900s, Pucón's economy centered on the timber industry, but the town's fate as a travel destination was sealed when the first hotel went up in 1923, attracting hordes of fishermen. Ten years later, the government built the stately Hotel Pucón, drawing hundreds more visitors each year, who at that time had to travel here by boat from Villarrica. Today there are many lodging options and even more adventure outfitters ready to fill your days.

It is important to note that the summer season, particularly from December 15 to the end of February, as well as Easter week, is jam-packed with tourists. Hotel and business owners gleefully take advantage of this and jack up their prices, sometimes doubling their rates during that time.

GETTING THERE **By Plane** Visitors normally fly into Temuco's **Manquehue Airport** and then arrange transportation for the 1- to 1½-hour ride into Villarrica or Pucón. Most hotels will arrange transportation for you, although it's usually at an additional cost. **Transfer & Turismo de la Araucanía** (ℂ **45/339900**), a minivan service at the airport, will take a maximum of 10 guests (minimum 4) to Pucón for $45. Pucón's new airport is now operational and equipped to handle jets, but for the time being, only two flights a week (on Fri and Sun) touch down here from Santiago, and only during the highest season, from mid-December to late February. Additional service is expected to be added as demand continues to increase; for fares and up-to-the-minute schedule information, contact **Lan** at (ℂ **600/526-2000;** www.lan.com).

By Car From the Panamericana Highway south of Temuco, follow the signs for Villarrica onto Ruta 199. The road is well marked and easy to follow. If coming from Valdivia, take Ruta 205 to the Panamericana Norte (Hwy. 5). Just past Loncoche, continue east, following signs for Villarrica and Pucón.

By Bus   Tur Bus (© **2/270-7500;** www.turbus.cl) offers service to Pucón from destinations such as Santiago, stopping first in Temuco and Villarrica. The trip is about 9 to 11 hours and generally a night journey; the cost is about $19 for an economy seat and $31 for an executive seat. **Buses JAC** (in Santiago, Av. Providencia 1072; © **2/235-2484**) has service from Santiago to Pucón every half-hour from its terminal at Bustamante and Aldunate (© **45/443693**).

VISITOR INFORMATION   The Chamber of Tourism (© **45/441671**) operates a helpful tourism office at the corner of Brasil and Caupolicán streets; it's open daily from 9am to 8pm December through March, and from 10am to 6:30pm the rest of the year. However, the staff does not speak English very well. The city of Pucón has an excellent website at **www.pucon.com**.

GETTING AROUND   There are dozens of tour companies providing transportation and tours to all points of interest around Pucón; they generally advertise everything in their front windows. However, this is another place where renting a car is a great option if you want to get out and leisurely see the sights. In Temuco, **Hertz** has an office at Las Heras 999 (© **45/441664**), and they operate a branch in Pucón at Ansorena 123—actually, an agency called **Enjoy Tour** © **45/441664.** In Pucón, try **Christopher,** in front of the supermarket (© **45/449013**); **Pucón Rent A Car,** Colo Colo 340 (© **45/443052**); or **SUP Comercial Rent A Car,** 191 Ansorena (© **45/444485**). Sierra Nevada, at the corner of O'Higgins and Palguin (© **45/444210**), also rents cars and mountain bikes. Rates start at $45 per day for a small car.

OUTDOOR ACTIVITIES

With so many outdoor adventures available here, it's no wonder there's a surplus of outfitters eager to meet the demand. When choosing an outfitter in Pucón, remember that you get what you pay for. Be wary of seemingly fly-by-night operations or those that treat you like just another nameless tourist. You want a memorable experience for the fun you've had, not for the mishaps and accidents. Most outfitters include insurance in the cost of a trip, but first verify what their policy covers.

For more things to see and do in this area, see "Hot Springs Outside Pucón" and "Natural Attractions Outside Pucón," later in this chapter.

TOUR OPERATORS   Be very careful when selecting a tour operator in Pucón because few are 100% competent, and some are downright dangerous or simply don't have the years of experience in the area to provide responsible service. Ask about your guide's familiarity with the tour you are proposing to take (unbelievably, a few operators have periodically sent guides on trekking expeditions without having actually gotten to know the trail first) and what kind of experience and/or qualifications your guide has.

Politur, O'Higgins 635 (© **45/441373;** www.politur.com), is a well-respected tour company that offers fishing expeditions, Mapuche-themed tours, and sightseeing trips around the Seven Lakes area, in addition to volcano ascents. They're slightly more expensive than other agencies but are worth it. **Outdoor Experience,** General Urrutia 592-B (© **09-7843139** or 09-4872414; outdoorexperience@hispavista.cl), is a tour company run by two bilingual Chileans who each boast impressive climbing and mountaineering resumes. The duo focuses on climbs to the top of all volcanoes in the Lake District, as well as rock climbing, rappelling, and ducky river trips. They can also arrange custom tours. What sets them apart is their small tour-group size and their unique trip to a private *araucaria* forest reserve, **Cañi.**

Aguaventura, Palguín 336 (© **45/444246;** www.aguaventura.com), is run by a dynamic French group, and their main focus is snowboarding in the winter with a shop that sells and rents boards, boots, and clothing; they also do volcano ascents with ski/snowboard descents, and rafting and kayaking, and they offer a half-day canyoneering and rappelling excursion. **Sol y Nieve,** O'Higgins and Lincoyán (© **45/441070;** www.chile-travel.com/solnieve.htm), has been on the scene for quite a while, offering rafting and volcano ascents as well as fishing, airport transfers, and excursions in other destinations around Chile; however, there have been some complaints recently of lackluster service.

Trancura, O'Higgins 211-c (© **45/441189;** www.trancura.com), sells cheap trips to the masses, and they are best known for their rafting excursions, which they've been doing forever. Beyond that, I do not recommend any other trips with this company because of their yearly roster of inexperienced guides hired on the cheap. They do have ski and bike rentals, however, with low prices.

SPANISH LESSONS If you are staying in Pucón longer than a few days and you'd like to learn a little of the local lingo, try **Language Pucón,** Uruguay 306 (© **45/444967;** www.languagepucon.com), which offers short but effective courses and home-stay opportunities. They also have a good book exchange in English and German.

SHOPPING You'll find shops everywhere in Pucón, but the best are on Fresia Street. One here stands out, the **DOMO,** 224 local 2 Fresia (© **45/444548**), a small gift shop specializing in preselected items from all over Chile, such as copper, wood, ceramics, alpaca, archaeological, Mapuche, and wool products.

BIKING Several outfitters on the main street, O'Higgins, rent bicycles by the hour and provide trail information and guided tours. Bicycle rentals run an average of $8 for a half-day. You can also just pedal around town, or take a pleasant, easy ride around the wooded peninsula.

CANOPY ⚡⚡ The newest available adventure for thrill-seekers, a canopy is much like a "flying fox," a swing through the tree tops suspended by a cable and secured by a harness. Anybody can do this, and it is a great half-day adventure. Book your trip at **Spirit Exploraciones,** Palguin 323 (© **45/442481;** www. spiritexplora.com).

CLIMBING THE VOLCANO ⚡⚡⚡ An ascent of Volcán Villarrica is perhaps the most thrilling excursion available here—there's nothing like peering into this percolating, fuming crater—but you've got to be in decent shape to tackle it. The excursion begins early in the morning, and the long climb requires crampons and ice axes. Note that the descent has traditionally been a combination of walking and sliding on your behind in the snow, but so many have done this that the naturally formed "luge" run is now enormous, slippery, and fast, and people have been hurting themselves on it lately—so be cautious. Volcán Villarrica is perpetually on the verge of exploding, and sometimes trips are called off until the rumbling quiets down. Tour companies that offer this climb are **Outdoor Experience, Politur,** and **Sol y Nieve** (see "Tour Operators," above). The average cost is $35 and does not include lunch.

FISHING ⚡ You can pick up your fishing license at the visitor center at Caupolicán and Brasil. Guided fishing expeditions typically go to the Trancura River or the Liucura River. See a list of outfitters above for information, or try **Off Limits,** Fresia 273 (© **45/441210** or 09/949-2481).

FOUR TRACK   These guided tours on four-wheel motorcycles are for people who either can't or don't want to walk through nature, and they are available in any kind of weather. Tours lead riders through native forests and, on clear days, to points with impressive volcano views. Only one company offers this excursion (about $12 an hour): **Ronco Track,** O'Higgins 615 (© **45/449597;** ronco track@hotmail.com).

GOLFING ☞   Pucón's private 18-hole **Península de Pucón** golf course is open to the playing public. For information, call © **45/441021,** ext 409. The cost is $42 for 18 holes. This is really the only way to get onto the private—and exclusive—peninsula that juts into the lake, by the way.

HIKING ☞☞   The two national parks, Villarrica and Huerquehue, and the Cañi nature reserve offer hiking trails that run from easy to difficult. An average excursion with an outfitter to Huerquehue, including transportation and a guided hike, costs about $22 per person. By far the best short-haul day hikes in the area are at Huerquehue and the Cañi nature reserve hikes.

HORSEBACK RIDING ☞   Half- and full-day horseback rides are offered throughout the area, including in the Villarrica National Park and the Liucura Valley. The **Centro de Turismo Huepil** (© **09/643-2673**) offers day and multiple-day horseback rides, including camping or a stay at the Termas de Huife, from a small ranch about a half-hour from Pucón (head east out of Pucón and then north toward Caburgua; take the eastern road toward Huife and keep your eyes open for the signs to Centro de Turismo Huepil). You'll need to make a reservation beforehand. All-inclusive multiple-day trips cost about $100 per person, per day. A wonderful couple, Rodolfo and Carolina, run this outfit. Rodolfo is a superb equestrian professor who used to train the Spanish Olympic team. Beginning riders are given an introductory course in the corral before setting out. Contact a tour agency for day rides in Villarrica Park, which go for about $60 for a full day. Tour agencies will also organize rides that leave from the **Rancho de Caballos** (© **45/441575**), near the Palguín thermal baths. If you're driving, the Rancho is at 30km (19 miles) on the Ruta International toward Argentina.

RAFTING ☞   Rafting season runs from September to April, although some areas might be safe to descend only from December to March. The two classic descents in the area are the 14km (8¾-mile) Trancura Alto, rated at Class III to IV, and the somewhat gentler Trancura Bajo, rated at Class II to III. Both trips are very popular and can get crowded in the summer. The rafting outfitter **Trancura** (see "Tour Operators," above) also offers an excursion rafting the more technical Maichin River, which includes a barbecue lunch. **Sol y Nieve** also offers rafting. The 3-hour rafting trip on the Trancura Alto costs an average of $20; the 3-hour Trancura Bajo costs an average of $8.

SKIING   The **Centro Esquí Villarrica** gives skiers the opportunity to schuss down a smoking volcano—not something you can do every day. There's a sizeable amount of terrain here, and it's all open-field skiing, but, regrettably, the owners **(The Grand Hotel Pucón)** rarely open more than two of the five chairs, due to nothing else but laziness. You'll need to take a chair lift to the main lodge, which means that nonskiers, too, can enjoy the lovely views from the lodge's outdoor deck. There's a restaurant, child-care center, and store. The Centro has a ski school and ski equipment rental; there are slightly cheaper rentals from Aguaventura, Sol y Nieve, and Trancura, among other businesses along O'Higgins. Lift ticket prices vary but average about $23. Most tour companies offer transport to and from the resort, and a shuttle goes every hour on the hour from The Gran Hotel Pucón. For more information, contact one of the tour operators above.

WHERE TO STAY

Pucón is chock-full of lodging options, nearly all of them good to excellent. If you're planning to spend more than several days in the region, you might consider renting one of the abundant *cabañas*. Keep in mind that Pucón is very busy during the summer, and accommodations need to be reserved well in advance for visits between December 15 and the end of February. Prices listed below show the range from low to high season; high season is from November to February, but verify each hotel's specific dates. You might consider visiting during the off season, when lodging prices drop almost 50%; November and March are especially good months to visit.

Expensive

Gran Hotel Pucón *(Kids)*   The Gran Hotel is a landmark built by the government in 1936 when fishing tourism began to take off in Pucón. It is a good choice for families, but otherwise I have mixed opinions about it. The owners renovated the premises fairly recently (and replaced a hideous peacock teal exterior with an insipid putty color), but one has the feeling they still have a long way to go, especially when it comes to service. The hotel's palatial hallways, stately dining areas, and lovely checkerboard patio give an aura of times gone by. Indeed, the old-world beauty of these common areas, with their marble and parquet floors, lofty ceilings, and flowing curtains, still looks scruffy. The rooms are not exactly noteworthy, but they are not bad, either: spacious, with comfortable beds and views of the volcano or the lake. The superior room has an alcove with one or two additional beds for kids; bathrooms are spacious and clean. The hotel is run somewhat like a cruise ship, with nightly dinner dances, stage shows, music, and comedy, as well as a team of activity directors who run a kids' "mini-club" and host classes for adults, such as cooking or tango. The hotel sits on the most popular beach in Pucón.

Clemente Holzapfel 190, Pucón. ©/fax **45/441001**, or 2/353-0000 for reservations (in Santiago). Fax 2/ 233-3174. www.granhotelpucon.cl. 145 units. $95–$160 double. Kids under 10 stay free in parent's room. AE, DC, MC, V. **Amenities:** Restaurant; outdoor cafe; bar; lounge; large outdoor pool and small indoor pool; health club; children's programs; concierge; tour desk; limited room service; laundry service; dry cleaning. *In room:* TV, minibar, safe.

Hotel Antumalal *(★★★ (Moments)*   The minute you arrive here, you know you've come upon something special. Perhaps it is the Antumalal's unique Bauhaus design and its lush, exotic gardens, or perhaps it's the sumptuous view of sunset on Lake Villarrica seen nightly through the hotel's picture windows or from its wisteria-roofed deck. Either way, this is simply one of the most lovely and unique hotels in Chile. Low-slung and literally built into a rocky slope, the Antumalal was designed to blend with its natural environment. The lounge is a standout, with walls made of glass and slabs of *araucaria* wood, goatskin rugs, tree-trunk lamps, and couches built of iron and white rope. It's retro-chic and exceptionally cozy, and the friendly, personal attention provided by the staff heightens a sense of intimacy with one's surroundings. The rooms are all the same size, and they are very comfortable, with honeyed-wood walls; a fireplace; a big, comfortable bed; and large panoramic windows that look out onto the same gorgeous view. Guests don't just walk into a room; they *sink* into it. The bathrooms have all been renovated recently and are sparkling clean. There's also a Royal Cottage for rent that comes with two bedrooms, a living room, and fireplace—perfect for families or as a romantic bungalow for two.

The owners are very involved in the day-to-day management of the hotel and will sit down with guests to help them plan their stay and arrange for any special requests. The bar is especially interesting, with high-backed leather chairs and a stone fireplace, and the dining room not only serves up a spectacular view, but it also serves some of the best food in Pucón. Well-kept terraced gardens zigzag down the lakeshore, where guests have use of a private beach. A kidney-shape pool is half-hidden under a lawn-covered roof, and the tennis courts are a short walk away. It's all fit for a queen—indeed, Queen Elizabeth graced the hotel with her presence several decades ago, as have Jimmy Stewart and Barry Goldwater.

Camino Pucón–Villarrica, Km 2. ℂ 45/441011. Fax 45/441013. www.antumalal.com. 16 units. $153–$212 double; from $380 Royal Cottage. Rates include full breakfast. AE, DC, MC, V. **Amenities:** Restaurant; bar; lounge; small outdoor pool; tennis court; room service; massage; laundry service.

Hotel del Lago 🅵 *Kids*   Pucón's sole five-star luxury hotel boasts a casino, the only cinema in town, and so many amenities that you might not feel like leaving the hotel. Attractively designed and a relatively new lodging option on the Pucón scene, the Hotel del Lago is airy and bright, with a lobby covered by a lofty glass ceiling. I recommend this hotel above the Villarrica Park Hotel for its central location and better design, though rooms do not have the lake views of that hotel. All the hotel's furnishings were imported from the United States, and the elegant, comfortable rooms are tastefully decorated with furniture and wood trim made of faux-weathered pine, accented with iron headboards, crisp linens, and heavy curtains colored a variety of creamy pastels, all very light and bright.

The bathrooms are made of Italian marble and are decently sized, as are double-size rooms—note that a double standard comes with two twins. The suites feature a separate living area. The Suite Volcán has the volcano view, but rooms facing west enjoy the late-afternoon sun. A concierge can plan a variety of excursions for guests, as well as transport to the ski center. The hotel offers many promotions and package deals from March to December, often dropping the double price to $110, so be sure to check their website for seasonal promotions.

Miguel Ansorena 23, Pucón. ℂ 45/291000. Fax 45/291200. www.hoteldellago.cl. 82 units. $120–$240 double; $200–$300 suite. Rates include buffet breakfast. AE, DC, MC, V. **Amenities:** 2 restaurants; bar; lounge; small indoor pool and large outdoor pool; state-of-the-art health club; spa; sauna; children's programs; game room; concierge; business center; room service; massage; babysitting; laundry service; dry-cleaning service. *In room:* TV, minibar, safe.

Hotel Huincahue 🅵 *Finds*   If you like to be in the center of town, steps from all the shops and restaurants, in a quiet and sophisticated setting, then this is your best bet. Pucón's newest hotel sits right on the main plaza and has an elegant, homey feel to it. From the cozy lobby lounge with a fireplace and adjoining library to the peaceful pool in the lovely garden, this place feels more like a private mansion than a hotel. Rooms have pleasant beige carpets and nice wrought-iron and wood furniture, and a few have spectacular views of the volcano (room no. 202 is best). Second-floor rooms have small balconies. The marble bathrooms are large and many have windows as well. The staff tries hard to accommodate, but their English is minimal, so be patient.

Pedro de Valdivia 375. ℂ/fax 45/443540 or 442728. www.hotelhuincahue.cl. 20 units. $85–$120 double. Rates include continental breakfast. AE, MC, V. **Amenities:** Restaurant; bar; lovely outdoor pool; room service; massage; babysitting; laundry service. *In room:* TV.

Moderate

Hotel & Spa Araucarias   The Hotel & Spa Araucarias is a good midrange option for its well-manicured grounds, indoor pool, outdoor deck, and extras such as an on-site gift shop. The size of the rooms is a little tight—not too much space to walk around in, but enough to open your suitcase. If you're looking for something a little more independent and spacious, try one of the four connected cabins in the back. The hotel has a "spa" room with a sauna and a heated indoor pool fitted with hydromassage lounges. The name comes from the *araucaria* trees that flank the entrance; there's also an *araucaria* sprouting from a grassy courtyard in the back. The hotel is in walking distance from the beach and is close to shops and restaurants.

Caupolicán 243, Pucón. ©/fax **45/441963**. www.araucarias.cl. 25 units. $60–$75 double. Rates include continental breakfast. AE, DC, MC, V. **Amenities:** Restaurant; lounge; heated indoor pool; Jacuzzi; sauna; massage. *In room:* TV.

La Posada Plaza ☆   This traditional hotel is housed in a 78-year-old home built by German immigrants, located on the main square 2 blocks from the beach. Everything about this old-fashioned hotel, from its exterior to its dining area, to its backyard swimming pool, is very attractive—except the rooms, that is, which are plain and inexplicably do not keep up the charm of the hotel's common areas. These old buildings always seem to come with fun-house floors that creak and slant in every direction. All in all, it's a comfortable enough place to hang your hat for the evening, and it is located on the plaza.

Av. Pedro de Valdivia 191, Pucón. © **45/441088**. Fax 45/441762. laposada@unete.com. 17 units. $42–$66 double. Rates include buffet breakfast. AE, DC, MC, V. **Amenities:** Restaurant; pool snack bar; lounge; large outdoor pool; laundry service. *In room:* TV.

Malahue Hotel ☆   This attractive, newer hotel is about a 15-minute walk from town, but it offers excellent value in handsome accommodations. It was designed to feel like a modern mountain lodge, made of volcanic rock and native wood, and is set on an open space in a residential area. The interiors are impeccably clean, and rooms are decorated with country furnishings. There's also a restaurant and a cozy lounge with a fireplace and couches. *Cabañas* have two bedrooms, a trundle bed in the living area, and a fully stocked kitchen. The location isn't ideal, but it is a good value nonetheless.

Camino Internacional 1615, Pucón. © **45/443130**. Fax 45/443132. www.pucon.com/malalhue. 24 units, 3 cabañas. $46–$70 double; $70–$98 cabaña. Rates include buffet breakfast. AE, DC, MC, V. **Amenities:** Restaurant; bar; lounge; room service. *In room:* TV.

Monte Verde Hotel & Cabañas ☆☆ (Kids)   Built in 2003 and tastefully designed using nearly every kind of wood available in the area (including recycled *alerce*), this six-room hotel is located about 6km (3¾ miles) from Villarrica, meaning you'll need a taxi or rental car to get here. The hotel and *cabañas* are perched on a hill to afford views of the volcano and the lake. The distance from town means no summer crowds, if you are here from December to February. All rooms are decorated differently; four have king-size beds and all but one have private balconies with lake views. The bathrooms are decorated with old-fashioned sinks and bathtubs obtained from a turn-of-the-20th-century hotel in Villarrica. Attentive service and a complimentary bottle of red wine upon arrival are welcoming touches. There is also a cozy lounge with wood-burning fireplace and board games; during the high season, there are kayaks and boats available for guest use at the beach below and an outdoor pool, whirlpool, and hot tub. There are 14 *cabañas* to choose from, and they all have three bedrooms and two bathrooms and can sleep two to seven guests. Reservations are necessary for *cabañas* at least a few months in advance, due to demand.

Camino Pucón-Villarrica Km 6. (C) **45/441351.** Fax 45/443132. www.monteverdepucon.cl. 6 units, 14 *cabañas.* $65–$100 double; $70–$170 *cabaña.* Rates include buffet breakfast. AE, DC, MC, V. **Amenities:** Lounge; room service.

Inexpensive

¡école! (C) (Value) Nearly 40 partners own this pleasant hostel, which offers small but clean and comfortable rooms with beds blanketed with goose-down comforters. ¡école! sees a predominantly international crowd, from backpackers to families traveling on a budget. It has a very good vibe throughout and a nice outdoor patio with picnic tables. The hostel provides great reading material in the small lounge, from travel guides to environment-oriented literature, to logging protest rosters. The hostel is part restaurant/part lodging/part ecology center, offering day trips to various areas, but especially to the private park Cañi, an *araucaria* reserve. It's very popular in the summer, when it's wise to book at least 1 or 2 weeks in advance. Note that some rooms are shared, meaning you may have to bunk with a stranger if the hostel fills up, although there are doubles located in the back for nonshared accommodations with a private bath.

General Urrutia 592, Pucón. (C)/fax **45/441675.** www.ecole.cl. 16 units. $30 double. Rates include continental breakfast. DC, MC, V. **Amenities:** Restaurant.

La Tetera (C) Rooms at La Tetera are simple but meticulously clean, and shared bathrooms are not much of an issue, as they are just outside your door. It's all squeezed in pretty tight, but guests have use of a private, sunny common area with chairs and a picnic table, and a short walkway connects to an elevated wooden deck. A Swiss-Chilean couple own La Tetera; they offer a book exchange and good tourism information, and will arrange excursions and help with trip planning. La Tetera (The Tea Kettle) lives up to its name, with two menu pages of teas, along with sandwiches, daily specials, and pastries. A common area next to the cafe has the only TV in the place. The staff can arrange for Spanish lessons, even if you're here for just a short time.

General Urrutia 580, Pucón. (C)/fax **45/441462.** www.tetera.cl. 6 units. $20–$33 double. Rates include continental breakfast. No credit cards. **Amenities:** Restaurant; bar (for guests only).

Refugio Peninsula Bed & Breakfast (C) Of the three inexpensive options mentioned here, this hostel has the best location, a half-block walk from the shore and just a 100m (328-ft.) walk from the main beach in Pucón. Tucked away on a quiet corner on the lush peninsula side of town, this brand-new hostel offers shared accommodations, a few doubles, and a *cabaña* for five with a kitchenette, and all its furnishings and interiors are fresh and new. Like ¡école! this hostel has an outdoor patio; it also has a cozy, wood-hewn restaurant and bar for meals and drinks. Shared rooms (some with three beds, some with five) mean that you will bunk with a stranger on busy nights, but here each room has a private bath, unlike its competitors. There are also two double rooms for couples or a single seeking privacy. Service here is friendly.

Clemente Holzapfel 11, Pucón. (C) **45/443398.** www.refugiopeninsula.cl. 8 units. $16 shared rooms; $32 double; $58 *cabaña* for 5. Rates include continental breakfast (except *cabaña*). No credit cards. **Amenities:** Restaurant; bar (for guests only).

Cabañas

Almoni del Lago Resort (C)(C) (Finds) Location is everything at the Almoni, with its lush, gorgeous grounds leading down to the lapping shores of Lake Villarrica just a few meters from the deck of your cabin. Cabins for two, four, and eight guests are available; ask for specials for multiple-day stays. Cabins are fully equipped, very comfortable, and elegant; guests are given their own remote gate opener to help control access. A kiosk sells basic food items and other sundries. Most *cabañas* have their own deck right on the water; others have a deck farther up the hill. Either way, the cabins are fairly close together, so you might end up getting to know your neighbor. Prices drop 50% in the off season.

Camino Villarrica a Pucón, Km 19. ⓒ **45/210676.** Fax 45/442304. www.almoni.cl. 8 *cabañas.* $47–$90 *cabaña* for 2. MC, V. **Amenities:** Large outdoor pool; tennis courts. *In room:* TV, kitchen.

Cabañas Ruca Malal 🗭   These custom-made, cozy wooden cabins are tucked away in a tiny forested lot at the bend where busy O'Higgins becomes the road to Caburga. The grounds, however, are peaceful, and they burst with bamboo, beech, magnolias, and rhododendron. The design of each cabin features log stairwells, carved headboards, and walls made of slabs of evergreen beech trunks cut lengthwise. They are well lit and have full-size kitchens and daily maid service. A wood-burning stove keeps the rooms toasty warm on cold days. In the center of the property is a kidney-shape swimming pool; there's also a Jacuzzi and sauna, but, unfortunately, you'll have to pay extra to use them. As with most cabins, those designed for four people mean one bedroom with a double bed and a trundle bed in the living area; book a cabin for six if you prefer two bedrooms. Those with a sweet tooth will delight with Ruca Malal's on-site chocolate shop.

O'Higgins 770, Pucón. ⓒ/fax **45/442297.** avalle@cepri.cl. 9 units. $36–$98 cabin for 4; $66–$110 cabin for 6. MC, V. **Amenities:** Lounge; small outdoor pool; Jacuzzi; sauna; laundry service. *In room:* TV, kitchen.

Las Cabañas Metreñehue 🗭 *Kids*   These pastoral *cabañas* are surrounded by dense forest and bordered by the thundering Trancura River, about a 10-minute drive from downtown Pucón, and are for those seeking a country ambience away from town. There are cabins built for seven guests; a few two-story cabins can fit eight. All are spacious and very comfortable, with wood-burning stoves, decks, and ample kitchens. Some come with bathtubs, and a few have giant picture windows; all have daily maid service. The two *cabañas* in the back have a great view of the volcano. Around the 3-hectare (7-acre) property are walking trails, a swimming pool, a volleyball court, a soccer field, and a river where guests can fish for trout. The cabins are popular with families in the summer, and sometimes large groups take advantage of the *quincho,* the poolside barbecue site. There's also mountain bike rental. The German owners are gracious and multilingual, and live in the main house (and reception area), near the cabins. Parties of two to five will have to pay a $110 six-guest rate during the summer.

Camino Pucón a Caburga, Km 10. ⓒ/fax **45/441322.** www.pucon.com/metrenehue. 7 units. $50–$110 for 2; $90–$110 for 6. AE, DC, MC, V. **Amenities:** Restaurant; large outdoor pool; bike rental; laundry service. *In room:* TV, kitchen.

Portal Pucón Cabañas *Kids*   Fourteen of these newer wooden cabins are spread out over a large, grassy lot overlooking Lake Villarrica, and the remaining five (built in 2003) are across the road that separates the cabins from the beach. They are comfortable and relatively inexpensive, and a good bet for families with kids, especially for the pool, play area, "kids' clubhouse," and babysitting service; daily maid service is also included. All cabins have tiny kitchens, living areas, wood-burning stoves, small decks with table and chairs, and sweeping views of the lake. However, five of the cabins *(cabañas chicas)* are large cabins split into two units, and are somewhat cramped. Solitary cabins for four are larger, but the view shrinks. The cabins on the lakefront are the most spectacular for their views and

have two bedrooms, one ensuite, the other with bunk beds, and there is also a sofa bed in the living room. The spacious property features walking trails, and there's also a private beach and docking area a 5-minute walk down the hill and across the road. Portal Pucón is a 3-minute drive from downtown.

Camino Pucón–Villarrica, Km 4.5. © 45/443322. Fax. 45/442498. www.portalpucon.cl. 19 units. $36–$64 for 2; $54–$105 for 4. AE, DC, MC, V. **Amenities:** Lounge; bar; large outdoor pool. *In room:* TV, kitchen.

WHERE TO DINE

Pucón has a good selection of cafes that serve *onces,* the popular late-afternoon coffee-and-cakes snack, in addition to a lunch menu. **Café de la "P,"** Lincoyán 395 (© **45/442018**), has a menu with sandwiches, cakes, coffee drinks, and cocktails. It's a nice place to unwind with a drink in the evening and is open until 4am in the summer. **La Suiza,** O'Higgins 116 (© **45/441241**), has a menu with everything from milkshakes to full-fledged entrees, and does a booming business with the Santiago crowd in the summer.

Patagonia, Fresia 223 (© **45/443165**), and **Patagonia Plaza,** Pedro de Valdivia 333 (© **45/444715**), are both great places to get a hot chocolate and a piece of cake on a rainy day or a multiflavored ice-cream cone in the heat of the summer. Patagonia Plaza is right off the main square and is charmingly designed using tree trunks that give it a feel like the house of the seven dwarfs.

Alta Mar SEAFOOD   Seafood is the specialty here, as you can tell by the marine decor. It's the best spot for seafood in Pucón, offering a wide range of fish usually served grilled, fried, or sautéed in butter and bathed in a sauce. Their ceviche is tasty, and so are the razor clams broiled with Parmesan cheese. Outdoor seating is available on the front deck during warm months.

Fresia 301. © 45/442294. Main courses $4–$8. AE, DC, MC, V. Daily noon–4pm and 7:30pm–midnight.

Antumalal 🎔🎔 *Moments* INTERNATIONAL   The Hotel Antumalal's restaurant serves some of the most flavorful cuisine in Pucón, with creative dishes that are well prepared and seasoned with herbs from an extensive garden. In fact, most of the vegetables used here are local and organic; the milk comes from the family's own dairy farm. Try a thinly sliced beef carpaccio followed by chicken stuffed with smoked salmon, grilled local trout, or any one of the pastas. There's a good selection of wine and an ultracool cocktail lounge for an after-dinner drink (but it's tiny and not a "happening" spot). It's worth a visit for the view of Lake Villarrica alone. This is our favorite dining experience in Pucón.

Camino Pucón–Villarrica, Km 2. © 45/441011. Fax 45/441013. Reservations recommended. Main courses $5–$9. AE, DC, MC, V. Daily noon–4pm and 8–10pm.

¡école! *Value* VEGETARIAN   This vegetarian restaurant includes one salmon dish among heaps of creative dishes like calzones, quiche, pizza, burritos, chop suey, and more. Sandwiches come on homemade bread, and the breakfast is the best in town, featuring an American-style breakfast as well as Mexican- and Chilean-style. ¡école! uses locally and organically grown products and buys whole-wheat flour and honey from a local farm. There are also fresh salads here. The outdoor patio is a lovely place to dine under the grapevine in good weather. The service is very slow and disorganized; they usually offer a shorter menu during the winter.

General Urrutia 592. ©/fax 45/441675. Main courses $3–$5. MC, V. Daily 8am–11pm.

Il Baretto 🎔🎔 PIZZERIA   Opened in 2004, this pizzeria is run by the same Uruguayan owners as La Maga, just across the street. Your meal will begin with delicious homemade breadsticks and a savory salsa of sun-dried tomatoes, olive oil, and garlic. Try any one of the pizzas on the menu, or create your own to be baked in the wood-burning oven. Go for one of the homemade pastas, or choose your own version by mixing and matching the sauces with the noodles. The calzones and a bottle of wine are a great snack to share, and for dessert, the tiramisu here is excellent. On a nice day, the patio tables are a great place to hang out and people-watch.

Fresia 124. ℂ/fax 45/443515. Pizzas $5–$12. MC, V. Daily noon–4pm and 7pm–midnight.

La Maga 𝕒𝕒 URUGUAYAN STEAKHOUSE   Undoubtedly the best *parrilla* in town, this restaurant originated in the beach town of Punta del Este, Uruguay. The food is excellent, especially the meat, chicken, and fish grilled on the giant barbecue on the patio. Order a bottle of wine and a large fresh salad, and watch the people go by the large picture windows overlooking the street. Try the grilled salmon with capers, if you're in the mood for fish. But, really, the best cuts here are the beef filets, known as *lomos,* served with mushrooms, Roquefort, or pepper sauce. The *bife de chorizo* (sirloin) is thick and tender. For dessert, the flan here stands out.

Fresia 125. ℂ 45/444277. Main courses $4–$8. AE, MC, V. Daily noon–4pm and 7pm–midnight.

La Marmita de Pericles 𝕒 FONDUE   Cozy and candlelit, La Marmita specializes in warm crocks of fondue, as well as the other Swiss favorite, *raclette.* Both involve a diner's participation, which usually makes for an amusing dinner—but if you are a fondue fan, you won't be as impressed here as in Europe, for example (the right cheeses aren't always available). Fondue can be ordered a variety of ways, with standard bread cubes, squares of breaded meat, or vegetables. A *raclette* runs along the same lines; diners heat cheese to eat with cured meats and potatoes; it's not as fun as fondue, but enjoyable nevertheless. Unfortunately, this restaurant closes during the winter, which is the perfect season for this kind of food.

Fresia 300. ℂ 45/441114. Fondue for 2 about $22. AE, DC, MC, V. Daily 7:30–11pm. Closed Apr–Nov.

Marmonhi 𝕒 *Finds* CHILEAN   If you'd like to have lunch with the locals, then this place, a good 20-minute walk from the center of town, is worth the hike. The food is typically Chilean, prepared by the amiable Elena, who runs a tight ship. Many of Pucón's residents stop by here to pick up lunch or dinner for their families, although the simple dining room is pleasant for a leisurely meal and there's a small patio for outdoor dining in good weather. Specials change daily, according to what Elena finds at the market. Vegetable or beef empanadas are a great start to the meal. Then order a big Chilean salad (fresh tomatoes and lots of sweet onion) and one of the special chicken or fish dishes. They're simply yet deliciously prepared: marinated and grilled and served with vegetables and rice. There's excellent baked lasagna as well. For dessert, have one of the decadent tarts that locals rave about, but skip the coffee, which is instant and tasteless.

Ecuador 175. ℂ 45/441972. Main courses $3–$7. AE, DC, MC, V. Daily noon–4pm and 7–10:30pm.

Puerto Pucón *Finds* SPANISH   Puerto Pucón pays homage to its owner's Spanish heritage through its design and well-made classics such as paella. Seafood is the focus here, and it is served in a multitude of ways: Have your razor clams, shrimp, and calamari sautéed in garlic or wrapped in a crepe and smothered in crab sauce. The atmosphere is typical Spanish, with white stucco walls, bullfight posters, flamenco-dancer fans, and racks of wine bottles; the fireplace is especially nice, and there's also a small bar. The sangria is excellent, and during warmer months, there's seating on the front deck, which can get packed.

Fresia 246. ℰ 45/441592. Main courses $6–$8. AE, MC, V. Daily 11am–3:30pm and 7–11:30pm (until 2am during summer).

Trawen ℰ VEGETARIAN This centrally located, almost all-vegetarian restaurant has tasty food and a lively atmosphere. Start your day off with a healthful breakfast of fresh juice, real coffee, granola, fruit and yogurt, and fresh whole-wheat bread. There is a large selection of delicious shakes, all made with fresh fruit. Try any one of the empanadas made with whole-grain dough—they are good value for their large size. They also have muffins and snacks to go. This is a good place on a sunny day for a beer on their sidewalk patio, after a trip up the volcano.

O'Higgins 311. ℰ/fax 45/442024. Main courses $5–$7. MC, V. Daily 8am–2am.

Viva Perú! ℰ *Kids* PERUVIAN This Peruvian restaurant is a favorite hang-out for locals, offering warm, personalized service and tasty cuisine. For solo travelers, there is bar seating, and there is a patio with a volcano view. The restaurant specializes in ceviche and seafood *picoteos* (appetizer platters), which make an excellent accompaniment to a frosty pisco sour. Daily fixed-price lunch specials include a mixed salad, entree (steamed or grilled fish, pork loin, or chicken), and coffee for about $5. The restaurant offers one of the few kid's menus in the area. Try the sugary-sweet Suspiro Limeño, a creamy Peruvian tra-ditional dessert.

Lincoyan 372. ℰ/fax 45/444025. Main courses $5–$7. AE, DC, MC, V. Daily noon–2am.

PUCON AFTER DARK

Pucón's **casino** can be found inside the five-star **Hotel del Lago** (see "Where to Stay," earlier in this chapter), with three gaming rooms and a bingo hall. There's a good bar here as well that appeals to all ages, and the place is open very late. The Hotel del Lago also has the town's only **cinema;** Monday to Wednesday there are two-for-one tickets, but just one movie is offered (call ℰ **45/291000,** or check the newspaper for listings). For bars, **El Bosque,** 524 O'Higgins (ℰ/fax **45/444025;** closed Mon), is a popular local hangout that is open from 6pm until around 3am, and has Internet access and a good fusion cuisine menu. **Mamas & Tapas,** O'Higgins 597 (ℰ/fax **45/449002**), is a recently renovated bar serving snacks and food; it has long been one of the most popular bars in Pucón. It gets packed in the summer and has excellent music, even with DJs during peak season.

HOT SPRINGS OUTSIDE PUCON

All the volcanic activity in the region means there's plenty of *baños termales,* or hot springs, that range from rustic rock pools to full-service spas with massage and saunas. Nothing beats a soothing soak after a long day packed with adven-ture. Also, like the Cañi Reserve, the hot springs make for a good rainy-day excursion.

Termas de Huife ℰ Termas de Huife, a relaxing escape for the body and mind, is popular with tourists and locals alike for its idyllic thermal baths and setting. Nestled in a narrow valley on the shore of the transparent River Liucura, Huife operates as a full-service health spa for day visitors and guests who opt to spend the night in one of their *cabañas* or suites. This is one of my favorite *ter-mas,* for both its cozy accommodations and gorgeous landscaping, complete with narrow canals that wind through the property and river-rock hot springs flanked by bamboo and palm fronds. The complex features two large outdoor thermal pools kept at 96°F to 98°F (36°C–37°C) and a cold-water pool, as well as private thermal bathtubs, individual whirlpools, and massage salons arranged around an airy atrium. The four-person *cabañas* and double suites are housed in shingled, rust-colored buildings along the river, about a 2-minute walk from the main building. All come with wood-burning stoves, and the *cabañas* have a living area. The bathrooms deserve special mention for their Japanese-style sunken showers and bathtubs that run thermal water. The only complaint I have about this place is that it can be busy during the day and night, and lots of families means lots of kids.

Road to Huife, 33km (20 miles) east of Pucón. Ⓒ/fax **45/441222**. www.termashuife.cl. 10 units. $118–$135 double. Day-use fee $9 adults, $4.30 children 10 and under. AE, DC, MC, V. Thermal baths daily 9am–8pm year-round. Take the road east out of Pucón toward Lago Caburgua until you see a sign for Huife, which turns off at the right onto an unnamed dirt road. Follow the road until you see the well-marked entrance for Termas de Huife. **Amenities:** Restaurant; cafeteria; 3 outdoor pools; exercise room; Jacuzzi; sauna; game room; massage. *In room:* TV, minibar.

Termas de Menetúe These thermal baths are better for a day visit than an overnighter because the cabins sit so far away from the complex. There are two pools here. The reception area and restaurant look out onto a giant grass-encircled swimming pool, and a short path takes visitors around to a woodsier setting, with one average-size pool serenaded by a gurgling waterfall. It's a relaxing, bucolic place with giant ferns and a gently flowing stream. The spa house has individual baths, but they're rather creepy and dark; better to join the floating masses in one of the outdoor pools. The pine cabins are for two to six people. They come with a fully stocked kitchen and wood-burning stove, and are a 5-minute walk from the baths. Menetúe rents out bicycles and can point out a few trails for walking. A restaurant serves decent Chilean cuisine, and there's a snack bar near the second pool.

Camino Internacional, Km 30. ⒸInternational/fax **45/441877**. www.menetue.com. 6 *cabañas*. $50–$64 *cabaña* for 2. Day-use fee $6.50 Apr–Nov; $8 Dec–Mar. No credit cards. Thermal baths Dec–Mar 9am–9pm; Apr–Nov 9am–6pm. **Amenities:** Restaurant; bar; 2 large outdoor pools; spa. *In room:* TV, kitchen.

Termas Los Pozones *(Finds)* Los Pozones is Huife's rustic neighbor, well known in the region for its cheaper prices, natural setting, and hours—they stay open 24 hours a day, year-round, for the (mostly) young adults (many of them local) who want to keep the party going after leaving the discos in Pucón. The hot springs are reached by walking down a long, steep path, which means a long, steep climb after your soak (there are plans for a cable-operated people-mover). One other drawback is the unsightly iron pipe that cuts through the property, bringing thermal water to its neighbor Huife. Los Pozones expanded in 2000 from two to six rock pools and has built three *cabañas* high above the springs across from the road. The simple but pleasant *cabañas* come with kitchens and have lovely views, although it's a walk to get to the springs.

Road to Huife, 34km (21 miles) from Pucón, just past Termas de Huife. No phone. $42–$58 *cabañas* for 4. Day-use fee $6. No credit cards. Thermal baths 24 hr. *In room:* Kitchen.

Termas San Luis *(Kids)* Located high in the saddle of the Curarrehue Valley, the Termas San Luis is popular for its well-built thermal pools and view of Volcán Villarrica, but mostly for the rare paved access road that gets you there. The compact resort is centered on two swimming pools built with stone tiles, one outdoor and the other covered by a fiberglass shell much like a greenhouse; both are surrounded by plastic lounge chairs for reclining after a long soak. If you'd like to spend the night, San Luis has six wooden cabins perched on a slope overlooking, unfortunately, the parking lot, although a few are hidden behind trees. The cabins sleep four to six guests, meaning one double bed, three singles, and a living-room trundle bed. They are bright and very pleasant but can get very cold in the winter unless the wood-burning stove is continually stocked. The spa house features a tiny sauna and a massage salon at an additional cost. There is a restaurant here as well.

Ruta Internacional Pucón, Km 27. **©** **45/412880.** www.termasdesanluis.cl. $100 double. Day-use fee $9 adults, $5 children, and $7 for a private bathtub. No credit cards. Thermal baths daily 9am–11pm summer; daily 10am–7pm winter. **Amenities:** Restaurant; large outdoor pool and large indoor pool; spa; sauna; limited room service; massage. *In room:* TV, kitchen.

NATURAL ATTRACTIONS OUTSIDE PUCON
PARQUE NACIONAL HUERQUEHUE
Smaller than its rivals Conguillío and Villarrica, though no less attractive, Parque Nacional Huerquehue boasts the best short-haul hike in the area, the **Sendero Los Lagos.** This 12,500-hectare (30,875-acre) park opens as a steeply walled amphitheater draped in matted greenery and crowned by a forest of lanky *araucaria* trees. There are a handful of lakes here; the first you come upon is Lago Tinquilco, which is hemmed in by steep forested slopes. At the shore, you'll find a tiny, ramshackle village with homes built by German colonists in the early 1900s. A few residents offer cheap accommodations, but the best place to spend the night is in a campground near the entrance or at the Refugio Tinquilco (see "Where to Stay," below).

There's a self-guided trail called **Ñirrico** that is a quick 400m (1,312-ft.) walk, but if you're up for a vigorous hike, don't miss the spectacular **Tres Lagos** trail that begins at the northern tip of Lake Tinquilco. The path first passes the **Salto Nido de Aguila** waterfall, then winds through a forest of towering beech, climbing to a lookout point with a beautiful view of Lago Tinquilco and the Villarrica volcano. From here the trail begins zigzagging up and up through groves of billowy ferns and more tall trees until finally (2–3 hr. later) arriving at the beautiful, *araucaria*-ringed **Lago Chico,** where you can take a cool dip. A relatively flat trail from here continues on to the nearby **Verde** and **Toro** lakes. Bring plenty of food and water, and come prepared with rain gear if the weather looks dubious.

On your way to or from the park, you can make a detour to the **Ojos de Caburga,** where two aqua-colored waterfalls crash into the tiny Laguna Azul. There are a few picnic tables here, and you can take a dip if the weather's nice. The turn-off point is about 15km (9¼ miles) from Pucón.

GETTING THERE & BASICS   The park is 35km (22 miles) from Pucón. Buses JAC has daily service to the park (several times per day, depending on the season), and most tour companies offer minivan transportation and will arrange to pick you up later, should you decide to spend the night. If you're driving your own car, head out of Pucón on O'Higgins toward Lago Caburga, until you see the sign for Huerquehue that branches off to the right. From here it's a rutted dirt road that can be difficult to manage when muddy. Conaf charges $5.75 for adults and $1.50 for kids to enter, and is open daily from 8:30am to 6pm.

WHERE TO STAY   Conaf has a campground near Lago Tinquilco and charges $18 per site, for a maximum of six people. The best option for a roof over your head is the attractive **Refugio Tinquilco** (**©** **2/777-7673;** fax 2/735-1187), a spacious lodge with bunks for $8 per person (you'll need your own sleeping bag), and regular rooms with complete bedding for $55 per double. They also have a good restaurant and offer full pension for an additional $9.

PARQUE NACIONAL VILLARRICA

This gem of a park is home to three volcanoes: the show-stealer Villarrica, Quetrupillán, and Lanín. It's quite a large park, stretching 61,000 hectares (150,670 acres) to the Argentine border and that country's Parque Nacional Lanín, and is blanketed with a thick virgin forest of *araucaria,* evergreen, and deciduous beech. A bounty of activities are available year-round, including skiing and climbing to the crater of the volcano (see "Outdoor Activities" under "Pucón," earlier in this chapter), hiking, horseback riding, bird-watching, and more.

The park has three sectors. Most visitors to the park head to **Sector Rucapillán** (the Mapuche's name for Volcán Villarrica, meaning House of the Devil). Volcán Villarrica is one of the most active volcanoes in the world, having erupted 59 times from the 16th century until now. There are two trails here, the 15km (9.25-mile) **Sendero Challupén** that winds through lava fields and *araucaria,* and the 5km (3-mile) **Sendero El Glaciar Pichilancahue,** which takes visitors through native forest to a glacier. The park ranger booth at the entrance can point out how to get to the trail heads. You'll also find the interesting **Cuevas Volcánicas** in this sector. Ancient, viscous lava that flowed from the volcano created underground tunnels, 400m (1,312 ft.) of which have been strung with lights and fitted with walkways that allow you to tour their dark, dripping interiors.

Visitors are provided with a hard hat; the cave's humid, cold air requires that you bring warm clothing, regardless of the season. There are also exhibits describing volcanism and bilingual tours. It's open daily from 10am to 8:30pm during the summer, and from 10am to 6:30pm during the winter; admission is a steep $10 for adults and $4.50 for children (© **45/442002**).

The second sector, **Quetrupillán,** is home to wilder, thicker vegetation and a multiple-day backpacking trail that wanders through virgin forest and past the **Termas de Palguín** (which is also accessible by road), a rustic hot springs. Here you'll also find several waterfalls, including the crashing **Salto el León.** There's a horse stable here (see "Horseback Riding" under "Pucón," earlier in this chapter) that offers trips around the area. There is also an excellent day hike and the region's best thermal baths here (see the Villarrica loop drive mentioned below). Finally, the third sector, **Puesco,** is accessed by Ruta 119 south of Curarrehue. There's a Conaf post and several hikes through the park's wildest terrain, including pine forests, lakes, and rugged mountains.

3 Siete Lagos: Panguipulli & Lican Ray

Panguipulli is 54km (33 miles) south of Villarrica; Lican Ray is 31km (19 miles) south of Villarrica

Few daylong sightseeing drives surpass the beauty of the **Siete Lagos (Seven Lakes)** region south of Pucón, where you can follow a half-paved, half-dirt loop around Lago Calafquén, with stops in the picturesque resort towns Panguipulli and Lican Ray. As its name implies, the region is home to seven lakes, one of which is across the border in Argentina, and all are set among rugged, verdant mountains that offer photo opportunities at every turn. (For more on the Argentina side of the Lake District, see chapter 9.) Now that Chile's newest and best hot springs, Termas Geométricas, have opened, it makes sense to make a detour here. This can be done by driving to Coñaripe and heading left toward Parque Nacional Villarrica (follow signs for the park or Pualafquén). For a more adventurous drive, and only if you have a rental car with high clearance (4×4 is necessary during inclement weather), drive the highly recommended loop through the national park from the other direction, as described below.

DRIVING THE SIETE LAGOS ROUTE & THE LOOP THROUGH VILLARRICA NATIONAL PARK

Renting a car is the best option here, but all tour companies can put this excursion together for you. Ideally, these drives are best when the sun is shining for maximum views; however, visiting the various hot springs and driving through dense forest is also a good way to pass a rainy day. For the Siete Lagos route, head south from Villarrica toward Lican Ray and then through Coñaripe, circling the lake until reaching Panguipulli. From here you take the paved road toward Lanco (although signs might say LICAN RAY as well) until you see the sign for Lican Ray and Villarrica. This rough dirt road continues to Villarrica (there's a good lookout point along the way) or forks to the right to Lican Ray, where you can again catch the paved road to Villarrica. Take a good look at the map before making any decisions; note that none of these roads is numbered or has a name. Of course, the trip can be done in the reverse direction, which might be more desirable for an afternoon soak at the hot springs just south of Coñaripe.

It's a little more difficult (read: potholes, slippery mud, and short, steep pitches), but the loop through Villarrica National Park is more desirable for its views of virgin forest of towering evergreen beech and monkeypuzzle (Araucaria) trees, a good day hike, and a visit to the Termas Geométricas. This route is for high-clearance vehicles (4×4 in wet conditions) and should be undertaken from the north through the south only. Leaving Pucón, head east toward Curarrehue and drive for 20km (12 miles), turning right at the sign for Palguín (30km/19 miles from Pucón). These hot springs have a small hotel and several thermal pools; however, the service here is surly and there are better hot springs in the area. Continue along the road until you reach the ranger station (37km/23 miles from Pucón; $3 per-person entrance fee). There is a full-day hike here, the Los Nevados (16km/10 miles; about 10 hr. round-trip and moderate), but a preferred and shorter hike can be found about midway between the ranger station and Coñaripe, the Pichillancahue trail (6.6km/4 miles; about 4 hr. round-trip). This trail winds through dense virgin forest of the unusual, spindly monkeypuzzle trees and has views of the surrounding volcanoes. The road from the ranger station to Coñaripe is about 27km (17 miles), with an obligatory stop at the most beautiful hot springs in the region, Termas Geométricas.

Termas de Coñaripe *Kids*   These *termas* boast a privileged location in a narrow valley hemmed in by lush, steep mountains and Lago Pellaifa. The full-service hot springs complex has lodging and a restaurant, whereas the

---

A Note on Camping

The road between Lican Ray and Coñaripe is full of campsites, some of which have showers and barbecue pits. Try **Cabañas and Camping Los Arrayanes Foresta** (© **45/431480** or **09/817-1796**; www.losarrayanesdel foresta.cl), 2km (1¼ miles) from Lican Ray, which has well-built sites and comfortable cabins for four guests (about $70–$85 during the summer, $50–$60 during winter), and cabins for 3 to 12 guests ($50 during winter and $200 during summer); check their website for exact prices at the time you'll be there.

Termas Geométricas is more remote and puts you in the middle of more natural surroundings (but with fewer services). Coñaripe is handsomely built, with touches of Japanese design. There are four outdoor pools, one with a slide, and one indoor pool with whirlpool lounges and a waterfall. A babbling creek meanders through the property. The thermal spa's on-site trout fishery is fun for kids, as they are allowed to feed the fish. Inside the lobby and the hallways, the floors are made of a mosaic of cypress trunks. Rooms are carpeted and spacious, and suites come with a queen-size bed. If you require quiet, you might not want a room near the busy pool. The *cabañas* come with two rooms with double beds and one with two twins.

Along with all this beauty and the deluxe amenities comes the inevitable crush during the summer months, and it's not unusual for these hot springs to see almost 1,000 visitors per day at peak high season from January 1 to February 15. There are so many people that guests who have booked a few days often leave early, shell-shocked. During this time, there is a self-service cafeteria to alleviate the packed dining room at lunch; a restaurant serves Chilean food year-round. Off-season crowds drop dramatically, and during the winter you might have the place to yourself.

Camino Coñaripe to Liquiñe at Km 15. © **45/431407** or 45/419488. Fax 45/411111. www.termasconaripe. cl. 10 units, 3 *cabañas*, 1 apt. $146–$183 double standard with full board; $223 cabin for 4. Day-use fee $9 adults, $5 children for use of outdoor pools, and an additional $3 for indoor pool. DC, MC, V. Thermal baths daily 9am–11pm year-round. **Amenities:** Restaurant; lounge; 4 outdoor pools and an indoor pool; tennis courts; exercise room; bike rental; game room; room service; massage; laundry service. *In room:* TV.

Termas Geométricas ✦✦✦ *Finds* I can't stop raving about these hot springs. If you have the time, try to plan a visit here because they are one of the best in Chile. Designed by famed Chilean architect Germán de Sol (architect of the Explora hotels), the hot springs are a sybaritic delight. More than a dozen pools, made of handsome gray slate tiles, descend an emerald, jungle-draped ravine, each one linked by a winding boardwalk. Each pool has a changing room and bathroom, with creative touches such as grass roofs and stream-fed sink taps, all very minimalist and decidedly Japanese influenced. It is so utterly relaxing here that you could float until your skin wrinkles like a prune. At the end of the gently sloping boardwalk, you will be taken aback by the sight of a tremendous, crashing waterfall that seems almost too perfect—it is such an ideal spot for a hot springs that it is hard to believe the area wasn't capitalized on earlier. There is a small restaurant that serves coffee, cakes, and cheese sandwiches; you might want to bring your own picnic lunch if you want something more filling. The hot springs are open at night, too, lit by tiny candles resting on the top of the pool walls. It's not cheap ($17 to enter), but it is money well spent.

12km (7½ miles) from Coñaripe on the road to Palguín. No phone. $17 per person, towel included. No credit cards. **Amenities:** Cafe; changing rooms.

LICAN RAY

This tiny resort town hugs the shore of Lago Calafquén, offering toasty beaches made of black volcanic sand and a forested peninsula for a leisurely drive or stroll. The lake is warmer than others in the region and is, therefore, better suited for swimming; you can also rent a boat here. The name comes from Lican Rayén, a young Mapuche woman from the area who is said to have fallen in love with a Spanish soldier. The town was founded as a trading post, and today there are about 3,000 permanent residents, except for the period from December 15 to February 28, when the population doubles with the arrival of summer vacationers.

The first weekend in January is the busiest time of year. There's also the **Noche Lacustre** the second week in February, when the bay fills with boats for a variety of contests and activities, followed by an evening fireworks display. Lican Ray is less crowded and less expensive than Pucón, and during the off season you'll practically have the place to yourself.

There are a few places to stay here: **Hotel Becker,** Manquel 105 (©/fax **45/ 431553;** koresbecker@hotmail.com), has modest but comfortable rooms, a restaurant, and a deck from which you can enjoy the lakefront view, charging $28 for a double in off season, $50 for a double in high season (includes breakfast). **Hostería Inaltulafquén,** Cacique Punulef 510 (© **45/431115;** fax 45/ 415813; jdf@universe.com), has good rooms and an even better dining area and deck, and it is ideally located across from the Playa Grande beach; it charges $30 to $50 per double. The *hostería* is run by two helpful Canadians, who also offer excursions. Another recommended hotel (but in Jan and Feb only) is the **Hotel San Agustín,** Chincolef 336 (© **45/431660;** fax 45/431042; millana@ctc internet.cl), a modern hotel with peaceful, airy rooms for $30 to $40 for a double (there's also a restaurant; no credit cards accepted). For dining, try the restaurant at the *hostería* or **Ñaños,** General Urrutia 105 (© **09/450-9449**), with an extensive menu that offers everything from barbecue meats to clay oven–baked pizzas, and a daily fixed-price lunch for $4. It also has outdoor seating during the summer but no lake view. For visitor information, go to Gral. Urrutia 310 (in front of the Plaza), January and February open daily 9am to 11pm; rest of the year open Monday to Thursday 9am to 1pm and 3 to 6pm, Friday 9am to 1pm and 3 to 5pm.

PANGUIPULLI

This little town with the impossible-to-pronounce name (try "pan-gee-*poo*-yee") is spread across a cove on the shore of its eponymous lake. During the summer, Panguipulli's streets bloom a riot of colorful roses, which the town celebrates in February during the **Semana de las Rosas (Rose Week)** festival. During January and February, the town holds regular folkloric festivals, art exhibits, concerts, and more. Panguipulli was founded as a timber-shipping port and today has nearly 10,000 residents. The town's primary attraction is its charming **Iglesia San Sebastián,** at Diego Portales and Bernardo O'Higgins (in front of the plaza). Mass is held from November to February Thursday and Saturday at 8pm, Sunday and holidays 8:30am and 11am; the church is open all day (no phone). The Swiss priest who initiated the building of this church in 1947 modeled its design after the churches from his native country, with two latticed towers painted in creamy beige and red and topped off with black-shingled steeples. For visitor information, go to O'Higgins and Padre Sigisfredo streets in front of the plaza (Jan–Feb open daily 9am–9pm; rest of the year open Mon–Fri 9am–6pm).

The town is better visited as a day trip, but there is a remote lodge here that is a wonderful place to hole up in the middle of a forest and take part in a variety of outdoor excursions. The lodge is the **Hotel Riñimapu** (©/fax **63/ 311388;** www.rinimapu.cl), located 27km (17 miles) south of Panguipulli and on the shore of Lago Riñihue. The Riñimapu draws guests from around the world for its fly-fishing, horseback riding, and hiking—but it is the tranquillity here that encourages guests to really lose themselves in the beauty of the surroundings. The woodsy lodge has 17 simple rooms, a restaurant, a bar, and a tennis court, and it charges $60 to $75 double, about $50 more for meals. To get here, head south out of Panguipulli on the paved-then-dirt road toward Lago

Riñihue, and continue for 20km (12 miles) until reaching the hotel; or contact the hotel for information about transfer shuttles from the Temuco or Pucón airports.

4 Valdivia (*

839km (520 miles) south of Santiago; 145km (90 miles) southwest of Pucón

Valdivia is a university town on the waterfront of a winding delta, and it often receives mixed reviews from visitors. I personally enjoy visiting this historic town and find that there is quite a bit to do and see in 1 day. If you are not planning to visit the coast near Santiago and you are in Pucón for several days, consider a quick visit here or an overnight stay. There are regal colonial homes here and a vibrant market on the water's edge, but it is as though every building from every decade from every architectural style were thrown in a bag, shaken up, and randomly scattered about the city. (Not that this doesn't happen in many Chilean cities, mind you.) Valdivia does have more charm and is far more interesting than Temuco and Puerto Montt, however, and there are many activities for kids here.

The city is energetic, full of life, and very tenacious. Valdivia has suffered attacks, floods, fires, and the disastrous earthquake of 1960 that nearly drowned the city under 3m (9¾ ft.) of water (the strongest earthquake ever recorded). During World War II, Valdivia's German colonists were blacklisted, ruining the economy. So if Valdivia looks a little weary—well, it's understandable. There are tours here to visit the tiny towns and ancient forts at the mouth of the bay that protected the city from seafaring intruders. The market, where fishmongers peddle their catch of the day and pelicans, cormorants, and fat sea lions wait for scraps, is a delight, and there are several good restaurants, opportunities to boat around the city's delta, and some of the best museums and galleries in Chile here, too.

Valdivia, with about 130,000 residents, is divided by a series of narrow rivers, notably the Río Valdivia and the Río Calle Calle, that wrap around the city's downtown area. These rivers have produced some of the world's top rowing athletes, and many mornings you can see spidery figures plying the glassy water. Across the Río Valdivia is the Isla Teja, a residential area that's home to the Universidad Austral de Chile. It is common to see students pedaling around town.

ESSENTIALS
GETTING THERE
BY AIR   Valdivia's **Aeródromo Pichoy,** ZAL (© **63/272295**), is about 32km (20 miles) northeast of the city; **Lan Express** (© **600/526-2000;** www.lan.com) has two daily flights from Santiago, one daily flight to Concepción, two weekly flights to Temuco, and one weekly flight to Puerto Montt. A **taxi** to town costs about $7, or you can catch a ride on one of **Transfer Valdivia's minibuses** for $4 (© **63/225533**).

BY BUS   The bus terminal is at Anwandter and Muñoz (© **63/212212**), and nearly every bus company passes through here; there are multiple daily trips from Pucón and Santiago (the average cost for a ticket from Santiago to Valdivia is $10; from Pucón to Valdivia, it is $4).

BY CAR   From the Panamericana Highway, take Ruta 205 and follow the signs for Valdivia. A car is not really necessary in Valdivia, as most attractions can be reached by boat, foot, or taxi. It's about a 2-hour drive from Pucón, 1½ hours from Temuco, and 3 hours from Puerto Montt.

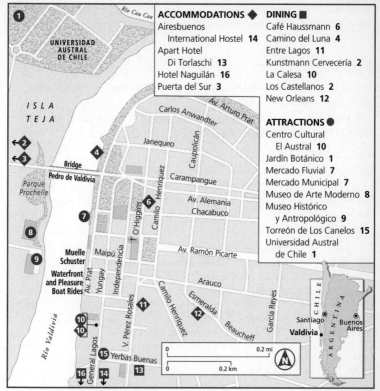

ACCOMMODATIONS ◆

Airesbuenos
International Hostel **14**
Apart Hotel
Di Torlaschi **13**
Hotel Naguilán **16**
Puerta del Sur **3**

DINING ■

Café Haussmann **6**
Camino del Luna **4**
Entre Lagos **11**
Kunstmann Cervecería **2**
La Calesa **10**
Los Castellanos **2**
New Orleans **12**

ATTRACTIONS ●

Centro Cultural
El Austral **10**
Jardín Botánico **1**
Mercado Fluvial **7**
Mercado Municipal **7**
Museo de Arte Moderno **8**
Museo Histórico
y Antropológico **9**
Torreón de Los Canelos **15**
Universidad Austral
de Chile **1**

VISITOR INFORMATION

Sernatur's helpful **Oficina de Turismo,** near Muelle Schuster at Arturo Prat 555 (② **63/215739**), has a well-stocked supply of brochures. The office hours from March to December are Monday to Thursday 8:30am to 5:30pm, and Friday from 8:30am to 4:30pm. January and February hours are Monday to Friday 8:30am to 7pm, Saturday and Sunday from 10am to 7pm. There's also an information kiosk at the bus terminal open daily from 8am to 9pm, and two websites with information at www.valdiviachile.cl and www.valdivia.cl.

SPECIAL EVENTS

The city hosts a grand yearly event, the **Verano en Valdivia,** with several weeks of festivities that begin in January, culminating with the **Noche Valdiviana** on the third Saturday in February. On this evening, hundreds of floating candles and festively decorated boats fill the Río Valdivia; in the evening, the city puts on a fireworks display. Note that Valdivia is crowded during this time, so hotel reservations are essential. For event info, check out www.munivaldivia.cl.

FAST FACTS: VALDIVIA

Car Rental   **Assef y Méndez Rent A Car** can be found at General Lagos 1335 (②/fax **63/213205**), and **Hertz** at Ramón Picarte 640 (②/fax **63/218316**); both have airport kiosks.

Currency Exchange   *Casas de cambio* can be found at **La Reconquista** at Carampangue 325 (② **63/213305**), but banks **Banco Santander-Santiago,**

Pérez Rosales 585, and **Corpbanca,** Ramón Picarte 370, have ATMs in addition to money exchange. **Redbanc** ATMs are in grocery stores, gas stations, and all banks throughout the city.

Hospital   The Clínica Alemana can be found at Beaucheff 765 (© **63/ 246100**).

Internet   Several spots for Internet access are near the plaza; try **Entel,** Vicente Pérez Rosales 601, #2.

Laundry   Self-service laundromats are **Lavamatic,** Walter Schmidt 305, #6 (© **63/211015**), and **Laverap,** Arauco 697, #2.

WHAT TO SEE & DO

The best tour is through Elisabeth Lajtonyi at **Outdoors Chile** (© **63/212931** or 09/444-3192; www.outdoors-chile.com). She can arrange your entire trip in Valdivia, from reserving hotels to airport transfers and personalized sightseeing tours.

BOAT TRIPS

A delightful way to explore the Valdivia region is with one of the many boat tours that depart from the pier Muelle Schuster at the waterfront, including yachts, catamarans, and an antique steamer. Tours are in full swing during the summer, and although there's limited service during the off season, it's possible for a group to hire a launch for a private trip. The most interesting journeys sail through the **Carlos Anwandter Nature Sanctuary** to the **San Luis de Alba de Cruces Fort** and to **Isla Mancera** and **Corral** to visit other 17th-century historic forts; both tours run about 5 to 6 hours round-trip and usually include meals. The Nature Sanctuary was created after the 1960 earthquake sank the banks of the Río Cruces, thereby spawning aquatic flora that, with the surrounding evergreen forest, is now home to more than 80 species of birds, including black-neck swans, red-gartered coots, and buff-necked ibis. Boating here is an excellent attraction for kids.

Embarcaciones Bahía (© **63/384727**) operates throughout the year with quick trips around Isla Teja ($5 per person), and tours to Isla Mancera and Corral (see "Niebla, Corral & Isla Mancera," below) can be arranged during the off season with a negotiated price or when there are enough passengers; children under 10 ride free. Other trips to Isla Mancera and Corral are offered by **Orión III** (©/fax **63/210533;** hetours@telsur.cl), which also includes a stop at the Isla Huapi Natural Park (also a Convention Center; www.islahuapi.com); the price is $25 per person, including lunch and snacks, and there are discounts for children under 10. By far the most luxurious is the **Catamarán Marqués de Mancera** (© **63/249191;** cmmancera@surnet.cl), which offers Isla Mancera and Corral tours with lunch and snacks included, and evening dinner cruises (only specially organized for large groups); both cost about $20 per person. The cheapest is the *Tatiana* (© **63/237104**), which leaves Valdivia for Corral at 1pm and returns at 6pm; the cost is $2.50 per person.

Go back in time on a journey aboard the *Vapor Collico* (© **63/222385**), a completely restored 1907 German steamer, with tours to the Nature Sanctuary and historical sightseeing journeys along the Río Calle Calle and the Collico area. There's a required minimum of 10 guests (or a negotiated fee), and reservations must be made at least 48 hours in advance ($35 per person, including lunch at an inland restaurant). For further information, check out the tourism board's website at **www.sernatur.cl**, under "Transporte Acuático" in the Valdivia section.

OTHER ATTRACTIONS

The bustling **Mercado Fluvial** ✮✮, at Muelle Schuster (Av. Prat at Maipú), is the principal attraction in Valdivia and is worth a visit for the dozens of fishermen who hawk fresh conger eel, hake, and spindly king crabs in front of colorful fruit and vegetable stands. Take a peek behind the fish stands to view the lanky pelicans and enormous sea lions barking for handouts. Across the street, the **Mercado Municipal** holds few attractions apart from a couple of souvenir shops and decent, inexpensive restaurants. Hours for the various shops here are erratic, but they are generally open Monday through Sunday from 9am to 7:30pm, closing at 9pm in summer, with some restaurants open later.

A block up from the waterfront, turn right on Yungay and head south until the street changes into **General Lagos** at San Carlos. A pleasant stroll for several blocks along General Lagos offers picturesque evidence of German immigration to the area through the stately, historic homes that dot the street. The houses, built between 1840 and 1930, belonged to affluent families, and many have been restored and maintained, despite the various earthquakes and other natural disasters that have beset them since construction.

Take a step back in time at the **Centro Cultural El Austral** ✮✮, Yungay 733 (© 63/213658), commonly known as the Casa Hoffman for the Thater-Hoffman family, who occupied the home from 1870 until 1980. It's open Tuesday through Sunday from 10am to 1pm and 4 to 7pm; admission is free. The first floor of this handsome building has been furnished to re-create the interior as it would have looked during the 19th century, complete with period antiques, paintings, and a few very garish chandeliers. Upstairs, the center holds temporary art exhibitions and painting, literature, and history classes. At the junction of General Lagos and Yerbas Buenas is the **Torreón de Los Canelos,** a 1781 defensive tower built to protect the southern end of the city—but if you're strapped for time, forget it.

ISLA TEJA

Isla Teja is a tranquil residential area that is also home to the Universidad Austral de Chile and a splendid history museum, the **Museo Histórico y Antropológico,** Maurice van de Maele ✮✮ (© 63/212872; www.museosaustral.cl). It's open December 15 to March 15 Monday through Sunday from 10am to 8pm, and the rest of the year Tuesday through Sunday from 10am to 1pm and 2 to 6pm; admission is $2 adults, 50¢ children 12 and under. To get there, cross the Pedro de Valdivia bridge, walk up a block, turn left, and continue for half a block. The museum is housed in the grand family home of Karl Anwandter, brewery owner and vociferous supporter and leader of German immigrants. Outside, two 19th-century carriages flank the entrance. Inside on the first floor is a varied collection of antiques culled from local well-to-do families and notable figures such as Lord Cochrane (the noted admiral who helped secure independence for Chile, Peru, and Bolivia), including furniture (even a double piano), photos, letters, medals, and everyday objects. There are also a few conquest-era artifacts, such as a Spanish helmet, as well as an excellent display of Mapuche Indian silverwork, textiles, and tools. An interesting collection of sepia-toned photos depicts settlers' images of Mapuches. Also along the waterfront, and occupying the old Kunstman brewery that was nearly demolished after the 1960 earthquake, is one of Chile's best art museums, the **Museo de Arte Moderno** (© 63/221968; www.macvaldivia.uach. cl), with excellent rotating displays of work by Chilean artists.

Leaving the museum, turn right and continue north on Los Laureles until you reach the **Universidad Austral de Chile.** Once inside the campus, the road veers right; follow it and the signs to the **Jardín Botánico** 𝒜𝒜, a lovely botanical garden created in 1957 that features a labeled collection of native trees and vegetation from every region in Chile and around the world. It's open from October 15 to March 15 daily from 9am to 7:30pm, from March 16 to October 14 daily from 9am to 5pm. Cut west through the campus to Calle Los Lingues and turn right until you reach the gated entrance to **Parque SAVAL** 𝒜, a sizeable park with rodeo stands, a children's playground, a picnic area, and a small lagoon. Admission is 50¢, kids 20¢, and it's open daily. From October to March, expositions, an arts and crafts fair, and agricultural demonstrations take place here.

NIEBLA, CORRAL & ISLA MANCERA

These three villages at the mouth of the bay were largely destroyed after the 1960 earthquake (on record as the strongest earthquake ever recorded). There's little left from that era, but what did survive were the relics of the 17th-century forts that once protected Valdivia from intruders, and a visit to these ancient relics, and the coastal views, makes for a very pleasant half-day trip—especially on a sunny day. If you are not planning to visit the coast near Santiago, do so here; there's enough to do and see to keep you occupied for at least a half-day, and Chile's only microbrewery is on the way back to town. Niebla lies 18km (11 miles) from Valdivia and is home to the **Castillo de la Pura y Limpia Concepción de Monfort de Lemus** (© **63/282084**), a defensive fort founded in 1671 and renovated in 1767. It's open December through February daily from 10am to 7pm, and March through November from 10am to 6pm, closed Monday; admission is $1, free for kids under 8. The fort is carved partially out of rock and features details such as cannons and a powder room, as well as a small museum. The town itself is mostly a hodgepodge of seafood restaurants (the best here is Los Castellanos; see "Where to Dine," below) and tiny houses with the most privileged views anywhere in Chile. There is a good beach for a stroll; enter to the left of the restaurant Las Terrazas.

To get there, take a private taxi for about $7, or grab a *colectivo* taxi (or micro) for $1 at the waterfront. In the summer, it is possible to take a tour boat to Niebla; in the off season, you'll need to take the road. The trip takes about 15 minutes.

Across the bay sits **Corral** (take a taxi to get here from Niebla) and the area's first and most powerful fort, the **Castillo San Sebastián de la Cruz,** built in 1645 and reinforced in 1764. The city itself is a picturesque jumble of brightly painted wooden homes and fishing boats, an old German colony that never really recovered from the tidal wave that wiped out most of the town. To get to Corral, take a tour boat from Valdivia during high season, or take a ferry from the fishing dock just before entering Niebla (let your bus or taxi driver know you're getting off there). The mock soldier battle that once was the highlight of this attraction has been put on hold due to overenthusiastic actors mishandling gun powder and shooting themselves in the foot; it remains to be seen if the ritual will continue anytime soon.

Either on the way to Corral or on the way back, ask to be dropped off at idyllic **Isla Mancera** (and ask to be picked up!) for a easy stroll and a visit to the fort **Castillo de San Pedro de Alcántara** (© **63/212872**). Admission is 80¢, and it's open from November 15 to March 15 daily from 10am to 7pm, and Tuesday through Sunday from 10am to 5pm the rest of the year. It was built in 1645 and restored in 1680 and again in 1762 to house the Military Government of Valdivia. Inside the grounds are the crumbling ruins of the San Francisco Convent and an underground supply room. It is possible to walk the circumference of the island in 20 to 30 minutes, and there is a site for picnics with great views.

WHERE TO STAY
EXPENSIVE

Hotel Naguilán ⭐ *Moments*   Although it sits about a 20-minute walk from the edge of downtown, the Hotel Naguilán boasts a pretty riverfront location and solid, attractive accommodations. The hotel is housed in an interesting structure (ca. 1890) that once held a shipbuilding business. All rooms face the Río Valdivia and the evening sunset; from here it's possible to watch waterfowl and colorful tugs and fishing skiffs motor by. The rooms are divided into 15 newer units in a detached building and 17 in an older wing. The newer "Terrace" units sit directly on the riverbank and feature contemporary floral design in rich colors, classic furniture, ample bathrooms, and a terrace patio. The older wing is more economical and features a few dated items, such as 1960s lime-green carpet, but the entire hotel is impeccably clean.

The staff offers professional and attentive service, and the hotel has a private dock from which guests board excursion boats. More than anything, though, the handsome design and great view make this hotel a winner. The Naguilán's restaurant, serving international cuisine, is one of the most attractive features of the property, with the river passing just outside the window.

General Lagos 1927, Valdivia. © 63/212851. Fax 63/219130. www.hotelnaguilan.com. 32 units. $90 standard double (older units); $101 double (newer units); from $132 suite. AE, DC, MC, V. **Amenities:** Restaurant; bar; outdoor pool; game room; concierge; room service; laundry service. *In room:* TV, minibar.

Puerta del Sur *Overrated* *Kids*   This quiet resort, just across the bridge on Isla Teja, offers all the amenities a guest would expect from a five-star hotel, but its drab decor and mediocre service don't quite live up to expectations. However, it does boast a gem of a location on the shore of the Nature Sanctuary. It's only about a 7-minute walk to downtown, but you'll feel miles away. All rooms come with views of the river and are fairly comfortable; double superiors are roomy, as are the sparkling bathrooms. This is one of the few hotels in Chile to offer doubles with either a queen-size or two full-size beds instead of singles. The suites come with giant, triangular picture windows, but are not much larger than a double superior.

Outside, a path winds past the pool and whirlpool to a private dock where guests can be picked up for boat tours or launch one of the hotel's canoes. There are also bikes available for guests at no extra charge. The airy lobby is set off by a second-story U-shape balcony and brocade couches next to two fireplaces. The hotel has a semiformal restaurant serving international cuisine. When making reservations, request promotional rates and ask about the discounted stays of 3 to 7 days that include some meals. Most room rates do not include breakfast.

Los Lingues 950, Isla Teja, Valdivia. © 63/224500, or 2/633-5101 for reservations (in Santiago). Fax 63/211046. www.hotelpuertadelsur.com. 40 units. $90–$140 double; from $193 suite. AE, DC, MC, V. **Amenities:** Restaurant; bar; large outdoor pool; tennis court; Jacuzzi; sauna; game room; room service; babysitting; laundry service. *In room:* TV.

MODERATE

Apart Hotel Di Torlaschi *Value* *Kids*   These fully equipped *cabañas* feature charming exteriors; pleasant, well-lit kitchens; and a decent location on a residential street near downtown. They're also quiet due to the grammar schools at the front and side that empty at the end of the day. The friendly owners and staff strive to make guests feel at home here, and offer a wealth of tourism information. The 16 wood *cabañas* are situated around a courtyard walkway planted with climbing ivy. Guests park just outside their door, and there is a security gate that shuts during the evening. Each *cabaña* is identical, with two bedrooms upstairs (one comes with a double bed and the other with two twins) and a sofa that unfolds into a bed downstairs, with a maximum of six guests allowed. Kitchens come with full-size fridge and microwave. These *cabañas* are popular with European visitors.

Yerbas Buenas 283, Valdivia. (© 63/224103. Fax 63/224003. www.aparthotelitaliano.cl. 16 *cabañas*. $43–$50 double. AE, DC, MC, V. **Amenities:** Tour desk; laundry service. *In room:* TV, kitchen.

INEXPENSIVE

Airesbuenos International Hostel *Value* This beautiful house is a historical monument in Valdivia and dates back to 1890. The young and friendly owner, Lionel Brossi, has meticulously restored the entire house and oversees the day-to-day operation of the hostel. There are special touches everywhere, which is rare when it comes to budget accommodations. A vintage staircase leads to 11 rooms of varying sizes, all with beautiful (and original) hardwood floors. Some of the rooms have bunk beds and are the top choice for traveling European and American backpackers; the bathroom in the hallway is clean and spacious. The five rooms with private bathrooms are pleasant and bright; the front room even has a balcony with river views. There's Internet access for guests in the foyer, and the owner will arrange free transportation from the bus station if you give him advance notice. The hotel is located about a 15-minute walk from the market and most restaurants.

General Lagos 1036, Valdivia. (©/fax 63/206304. www.airesbuenos.cl. 11 units. $15 per person in a shared room; $30 double with private bathroom; $24 single; $39 triple. All rates include breakfast. AE, DC, MC, V. **Amenities:** Lounge.

WHERE TO DINE

For an inexpensive meal, try the **Municipal Market** near the waterfront at Yungay and Libertad, where you'll find several basic restaurants with fresh seafood and Chilean specialties.

Café Haussmann *Moments* CAFE The Haussmann is known for its *crudos* (steak tartare and raw onion spread on thin bread), which it has served since opening its doors in 1959. This tiny, old-fashioned cafe has just four booths and a counter, and is frequently packed with downtown workers. There are no frills, but there are good sandwiches, local color, and Kunstmann beer on tap.

O'Higgins 394. (© 63/202219. Sandwiches $1.80–$5. MC, V. Mon–Sat 8am–9pm (summer until midnight).

Camino de Luna SEAFOOD The Camino de Luna serves excellent seafood and other dishes aboard a floating restaurant moored at the waterfront. The menu includes delicious fare such as seafood crepes, abalone stew, and *congrio* steamed in wine, bacon, asparagus, and herbs, as well as Greek and chef salads and a long list of terrific appetizers. Inside, the well-appointed, candlelit tables are much nicer than the pea-green facade and red Coca-Cola neon outside would indicate. The restaurant does sway when vessels speed by, but not much.

Costanera at Arturo Prat. (© 63/213788. Main courses $6–$10. AE, DC, MC, V. Daily 12:30–11:30pm.

Entre Lagos *Value* CAFE Entre Lagos is one of the best-known shops in the region for its mouthwatering chocolates and colorful marzipan, and its neighboring cafe is equally good. Nothing on the menu is short of delicious, from the juicy sandwiches and french fries down to the heavenly cakes and frothy cappuccinos. The restaurant serves a dozen varieties of crepes, such as ham and cheese, and abalone and shrimp in a creamy crab sauce. Entre Lagos is a great spot for lunch or to relax for an afternoon *once* or coffee. It also offers a set menu for $6 that includes a main dish, dessert, and coffee.

Pérez Rosales 640. ⓒ 63/218333. www.entrelagos.cl. Main courses $4–$8. AE, DC, MC, V. Daily 9am–10pm.

Kunstmann Cervecería GERMAN PUB   This is a nice place to stop on the way back from Niebla (see "Niebla, Corral & Isla Mancera," above); it's a 10-minute drive from town. The popular Kunstmann brewery serves four varieties of beer on tap (they'll let you sample before ordering) in a newer, microbrew-styled restaurant with wooden tables and soft, yellow light. The hearty fare includes appetizer platters of grilled meats and sausages, German-influenced dishes such as smoked pork loin with cabbage, and sandwiches, salads, and spaetzle. Kunstmann also has a small on-site brewery museum.

950 Ruta T-350. ⓒ/fax **63/292969.** www.cerveza-kunstmann.cl. Main courses $5–$10. DC, MC, V. Daily noon–midnight.

La Calesa ⓚ *Finds* PERUVIAN   Owned and operated by a Peruvian family, the cozy La Calesa features spicy cuisine served in the old Casa Kaheni, a gorgeous 19th-century home with high ceilings, wood floors, and antique furnishings. The menu features Peruvian fare along with several international dishes. Standouts include grilled beef tenderloin and sea bass in a cilantro sauce; *ají de gallina,* a spicy chicken and garlic stew with rice; and any of the nightly specials. The pisco sours are very good, as is the wine selection. There's also a great wooden bar lit by giant windows looking out onto a garden and the river.

Yungay 735. ⓒ **63/225467.** Dinner reservations recommended. Main courses $8–$12. AE, DC, MC, V. Daily 12:30–3:30pm and 8pm–midnight.

Los Castellanos ⓚ *Moments* SEAFOOD   If you're hankering for seafood while enjoying an ocean view, then drive or take a taxi to Niebla (a 20-min. trip). Los Castellanos sits on a hill overlooking the bay and is elegantly decorated with handsome wood floors and large picture windows overlooking the water. Always be sure to ask what fish arrived that morning and order accordingly. Usually, there's an excellent salmon carpaccio and a sampler seafood plate that may include scallops, mussels, shrimp, and other delicacies. For the main course, you can't go wrong with any of the fresh grilled fish such as congrio eel, salmon, or tuna. There are over 110 wines to choose from, and the bartender whips up a mean pisco sour here. The waiters are rather slow and they speak no English, so be patient; the views and the food are worth the effort.

Antonio Ducce 875 in Niebla. ⓒ **63/282082.** Reservations recommended in high season. Main courses $8–$11. No credit cards. April–Nov Tues–Sat 12:30–3:30pm and 7:45–11pm, Sun 12:30–3:30pm; Dec–Mar daily 12:30–3:30pm and 7:45–midnight.

New Orleans INTERNATIONAL   This is Valdivia's most popular restaurant, tucked away on a side street a few streets in from the river, and it seems to always be busy. There's a pleasant outdoor patio with tables very close together and a charming dining room with more spacious seating. The food here is consistently good and fresh, and the menu changes often. Main courses often include pastas, grilled salmon or tuna, chicken, and steak. This is a loud, boisterous place, often filled with families with children early in the evening. Later, the atmosphere is more publike.

Esmeralda 682. ⓒ **63/218771.** Dinner reservations recommended. Main courses $9–$13. AE, DC, MC, V. Mon–Fri noon–4pm and 7pm–midnight; Sat 5pm–midnight. Closed Sun.

5 Puyehue ⟨★

Termas de Puyehue is 73km (45 miles) east of Osorno; 95km (59 miles) west of Antillanca; 93km (58 miles) west of the Argentine border

This region is home to the long-standing **Termas de Puyehue** spa, the **Antillanca** ski and summer resort at the base of the Casablanca Volcano, and one of Chile's underrated national parks, **Puyehue.** It is a remarkably beautiful area, with thick groves of junglelike forest, emerald lakes, picture-perfect volcano backdrops, waterfalls, and roads narrowed by overgrown, enormous ferns. You won't find a tourist-oriented town here, such as Pucón or Puerto Varas, but there are several good lodging options in the area. You'll also find a fair number of outdoor activities, scenic drives, and one of the best lookout points in Chile, which can reached by car during the summer.

The Puyehue area is best suited as a diversion for travelers on their way to Argentina. I strongly recommend this journey; it is one of my favorite excursions in Chile, and visitors can even complete a "loop" through the lake districts of Argentina and Chile by booking a one-way ticket to Bariloche via the popular "lake crossing" (see "Parque Nacional Vicente Pérez Rosales & the Lake Crossing to Argentina," below) and later returning to Chile via bus (or tour) to Puyehue, passing first through Villa la Angostura at the Argentina-Chile border and crossing at the international pass Cardenal Antonio Samoré, or vice versa. The scenery is just breathtaking.

The road from Osorno to Puyehue is rather flat and banal, but the scenery viewed when crossing from Villa Angostura to Puyehue is stunning. Note that during the winter, chains might be required when crossing the border. The city of Osorno is considered by Chileans as one of the least attractive cities in Chile, so consider it a transportation hub only.

GETTING THERE
BY PLANE **Lan Airlines** (© **600/526-2000;** www.lan.com) serves Osorno's **Aeródromo Cañal Bajo** (© **64/247555**), with two daily flights from Santiago; one flight stops first in Temuco. Osorno is a 1-hour drive from Puyehue. Lan has more frequent flights from Santiago to Puerto Montt (PMC), which is about a 2-hour drive from Puyehue.

BY BUS Bus service from Osorno is provided by **Buses Puyehue,** with four daily trips to and from Puyehue, departing from the Mercado Municipal at Errázuriz 1300 (© **64/201237**). A better option is one of the colectivos from the Mercado Municipal, which makes more frequent trips. From Bariloche, Argentina, **Andes Mar** and **Río de la Plata** buses head to Osorno and stop along the highway near Puyehue or directly at the Hotel Termas de Puyehue. If you're trying to get to Puyehue from Puerto Montt, you'll need to transfer at Osorno. From Santiago, the buses run by **Tas Choapa** (to Bariloche) depart Monday, Wednesday, and Friday, heading for Bariloche; they'll drop you off in Puyehue. From Puerto Varas, an excellent bilingual service offered by **LS Travel** (San José 130, Puerto Varas; © **65/232424;** www.lstravel.com) takes visitors to Bariloche, leaving at 9:30am, stopping for a swim at the Termas Puyehue, passing through Villa la Angostura and on to Bariloche. The tour agency has an office in Bariloche (Mitre 83; © **02944/434111**). The cost is about $100 per person, minimum two guests (cheaper prices for groups), and includes entrance fees and lunch.

BY CAR Termas de Puyehue is about 75km (47 miles) east from Osorno via Ruta 215. The border with Argentina, Control Fronterizo Cardenal Antonio

Samoré, is open daily November through March from 8am to 9pm, and April through October from 8am to 7pm. The road is a bit curvy, and there are some potholes on the Chilean side, so plan on driving slowly.

EXPLORING PUYEHUE NATIONAL PARK

Puyehue National Park (www.parquepuyehue.cl) is one of Chile's best-organized national parks, offering a variety of trails to suit all levels, well-placed park information centers, lodging, camping, restaurants, and hot springs. The 107,000-hectare (264,290-acre) park sits between the Caulle mountain range and the Puyehue Volcano, and is divided into three sectors: **Anticura, Aguas Calientes,** and **Antillanca.** Visitors head east toward Argentina to access Anticura, where they'll encounter a park ranger information station just before the border, as well as trail heads for day hikes and the 16km (10-mile) backpacker's trail up and around the Puyehue Volcano. There's also a self-guided, short hike to the Salto del Indio waterfall, where you'll see 800-year-old evergreen beech trees, known locally as *coigüe.*

To get to Antillanca, visitors pass first through the Aguas Calientes sector, where there are hot springs, 28 rustic cabins (five beds in each; all with kitchenettes) a restaurant, campgrounds, and a park information center (© **64/ 331710** or 64/331711). The most popular excursion in this region is the ascent to a spectacular lookout point atop the Raihuén crater, reached by foot or vehicle about 4km (2½ miles) past the Antillanca hotel and ski resort. This *mirador* can be reached only during temperate months (or during ski season via the center's ski lift) and is not worthwhile on a heavily overcast day. The view stretches into Argentina. The park ranger information stations are open daily from 9am to 1pm and 2 to 6pm, or contact Conaf (© **64/1974573**). They sell an information packet about the region's flora and fauna, and issue fishing licenses. For information about day visits to the hot springs at Termas de Puyehue or Aguas Calientes, see "Where to Stay & Dine," below. To get here, you need to catch a bus in Osorno or book a tour with an operator out of Temuco, Puerto Montt, or Puerto Varas.

OTHER ATTRACTIONS

Along the road to Puyehue, at about Km 25 on Ruta 215, just before the ramshackle town of Entre Lagos, is Chile's first car museum, the well-designed **Auto Museum Moncopulli** (© **64/204200;** www.moncopulli.cl). Admission is $2.50 adults, $1.70 students, and 85¢ kids; it's open from April to October Tuesday through Sunday from 10am to 6:30pm, and from November to March Tuesday through Sunday from 10am to 8pm. Owner Bernardo Eggers has assembled a collection of 42 Studebakers from the years 1928 to 1964, plus other vehicles, such as a 1928 Model A fire engine.

WHERE TO STAY & DINE

Aguas Calientes Turismo y Cabañas   These A-frame cabins are a cheaper alternative to Termas de Puyehue and are owned by the same company. There's a hot spring/spa facility here, included in the price of the *cabañas,* and it can be used for the day for a fee. The *cabañas* sleep four to eight guests and are simple affairs with fully stocked, plain but decent kitchenettes (and *parrillas* for barbecues on the balcony). The drawback here is that the beds are really crammed into small spaces. A cabin for five, for example, has one bedroom with a double bed, and three twins in the living room that leave little room for the dining table. Ask for a cabin with two floors; those come with separate living/eating areas. All cabins come with decks and a barbecue. There are also two nicely developed campgrounds here called Chanleufú and Los Derrumbes, with barbecue pits, free firewood, thermal spa with mud, hydrotherapy, and hot showers (Los Derrumbes $18 for four campers, $4 each extra camper; Chanleufú $23 for four camper, $4 each extra camper).

The hot springs facility features indoor and outdoor pools (the outdoor pool is far nicer); there is also a picnic area. Day-use fees are $6 adults, $2.50 kids for the indoor pool; $1.50 adults, 70¢ kids for the outdoor pool. A private herbal bath costs $11. There is also massage for $21 an hour.

Camino a Antillanca, Km 4. ℂ/fax **64/236988** or 64/331700. www.puyehue.cl. 26 *cabañas*. $57 cabin for 2; $69 cabin for 4; $82 cabin for 5. AE, DC, MC, V. **Amenities:** Large outdoor pool and indoor pool; Jacuzzi; massage. *In room:* TV, kitchen.

Antillanca Hotel and Tourism Center 𝓕

The Antillanca Hotel is really nothing to write home about, but the lovely surroundings and the ski/summer resort is really one of Chile's gems—if you can hit it on a good weather day. The resort is open year-round, offering trekking, fishing, mountain biking, canoeing, and ascents of Volcán Antillanca in addition to skiing. The ski resort is a local favorite, tiny but steep, with three T-bar lifts and one chair lift. Heavy, powdery snowfall makes for great skiing, but often a storm or *puelche* (a freezing western wind) blows in, essentially ruining the day; also note that car chains are often required during the winter, but they can be rented from a guard's post before driving up the winding road. A lookout point boasts one of the most magnificent views in Chile. Additionally, you will see very few foreign visitors here.

The hotel could really stand to renovate its rooms, especially considering the price. Couples would do well to view the options, as the only room that comes with a double bed also comes with two twins and is considered a quadruple. The rooms are fairly spacious, but many are nothing more than dormitory style, with four bunks to a room and early '80s furniture.

If you're looking for something cheaper, you might consider the *refugio*, the slightly shabby, older wing of the hotel popular with students and young adults for its rooms costing about a third less. The split-level lobby/restaurant/bar/lounge area is a delight, however, cozy and with character derived from pillars made of tree trunks that still have branches and a giant fireplace. There's also a deck for sunbathing and complimentary use of mountain bikes for registered guests.

You may even choose to stay at the Termas de Puyehue down the road and end your day with a soak in that hotel's hot springs spa (see below).

Ski Resort: Lift tickets Monday through Friday cost $26 adults ($20 halfday), $17 students; Saturday and Sunday and holidays cost $30 adults ($21 halfday), $17 students. Ski and snowboard equipment rental is available and sold in packages that include a lift ticket for $41 adults and $28 students. If you're not skiing but want to ride a chair lift to the top, the cost is $6.

Road to Antillanca, at about 12km (7½ miles) past Ñilque, or (in Osorno) O'Higgins 1073. ℂ/fax **64/235114.** www.skiantillanca.com. 73 units. $55–$70 double standard; $80–$120 double superior. AE, DC, MC, V. **Amenities:** Restaurant; bar; lounge; exercise room; sauna; game room; room service; laundry service.

Termas de Puyehue 𝓕 (Kids)

The first thing you'll notice about this classic, grand hotel is its size; the entrance's stone facade alone nearly dwarfs guests as they enter. Termas de Puyehue is more aptly called a lodge, for its lofty ceilings, giant stone fireplaces, wood walls and floors, and country setting. The compound features a view of Lake Puyehue and two attractively designed, enormous thermal pools, as well as massage rooms, mud baths, herbal baths, saunas, game rooms, and more. Termas de Puyehue was built between 1939 and 1942, and has undergone recent substantial renovations as well as the addition of 55 brand-new elegant and roomy suites. Standard double rooms are disappointing, which is surprising for a hotel that esteems itself so highly. Perhaps the best lodging unit is their converted home on the shore of the lake.

This resort is a good option for skiers at Antillanca, or as a stop on the way to Argentina for a soak and lunch, because a night here as a "destination" is an overrated experience. The staff has no concept of customer service, and problems with plumbing have annoyed guests. But the activities and excursions offered, including horseback riding, trekking, mountain biking, windsurfing, fishing, tennis, and farm tours through organic gardens (all for an extra cost) might make a stay worthwhile. The spa facilities (which you can use even if you don't stay here) are more upscale than those at Aguas Calientes, including an attractive "tropical" indoor pool under a glass roof. The costs charged to day visitors are indoor pool, $15 adults, $10 kids; outdoor pool, $10 adults, $6 kids. Hours are: indoor pool daily 8am to 9pm (summer), 8am to 8pm (rest of the year); spa 9am to 8pm (all year). Herbal, mud, sulfur, and marine salt baths run $20 to $40 (reflexology and herbal therapy $10). Guests take their meals at either the cafeteria, the casual eatery, or the semiformal restaurant. There's also a cozy bar and a lounge with a giant stone fireplace.

Ruta 215, Km 76. (C) 2/293-6000. Fax 2/283-1010, 64/23281 in Osorno. www.puyehue.cl. 130 units (55 completely new). $90 standard double; $115 double with view of the forest; $142 double with view of the volcano. Rates include buffet breakfast. AE, DC, MC, V. **Amenities:** 3 restaurants; bar; lounge; large outdoor pool and large indoor pool; tennis courts; gym; spa; Jacuzzi; sauna; limited watersports equipment rental; bike rental; game room; shopping arcade; gift shop; room service; massage; laundry service; dry-cleaning service; free Internet; library. *In room:* TV, minibar.

6 Frutillar, Puerto Octay, Puerto Varas ⓐⓐ, Lago Llanquihue, Ensenada, Parque Nacional Vicente Pérez Rosales & the Lake Crossing to Argentina

Lago Llanquihue is the second-largest lake in Chile, a body of clear, shimmering water whose beauty is surpassed only by the 2,652m (8,699-ft.), perfectly conical, snowcapped Volcán Osorno that rises from its shore. The peaks of Calbuco, Tronador, and Puntiagudo add rugged beauty to the panorama, as do the rolling, lush hills that peek out from forested thickets along the perimeter of the lake. The jewel of this area is without a doubt the 231,000-hectare (570,570-acre) Vicente Pérez Rosales National Park, the oldest park in Chile and home to Volcán Osorno and the strangely hued emerald waters of Lago Todos los Santos.

This splendid countryside and the picturesque, German-influenced architecture of the homes and villages that ring Lago Llanquihue draw thousands of foreign visitors each year. Many adventure-seekers come to take part in the vast array of outdoor sports and excursions to be had here, including fly-fishing, rafting, volcano ascents, trekking, and just sightseeing. Puerto Varas is similar to Pucón, in that it offers a solid tourism infrastructure, with quality lodging and restaurants, nightlife, and several reliable outfitters and tour operators. I urge visitors to lodge in Puerto Varas, Frutillar, or Ensenada instead of Puerto Montt, as these three towns are far more attractive and closer to natural attractions than Puerto Montt. Puerto Octay, about 46km (29 miles) from Puerto Montt, is the most remote lodging option, a sublime little village with one lovely lodge on the shore of the lake.

A Health Warning

Every January, this region is beset by horrid biting flies called *tábanos*. Avoid wearing dark clothing and any shiny object, which seem to attract them; they are also more prevalent on sunny days.

FRUTILLAR & PUERTO OCTAY ℛ

58km (36 miles) south of Osorno; 46km (29 miles) north of Puerto Montt

Frutillar and Puerto Octay offer a rich example of the lovely architecture popular with German immigrants to the Lago Llanquihue area, and both boast dynamite views of the Osorno and Calbuco volcanoes. The towns are smaller than Puerto Varas and less touristy. For a soft adventure, the towns make an excellent day trip, and the coastal dirt road that connects the two is especially beautiful, with clapboard homes dotting the green countryside—bring your camera. Apart from all this scenic beauty, there are a few museums documenting German immigration in the area.

Frutillar was founded in 1856 as an embarkation point with four piers. Later, the introduction of the railway created a spin-off town that sits high and back from the coast, effectively splitting the town in two: Frutillar Alto and Bajo, meaning "high" and "low," respectively. You'll drive straight through the ugly Alto section, a ratty collection of wooden homes and shops.

Puerto Octay was founded in the second half of the 19th century by German immigrants; folks in the region know it for a well-stocked general goods store—the only one in the region—run by Cristino Ochs. In fact, the name *Octay* comes from "donde Ochs hay," roughly translated as "you'll find it where Ochs is." Today there are only about 3,000 residents in this quaint little village, which can be reached by renting a car or with a tour (or bus if staying here). Two helpful websites are www.frutillar.cl and www.puertooctay.cl.

ESSENTIALS

VISITOR INFORMATION   The **Oficina de Información Turística** is located along the coast at Costanera Philippi (© **65/421080**); it's open January through March daily from 8:30am to 1pm and 2 to 9pm. The **Oficina de Turismo Municipal** is open year-round and can be found at Av. Bernardo Philippi 753 (open daily 8am–1pm and 2–5:30pm; © **65/421685;** www.frutillar chile.info).

GETTING THERE   See the information under the "Puerto Varas" section, below.

WHAT TO SEE & DO

Excursions to **Parque Nacional Vicente Pérez Rosales** from Frutillar can be arranged by your hotel with a company such as **Alsur Expediciones** or **Aquamotion** out of Puerto Varas (see "Outdoor Activities" under "Puerto Varas," later in this chapter). In Frutillar, spend an afternoon strolling the streets and enjoying the town's striking architecture. The town really gets hopping during the last week of January and first of February when it hosts, for 10 days, the **Semanas Musicales,** when hundreds of Chilean and foreign musicians come to participate in various classical music concerts. Call the administration in Osorno © **64/245677;** tickets are never hard to come by.

The two most-visited attractions in town are **the Museo de la Colonización Alemana de Frutillar** and the **Reserva Forestal Edmundo Winkler.** The museum (© 65/421142) is located where Arturo Prat dead-ends at Avenida Vicente Pérez Rosales. Admission is $2.50 adults, 85¢ kids 12 and under; it's open from April to November daily from 10am to 1:30pm and 3 to 6pm, and from December to March daily from 9:30am to 1:30pm and 3 to 8pm. It features a collection of 19th-century antiques, clothing, and artifacts gathered from various immigrant German families around the area.

The *reserva* is run by the University of Chile and features a trail winding through native forest, giving visitors an idea of what the region looked like before immigrants went timber crazy and started chopping down trees. It's open year-round Monday to Friday from 8am to 5pm, Saturday 8am to 6pm, Sunday 10am to 6pm; admission costs $1.80 for adults and 80¢ for kids. To get there, you'll have to walk a kilometer up to the park from the entrance at Calle Caupolicán at the northern end of Avenida Philippi. You might also consider paying a visit to the town **cemetery,** which affords a panoramic view of the lake. To get there, continue farther north up Avenida Phillipi.

WHERE TO STAY

Hotel Ayacara ★★ *Finds*   The Ayacara is a top choice in Frutillar, housed in a superbly renovated 1910 antique home on the coast of Lago Llanquihue. The interior of the hotel is made of light wood, and this, coupled with large, plentiful windows, translates into bright accommodations. The rooms come with comfy beds, crisp linens, wood headboards, country furnishings, and antiques brought from Santiago and Chiloé. The Capitán room is the largest and has the best view. An attractive dining area serves dinner during the summer, and there's a small, ground-level outdoor deck and a TV/video lounge. The staff can arrange excursions around the area; fly-fishing excursions are their specialty.

Av. Philippi 1215, Frutillar. ©/fax 65/421550. www.hotelayacara.cl. 8 units. $45–$100 double; $75–$100 Capitán double. Rates include breakfast. AE, DC, MC, V. **Amenities:** Restaurant (all year); bar; tour desk.

Hotel & Cabañas Centinela ★★ *Moments*   At the tip of a peninsula, at the end of a lush tree-lined dirt road, 10 minutes from town and right on the lake, you'll find this hidden gem with its own private beach. Originally built in 1914 as a bordello, it has long since been turned into a homey lodge with 12 rooms and 18 *cabañas*. Rooms in the main building are quaint, with thick beige berber carpets, down comforters, and antique furnishings. The new bathrooms are of varying sizes, simple and very clean. The downstairs living room has a beautiful fireplace; there's a satellite TV and free Internet access as well. The restaurant serves excellent Chilean cuisine cooked by a well-known chef, Juan Pablo Moscoso; there's a daily fixed-price three-course meal for $14 for lunch and dinner. This place exudes charm, not luxury; there's no spa, but there's a rustic wood-fired hot tub. Six of the *cabañas* sit right on the water's edge; request nos. 21 to 26 when making your reservations, and you'll have the best views. The 12 A-frame *cabañas* that sit back from the water are pleasant for families and come with kitchenettes; all the *cabañas* have rather small bathrooms. The hotel's friendly staff can arrange for fishing trips, including fly-fishing expeditions; they can also arrange for transfers from the airport.

Península de Centinela, Puerto Octay. ©/fax 64/391326. www.hotelcentinela.cl. 30 units. $82–$100 double; from $80 *cabaña* for 4 people; $100 *cabaña* for 6 people. Rates include full breakfast. AE, DC, MC, V. **Amenities:** Restaurant; lounge; Jacuzzi; limited watersports equipment rental. *In room:* Fridge (in *cabañas* only).

Hotel Elun ★★   This four-star, azure-colored hotel is a good bet for anyone seeking modern accommodations, a room with a view, and a quiet, forested location. The hotel, opened in 1999, is made almost entirely of light, polished wood and was designed to take full advantage of the views. The lounge, bar, and lobby sit under a slanted roof that ends with picture windows; there's also a deck, should you decide to lounge outside. Double standard rooms are decent size and feature berber carpet and spick-and-span white bathrooms. The superiors are very large and come with a comfy easy chair and a table and chairs. Room no. 24 looks out over Frutillar. The hotel is attended by its owners, who will arrange excursions. A restaurant serves dinner during the summer, and breakfast can be ordered in your room.

200m (656 ft.) from start of Camino Punta Larga, at the southern end of Costanera Phillipi, Frutillar. ℂ/fax 65/420055. www.hotelelun.cl. 14 units. $60–$75 double. Rates include breakfast. DC, MC, V. **Amenities:** Restaurant (summer only); lounge; mountain bike rental; tour desk; room service; laundry service. *In room:* TV.

Hotel Residenz Am See *Value* This pleasant wooden hotel is a steal in the low season when you factor in the lakefront view and its clean, comfortable accommodations. Run by an elderly German couple, the Residenz has rooms that range in size, and a few of the doubles are large enough to fit an extra twin bed. The rooms that look out onto the lake are slightly more expensive than those facing the back, but the rooms in the back receive glorious afternoon sun. The owners have a shop selling arts and crafts, and have decorated the place with woven wall hangings that are for sale. Downstairs there's a tea salon where guests are served German breakfast; in the afternoon, folks drop by for tea and home-made *kuchen*, bread, pâté, and marmalade. They also arrange excursions.

Av. Philippi 539, Frutillar. ℂ 65/421539. Fax 65/421858. ciberg@123mail.cl. 6 units. $36–$57 double; from $71 suite. Rates include German breakfast. AE, DC, MC, V. **Amenities:** Restaurant. *In room:* TV.

Hotel Salzburg & Klein Salzburg *Kids* Both hotels share the same owner. The Hotel Klein Salzburg is housed in a large wooden home built in 1911 and painted a spruce blue and white. It sits on the lakefront, but only one room has a view—the VIP room, which is larger than the rest and has a small balcony. The hotel has a lot of antique charm, complete with creaky wooden floors, but the decoration is as sugary sweet as the delicious cakes and tortes it serves in its tea-room: flowered wallpaper, duck motifs, and pink trim, all a tad cutesy, but not too overbearing. There are two little rooms for kids. For the price, you'd be bet-ter off at the Hotel Salzburg. Located higher up from the shore, the Salzburg has the edge on decor, and there are cabins, too, and a spacious, grassy complex with a kidney-shape pool and outdoor oversize chess game (though Klein guests may use the amenities here).

Av. Philippi 663, Frutillar. ℂ 65/421589. Fax 65/421599. www.salzburg.cl. 8 units (Klein); 31 units (Salzburg). $55–$58 double, $65 suite (Klein); $55 double, $70 cabin for 6 (Salzburg). Rates include German breakfast. AE, DC, MC, V. **Amenities:** Restaurant; bar; pool; gym; sports court; laundry. *In room:* TV.

Hotel Villa San Francisco *Finds* The Villa San Francisco sits high on a cliff and features a layout similar to the Hotel Elun (see above), with rooms that all face the lake, some with a view of the volcano. All of the rooms are identical, deco-rated with simple but attractive furnishings that include comfortable beds and wicker headboards. Some guests might find the rooms a little on the small side, but most come with a terrace and four have corner windows. The new owners of this hotel have invested a great deal in gardens that surround the property. There's also a great barbecue area that sits on a grassy perch looking straight out toward the volcano, as does a pleasant glass-enclosed dining area. The staff will arrange excursions around the area for guests.

Av. Philippi 1503, Frutillar. ℂ/fax 65/421531. iberchile@telsur.cl. 15 units. $60–$75 double. AE, MC, V. **Amenities:** Restaurant; bar. *In room:* TV.

WHERE TO DINE

Club Alemán GERMAN/CHILEAN   Nearly every city in the Lake District has a Club Alemán, and Frutillar is no exception. You'll find a few German dishes here, such as pork chops with sauerkraut, but the menu leans heavily toward traditional Chilean fare. Periodically, game specials such as duck and goose are on the menu, and there are set lunch menus for $6 on weekdays and $10 on Sunday that include a choice of fish or meat. The atmosphere here is congenial, and the service is very good.

San Martín 22. Philippi 47 *©* 65/421249. Main courses $4–$10. AE, DC, MC, V. Daily noon–4pm and 7:30pm–midnight.

El Ciervo CHILEAN   This newer restaurant specializes in smoked meats and game, and lives up to its name (which means "deer" in Spanish) by offering a tasty grilled venison in pepper sauce. There are other delights, such as smoked pork chops Kassler with mashed potatoes and sauerkraut, filet mignon in a mushroom sauce, and pork leg pressure-cooked to tenderness and served with applesauce. Mounted deer antlers don't do much to add to the cold atmosphere. It's a good spot for lunch, as it serves lighter fare such as sandwiches. The specialties here include venison bourguignon and hazelnut venison, with potatoes, red cabbage, and apples.

San Martín 64. *©* 65/420185. Main courses $6–$15. No credit cards. Mar–Nov noon–6pm; Dec–Feb 11am–midnight.

PUERTO VARAS ☆☆

20km (12 miles) north of Puerto Montt; 996km (618 miles) south of Santiago

Puerto Varas is one of Chile's most charming villages, located on the shore of Lago Llanquihue. Like Pucón, it is an adventure travel hub, and it is also the gateway to the **Parque Nacional Vicente Pérez Rosales** (see "Parque Nacional Vicente Pérez Rosales & the Lake Crossing to Argentina," above). Unlike its neighbor Puerto Montt, 20 minutes away, it is a spruce little town, with wood-shingled homes, a rose-encircled plaza, a handsomely designed casino, and an excellent tourism infrastructure that provides all the necessary services for visitors without seeming touristy. It can get crowded during the summer months, but not as busy as Pucón; seemingly because of its distance from Santiago. The city was built by the sweat and tenacity of German immigrants, and later it became a port for goods being shipped from the Lago Llanquihue area to Puerto Montt (mostly timber). Today most of the area's middle- and upper-middle-class residents call Puerto Varas home and commute to Puerto Montt and other surrounding places for work.

ESSENTIALS

VISITOR INFORMATION   The **Casa del Turista** tourism office can be found at the pier on the shore (*©* 65/237956; www.puertovaras.org) and is open daily from December to March from 9am to 10pm, and the rest of the year daily from 9am to 1:30pm and 3 to 7pm.

SHOPPING   There is an **arts and crafts fair** on the Del Salvador street side of the plaza. For high-end arts, clothing, and jewelry, go to **Primitiva,** Santa Rosa 302, or **Vicki Johnson,** Santa Rosa 318. The little wagons at the shore in front of the pier offer arts and crafts, but hours are erratic and most are open during the summer only.

MONEY EXCHANGE   **Travel Sur** exchanges dollars at its office on San José 261 (*©* 65/236000).

GETTING THERE   By Plane   El Tepual airport (© **65/294161**) is almost equidistant from Puerto Montt and Puerto Varas; it's about 25km (16 miles) from the airport to Puerto Varas. A taxi from the airport costs $15 to $22, or you can arrange a transfer with **ETM,** by either calling ahead or approaching their booth at the airport (© **32/294294**). They charge $20 for a car for a maximum of three people. Because there are fewer flights here, there normally are a few people waiting for a transfer, so the price can drop if there are others. **LanExpress** serves the El Tepual airport with 7 to 10 daily flights from Santiago. **Sky Airlines** (© **600/600-2828;** www.skyairline.cl) also has service to the El Tepual airport. Ask your hotel about a transfer shuttle, as many include one in their price.

By Bus   The following buses offer service to and from major cities in southern Chile, including Santiago: **Buses Cruz del Sur,** San Francisco 1317 and Walker Martínez 239 (© **65/236969** or 65/231925); and **Buses Tas Choapa,** Walker Martínez 320 (© **65/233831**). Buses **Tas Choapa** and the Argentine company **Andesmar,** Walker Martinez 320 (© **65/233831;** www.andesmar.com.ar), have service to Bariloche, Argentina (Tas Choapa Thurs–Sun; Andesmar on Mon, Wed, and Fri). **Bus Norte,** Walker Martínez 239, has daily service to Bariloche (© **65/236969**).

By Car   Puerto Varas is just 20km (12 miles) north of Puerto Montt and 88km (55 miles) south of Osorno via the Panamericana. There are two exits leading to Puerto Varas, and both deposit you downtown. To get to Frutillar, you need to get back on the Panamericana, go north, and take the exit for that town. There is about a 70¢ toll to enter the off-ramp, and another toll for about $1 to enter Puerto Montt.

GETTING AROUND   By Bus   Buses Cruz del Sur offers transportation to Chiloé and nearly 20 daily trips to Puerto Montt, leaving from an office in Puerto Varas, at Walker Martínez 239 (© **65/236969** or 65/231925). There are also cheap minibuses that leave frequently from the corner of Del Salvador and San Pedro across from the pet shop, leaving you at the bus terminal in Puerto Montt. You'll also find minibuses at San Bernardo and Walker Martínez that go to Ensenada, Petrohué, and Lago Todos los Santos every day at 9:15am, 11am, 2pm, and 4pm. **Andina del Sud,** Del Salvador 72 (© **65/232811;** fax 65/232511; www.andinadelsud.com), has daily trips to this area as well.

By Car   Renting a car is perhaps the most enjoyable way (but also the most expensive) to see the surrounding area. Try **Adriazola Turismo Expediciones,** Santa Rosa 340 (© **65/233477;** adriazolaflyfishing@yahoo.com); **Hunter Rent a Car,** San José 130 (© **09/920-6888;** www.lstravel.com); **Jardinsa,** Mirador 135 (©/fax **65/235050;** www.jardinsa.cl); or **Travel Sur** at San José 261 (© **65/236000;** www.travelsur.com).

WHERE TO STAY

You'll find hotels and hostals in the town center area. Along the coast (both the Puerto Chico coast and all the way to Ensenada), it's mostly *cabañas,* cabins for two to eight people with living spaces and kitchenettes. The following are the best hotels available in the area, plus a couple of *cabañas* along the coast for those who want quiet accommodations in more bucolic settings. Ask where the *cabaña* is located on the complex when booking because many are filed in a row from the shore, meaning only the first two *cabañas* have a view. Also, some *cabañas* consider a foldout couch bedding for two.

Expensive

Gran Hotel Colonos del Sur & Hotel Colonos de Sur Express ★★

Boasting a waterfront location next door to the casino and charming German colonial architecture, the Colonos del Sur is a standard favorite among travelers to Puerto Varas and one of the nicer hotels in town. However, the hotel recently acquired another hotel and renovated the premises, calling it the Express, and this hotel is where you'll find the best panoramic views, cheery interiors, and an outdoor pool. Really, these factors give the Express an edge (and the lower price helps, too), even if the rooms at the Gran Hotel are a bit more sophisticated and the Gran is more centrally located. You can't miss the Express: a red-and-white building perched high on the hills just above downtown, with the giant sign HOTEL affixed to the roof. The corner rooms offer the best views, so try to get one. At the Gran, the common areas are large and plentiful, and the interiors have an old-fashioned country decor. The tea salon here is one of the best in Puerto Varas, and it is a good place to sample Chile's famous *onces* (high tea). Doubles with a lake view are slightly larger, for the same price; others face the casino and are not much of a value for the price. The large suites have wraparound windows, sparkling bathrooms, and extra touches like crocheted bedspreads.

Gran Hotel: Del Salvador 24, Puerto Varas. ✆ **65/233369**, or for reservations 65/233039. Fax 65/233394. www.colonosdelsur.cl. 60 units. $85–$110 double; from $160 suite. AE, DC, MC, V. **Amenities:** Restaurant; lounge; bar; small indoor pool; sauna; room service; laundry service; dry-cleaning service. *In room:* TV, minibar, safe. Hotel Colonos de Sur Express: Estación 505. ✆ **65/235555.** www.colonosdelsur.cl. $60 double. AE, DC, MC, V. **Amenities:** Restaurant; bar; outdoor pool; laundry. *In room:* TV.

Hotel Cabañas del Lago ★★ *Kids*

Recent renovations and sweeping views of Puerto Varas and Volcán Osorno make Hotel Cabañas del Lago the highest-quality lodging available in town. The lakeview and park suites are luxuriously appointed and colossal in size; one could get lost in the bathroom alone. A junior suite is a slightly larger double and might be worth booking for the larger windows and better decorations. Doubles are not overly spacious and have cramped bathrooms, but curtains and bedding have been updated. Doubles with a lake view are the same price as rooms that overlook the *cabañas.*

The hotel takes advantage of its location with lots of glass in its attractive lounge and restaurant, which, like all the rooms, sports a country decor. The common areas have the feel of a mountain lodge, complete with deer-antler chandeliers. There's also a large sun deck. The small two- to five-person *cabañas* are not as pleasant as the hotel rooms but are a bargain for a family of four, if you're willing to be a bit cramped. The excellent **El Mirador** serves wild game and other daily specials from an extensive menu. The hotel is a 2-block walk up from town.

Klenner 195, Puerto Varas. ✆ **65/232291.** Fax 65/232707. www.cabanasdellago.cl. 125 units, 13 *cabañas.* $99–$125 double; $125–$150 junior suite; $89–$90 *cabañas* for up to 4 people. Rates include buffet breakfast. AE, DC, MC, V. **Amenities:** Restaurant; bar; lounge; indoor heated pool; sauna; game room; room service; babysitting; laundry service. *In room:* TV.

Moderate

Cabañas Altué ★ *Finds*

Located at the quiet end of the beach in Puerto Chico, about a 5-minute drive from downtown Puerto Varas, these *cabañas* have lovely views (but not of the volcanoes) and are situated among one of the most impressive arboreal gardens in the region. Guests arrive at a circular driveway ringed with roses and fronted by a huge magnolia tree; the *cabañas* themselves are surrounded by *araucaria,* pine, *alerce,* and more. The nine cabins are perched above the beach behind a row of eucalyptus trees, with a vista of Puerto Varas and the beach. The cabins were freshly painted recently and are decent and comfortable, with a separate kitchen/dining room and a deck. Nearly every plant or tree in the surrounding garden is unique, often from other regions in Chile. This is a place for those who want direct beach access, fragrant surroundings, and an address outside town. It's about a 25-minute walk to town, but there are several good restaurants nearby.

Av. Vicente Pérez Rosales 1679, Puerto Varas. ℂ/fax **65/232294**. www.altue-chile.cl. 9 units. $40–$63 *cabañas* for 2–3; $70–$100 *cabañas* for 4–6. AE, DC, MC, V. **Amenities:** Laundry. *In room:* TV.

The Guest House 𝒦𝒦 *Finds*   Owned and operated by Vicki Johnson, an American who owns the crafts and foods store downtown (see "Shopping," above), this bed-and-breakfast is a more intimate hotel, located in a quiet residential area about a 4-block walk from the plaza. The hotel is housed in a 1926 renovated mansion, and, like most bed-and-breakfasts, the lodging experience here is a little like staying in one of your friends' homes, with a comfy living area decorated with art that has been collected, not store bought, and a collection of reading material; a dining area with one long, family-style table; and a big kitchen where you are given the opportunity to help out with the cooking, if you so wish. What's also special about the location of this B&B is that nearly all the homes that surround it are the lovely shingled style popular at the time of this home's inception. The rooms have high ceilings, comfortable beds, and a simple, clean decor.

O'Higgins 608, Puerto Varas. ℂ **65/231521**. Fax 65/232240. www.vicki-johnson.com/guesthouse. 10 units. $60 double standard. Rates include continental breakfast. AE, MC, V. **Amenities:** Room service; laundry; yoga and cooking classes.

Hotel Bellavista 𝒦𝒦 *Value*   Another waterfront hotel with gorgeous views, the Bellavista recently renovated all of its guest rooms, giving it the edge on its competitors, Colonos and Cabañas del Lago (it used to be in competition with the Hotel Licarayen). The hardwood floors here aren't as cozy as the carpeted rooms found in other hotels; however, the fresh linens and handsome earth-toned decor is quite sophisticated, and their restaurant and bar is an inviting place to while away an hour with a coffee and admire the view of the volcano. There is also a cozy fireside lounge. There are four larger guest rooms that face a forested cliff for those seeking quieter accommodations, and, best of all, the duplex apartments for five to six people are the best in town: duplexes with two-storied, panoramic windows, good deals for a group of friends or families with kids. The Bellavista's restaurant has a good range of international dishes.

Av. Vicente Pérez Rosales 60, Puerto Varas. ℂ **65/232011**. Fax 65/232013. www.hotelbellavista.cl. 50 units. $96 double; from $137 suite; $143 duplex. Rates include buffet breakfast. AE, DC, MC, V. **Amenities:** Restaurant; bar; lounge; sauna; laundry service. *In room:* TV, minibar, hair dryer, safe.

Hotel El Greco 𝒦 *Value*   This is an excellent value in Puerto Varas, for both its low price and its delightful interiors. A block's walk from downtown, the hotel is an antique, shingled home painted lemon and lilac. A comfortable living area is packed with antiques, magazines, and photo books, and there's a small dining area. The rooms are small and simply decorated; try not to get one of the two rooms by the stairs because you'll have to listen to people ascending and descending all morning. The bathrooms are cramped, too. But the flair this little place has (the walls are crowded with dozens upon dozens of paintings by local artists) and the friendly owner make you feel at home. The staff here organize excursions, especially cultural and archaeological.

Mirador 134, Puerto Varas. ℂ **65/233388**. Fax 65/233380. www.hotelelgreco.cl. 12 units. $30–$50 double. Rates include continental breakfast. AE, DC, MC, V. **Amenities:** Restaurant; laundry. *In room:* TV.

Hotel Licarayen ⚘ *Value*   This is another value in Puerto Montt, for its comfortable accommodations, waterfront views, and central location. The lobby and rooms are cheery and well lit. Double superior rooms come with lake views and balconies. Superiors are also substantially larger than standards and come with big, bright bathrooms; if you've booked a standard double, ask for an upgrade for the same price during slow months. Only a few standards have lake views, so ask for one; suites are ample and come with a couch. The hotel may not have the antique character of Colonos del Sur (see above), but the quality is not far behind. There's a pleasant dining area for breakfast. The hotel sits on the main plaza and is close to everything. The service is cordial and professional.

San José 114, Puerto Varas. ✆ 65/232305. Fax 65/232955. www.hotelicarayen.cl. 23 units. $55–$78 double standard. Rates include continental breakfast. AE, DC, MC, V. **Amenities:** Sauna; room service. *In room:* TV.

Inexpensive

Casa Margoya   This is a budget/backpacker's hostal in a well-situated area on Santa Rosa, close to everything. It's on the second floor, and there's a central living area with large tables and couches, and a kitchen that is open for guest use. It's a comfortable place and the service is friendly. There are five rooms, two of which have one double bed; the rest are shared accommodations that range in price according to the number of beds in the room. Bathrooms are clean but communal. This is a good place to meet other travelers. Breakfast is not included.

Santa Rosa 318, Puerto Varas. ✆ 65/346433. 5 units. $22 double; $11–$13 per person for shared rooms. No credit cards. **Amenities:** Kitchen. *In room:* No phone.

WHERE TO DINE & DRINK

Puerto Varas has many good to excellent restaurants, but the service in this area tends to be slow, so have patience. In addition to the restaurants below, there is **Pim's,** San Francisco 712, a country/western-style pub with burgers, sandwiches, American-style appetizers like buffalo wings, and salads. It is popular with locals and the nighttime ambience is very lively (✆ 65/233998).

Two other good spots for a drink at night are the **Barómetro,** San Pedro 418 (✆ 65/236371), with a wood-hewn bar and tree-trunk tables, a cozy atmosphere, and snacks; and the **Garage** (no phone; located on San José St. next to the Copec gas station), a two-story place with wood tables and electronic music that is popular with adults in their 20s and 30s.

Café Dane's ⚘ *Value* CHILEAN CAFE   It's often hard to get a table during the lunch hour in this extremely popular restaurant. Dane's serves inexpensive, hearty food in good-size portions, plus mouthwatering desserts. The interior is simple and unassuming, and much of the food is standard Chilean fare, all of it good or very good. The fried empanadas, especially shellfish, deserve special mention. Dane's serves a daily set menu for $6 Monday through Saturday and $9 on Sunday, as well as a special dish, or *plato del día,* for $3.50. It's less busy before 1pm or after 3pm. You can also buy food to go from the front counter.

Del Salvador 441. ✆ 65/232371. Main courses $3.50–$8; sandwiches $2–$5.50. No credit cards. Daily 8am–11pm.

Café Mamusia *Value* CHILEAN CAFE/BAKERY   The Mamusia is locally renowned for its delicious chocolates and pastries. The atmosphere is somewhat like a tearoom or ice-cream parlor, but there are delicious sandwiches and full meals throughout the day as well. Café Mamusia is also a good place for breakfast and serves a continental version for $5. Typical Chilean favorites such as *pastel de choclo* and *escalopas* are served here, as well as lasagna, pizza, and grilled meats and fish; sandwiches come on homemade bread.

San José 316. No phone. Main courses $5–$8; sandwiches $5.50. MC, V. Summer daily 8:30am–2am; winter Mon–Fri 9am–10:30pm, Sat–Sun 10am–11pm.

Club Alemán GERMAN/CHILEAN   This Club Alemán seems to offer more German specialties than its fellow clubs, with goose, duck, and bratwurst served with onions, potatoes, and applesauce; pork chops with caramelized onions and sauerkraut; goulash with spaetzle; steak tartare; and other dishes, in addition to Chilean favorites. Sandwiches are much cheaper than main dishes ($3–$6) and are substantial. There are also appetizing desserts, such as crepes *diplomático,* with bananas, ice cream, and chocolate sauce.

San José 415. ⓒ 65/232246. Main courses $8–$13. DC, MC, V. Daily 11am–midnight.

Club de Yates ⍟   Like its counterpart in Puerto Montt, this brand-new restaurant sits over the water on stilts, affording excellent views of Volcano Osorno and giving the sensation of being on a ship. The food here is better than the at Puerto Montt branch, although there are better restaurants in town in terms of food quality. Club de Yates specializes in seafood, and the lengthy menu offers just about every kind of fish or shellfish cooked every way: grilled, sautéed, or fried, with sauces and your choice of a side dish. There are also good appetizers, such as Parmesan razor clams and, occasionally, *locos,* or abalone, and they serve enough meat dishes to satisfy those who aren't in the mood for seafood. The dining area is semiformal, with high ceilings and an airy atmosphere, but it is pleasurable and doesn't feel cold. Club de Yates often holds special events and large-scale lunches for cruise travelers who've docked in Puerto Montt, so they sometimes close to the public. This is a good restaurant if you are lodging downtown and do not feel like going very far.

Santa Rosa 161. ⓒ 65/232000. Main courses $7–$13. AE, DC, MC, V. Daily 11:30am–3:30pm and 7pm–1am.

Color Café ⍟ INTERNATIONAL   The Color Café calls itself a wine restaurant, for it has more than 100 top wines on offer, plus a diverse menu. Clean, crisp interiors offset by contemporary oil paintings, a long bar, and a blazing, wood-burning stove set the ambience here. It's a bit of a walk from the town center (about 15–20 min.). The periodically changing menu features good bistro-style cuisine, including Caesar salads, soups, quiches, pastas, and main courses such as venison in a berry sauce and salmon tataki. This is a good place for a cocktail and an appetizer of regional smoked salmon.

Los Colonos 1005. ⓒ 65/234311. Main courses $6–$11. AE, DC, MC, V. Dec–Mar daily noon–2am; Apr–Nov daily 8pm–midnight.

Ibis ⍟⍟ INTERNATIONAL/CHILEAN   This popular restaurant specializes in seafood and is one Puerto Varas's best. Like a few of the aforementioned restaurants, it is about a 10-minute walk from the town center. On offer is creative cuisine and a vast menu with dishes such as flambéed Ecuadorian shrimp in cognac; pistachio salmon; beef filet in a sauce of tomato, garlic, and chipotle pepper; and lamb chops with mint sauce. To begin, try a shellfish appetizer that the chef brings in fresh from the coast, and end the meal with crêpes suzette. The eating area is small but warm and is decorated with crafts-oriented art; there's also a bar here. During the day, there is pleasant outdoor seating that overlooks the lake. The wine list also merits mention for its variety.

Av. Vicente Pérez Rosales 1117. ⓒ 65/232017. Main courses $7–$13. AE, DC, MC, V. Daily 1:30am–3:30pm and 7pm–1am.

La Cucina d' Alessandro ✦ PIZZA/PASTA   The authentic, fresh pastas and thin-crust pizzas at this restaurant are excellent because they are made by an Italian family who emigrated to Puerto Varas only a few years ago, bringing with them Italian gastronomy know-how. The pizzas are what really shine here, and their special two-for-one pizza offer from 4 to 8pm every day makes this restaurant a good value. The restaurant has a cozy atmosphere and is housed in a typical shingled home across from the beach. There are a few wooden tables that are large enough for groups of six to eight diners. It's a 15-minute walk from downtown. Apart from pasta and pizza, La Cucina has good seafood dishes, and it is open all day. It's a tiny restaurant, so make reservations for dinner and come early for lunch.

Av. Costanera. ✆ 65/310583. Main courses $5–$9. No credit cards. Daily noon–midnight.

Mediterráneo ✦ *Moments* INTERNATIONAL   Boasting an excellent location right on the Costanera, this restaurant has a glass-enclosed terrace with water views. The cheerful orange tablecloths add to its brightness, as does the pleasant waitstaff. Mediterráneo is known for its imaginative dishes (think Chilean-Mediterranean fusion) that change weekly. The owners use mostly local produce, including spices bought from the Mapuche natives. Here, you'll find big, fresh salads mixing such ingredients as endives, Swiss cheese, anchovies, olives, and local mushrooms. For the main course, the venison here is excellent, served with a yummy zucchini gratin. Other standouts are the fresh seabass with a caper white-wine sauce, and a delicious lamb cooked in a rosemary wine reduction and served with roasted potatoes. For dessert, try one of the fruit sorbets.

Santa Rosa 068, corner of Portales. ✆ 65/237268. AE, DC, MC, V. Main courses $4–25. Apr–Nov daily noon–3:30pm and 7:30–11pm; Dec–Mar daily 10am–2am.

Merlín ✦✦✦ *Finds* CHILEAN   Merlín is the finest restaurant in Puerto Varas and the one I recommend first to visitors. The German chef who has been running this restaurant for more than a decade changes the menu seasonally but always employs creative recipes using only local (and mostly organic) ingredients. Merlín is housed within an old wood-shingled home that has been stylishly refurbished; the front dining area is bright and cheerful, and though the back is darker, it overlooks a lush garden. There's a more casual bar/dining area, but this restaurant doesn't really fill up except on weekends and during the summer, so it's usually empty. Example menu items are roast pork loin with a cilantro sauce and cabbage, curried abalone and shrimp, toasted goat cheese and peach compote on arugula, and rabbit stew. I don't recommend any of the cream soups, however. There is also a good wine list and a romantic ambience.

Imperial 0605. ✆ 65/233105. Reservations recommended. Main courses $10–$15. AE, DC, MC, V. Daily noon–3pm and 7pm–midnight.

WHAT TO SEE & DO
A Walk Around Town   Puerto Varas is compact enough to explore by foot, which is the best way to view the wooden colonial homes built by German immigrants from 1910 until the 1940s. Eight of these homes have been declared national monuments, yet there are at least a dozen more constructed during the period of expansion that began with the installation of the railroad connecting Puerto Varas with Puerto Montt.

Walk up San Francisco from Del Salvador until reaching María Brunn, where you turn right to view the stately **Iglesia del Sagrado Corazón de Jesús,** built between 1915 and 1918. The neo-Romantic design of the church, made entirely of oak, was modeled after the Marienkirche in the Black Forest. Continue along María Brunn and turn right on Purísima, where you'll encounter the first group of colonial homes. The first is **Gasthof Haus** (1930), now run as a hotel; then **Casa Yunge** (1932), just past San Luis on the left; and on the right, **Casa Horn** (1925) where you turn left. If you'd like to see more, walk to Calle Dr. Giesseler and turn right, following the train tracks for several blocks, passing the **Casa Opitz** on the right (1913, and now a hotel) until you see **Casa Maldonado** (1915) on the left.

Turn left on Nuestra Señora del Carmen to view the five homes left and right, including the **Casa Jüptner** (1910). Double back and continue along Dr. Giesseler, turn left on Estación and then right on Decher, passing the **Casa Emhart** (1920) and several other homes on the left. Continue through the forested road that winds up the hill to reach **Parque Philippi** (home to the giant cross, which is lit up at night and can be seen from downtown Puerto Varas), where you'll find an excellent lookout point. Double back, and turn left on Bellavista, right on Klenner, and left on Turismo; at the corner sits the eclectic **Casa Kuschel** (1910), with its Bavarian baroque tower. At the end of Turismo is the Avenida Costanera; turn right and take a stroll down the boardwalk.

Casino   At night, the stately **Casino Puerto Varas,** Del Salvador 021 (✆ 65/346600; www.casino.cl), gives visitors a chance to depart with their travel money (or hopefully win enough for a hotel upgrade) via slot machines and gaming tables offering blackjack, baccarat, roulette, and more. The gaming salon is open daily from noon to 7am, the slot machine floor from noon to 5am, and every Monday the minimum bet drops to $1.50, roulette to 30¢. The casino's bar and restaurants are open from noon to 4am, if you're looking for a midnight snack. It's quite an exciting place to be on weekends, and the decor is stylish in a way that Las Vegas should strive to be more like.

OUTDOOR ACTIVITIES
TOUR OPERATORS & OUTFITTERS   Tour companies and outfitters have changed ownership over the past few years, but, thankfully, these companies have matured and I can now recommend several with a clear conscience. **Aquamotion Expediciones,** San Francisco 328 (✆ 65/232747; fax 65/235938; www.aquamotion.cl), is a professional, competent operation with a bilingual staff that can organize trekking, rafting the Petrohué, horseback riding, canyoneering, photo safaris, journeys to Chiloé, and much more. They also custom-plan excursions and offer packages that include accommodations; and they are better than their competition, CTS, across the street. **Tranco Expediciones,** San Pedro 422 (✆/fax 65/311311; www.trancoexpediciones.cl), and Aquamotion Expediciones both offer ascents of Volcano Osorno, for about $180 for two, which includes gear, lunch, and transportation. They also offer an alternative photography-oriented walk on the volcano for $73 per person.

For city tours and sightseeing tours around the Lake District, including trips to Frutillar, Puyehue, and Chiloé, try **Andina del Sud,** Del Salvador 72 (✆ 65/232811; fax 65/232511; www.andinadelsud.com). Andina del Sud is the company that provides boat excursions on Lago Todos los Santos and the Chilean leg of the lake crossing to Argentina (for information, see "Parque Nacional Vicente Pérez Rosales & the Lake Crossing to Argentina," earlier in this chapter).

For trips to Bariloche via road, contact **LS Travel,** San José 130, Puerto Varas (✆ 65/232424; www.lstravel.com).

BOATING During the summer, it is possible to rent kayaks and canoes at the pier, located near the main plaza. For a sailing cruise around Lago Llanquihue, try **Motovelero Capitán Haase** (© 65/235120; fax 65/235166; www.team building.cl). The amicable owner and captain offers one daily cruise aboard his "antique" yacht (built in 1998 to resemble a turn-of-the-20th-century boat) using antique designs. You can't miss it moored in the bay. "Sunset with the Captain," from 6:30 to 9:30pm, is a quiet, romantic trip using sails and no motor; the cost is $25 per person, which includes an open bar. Inquire about charters if you have a large group.

KAYAKING Ko'Kayak, a small outfit run by French kayak enthusiasts, is the best choice for kayaking both for the day and for multiple-day kayak/camping trips. They have a base in Ensenada at Km 40, but make a reservation at their main office at San José 320 (© 65/511648; www.kokayak.com).

FISHING This region is very popular for fly-fishing, principally along the shores of Río Puelo, Río Maullín, and Río Petrohué—but there's fish in the lake, too. The best and most exclusive fishing expeditions are offered to guests at the Yan Kee Way Lodge (see "Where to Stay," below). There's also **Gray's Fly-Fishing Supplies,** which has two shops, at San José 192 and San Francisco 447 (© 65/310734; www.grayfly.com). Gray's is a central hub for information, gear, and fishing licenses, and they can arrange day trips for river and lake fishing. Another good option for day trips is **Adriazola Fly Fishing,** Santa Rosa 340 (© 65/233477; www.adriazolaflyfishing.com). The owner, Adrian, will custom-arrange any fly-fishing and trolling day tour with a bilingual guide. Both outfitters charge around $130 for a half-day and $300 for a full day (for two guests, including transportation, boat, lunch, wine, and fishing guides).

The exclusive, full-service **Río Puelo Lodge** (© 2/229-8533 in Santiago; fax 2/201-8042; www.riopuelolodge.cl) caters to fly-fishermen and hunters, but also offers horseback riding, boat rides, water-skiing, and more. The stately wood-and-stone lodge is tucked well into the backcountry on the shore of Lago Tagua Tagua, and it caters mainly to groups of guys who come to have fun in the backcountry. Packages average around $350 per person, per day, including meals, open bar, guide, boats, horseback riding, trekking, and heated pool. Ask about discounts for groups.

HORSEBACK RIDING **Campo Aventura,** San Bernardo 318, Puerto Varas (©/fax 65/232910; www.campo-aventura.com), offers horseback riding year-round, leaving from their well-designed camp in Valle Cochamó, south of the national park. Both day and multiple-day trips can be planned with the outfitters, with lodging in rustic shelters they have set up along the trail. Gear and bilingual guides are provided, and multiple-day trips are all-inclusive. Other tour companies, such as **Aquamotion** (see "Tour Operators & Outfitters," above), offer day horseback-riding trips in Vicente Pérez Rosales National Park, among other areas for the day. Horseback riding through a forested area is a good option for a rainy day—just throw on a waterproof jacket and pants, and let the horse walk through the mud for you.

RAFTING Few rivers in the world provide rafters with such stunning scenery as the Río Petrohué, whose frothy green waters begin at Lago Todos los Santos and end at the Reloncaví Estuary. Rafters are treated to towering views of the volcanoes Osorno and Puntiagudo. The river is Class III and suitable for nearly everyone, but there are a few rapids to negotiate with sudden bursts of heavy paddling, so timid travelers might consult with their tour agency before signing up. For rafting, go to **AlSur Expediciones,** Del Salvador 100 (© **65/232300;** www.alsurexpeditions.com).

A SIDE TRIP FROM PUERTO VARAS TO ENSENADA

Ensenada is a tiny settlement at the base of Volcán Osorno. Its proximity to Petrohué and Lago Todos los Santos makes it a convenient point for lodging if you plan to spend a lot of time around the Vicente Pérez Rosales National Park. There is no town to speak of here, just a few vacation rentals, hotels, and a couple of shops. About 4km (2½ miles) outside Puerto Varas on the way to Ensenada is a Chilean rodeo *medialuna* (half-moon), where events are held during February and on Independence days, September 18 and 19. Check with the visitor's office if you are here during that time for this not-to-miss event that provides an in-depth look into Chilean rural culture.

GETTING THERE   If you have your own vehicle, take the coastal road east out of Puerto Varas and continue for 46km (29 miles) until you reach Ensenada. In Puerto Varas, you'll find minibuses at the intersection of San Bernardo and Martínez that go to Ensenada, Petrohué, and Lago Todos los Santos every day at 9:15am, 11am, 2pm, and 4pm. **Andina del Sud,** Del Salvador 72 (© **65/ 232811;** www.andinadelsud.com), has daily trips to this area as well.

WHERE TO STAY

There are many *cabañas* on the shore; the **Cabañas Bahía Celeste** stand out. These self-service units have lake views, living areas, and kitchens for travelers seeking a little more freedom (although there are a few restaurants here if you would like to dine out at night). The *cabañas* are attractive stone-and-wood units on the lakeshore for two, four, or six guests. There is also maid service, and each one comes with a wooden deck (© **09/873-6568;** www.bahiaceleste.cl; prices are $100 cabin for two, $115 cabin for four, and $143 cabin for six).

As is true with the majority of hotels in rural settings (ecolodges, for example), the hotels in this area do not have TVs.

Hotel Ensenada 🔆 *Value*   The Hotel Ensenada is a veritable museum, with a lobby jam-packed with colonial German antiques. The hotel itself is a living antique, built more than 100 years ago. Although it offers an acceptable level of comfort, the rooms do reflect the hotel's age. It's such a fun place, though, that most visitors, many of them foreigners, don't seem to mind. All rooms on the second floor have private bathrooms, and, for the most part, the rest share with just one other room. Rooms are sparsely decorated. If they're not too full, ask to see several rooms, as each one is differently sized. The hotel is situated on a 500-hectare (1,235-acre) private forest that's perfect for taking a stroll or riding a bike—which comes free with the room—and there's a tennis court, canoes, and motorboats. The old-fashioned kitchen serves simple Chilean cuisine with vegetables straight from the garden.

Ruta Internacional 225, Km 45. © 65/212017. Fax 65/212028. www.hotelensenada.cl. 23 units. $60 double; $90 double with volcano view. AE, DC, MC, V. Closed Mar–Sept. **Amenities:** Restaurant; lounge; breakfast.

Yan Kee Way Lodge 🔆🔆🔆 *Moments*   The name "Yan Kee Way" is a play on words, a gringo's pronunciation of Llanquihue, and, coincidentally, it's owned and managed by an American. The lodge is luxury at its finest, and it is patronized by wealthy entrepreneurs, military generals, actors, sports stars, and more—most of them Americans. The owner could not have chosen a more picture-perfect site: nestled in a thick forest of cinnamon-colored *arrayán* trees on the shore of Lago Llanquihue, and facing the astounding view of Volcano Osorno directly in front of the lodge.

The Yan Kee Way Lodge takes just eight fisherman on outings per day (the lodge capacity is higher, however) via inflatable boats, horseback, or walk-and-wade fishing. The best fishing season is from November to early May, yet fisherman have done well year-round—in fact, this lodge offers the best fly-fishing opportunities in the area because they can get to areas that are inaccessible to other fly-fishing operations. The hotel complex has independent units in standard rooms, two-story bungalows, and apartments; the latter are very spacious and good for a family or group of friends. Blending with the surroundings, each elegant building here is painted in tones of terra cotta and forest green, with contemporary decor such as ebony leather couches and furniture, and art imported from Mexico and Argentina. Service is attentive and very friendly, and the owner strives to provide the very best, including an extensive wine cellar with rare wines, a wine-tasting cave, and the region's finest restaurant, Latitude 42 (see below).

Yan Kee Way is not just a fly-fishing lodge, however, and they offer sport adventure all-inclusive packages, including rafting, mountain biking, hiking, and horseback riding. An on-site sommelier offers wine-tastings sessions. At the end of the day, many guests unwind in the spa or in the two wood-fired hot tubs that face the lake and the volcano.

Road to Ensenada east of Puerto Varas, Km 42. © 65/212030. Fax 65/212031. www.southernchilexp.com. 18 units. $175–$250 single; $200–$300 double; $318 per person, per day, all-inclusive sport adventure package, which includes all meals and house wines with dinner. AE, DC, MC, V. **Amenities:** Restaurant; bar; lounge; exercise room; spa; Jacuzzi; sauna; watersports equipment; room service; massage; laundry service; wine-tasting cellar; cigar bar; free Internet access. *In room:* Fridge, hair dryer, safe.

WHERE TO DINE

Latitude 42 ★★★ *(Moments* INTERNATIONAL   This is one of the finest restaurants in Southern Chile, located right on the lake overlooking the volcano. The elegant decor features marble and brass chandeliers, fireplaces made of volcanic rock, orangey leather chairs, picture windows overlooking the water, a basement "cave" for wine tasting, and a cigar bar that sells Havanas. Service is superb. The chef uses only the highest-quality produce, mostly local and organic, to create the most tantalizing dishes. The salmon is smoked in-house using apple cider, and the meat is aged on the premises. Fish is brought daily from Puerto Varas and Puerto Montt, usually sea bass, salmon, and conger eel. Specials change daily and the entire menu changes occasionally throughout the year. The cellar houses outstanding wines, an impressive collection from over 40 vineyards. Pastries and desserts are also terrific; even the heavenly chestnut ice cream is homemade. The menu is surprisingly economical for the high quality of this restaurant. It is a good idea to make a reservation if you are not staying in the lodge.

In the Yan Kee Way Lodge, Road to Ensenada, east of Puerto Varas, Km 42. © 65/212030. Main courses $10–$20. AE, DC, MC, V.

PARQUE NACIONAL VICENTE PEREZ ROSALES & THE LAKE CROSSING TO ARGENTINA
WHAT TO SEE & DO

About 65km (40 miles) from Puerto Varas sits Chile's oldest national park, Vicente Pérez Rosales, founded in 1926. It covers an area of 251,000 hectares (619,970 acres), incorporating the park's centerpiece, **Lago Todos los Santos, Saltos de Petrohué,** and three commanding **volcanoes:** Osorno, Tronador, and Puntiagudo. The park is open daily from December to February 8:30am to 8pm, March to November 8:30am to 6:30pm; admission to Saltos de Petrohué is $3.30 adults, $2.50 kids. Conaf's **information center** (© **65/486115**) can be found toward the end of the dirt road.

Tips **Get on the Road**

I have found that a better way than boat to travel from Puerto Varas to Bariloche is via the international highway (which is dirt is some areas), passing for a stop at Termas de Puyehue, driving through the high Andes, dropping in through the picturesque village of Villa la Angostura, and finally circumnavigating the lake to arrive at Bariloche. Your car-rental agency can arrange the paperwork for you, or try a service such as **LS Travel** (see "Puyehue," earlier in this chapter).

By far the most popular excursions here are boat rides across the crème de menthe–colored waters of **Lago Todos los Santos,** and there are several options. **Andina del Sud** offers a 30-minute sail around Isla Margarita during the summer for only $10 per person, and a 1¾-hour sail to Peulla for $40, with the option of lodging overnight at the Peulla Hotel. Travelers may then return or continue on to Bariloche with the Argentine company Cruce de Lagos (www.crucedelagos.cl). Andina del Sud has a ticket office at the pier and an office in Puerto Varas, at Del Salvador 72 (℃ **65/232811;** $140–$160). This is a very popular journey; however, it is touristy, and though the trip to Bariloche offers rugged, panoramic views, the trip is not worth the money on stormy days. And a bit of the cattle herd mentality exists here as tourist-weary guides shuttle passengers in and out quickly. The ferry portions of this journey are broken up by short bus rides from one body of water to the other.

There are relatively few hiking trails in this national park. The shortest and most popular trail leads to the **Saltos de Petrohué,** located just before the lake (admission $3). Here you'll find a wooden walkway that has been built above the start of the Río Petrohué; from here it is possible to watch the inky-green waters crash through lava channels formed after the 1850 eruption of Volcán Osorno. Apart from the one perfect photo opportunity of the crashing emerald water with the volcano in the background, there isn't really much to see here. If you're serious about backpacking, pick up a copy of the map *Ruta de los Jesuitas* for a description of longer trails in the park, one of which takes you as far as Lago Rupanco and Puerto Rico (the town, not the Caribbean island), where you can catch a bus to Osorno. Day hikes take visitors around the back of Volcán Osorno. One of my favorite treks here is a 1-night/2-day trek to the **Termas del Callao** thermal baths, the trail head of which is accessible only by boat. You can hire one of the boats at the dock (six-person maximum, $50), or arrange a trip with **Expediciones Petrohué,** which will get you a guide and take care of gear and meals for the overnight stay. There is a rustic cabin at the hot springs; check with Expediciones before leaving for this trip to see if it is already booked. They also have rafting, 4×4 photo safaris, climbing, trekking, fly-fishing, and canyoneering opportunities. Expediciones organizes excursions for guests of the hotel and also for day visitors (Petrohué s/n, Ruta 225, Km 64, Parque Nacional; ℃ **65/212045;** www.Petrohué.com), plus they have bike rentals.

There is a new **Volcán Osorno Ski Resort** *(★* on the western slope of the volcano, with two basic chair lifts and a T-bar in terrain. It's a tiny resort, with only 600 hectares (1,482 acres) of terrain, but there are sweeping views and runs apt for every level. This is not a ski resort that travelers head to Chile specifically for, such as Valle Nevado or Portillo; it's more of a novelty for those in the area during the mid-June to early October season. The snow can be bulletproof sometimes, as this side of the lake receives a lot of wind, and all the terrain is above tree level. The resort offers packages that include transportation from Puerto Varas, lift ticket, lunch, and rentals for $52 for 10 people minimum (e-mail or call because they usually have groups organized that you can join; © **65/233445;** www.volcan osorno.com). Located at the park ranger station on the mountain, on the road that detours off the road to Puerto Octay.

WHERE TO STAY

Hotel Peulla 🎿 *(Finds)*   Passengers on the 2-day journey to Bariloche stop for the night at this giant lodge, which sits on the shore of Lago Todos los Santos inside the Vicente Pérez Rosales National Park. It's possible to spend several days here if you'd like, to take part in trekking (limited), fishing, kayaking, and horseback riding in the area. The lodge's remoteness is perhaps its biggest draw, surrounded as it is by thick forest and not much else. Built in 1896, the Peulla is a mountain lodge, with enormous dining rooms, roaring fireplaces, and lots of wood. It's an agreeable place, with a large patio and sprawling lawn, though it is older and not as exclusive as the price suggests. Guest rooms haven't really changed since the hotel was built; they are simple and slightly dark, with hardwood floors. Try reserving rooms at a lower rate through a travel agency.

Lago Todos los Santos. ©/fax **2/889-1031** in Santiago. www.crucedelagos.cl. 72 units. $137 double. AE, MC, V. **Amenities:** Restaurant; bar; gym; watersports equipment; game room; Internet access. *In room:* Satellite TV.

Petrohué Hotel & Cabañas 🎿🎿   The brand-new Hotel Petrohué (built to replace the old lodge that recently burned to the ground) is recommended because it puts travelers right where the outdoor action is, without having to commute from Puerto Varas every day to the park—and the hotel has an excursion outfitter with a range of daily activities. It sits perched above the shore of Todos los Santos Lake, within the confines of the National Park, meaning it gets busy when the lake crossing boat pulls in with a horde of people (but this doesn't last very long, as they're bussed out quickly). The forested location is gorgeous, even on a rainy day. The Petrohué Hotel & Cabañas is a tad austere, given its absence of homey touches such as artwork or plants, but the contemporary design of its interiors (stone, heavy wood beams, fresh white couches) is attractive, and the rooms are very comfortable, with crisp linens and panoramic windows. What's an even better idea is bunking up in one of their four cozy *cabañas* a little closer to the shore, all of which come with kitchenettes and maid service. This way you do not have to depend on the restaurant for all of your meals.

Petrohué s/n Ruta 225, Km 64, Parque Nacional. © **65/212025.** www.Petrohué.com. 13 units; 4 cabins. $139 double, $161 double with half-board; $132 cabin for 2; $180 cabin for 8. AE, MC, V. **Amenities:** Restaurant; bar; lounge; outdoor pool; outdoor excursions; boat; room service; laundry service. *In room:* Kitchenette (*cabañas*).

7 Puerto Montt

20km (12 miles) south of Puerto Varas; 1,016km (630 miles) south of Santiago

This port town of roughly 155,000 residents is the central hub for travelers headed to Lagos Llanquihue and Todos los Santos, Chiloé, and the parks Alerce Andino and Pumalín. It is also a major docking zone for dozens of large cruise companies circumnavigating the southern cone of South America and several ferry companies with southern destinations to Laguna San Rafael National Park and Puerto Natales in Patagonia.

There isn't much to see or do here, and most visitors head straight out of town upon arrival, but Puerto Montt's small downtown offers a quick, pleasant stroll on a sunny day, and there is an extensive outdoor market that sells Chilean handicrafts.

Puerto Montt was founded in 1853 by German immigrants and their stalwart promoter Vicente Pérez Rosales, who named the town after another promoter of immigration, President Manuel Montt. The waterfront here was rebuilt after the devastating earthquake of 1960, which had destroyed the city's port, church, and neighborhood of Angelmó. Today it is the capital of Chile's Southern Lake District, a thriving city that invests heavily in salmon farming, shipping, and tourism.

ESSENTIALS
GETTING THERE
BY PLANE   Puerto Montt's **El Tepual** (PMC) airport (© 65/294161) is currently served by airlines **LanExpress** (© 600/526-2000; www.lan.com) and **Sky** (© 600/600-2828; www.skyairline.cl), with multiple daily flights to Santiago, Punta Arenas, Balmaceda (Coyhaique), and Temuco. **Aero Taxi,** Antonio Varas 70 (©/fax 65/252523), has two daily flights to Chaitén, and the cost is $115 round-trip. This is a deal because the ferry to Chaitén takes 10 hours. An **ETM bus** from the airport to the city's downtown bus terminal costs $1.50; a taxi costs $9. Agree on the fare before getting into the cab. There are **several car-rental** agencies at the airport, including Hertz and Avis.

BY BUS   Puerto Montt's main terminal is at the waterfront (Diego Portales s/n), a 10- to 15-minute walk from downtown, or there are taxis to transport you. Regular bus service to and from most major cities, including Santiago, is provided by **Cruz del Sur** (© 65/254731), **Tur Bus** (© 65/253329), **Tas Choapa** (© 65/254828), and **Bus Norte** (© 65/252783).

BY CAR   The Panamericana Highway ends at Puerto Montt.

VISITOR INFORMATION
The municipality has a small **tourist office** in the plaza at the corner of Antonio Varas and San Martín (© 65/261823); it's open December through March daily from 9am to 9pm, and April through November Monday through Friday from 9am to 1pm and 2:30 to 7pm, Saturday and Sunday from 9am to 1pm. There is a largely unhelpful tourism kiosk in the main plaza (© 65/261808; turismomontt@puertomonttchile.cl).

ORIENTATION
Puerto Montt is divided into *poblaciones,* or neighborhoods, scattered around the city's hilltops. From the city center to the east is the **Pelluco** district, where many of the city's good restaurants can be found, and to the west is the district **Angelmó,** with the city's fish market, port departures, and Feria Artesanal with great shopping; the two districts are connected by the coastal road Diego Portales. The city center is laid out on a grid system that abuts a steep cliff.

GETTING AROUND
BY FOOT   The city center is small enough to be seen on foot. The crafts market and fish market in Angelmó are a 20-minute walk from the center, but you can take a cab. You'll need a taxi to reach the Pelluco district.

BY BUS   **Buses Cruz del Sur** (© 65/254731) leaves for Puerto Varas 19 times daily from the bus terminal, and so do the independent white shuttle buses to the left of the coaches; look for the sign in the window that says PUERTO VARAS. Cruz del Sur also serves Chiloé, including Castro and Ancud, with 25 trips per

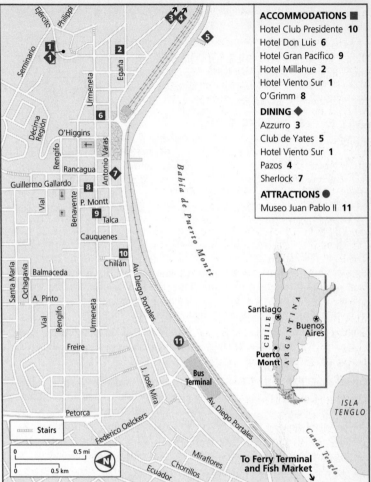

Puerto Montt

ACCOMMODATIONS ■
Hotel Club Presidente **10**
Hotel Don Luis **6**
Hotel Gran Pacífico **9**
Hotel Millahue **2**
Hotel Viento Sur **1**
O'Grimm **8**

DINING ◆
Azzurro **3**
Club de Yates **5**
Hotel Viento Sur **1**
Pazos **4**
Sherlock **7**

ATTRACTIONS ●
Museo Juan Pablo II **11**

day. **TransChiloé** (© **65/254934**) goes to Chiloé seven times per day from the terminal.

BY CAR   This is one of those places where renting a car can come in handy, given the ample sightseeing opportunities and pleasant drives in the area. Local car-rental agencies in Puerto Montt include **Hertz,** Antonio Varas 126 (© **65/ 259585;** www.hertz.com); **Avis,** Urmeneta 1037 (©/fax **65/253307;** www.avis. com); **First,** Av. Urmeneta 252 (©/fax **65/252036;** firstptomontt@surnet.cl); and **Econo Rent,** Av. Ejército 600 (© **65/254888;** econorent@telsur.cl). Hertz and Avis rent cars to travelers who wish to drive south along the Carretera Austral (see the "Driving the Carretera Austral" section in chapter 17, beginning on p. 393), and they can arrange to have the vehicle dropped off in Coyhaique. Some companies insist that you rent a 4×4 for the Carretera Austral (the importance of this during the summer is debatable; during the winter it could help if the road turns muddy). Calling the local office of each company is usually the best way to get bargain rates, but in general the rental drop-off fee is $500, in addition to the daily cost.

SPECIAL EVENTS

During the second week of February, the city holds its annual **Semana Puertomontina,** with weeklong festivities that culminate in a fireworks display over the bay. The festival celebrates Puerto Montt's anniversary. Throughout the summer, the city holds arts and crafts exhibits in public plazas.

FAST FACTS: PUERTO MONTT

Currency Exchange   You can exchange currency at **Trans Afex,** Av. Diego Portales 516; **Cambios Inter,** Paseo Talca 84 (© 64/343683); **La Moneda de Oro,** in the bus terminal, Office #37; and **Eureka Tour,** Guillermo Gallardo 65. Exchange houses are generally open Monday through Friday from 9am to 1pm and 2 to 6pm, Saturday from 9am to 2pm. For ATMs, look for banks at Urmeneta and Guillermo Gallardo downtown. Banks are open Monday through Friday from 9am to 2pm.

Hospital   Try either **Hospital Base,** Seminario, s/n (© 65/261100), or **Hospital de la Seguridad,** Panamericana 400 (© 65/257333).

Internet Cafe   Internet cafes come and go quickly, so it's best to walk Urmenta street and look for a sign or ask at your hotel. Try **Arroba Cibercafé,** Guillermo Gallardo 218 #A, or **New Ciber,** San Martín 230. Internet service costs $1.50 per hour, but many hotels are slowly adding free access for guests.

Laundry   **Anny,** San Martín 167 (© 65/255397); **Lavaseco Arcoiris,** San Martín 230; and **Lavatodo,** O'Higgins 231, are all spots to do your wash.

WHAT TO SEE & DO

Museo Juan Pablo II   This museum contains a medley of artifacts culled from this region. There's an interesting interpretive exhibit here of the Monte Verde archaeological dig that found bones estimated to be 12,000 years old. There's also an open-air railway exhibit next to the museum, but truthfully, the museum is worth a visit only if you have time to kill.

Av. Diego Portales 991. © 65/344457. Admission 90¢. Mon–Fri 9am–7pm; Sat–Sun 10am–6pm.

TOUR OPERATORS & TRAVEL AGENCIES   **Ace Turismo,** Antonio Varas 445 (© 65/254988 or 09/707-9445), offers just about everything you could want, including tours to Vicente Pérez National Park, the Termas de Puyehue, and Chiloé; sightseeing tours around the circumference of Lago Llanquihue; 2-night treks around Volcán Osorno with an overnight in a family home; and more.

Andina del Sud, Antonio Varas 437 (© 65/257797; fax 299015; www.andina delsud.cl), is the tour agency with the monopoly on Lago Todos los Santos for the lake crossing to Bariloche; they also offer city tours and sightseeing journeys, and transportation service to attractions. **Travellers,** Av. Angelmó 2456 (© 65/262099; fax 65/258555; www.travellers.cl), is somewhat like a one-stop travel shop, with information and booking arrangements with nearly every outfitter, hotel, and program around Chile. Their location is far from the city center, though it is close to the arts and crafts market Feria Artesanal de Angelmó. They have a book exchange here, too.

SHOPPING   Puerto Montt is a great place to pick up souvenirs. On Avenida Angelmó, from the bus terminal to the fish market, is the **Feria Artesanal de Angelmó** ✿ (open daily 9am–7pm, 9pm in the summer), with dozens of stalls and specialty shops that peddle knitwear, ponchos, handicrafts, jewelry, regional foods, and more from areas around the Lake District, including Chiloé. It's about a 20-minute walk from the plaza, or you can take a taxi. There is also a large, tacky shopping mall south of the main plaza, with national and international chains.

WHERE TO STAY
EXPENSIVE
Hotel Club Presidente ⚘   This well-tailored hotel's classic, nautical-themed design appeals equally to executives and tourists, and handy kitchenettes give guests a little extra freedom. Located on the waterfront, in a central location close to shops, the Presidente is on busy Avenida Portales, but double-paned windows keep noise to a minimum. All rooms have either queen-size or king-size beds. The doubles are spacious, but the superiors are much larger and worth the extra $5; they also have ocean views. Most come with a small loveseat and a table and chairs. The rooms are decorated with creams and terra cotta, striped curtains, and nubby bedspreads. A breakfast buffet is served daily in the comfortable restaurant/bar on the eighth floor.

Av. Diego Portales 664, Puerto Montt. ⓒ **65/251666.** Fax 65/251669. www.presidente.cl. 50 units. $55–$110 double. Rates include buffet breakfast. AE, DC, MC, V. **Amenities:** Restaurant; bar; small heated pool; sauna; business center; laundry service. *In room:* TV, kitchenette, safe.

Hotel Don Luis   The Don Luis offers comfortable accommodations with traditional decor. For the price, you'd do better staying at the Club Presidente (see above), but occasional discounts might make this hotel more attractive. The lobby has glass walls, shiny white floors, and English-style furniture. The hotel renovated its rooms and sparkling-white bathrooms in 2000, but not the carpet, which could stand to be replaced. Corner rooms and those on the seventh and eighth floors have the best views. Junior suites have a terrace, and superiors come with a queen-size bed. The hotel often caters to executives and conventioneers.

Calle Urmeneta and Quillota 146, Puerto Montt. ⓒ **65/259001.** Fax 65/259005. www.hoteldonluis.cl. 60 units. $85–$120 double; $130 suite. Rates include buffet breakfast. AE, DC, MC, V. **Amenities:** Restaurant; bar; lounge; exercise room; sauna; small business center; room service; laundry service. *In room:* TV.

Hotel Gran Pacífico ⚘   Opened in late 2001, the Gran Pacífico is the city's only luxurious hotel, and its imposing 10-story structure towers over the waterfront. The Art Deco lobby is sleek and modern, with lots of wood and marble. The rooms follow the same motif and are spacious, modern, and very bright. They have wood headboards, off-yellow wallpaper, and large-screen TVs. Those overlooking the water have breathtaking views (request an upper-level ocean-view floor when you check in). The marble bathrooms are a tad small, but the size of the room makes up for it. For such a high-caliber hotel, the staff is not too efficient, nor do they speak much English, so be patient.

Urmeneta 719, Puerto Montt. ⓒ **65/482100.** Fax 65/292979. www.hotelgranpacifico.cl. 48 units. $125 double. AE, DC, MC, V. **Amenities:** Restaurant; bar; lounge; exercise room; sauna; business center; room service; laundry service. *In room:* TV, minibar, safe.

Hotel Viento Sur ⚘   The main body of this appealing bed-and-breakfast-style hotel is within an 80-year-old home clinging to a cliff, with a decade-old, added-on wing below that keeps with the architectural uniformity of the establishment. The hotel has luminous blond-wood floors and is brightly lit by a generous supply of windows that look out over Puerto Montt's bay. The rooms are unique, each with a folk-art and nautical theme, but simple and not luxurious at all. The upstairs rooms in the old house have tall ceilings, the rooms in the lower wing have the cozy feel of a ship's cabin, and rooms on the fourth floor have terraces or balconies. Doubles come in standard and superior, and nearly all have a view of the bay. A large patio juts out from the front of the hotel.

One of the perks at the Viento Sur is the delicious breakfast buffet served in the restaurant, which is locally considered one of the best in Puerto Montt (see "Where to Dine," below).

Ejército 200, Puerto Montt. © 65/258701. Fax 65/314732. www.hotelvientosur.cl. 27 units. $84–$90 double standard; $95–$98 double superior. Rates include buffet breakfast. AE, DC, MC, V. **Amenities:** Restaurant; sauna; laundry service. *In room:* TV.

O'Grimm   One of the city's most established hotels, the O'Grimm is run by a friendly English-speaking staff and is adjacent to the popular O'Grimm Pub. Rooms are of varying sizes and all come with sleek black and gray furniture and dark satinlike bedspreads. There's no view to mention, really, and the rooms are not as inviting as the price may suggest. Bathrooms are small and aging, but clean. The restaurant, pub, and bustling atmosphere downstairs are pleasant, and there's live music several nights of the week.

Guillermo Gallardo 211, Puerto Montt. © 65/252845. Fax 65/258600. www.ogrimm.com. 26 units. $65–$100 double; from $110 suite. AE, DC, MC, V. **Amenities:** Restaurant; bar; business center with Internet access. *In room:* TV, safe, minibar.

MODERATE

Hotel Millahue   This older hotel is not particularly fancy, but it does offer clean, large double rooms and friendly service. All double rooms are sized differently but priced the same, and rooms on the fourth and fifth floors are the nicest, especially those whose numbers end in 06 and 07. There's a dining area for breakfast and hearty, set-menu Chilean meals, should you decide to eat in. Beds are average but offer standard comfort. The hotel is run by its owner, a friendly woman who strives to make guests feel at home.

Copiapó 64, Puerto Montt. © 65/253829. Fax 65/256317. www.hotelmillahue.cl. 25 units. $30–$45 double. Rates include breakfast. MC, V. **Amenities:** Restaurant; laundry service.

WHERE TO DINE

Puerto Montt is Chile's seafood capital. If you're feeling adventurous, try a Chilean favorite, such as abalone, sea urchin, or the regional barnacle. And where better to see, smell, and taste these fruits of the sea than the **Fish Market of Angelmó,** located at the end of Avenida Angelmó, where the artisan market terminates? It's open Monday through Sunday from 10am to 8pm during the summer, until 6pm during the winter. Like most fish markets, it's a little grungy, but it's a colorful stop nevertheless and there are several restaurant stalls offering the freshest local specialties around. *A word of caution:* There have been reports that a few food stalls like to overcharge tourists, so double-check your bill with the menu.

Apart from the restaurants below, there are a handful of inexpensive cafes in Puerto Montt, including **Café Central,** Rancagua 117 (© 65/482888); **Dino's,** Antonio Varas 550 (© 65/252785); and **Super Yoco,** Quillota 245 (© 65/252123), which has lunches, empanadas, and appetizer platters. If you're in the mood for pizza, try **Di Napoli,** Av. Guillermo Gallardo 118 (© 65/254174).

Azzurro 🞓 ITALIAN   Fresh pasta served in rich sauces is this Italian eatery's mainstay, but that's not all they serve—the stuffed Roquefort chicken and pizzas are also very good. The folk-artsy blue dining area has a fun, pleasant atmosphere. The pastas are very good, such as lasagna, fettuccine, or cannelloni stuffed with crab and spinach, or with ricotta, walnuts, eggplant, and fresh basil, and bathed in a choice of 11 sauces.

Av. Inés Gallardo 146, Pelluco. © 65/318989. Reservations recommended on weekends. Main courses $7–$11. MC, V. Mon–Sat 1–3:30pm and 8pm–midnight; Sun 1–3:30pm.

Club de Yates 🆀 SEAFOOD   The light-blue Club de Yates looks like a traditional seafood restaurant that sits out over the water like a pier. Inside, though, the atmosphere is white tablecloths, candlesticks, and sharp waiters in bow ties; it's one of the more elegant dining areas in town. This is a good place to come if you're looking for typical Chilean seafood dishes, such as razor clams broiled with Parmesan or sea bass *Margarita,* which is a creamy shellfish sauce. It has a great waterfront view and is located about 1km (½ mile) from the plaza toward Pelluco.

Av. Juan Soler Manfredini 200. © 65/82810. Main courses $20–$25. AE, DC, MC, V. Daily noon–4pm and 7:30pm–midnight.

Hotel Viento Sur 🆀 CONTEMPORARY CHILEAN   The main reason to come here is for the intimate dining area with its expansive view of the bay—if you get a table near the window, that is. The restaurant is built of polished blond wood, with linen tablecloths and a nautical theme. Tasty dishes include beef tenderloin and cilantro rice, saffron conger eel, and chicken marinated in port with almonds. A most unusual dish is the exquisite smoked salmon soup with spinach. Although there are set hours for dining, the restaurant serves cocktails, tea, and cakes all day, should you be looking for a good place to take a break. There's also a tiny bar here.

Ejército 200. © 65/258701. Main courses $5–$10. AE, DC, MC, V. Daily 7am–3pm and 6:30–11pm.

Pazos CHILEAN   This is the place to come if you're interested in sampling *curanto* but don't have time to make it to Chiloé. *Curanto* is that island's specialty, a mixture of mussels, clams, sausage, chicken, pork, beef, and a gooey pancake steamed in a large pot and served with a cup of broth. Pazos also serves a variety of other seafood items, such as sea urchin omelets and the shellfish cornucopia, *sopa marina.* The restaurant is on the waterfront in Pelluco, in a 90-year-old home. It's very popular with summer visitors to Puerto Montt.

Liboro Guerrero 1, Pelluco. © 65/252552. Main courses $8–$12. AE, DC, MC, V. Daily 12:15–3pm and 8:15–10pm.

Sherlock 🆀 *(Finds* CHILEAN/PUB   The newest and most happening place in Puerto Varas is this centrally located pub, cafe, and restaurant all rolled into one. There's lots of charm, a nice bar, and wood furniture, and it fills with locals at all hours of the day. This is a good place to get some local color, and they serve excellent homemade Chilean cuisine and delicious sandwiches. Try the albacore steak with a Chilean tomato-and-onion salad or the Sherlock sandwich with beef strips, tomato, corn, cheese, bacon, and grilled onion.

Two locations: Antonio Varas 542 and Rancagua 117. © 65/288888. Main courses $6–$10; sandwiches $3–$5. MC, V. Daily 9am–2am.

8 Ferry Crossings to the Carretera Austral & Sailing to Patagonia Through the Fjords

Few fjordlands in the world surpass the elegant beauty of Chile's southern region. The entire coast of Chile is composed of thousands of little-explored islands, canals, and sounds. **Navimag** offers a popular sailing trip through the southern fjords to Puerto Natales in Patagonia. The company also offers journeys to the Laguna San Rafael Glacier, as does the freight ferry **Transmarchilay** and the luxury liners *Skorpios* and *Patagonian Express* (which leaves from Puerto Chacabuco). Both cruises are unforgettable.

For information about the journey to the Laguna San Rafael Glacier, see chapter 17.

Navimag Ferries *Moments* Navimag offers a sensational 3-day/3-night journey through the southern fjords to **Puerto Natales,** near Torres del Paine National Park (the trip can also be done in the reverse direction—see the section on Puerto Natales in chapter 18 for departure dates and times). Navimag's ship, M/N *Magallanes,* is a passenger and freight ferry with a variety of cabins, from basic shared accommodations to higher-end cabins. The cruise is unforgettable not only for the spectacular views it offers, but also for the camaraderie that occurs among the passengers. The ship sails through fjords and channels, past coves, and across the Golfo de Penas, or "Gulf of Grief," where, depending on climatic conditions, passengers may experience seasickness.

The *Magallanes* leaves Puerto Montt every Monday at 4 pm and arrives at Puerto Natales on Thursday. The return trip leaves Puerto Natales on Friday at 6am (check-in is Thurs at midnight) and arrives back here on Monday at 6am.

Cabin prices include all meals. Check to see if your cabin has a private bathroom and interior or exterior windows. You may have to share with strangers unless you fork over the entire price of a Cabin Triple A ($1,600 for 2). Other rates are $360 to $415 per person, quadruple occupancy. Prices drop from here all the way down to $250 per person, but be forewarned that the very cheapest bunks are booked by young backpackers and are separated only by curtains. Prices drop for off-season travel (quadruples start from $200); check Navimag's website for specials from April to October.

Offices in Puerto Montt at Av. Angelmó 2187 in the Terminal de Transbordadores ((C) **65/432300**; fax 65/276611) and Santiago at El Bosque Norte 0440 ((C) **2/442-3120**). In Chaitén, call (C) **65/731570**. www.navimag.com. AE, DC, MC, V.

FERRY SERVICES Puerto Montt is the hub for all ferry companies. If you are planning a trip down the Carretera Austral, you'll need to travel to or from Puerto Montt or Chiloé by ferry (unless you enter through Argentina). During the summer, passengers and autos can cross into Pumalín Park and Caleta Gonzalo by ferry. This route is preferred but available only from December to March. For information about ferry crossings to Caleta Gonzalo, see the section on Pumalín Park in chapter 17, beginning on p. 397. Navimag is talking about canceling their ferry, so check their website for updated news. Of course, if this happens, visitors will be able to cross with vehicles only during the summer.

Throughout the year, Transmarchilay and Navimag offer service to Chaitén at the Carretera Austral, from Puerto Montt; Transmarchilay also offers three trips a week from Castro, on the island of Chiloé to Chaitén.

Navimag's (see above) ferries to **Chaitén** leave once a week (usually Sun) during the summer; call for days because they tend to vary. The trip takes 10 hours and costs $25 per person for the right to stay in the salon with tables and chairs, or $30 per person for a semireclining seat.

Transmarchilay, in Puerto Montt at Av. Angelmó 2187, Terminal de Transbordadores ((C) **65/270416;** fax 270414; www.transmarchilay.cl), is, unfortunately, active only during January and February. Their ferry crossings to **Chaitén,** aboard the ship *Pincoya,* leave Monday at noon and Tuesday, Thursday, and Friday at 8pm for $20 per passenger and an additional $110 for autos; bikes are charged $11. The trip takes 10 hours, and passengers sleep in reclining seats. From Chaitén, the return trips depart on Monday, Wednesday, and Sunday at 10pm, and Friday at 9am. From Castro, Chiloé, the ferry leaves Wednesday, Saturday, and Sunday at 9am.

16

Chiloé

The "Grand Island of Chiloé" is a land of myths and magic—of emerald, rolling hills shrouded in mist, and tiny, picturesque coves that harbor a colorful palette of wooden fishing skiffs. This is Chile's second-largest island, located south of Puerto Montt with an eastern coast that faces the Gulf of Ancud and a western, wet Pacific shore. With the exception of a few small towns, the landscape here by and large is pastoral, with a deference to development that tends to make the visitor feel as if he has been transported back a century. Across the island, antique wooden churches modeled after a Bavarian, neoclassic style appear like a beacon in every bay; they are so lovely and architecturally unique that UNESCO recently deemed them World Heritage Monuments.

Visually appealing as it is, Chiloé is truly defined by its people, the hardy, character-rich Chilotes who can still be seen plowing their fields with oxen or pulling in their catch of the day the same way they have for centuries. Spanish conquistadors occupied Chiloé as early as 1567, followed by Jesuit missionaries and Spanish refugees pushed off the mainland by Mapuche Indian attacks. For 3 centuries, Chiloé was the only Spanish stronghold south of the Río Biobío, and its isolation produced a singular culture among its residents, who, after so much time, are now a *mestizo* blend of Indian and Spanish blood. The Chilotes' rapid and closed speech, local slang, mythical folklore, and style of food, tools, and architecture was and still is uniquely different from

their counterparts on the mainland. The downside of Chiloé's limited contact with the outside world is a dire poverty that has affected (and continues to affect) many of the island's residents. Most families eke out a living by relying on their own garden patch and livestock, animals that can be seen pecking and grazing along the side of the road. Off the main highway, it is as common to see residents traveling on horseback or by fishing boat as it is by vehicle.

I recommend a day or overnight trip to Chiloé rather than spending time in the grimy environs of Puerto Montt, but with one caveat: It is essential to rent a car. While the principal cities **Ancud** and **Castro** offer much to see and can be easily reached by bus, the true pleasure of visiting Chiloé is losing yourself on backcountry roads and discovering picturesque little bays and lookout points that are otherwise inaccessible by bus, and stopping at roadside stands for local cheese, fresh fish, and other delicacies. This chapter covers the highlights here, but the island is easy to navigate with a road map. (See "Driving to & Around Chiloé," below). Chiloé also boasts the **Chiloé National Park,** where visitors can indulge themselves with a walk through primordial old-growth rainforest that once blanketed the island. The island's tourism infrastructure is improving, but as of yet, visitors should expect to find modest accommodations. The tedious rain that falls more than half the year here makes for soggy shoes and limited views; nevertheless, Chiloé rates as one of Chile's top attractions for its cultural value and natural beauty. Few visitors to Chile are aware of this.

Useful websites for information about Chiloé are **www.chiloe.cl** and **www. interpatagonia.cl**.

EXPLORING THE ISLAND

Most visitors use Castro as a central base for exploring the island. I wouldn't really recommend a stay in Ancud unless you are short on time. Quellón is considered primarily a ferry departure point for Chaitén on the Carretera Austral (see chapter 17). On a clear day—not very often—one can see Volcán Osorno and the towering, snowcapped Andes in the distance.

You'll need a day or 2 to explore Castro, Dalcahue, Achao, and Conchi; a day to see the national park (more if you wish do a long hike or camp out); and about a half-day to see Ancud (with a stop in Chacao).

GETTING TO THE ISLAND

By Boat　There's been talk of building a bridge between the mainland and Chiloé, but until then, two ferry companies operate continuously between Pargua (on the mainland) and Chacao (on the island), shuttling passengers and vehicles. If you are taking a bus to Chiloé, you won't need to worry about paying the fare because it's included in the price of the bus ticket, but if you've rented a car, the cost is $12 one-way. The ride lasts 30 to 40 minutes. (And, yes, there are toilets on board the ferry.)

By Bus　Several companies provide service to Ancud, Castro, and Quellón from Puerto Montt, and even Santiago and Punta Arenas. In Puerto Montt, daily departures for Ancud and Castro leave from the bus terminal. **Cruz del Sur** (© 65/254731; www.busescruzdelsur.cl/Itinerarioset.html) has 18 trips per day, **TransChiloé** (© 65/254934) has seven trips per day, and **Queilén Bus** (© 65/253468) has eight trips per day. From Puerto Varas, try **Cruz del Sur** at San Francisco 1317, with five trips per day (© 65/236969). **Cruz del Sur**

Tips　Driving to & Around Chiloé

Chiloé is a sightseer's paradise and, therefore, it is highly recommended that visitors rent a vehicle. You will be able to cover more ground and take full advantage of seemingly endless photo-worthy vista points, historic churches, and picturesque little villages. Hopping from island to island in a vehicle is a snap, and visitors can pack a lot of action into just one day. You will need to rent a car at the airport, in Puerto Montt or Puerto Varas, because there is no rental service available in Chiloé. Car rental information for Puerto Montt and Puerto Varas is listed under their individual listings (p. 371 and 358, respectively).

Local bus service from town to town is frequent and inexpensive. More information about bus service can be found in the sections for each specific town below. If you're driving your own rental car onto the ferry, don't line up behind the trucks and buses, but go to the front of the line and park to the left—that will make you visible to the ferry attendants, and they'll squeeze you onto the next available ferry.

Gas stations are sporadic. Fill up in Puerto Montt or Puerto Varas, and again in Ancud. If visiting the national park, fill up in Castro or Conchi.

Chiloé

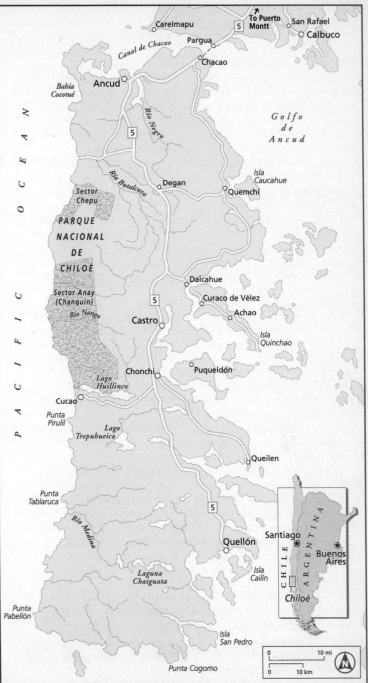

Chiloé's World Heritage Churches

Designated World Heritage Sites by UNESCO in 2002, the nearly 150 churches of Chiloé are without a doubt the island's most unique attractions, and they are wholly unlike anything found on the mainland. Built entirely of wood, the humble—and yet striking—churches represent a rare form of architecture brought about by the fusion of European and indigenous cultural traditions, namely those of the Jesuit missionaries of the 17th and 18th centuries and the island's early inhabitants, the Mapuches, the Cunco, and the Chonos.

Jesuit missionaries first arrived on the island in 1608, conducting circular missions throughout the island wherein they traveled the archipelago throughout the year, stopping for several days at a mission site and spreading their brand of religion. But unlike other missionary groups, the Jesuits attempted to learn the languages and the cultural traditions of those they were hoping to convert. Thus, it was both their respect for traditional building methods and the Jesuits' absence for much of the year that afforded the indigenous peoples of the island the opportunity to lay such a heavy influence on the construction of each church.

The styles and layouts of the churches can be traced back to Europe: **Chonchi's** represents classicism, the church in **Nercon** is Renaissance, and in **Achao** you'll find baroque. However, the interiors and the locations chosen for each church reflect the inspiration of their local indigenous builders. A close look inside each church offers numerous examples of techniques that were borrowed from shipbuilding, such as wooden pegs and joints instead of nails. The center of the roof, if imagined inverted, often resembles the hull of a boat. Moreover, nearly all the chapels in Chiloé face the water, with central towers that functioned as beacons for sailors. The influence of the island's early maritime inhabitants continues to be a point of pride for those that call it home.

Although each church shares the same facade of semicircular arches, each church varies greatly in color and size, the latter representing what type of festivals were to be had at the church. The church at Achoa is the oldest, but the church at Tenaún, with its royal blue exterior upon which are painted two large white stars, is probably the most impressive. Don't miss a stop at one while here in Chiloé.

(✆ 2/779-0607) offers three services per day from Santiago to Chiloé; the trip takes about 15 hours. Buses ride over on the ferry; you can remain in your seat or step out and walk around.

1 Ancud

95km (59 miles) southeast of Puerto Montt; 146km (91 miles) north of Castro

Ancud is Chiloé's largest city, founded in 1767 as a defensive fort to monitor passing sea traffic to and from Cape Horn. It was for many years the capital of Chiloé until the provincial government pulled up stakes and moved to Castro in

1982. Ancud is a bustling, rambling port town with much to see, but Castro is a more convenient base if you want to reach the island's outlying areas. This was the last Spanish outpost in Chile, and visitors can view the fort ruins here; there's also a good museum depicting Chilote history and culture.

GETTING THERE & DEPARTING   By Bus   For regular bus service from Puerto Montt to Ancud, see "Getting to the Island," above. Ancud has a central bus station, the **Terminal Municipal,** at the intersection of Avenida Aníbal Pinto and Marcos Vera; from here, you'll need to take a taxi to the center of town, or a local bus headed toward the plaza. Frequent buses leave from this station for destinations such as Castro, Dalcahue, and Quellón; try **Cruz del Sur/Transchiloé** (© 65/622265) or **Queilén Bus** (© 65/621140).

By Car   Ruta 5 (the Panamericana Hwy.) is a well-paved road that links Ancud with nearly every city on the island. The paved highway ends just south of Quellón.

ORIENTATION   Ancud is spread across a tiny peninsula, with the Canal de Chacao to the east and the Golfo de Quetalmahue to the west; it is 27km (17 miles) from the Chacao ferry dock. The city is not laid out on a regular grid pattern, and its crooked streets might easily confuse anyone driving into the city. Avenida Aníbal Pinto is the main entrance road that funnels drivers into the center of town. Most attractions are located within several blocks of the plaza.

Visitor Information   Sernatur's office is on the plaza, at Libertad 655 (© 65/622800; fax 65/622665). It's open daily from 8:30am to 7pm during January and February; the rest of the year it's open Monday through Thursday from 8:30am to 5:30pm, Friday from 8:30am to 4:30pm, and closed on weekends.

SPECIAL EVENTS   From the second week in January to the last week of February, the city hosts the "Different and Magical Summer of Ancud." The event kicks off with classical music concerts and a 3-day food and folklore festival at the Arena Gruesa (third week in Jan) and a shore-fishing contest (second week of Feb), and culminates with a fireworks display, again in Arena Gruesa (third week of Feb). For more information, call © 65/628163 (municipal tourism information) or Sernatur (© 65/622800).

FAST FACTS: ANCUD

Currency Exchange   There are no places to exchange money here, but there are a couple of ATMs on Ramírez, near the plaza.

Ferry   Ferry tickets are paid on board; for information, call **Navimag** (© 65/682207) or **Transmarchilay** (© 65/270416). Offices are located in Quellón.

Hospital   The hospital is at Almirante Latorre 301 (© 65/622356).

Internet Access   Internet access can be found at **Entel,** on Pudeto 219 (on the Plaza, near Correos de Chile).

Laundry   Laundry services are available at the **Clean Center,** Pudeto 45, half a block from the plaza.

WHAT TO SEE & DO

Fuerte San Antonio   Built in 1770 and fortified with cannons aimed at the port entrance, Fort San Antonio was Spain's last stronghold in Chile after the War of Independence. The Spanish flag last flew here on January 19, 1826, and just 6 days later, Peru's El Callao surrendered, ending Spanish rule in South

America forever. Okay, it's not much, but the site affords a sweeping ocean view, and the Hostería Ancud is next to the site if you're looking for a place for lunch.

San Antonio and Cochrane (below Hostería Ancud). No phone. Free admission.

Museo Regional de Ancud Audelio Bórquez Canobra *★★* *Kids* This handsome, well-designed museum features a wide variety of exhibits related to the history and culture of Chiloé. The museum includes a large courtyard with sculptures depicting the mythological characters that form part of Chilote folklore. Inside you'll find interactive displays designed for kids and a variety of archaeological items, such as Indian arrowheads and nautical pieces, as well as displays explaining the farming and wool-production techniques used by Chilotes. A new permanent exhibit covers the entire span of Chiloé's history from the pre-Columbian era to the 20th century. Temporary exhibits display photography, sculpture, and contemporary art.

Libertad 370. © 65/622413. Admission $1 adults, 50¢ children. Jan–Feb Mon–Sun 10am–7:30pm; Mar–Dec Tues–Fri 10am–5:30pm, Sat–Sun 10am–2pm.

SHOPPING

For a selection of regional handicrafts, including knitwear, baskets, local foodstuffs, and carved wooden utensils and crafts, try the **Fería Rural y Artesanal,** between Prat and Dieiocho streets (no phone; open Mon–Sat 8am–9:30pm, Sun and holidays 8:30am–7:30pm). For mouthwatering smoked salmon and other local foodstuffs, stop on your way in or out of Chiloé at **Die Raucherkate,** a German-owned smokery located about 2km (1¼ miles) before the Chacao ferry dock (© 09-4445912). There is a SMOKED SALMON sign that can be easy to miss, so keep your eyes peeled.

WHERE TO STAY

Caulín Lodge *Finds* *Kids* *★★* The Caulín Lodge is not a woodsy hotel, but eight cabins fronting an isolated beach and backed by a forest called the Fundo Los Cisnes, a private ecological reserve. These combining factors make Caulín the best choice for visitors who seek quiet, undeveloped surroundings. The cabins at Caulín are more suitable for visitors with a private vehicle because the hamlet of Caulín is about 25km (16 miles) from Ancud, although taxi service is available for a moderate $10. All wooden cabins face a splendid estuary that's home to flamingos and black-necked swans; the cabins are rustic but comfortable and clean, and have kitchens. Cabins have two or three bedrooms, one with a full-size bed and the other(s) with a twin and a bunk bed. The spacious living area has wood floors and is warmed by a *cancahua,* a ceramic fireplace typical of the region. There is a wood-hewn, cozy pub/restaurant, although a few minutes' walk down the beach sits the popular Ostras Caulín (see "Where to Dine," below).

Road to Caulín, 9km (5½ miles) from port of Chacao. © 09/3301220. www.caulinlodge.cl. 8 cabins. $50–$100 cabin. AE, DC, MC, V. **Amenities:** Restaurant; outdoor pool; tennis court; sauna; horseback riding. *In room:* Kitchen, fireplace.

Hostal Lluhay This hostal is 1 block from the pier (300m/984 ft. from downtown), and it caters to a predominately international crowd. Rooms are slightly dark and very humble, but many bathrooms have been newly tiled. The open lounge has a fireplace and a picture window that looks out onto the sea, which should make you overlook an occasional hole in the burgundy carpet. The couple who own the Lluhay couldn't be nicer; they like to chat and show off their 200-year-old piano and antique Victrola.

Lord Cochrane 458, Ancud. ℂ/fax **65/622656.** www.hostal-lluhay.cl. 17 units. $20–$30 double. No credit cards. **Amenities:** Lounge. *In room:* TV, no phone.

Hostería Ahui This weatherbeaten, shingled, two-story hotel has midrange-quality rooms and views of the ocean, and is only 1 block from downtown. Rooms are sunny, and though the furnishings and bedding are of average quality, this is a good choice for travelers on a budget. A dining area and lounge are more spacious than similar spaces in other hotels around town, giving guests a bit more breathing room. The staff is open to negotiating a lower price, especially in low season, so it's worth bargaining once you get here.

Costanera 906, Ancud. ℂ/fax **65/622415.** 22 units. $24 double. Kids stay free in parent's room. No credit cards. **Amenities:** Lounge. *In room:* TV, no phone.

Hostería Ancud 🏨🏨 Part of the Panamericana Hoteles chain, the Hostería Ancud is as upscale as it gets in Ancud, and it is the logical choice for travelers who are not comfortable sleeping in a hostel or a funky little hotel. It fronts the Gulf of Quetalmahue and is next to the ruins of the old Fort San Antonio. All rooms come with a partial view of the ocean, as does the airy, split-level lounge and restaurant and the large outdoor deck. Rooms are tight but offer all the necessary comforts. The interior bedroom walls are made of polished alerce logs, and the lobby is adorned with woodcarvings from the region. The *hostería* also has one of the better restaurants in town (see "Where to Dine," below), as well as a cozy bar with a giant fireplace.

San Antonio 30, Ancud. ℂ **65/622340.** Fax 65/622350. www.hosteriancud.com. 24 units. $42–$74 double ($100 high season). AE, DC, MC, V. **Amenities:** Restaurant; bar; lounge. *In room:* TV.

"See Food" Everywhere: What to Eat on Chiloé

Part of the experience in Chiloé is sampling the local specialties of fish and shellfish dishes the Chilotes have invented over time. You'll commonly see dried and smoked mussels hanging in markets, but I haven't had the courage to try them yet. Another common sight (though common throughout Chile) is the *cochayuyu,* dried seaweed tied in bundles that Chileans use for stew. Chile's plentiful salmon farms are across the sound in the Andean fjords, and Chiloé has several oyster farms along its coast, so you'll see both items frequently on the menu.

Cancato Salmon stuffed with sausage, tomatoes, and cheese and steamed in tinfoil.

Carapacho A rich crab "casserole" with a breaded crust.

Curanto Perhaps the most famous dish here in Chiloé, traditionally prepared in a hole in the ground (similar to a New England clambake). First, hot rocks are placed in the hole and then layered with mussels, clams, beef, pork, chicken, sausage, and potatoes, and topped off with tasteless, chewy pancakes called *milcaos.* Of course, most restaurants cook this dish in a pot and often call it *pulmay;* it is then served with a cup of broth. You are supposed to take a bite and then sip the broth; I recommend you just pour the broth over the meat and fish for a tastier meal.

Hotel Galeón Azul ⭑   Like the Hostería Ancud, this hotel's strength is its location—perched high on a cliff above the sea—and although the rooms are not nearly as nice, some travelers prefer the character of this bed-and-breakfast to that of the Ancud. With porthole windows, a nautical motif, and curved walls, the big, sunflower-yellow hotel feels somewhat like a ship—an aging ship, that is. Upstairs an intriguing, narrow hallway has a high ceiling that peaks into skylights. The hotel is next to the regional museum; large windows look out onto the museum's sculpture garden. The rooms have recently been recarpeted and bathrooms fitted with new showers; however, rooms are still drab and lifeless. The most attractive part of the hotel is its sunny restaurant, with glass walls that look out onto the ocean.

Av. Libertad 751, Ancud. ℭ 65/622543. Fax 65/622567. www.hotelgaleonazul.cl. 16 units. $49–$70 double. No credit cards. **Amenities:** Restaurant. *In room:* TV, no phone (some).

WHERE TO DINE

For good, inexpensive seafood meals, including Chilote dishes such as *curanto, carapacho,* and *cancato,* try **La Pincoya,** Av. Prat 61 (ℭ **65/622613**), which also offers views of fishermen at the pier engaging in hectic business from their colorful fishing skiffs. One restaurant popular with tourists and locals alike is **Sacho** (ℭ **65/622260**), which can be found inside the somewhat grungy market (Local 7). Across from the market is **El Cangrejo,** Dieciocho 155 (ℭ **65/623091**), which serves dishes such as crab *carapacho* in a kitschy ambience. Reservations at these establishments are neither necessary nor accepted.

Galeón Azul ⭑ CHILEAN   The Galeón's yellow-painted dining area has sweeping ocean views, so be sure to get a table that sits up against the front windows. The menu here features several Chilote specials such as *curanto,* as well as the standard Chilean fish and meat grilled and served with a choice of sauces. Try the salmon stuffed with ham and mushrooms or the garlicky *locos* (abalone).

Av. Libertad 751. ℭ 65/622543. Main courses $5–$9. No credit cards. Daily 11am–3pm and 7–11pm.

Hostería Ancud ⭑⭑ INTERNATIONAL/CHILEAN   The expansive dining area here commands a superb view of the ocean, and there are good offerings from the menu that mix Chilean specialties with international dishes. Seafood such as oysters on the half-shell and king crab are offered as appetizers, as well as king crab casserole and conger eel with sea urchin sauce for entrees. Meat dishes include pork loin with mustard sauce and risotto. There's also a bar for a quiet evening drink. If weather permits, you can watch the sunset from the deck.

San Antonio 30. ℭ 65/622340. Main courses $5–$10. AE, DC, MC, V. Daily noon–11pm.

Kurantón ⭑ CHILEAN   As the name implies, this restaurant specializes in *curanto.* Other standards include *paila marina* (a fish stew), but what really stands out is their luscious, creamy *carapacho* that is speckled with crabmeat. The walls of Kurantón are covered with old photos, making for an amusing place to split a bottle of wine and sample local specialties.

Prat 94. ℭ 65/623090. Main courses $5–$10. V, MC. Daily noon–10pm.

La Candela ⭑ CHILEAN   This recently opened restaurant is a gringo favorite and a good place to stop in for a drink—just don't expect it to be quick because service can be painfully slow. The mood is mellow and the music low enough to allow for good conversation. Tuck into one of two reading nooks and flip through one of their English-language magazines and order a Beso de Abeja, a cocktail with rum, cream, and a kiss of honey. Tapas and more substantial plates are also available, including many vegetarian items.

Libertad 599. © **65/629995**. Main courses $5–$9. No credit cards. Mon–Sat 10am–4pm and 6pm–midnight for food service, all day for drinks (hours for food service are often erratic).

Ostras Caulín ⭐ *Finds* CHILEAN/OYSTERS   Oyster lovers won't want to miss this tiny restaurant on the shore of Caulín, about 9km (5½ miles) from Chacao and 25km (16 miles) from Ancud (from the ferry, follow the signs and turn right onto a gravel road). The restaurant, with its hardwood floors and cheery red tablecloths, sits on an estuary where they farm their own oysters, and they offer three sizes: *especial, extra,* and *exportación,* all on the half-shell and all exceptionally fresh. The menu is really just oysters served fried, stewed, and cocktailed, but there is salmon and beef stew, too. Afternoon tea is served with cakes and sandwiches daily from 3 to 7pm. The restaurant caters almost exclusively to visiting foreigners, so don't expect to mingle with locals here.

On the shore in Caulín. ©/fax **09/643-7005**. www.ostrascaulin.cl. Main courses $5–$9. AE, DC, MC, V. Daily 8am–10pm (until midnight Jan–Feb).

Pastelería Pedersen ⭐ *Finds* CAFE/PASTRIES   This is the place to blow your diet. There are plenty of cakes and numerous tarts to choose from, but it's the raspberry-topped cheesecake, a perennial favorite, that often sells out. They serve a rare cup of decent Joe, too. The pastry house is located in an old home with plenty of windows to watch a storm come in over the sea.

Cochrane 470. © **65/622642**. Slice of cake $1.50. No credit cards. Daily noon–7pm.

2 Castro

146km (91 miles) south of Ancud; 99km (61 miles) north of Quellón

Castro is spread across a promontory on the eastern shore of Chiloé, midway between Ancud and Quellón. It is the capital of Chiloé, and Chile's third-oldest city, with about 29,000 inhabitants. Visitors to the island often choose Castro as a base for its central proximity to many attractions. Not the most architecturally charming of all towns, Castro's shores are nonetheless interesting for their rickety homes on stilts, known as *palafitos,* and the main church painted as colorfully as an Easter egg.

ESSENTIALS
GETTING AROUND   By Bus   You'll find the bus terminal at the corner of Esmeralda and Sotomayor. For buses to Dalcahue and Isla Quinchao, take **Buses Arriagada,** San Martín 681; for Dalcahue and Chonchi, take **Colectivos** from the Terminal Municipal; for Isla Lemuy, take **Buses Gallardo** from its office at San Martín 681; and for transportation to the national park, take **Buses Arroyo** or **Buses Ojeda** from the Terminal Municipal. The majority of these bus companies are independently owned and operated, so it's difficult to obtain reliable information about schedules and fares in advance. We recommend showing up at the terminal or checking at the tourist information kiosk (see "Visitor Information," below) to ask questions or book a tour.

By Car   To get to Castro from Ancud, head south on the island's only highway for 146km (91 miles), and from Quellón, north on the highway for 99km (61 miles).

VISITOR INFORMATION   A tiny privately run **tourism kiosk** on the main plaza offers a fairly poor selection of information. During the summer, the kiosk is open all day, but during the winter it can close unexpectedly. A better source for information is Sernatur in Ancud.

SPECIAL EVENTS A weeklong gastronomic celebration takes place the third week in February, known as the **Festival Costumbrista Chilote.** If you like to eat, this enormous feast could very well be the highlight of your trip to Chiloé. The festival centers on traditional food and Chilote culture and mythological folklore, with men roasting meat over open fires and *curanto* simmering in grand cauldrons. Come hungry. For more information, call © **65/633760.**

FAST FACTS: CASTRO

Currency Exchange **Julio Barrientos,** Chacabuco 286 (© 65/635079), is open Monday through Friday from 9am to 1pm and 3 to 7pm, Saturday from 9am to 1pm; from December to March, they do not close for lunch. There are several ATMs in the downtown area.

Hospital Castro's hospital is **Augusta Rifat,** located at Freire 852 (© **65/ 632444**).

Internet Access **Hostería Castro** (see "Where to Stay" below) offers Internet access for its guests free of charge. If you're not staying there, try **Café de la Brújula,** O'Higgins 308 (© 65/633229), open daily from 9am to 2am, or even better, the **Entel** office at Bernardo O'Higgins 480 (© **65/620271**), open daily from 10am to 6pm.

Laundry **Clean Center** is located at Balmaceda 230 (© 65/633132).

Travel Agency LanChile's representative is **Turismo Pehuén,** Blanco 299 (© 65/635254; www.turismopehuen.cl), open Monday through Friday from 9am to 1:30pm and 3 to 7pm, Saturday from 10am to 1pm, closed Sunday.

WHAT TO SEE & DO IN CASTRO

You might begin a tour of Castro at the plaza and the neo-Gothic **Iglesia de San Francisco** 🌟🌟 church, painted in lilac and peachy-pink for Pope John Paul II's visit in 1987. Impossible to miss, the 1912 national monument glows on a dreary, gray Chiloé day (which is pretty much three-quarters of the year).

From there, head down Esmeralda toward the waterfront and drop by the town's small **Museo Municipal de Castro** 🌟, half a block from the plaza (© 65/ 635967). It's open from January to February Monday through Saturday from 9:30am to 7pm, and Sunday from 10:30am to 1pm; from March to December Monday through Friday from 9:30am to 1pm and 3 to 6:30pm, Saturday from 9:30am to 1pm, and closed on Sunday. Admission is free, although a donation is encouraged. This earnest, small museum features displays of Chilote farming and household wooden implements that take visitors back in time to days when day-to-day living could be an arduous chore. There are also Indian artifacts such as arrowheads, bones, and *boleadoras;* scale models; as well as a dramatic photographic exhibit of the damage done to Castro after the 1960 earthquake and flood.

Castro's curious *palafitos,* ramshackle houses built near the shore but atop stilts over water, are a colorful attraction and a tourism favorite, in spite of the fact that locals consider palifitos a somewhat unsanitary mess. There are four main spots to view these architectural oddities. The first two sites are at the town entrance, the third site is on the coast at the end of San Martín, and the fourth is at the cove of the Castro Fjord, on the way out of town on Ruta 5.

A short taxi ride will take you to the **Parque Municipal,** home to the Costumbrista Festival in February and the **Museo de Arte Moderno (MAM;** © 65/ 635454). Admission is free, and it's open daily January and February from 10am to 6pm; November, December, and March from 11am to 2pm. It's closed April through October, but opening hours can randomly change. If the museum is closed, call to arrange a private viewing. If the weather is clear, visitors to the park are treated to stretching views of Castro and the Andes. MAM, housed in several renovated shingled barns, is one of the only contemporary art museums in the country, and it often hosts exhibitions by some of Chile's most prominent artists.

SHOPPING

The **Fería Artesanal,** on Lillo at the port, brings together dozens of artisans who offer a superb selection of hand-knitted woolen goods and handicrafts. Here you'll find the island's typical tightly woven ponchos; the raw wool used makes them water resistant. Vendors open their booths independently, and hours are roughly from 10am to 5pm April through November, and from 10am to 9pm December through March.

WHERE TO STAY

Hostal Kolping ⭐ *Value*   This hostal is a great value for the price, and really the best place to stay if you're looking for inexpensive lodging. The rooms are sunny and immaculately clean, and they come with beds with thick foam mattresses that are adequately comfortable. The rooms are all rather nondescript, but they are reasonably spacious and so are the bathrooms. A cheery dining area brightens a gloomy weather day.

Chacabuco 217, Castro. ℂ/fax 65/633273. kolpingcastro@surnet.cl. 11 units. $25–$40 double. No credit cards. **Amenities:** Lounge. *In room:* TV.

Hostería Castro ⭐   This *hostería* is about as upscale as hotels get in Castro. Built in 1970, the Hostería Castro is solidly comfortable and clean, offering all the standard amenities of a midrange hotel; however, the rooms are cramped, and in more than a few it is difficult to walk around the bed. Ask to see several rooms, if you can, because a few are larger. Probably the best feature of the hotel is its cast-iron fireplace in the bar for cozying up with a pisco sour, and the decent bar/disco downstairs. The hotel overlooks the ocean, but only the rooms on the eastern side (rooms ending in odd numbers) have views of the water; rooms on the western side have a leafy view of a stand of trees. The white-tiled bathrooms are ample. The A-frame, shingled roof has a lengthy skylight that brightens the interior hallways. Service is friendly, and the bar is popular with traveling Europeans, as is Las Araucarias restaurant (see "Where to Dine," below). There's also a computer with free Internet access for guests.

Chacabuco 202, Castro. ℂ 65/632301. Fax 65/635688. www.hosteriadecastro.cl. 29 units. $50–$65 double. AE, DC, MC, V. **Amenities:** Restaurant; bar; room service; laundry service. *In room:* TV.

Hotel Casita Española   All 14 rooms are exactly the same here, set up motel-like with two stories. The lobby faces the street, but the rooms are reached via a pretty walkway sandwiched between a tall residential building and the hotel. You won't be wowed when you walk into your room, but the quality is about par for the price: thick foam mattresses, drab but decent decor, a tiny desk used primarily as a TV stand, and okay bathrooms with tubs (many bathrooms in town come with showers only). There's an eating area next to the reception area for breakfast.

Los Carrera 359, Castro. ℂ/fax 65/635186. www.hosteriadecastro.cl (click on "Bed & Breakfast"). 14 units. $34–$40 double. AE, MC, V. **Amenities:** Lounge. *In room:* TV.

Unicornio Azul *Overrated*   Many people say this is the best place to stay in Castro—but we'll let you be the judge. It's a fun place to stay, but don't expect regal comfort. Certainly, the hotel has character; it's housed in a pretty Victorian on the waterfront, with funky interiors decorated with framed prints of unicorns. But the quality the Unicornio Azul seems to promise from the lobby falls short once you step into the rooms. The best rooms sit high above the main building facing out toward the water, and they come with tiny balconies and wooden floors. But they're unremarkable, and you have to hike up a long flight of stairs to get to them. Downstairs rooms are darker but newly carpeted, and a few come with bathtubs, unlike the rooms upstairs, which have showers only. The exterior is painted as pink as a Mary Kay Cadillac, and many of the wooden beams and floor-runner carpets are sugary shades of pink, too. The owners of this hotel also own Ancud's Hotel Galeón Azul (p. 384).

Pedro Montt 228, Castro. ✆ **65/632359.** Fax 65/632808. www.hotelunicornioazul.cl. 18 units. $58–$85 double. No credit cards. **Amenities:** Restaurant; bar. *In room:* TV, no phone (some).

WHERE TO DINE

Años Luz Chiloé ✦ *Value* INTERNATIONAL/PUB   Right on the main plaza, this is the newest and most happening place in Castro. The attractive main dining area, with its hardwood floors, has windows looking out onto bustling San Martín Street, where locals sip coffee, pisco sours, and beer. A simple but delicious selection of salads, sandwiches, and a few meat dishes are served. The smoked salmon salad is yummy, with lots of fresh green lettuce and locally smoked salmon, and the steak and fries is the top choice for a main course. The back area has more of a pub feel, with tables closer together and local Castro "yuppies" drinking pint-size beers. The unusual bar area is carved out from a real wooden boat.

San Martín 309. ✆ **65/532-700.** Main courses $4–$8. MC, V. Daily 9:30am–midnight (Sat–Sun until 2–3am).

Café La Brújula del Cuerpo CAFE   This sizeable cafe on the plaza (the name translates as "the Body's Compass") is the social center for residents of Castro. It's perennially active thanks to its friendly service and extensive menu offering sandwiches, salads, main dishes, ice cream, desserts, espresso, and delicious fresh juices. The cafe/restaurant is open all day, and you'll often find travelers writing out postcards here. There's also one computer for Internet use.

O'Higgins 308. ✆ **65/633229.** Main courses $4–$7; sandwiches $2–$4. MC, V. Daily 9am–2am.

Las Araucarias ✦ INTERNATIONAL/CHILEAN   Las Araucarias is Hostería Castro's restaurant, and it is one of the top places to dine in town. The atmosphere is better during lunchtime, with the view and the airy interiors brought on by the two-story-high ceilings and a wall of windows; at night the dining room's airiness seems to encourage echoes, but it is comfortable nevertheless. The menu is steak and seafood, featuring Chilean classics and Chiloé specialties such as *carapacho* and *curanto*. There's also a wide selection of meat dishes, such as filet mignon wrapped in bacon and served with sautéed vegetables. You might want to call ahead; the hotel often has a buffet special that is usually themed (German food, for example), and although it is quite good, it might not be what you're in the mood for.

Chacabuco 202. ✆ **65/632301.** Fax 65/635688. Main courses $5–$9. AE, DC, MC, V. Mon–Sat noon–midnight; closed Sun.

Octavio ✦✦ CHILEAN   Octavio has the best atmosphere in Castro, with a wood-shingled, airy dining area that sits directly over the water, and a panorama of windows showcasing the view. Octavio specializes in Chilote specials—it's known around town for its *curanto*. It also serves seafood specials such as *mariscal*, a shellfish stew made with onion and cilantro, and other typical Chilean dishes, such as breaded cutlets and filet mignon. Fish is delivered daily. This place has a simple menu and simple food, but it is all very good, including a few sandwiches and soups if you don't want to have a full meal. Octavio is typically more popular with visitors to Castro, while Sacho (see below) is more popular with locals, most likely because it is cheaper.

Pedro Montt 261. ℂ 65/632855. Main courses $6–$9. No credit cards. Daily 10am–midnight.

Sacho ⋇ *Value* SEAFOOD/CHILEAN   It's doesn't have the most eye-catching ambience, but Sacho serves some of the best cuisine in Castro, a fact clearly evident by the throngs of locals who patronize the restaurant daily. The upstairs dining room has large windows and a view of the water. The specialty here is seafood, and they serve the most inexpensive abalone *locos* I've seen anywhere in Chile. Try starting off with a plate of clams Sacho raw, steamed, or broiled and served with onion, lemon, whiskey, and Parmesan; then follow it up with a *cancato*. Typically the only fish served here is *congrio* (conger eel) and salmon, but they do have hake and sea bass from December to March.

Thompson 213. ℂ 65/632079. Main courses $5–$7. No credit cards. Mar–Dec daily noon–4pm and 8pm–midnight; Jan–Feb daily noon–midnight

3 Excursions Outside Castro

Few Chilean towns surpass the entrancing beauty of **Dalcahue, Achao,** and **Curaco de Vélez,** the latter two located on the **Isla Quinchao.** The towns and the countryside separating them are Chiloé highlights, offering lush scenery and a glimpse into the Chilote's culture and day-to-day life.

Just off of Ruta 5, the island's only major highway, **Dalcahue** is a little town whose prosperity is best illustrated by the hustle and bustle of salmon industry workers at the pier, unloading and loading crates of fish byproducts to be processed. Dalcahue's other thriving industry (although to a smaller scale) is its **Feria Artesanal** ⋇⋇, located at the waterfront about 2 blocks southwest of the plaza. Every Thursday and Sunday, artisans drive or paddle in to Dalcahue from the surrounding area to hawk their knitwear, baskets, hand-carved wood items, clothing, and more. At the plaza sits one of the larger Chiloé churches, with scalloped porticos. Across the plaza, on the corner, you'll find the tiny **Museo Histórico Etnográfico** ⋇, Pedro Montt 105 (ℂ 65/641214); it's open daily from 10am to 6pm, with a cluttered array of stuffed birds and Indian and colonial-era artifacts. For directions to Dalcahue, see "Essentials" under Castro, above. All transportation stops in Dalcahue first before crossing over to Quinchao.

Several blocks away at Dalcahue's pier is the ferry to **Isla Quinchao.** The ferry makes the 5-minute ride almost continuously from 7am to 10:30pm every day ($8 for cars round-trip). This is one of Chiloé's most populated islands, a magical landscape of plump, rolling hills, where smoke slowly wafts from clapboard homes and Chilote farmers can be seen tilling their land with oxen and a plow. The island also affords the visitor with spectacular views of the Gulf of Ancud and the scattered, pint-size islands that sit between the Isla Quinchao and the mainland.

The first town you'll encounter upon exiting the ferry is **Curaco de Vélez,** a historic village whose former prosperity brought about by wool production and whaling can be witnessed through the grand, weatherbeaten homes that line the streets. If you are hungry and are feeling adventuresome, follow the yellow

OSTRAS street signs to an open-air restaurant across the street from the water. Here you can slurp three different kinds of oysters, shucked right in front of you, for a quarter of the price you would pay back home.

Continue southeast along the island's single, unnamed main road to **Achao,** a former Jesuit colony founded in 1743 and home to the oldest church in Chiloé. Made entirely of cypress, alerce, and mañío, this church is as plain as a brown paper bag from the outside, but one step inside and all impressions change due to its multicolored interiors and whimsical decorations. Take a walk along the water-front for people- watching, and bring your camera for the photo op along the shore, where red, yellow, and sky-blue fishing boats bob and dance in the bay. Throughout the Island of Quinchao, you'll find wooden gazebos atop well-designed lookout points along the road. Here's hoping the weather allows you to take full advantage of them. The homes in Achao are characterized by the region's penchant for adapting shingles into a variety of geometrical patterns, from concave to convex, circular to triangular, all nailed tightly together to keep the rain out.

I recommend that you make the aforementioned destinations a priority, but if you still have enough time, try to make it to Conchi. Located about 32km (20 miles) south of Castro, on the main highway, this pleasant town is home to the best-preserved 18th-century buildings on the island. The early prosperity brought on by the timber export industry (mostly cypress) at that time is reflected in the handsome wooden houses and buildings around town. Made from fermented cow's milk, *Licor de Oro* is as much a cultural experience as it is an intoxicating elixir. Conchi has created a cottage industry out of this liqueur's production, and drinking it here is the norm. Made with fruits, herbs, or, in some cases, sugar and egg (think egg nog), the liqueur isn't as bad as you might think, and it makes for a fun activity on a rainy day. You'll find it at Conchi's *Fería,* located on the corner of Irarrázaval and Canessa streets.

PARQUE NACIONAL DE CHILOE

Chiloé National Park, on the western coast of Chiloé, covers 43,000 hectares (106,000 acres) and is divided into three sectors: **Chanquin, Middle,** and **North.** This park's strong suit is its **short hikes** that allow you to savor the best the park has to offer; in fact, the 19km (12-mile) backpacker's hike is disappointing. Lodging at the park is a super deal, too, with attractive cabins for about $40 a night. The Chanquin sector is connected by a dirt road that branches off Ruta 5, about 35km (22 miles) south of Castro; this is where you'll find the Conaf ranger station and a visitor center. This is the only truly suitable part of the park for visiting, due to its easy access and good trail conditions (unlike the North, or "Chepu," sector). The Middle section (also referred to as Metalqui) is a protected island with a large sea lion colony, but visitors are not allowed there.

For transportation to the national park, take **Buses Arroyo** or **Buses Ojeda** (no phone) from the Terminal Municipal. Buses depart once daily in low season and twice daily in high season, though schedules vary. The park is wild and wet—very, very wet, but it is one of the few places to see old-growth, thick rain-forest bordering the coast. Many backpackers come in the summer to hike through the park's forest and along vast stretches of sandy beach that often peak into sand dunes.

Visitors first arrive at the tiny village of **Cucao,** the gateway to the national park, which was devastated by a 1960 tidal wave; today it is a collection of rick-ety homes. This is where you'll find the four **Cabañas Conaf,** each for six guests,

and they have kitchenettes, so come prepared (© **65/532502;** pnchiloe@
conaf.cl). After the suspension bridge, visitors will find the park interpretation
center run by Conaf (Chile's national park service), which has environmental
displays and information about hiking trails. From here hikers have an option
of three trails. The short, though very informative (English-language signs are
here) 770m (2,926 ft.) **Sendero El Tepual** winds through thick, humid tepú
forest. The **Sendero Dunas de Cucao** is about 1.5km (a little less than 1 mile),
and it passes alternately through dense vegetation and open stretches of sand
dunes blanketed in golden grass.

Vast and desolate, this stretch of coastline is one of the most beautiful in
Chile. If you are lucky and arrive at low tide, a handful of locals might be here
digging *machas,* or razor clams, out of the sand, which they sell to buyers all the
way to Puerto Montt. There is a 20km (12-mile) backpacker's trek via a long
trail on the coast, which weaves in and out of evergreen forest and sandy beach
until arriving at Conaf's backcountry refuge, **Cole-Cole.** In truth, the hike is
overrated, but backpackers will enjoy camping out in this lovely environment.
From here it's another 2 hours to Conaf's other refuge, **Anay.** The refuges are in
bad condition, and it is recommended that you bring a tent. Parque Nacional
Chiloé has a variety of campsites, and it is open every day from 9am to 7:30pm;
admission is $1.50 adults, free for children. For park info, contact Hernán
Rivera (© **65/532502;** hrivera@conaf.cl).

SPORTS, GUIDED TOURS & OTHER ACTIVITIES

Turismo Pehuén, Blanco 299 in Castro (©/fax **65/635254;** www.turismo
pehuen.cl), is the most reliable, respected agency in Chiloé, offering a variety of
tours in the area that include hiking in the national park and guided visits to
Dalcahue and Achao; and, during the summer only, horseback riding, boat
tours, and overflight tours that give passengers an aerial view of the island. It's
really the most complete tour agency; however, **Queilén Bus,** Villa Llau Llau s/n
(© **65/632594;** fax 635600; queilenbus@surnet.cl), also offers guided tours
around the area.

The calm, fairy-tale bays and coves of Chiloé and the emerald Andean fjords
across the sound render this region the best region in Chile for **sea kayaking**
and **boating.** I strongly recommend that visitors interested in this sport consider
the following two excellent tour operators that offer trips for several days or
longer. These operators can customize trips according to your experience and
stamina; in many cases, you don't need kayak experience at all, just a willingness
to learn. Here are my picks:

Altué Expeditions is Chile's foremost tour operator for trekking, horseback
riding, and kayaking, and their kayak center on the shore of Dalcahue, one of the
prettiest areas of Chiloé, is the ideal base for practicing the sport. The center has
a Chiloé-style shingled and very attractive lodge for overnight stays, and they plan
longer journeys that include the Andean fjords and hot spring visits, using a
Chilote boat as a support vessel (camping at night). There's a hot tub at the lodge,
and they treat guests to a typical *curanto* meal while visiting. The superb crew is
not only knowledgeable, but friendly, too. Trips around Chiloé archipelago last 3
nights and 4 days; trips including the Andean fjords last 8 nights and 9 days. Call
or e-mail for pricing information, as group size is a factor in cost (© **2/233-2964**
in Santiago, or 65/641110 in Chiloé; www.seakayakchile.com).

For kayaking, and especially sailing and soft-adventure nature and cultural
tours, try the top-notch operation **Austral Adventures** (© **65/625977** or

09/642-8936; www.austral-adventures.com). The North American/Chilean outfit specializes in luxury excursions around Chiloé and the Andean fjords, with a round-trip Lake District–Chiloé–Pumalín–Lake District circuit, aboard their refitted Chilote boat *Cahuella*. They also pick up in Puerto Montt. Their guides are exceptional: three biologists and one anthropologist/ornithologist, plus gourmet food and wine for a maximum of seven guests. AA offers some day options for $28 per person from Ancud: coastal hike and penguin colony (minimum four guests), and sea kayaking the Ancud bay (minimum three guests) for those short on time. They also offer a 2-night/3-day kayak trip around Chiloé with lodging in rustic homes for $260 per person (minimum two guests).

17

The Carretera Austral

South of Puerto Montt, the population thins and the vegetation thickens. This is the region of northern Patagonia that is commonly called the "Carretera Austral," named for the dirt road that runs south to the city of Coyhaique and terminates farther south at Villa O'Higgins between 48 degrees and 49 degrees latitude. The Carretera Austral opened little more than a decade ago to the traveling public; it is a 1,240km (769-mile) dirt-and-gravel road that bends and twists through thick virgin rainforest, past glacial-fed rivers and aquamarine lakes; jagged, white-capped peaks that rise above open valleys; and precipitous cliffs with cascading ribbons of waterfalls at every turn. If you like your scenery remote and rugged, this is the place for you. The region doesn't offer a grand national park like Torres del Paine, but in many ways, a journey down this "highway" is *the* quintessential Chilean road trip, and many of its natural attractions are as stunning as any you'll find farther south. There are also some of the country's best fly-fishing lodges, one of the world's top rivers for rafting, a gorgeous hot springs hotel, and a sailing journey to one of Chile's most awe-inspiring glaciers. It is also home to fjords that are ideal for kayaking, and the rainforest jungle of Pumalín Park.

The Carretera Austral runs from **Puerto Montt** in the north to **Villa O'Higgins** in the south, and passes through two regions: the southern portion of the **Región de Los Lagos** and the **Región de Aysén,** whose capital city, **Coyhaique,** is home to almost half the population in the area. In the past, the entire region was accessible only from other locations by ferry or plane, and vehicles servicing the tiny villages and fishing hamlets that make up the area's civilization had to enter from Argentina. It's no wonder they call it the "last frontier."

The road exists thanks to ex-dictator Augusto Pinochet, who, concerned about a very real threat of war with Argentina in the 1970s, sought to fortify Chile's presence in this isolated region. Construction of the Carretera Austral began in 1976 but wasn't fully completed until 1999, at a staggering cost: more than $300 million (and counting) and the lives of more than two dozen men.

1 Driving the Carretera Austral ★★

Although it is possible to reach most destinations in this region by ferry, bus, or plane, road improvements and an expansion of services mean an increasing number of travelers are choosing to drive the Carretera Austral. It's not as enormous an undertaking as it sounds, but it can be costly, especially when you factor in the cost of ferry rides, drop-off fees (about $500), and gas.

Several agencies in Puerto Montt and Coyhaique offer one-way car rentals, and some allow you to cross into Argentina or leave the car as far away as Punta Arenas, Chile. (See "Essentials" under "Puerto Montt," in chapter 15.) Alternatively, you could rent a car in Coyhaique and drive north, stopping in Puyuhuapi and on to Futaleufú. Although you'd have to backtrack to Coyhaique to return the car, this is a less expensive option. (See "Coyhaique," later in this chapter, for information.)

The most troublesome considerations are flat tires, slippery roads, and foul weather, any of which can strike at any time.

ESSENTIALS

FERRY CROSSINGS   It is recommended that all travelers make a reservation for ferry service, as they tend to fill up, even during the low season. The trip from Puerto Montt to Chaitén requires a ferry crossing (in operation all year by Transmarchilay). See "Ferry Crossings to the Carretera Austral & Sailing to Patagonia Through the Fjords" in chapter 15, p. 375, for information on ferries to Chaitén.

GAS   Service stations can be found at reasonable intervals, and some smaller towns such as Futaleufú sell gas in jugs from stores or private residences, but some travelers feel safer carrying a backup canister of fuel. Canisters can be purchased from any service station.

CROSSING INTO ARGENTINA   Drivers who head into Argentina must prove that they are the owner of their car, or have their rental agency set up the proper paperwork, which must be completed by your agency 48 hours in advance, to show you are driving a rental car. There's also an extra insurance that usually has to be purchased, averaging around $150 per car. Drivers must fill out a detailed form and are then given a copy to carry with them until crossing back into Chile.

ROAD CONDITIONS   The Carretera Austral is made entirely of dirt and gravel, which can get slippery during a storm. A 4×4 vehicle isn't necessary but can help, especially if snow is in the forecast. Some rental agencies insist that you rent a truck with high clearance. Giant potholes are the exception, not the norm, but they can cause a car to spin out or even flip if driving too fast. For this reason, drivers are cautioned to keep their speed between 40kmph (25 mph) and 60kmph (37 mph). When it's wet or the road curves, you need to slow down even more.

HITCHHIKERS   Road courtesy dictates that you might have to pick up a hitchhiker or two along the way. Most hitchhikers are humble local folk who simply do not have the means to get from place to place (during the summer many foreign backpackers try to get a lift, too). Use your own judgment. You should always lend a hand to anyone whose car has broken down.

GETTING AROUND BY BUS

There is inexpensive, frequent summer service and intermittent winter service to and from destinations along the Carretera Austral for those who choose not to drive. It takes longer, and you won't have the opportunity to stop at points of interest along the way; however, every town has a tour operator that can usually get you to outlying sites for day trips. Also, the breathtaking scenery never fails to dazzle, even if you can't get off the bus.

For the 5-hour journey from Puerto Montt to Hornopirén (for the summer-only ferry to Caleta Gonzalo), take **Buses Fierro** (© **65/289024** or 65/253022), which leaves from the main bus terminal two times daily. The bus makes one 30-minute ferry crossing before landing in Hornopirén (cost is $3). From there you

The Carretera Austral

Santiago

Buenos Aires

Map Area

Lago Llanquihue

Lago Nahuel Huapi

Puerto Varas

San Carlos de Bariloche

Puerto Montt

Parque Nacional Alerce Andino

La Arena

Pargua

Chacao

Caleta Puelche

Hornopirén

El Bolsón

Ancud

Golfo de Ancud

PARQUE NACIONAL PUMALÍN

Castro

Caleta Gonzalo

ISLA GRANDE DE CHILOÉ

Esquel

Chaitén

Quellón

Lago Yelcho

Futaleufú

Villa Santa Lucía

Tecka

Palena

Lago Gral. Vintter

Lago Palena

José de San Martín

Puerto Púyuhuapi Lodge & Spa

Puerto Puyuhuapi

PARQUE NACIONAL QUEULAT

PARQUE NACIONAL ISLA MAGDALENA

La Tapera

Puerto Cisnes

Parque Nacional Isla Guamblin

Puerto Aisén

RESERVA NACIONAL LAS GUAITECAS

Puerto Chacabuco

Coyhaique

Lago Atravesado

Lago Elizalde

Balmaceda

Lago General Carrera

Lago Buenos Aires

Chile Chico

Perito Moreno

Laguna San Rafael

PARQUE NACIONAL LAGUNA SAN RAFAEL

Lago Cochrane

Golfo de Penas

Cochrane

Lago Pueyrredón

Puerto Yungay

- - - Ferry route

0   50 mi

0   50 km

Villa O'Higgins

PACIFIC OCEAN

CHILE

ARGENTINA

395

take another ferry to Caleta Gonzalo, where buses meet ferry arrivals for the journey to Chaitén. Buses from Chaitén leave for Futaleufú an average of five to six times per week during the summer, and about three times per week during the winter.

Buses from Chaitén to Coyhaique, stopping first in Puyuhuapi, leave up to four times per week year-round. For information about buses from Chaitén, see "Getting There" under "Chaitén," below. Note that bus schedules are subject to change without notice.

2 Parque Nacional Alerce Andino ★★

46km (29 miles) southeast of Puerto Montt

The Carretera Austral is also known as Ruta 7, and it begins just outside the city limits of Puerto Montt, following the coast of Reloncaví Sound until it reaches **Parque Nacional Alerce Andino,** one of Chile's little-known national parks. You won't find wild, extreme adventure here; instead, indulge in quiet walks or canoe rides through dense forest. This 39,255-hectare (96,960-acre) park is home to the *alerce,* which is often compared to the sequoia for its thick diameter and height. These venerable giants can live more than 3,000 years, making them the second-oldest tree, after the American bristlecone pine. The *alerce* was designated a national monument in 1976, and heavy fines are levied against anyone caught harming or cutting one down. Other species in the park include evergreen beech, *mañío, canelo, ulmo,* and thick crops of ferns. It can get pretty wet here year-round, so bring rain gear just in case.

The park itself is serviced by a rough dirt road that leads to a **Conaf guard station** in what's known as the **Chaica sector,** where there is a campground and the trail head for the half-hour round-trip walk to a waterfall and a fenced-off 3,000-year-old *alerce* tree. The walk to Laguna Chaiquenes is about 5.5km (3½ miles), and to Lago Triángulo about 10km (6¼ miles) from the campground. Roads, trails, and campgrounds are often washed out or impeded by falling trees. Be sure to check the park's condition before heading out. For more information, contact the Conaf office in Puerto Montt at Ochagavía 464 (© **65/486115;** www.conaf.cl).

The park's second sector, **Laguna Sargazo,** is at Lago Chapo, and it also has campgrounds and two muddy trails for day hikes through the park's rainforest, a section of which has a thick stand of alerce trees. Though this sector sees fewer visitors, it is more difficult to get to if you do not have your own vehicle because buses go only as far as the pueblo Correntoso, a 2-hour walk from the park entrance (although it is possible to arrange a tour; see "Getting There," below). At the park ranger station here, it is possible to rent canoes for a paddle across Lago Chapo.

GETTING THERE   If you're driving, head south on Ruta 7, winding past tiny villages on a gravel road until you reach Chaica, about 35km (22 miles) from Puerto Montt, where a sign indicates the road to the park entrance at the left. The park ranger station is open from 9am to 5pm, so leave your car outside the gate if you plan to return later than 5pm. Travelers without a vehicle can take **Buses Fierro** (© **65/289024** or 65/253022) headed in the direction of Hornopirén from the main terminal in Puerto Montt (ask to be dropped off at Chaica); however, the bus (three daily services), which costs $1.30, leaves visitors at an entrance road 4km (2½ miles) from the park ranger station. You might consider hiring a tour operator to take a day trip or possibly to organize an advance pickup date if you plan to camp. To get to the Lago Chapo sector, head south on Ruta 7 for about 9km (5½ miles) to Chamiza; just before the bridge, take a left toward the town Correntoso and drive 19km (12 miles) to the park entrance. **Buses Fierro** (© 65/289024 or 65/253022) has two daily trips, costing $1.50, to Correntoso that leave from the main terminal in Puerto Montt; from here, it's a 2-hour walk to the park entrance. For tours to either of the park's sectors, try **Andina del Sud,** in Puerto Varas at Del Salvador 72 (© 65/232811; www.andinadelsud.com); the company's main office is in Puerto Montt at Antonio Varas 437 (© 65/257797).

WHERE TO STAY

Alerce Mountain Lodge 🏔🏔 (Finds) This quiet, remote lodge sits on the shore of a small lake—which must be crossed by a hand-drawn ferry—at the edge of the national park and is surrounded by dense stands of stately 1,000-year-old *alerce* trees. This is where you go to get away from crowds.

The lodge is about an hour and 45 minute's drive from Puerto Montt (they provide free transportation from there) and is built almost entirely of handcrafted *alerce* logs, with giant trunks acting as pillars in the spacious, two-story lobby. The woodsy effect continues in the cozy rooms, which are decorated with local crafts and feature forest views. The cabins have a view of the lake and come with a living room and two bedrooms, and accommodate a maximum of six guests. One of the highlights at this lodge is that the surrounding trails are not open to the general public, so you'll have them to yourself. Bilingual guides lead horseback rides and day hikes that can last as long as 7 hours or as little as a half-hour.

Carretera Austral, Km 36. ©/fax 65/286969. www.mountainlodge.cl. 11 units, 3 *cabañas*. All-inclusive packages run per person, double occupancy: 2 nights/3 days $460; 3 nights/4 days $680. Inquire about other packages and off-season discounts. AE, DC, MC, V. **Amenities:** Restaurant; bar; Jacuzzi; sauna; game room.

3 Pumalín Park 🏔🏔

The Pumalín Park Project, the world's largest private nature reserve, spans roughly 295,000 hectares (728,650 acres) and incorporates temperate rainforest, glaciers, fjords, thundering waterfalls and rivers, and stands of ancient *alerce* trees. It's a marvelous place that exists thanks to American millionaire and philanthropist Douglas Tompkins, who bought his first chunk of land here in 1991.

Although any nature-lover would be led to believe Tompkins did Chileans and the world a favor by spending his money on this ecological cause, the move did not sit well with the Chilean government, which was uneasy with the foreign ownership of so much land, especially because it stretched from the Pacific Ocean to the Argentine border. But the absurdity of the criticism brought forth by the government (which led a kind of smear campaign against Tompkins) and the roadblocks they threw in Tompkins's way were really just a thinly veiled desire to develop the land and sell portions of it to corporations intent on destroying one of Chile's few remaining old-growth forests.

Years have passed, the public and the government have slowly grown to accept the project, and today Pumalín boasts a growing number of visitors. Tompkins plans to eventually donate this park to the Fundación Pumalín (known as the Conservation Land Trust) and run it as a national park under a private initiative. The facilities here are superb, really the best you'll find in any park or reserve in Chile, with elegantly designed cabins, well-groomed campgrounds, and a cafe selling tasty meals.

The park is divided into a north and south section; the first is accessible via Hornopirén (which can be reached by vehicle or bus), but from here there is no infrastructure and access to the region's trademark fjords and the Cahuelmó hot springs is by rented boat or tour only (see "Organized Tours," below). The southern section is where travelers will find **Caleta Gonzalo** and the **main information center,** with lodging, campsites, park information, and a store selling locally produced crafts. Caleta Gonzalo is reached by ferry from Hornopirén in January and February, and by Chaitén year-round. This is where visitors can explore a rainforest bursting with life via one of the several trails in the area.

Pumalín makes for an excellent introduction to the Carretera Austral; however, outside of the summer months, torrential downpours can go on for days, even in the middle of summer. Most visitors spend only a day or 2 here, unless they are part of an organized boat/kayak tour.

PARK INFORMATION

For advance information about Pumalín Park, call their U.S. office at (© **415/ 229-9339;** pumalin@earthlink.net; www.parquepumalin.cl). Travelers coming from the north should stop at Pumalín's office in Puerto Montt at Buin 356 (© **65/250079**); those coming from the south should stop at the park's office in Chaitén at O'Higgins 62 (© **65/731341**).

GETTING HERE

Hornopirén can be reached by private vehicle; take Ruta 7 south from Puerto Montt for 45km (28 miles) until reaching La Arena, from which there is a 30-minute-long ferry that leaves nine times per day, year-round, to Puelches. From here it is 55km (34 miles) to Hornopirén. Bus service to Hornopirén is offered from the Puerto Montt bus station by **Buses Fierro** (© **65/253022**), leaving three times per day (twice on Sun).

To get to Caleta Gonzalo and the southern section of the park, travelers can come from Chaitén in the south (see "Chaitén," below), or by a 6-hour ferry ride from Hornopirén. During January and February, the ferry leaves daily at 4pm from Hornopirén and 9am from Caleta Gonzalo; it takes 5 hours and costs $13 per person, plus $80 for a private vehicle. Outside of January and February, visitors will need to go first to Chaitén to visit Pumalín. Reservations are necessary for vehicles; contact Transmarchilay at Av. Angelmo 2187 (© **65/270430;** www.transmarchilay.cl).

WHAT TO SEE & DO

The kayak and boat trip I took in the northern Pumalín region several years ago is one of my most memorable journeys ever taken in Chile. With so few people here, it feels as if you've discovered a magic kingdom that you have all to yourself. The fjords that plunge into the sea rival Norway's and are simply magnificent, and the remote, natural hot springs make for a divine way to end the day, especially if you've been kayaking. Of course, it rains profusely at times, and that can test your patience, especially when setting up camp. If you cannot stand the mud and watching your fingers turn to prunes, consider a boat trip with interior sleeping arrangements.

HIKING At Caleta Gonzalo, trails include the 3-hour round-trip **Sendero Cascada,** which meanders along a footpath and elevated walkways through dense vegetation before terminating at a crashing waterfall. The **Sendero Tronador,** 12km (7½ miles) south of Caleta Gonzalo, takes visitors across a suspension bridge and up, up, up a steep path and wooden stepladder to a lookout point, with views of Volcán Michimahuida, then down to a lake with a campground, taking, round-trip, about 3½ hours. The **Sendero Los Alerces** is an easy 40-minute walk through old stands of *alerce.*

OTHER ACTIVITIES Pumalín offers **horse pack trips** and trips to the remote **Cahuelmó Hot Springs,** all with advance reservation only. You can also tour an **organic farm** or sign up for **boat trips** around the fjord and to the sea lion rookery; there are also flights over the park. For more information and reservations, contact the official outdoor operator for the park, **Alsur Expeditions** (see below).

ORGANIZED TOURS The northern section's hot springs and renowned fjords are accessible only by boat tour. Tours can include kayaking, overnight camping or ship-based lodging, and hiking. The park's "official" tour operator is **Alsur Expeditions,** in Puerto Varas at Del Salvador 100 (ℂ/fax **65/232300;** www.alsurexpeditions.com), which has horseback-riding and trekking tours, specializing in sailing, aboard their small yacht (Puerto Montt–Chiloé–Pumalín) or kayaking, using a Chiloé-style support boat. However, the best sea kayaking is with **Altue Sea Kayaking,** based out of Santiago at Encomenderos 83, Las Condes (ℂ **2/232-1103;** www.seakayakchile.com), with outstanding kayak trips around Pumalín, which they normally combine with a kayak tour of Chiloé (where they own a coastal lodge). Altue also has a motorized support vehicle. **Austral Adventures,** Lord Cochrane 432, Ancud (ℂ **65/625977;** www. austral-adventures.com), an American-owned operation based out of Chiloé, specializes in sailing, bird-watching, and fly-fishing journeys from Puerto Montt to Pumalín, including Chiloé, aboard their newer Chiloé-style boat. Lastly, the company **Yak Expeditions** is concentrated solely on kayaking and getting from one place to another by kayak and without a support boat. It is a quieter, more activity-oriented journey, with camping as lodging where there are no lodges (ℂ **2/227-0427** or 09/299-6487; www.yakexpediciones.cl).

WHERE TO STAY & DINE

Cabañas Caleta Gonzalo ✦✦✦ These stylishly designed yet rustic cabins are built for two to six guests and feature details like nubby bedspreads, gingham curtains, and carved wood cabinets. Only one comes with a kitchen, the "family" cabin at Reñihué, a more remote cabin with fishing access that goes for $100 for five. The cabins are small but very cozy, with a double bed and twin on the bottom floor and two twins above in a loft; all are bright.

The sites at **Camping Pumalín,** on the beautiful Fiordo Reñihué, are well-kept rooms with a fire pit (firewood costs extra), a sheltered area for cooking, bathrooms with cold-water showers, and an area for washing clothing; the cost is $2.50 per person. About 14km (8¾ miles) south of Caleta Gonzalo is the **Cascadas Escondidas Campground,** with sheltered tent platforms, picnic tables, cold-water showers, bathrooms, and the trail head to three waterfalls. The cost to camp here is $10 per tent. There are more than 20 campsites throughout the park, many of them accessible by boat or by backpacking trail; consult the park for more information.

Caleta Gonzalo s/n. ℂ **65/250079,** or 415/229-9339 in the U.S. reservasalsur@surnet.cl (reservations). 6 units. $91 double; $10 each additional guest. AE, DC, MC, V. **Amenities:** Restaurant.

4 Chaitén

420km (260 miles) north of Coyhaique

Chaitén is a sleepy hamlet that serves as a jumping-off point for exploring Pumalín, Futaleufú, and the Carretera Austral. There's not much to see or do here, but it is a solid service center and it is the only way of reaching Pumalín Park during the low season. Visitors who choose to drive the Carretera Austral from north to south will also need to begin here during the low season. The town's main attraction is the view of **Volcán Michimahuida** in the distance, although perennial wet weather often impedes visibility of anything except the puddled, potholed streets.

GETTING THERE

BY BOAT **Transmarchilay,** at Corcovado 266 in Chaitén (✆ **65/731272**) and Angelmó 2187 in Puerto Montt (✆ **65270430;** www.transmarchilay.cl), has four weekly trips from Puerto Montt (10 hr.) and three weekly trips from Castro, Chiloé (7 hr.); the cost is about $25 one-way.

BY AIR Travelers who can afford it and who are without a vehicle are better off flying from Puerto Montt to Chaitén (if weather permits) for the short, 35-minute journey and the sweeping views. Try **Aerotaxis del Sur,** Carrera Pinto and Almirante Riveros (✆ **65/731315;** www.aerotaxisdelsur.cl), with one daily flight; or try **Aeropuelche** at Corcovado 218 in Chaitén (✆/fax **65/731800**), or in Puerto Montt at Baquedano 199 (✆ **65/435827**). The cost is around $60 per person one-way.

BY BUS Bus schedules in this region are always subject to change, and both **Chaitur,** Diego Portales 350 (✆/fax **65/731429;** nchaitur@hotmail.com), and **B&V Tours,** Libertad 432 (✆ **65/731390**), have information about service to destinations such as Caleta Gonzalo, Futaleufú, Puyuhuapi, and Coyhaique. Buses to all destinations leave daily from December to March; from April to November, buses to Futaleufú leave six times weekly, as do buses to Caleta Gonzalo, and four times weekly to Coyhaique, with a stop at Puyuhuapi.

VISITOR INFORMATION & TOUR OPERATORS

Sernatur has an office at Av. Bernardo O'Higgins 254 (✆ **65/731082;** www.sernatur.cl), open Monday to Thursday 8:30am to 5:30pm and Friday 8:30am to 4:30pm. There is a municipal visitor information kiosk on the Costanera during the summer. Another good source of information is the **Pumalín Park office** in Chaitén at O'Higgins 62 (✆ **65/731341**). For tours, **Chaitur,** Diego Portales 350 (✆ **65/731429;** nchaitur@hotmail.com), is the only serious agency in town, and they offer trips to Yelcho Glacier and Pumalín Park, horseback riding, rock climbing, kayaking, and even mountain biking to destinations as far away as Coyhaique.

WHERE TO STAY

Hostal Puma Verde ★★★ 𝑉𝑎𝑙𝑢𝑒 Owned and operated by the Pumalín Park Project, this stylish, wood-shingled hostal is the best lodging option here in Chaitén, and its "apartment" is a steal for groups of four or five guests. The Pumalín office, information center, and gift shop are here as well. Guest rooms are small, but they are fitted with contemporary decorations and linens in cream and forest green, and are exceptionally cozy. There is a gourmet kitchen made of wood and brass, a dining area where guests can take meals, a lounge with soft couches and a fireplace, a good place to curl up on a cold, wet day. The complex has one double, two triples (that are shared with strangers if not filled by one group), and an apartment for a maximum of five, with kitchen facilities (a steal at $86).

O'Higgins 54, Chaitén. ✆/fax **65/731184.** www.parquepumalin.cl. 4 units. $50 double. Rates include breakfast (except apt). AE, DC, MC, V. **Amenities:** Lounge; room service; laundry.

Hostería Los Coihues (★ (Value   This is one of the nicer hotels in Chaitén, and it's downright cheap. The unassuming log-cabin building sits several blocks back from the waterfront and has a comfortable dining area/lounge with windows facing Volcán Corcovado. The rooms have wood floors, not carpet or rugs, but the heat is kept at a level that keeps the interiors toasty, and the bathrooms are sparkling clean. Doubles have a full-size bed or two twins, and triples have a twin and a bunk bed. Daily excursions are available for an additional cost. Packages include transportation from and to the Chaitén airport, so ask for other arrangements if you plan to arrive by ferry or catamaran.

Pedro Aguirre Cerda 398, Chaitén. ℰ/fax 65/731461. www.tierranativa.cl/hosteria/host.htm. 16 units. $50 double with breakfast. AE, DC, MC, V. **Amenities:** Restaurant; lounge; tour desk.

Hotel Mi Casa (★ (Kids   The Hotel Mi Casa is a traditional hotel perched on a hill just above town, offering a direct view of Volcán Corcovado, the colorful rooftops below, and the nightly sunset taken in from a winding deck. The plain guest rooms are nothing to go wild about, but the friendly service, decent restaurant, and extra amenities give it a slight edge above several of its competitors. Two rooms have a double bed and an extra twin for parents traveling with a child. Although many have thin carpet, the rooms are large enough and kept toasty warm. A winding path out back leads to a gym with weights, a Ping-Pong table, a sauna, and massage cabin. One sitting area in the hotel has a TV. A fun extra is the hotel's *quincho,* where they often host lamb, beef, and pork barbecues grilled the Chilean way, on a spit over a roaring fire. Internet access is available for guests for a small fee. The hotel arranges transfers from the airport, fly-fishing and hunting expeditions, and tours to Palena, Futaleufú, Puyuhuapi, and Pumalín.

Av. Norte 206, Chaitén. ℰ/fax 65/731285. www.hotelmicasa.cl. 18 units. $20–$45 double. Rates include full breakfast. No credit cards. **Amenities:** Restaurant; bar; gym; exercise room; sauna; massage. *In room:* No phone.

Hotel Schilling   The Hotel Schilling has a bright, cheery lobby and a waterfront location, but the rooms are dowdy and not a great value. Nevertheless, it's still one of the better hotels in Chaitén, and it's possible to negotiate the price, especially in the off season or for multiple-day stays. The decor consists of colorful velveteen bedspreads and frilly lamps, and rooms can be cold, as they are heated only by a wood-burning stove in the hall; a few come with a TV. There's a nice dining area and bar on the bottom level, but if you can afford it, try another hotel first.

Av. Corcovado 230, Chaitén. ℰ/fax 65/731295. constsch@telsur.cl. $25–$35 per person. No credit cards. **Amenities:** Restaurant; bar; lounge; laundry. *In room:* TV (some).

Residencial Astoria   If you can get past the dark, musty bottom floor, this *residencial* is a good bet for cheap accommodations. There are two bedrooms on the first level, but stay instead on the sunny second floor, which has a giant living room with windows that face out over the ocean (and a Copec gas station). Low ceilings, especially in the shower, are inconvenient for anyone over 1.8m (6 ft.) tall. The rooms are not heated, and the walls are thin, but this *residencial* is very clean, its beds are comfortable, and you can't beat the price

Av. Corcovado 442, Chaitén. ℰ/fax 65/731263. 9 units. $12–$15 private bathroom; $9–$13 shared bathroom. No credit cards. **Amenities:** Lounge.

WHERE TO DINE

Hotel Mi Casa Restaurant (★ CHILEAN   This restaurant has a sweeping view of Chaitén and the waterfront, and its dining room is nicer in the day than the evening, when fluorescent lights go on. The menu features simply prepared

Chilean dishes, such as filet mignon with mashed potatoes, *cazuela* stew, and occasional *curantos*. All the food is organic, however, and the staff will arrange a special lamb barbecue for couples and groups, if you call ahead.

Av. Norte 206. ℰ/fax 65/731285. Main dishes $4–$10. No credit cards. Daily 9am–10pm year-round (although hours can be spotty during the dead of winter).

Restaurant Brisas del Mar CHILEAN This is one of Chaitén's better restaurants, but it's open only during the summer. Brisas del Mar sits on the waterfront and has a sunny, semicasual dining area. The menu offers a typically Chilean selection of seafood and meats.

Av. Corcovado 278. ℰ 65/731266. Main courses $4–$8. No credit cards. Jan–Feb daily 8:30pm–1am.

Restaurant Flamengo CHILEAN The best thing that can be said about the Flamengo is that it is open all day, year-round. However, it's expensive, given the simple dishes it serves and its casual atmosphere. Flamengo offers grilled meats, fish, and chicken with a choice of a dozen sauces and often has shellfish specials during the summer.

Av. Corcovado 218. ℰ 65/731800. Main courses $6–$12. No credit cards. Daily 8:30am–1am high season; daily 10am–11pm low season.

5 South from Chaitén: Futaleufú ⭑

155km (96 miles) southeast of Chaitén

The road south between Chaitén and Villa Santa Lucía, where drivers turn for Futaleufú, passes through mountain scenery that affords direct views of Volcán Michimahuida rising high above the wilderness, Yelcho Glacier, and Lago Yelcho. At 25km (16 miles), you'll arrive at Amarillo, a tiny village and the turnoff point for the 5km (3-mile) drive to Termas de Río Amarillo.

Termas de Río Amarillo This hot springs has a large temperate pool along with several outdoor and private indoor pools. Check out Pumalín's website for updated information about their new trail to the Amarillo Valley that, in 2 hours, will take you to one of best campgrounds in the area, with extensive alpine and glacier views. Or lodge at the modest, family-run **Cabañas y Hospedaje Los Mañíos,** about 100m (328 ft.) from the hot springs, for about $15 per person, or $50 for a cabin for four, $65 for a cabin for six (ℰ **65/731210**).

No phone. $3.30 adults, $1.70 children 12 and under; $4 for camping. Nov–Apr daily 9am–8pm; Mar–Oct daily 9am–6pm.

CONTINUING ON TO FUTALEUFU

Farther south, the road curves past the northern shore of Lago Yelcho and the Yelcho en la Patagonia Lodge (see below), and at 60km (37 miles) crosses the Puente Ventisquero, which bridges a milky green river; this is where you'll find the trail head to **Yelcho Glacier.** To get there, take the short road before the bridge and then walk right at the almost imperceptible sign indicating the trail. A muddy 1½-hour hike takes you through dense forest to Yelcho Glacier.

At Villa Santa Lucía, the Carretera Austral continues south to Puyuhuapi, but visitors should not miss a stay, or at the very least, a detour, to Futaleufú, an idyllic mountain town with adventure activities and one of the most challenging rivers to raft in the world. The road to Futaleufú is worth the trip itself for its majestic views at every turn, first winding around the southern end of Lago Yelcho before passing the Futaleufú River and lakes Lonconao and Espolón, and on to the emerald valley surrounding the town of Futaleufú.

AN ADVENTURE LODGE

Yelcho en la Patagonia Lodge 🐸🐸 *Finds*   The Yelcho Lodge is a remote tourism complex on the shore of the Lake Yelcho, a beautiful emerald lake bordered by tall peaks crowned with glaciers. It is the region's only complete resort, with woodsy, attractive accommodations and a full range of excursions, especially fly-fishing. Yelcho offers three options: suites, *cabañas* for four to six guests, and 15 well-equipped campsites complete with barbecues. The white, shingled *cabañas* come with spacious kitchens, but there's also a restaurant that serves gourmet cuisine as well as barbecue roasts. The cabins have a deck and barbecue and a view of the lake seen through a stand of *arrayán* trees; note that cabins for six mean two sleep in the living area. The lodge and the indoor accommodations have handsome two-tone floors made of *mañío* and *alerce.* The lodge offers excursions with bilingual guides for fly-fishing the Yelcho River and Lago Yelcho, locally renowned for its plentiful salmon and trout. Apart from fly-fishing (which costs $120 with boat and guide for 8 hr. for two people; $60 for 4 hr.), the lodge also has treks to Yelcho Glacier, mountain biking, horseback riding, and visits to the Río Amarillo hot springs, Futaleufú, Chaitén, and Pumalín. The lodge will pick you up from nearly any nearby location.

Lago Yelcho, Km 54, Carretera Austral, Región X. ✆ 65/731337, or 2/1964187 in Santiago. www.yelcho.cl. 8 suites, 6 *cabañas,* 15 camp sites. $80 double; $100 triple; $150 *cabaña* for 4; $32 camping for 4. Rates include full breakfast. AE, DC, MC, V. **Amenities:** Restaurant; excursions.

FUTALEUFU 🐸🐸🐸

155km (96 miles) southeast of Chaitén; 196km (122 miles) northeast of Puyuhuapi

Futaleufú is one of the prettiest villages in Chile, a town of 1,200 residents who live in colorful clapboard homes nestled in an awe-inspiring amphitheater of rugged, snowcapped mountains. Futaleufú sits at the junction of two rivers, the turquoise Río Espolón and its world-renowned cousin, the Río Futaleufú, whose white-water rapids are considered some of the most challenging on the globe. Every November to April, this quaint little town becomes the base for hundreds of rafters and kayakers who come to test their mettle on the "Fu," as it's colloquially known, although just as many come to fish, hike, mountain-bike, paddle a canoe, or raft the gentler Río Espolón. Futaleufú is just kilometers from the Argentine border; it's possible to get here by road from Puerto Montt by crossing into Argentina, a route sometimes preferred for its paved roads.

Note that there are no banks or gas stations here in Futaleufú. Residents do, however, sell gas out of wine jugs and other unwieldy containers; just look for signs advertising BENCINA.

GETTING THERE & AWAY

BY PLANE   **Aerotaxis del Sur** offers two air-taxi charter flights from Puerto Montt and even Chaitén, weather permitting (✆ 65/252523 in Puerto Montt, or 65/731268 in Futaleufú; www.aerotaxisdelsur.cl). It's entirely feasible to fly into Esquel in Argentina from Buenos Aires and then travel by road 65km (40 miles) to Futaleufú; just be sure to factor in the possible delay at the border crossing and give yourself plenty of time to make the journey (3–4 hr.).

BY BUS   From Chaitén, there's a daily van service that departs from the **Chaitur** office at O'Higgins 167 (✆ 65/731429; nchaitur@hotmail.com) every afternoon at 3pm for the 4-hour journey ($10). There isn't a bus terminal here, so ask at your hotel or call each company for schedules, locations, and prices. Winter service is sketchy; try calling **B&V Tours** in Chaitén to see if they have an upcoming trip (✆ 65/731390).

BY CAR   From Chaitén, take Ruta 7 south and go left to Ruta 235 at Villa Santa Lucía. The road winds around the shore of Lago Yelcho until Puerto Ramírez, where you head northeast on Ruta 231 until you reach Futaleufú.

WHAT TO SEE & DO

Futaleufú was put on the map by travelers with one goal in mind: to raft or kayak the internationally famous Class V waters of the village's namesake river—although just as many come to enjoy the opportunities to fly-fish, horseback-ride, or just hang out amid the pristine alpine setting here. The Futaleufú is one of the most challenging rivers in the world. You've got to be good—or at least be experienced—to tackle frothing white-water so wild that certain sections have been dubbed "Hell" and "The Terminator." But rafting and kayaking companies will accommodate more prudent guests with shorter sections of the river, and the nearby Río Espolón offers a gentler ride. A paddling trip in this region is undoubtedly one of the best far-flung adventures a traveler can have in Chile.

For **fishing licenses,** go to the municipal building at O'Higgins 596 (© **65/ 721241**); it's open April to November Monday through Friday from 8am to 1:30pm and 2:30 to 5pm, December to March Monday through Friday 9am to 7pm (outside the Municipalidad). For more information on fishing, see the "Fly-Fishing Lodges in the Northern Patagonia Region" section below.

WHERE TO STAY IN THE AREA

Really, most visitors to this area join one of the organized trips mentioned in the "Rafting on the Rio Futaleufú" box, above. Those with a rental vehicle will find a few local cabins for rent during the summer in town, although for hotels it is slim pickings here, and you'll be charged a lot for what you get. Outside Futaleufú, there are several options for lodging, including campsites that dot the road between here and Villa Santa Lucía. If you'd like to do a little fishing, check out the **Hostal Alexis** (© **65/731505**), located just before Puerto Ramírez and situated on the grassy bank of Lago Yelcho. There's a hotel in an old converted farmhouse and a dozen campsites with wooden half-walls that protect sites from the wind. You can fish directly from the shore here, but the owners also offer fishing excursions. Open from November to April only; $28 double.

Hostería Río Grande ⭐   This wooden, two-story *hostería* is popular with foreign tourists for its outdoorsy design and especially its restaurant and pub. It's one of the better hotels in town, but it has lost a lot of its energy of late, and it could really stand to be upgraded, as the rooms seem expensive for their dull, standard furnishings and office-building carpet. However, the atmosphere is relaxed and guests can expect a standard level of comfort. There's also an apartment (but no kitchen) for six guests. The Río Grande's restaurant is the unofficial hangout spot in town, and it has a nice atmosphere for relaxing with a beer. There's seafood throughout the week, but try to make it on Wednesday and Saturday, when the restaurant receives its fresh fish delivery by air.

O'Higgins 397, Futaleufú. ©/fax 65/721320. www.pacchile.com. 10 units, 1 apt for 6. $80 double. AE, DC, MC, V. Hotel and restaurant closed June–Oct. **Amenities:** Restaurant; bar; extensive watersports equipment rental; mountain bike rental. *In room:* No phone.

Posada Ely   The friendly woman who owns and runs Posada Ely offers decent but no-frills accommodations in an old, shingled building. The rooms are somewhat cramped and the floors squeak, but that's pretty common for lodging in this price range for this town. Two of the rooms share a bathroom. Guests take breakfast in a downstairs living room that also acts as a lobby.

Rafting on the Rio Futaleufú

The Futaleufú River is known as one of the best white-water rivers in the world, and an adventure down the rapids here rates as one of the highlights of a Chilean holiday. Tour operators can organize hard adventure rafting expeditions, or shorter rafting on more mellow sections of the Futaleufú. There is also the Epsolon River closer to town, which is suitable for light day rafting and kayaking trips (the **Hostería Río Grande,** see below, has sit-on-top kayak day rentals for the Epsolon). The following three outfitters are the best around, and they offer weeklong all-inclusive packages that cost around $2,500 to $3,000.

The rafting and kayaking company with the most experience and local knowledge is **Expediciones Chile,** run by American Olympic kayaker Chris Spelius. This outfit has one of the best-run all-inclusive trips here, with a series of lodges both in Futaleufú and in the surrounding backcountry; they're based at the three-story town house **Adventure Lodge,** Gabriel Mistral 296 (© **800/488-9082** in the U.S., or 65/721386 in Futaleufú; www.exchile.com). Expediciones Chile is, however, less of a lodge and more of an interconnected series of properties that include camping and the get-away-from-it-all cabins **CondorNest** at Tres Campos. These backcountry cabins are serviced by a staff that leaves every evening to ensure absolute privacy, and there are wood-fired saunas and massage service on premises. Depending on your desire, Expediciones Chile can organize a week that can include rafting, kayaking, horseback riding, hiking, and fly-fishing. Contact them ahead of time for day trips if you are short on time.

Another outstanding pick is the all-inclusive rafting outfit **Earth River Expeditions,** with a 400-hectare (1,000-acre) private ranch outside of Futaleufú fitted with camp-style lodging in lofty treehouses and "cliff dwellings" with tent platforms and sweeping views (180 Towpath Road, Accord, NY 12404; © **800/643-2784**; www.earthriver.com). They've been around for more than a decade, and, like Expediciones Chile, they boast superb guides whose local knowledge is as keen as their concern for safety. They also have outdoor hot tubs and massage services.

Lastly, try the rafting pros **Bío Bío Expeditions** (© **800/246-7238** in the U.S.; www.bbxrafting.com), a U.S.-based company with a passion for the Futaleufú. Like the other two outfits mentioned above, Bío Bío utilizes riverfront lodging in the form of camping (on forest-canopied tent platforms) and cabins, and they combine a full-day horseback ride to a glacier to raft the river that runs from it. They also have a sauna and yoga classes.

Balmaceda 409, Futaleufú. © **65/721205.** Fax: 65/721308. 5 units. $15–$35 double. Rates include continental breakfast. No credit cards. **Amenities:** Lounge. *In room:* No phone.

Posada La Gringa *(Finds* This attractive German-style clapboard hotel sits on a large, grassy property with excellent views of the countryside stretched out before it. It is a cozy little place that makes you feel as if you are visiting someone's home, not a hotel. With well-maintained, clean, pleasant rooms, the hotel is open from November to March only, and the owner, "La Gringa," serves an excellent breakfast. There are rumors that the owner is trying to sell this property, so it is anyone's guess how long it will be open.

Sargento Aldea s/n, corner of Aldea, Futaleufú. (*C*) **65/721260**, or 2/2359187 in Santiago. www.lagringa hostal.homestead.com/f.html. 5 units. $75 double. Rates include full breakfast. No credit cards. Closed Apr–Oct. **Amenities:** Lounge. *In room:* No phone.

WHERE TO DINE IN THE AREA

The **Hostería Río Grande** is really the only decent place to eat in town (see above), but there's **Restaurant Skorpion's,** Gabriela Mistral 255 ((*C*) **65/721228**), which offers about four choices per day of simple meat and seafood dishes (no credit cards accepted; daily 11am–2am). **Restaurante Futaleufú,** Pedro Aguirre Cerda 407 ((*C*) **65/721265**), has a short menu with 10 or so simple dishes that all cost the same ($5; no credit cards accepted). Sample items include homemade spaghetti and chicken stewed with peas; there's also a range of sandwiches (daily 11am–1:30am).

FLY-FISHING LODGES IN THE NORTHERN PATAGONIA REGION

Anglers around the world consider Patagonia to be one of the last great regions for fly-fishing, especially now that fishing clubs, lodges, and private individuals have bought up stretches of some the best rivers in the U.S., strictly limiting access to some of the sweetest spots for casting a line. Some of the highest trout-yielding rivers in Patagonia see only a few dozen or so fly-fisherman per year, and, therefore, angling fanatics, some of Hollywood's biggest stars, and many international political bigwigs (such as ex-president George H. W. Bush, Michael Douglas, Robert Redford, and Harrison Ford) pay a visit here to escape the crowds and savor the sensation of being at one with nature. The following list is a guide to the best lodges from Puerto Montt to Coyhaique. They aren't cheap; most run from $250 to $600 per night per person, everything included (nonfishing spouses sometimes pay less; and some offer "father-son" deals, so ask before booking). All of the following lodges rate three Frommer's stars (our highest ranking) for their one-of-a-kind location, direct access to prize streams and lakes, service, and friendliness.

El Patagon Lodge ✮✮✮   Owned and operated by the first-class Yankee Way Lodge near Puerto Varas, El Patagon is nestled in the temperate rainforest south of Futaleufú and Palena, and it is a remote, rustic version of the aforementioned lodge. The area's trout-filled streams and lakes draw other fly-fishing guides with clients who must drive hours to reach the region, making this lodge's immediate access a bonus for longer fishing days. In fact, the American owners of this lodge purchased the land from a float pilot and fly-fishing enthusiast who sold his map of "secret" fishing spots along with the property. The property houses four wood-hewn cabins for a total of eight fly-fishing guests, plus an Oregon yurt dining room, and a sauna and hot tub perched high above the Figueroa River. There are also multiple-day fishing journeys outside the property, with horseback rides to remote fishing streams, and stays that combine local Chilean accommodations.

Región X, Latitude 44. (*C*) **65/212030.** www.southernchilexp.com. 7-night all-inclusive packages cost, per person, around $3,000–$4,000 for fly-fishing; $2,220 for sport packages. AE, DC, MC, V. **Amenities:** Restaurant; bar; lounge; sauna; hot tub. *In room:* No phone.

Heart of Patagonia Lodge ★★★   This lodge pulled up stakes recently and reopened with the same name and staff at a property closer to the two major rivers in the region, the Río Simpson and Manihuales. It is another American-owned lodge, this time an ex-editor of *Angling Report*, John Jenkins, who settled in this region in the late 1980s. The Heart of Patagonia caters predominately to foreigners. Jenkins decided to move his business from the outskirts of Coyhaique to save on drive time and take advantage of the morning and evening hatch; however, the lodge is still close enough to town, if that is important to you. The lodge is in a remodeled home built in the 1930s by an Austrian immigrant, and the owner has maintained the old-fashioned style with antiques and other homey touches. The lodge has good Chilean food as well as hiking and horseback riding options (it's probably the best lodge for those with nonfishing spouses).

18km (11 miles) from Puerto Aysén, road to Coyhaique. ✆ 67/334906. www.heartofpatagonia.com. 6 units. 7-night all-inclusive packages $3,995 (double occupancy with guide), $4,250 (single occupancy with guide) per person; $3,200 a week for nonanglers. No credit cards. **Amenities:** Restaurant; lounge. *In room:* No phone.

Isla Monita Lodge ★★★ *Moments*   What is more exclusive than a fly-fishing lodge on a 112-hectare (277-acre) private island? This is not a lodge that is dependent on just one or two rivers; instead, the Isla Monita has access to some of the most diverse fly-fishing conditions found in Chile: the rivers Futaleufú, Palena Yelcho, Malito, and Verde, not to mention the lake the lodge sits on, the profoundly blue Lake Yelcho. All rivers are within a short drive from the lodge, and there are wading and floating excursions (32 boats in all) available. The lodge is owned by Chris Brown, an Englishman who has run this lodge since 1990, and there is room for just 12 guests. The idea at Isla Monita is that guests feel as if they are in their own home, and good food, privacy, and friendly service are the lodge's trademark. To get here, guests cross the lake by boat. Prices are higher from January to March.

Lago Yelcho, Futaleufú, Región X. ✆ 800/245-1950 in the U.S., or 2/203-0023. www.islamonita.cl. 7-night all-inclusive packages cost, per person, $4,150 Jan–Mar, $2,800 Nov–Dec and Apr. **Amenities:** Restaurant; bar; lounge. *In room:* No phone.

Juncales Lodge ★★★   One-hundred percent Chilean—that is the idea here at Juncales. Every member of the staff here must be from the region, using the logic that only locals can show you the richest spots for fly-fishing trout and salmon, and provide guests with a more "authentic" experience. The lodge is located in undoubtedly one of the best regions for fly-fishing, with access to the rivers Correntoso, Futaleufú, and Révolver, and the Black and White lakes. Guides take guests to a different location every day, unless the fishing is particularly good in one spot, and they have a dock moored with motor boats and MacKenzies for float trips. This is one of the newer lodges in the area, founded in 2001, and the lodge focuses on comfort more than luxury, with a capacity of 10 guests (it is also cheaper than the other lodges). The cuisine here is decidedly Chilean, using local recipes and ingredients.

Near Lago Yelcho, Región X. ✆ 800/560-8877 in the U.S., or 2/201-8571 in Santiago. www.juncaleslodge.cl. 7-night all-inclusive packages run $3,500 per person. AE, DC, MC, V. **Amenities:** Restaurant; bar; laundry.

La Posada de los Farios ★★★   Founded by a North American who came to Chile 16 years ago as a guide and never left, this lodge specializes in "farios," or brown trout. The lodge is north of Coyhaique, in a refashioned country home on a private, tranquil ranch, and it caters predominately to foreigners. Nevertheless, the lodge keeps its roots firmly planted in the local culture, serving hearty Chilean cuisine and giving guests close access to rural folk whose traditional way of life has long disappeared in other parts of the world. Los Farios has a capacity of just six guests, who not only can take advantage of fishing rivers and lakes that are the secret of the guides, but also can navigate the fjords of Queulat National Park for saltwater fishing, if they are so interested. The lovely American/Chilean couple who run this lodge provide very friendly, personal attention, and they arrange activities such as horseback riding, bird-watching, and more for nonfishing guests. The lodge is open from November to April.

Casilla 104, Coyhaique. © **800/669-3474** in the U.S., or 67/236402. www.chilepatagonia.com. 5-night all-inclusive packages are, per person based on double occupancy, $2,915; nonanglers pay $1,650. AE, MC, DC, V. **Amenities:** Restaurant; laundry. *In room:* No phone.

6 Puyuhuapi (⚑

198km (123 miles) south of Chaitén; 222km (138 miles) north of Coyhaique

Just south of Villa Santa Lucía is the end of Chile's X Región Lake District (also called Región de Los Lagos) and the beginning of XI Región, better known as Región de Aysén. South of here you enter a flat valley and the utilitarian town La Junta. The only thing of any interest there is a gas pump and well-stocked store. The view begins to pick up farther along, until the scenery goes wild as the valley narrows and thick green rainforest rises steeply from the sides of the road, just outside the entrance of Parque Nacional Queulat. When the valley opens, the Seno Ventisquero (Glacier Sound) unfolds dramatically, revealing the charming town of Puerto Puyuhuapi on its shore.

Puerto Puyuhuapi was founded by four young German immigrant brothers and their families who set up camp here in 1935. They ran a surprisingly successful **carpet factory,** whose humble, shingled building you can still visit Monday through Friday from 8:30 to noon and 3 to 7pm, Saturday and Sunday 9am to noon. Admission is free (© **67/325131;** www.puyuhuapi.com). It really is worth a visit.

The most popular attractions in this region are **Parque Nacional Queulat** and the five-star **Patagonia Connection Puyuhuapi Lodge & Spa** (see "Outside Puerto Puyuhuapi," below), just south and on the other side of the sound, a 5-minute boat ride away. If the Patagonia Lodge's prices are beyond your limit, you might opt to stay at a more economical hotel in Puerto Puyuhuapi or, during the off season, at El Pangue *cabañas,* and take a soak in the hot springs for the day. You can then spend the following day at Parque Nacional Queulat.

PARQUE NACIONAL QUEULAT

Parque Nacional Queulat is one of Chile's least-explored national parks, due to its dense concentration of virgin rainforest—in fact, some areas of this park have not been visited by any human. Yet what makes this park so special is that you can drive through the heart of it, and there are several lookout points reached by car or a brief walk. Be sure to keep your eyes open for the *pudú,* a miniature Chilean deer that is timid but can, with luck, be seen poking its head out of the forest near the road.

The 154,093-hectare (380,610-acre) park has several access points but few trails and no backpacking trails. If entering from the north, you first pass a turnoff that heads to the shore of **Lago Risopatrón** and a very attractive camping spot that charges $9 per site ($1.50 for firewood and $4 for a short boat ride). There's a 5.8km (3½-mile) round-trip trail here that leads trekkers through rainforest and past Lago Los Pumas (a 4-hr. hike). Continuing south of Puerto Puyuhuapi, visitors arrive at the park's star attraction, the **Ventisquero Colgante,** a tremendous U-shape river of ice suspended hundreds of feet above a sheer granite wall. From the glacier, two powerful cascades fall into Laguna Témpanos below. Visitors can drive straight to a short trail that takes them to the glacier's lookout point at no charge. To get closer, cross the hanging bridge that's before the campground and take the **Sendero Mirador Ventisquero Colgante,** a moderate 3- to 4-hour hike (3.5 km/2¼ miles) that takes you to the lake below the glacier. The park service Conaf offers boat rides in this lake for about $4 per person; the park station is open daily November through March from 8:30am to 9pm, and April through October from 8:30am to 5:30pm. To camp in this area, the park charges $9 per site. For more information, contact Conaf's offices in Coyhaique at © 67/212225 or 65/212142; www.conaf.cl.

Traveling farther south, the scenery becomes more rugged as the road takes visitors up the Cuesta de Queulat and to views of glacier-capped peaks, and then down again where the road passes the trail head to the **Sendero Río Cascada.** Even if you don't feel like walking the entire 1.7km (1-mile) trail, at least stop for a quick stroll through the enchanting forest. The trail leads to a granite amphitheater draped with braided waterfalls that fall into an ice-capped lake. Note that Conaf is slow moving when it comes to clearing trails of fallen trees, especially on the Río Cascada trail. If you're able, you can scramble over the trees, but it takes some maneuvering that will tack extra time onto your journey. Check with Conaf at the Ventisquero Colgante entrance for the status of a trail, or factor obstacles into your trip time. The station is open daily November through March from 8:30am to 9pm, and April through October from 8:30am to 5:30pm (© **67/212225** or 65/212142).

WHERE TO STAY & DINE
IN PUERTO PUYUHUAPI

Try **Café Restaurant Rossbach,** Aysén s/n, next to the carpet factory (© **67/ 325203**), if you're looking for something to eat—cakes are the specialty here. **El Pangue** has a restaurant, but it's 18km (11 miles) away. Call beforehand to see if you can get a table (see "Outside Puerto Puyuhuapi," below).

Hostería Alemana *(finds)*   The German woman who runs this hotel emigrated to Puerto Puyuhuapi more than 50 years ago, and her roots are reflected in the style of the establishment, including delicious breakfasts with sliced meats and *kuchen.* The hotel is in a well-maintained, flower-bordered antique home that just got a fresh coat of paint this year. Only one room comes with a private bathroom, and one triple comes with a wood-burning stove. All are spacious and scrubbed.

Av. Otto Uebel 450, Puerto Puyuhuapi. © **67/325118.** Hosteria_alemana@entelchile.net. 6 units. Oct–Apr $90 double, $60 single; May–Sept $20 per person. Rates include full breakfast and dinner. No credit cards. **Amenities:** Lounge. *In room:* No phone.

Residencial Marily   Just across the street from the Hostería Alemana is this inexpensive *residencial.* The place doesn't have much style, but it is clean and the beds are surprisingly comfortable. The floors are wood, the walls mauve and light blue, and some rooms share a bathroom; there is a TV in the lounge. Really, the only truly interesting thing about this place is the stuffed puma in the living room.

Av. Otto Uebel s/n, Puerto Puyuhuapi. © **67/325201.** Fax 67/325102. 7 units. Per person $12 private bathroom; $10 shared bathroom. Rates include breakfast. No credit cards. **Amenities:** Lounge. *In room:* No phone.

OUTSIDE PUERTO PUYUHUAPI

Hotel y Cabañas El Pangue *(Kids) (Finds)* El Pangue is located just kilometers from the edge of Parque Nacional Queulat, 30m (98 ft.) from Lago Risopatrón, and 18km (11 miles) from Puerto Puyuhuapi. Dense rainforest encircles the complex; a winding stream provides a fairy-tale spot for a quiet walk or a quick dip. What I love most about this hotel are the tremendous *nalca* plant leaves around the property, some so large they'd serve as an umbrella. The staff is friendly and facilities are of good quality, and although the lodge focuses heavily on fly-fishing from November to May, other excursions include mountain biking, hiking, canoeing, and boat rides. Guided fly-fishing is offered here and around the region; this lodge sees more Chilean guests than most lodges that offer fly-fishing. I wouldn't fly from the U.S. solely to visit this property, but if you are driving the Carretera Austral, this is a good spot for a night or two.

Lodging consists of cozy, attractive wood-paneled rooms that fit two to three guests. There is also one "house" with kitchen for seven guests; all cabins have kitchens. The open-room, split-level cabins have a small table and chairs and an extra bed/couch; bathrooms have sunken tubs. The main building houses an excellent restaurant, game room, and lounge; outside is a *quincho* where there are frequent lamb barbecues. As on a ranch, there are ducks, geese, pheasants, and chickens squawking from a fenced-in area. Off-season rates drop dramatically.

Carretera Austral Norte, Km 240, Región XI. ℂ/fax 67/325128. www.elpangue.cl. 12 units. 4 *cabañas* for 5 people, $92–$141; 8 exterior rooms $55–$89 double. Rates include buffet breakfast (*cabañas* excluded). AE, DC, MC, V (only during high season). **Amenities:** Restaurant; bar; lounge; outdoor heated pool; Jacuzzi; sauna; limited watersports equipment; mountain bike rental; game room; business center; room service; laundry service; Internet.

Patagonia Connection Puyuhuapi Lodge & Spa *(Moments)* This region's top attraction is an extraordinary place to spend the night or visit for the day. The former Termas de Puyuhuapi Spa & Hotel is perhaps the best hotel/thermal spa complex in Chile, and it draws visitors from all over the world for its remote, magnificent location, elegant design, thermal pools, and full-service spa. The hotel is nestled in thick rainforest on the shore of the Seno Ventisquero; to get here, guests must cross the sound via a 5-minute motorboat ride. There visitors find an indoor complex with a giant pool, whirlpools, steam baths, spa, and three open-air pools, one a rock pool framed by ferns.

The Termas was just a handful of ramshackle cabins until German pioneer Eberhard Kossman bought the property and built this handsome complex of shingles and glass; the only remaining original building is one of the *cabañas*, which is probably the least appealing lodging option. Nine large suites are on the shore, and they come with a deck that hangs out over the water during high tide. There are six newer, and smaller, nonsmoking suites that come with a more stylish decor (especially the "Captain's Suite"). Other options include duplexes, but they do not come with a kitchen stove or a view.

Of special note is the superb cuisine served here. Outside, a winding path takes guests to two short hikes through the rainforest, and there's a pier where you can drop a kayak in the sound. But the big outdoor attractions here are Puyuhuapi's fly-fishing expeditions and the connection with *Patagonia Express*, a boat that takes visitors to Laguna San Rafael Glacier (see "Puerto Aysén, Puerto Chacabuco & Laguna San Rafael National Park," later in this chapter). Both are sold as packages. Guests typically fly into Balmaceda (Coyhaique) and transfer to the lodge by vehicle. On the return trip, they board the *Express* for a visit to the glacier and get dropped off in Puerto Chacabuco for the night, then go back to the airport. If you're not staying at the hotel but want to use the facilities, there's an average charge of $24 for day use, more for sauna use or a massage ($25 each one). This is a soft-adventure destination, which won't be satisfying for visitors seeking active travel that is heavy on physical exertion.

Puerto Puyuhuapi, Región XI. ©/fax in Santiago **2/225-6489,** or 67/325103 in Puyuhuapi. www.patagonia-connection.com. 33 units. $120–$140 double, meals not included. 3-night packages including the cruise to Laguna San Rafael cost about $1,300 per person ($870 low season); half-price for kids. AE, DC, MC, V. **Amenities:** Restaurant; bar; lounge; large indoor pool and 3 outdoor pools; spa; Jacuzzi; thermal pools; sauna; massage.

7 Coyhaique

222km (138 miles) south of Puyuhuapi; 774km (480 miles) north of Cochrane

The province of Aysén includes the capital city Coyhaique and a handful of natural reserves whose rivers and lakes draw thousands every year for superb fly-fishing opportunities. Visitors who are not traveling the Carretera Austral can fly into Coyhaique from Santiago or Puerto Montt; travel to southern Patagonia from here requires that you fly again to Punta Arenas, unless you have your own car and plan to take the long and gravelly road through flat Argentine Pampa.

Driving south out of Parque Nacional Queulat, the scenery provokes oohs and ahhs at every turn. The pinnacle of Cerro Picacho comes into view before you enter Villa Amengual, a service village for farmers. The scenery is sadly marred at times by the terrible destruction caused by settlers who burned much of the area for pastureland. Tall, slender evergreen beech tree trunks bleached silver from fire can still be seen poking out from regrowth forest or littered across grassy pastures in a messy testament to these fires.

The road passes through rinky-dink towns such as Villa Mañihuales before arriving at a paved road that appears like a heaven-sent miracle after hundreds of kilometers of jarring washboard. At a junction south of Mañihuales, drivers can head to Puerto Aysén and Puerto Chacabuco, the departure point for boat trips to Laguna San Rafael and Puerto Montt, and then southeast toward Coyhaique, passing first through the Reserva Nacional Río Simpson.

Coyhaique is an urban city plopped down in the middle of wild Patagonian terrain, and it is unfortunate that city planners failed to adapt the community's design to complement such a stunning location. As it stands, Coyhaique is an ugly mishmash of homes and businesses that sprawl beneath a towering basalt cliff called Cerro Mackay, and it is surrounded by green rolling hills and pastures. This region of Patagonia always takes a backseat to its southern counterpart around Torres del Paine, yet outside of Coyhaique, new expeditions to unexplored areas seem to open up every year, and because of this it seems easier to get farther away from the crowds than in the south. The city is home to almost half the population of the entire Aysén region—about 44,000 residents. Coyhaique is the only place where you'll find a full range of services—most important, banks. The city also sits at the confluence of the Simpson and Coyhaique rivers, both renowned for trout and salmon fishing and the reason so many flock to this region. The other prime attraction here is the Laguna San Rafael Glacier, a colossal glacier that can be visited on a modest ship or a luxury liner from Puerto Chacabuco; there are also fly-overs that provide unforgettable memories. Beyond fishing, visitors can choose from a wealth of activities within a short drive of the city.

ESSENTIALS
GETTING THERE & AROUND

BY PLANE   Coyhaique's **Aeropuerto de Balmaceda** (no phone) is a gorgeous 1-hour drive from downtown. This is where the large jets arrive. **Lan Airlines** has two to three daily flights from Santiago, with a stop in either Puerto Montt or Temuco (there are no nonstops from Santiago); there's also one weekly flight from Punta Arenas. The Lan office is at General Parra 402 (© **600/526-2000** toll-free; www.lan.com). **Sky Airlines** has one daily flight, with a stop in Puerto Montt (Prat 203; © **67/240827** in Coyhaique, or 600/600-2828 toll-free; www.skyairline.cl).

Charter flights (all small propeller planes) to closer destinations such as Villa O'Higgins, Chile Chico, and Cochrane leave from the **Aeródromo Teniente Vidal** (no phone) 7km (4¼ miles) outside town. Two charter flight companies offer tourist overland flights, even over the Laguna San Rafael Glacier. Both are the same in terms of price and quality (about $1,000 for 3 hr. for one to five people): **Aerohein,** Baquedano 500 (© **67/232772** or 67/252177; www.aerohein. cl), or **Empresas Don Carlos,** Baquedano 315 (© **67/231981** or 67/233372; www.doncarlos.cl).

BY BOAT   Some travelers arrive at Puerto Chacabuco by boat from Puerto Montt and then transfer to Coyhaique (although the scrappy port is a disappointing first impression—hang on, the scenery improves!). It is 67km (42 miles) to Coyhaique. For schedule information, see "Puerto Aysén, Puerto Chacabuco & Laguna San Rafael National Park," later in this chapter. Ferry company offices in Coyhaique are at **Transmarchilay,** Av. 21 de Mayo 447 (© **67/ 231971;** www.transmarchilay.cl), and **Navimag,** Ibáñez 347 (© **67/233386;** www.navimag.cl).

BY BUS   Coyhaique has a bus terminal at Lautaro and Magallanes streets, but many companies use their own office for departures and arrivals. For buses with a final destination in **Chaitén,** try **Buses Becker,** Presidente Ibáñez 358 (© **67/ 232167;** busesbecker@123.cl), which leaves on Monday, Thursday, and Saturday at 8am ($25 one-way). For **Cochrane,** take **Buses Don Carlos,** Baquedano 315 (© **67/231981;** www.doncarlos.cl), which leaves on Tuesday, Thursday, and Saturday at 9:30am ($16). For **Puerto Aysén** and **Chacabuco,** take **Suray** with 20 trips per day, at Prat 265 (© **67/238387**), or **Interlagos** at the

---

Car Rental for Local Trips & the Carretera Austral

Car rental is very expensive here, and most require that you rent a truck if heading anywhere off paved roads (about $100 per day for a truck, $125 for a 4×4). **Hertz** (Av. Baquedano 457 and the Balmeceda airport; © **2/ 496-1111;** www.hertz.cl) or **Budget** (Errázuriz 454 and the Balmeceda airport; © **67/255171;** www.budget.cl) are here. For local rental, try: **AGS Rent a Car,** Av. Ogana 1298, and at the airport (©/fax **67/231511;** agsrentacar@entelchile.net); **Rent a Car Aysén,** Francisco Bilbao 926 (© **67/ 231532**); **Turismo Prado,** Av. 21 de Mayo 417 (© **67/231271;** fax 67/213817; ventas@turismoprado.cl); **Ricer Rent a Car,** Horn 48 (©/fax **67/232920**); or **Automundo AVR,** Francisco Bilbao 510 (© **67/231621;** fax 67/231794; wfritsch@patagoniachile.cl). If you can't find what you want with these companies, request a list from the visitor center, as there are many independent offices that rent cars here in Coyhaique.

Coyhaique

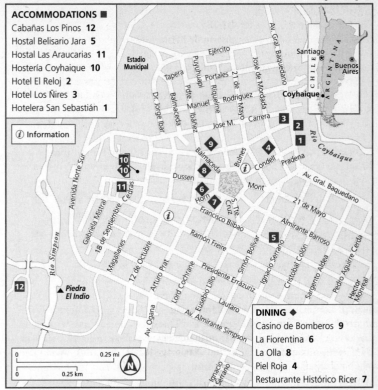

ACCOMMODATIONS ■

Cabañas Los Pinos **12**
Hostal Belisario Jara **5**
Hostal Las Araucarias **11**
Hostería Coyhaique **10**
Hotel El Reloj **2**
Hotel Los Ñires **3**
Hotelera San Sebastián **1**

(i) Information

DINING ◆

Casino de Bomberos **9**
La Fiorentina **6**
La Olla **8**
Piel Roja **4**
Restaurante Histórico Ricer **7**

Terminal (similar frequencies; *©* **67/240840;** www.turismointerlagos.cl). For **Puerto Ibáñez,** try **Minibus Don Tito,** Pasaje Curicó 619 (*©* **67/250280**).

BY CAR Heading south on Ruta 7, the highway comes to a fork—one paved road and one dirt. The choice here is clear, especially if you've been driving on gravel all day. The well-signed, paved route heads first toward Puerto Aysén and then heads southeast for a beautiful drive through the Río Simpson National Reserve before hitting town. At the city entrance, a sign points left for the center of town.

VISITOR INFORMATION

A very helpful bilingual staff can be found at the **Sernatur** office at Bulnes 35 (*©* **67/231752** or 67/240290; www.sernatur.cl); it's open January through February Monday through Friday from 8:30am to 8:30pm, Saturday and Sunday from 11am to 6pm; and March through December Monday through Friday from 8:30am to 5:30pm. Sernatur produces a glossy magazine packed with information about the region and full listings of services. For information about the surrounding natural parks and reserves, you can try **Conaf**'s office at Los Coigües s/n (*©* **67/212125;** www.conaf.cl).

ORIENTATION

Coyhaique has a disorienting pentagon-shape plaza and many one-way streets that can easily confuse a visitor with a rental car. Most services and hotels are near the plaza, and you'll find it convenient to stick to walking when in the city. The rest of the city is on a regular grid pattern.

FAST FACTS: Coyhaique

Currency Exchange Options include **Turismo Prado,** Av. 21 de Mayo 417 (© 67/231271), and **Emperador,** Freire 171 (© 67/233727). Both are open Monday to Friday 9am to 1:30pm and 3 to 7pm, Saturday 9am to 2pm.

Fishing Licenses **Departamento de Tránsito Municipalidad de Coyhaique,** Bilbao 357 (© 67/231788), open Monday to Friday from 9am to 1pm.

Hospital The city's Regional Hospital is at Jorge Ibar 0168 (© 67/219100). For emergencies, dial © **131** as in every city in Chile.

Internet Access **Entel** has Internet access and a calling center at Prat 340.

Laundry Try **Lavaseco All Clean,** General Parra 55, #2 (© 67/219635).

Outdoor & Fishing Gear Go to **Ferretería La Nueva,** Condell 150 (© 67/231724; no licenses given out here).

Post Office **Correos de Chile** is at Cochrane 226 (© 67/231787).

WHAT TO SEE & DO IN COYHAIQUE

Museo Regional de la Patagonia ⊛ This small museum doesn't rank as one of Chile's finest, but it does offer information about regional flora and fauna, with stuffed birds, armadillos, and turtles; rock and petrified wood samples; and an ethnographic exhibit featuring photographs, colonial machinery, and other antique items. There is also a photo exhibit of workmen building the Carretera Austral.

Av. Lillo 23, corner of Baquedano. © 67/213175. Admission 70¢ adults, free for kids. Mid-Dec to Feb daily 8:30am–8pm; Mar to mid-Dec Mon–Fri 8:30am–1:30pm and 2:15–5:30pm.

Reserva Nacional Coyhaique ⊛ You don't need to go far in Coyhaique to surround yourself in wilderness. This little reserve (2,670 hectares/6,595 acres) is just under 5km (3 miles) from town on the road to Puerto Aysén and is a good place to go for a light walk through native forest, have a picnic, or pitch a tent. A ranger station at the entrance has complete trail information. From here, a short trail leads to a campground and then continues to Laguna Verde, with picnic and camping areas. There is a longer trail called the Sendero Las Piedras, which rewards hikers with wide-open views of the surrounding area and city below. The reserve's proximity to the city means it's entirely feasible to walk there.

5km (3 miles) from Coyhaique on the road to Puerto Aysén. © 67/212225. www.conaf.cl. Admission $1 adults, 30¢ kids; camping $6. Nov–Mar daily 8:30am–9pm; Apr–Oct daily 8:30am–5:30pm.

Reserva Nacional Río Simpson The only way to really see this reserve is by car—which you'll do anyway if you take the road from Coyhaique to Puerto Aysén. The road winds along the shore of the Río Simpson, passing through impressive scenery and offering two crashing waterfalls, the Bridal Veil and the Virgin, which are signposted. There's also a museum here without anything of much interest and an information center. Unfortunately, trails in this reserve are not regularly maintained and are, therefore, tough to hike; inquire at the information center as to their status.

Road to Puerto Aysén, Km 37. © 67/21222. www.conaf.cl. Admission $1 adults, 30¢ kids; camping $6. Nov–Mar daily 8:30am–9pm; Apr–Oct daily 8:30am–5:30pm. Information center daily 8:30am–1:30pm and 2:15–6:30pm.

OUTDOOR ACTIVITIES IN THE AREA

TOUR OPERATORS   Tour operators plan day trips, multiple-day trips, and full expeditions to areas as far as the Southern Ice Field. **Adventure Expeditions Patagonia,** Riquelme 372 (© 67/219894; www.adventurepatagonia.com), can put together unforgettable expeditions to areas rarely seen by travelers, including a hut-to-hut hiking expedition along the Aysén Glacier, a 14-day horseback-riding trip along the Pioneer Trail, and an "Ice to Ocean" 11-day horseback, hiking, and rafting adventure; they are highly recommended and they have an excellent staff of guides. **Andes Patagónicos,** Horn 48, #11 (© 67/216711; fax 67/216712; www.ap.cl), has tours around Coyhaique such as trips to the Lake Carrera and its Marble Cathedrals; 5-day journeys to Caleta Tortal with stops at archaeological sites, immigrant posts, glaciers, and rivers; 1-day and multiple-day fly-fishing tours; trips to the Laguna San Rafael and Termas de Puyuhuapi; and more. For a private fly-fishing guide, try **Expediciones Coyhaique,** Portales 195 (©/fax **67/232300;** juliomeier@patagoniachile.cl). For sightseeing trips along the Carretera Austral and to Puerto Aysén, and trips to view Telhuelche Indian rock, try **Turismo Prado,** 21 de Mayo 417 (©/fax **67/231271;** ventas@ turismoprado.cl).

FISHING   Since their introduction in the late 1800s, trout and salmon have thrived in the crystalline waters in southern Chile, but nowhere in the country has fly-fishing taken off as it has here in the Aysén region. The burgeoning number of fly-fishing guides alone bears testament to the truth of this region's claim as one of the premier fishing destinations on the globe, drawing thousands of anglers from around the world to reel in 3-, 5-, and even 10-pounders. Even if you've never fished before, this might be your opportunity to give it a go. Each tour operator has a list of their own fly-fishing guides in the Aysén region, some of whom work independently. If you're coming here mainly to fly-fish, there are several full-service luxury lodges in the region. All have on-site guides, both Chilean and foreign, especially American. Most offer activities for nonangling spouses and friends (see the "Fly-Fishing Lodges in the Northern Patagonia Region" section on p. 406).

Tour operators organize day, multiple-day, and weeklong excursions to fly-fishing spots such as the Simpson, Baker, and Nirehuao rivers, and Bertrand and General Carrera lakes. Some combine excursions with other activities, such as horseback riding or hiking.

HORSEBACK RIDING   Trips often head to the Coyhaique Reserve and Lago Margaritas, but tour companies offer a variety of destinations. Some arrange all-inclusive, multiple-day trips; for this, try **Andes Patagónicos,** Horn 48, #11 (© **67/216711;** www.ap.cl).

SKIING   It's not a world-class ski resort (two T-bars are the lift service), but it can be fun to visit if you're here from June to September. The **Centro de Esquí El Fraile** (© **67/1983007**) is located 29km (18 miles) from Coyhaique, offering five ski runs serviced by two T-bars. It's a tiny resort but can make for a fun day in the snow, and it's one of the few resorts in Chile that has tree skiing. There are also cross-country skiing opportunities here. Tickets cost about $23 per day, and it's possible to rent equipment for an average of $20. **Andes Patagónicos** can get you there (see "Tour Operators," above).

WHERE TO STAY

There are many clean hostals in Coyhaique that are very inexpensive, but they're pretty basic and rooms are small; also, most have shared bathrooms and you must bring your own towel. Try the friendly **Hospedaje María Ester,** Lautaro 544 (ⓒ/fax **67/233023;** www.hospedajemariaester.cl), a family home with kitchen facilities for $8.50 per person, $20 double with shared bathroom, and $25 for a double with private bathroom. **Hospedaje Lautaro,** Lautaro 269 (ⓒ **67/238116**), also offers kitchen facilities, though it's usually closed during the winter.

EXPENSIVE

Cabañas Lodge La Pasarela 𝘼𝘼 *(Moments)*   These attached rooms and cabins nestled on the shore of Río Simpson (on the fork with Río Coyhaique) are good for those who'd like a more rural surrounding not too far from town. The complex is on the other side of the river, away from the main road, and to get there guests must first cross a wooden suspension bridge. Cabañas La Pasarela is geared toward fly-fishermen, with private guides from Chile and the United States. But guests also like this lodge because you can fish right at the bank of the Río Simpson outside your door. The cozy restaurant is one of the best in town, and the fireside bar is a great place to unwind with a drink. All of the structures are made of cypress logs and have black, shingled roofs. In 2002, the main lobby, bar, and restaurant areas were refurbished and are now a bit more elegant than before, but the rooms are a bit on the dark side, with the exception of the new suites, which are worth a splurge for their pleasant decor, queen-size beds, and extras like a minibar. A pebbled walkway goes up to four A-frame *cabañas.* Note that you've got to be family or really good friends to rent one of the cabins because three twins are in the bottom living area next to the kitchen. They arrange bilingual fly-fishing tours: $350 a day for two people, including transportation, fishing licenses, and lunch. La Pasarela is closed between May and September.

Km 2, road to Puerto Aysén, Coyhaique. ⓒ **67/240700.** www.lapasarela.cl. 11 units. Apt $200 for 8; $60–$95 double; $130 cabin for 5; $80 suite. Rates include buffet breakfast. AE, DC, MC, V. **Amenities:** Restaurant; bar; lounge. *In room:* TV.

Hostal Belisario Jara 𝘼 *(Value)*   This boutique hotel is Coyhaique's best lodging option. The charming architectural design features honey-colored wood frames nailed together in varying angles, giving every room and sitting area a unique size and shape. A twisting hallway winds around the rooms, and the roof is a cupola topped off with a steeple and weathervane. The hotel is made of army-green stucco and windows aplenty, so it's bright and airy, and the crisp, white walls are accented here and there with local arts and crafts. Rooms are average size, some brighter than others, and all have carpeted floors. The softly lit, cozy dining area/bar is the highlight of the hotel, with a wooden table and chairs for relaxing fireside. French doors open out onto the front garden; the hotel sits on a busy street but is set back far enough so that you do not notice. The hotel has an apartment on the second floor of an old home on the main road, separate from the main building, that comes with a kitchen and can fit up to six. The hotel can arrange fly-fishing tours, car rental, and other expeditions.

Francisco Bilbao 662, Coyhaique. ⓒ/fax 67/234150. www.belisariojara.itgo.com. 10 units. $60–$75 single; $75–$90 double. Rates include buffet breakfast. No credit cards. **Amenities:** Bar; lounge; laundry service. *In room:* TV.

Hotel Coyhaique *(Kids)* *(Overrated)*   This ex-*hostería* is Coyhaique's largest hotel, and it sits in a quiet part of town surrounded by an unkempt, overgrown garden. Though it is a more traditional hotel than most in Coyhaique, the so-so quality offered by the Hotel Coyhaique makes it seem as if it has fallen on hard times but can't bear to lower its prices to reflect this. For the price, you'd be better off at La Pasarela or the Belisario Jara. However, the hotel has its own boat service to Laguna San Rafael Glacier, called the Iceberg Expedition, that is available for guests only. Their Patagonia Flash, a 3-day program with a visit to San Rafael, costs $600 per person based on double occupancy. Guest rooms are clean. Doubles come in two sizes: the matrimonial double with a full bed is larger than the double with two twins. A dark-wood lobby leads into the bar, and around the corner is a semiformal restaurant; there's a more casual restaurant downstairs with great views of the countryside. Outside there's a kidney-shape pool and lots of grass for kids to romp around. The hotel offers packages that include lodging, most meals, and various excursions; contact the hotel for details.

Magallanes 131, Coyhaique. ℂ **67/231137.** Fax 67/233274. www.hotelsa.cl. 40 units. $87–$110 single; $90–$120 double. Rates include buffet breakfast. MC, V. **Amenities:** 2 restaurants; bar; lounge; outdoor pool; tour desk; room service; laundry service; nonsmoking rooms; transfers. *In room:* TV, minibar.

MODERATE

Cabañas Los Pinos ⋆ *(Finds*   These handcrafted log cabins are nestled in a pine forest on the shore of Río Simpson, about a 5-minute drive from downtown. There are cabins for three, four, or six people with a wood-burning stove; the cabin for six has one bedroom with a full-size bed and one with two bunks. The cabins for four are a little tight, but the charm of the place makes up for it. The cabin for six comes with a kitchen; the other two cabins share a separate eating area, which guests usually don't mind, considering the eating area is an idyllic little cabin with a beautiful view, great cooking facilities, and two tables for four. The couple who own and run the property are very friendly, and they have a vehicle for excursions; however, without an e-mail address or fax number, it can be difficult to make a reservation.

Camino Teniente Vidal Km 1.5, Parcela 5, Coyhaique. ℂ **67/234898.** 4 units. $50–$65 cabin for 3–4; $65–$75 cabin for 4–5; $75–$85 cabin for 6. No credit cards. **Amenities:** Restaurant. *In room:* TV, no phone.

Hotel El Reloj   This bed-and-breakfast-style hotel is housed in a forest-green-and-lemon old home flanked by two *lenga* trees. The hotel is surrounded by an abundance of greenery, which is pleasant, but it shades the windows, so the rooms are fairly dark. The rooms are a little on the small side but are appealing; some have stone walls, and all have old wood floors. It's a cozy enough place and very clean. There's a common living area and a small restaurant serving local fare, such as wild hare, sheep cheese, and fresh salmon. The restaurant is open to the public, but limited seating keeps the numbers low.

Av. Baquedano 828. ℂ/fax **67/231108.** htlelreloj@patagoniachile.cl. 13 units. $50–60 single; $75–$90 double. Rates include buffet breakfast. No credit cards. **Amenities:** Restaurant; lounge; bar; room service; laundry. *In room:* TV.

Hotelera San Sebastián ⋆   This hotel's mustard exterior is so nondescript you might miss it the first time you pass by. But don't let the outside fool you: Inside, each room offers high-quality interiors, and all but one have lovely views of the Coyhaique River meandering through grassy countryside. The hotel has been recently renovated, and the spacious bedrooms are tastefully painted in rose and cream, with matching linens and curtains, and are impeccably clean, as are the bathrooms. The hotel is on a busy street, but it sits back, tucked away between two buildings and, therefore, is very quiet. Again, it's difficult to make a direct reservation here, as there is no fax or e-mail address.

Av. Baquedano 496, Coyhaique. © 67/233427. 7 units. $55–$65 double. Rates include buffet breakfast. No credit cards. **Amenities:** Restaurant. *In room:* TV.

Hotel Los Ñires ☆ The Hotel Los Ñires is a good midrange choice, offering clean, bright rooms with decent, average furnishings. The rooms are average size, but if you want extra space, the staff can put a full-size bed in a room built for a triple (triple rate is $60–$75). The hotel has a large restaurant on the bottom floor that is open to the public, but guests take their breakfast in a sunny dining area off the lobby. The hotel's wood facade repeats itself indoors, with wood slat paneling. This hotel is owned by the Don Carlos charter plane service, which has overflights of Laguna San Rafael, and they can put together packages for guests including this service.

Av. Baquedano 315, Coyhaique. © 67/232261. Fax 67/233372. www.doncarlos.cl/hotel.htm. 21 units. $40–$50 single; $50–$60 double. Rates include continental breakfast. AE, DC, MC, V. **Amenities:** Restaurant; bar. *In room:* TV.

INEXPENSIVE

Hostal Las Araucarias The Hostal Las Araucarias sits on a quiet street across from the Hostería Coyhaique's large garden park. This slightly weathered hostel is slowly getting a makeover, but they would do well to start with their facade, as it is still somewhat unwelcoming. There's an upstairs sitting area and a downstairs dining area that feels a bit like someone's own living room. The woman who owns and runs this hostel is very welcoming, yet the price is too high for what you get.

Obispo Vielmo 71, Coyhaique. © 67/232707. contacto@hostalaraucaria.cl. 8 units. $25 single; $40 double. Rates include buffet breakfast. No credit cards. *In room:* TV.

WHERE TO DINE

There are several cafes downtown that are good for a quick bite, such as **Café Oriente** (© 67/231622), Condell 201, with pizzas and sandwiches. The **Cafetería Alemana** (© 67/231731) is a very nice cafe almost next door, at Condell 119. It serves German specialties such as *kuchen* and steak tartare, as well as sandwiches, pizzas, and a good fixed-price lunch for $5.

Casino de Bomberos *(Finds* CHILEAN Chile's volunteer firemen need some way to make a buck, and here's their solution: Open a cafe in the fire station. The atmosphere is plain but fun, and the menu features classic dishes like roasted chicken and calamari with tomato sauce. The food is tasty and the fixed-price lunch is a steal at $5, including a salad, soup, main dish, and dessert. On Sunday, there are baked and fried fresh empanadas.

General Parra 365. © 67/231437. Main courses $6–$9. No credit cards. Daily noon–4pm and 7pm–midnight.

Hostería Coyhaique INTERNATIONAL/CHILEAN This spacious, semiformal restaurant features an extensive menu serving international and Chilean fare, including pastas, salads, grilled meats, and pan-fried seafood, with a choice of sauces such as garlic or peppercorn. Nevertheless, the food is unremarkable for the price; better to try their casual restaurant downstairs, with a cozier ambience and valley view. Most travelers eat at this restaurant only when lodging here at the hotel.

Magallanes 131. © 67/231137. Main courses $11. MC, V. Daily 8am–midnight.

La Fiorentina *(Value* PIZZA/CHILEAN La Fiorentina serves a long list of pizzas and hearty, home-style dishes that can even be ordered to go—and stays open all day. The fixed-price lunch offers two selections and costs $4; it's very popular with the locals, who usually sit alone at lunchtime with their eyes glued to the TV blaring in one eating area. The atmosphere is very, very casual, but the service is friendly and attentive.

Arturo Prat 230. © 67/238899. Individual pizzas $3–$4.50. MC, V. Mon–Sat 9am–midnight; Sun 10am–11pm Jan–Feb only.

La Olla CHILEAN   This tiny restaurant offers a brightly lit, semicasual dining area with floral tablecloths and attentive service. La Olla looks as though it promises more, but the menu is surprisingly brief. The fare is typical Chilean, with classics such as beef tenderloin and fried conger eel paired with the usual french fries or mashed potatoes. The food is hearty and good, but too simple. There is, however, a decent paella on Sunday. The two owners are usually on hand, and they are exceptionally friendly.

Prat 176. ©/fax 67/242588. Main courses $5–$8.50. AE, DC, MC, V. Daily 11am–11pm.

La Pasarela ✿ CHILEAN   La Pasarela is about the best thing going in town. To get here, you need to take a taxi ride just outside town and across a wooden suspension bridge. The atmosphere is great: stone walls, wood beams, a roaring fireplace, and a comfortable bar for relaxing with a pisco sour. Through the windows, diners watch the Río Simpson rush by. The Pasarela is part of a *cabaña*/hotel complex and usually whips up specials according to the guests' whims. Standbys include grilled meats and pastas. There is usually a fixed-price meal for lunch and dinner, including appetizer, main dish, dessert, and coffee, for about $10 for lunch and $12 for dinner. Diners who are not lodging at La Pasarela must always call ahead for a reservation for dinner.

Road to Puerto Aysén, Km 2. © 67/240700. Reservations required. Main courses $8–$11. AE, DC, MC, V. Daily 7:30am–midnight.

Piel Rojo ✿✿   This pub is the best spot for a casual dinner such as quesadillas, burgers, sandwiches, pastas, and more. The funky interiors are embellished with iron and stained-glass lamps, tree-trunk tables and chairs, low lighting, and a long, winding wooden bar that is perfect for a solo traveler looking for a quick meal. Piel Rojo is a good all-in-one place to grab a bite, relax with friends, have a few drinks—or go all night in the disco, as it stays open very late.

Moraleda 495. © 67/237832. Main courses $5–$10. AE, DC, MC, V. Kitchen daily 5pm–midnight (bar and disco until 4am).

Restaurant Histórico Ricer ✿ *Kids* CHILEAN/INTERNATIONAL   This restaurant is a favorite with traveling gringos, and just about everyone else in town, too. The large, pub-style restaurant is fashioned of logs, and a handcrafted wood staircase leads to a mellower, slightly more formal dining area upstairs. All in all, the food is decent, although terribly overpriced, and the service is absentminded: Waitresses tend to group at the cash register and gossip rather than wait on tables. The fixed-price menu is a good deal at $7 and includes an appetizer, main course, and dessert, and the restaurant stays open very late.

Horn 48. © 67/232920. www.ap.cl/restaurante.htm. Main courses $5–$15. AE, DC, MC, V. Daily 8:30am–2am (to 3am in summer).

SOUTH FROM COYHAIQUE
A SIGHTSEEING EXCURSION AROUND LAGO ELIZALDE

The Seis Lagunas (Six Lagoons) and Lago Elizalde region just south of Coyhaique offers a sightseeing loop that passes through fertile, rolling farmland and forest, and past several picturesque lakes, all of which are known for outstanding fly-fishing. This area is little visited and is a great place to escape the crowds. If you're tempted to stay and fish for a few days here, there are lodges that cater to this sport, described in "Fly-Fishing Lodges in the Northern Patagonia Region" on p. 406. If you rent your own car, pick up a good map because many of these roads have no signs.

Leaving Coyhaique via the bridge near the Piedra del Indio (a rock outcrop that resembles the profile of an Indian), head first to Lago Atravesado, about 20km (12 miles) outside town. The road continues around the shore and across a bridge, and enters the Valle Laguna. From here, you'll want to turn back and drive the way you came until you spy a road to the right that heads through country fields, eventually passing the "six lagoons." Take the next right turn toward Lago Elizalde. This pretty, narrow lake set amid a thick forest of deciduous and evergreen beech is a great spot for picnicking and fishing. There is often a boat-rental concession here in the summer. There's a lodge here, but it's open only occasionally, usually when it books a large group. From here you'll need to turn back to return to Coyhaique; follow the sign for Villa Frei, which will lead you onto the paved road to Coyhaique instead of backtracking the entire route. Keep an eye open for El Salto, a crashing waterfall that freezes solid in the winter.

LAGO GENERAL CARRERA & THE MARBLE CATHEDRALS

The Lago General Carrera straddles the border of Argentina (where it is known as Lago Buenos Aires) and is Chile's largest lake. There are two reasons to pay a visit here: the robin's-egg-blue hue of the water and the "Marble Cathedral," a series of limestone caves polished and sculpted by centuries of wind and water whose black-and-white swirls are a magnificent contrast to the blue water below. Those with extra time and a rental vehicle might consider continuing on around the lake on a sightseeing drive, from the Marble Cathedral at Puerto Río Tranquilo south and then northeast to Chile Chico. From here, travelers must put their vehicle on a ferry, which crosses the lake and lands in Puerto Ibañez, from where drivers continue north to Coyhaique (reservations for vehicles are a good idea; contact **Motonave Pilchero;** © **67/233466;** $4 passengers, $35 vehicles; one daily round-trip service Mon, Tues, Wed, and Fri only from Puerto Ibáñez). This journey is for independent travelers with a good map and ample time, as you will need to spend the night somewhere along the way, most likely in Chile Chico. Try the charming **Hostería de la Patagonia,** just outside town on the Camino Internacional (© **67/411337**), with an in-house restaurant. It charges $22 per double; no credit cards accepted.

If you're looking for a day trip, however, a boating excursion to the Marble Cathedrals is a very interesting option—but at 223km (138 miles) from Coyhaique along a paved, then dirt, road, it's a long round-trip drive to get to the dock in Puerto Tranquilo. A charter boat service takes visitors around and inside the marble caves for a half-day journey. You could plan a picnic and kick back along the shore.

AN ADVENTURE LODGE NEAR LAKE CARRERA

The Terra Luna Lodge ⟨★★★⟩ *Kids* This remote adventure lodge is owned by the French-Chilean outfitter company Azimut, which offers every kind of excursion throughout Chile. The lodge sits on a grassy slope above the robin's-egg-blue waters of Lake Carrera, and it is the only lodging in the area. What is special about this lodge are the 1- to multiple-day excursions to glaciers, rivers, and jagged northern Patagonia scenery that are, thankfully, devoid of other tourists. Because the owners are renowned mountaineers and outdoors-lovers, they can arrange serious hardcore adventure trips scaling regional peaks, long treks to glaciers, or rafting trips to the white-water rapids of Río Baker—but there are gentler hikes, horseback riding, and mountain biking as well. The lodging options consist of a spacious pine lodge with doubles and triples, a bungalow for four with a kitchenette and another for two with a whirlpool, a "family" house for two to eight guests seeking total independence, and a low-cost cabin with bunks for two.

Km 1.5, Camino Puerto Guadal-Chile Chico. In Santiago, General Salvo 159, Providencia. © 2/2351519. www.terra-luna.cl. 4 apts, with 3 rooms each. 1 cabin for 2, 1 cabin for 4, 1 for 7. $80 double (each room from the apt can be paid as a double room); $120 for 4 people. All rates include breakfast. All-inclusive packages run an average of 4 days/3 nights at $890 per single, $690 per double. AE, MC, V. **Amenities:** Restaurant; Jacuzzi; sauna; kayak and bike rental; laundry service.

8 Puerto Aysén, Puerto Chacabuco & Laguna San Rafael National Park ★★

Puerto Aysén is 68km (42 miles) west of Coyhaique

Puerto Aysén was a vigorous port town until the 1960s, when silt filled the harbor and ships were forced to move 16km (10 miles) away to Puerto Chacabuco. Puerto Aysén still bustles, but it really offers few attractions to the visitor. The same could be said for Puerto Chacabuco; however, the majority of visitors to this region pass through here at some point to catch a ship or ferry to Laguna San Rafael Glacier or to Puerto Montt. Most travelers arriving by ferry from Puerto Montt head straight to Coyhaique, and vice versa, but the full-day ferry ride to Laguna San Rafael leaves early and returns late, so many travelers find it convenient to spend a night here in Puerto Chacabuco.

It's recommended that you at least take a day trip to Puerto Aysén and Puerto Chacabuco, more than anything for the beautiful drive through the Reserva Nacional Río Simpson and the equally beautiful view of Aysén Sound at the journey's end. That said, both towns are a little scrappy, but the Hotel Loberías del Sur (see "Where to Stay & Dine," below) is a good spot for lunch before heading back to Coyhaique. If you don't have your own transportation, you can try **Buses Suray,** Eusebio Ibar 630 (© **67/336222**). The best bet is to call **Patagonia Austral,** Condell 149, #2 (©/fax **67/239696**; ventas@australpatagonia.cl), which offers day trips around this area, especially bird-watching tours. The tours operate from November 15 to March 15 only, but the agency will arrange trips any time of the year for small groups. **Turismo Rucaray,** in Puerto Aysén at Teniente Merino 668 (© **67/332862**; fax 332725; rucaray@entelchile.net), offers other excursions around the area and sells ferry tickets.

For more information, there's a good website crammed with information about Aysén at www.puntoaisen.cl.

PARQUE NACIONAL LAGUNA SAN RAFAEL ★★★

If you're not planning a trip to Patagonia, Laguna San Rafael National Park is a must-see. It's the foremost attraction in the Aysén region, drawing thousands of visitors each year to be dazzled by the tremendous vertical walls of blue ice that flow 45km (28 miles) from the Northern Ice Field and stretch 4km (2½ miles) across the Laguna San Rafael. Around these walls, thousands of aquamarine icebergs float in soupy water, forming jagged sculptures. If you're lucky enough, you'll see a few crash off the iceberg in a mammoth kerplunk.

The glacier is actually receding, and quite quickly. The first explorers here in 1800 described the glacier as having filled three-quarters of the Laguna; when you're here, you can appreciate how much has disappeared.

Laguna San Rafael National Park is a staggering 1.7 million hectares (4 million acres). Most of the park is inaccessible except by ship, on which visitors slowly cruise through narrow canals choked with thick vegetation. Like Torres del Paine, Laguna San Rafael is a UNESCO World Biosphere Reserve. Visitors set sail in Puerto Chacabuco or Puerto Montt aboard an all-inclusive luxury liner or modest ferry for day and multiple-day trips. The ship anchors near the glacier and passengers board zodiacs (inflatable motorized boats) for a closer look at the icebergs and the glacier, which in some places rises as high as 70m (230 ft.). A smaller fraction of visitors book an overflight excursion for a bird's-eye view of the glacier's entirety, which includes a touchdown at the park's center near the glacier for an hour-long visit.

It rains endlessly in this national park, but that's not a reason to cancel a trip to the glacier. Although this region sees heavy rainfall throughout the year, your best bet for clear skies is from November to March. Even on foul-weather days, the glacier is usually visible, as the clouds tend to hover just above it. Bring protective rain gear just in case, or inquire when booking a ticket, as many companies provide guests with impermeable jackets and pants.

Conaf administers the park and charges a $4 admission fee (ferry passengers do not pay; only those landing in planes do, but please donate something at the park ranger station anyway, as every little bit of funds helps). Conaf offers several services at the park, including a boat ride near the glacier for $40 per person, and five sites for camping ($4 per tent).

FERRY JOURNEYS THROUGH THE FJORDS TO LAGUNA SAN RAFAEL ★★★

This extraordinary journey is about a 200km (124-mile) sail from Puerto Chacabuco, but many visitors leave from Puerto Montt for a round-trip journey or to disembark in Puerto Chacabuco. Some visitors plan a multiple-day journey to Laguna San Rafael as the focal point of a trip to Chile. When booking a trip, consider the journey's length and whether you will be traveling at night and, therefore, missing any portions of scenery. If you're doing a loop, you should be able to see everything.

Catamaranes del Sur ★
This catamaran service to Laguna San Rafael also owns the hotel at the port in Chacabuco, the Hostería Loberías del Sur, and they offer packages that include a stay here or 1-day journeys for travelers not lodging at the hotel. Catamaranes has their own private park, Aikén del Sur, which they visit for a half-day tour included in their 2- to 3-night packages. Also included in their packages is a typical Patagonian lamb barbecue. The company has a fleet of ships that are smaller and, therefore, offer a more personalized experience than the large Navimag ships, making this a good choice for day trips to the Laguna (the price is slightly higher than with Navimag). I don't recommend their 3-night packages because lodging is at their hotel in Puerto Chacabuco, and there isn't enough to see here to warrant more than a 1-night stay. Trips include all meals, an open bar, and inflatable zodiac boat rides near the glacier.

In Santiago, Pedro de Valdivia 0210. ℂ 2/231-1902. Fax 2/231-1993. www.catamaranesdelsur.cl. AE, DC, MC, V. Day trips $299 adults, $100 children; 3-night packages $860 per person, double occupancy. Includes all meals, open bar, and excursions.

Navimag Ferries ★ (Value)
Navimag offers passenger and cargo ferry service to Laguna San Rafael. There are several embarkation options here. Navimag's ship *Puerto Edén* leaves from Puerto Montt, arrives in Puerto Chacabuco the next day and the Laguna San Rafael the following day, and then returns to Chacabuco

and back to Puerto Montt. You can get on or off at Puerto Chacabuco for a cheaper, shorter trip. Like the rest of the companies, guests are taken close to the icebergs aboard a dinghy. There are cabins for four with a private or shared bathroom, and with an exterior or interior view. All lodging options are cabins. Prices include meals, lodging, and excursions. Vehicles cost $150 one-way from Puerto Montt to Chacabuco.

Offices in Puerto Montt at Av. Angelmó 2187 in the Terminal de Transbordadores, 🕿 65/432300; in Santiago at El Bosque Norte 0440, 🕿 2/442-3120, fax 2/2035025; in Chaitén, Ignacio Carrera Pinto 188, 🕿 65/731570, fax 65/731571; and in Coyhaique, at Presidente Ibáñez 347, 🕿 67/233306, fax 67/233386. www.navimag.cl (online tickets). AE, DC, MC, V. Prices vary but average $310–$500 per person for the 4-night round-trip journey from Puerto Montt. The 2-night round-trip journey from Puerto Chacabuco costs about $100–$265 per person.

Patagonia Express ★★   Patagonia Express works in conjunction with the Patagonia Connection Lodge (former Termas de Puyuhuapi; see "Where to Stay & Dine" under "Puyuhuapi," above), leaving from Puerto Chacabuco and including a 2-night stay at the hotel and 1 night in Puerto Chacabuco. This is another premium excursion with sharp service and wonderful accommodations, but unlike Skorpios, you do not spend the night onboard the ship. Departs Tuesday and Saturday from September to April.

In Santiago, Fidel Oteíza 1921, #1006. 🕿 2/225-6489. Fax 2/274-8111. www.patagonia-connection.com. AE, DC, MC, V. Prices average $1,000 per person for the 3-night package, including 1 night in Puerto Chacabuco and 2 nights at the Patagonia Connection Lodge; half-price for kids under 16. Includes all meals and excursions.

Skorpios ★★★   Skorpios is the upscale cruise service to Laguna San Rafael, offering deluxe onboard accommodations, great food, and all-around high quality. The wood-hewn cabins come with berths or full-size beds (or both, for families), in standard rooms or suites. There are two ships here: the *Skorpios I* and *II*, for 68 and 130 people, respectively, although the trips are not usually heavily booked. Skorpios offers 7-day cruises leaving from Puerto Montt and 4-day cruises from Puerto Chacabuco. The 7-day takes visitors first along the eastern coast of Chiloé near Castro, then down to the glacier. On the return trip, the ship detours up the Fjord Quitralco to visit the remote hot springs there. Heading back to Puerto Montt, the ship cruises along the southern coast of Chiloé, stopping in Castro for an afternoon excursion. The 4-day journey also includes a stop at the hot springs. Skorpios offers service from September to May.

In Santiago, Augusto Leguía Norte 118, Las Condes. 🕿 2/231-1030. Fax 2/232-2269. In Puerto Montt, Av. Angelmó 1660. 🕿 65/256619. Fax 65/258315. www.skorpios.cl. AE, DC, MC, V. Cost for the 7-day/6-night journey is $760–$3,000 per person; the 4-day/3-night journey is $480–$1,800 per person. Prices include all meals, drinks, and excursions, and vary from high season to low season. Half-price for kids under 12 years when they room with their parents.

OVERFLIGHT TRIPS TO THE LAGUNA SAN RAFAEL

Two companies arrange overflight trips to the Laguna San Rafael, which include a few hours near the glacier. It is a spectacular experience to view the glacier in its entirety (which means you won't want to do this trip on a cloudy day). These are charter flights, so you'll have to get a group together or fork over the entire price. Try **Flota Don Carlos,** Subteniente Cruz 63 (🕿 67/231981; www.doncarlos.cl; $1,100 for seven passengers), or **Aerohein,** Baquedano 500 (🕿 67/232772 or 67/252177; www.aerohein.cl; $740 for five passengers).

Where to Stay & Dine

Hotel Loberías del Sur ★ *Kids*   Puerto Chacabuco's shabbiness belies its lovely location on the shore of Aysén Sound, and, thankfully, this hotel does it justice with wraparound windows in a large dining area and lounge. The Loberías del Sur is the obvious choice for its location right above the pier and because it is the only decent hotel in Puerto Chacabuco. This is where most travelers with ferry connections spend the night when they don't want to make the early morning journey from Coyhaique. It's a large complex with a garden and a kid's play area. The rooms have been recently renovated with new wallpaper, paint, and linens, as have the bathrooms. Even if you're not planning on staying here, stop by for a seafood lunch or pisco sour before heading back to Coyhaique.

Carrera 50, Puerto Chacabuco, Región XI. Ⓒ **67/351115.** Fax 67/351188. www.catamaranesdelsur.cl/indexlober.htm. 60 units. $80–$130 double. Rates include buffet breakfast. DC, MC, V. **Amenities:** Restaurant; bar; lounge; gym; sauna; game room; gift shop; room service; laundry service. *In room:* TV.

Patagonia, Tierra del Fuego & Antarctica

Few places in the world have capti-vated the imagination of explorers and travelers like Patagonia and Tierra del Fuego. It has been 4 centuries since the first Europeans sailed through on a boat captained by Ferdinand Magel-lan. And yet this vast, remote region is still, for the most part, unexplored. Sailors from around the world con-tinue to test their luck and courage in these harrowing straits and fjords. Mountaineers stage elaborate excur-sions through rugged territories, only to be beaten back, like their predeces-sors, by unrelenting storms. A traveler can drive for days without seeing another soul on the vast Patagonian Pampa, his perception of time and dis-tance so warped that he believes he is the only human left on the planet. What seduces so many people to Patagonia is the idea of the "remote"—indeed, the very notion of

traveling to The End of the World. It is a seduction, but also an illusion. After all, people do live here—very few people, but those who do are hardy survivors.

A harsh, wind-whipped climate and Patagonia's geological curiosities have produced some of the most beautiful natural attractions in the world: the granite towers of Torres del Paine and Los Glaciares national parks, the Southern and Northern Ice Fields with their colossal glaciers, the flat Pampa broken by multicolored sedi-mentary bluffs, and the emerald fjords and lakes that glow an impossible sea-foam blue. In the end, this is what compels most travelers to plan a trip down here. Beyond landscapes, the region's "cowboys" (called *gauchos* in Argentina and *baquedanos* in Chile) lend a certain air of romanticism.

EXPLORING THE REGION

Patagonia and Tierra del Fuego are surprisingly easy to travel. It's entirely feasi-ble to plan a circuit that loops through, for example, Ushuaia, Punta Arenas, Torres del Paine, and then El Calafate and El Chaltén. There's so much to see and do here, you'll really want to include a visit to this region in your trip to Argentina or Chile, if possible. How much time you plan on spending in Patag-onia is entirely up to you. If you're planning a backpacking trip in Torres del Paine, for example, you'll want to spend between 5 and 10 days there—however, those with plans for a few light walks and sightseeing drives in that national park might find that 4 days are enough. A quick trip to Patagonia might include 2 days in El Calafate, 3 in Torres del Paine, and 2 in Punta Arenas. A longer jour-ney could begin with several days in El Chaltén, 2 in El Calafate, 5 in Torres del Paine, 2 in Punta Arenas, and a flight or cruise to Ushuaia for 3 to 4 days.

Prices jump and crowds swell from early November to late March, and some businesses open during this time frame only. The busiest months are January and February, but these summer months are not necessarily the best months to

Calling Between Chile & Argentina

One would think that two neighboring countries would offer low telephone rates for calls made from one to the other, but not so with Chile and Argentina. Visitors can expect to pay the same or higher rates as a call to the U.S., often around $1 per minute. When calling from Argentina to Chile, first dial **00-56,** then the area code and number. The prefix for Chilean cellphones is **09,** but callers from Argentina have to drop the 0; so to call a Chilean cellphone from Argentina, dial **00-56-9,** then the number.

When calling from Chile to Argentina, you must first call whichever carrier you're using (ask your host, your hotel, or at a calling center for the carrier prefix, usually either **123, 181,** or **188**), followed by **0-54,** then the area code and number. Argentine area codes always begin with a 0 prefix, which you'll drop when dialing from Chile. For example, if dialing from Punta Arenas, Chile, to Ushuaia, Argentina, you'll dial 123 (or whichever carrier you're using), then 0-54-2901 and the number. When dialing Argentine cellphone numbers (which begin with 15), drop the 15 and replace it with the region's area code.

visit Patagonia, as calmer weather prevails from mid-October to late November, and from mid-March to late April.

1 Punta Arenas, Chile

254km (158 miles) southeast of Puerto Natales; 3,090km (1,916 miles) south of Santiago

Punta Arenas, with a population of 110,000, is the capital of the Magellanic and Antarctic Region XII, and it is Patagonia's most important city. The streets here hum with activity, and its airport and seaports bustle with traffic. The town has made a living from carbon mines, wool production, petroleum, and fishing, and as a service center for cargo ships.

Punta Arenas's earliest wealth is reflected in the grand stone mansions that encircle the main plaza, which were built with earnings from the sheep *estancias,* or ranches, of the late 1800s. Gold fever followed, and then flight from World War I, when hundreds poured into the region from Yugoslavia, Russia, Spain, and Italy. Today Punta Arenas's streets are lined with residential homes with colorful, corrugated rooftops, business offices and hotels downtown, and an industrial port. The city considers itself somewhat of an independent republic due to its isolation from the rest of Chile, and this, in turn, has affected the personality of its people, an indefatigable bunch who brace themselves every summer against the gales that blow through this town like a hurricane. The wind, in fact, is so fierce at times that the city fastens ropes around the plaza for people to hold on to. If that weren't enough, residents here now have to contend with a paper-thin ozone layer, which nearly dissipates around November.

The history of this region and the extremity of Punta Arenas's climate, as well as its position overlooking the renowned Magellan Strait, make for a fascinating place to explore. Plan on spending at least one night here, but keep in mind that there is enough to do here to fill 2 days, if you have the time.

GETTING THERE

BY PLANE Punta Arenas's **Aeropuerto Presidente Ibáñez** is 20km (12 miles) north of town, and, depending on the season, it's serviced with up to 10

Patagonia

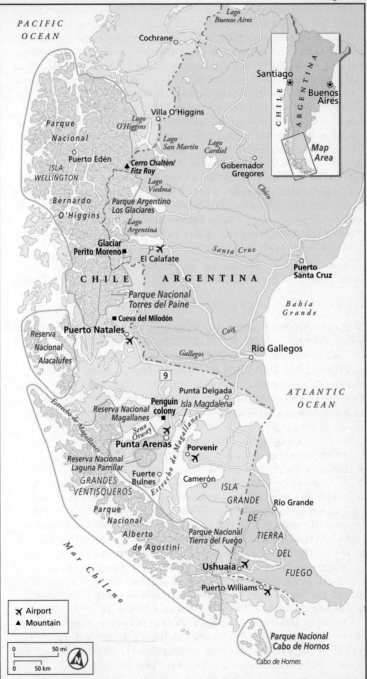

PACIFIC
OCEAN

Lago
Buenos Aires

Cochrane

Parque
Nacional

Puerto Edén

ISLA
WELLINGTON

Lago
O'Higgins

Villa O'Higgins

Lago
San Martín

Lago
Cardiel

Bernardo

O'Higgins

▲ Cerro Chaltén/
Fitz Roy

Lago
Viedma

Parque Argentino
Los Glaciares

Lago
Argentina

Gobernador
Gregores

Chico

Glaciar
Perito Moreno ■

✈
El Calafate

Santa Cruz

Puerto
Santa Cruz

CHILE : ARGENTINA

Parque Nacional
Torres del Paine

■ Cueva del Milodón

Bahía
Grande

Reserva

Nacional

Alacalufes

Puerto Natales
✈

Coig

Gallegos

Río Gallegos

9

Punta Delgada

Penguin
colony ■

Isla Magdalena

ATLANTIC
OCEAN

Reserva Nacional
Magallanes

Seno
Otway

✈

Punta Arenas

Porvenir
✈

Reserva Nacional
Laguna Parrillar

GRANDES
VENTISQUEROS

Fuerte
Bulnes

Camerón

ISLA

GRANDE

Río Grande

Parque
Nacional

Alberto
de Agostini

DE

TIERRA

DEL

FUEGO

Parque Nacional
Tierra del Fuego

Mar Chileno

Ushuaia ✈

Puerto Williams ✈

✈ Airport
▲ Mountain

0   50 mi
0   50 km

Parque Nacional
Cabo de Hornos

Cabo de Hornes

Map Area inset

PACIFIC OCEAN

Santiago ✪

Buenos
Aires ✪

CHILE

ARGENTINA

Map
Area

flights per day from Santiago (all stop in Puerto Montt). **Lan Express,** Lautaro Navarro 999 (© 600/661-3000 or 61/241100), has the most flights per day, but they are also the most expensive; they also have a Saturday flight from Balmaceda. **Sky Airline,** Roca 935 (© 600/600-2828; www.skyairline.cl), has two flights per day; and new on the scene is the Argentine airline **Aerolineas del Sur,** Pedro Montt 969 (© 210-9000), with one flight from Santiago per day. Lan Express has a daily flight to Ushuaia, as does the regional **Aerovías DAP,** O'Higgins 891 (© 61/223340; www.aeroviasdap.cl), with flights to and from Ushuaia every Tuesday and Friday from November to March; it also has daily service to Porvenir and the only air service to Puerto Williams, and Puerto Natales to Calafate (Nov–Mar only Mon–Fri). From November to March, DAP offers an unforgettable adventure to Cape Horn, with an overland flight and option to stay in Puerto Williams; the cost is $300 and the flight leaves on Sunday, Monday, and Wednesday. To get to Punta Arenas, hire a taxi for about $8 or take one of the transfer services there (which can also arrange to take you back to the airport; their booths are at the baggage claim area). **Buses Transfer Austral** (© 61/229613) has door-to-door service for $5 per person; **Buses Pacheco** (© 61/242174; www.buses pacheco.com) has service to its station at Colón 900 for $2.50.

BY BUS From Puerto Natales: **Bus Sur,** José Menéndez 565 (© 61/244464), has four daily trips; **Buses Fernández,** Armando Sanhueza 745 (© 61/221429;

Cruising from Punta Arenas to Ushuaia

Mare Australis operates an unforgettable journey between Punta Arenas and Ushuaia aboard its ship, the M/V *Mare Australis.* This cruise takes passengers to remote coves and narrow channels and fjords in Tierra del Fuego, and then heads into the Beagle Channel, stopping in Puerto Williams on Isla Navarino and later Ushuaia, Argentina. The trip can be done as a 7-night, 8-day round-trip journey; a 4-night one-way from Punta Arenas; or a 3-night one-way journey from Ushuaia. I recommend that you take just the one-way journey, leaving you to explore a new city and then travel by air or land from there.

What is unique about this cruise is the intimacy of a smaller ship and its solitary route that takes passengers to places in Tierra del Fuego that few have a chance to see. Passengers are shuttled to shore via zodiacs (motorized inflatable boats) for two daily excursions that can include visits to glaciers or a sea elephant rookery, walks to view elaborate beaver dams, or horseback rides. There are several excellent bilingual guides who give daily talks about the region's flora, fauna, history, and geology. Service aboard the *Mare Australis* is excellent, and the food is quite good. The accommodations are comfortable, ranging from suites to simple cabins. All-inclusive, per-person prices (excluding cocktails) range from $785 to $1,903 one-way from Punta Arenas and $1,152 to $2,537 round-trip. This cruise operates from early October to late April. For reservations or information, contact their U.S. offices in Miami at 4014 Chase Ave., Suite 202 (© 877/678-3772; fax 305/534-9276); in Santiago at Av. El Bosque Norte 0440 (© 2/442-3110; fax 2/203-5173); and in Punta Arenas at Av. Independencia 840 (© 61/224256); or visit www.australis.com.

ACCOMMODATIONS ■
Cabo de Hornos Hotel **7**
Hostal de la Avenida **15**
Hostal Oro Fuegino **11**
Hostal del Sur **14**
Hotel Calafate **10**
Hotel Finis Terrae **12**
Hotel Isla Rey Jorge **2**
Hotel José Nogueira **8**
Tierra del Fuego **13**

DINING ◆
Brocolino **6**
La Pérgola **9**
Remezón **1**
Sotitos **4**
Puerto Viejo **3**
ATTRACTIONS ●
City Cemetery **17**
Instituto de Patagonia **18**
Museo Naval y Marítimo **5**
Museo Salesiano
  Maggiorino Borgatello **16**
Palacio Sara Braun **8**

www.busesfernandez.com), has seven daily trips; **Buses Transfer Austral,** Pedro Montt 966 (© **61/229613**), has two daily trips; and **Buses Pacheco,** Av. Colón 900 (© **61/242174;** www.busespacheco.com), has three daily trips. The cost is about $5 and the trip takes 3 hours.

To and from Ushuaia, Argentina: **Buses Tecni Austral,** Lautaro Navarro 975 (© **61/222078**), and **Buses Ghisoni,** Lautaro Navarro 971 (© **61/223205**), leave Punta Arenas Tuesday, Thursday, Saturday, and Sunday, and return from Ushuaia on Monday, Wednesday, and Saturday; the cost for either is $35. **Buses Pacheco,** Av. Colón 900 (© **61/242174**), has direct service to Ushuaia on Thursday and Sunday, and returns on Friday and Monday for $33; they also have service to Ushuaia with a stop first in Río Grande for the same price, leaving Monday, Wednesday, and Friday, and returning on Tuesday, Thursday, and Saturday. Buses cross through Porvenir or Punta Delgada. The direct trip to Ushuaia takes about 12 hours.

BY CAR Ruta 9 is a paved road between Punta Arenas and Puerto Natales. Strong winds often require that you exercise extreme caution when driving this route. To get to Tierra del Fuego, there are two options: Cross by ferry from Punta Arenas to Porvenir, or drive east on Ruta 255 to Ruta 277 and Punta Delgada for the ferry crossing there (for more information, see "The Far South: Puerto Williams, Chile," later in this chapter).

CAR RENTAL The following rental agencies have offices in town and kiosks at the airport: **Hertz,** O'Higgins 987 (© **61/248742;** www.hertz.com); **Lubac,**

Magallanes 970 (© 61/242023); **Budget,** O'Higgins 964 (© 61/202720; www.
budget.com); **Emsa,** Roca 1044 (© 61/241182); and **Rus Rent a Car,** Av.
Colón 839 (© 61/221529; www.rusrentacar.cl.

GETTING AROUND

Punta Arenas is compact enough to explore on foot; however, taxis are plentiful
and you can hail one off the street. Travel anywhere within the city limits will
not cost more than $3; always confirm the fare with your driver before getting
in the car. Buses are also abundant and run either north-south on calles Bulnes
and Noguiera or east-west along Independencia. Bus fare is about 70¢.

VISITOR INFORMATION

There's an excellent **Oficina de Turismo** (© 61/200610) inside a glass gazebo
in the Plaza de Armas. The staff is helpful, and they sell a wide range of historical and anthropological literature and postcards. The office is open from
December to March Monday through Friday from 8am to 8pm, Saturday from
9am to 6:30pm, and Sunday from 9am to 2pm. The rest of the year, it is open
Monday through Friday from 8am to 7pm only, and Saturday from 9am to
6:30pm (except May–Sept, when it closes on Sat and at 5pm on weekdays). **Sernatur**'s office at Hernándo de Magallanes 960 (© **61/248790;** www.sernatur.
cl), on the other hand, is harried and inattentive; it's open Monday through Friday from 8:15am to 12:45pm and 2:30 to 7pm.

FAST FACTS: **Punta Arenas**

Currency Exchange Exchange money at **La Hermandad,** Lautaro Navarro
1099 (© 61/248090); **Cambios Gasic,** Roca 915, #8 (© 61/242396); **Cambio
de Moneda Stop,** José Nogueira 1168 (© 61/223334); or **Scott Cambios,**
corner of Avenida Colón and Magallanes (© 61/244464). Casas de cambio
are open Monday through Friday from 9am to 1pm and 3 to 7pm, and
Saturday from 9am to 1pm. For banks with 24-hour ATMs, go to **Banco
Santander,** Magallanes 997 (© 61/247145); **Banco de Chile,** Roca 864
(© 61/206033); or **Banco de A. Edwards,** Plaza Muñoz Gamero 1055 (© 61/
241175). Banks are open Monday through Friday from 9am to 2pm.

Hospital The local hospitals are **Hospital de las FF. AA. Cirujano Guzmán,**
Avenida Manuel Bulnes and Guillermos (© 61/207500), and **Clínica Magallanes,** Av. Manuel Bulnes 1448 (© 61/211527).

Internet Access Try **Telefónica,** Bories 798 (© 61/248230), or better yet,
Calafate, Magallanes 22 (© 61/241281). Internet service costs an average
of $3 per hour.

Laundry Try **Lavandería Antártida,** Jorge Montt 664; **Autoservicio Lava-
sol,** O'Higgins 969; **Lavandería Lavasuper,** José Nogueira 1595; or **Limpec,**
21 de Mayo 1261.

Pharmacy Go to **Farmacias Ahumada,** Bories 950 (© 61/245188); **Farmacias Cruz Verde,** Bories 858 (© 61/246572); or **Farmacia Salco,** Bories 970
(© 61/229227).

Post Office The central post office is at José Menéndez and Bories (© 61/
222210); hours are Monday through Friday from 9am to 6pm, and Saturday from 9am to 1pm.

WHAT TO SEE & DO IN PUNTA ARENAS

There are a surprising number of activities and sights to fill your day(s) while in Punta Arenas, the reason I recommend you stay here 1 night at the very least. Begin your tour of Punta Arenas in the **Plaza Muñoz Gamero,** where you'll find a bronze **sculpture** of Ferdinand Magellan donated by the region's long-ago wool czar José Menendez. Magellan is surrounded by lounging native Indians, one of whom has a shiny toe polished by the hundreds of visitors who kiss the nub each year; local lore here says that if you kiss the toe, you'll be lucky enough to visit Patagonia once again. The tranquil little plaza, delineated by cypress and other regional trees, has a visitor's center gazebo, and several vendors here display crafts and souvenirs for sale. Around the plaza are old Punta Arenas's principal **mansions and edifices** from its pioneering days, which have, fortunately, been well kept over the decades. From the plaza on Avenida 21 de Mayo, head north toward Avenida Colón for a look at the **Teatro Municipal,** designed by the French architect Numa Mayer and modeled after the Teatro Colón in Buenos Aires. Head down to the waterfront and turn south toward the pier, where you'll find a 1913 clock imported from Germany that has a complete meteorological instrumentation and hands showing the moon's phases and a zodiac calendar.

City Cemetery ⊛   They say you can't really understand a culture until you see where they bury their dead, and in the case of the cemetery of Punta Arenas, this edict certainly rings true. The City Cemetery was opened by the Governor Señoret in 1894 and is fronted by a giant stone portico donated by Sara Braun in 1919. Inside this necropolis lies a veritable miniature city, with avenues that connect the magnificent tombs of the region's founding families, settlers, and civic workers, and a rather solemn tomb where lie the remains of the last Selk'-nam Indians of Tierra del Fuego. The Alice-in-Wonderland cypress trees that line the tombs make for a surreal atmosphere. If you can, organize a city tour so that a guide may delve into the fascinating history behind the lives of the pioneers and Indians buried here. It's about a 20-minute walk from the plaza.

Av. Manuel Bulnes and Angamos. No phone. Free admission. Daily Oct–Mar 7:30am–8pm; Apr–Sept daily 8am–6:30pm.

Instituto de Patagonia/Museo del Recuerdo ⊛   The Instituto de Patagonia is run by the University of Magallanes and directed by the region's chief historian, Dr. Mateo Martinic. Here you'll find an engaging exhibit of colonial artifacts called the Museum of Remembrances. Antique machinery and horse-drawn carts are displayed around the lawn and encircled by several colonial buildings that have been lifted and transported here from ranches around the area. One cabin shows visitors what home life was like for a ranch hand, another has been set up to resemble a typical dry goods store, another is a garage with a 1908 Peugeot, and another is a carpenter's workshop. There's a library on the premises with a collection of books and maps on display and for sale. To get into the colonial buildings, you'll need to ask someone in the museum's office to unlock them for you. The museum is about 4km (2½ miles) out of town, so you'll need to take a taxi. The Zona Franca (a duty-free shopping center) is just down the street, so you could tie in a visit to the two.

Av. Manuel Bulnes 01890. ⒸⒻ **61/217173.** Admission 70¢. Mon–Fri 8:30am–noon and 2:30–6pm; Sat 8:30am–noon; erratic hours and closing policies on Sun, so call ahead.

Museo Naval y Marítimo   Punta Arenas's tribute to its seafaring history is this Naval and Maritime Museum. Here you'll find photos depicting the various ships and port activity over the past century, as well as small ship replicas and other artifacts. This museum is really recommended only for those with a strong interest in nautical-related items.

Pedro Montt 981. No phone. Admission $1. Tues–Sat 9:30am–12:30pm and 3–6pm.

Museo Salesiano Maggiorino Borgatello ★★ *(Kids*

This mesmerizing museum offers an insight into the Magellanic region's history, anthropology, ecology, and industrial history. That said, the lobby-level floor is packed with a fusty collection of stuffed and mounted birds and mammals that at turns feels almost macabre, considering that many have lost their shape; nevertheless, it allows you to fully appreciate the tremendous size of the condor and the puma. Several rooms in the museum display Indian hunting tools, ritual garments, jewelry, an Alacalufe bark canoe, and colonial and ranching implements, as well as the inevitable religious artifacts from the Catholic missionaries who played such a large role in the deterioration of native Indians' culture. Perhaps some of the most intriguing items on view here are the black-and-white photos of the early missionary Alberto d'Agostini, whose collection is a rare documentation of the native cultures who have since disappeared from this region. There's a petroleum display that will appeal only to anyone interested in that subject.

Av. Manuel Bulnes and Maipú. © 61/221001. Admission $2.25. Tues–Sun 10am–12:30pm and 3–6pm.

Palacio Sara Braun and Museo Regional Braun Menéndez ★★ *(Moments*

These two attractions are testament to the staggering wealth produced by the region's large-scale, colonial-era sheep and cattle *estancias*. The museums are the former residences of several members of the families Braun, Nogueira, and Menéndez, who believed that any far-flung, isolated locale could be tolerated if one were to "live splendidly and remain in constant contact with the outside world." And live splendidly they did in these veritable palaces. The Palacio Sara Braun is now partially occupied by the Hotel José Nogueira and the Club de la Unión, a meeting area for the city's commercial and political leaders. Sara Braun, who emigrated from Russia with her brother Mauricio Braun, was the widow of the shipping, wool, and cattle magnet José Nogueira. The Museo Regional Braun Menéndez is the former residence of Mauricio Braun and Josefina Menéndez, a marriage that united the two largest fortunes in the Magellanic region. With the falling price of wool and the nationalization of *estancias* during the early 1970s, the families lost a large percentage of their holdings, and their descendants have relocated to places such as Buenos Aires.

The homes are national monuments, and both have been preserved in their original state, which allows visitors to appreciate the finest European craftsmanship available at the end of the 19th century. French architects planned the neoclassical exteriors, and craftsmen were brought from Europe to sculpt marble fireplaces and hand-paint walls to resemble marble and leather. The interior fixtures and furniture were also imported from Europe, including gold and crystal chandeliers, tapestries from Belgium, Arabian tables inset with abalone, stained-glass cupolas, English and French furniture, hand-carved desks, and more. For some visitors, the knowledge that these families single-handedly exterminated the Native Indians in the region on their quest for wealth may temper the appreciation for the grandeur of these palaces. The Museo Menéndez also has a salon devoted to the ranching and maritime history of the region. Tours are conducted in Spanish; however, the museums offer literature in English.

Palacio Sara Braun: Plaza Muñoz Gamero 716. © 61/248840. Admission $1.50 adults, free for those under 16. Mon–Fri 11am–1pm and 4–8:30pm; Sat 10:30am–1pm and 8–10pm.

Museo Regional Braun Menéndez: Magallanes 949. (*C*) **61/244216.** Admission $1.15 adults, 60¢ children under 16. Sun and holidays free. Nov–Apr Mon–Fri 10:30am–5pm; Sat–Sun 10:30am–2pm; May–Oct daily 10:30am–2pm.

SHOPPING

Punta Arenas is home to a duty-free shopping center called the **Zona Franca,** with several blocks of shops hawking supposedly cheaper electronics, home appliances, imported foodstuffs, sporting goods, perfumes, clothing, toys, booze, and cigarettes. The savings here are negligible, except for on alcohol, and the selection isn't what you'd hope for, although there certainly is a lot on offer, including a few supermarkets. However, this is a good place to stock up on supplies if you're planning a backpack trip to Torres del Paine—otherwise, forget it. The Zona Franca is located on Avenida Manuel Bulnes, just outside town. Because of its proximity to the Museo del Recuerdo (see "What to See & Do in Punta Arenas," above), you might want to tie a visit in here with that attraction; take a taxi to get there. It's open Monday through Saturday from 10am to 12:30pm and 3 to 8pm, and closed Sunday and holidays.

For regional crafts, try the good selection available at **Chile Típico,** Carrera Pinto 1015 (*C* **61/225827**), or **Artesanía Yoyi,** Av. 21 de Mayo 1393 (*C* **61/ 229156**). Both have knitwear, carved-wood items, lapis lazuli, and more. For high-end, artsy-craftsy household items such as picture frames, candles, throws, curtains, and the like, try **Almacén Antaño,** Colón 100 (no phone).

EXCURSIONS OUTSIDE PUNTA ARENAS
TOUR OPERATORS

Many tour operators run conventional city tours and trips to the penguin colonies, as well as short visits and multiday, all-inclusive trekking excursions to Torres del Paine National Park; however, for excursions within the park I recommend that you stick with one of the outfitters listed under tour operators in the Puerto Natales section. A city tour here provides the historical background to this region and undoubtedly enriches a visitor's understanding of the hardship the immigrants and native Indians faced during the past century.

Turismo Yamana, Errázuriz 932 (*C* **61/710567;** www.yamana.cl), offers thrilling kayak trips on and around the Strait of Magellan and Tierra del Fuego for multiple days with a support boat (about $3,245 per person for an all-inclusive 8 days, two persons; $2,934 per person for three to four people). Multiple-day trips take kayakers to elephant seal and penguin colonies, and through fjords and past glaciers. The company also offers multiple-day trips to Lago Blanco in Tierra del Fuego for trekking, horseback riding, and fishing.

Turismo Comapa, Magallanes 990 (*C* **61/200200;** www.comapa.com), is the leader in town for conventional tours such as city tours and visits to the penguin colonies. City tours last approximately 3 hours. **Turismo Viento Sur,** 585 Fagnano (*C* **61/226930;** www.vientosur.com), is another respected company offering excursions in and around Punta Arenas, including a trip to the little-known Pali Aike National Park. Viento Sur also has half-day and full-day kayaking trips with qualified guides.

FUERTE BULNES

In 1843, Capt. Juan Williams, the naturalist Bernardo Philippi, 16 sailors and soldiers, and 2 women set sail from Ancud in Chiloé to the Strait of Magellan to plant the Chilean flag in this region before European colonists could beat them to it. They chose a rocky promontory that dominated the strait and named it **Fuerte Bulnes.** Although this promontory was strategically appropriate for monitoring seafaring traffic, the location proved undesirable, and they pulled up stakes and moved 25km (16 miles) north, founding what is today Punta Arenas. In recognition of the historical value of Fuerte Bulnes, the Chilean government reconstructed the site in 1943, its centenary anniversary, and made it a national monument. Here you'll find reproductions of the log cabins that housed the settlers, a chapel, and several cannons. There are no set hours, and admission is free.

Just before Fuerte Bulnes is a short road leading to **Puerto Hambre.** The site was founded as Rey Felipe by Pedro Sarmiento de Gamboa in 1584, and settled by 103 colonists who were tragically stranded after tremendous storms prevented their ships from returning to shore. The name Puerto Hambre (Port Hunger) was given by the British captain Thomas Cavendish, who found only one survivor when he docked here in 1587 (the rest had died of starvation and exposure). In 1993, the Chilean ambassador José Miguel Barros found the plan for Rey Felipe in the library of the Institute of France in Paris, and it is the oldest known document of urban history in Chile. The only thing you'll find here is a plaque and the remains of a chapel, but imagining yourself in the place of these settlers on this forsaken plot is worth the visit—if you have enough time and are running out of things to see near Punta Arenas. Admission for both Fuerte Bulnes and Puerto Hambre is free, with unspecified hours. To get here, sign up for a tour with Comapa or Viento Sur (see above).

PENGUIN COLONIES AT SENO OTWAY & ISLA MAGDALENA

One of the highlights of a visit to Punta Arenas is a trip to the penguin colonies at Seno Otway or Isla Magdalena. Both colonies allow visitors to get surprisingly close to the amusing Magellanic penguins (also called jackass penguins for their characteristic bray) at their nesting sites. But this happens only during their natural nesting cycle from October to March—and even by early March, they've all pretty much packed up and headed north. November to February provides the best viewing. Isla Magdalena is by far the best place to view the penguins (with an estimated 150,000 in one colony, as compared to 3,000 at Seno Otway). But the trip here involves a ferry ride and will take up more of your time.

Penguins form lifelong partnerships and divide their chores equally: Every morning around 10am and in the afternoon around 5pm, the penguin couples change shifts—one heads out to fish, the other returns from fishing to take care of their young. When this changing of the guard begins, the penguins politely line up and waddle to and from the sea.

Seno Otway is accessible by road about 65km (40 miles) from Punta Arenas. A volunteer study group has developed the sight with roped walkways and lookout posts, including a peek-a-boo wall where you can watch the penguins diving into the ocean. Tours are offered in four languages, and there is a tiny cafe here, too. It's open daily from October 15 to March 31 from 8am to 8:30pm. The best time to visit is between 9 and 10am and 5 and 7pm, when the majority of activity takes place (the crowds of visitors are thinner during the morning shift). The cost of a tour here is about $10 to $12, plus a $4 entrance fee (free for kids; ✆ **61/224454**). Take Ruta 9 toward Puerto Natales, then turn left on the dirt road that branches out near the police checkpoint. Keep your eyes open for the ostrichlike Darwin's rhea on the ride here.

Isla Magdalena is much larger than Seno Otway, with an estimated 150,000 penguins sharing nesting space with cormorants. These penguins are more timid than those at Seno Otway, but the sight of so many of these birds bustling to and fro is decidedly more impressive. To get here, you need to take a ferry, which makes for a pleasant half-day afternoon excursion. **Turismo Comapa,** Av. Magallanes 990 (© **61/200200;** www.comapa.com), puts this tour together. Its boat, the *Barcaza Melinka,* departs from the pier at 3:30pm and returns at 8:30pm on Tuesday, Thursday, and Saturday from December to February ($28 for adults, $13 children under 12).

SKIING IN THE AREA

Punta Arenas has a ski resort that operates from mid-June to mid-September: the **Centro de Esquí Cerro Mirador,** situated at the border of the Reserva Nacional Magallanes. If you're here during the season, this little resort is a fun place to spend the afternoon, notable more than anything else for its view of the Strait of Magellan, Tierra del Fuego, and—on a clear day—Dawson Island. During the summer, they often run their only chair lift to carry you to the top of the peak, or you can hike the hill yourself. The resort has 10 runs, ski rental, and a cafeteria. Ski lift tickets cost about $18; a ski rental package is $22. The resort (© **61/241479**) is very close to town; to get here, take a taxi.

WHERE TO STAY

In general, lodging in Punta Arenas is somewhat expensive for the caliber of accommodations available; however, its strong suit is its abundance of simple and economical hostels. Note that price ranges reflect the low to high season—high season being from October 15 to April 15—and that each hotel is willing to negotiate a price, especially if you book the more expensive hotels with a travel agent. Always ask for "promotional rates" when calling a hotel, and check the hotel's website (when available) for Internet-only discounted rates.

EXPENSIVE

Hotel Finis Terrae 🗲🗲   This hotel is very popular with foreigners, especially Americans, and it's part of the Best Western chain. The well-lit accommodations here are very comfortable, with king-size beds in double rooms and a softly hued decor in peach and beige, with wood trim and wooden headboards. And although Richard Gere stayed here in November 2002 (he chose the spacious fifth-floor suite with a whirlpool tub and minibar) on his way to Antarctica to film a documentary, the rooms are by no means luxurious. The singles here are tiny, so be sure to ask for a larger double for the single price, which they will likely agree to, especially during slower months. The simple yet panoramic penthouse restaurant has an enormous A-frame ceiling fronted with windows on both ends that look out over the city and the Strait of Magellan. There's an adjoining lounge where visitors can relax and order a drink. The view from these two salons is undoubtedly the best in Punta Arenas.

Av. Colón 766, Punta Arenas. © 61/228200. Fax 61/248124. www.hotelfinisterrae.com. 64 units, 2 suites. $140–$160 double; $170–$210 superior suite. Rates include buffet breakfast. AE, DC, MC, V. **Amenities:** Restaurant; lounge; room service; laundry service. *In room:* TV, minibar, safe.

Hotel Isla Rey Jorge 🗲🗲 *(Finds*   This hotel is housed in an antique English-style mansion, 2 blocks from the plaza. There's a compact lounge lit by a pergola-like glass ceiling, decorated with a blue country-style theme. Altogether, it's a lovable little hotel. The snug rooms (some are quite small) with angled eaves are just slightly dark but kept toasty warm. Rooms have a classic, executive-style decor, in navy blue and burgundy offset with brass details. The junior suites are the most spacious, with king-size beds and whirlpool tubs. The friendly staff let it be known that they rarely charge the advertised price, so always ask for a discount. Downstairs, in what was the brick-walled cellar, is an intimate restaurant and a popular pub where they serve, among more standard fare, regional dishes such as Calafate (a wild berry) mousse and grilled beaver.

Av. 21 de Mayo 1243, Punta Arenas. ©/fax 61/248220. www.islareyjorge.com. 25 units. $150–$110 double; from $189 junior suite. Rates include buffet breakfast. AE, DC, MC, V. **Amenities:** Restaurant; pub; room service; laundry service. *In room:* TV.

Hotel José Nogueira ✪✪✪ (Moments) The best hotel in town is in this partially converted neoclassical mansion once owned by the widow of one of Punta Arenas's wealthiest entrepreneurs; half of the building is still run as a museum. The mansion was built between 1894 and 1905 on a prominent corner across from the plaza, with materials imported entirely from Europe. The José Nogueira is appealing for its historical value but also offers classic luxury. The rooms here are not as large as you would expect, but high ceilings accented by floor-to-ceiling curtains compensate for that. All are tastefully decorated, with Oriental rugs and lithographs of local fauna; the marble bathrooms are sparkling. The Nogueira's singles are unusually spacious. The suites have ample bathrooms with Jacuzzi tubs and a living area in the open bedroom. Keeping with the old-fashioned theme, the maids here dress in long smocks. The mansion's old "winter garden" is now a restaurant, La Pérgola, housed under the Nogueira's glass-enclosed terrace. Downstairs is a popular pub in what once was the wine cellar.

Bories 959, Punta Arenas. © 61/248840. Fax 61/248832. www.hotelnogueira.com. 25 units, 3 suites. $115–$179 double; $135–$255 suite. Rates include buffet breakfast. AE, DC, MC, V. **Amenities:** Restaurant; bar; room service; laundry service. *In room:* TV, minibar.

Tierra del Fuego ✪ (Value) If you're looking for good value in this price category, then look no further. The Tierra del Fuego offers some of the most spacious accommodations in Punta Arenas, especially if you request the second-floor rooms that come with kitchenette at no extra charge. Rooms are comfortable, but don't expect much elegance: brown carpet, flowery bedspreads, and dark wood furniture. The marble bathrooms are clean but small. The focus of the hotel is the ground-floor pub that pulls in many of the city's young professionals and visiting businessmen. It gives the hotel a vibrant, youthful atmosphere. There's also a computer with Internet access available to guests for a small fee.

Colon 716, Punta Arenas. ©/fax 61/226200. www.puntaarenas.com. 26 units. $98 double; from $130 suite. Rates include buffet breakfast. AE, MC, V. **Amenities:** Restaurant; pub; room service; laundry service. *In room:* TV, dataport, minibar, hair dryer.

MODERATE

Hostal de la Avenida ✪ This olive-colored, homey hostel looks as though it were run by a little old lady, judging by the sugary dining area decorated in floral prints and porcelain figurines. Some of the rooms are very dark; however, the management has seen to small details like fruit on the nightstand, a complimentary toothbrush, and a well-priced minibar. Most rooms face a plant-filled "garden"; ask for one of the four rooms upstairs that receive more light. Rooms are simple, with brick walls, and the breakfast is hearty.

Av. Colón 534, Punta Arenas. ©/fax 61/247532. 7 units. $50–$60 double. Rates include continental breakfast. AE, DC, MC, V. **Amenities:** Lounge. *In room:* TV, minibar.

Hostal Oro Fueguino ✪ (Value) This hostal is a favorite with backpackers and budget travelers for its clean, comfortable rooms and friendly service. The interiors here are painted vibrant colors and decorated with folk art, and there are rooms for doubles, triples, and quadruples—all with private bathrooms. Their plant-filled, colorful dining room and lounge is a cozy spot to relax. The hostal is a 5-block walk up from the plaza; look for the bright yellow-and-aqua exterior.

Fagnano 356. ⓒ **61/249401.** www.orofueguino.cl. 12 units. $52 double with private bathroom; $40 double with shared bathroom. Rates include continental breakfast. AE, DC, MC, V. **Amenities:** Lounge; laundry. *In room:* TV.

Hotel Calafate ⚘ *Value*   A central location and a full-service, 24-hour Internet cafe on the first floor make the Hotel Calafate a good value in Punta Arenas. This is really the only moderately priced "hotel" (as opposed to a funkier hostel) in the city, and, therefore, rooms feature comfortable mattresses rather than foam beds, and a more standardized hotel design that is a little on the frilly side nonetheless. Most doubles, triples, and quadruples are reasonably spacious (some with private bathrooms, some with shared); however, there are two tiny rooms that go for just $13 per person. The staff is helpful in assisting with travel plans.

Magallanes 22, Punta Arenas. ⓒ **61/241281.** www.calafate.cl. 19 units. $53 double with private bathroom; $38 double with shared bathroom. Rates include continental breakfast. AE, DC, MC, V. **Amenities:** Internet cafe. *In room:* TV.

INEXPENSIVE

Hostal del Sur *Value*   This little hostal is tucked away on a residential street among a grove of pine trees, and it has been popularized by word of mouth. It is more of a family-style hostal, with exceptionally pleasant service and a friendly yellow Labrador that welcomes you at the door. Simple yet clean rooms and private bathrooms in every room make this hostal a good value.

Mejicana 151, Punta Arenas. ⓒ **61/227249.** Fax 61/249401. 8 units. $30 double. No credit cards. **Amenities:** Lounge. *In room:* TV.

WHERE TO DINE

There are plenty of good restaurants in Punta Arenas, most of which serve local fare such as lamb, king crab, and shellfish. All major hotels have decent restaurants, if you feel like dining in. For a quick bite, try the casual cafe **Patiperros,** Av. Colón 782 (ⓒ **61/245298**), open daily from 11am to 1am. A local favorite, although slightly overpriced, is the diner-style **El Mercado,** Mejicana 617 (ⓒ **61/247415**). If you're not planning a trip to Chiloé, you might want to try El Mercado's version of that island's specialty: *curanto,* a heaping surf-and-turf platter with tomato broth. The liveliest cafe for drinks or sandwiches is the **Pub 1900** (corner of Bories and Colón; ⓒ **61/242759**); it is the social center for townsfolk here. The best casual spot for dinner and a pint of beer is **Santino,** Colón 657 (ⓒ **61/220511**), a spacious pub/restaurant that is the happening spot at night; they have sandwiches and simple Chilean dishes like *lomo a lo pobre,* that heart attack on a plate dish of steak, fries, and a fried egg.

Brocolino ⚘⚘ REGIONAL/PASTA   One of the city's better restaurants, Brocolino features food that is Italian and French by genre, but made with mostly regional ingredients; all are elegantly presented and utterly delicious. The quirky menu is described by the chef as offering "sensual" food, such as the Aphrodisiac Raviolis or the Promiscuous Crayfish. Other highlights are the roast Patagonian lamb and the pasta "roll," something akin to a crepe stuffed with spinach and king crab, or the steak with pistachio sauce.

O'Higgins 1049. ⓒ **61/710479.** Main courses $7–$13. AE, DC, MC, V. Daily 11am–midnight.

La Pérgola ⚘ REGIONAL   La Pérgola is located inside the glass-enclosed, vine-draped "winter garden" that once was part of the stately mansion owned by Sara Braun, now part of the Hotel José Nogueira. The ambience is as lovely as the cuisine; and the long days of summer mean diners can enjoy the well-lit glass pergola until 11pm. The menu provides photos of each dish, including king crab quiche, curried lamb with glazed carrots, filet mignon in three sauces, and pork loin in a cherry sauce. There's even salmon sashimi. An ample wine list and desserts such as tiramisu round out the menu.

Bories 959. ℂ **61/248840.** Main courses $9–$13. AE, DC, MC, V. Daily noon–3:30pm and 7:30pm–midnight.

Puerto Viejo ★★ *Kids* SEAFOOD   Located at the old port of Punta Arenas (hence its name), this newer restaurant serves outstanding seafood dishes and fresh pastas. The modern, nautically themed design—with a faux ship's bow and fish nets strewn above tables—provides a casual ambience that will appeal to kids, too. The fresh-from-the-ocean seafood is delicately prepared and served by helpful, gracious waiters. This is where you should sample a cold plate of king crab, or other highlights such as abalone casserole, a savory conger eel "Mediterranean" made with tomatoes and artichoke hearts, or hake with cider sauce. The bright, airy interiors make this a good spot for lunch.

O'Higgins 1205. ℂ **61/225103.** Main courses $6–$12. AE, DC, MC, V. Daily 12:30–3:30pm and 7–11:30pm.

Remezón ★★ *Finds* CONTEMPORARY/REGIONAL   One of the best restaurants in the region, Remezón breaks from the traditional mold with a warm, intimate dining area decorated with a jumble of art and slightly kitschy items that are as personal as the chef's daily changing menu. The food is, in a word, divine—not too pretentious, but always prepared with fresh regional vegetables, seafood, and meats seasoned to delicious perfection. Sample dishes include broiled Parmesan scallops; calamari, zucchini, and avocado salad; goose marinated in pisco and lemon; and crepes stuffed with king crab and cream. There are also exotic items such as guanaco and ñandú. My only complaint is that their wine list is overpriced and of mediocre quality. Remezón is about a 4-block walk from the plaza. Don't miss their calafate-berry piscos.

Av. 21 de Mayo 1469. ℂ **61/241029.** Main courses $8–$13. AE, DC, MC, V. Daily noon–3pm and 7:15pm–midnight. Closed Mon Apr–Sept.

Sotitos ★ CHILEAN   Don't be fooled by the plain green front and weathered sign: Sotitos has handsome semiformal interiors with brick walls and white linen tablecloths. If you're looking for traditional Chilean cuisine, this is your restaurant. Sotitos offers more than most Chilean restaurants, including steak and seafood, local baked lamb, Valencia shellfish rice (which must be ordered ahead of time), pastas, and fresh salads. The key is that everything is of high quality, regardless of how simple the dish. The service here is attentive but not overbearing. On Friday, Saturday, and Sunday, the restaurant fires up their *parrilla* (grill) for barbecued meats. There's a nonsmoking section up front, but it's usually empty.

O'Higgins 1138. ℂ **61/221061.** Main courses $6–$13. AE, DC, MC, V. Mon–Sat 11:30am–3pm and 7–11:45pm.

PUNTA ARENAS AFTER DARK

The city has a handful of good bars and pubs, plus a few discos, which I recommend only if you like to hang out with teenagers and listen to bad techno music. One of the most popular pubs is **Santino** (see above under "Where to Dine"), and it is especially suitable for large groups; or try the more intimate ambience of the **La Taberna** (ℂ **61/248840**) cellar bar, below the Hotel José Nogueira at the corner of Bories and Sequel across from the plaza; appetizers are available. Another popular spot is the **Pub 1900** (ℂ **61/242759**), at the corner of Avenida Colón and Bories; yet another pub is the **El Galeón**, Av. 21 de Mayo 1243, below the Hotel Isla Rey Jorge (ℂ **61/248220**). The **Cabo de Hornos Hotel** (ℂ **61/242134**), on the plaza, has a 1960s-chic bar but a decidedly more somber atmosphere. The **Cine Estrella,** Mejicana 777 (© **61/225630**), is the only cinema in town; call or check newspaper listings for what's playing.

2 Puerto Natales, Chile

254km (158 miles) northwest of Punta Arenas; 115km (71 miles) south of Torres del Paine

Puerto Natales is a rambling town of 15,000, spread along the sloping coast of the Señoret Canal between the Ultima Esperanza Sound and the Almirante Montt Gulf. This is the jump-off point for trips to Torres del Paine, and many visitors to the park will find themselves spending at least 1 night here. The town itself has grown recently to accommodate more tourism-oriented businesses, but it is still really nothing more than a small center with rows and rows of weather-beaten tin and wooden houses. Puerto Natales has a frontier-town appeal, and it boasts a stunning location with grand views out onto a grassy peninsula and glacier-capped peaks in the distance. From May to September, the town virtually goes into hibernation, but come October, the town's streets are crowded with international tourists decked out in parkas and hiking boots on their way to or back from the park.

Puerto Natales was founded in 1911 as a residential center and export port for local sheep ranches. Tourism has now replaced wool as a dominant economic force, evident by the plethora of hostels, restaurants, and tour companies found here.

ESSENTIALS
GETTING THERE & GETTING AROUND
BY PLANE   The tiny Puerto Natales airport (no phone) has only one scheduled flight per day, and that is a nine-passenger propeller plane from El Calafate. Contact **Aerovías DAP,** in Punta Arenas, at O'Higgins 891 (© **61/223340;** www.aeroviasdap.cl), for information and reservations. At this writing, the one-way fare is $54 for the short hop to Argentina. A taxi from Puerto Natales to the airport costs $2 and is only a 5-minute drive. Windy days may affect flight schedules.

BY BUS   Puerto Natales is the hub for bus service to Torres del Paine National Park and El Calafate, Argentina. For information about bus service to and from Torres del Paine, see "Parque Nacional Torres del Paine," later in this chapter. There are frequent daily trips between Punta Arenas and Puerto Natales. In Puerto Natales, each bus company leaves from its own office.

To and from Punta Arenas   **Buses Fernández,** at Ramirey and Esmeralda streets (© **61/411111**), has seven daily trips; **Bus Sur,** Baquedano 558 (© **61/242174**), has five daily trips; **Buses Pacheco,** Baquedano 244 (© **61/414513**), has three daily trips (and the most comfortable buses); and **Transfer Austral,** Baquedano 414 (© **61/412616**), has two daily trips. The trip takes about 3 hours and the cost is about $6 one-way. Reserve early during the busy season, as tickets sell out fast.

To El Calafate, Argentina   **Buses Zaahj,** Arturo Prat 236 (© **61/412260;** www.turismozaahj.co.cl), leaves daily at 9am; **Bus Sur,** Baquedano 558 (© **61/411859;** www.bus-sur.cl), leaves at 9am Monday, Wednesday, and Friday, and returns at 8am Tuesday, Thursday, and Saturday; and **Cootra,** Baquedano 244 (© **61/412785**), leaves at 6:30am daily. The cost is $15 to $22 one-way. The trip takes 5 to 6 hours, depending on the traffic at the border crossing. Note that most of this voyage is on unpaved dirt roads.

BY CAR   Ruta 9 is a paved road that heads north from Punta Arenas. The drive is 254km (158 miles) and takes about 2½ to 3 hours. If you're heading in from El Calafate, Argentina, you have your choice of two international borders: Cerro Castillo (otherwise known as Control Fronterizo Río Don Guillermo) or Río Turbio (otherwise known as Controles Fronterizos Dorotea y Laurita Casas Viejas), both are the same in terms of road quality; however, Río Turbio is busier, with Chileans heading to Argentina for cheaper goods. Both are open 24 hours from September to May, and daily from 8am to 11pm the rest of the year. Gas is much cheaper in Argentina, so fill up there.

Car rentals in Puerto Natales are offered by **Motorcars,** Encalada 330, #2 (© **61/413593**), and **EMSA** (an Avis representative), Av. Manuel Bulnes 632 (© **61/410775**).

BY BOAT   **Navimag** runs a popular 3-night ferry trip between Puerto Natales and Puerto Montt, cruising through the southern fjords of Chile. This journey passes through breathtaking (though repetitive) scenery, and it makes for an interesting way to leave from or head to Chile's Lake District. The trip is described in chapter 15, under "Ferry Crossings to the Carretera Austral & Sailing to Patagonia Through the Fjords." Navimag leaves every Thursday evening; its offices are at Manuel Bulnes 533 (© **61/414300;** www.navimag.com).

ORIENTATION

Puerto Natales is built on a grid pattern, and you'll spend most of your time within a 5-block radius. There is the main plaza, Plaza de Armas, along which runs Calle Eberhard, the street where you'll find the post office and the town's yellow cathedral. Calle Eberhard dead-ends a block away at Blanco Encalada; this street, Avenida Manuel Bulnes (1 block to the right), and Baquedano (1 block up from Blanco Encalada) are the principal streets, with most of the supermarkets, banks, and tourism-oriented businesses. Along the shore of Puerto Natales runs Pedro Montt, also called the Costanera, which is an excellent place for a stroll.

VISITOR INFORMATION

Sernatur operates a well-stocked office on the Costanera at Pedro Montt and Philippi (© **61/412125;** www.sernatur.cl); it's open October through March Monday through Friday from 8:30am to 8pm, Saturday and Sunday from 9:30am to 1pm and 2:30 to 6:30pm; April through September, it's open Monday through Friday from 8:30am to 1pm and 2:30 to 6:30pm, closed Sunday and holidays. Better yet is the **Municipal Tourism office,** tucked in a corner of the historical museum at Bulnes 285 (© **61/411263**), with a wealth of information on lodgings, restaurants, and day trips; the staff here is far more helpful than at Sernatur. **Conaf** has its park headquarters at O'Higgins 584 (© **61/ 411438;** www.conaf.cl), but you'll get better park information from a tour operator (see "Tour Operators & Adventure Travel Outfitters," below).

FAST FACTS: Puerto Natales

Camping Equipment If you don't feel like lugging your own camping gear down here, there are several agencies that rent equipment. Typical daily rental prices are two-man tents for $6, sleeping bags $2, stoves $1.50, sleeping mats $1.50, and backpacks $3. During the high season, it's best to reserve these items. The newest rental agency, **La Maddera,** Arturo

Prat 297 (© **61/413318**), is recommended for its high-quality equipment, or try **Casa Cecilia**, at Tomas Rogers 60 (© **61/411797**).

Currency Exchange There are several exchange houses on Blanco Encalada; try **Mily**, Blanco Encalada 183, and their other office on the same street, at no. 266 (© **61/411262**; open Mon–Sat 10am–8pm). ATMs can be found at **Banco de Santiago** at the corner of Blanco Encalada and Bulnes, and **Banco Chile** at Bulnes 544.

Hospital Frankly, the town's public hospital is horrible. It's on the corner of Pinto and O'Higgins (© **61/411583**). For major medical emergencies, it's best to get yourself to Punta Arenas.

Internet Access **Turismo Mily**, Blanco Encalada 183; **Explor@Dores**, 226 Eberhard; and **Chilnet**, 343 Manuel Bulnes, have Internet services. Connections in Puerto Natales are excruciatingly slow.

Laundry Try **ServiLaundry**, Av. Manuel Bulnes 513 (no phone). Hours vary, but it's open more or less Monday through Saturday from 9am to 1pm and 2 to 8pm.

Pharmacy **Farmacias Marisol** is at Baquedano 331 (© **61/411591**).

Post Office The post office is on the Plaza de Armas next to the cathedral (no phone; open Mon–Fri 9am–6pm, Sat 9am–1pm).

EXCURSIONS OUTSIDE PUERTO NATALES
CUEVA DE MILODON

In 1896, local resident Captain Eberhard found a scrap of hairy skin and a few bones in a large cave near his property that were later determined to be from a *Milodon,* a prehistoric ground sloth. The story of the *Milodon* was popularized by Bruce Chatwin's travelogue *In Patagonia.* Although the *Milodon* is depicted in a full-size replica at the cave's entrance, most of the *Milodon's* remains were shipped off to London, which means the real attraction is the 30m-high (98-ft.), 200m-deep (656-ft.) cave itself, which has a weird, shaggy roof and is surrounded by interesting conglomerate rock formations. There's an interpretative center with a few *Milodon* bones and a display showing the geological formation of the cave, as well as a historical display of the Indians who inhabited this and nearby caves as far back as 12,000 years ago. A new, modern restaurant was recently installed and was designed to reflect the shape of the cave; nonetheless, this attraction is recommended only if you happen to be passing by, or if you've run out of things to do in Puerto Natales. The cave is located 24km (15 miles) north of Puerto Natales, so you'll need your own car or a tour to get here. To get here, take the road to Torres del Paine; at 20km (12 miles), turn left, and then drive for 4km (2½ miles) to the cave's turn-off. The site is managed by Conaf and open daily from 8:30am to 7pm; admission is $4.50 adults, $2.50 children (© 61/411438 in Puerto Natales).

SAILING TO PARQUE NACIONAL BERNARDO O'HIGGINS

This national park, tremendous in its size, is largely unreachable except for boat tours to the glaciers Balmaceda and Serrano, tours that involve kayaking (for kayaking trips, see Bigfoot Expeditions under "Tour Operators & Adventure Travel Outfitters," below), and the new Skorpios journey to the grand Pio XI glacier (see below). A low-key, traditional day trip takes travelers to the Serrano and Balmaceda glaciers, with a stop at the Monte Balmaceda Hostel and a short walk along the glacier and its iceberg-studded bay. The best option is to take this journey on your first day, and continue on with a zodiac ride to Torres del Paine, or vice versa (see "Getting There & Away" under "Parque Nacional Torres del Paine," later in this chapter). The ride kicks off with a trip past the old mutton-canning factory, an *estancia,* and a cormorant nesting site, among other sites of interest. The return trip is a straight shot back to Natales—which can be repetitive, so bring a book in the event of boredom or bad weather.

Turismo 21 de Mayo, Eberhard 560 (© **61/411978;** www.turismo21de mayo.cl), has a cutter and a yacht, and leaves daily November through March and every Sunday from April to October (other days dependent on demand). The trip leaves at 8am, arriving at Serrano Glacier at 11:30am, where it stays for 1½ hours, returning at 5pm. They also offer custom-made charter rides for groups. **Nueva Galicia,** Eberhard 169 (© **61/412352;** nuevagalicia@terra.cl), takes visitors along a similar route aboard its wooden yacht of the same name, leaving at 7:45am and arriving at Serrano Glacier at 11am for a half-hour, then across the adjoining river to its lodge, the Hostería Monte Balmaceda. There visitors can take a walk around the self-guided nature trail, have lunch in the restaurant, and reboard, arriving at Puerto Natales at 5:30pm. Please note that the restaurant here normally serves tough, tasteless food, so you may consider bringing a picnic, especially if the weather is pleasant.

The luxury cruise company **Skorpios,** Agosto Leguia Norte 118 (© **2/231-1030;** www.skorpios.cl), has an all-inclusive 6-day journey from Puerto Natales to Pio XI Glacier, the largest and only advancing glacier in the Southern Hemisphere. This glacier measures an astounding 6km (3¾ miles) in length and peaks in height at 75m (246 ft.); it is also the least-visited glacier, and this alone makes a visit all the more special. The size of the Pio XI simply dwarfs other glaciers, such as Glacier Grey in Torres del Paine, providing an awe-inspiring experience. The ship also sails through fjordland offering viewings of local flora and fauna and the opportunity to conduct short hikes. I recommend this journey for travelers who are not very physically active and who don't want to miss a visit to Torres del Paine but wish to add on a special journey to an out-of-the-way destination. Active travelers might get bored on a 6-day sailing journey.

TOUR OPERATORS & ADVENTURE TRAVEL OUTFITTERS

The many tour operators in Puerto Natales can be divided into two groups: conventional sightseeing day tours to Torres del Paine, Perito Moreno Glacier in Argentina's Los Glaciares National Park, the Cueva de Milodon, the Nordenskjold Trail, and the icebergs at Lago Grey; and adventure travel outfitters that arrange multiday, all-inclusive excursions, including trekking the W or the Circuit (see "Trails in Torres del Paine," later in this chapter) and climbing in Torres del Paine, kayaking the Río Serrano in Parque Nacional Bernardo O'Higgins, and taking horseback trips. Keep in mind that it's very easy to arrange your own trekking journey in Torres del Paine; the bonus with these outfitters is that they carry the tents (which they'll set up) and food (which they'll cook). They also will pick you up from the airport and provide guided information about the flora and fauna of the park.

CONVENTIONAL DAY TOURS These tours are for people with a limited amount of time in the area. Tours typically leave at 7:30am, return around 7:30pm, and cost about $30 per person, not including lunch or park entrance fees. For day tours, try **Turismo Mily,** Blanco Encalada 266 (© **61/411262**), or

Viaterra, Bulnes 632 (© **61/410775;** www.viaterra.cl); Viaterra has transfers from Punta Arenas directly to the park on a charter basis. Probably the most interesting way to see the Cueva de Milodon is with **Estancia Travel** (© **61/ 412221;** www.estanciatravel.com), which offers a horseback-riding trip there for $69, including transfers, equipment, a bilingual guide, snacks, and a horse you'll feel comfortable with.

ADVENTURE TRAVEL Apart from the local guiding outfitters here in Puerto Natales, several American and Chilean companies offer well-planned trekking excursions in Torres del Paine, specifically **Mountain-Travel Sobek** and **Cascada Expediciones** (both have bases here; see "The Active Vacation Planner," in chapter 11, for more information). Mountain-Travel has multiple-day trekking journeys around Torres del Paine; Cascada operates from their base at Hostería los Torres, where they have dome-shape cabins for lodging before or after a trekking journey. Most of the following operators offer custom packages. **Bigfoot Expeditions,** Bories 206 (© **61/413247;** www.bigfootpatagonia.com), is one of the most respected local outfitters for climbing, mountaineering, and kayaking; they also own the concession for the unforgettable ice walk across Glacier Grey (described in "Parque Nacional Torres del Paine," below). One of their most popular trips is a 3-day kayak descent of the River Serrano, with a paddle around Serrano Glacier. **Antares,** Barros Arana 111 (© **61/414611;** www.antarespatagonia.com), focuses on the "softer" (meaning less strenuous and/or technical) side of adventure travel, with a variety of multiday trekking journeys through the park that can include horseback riding, kayaking, and sailing; and they have an office in the U.S. (© **415/703-9955**). **Chile Nativo Expeditions**, Eberhard 230 (© **61/411835;** www.chilenativo.com), offers high-end trekking, bird-watching, and horseback-riding adventures outside of the more "touristy" areas. **Onas,** Blanco Encalada and Eberhard (©/fax **61/414349;** www.onaspatagonia.com), has a half-day zodiac trip down the Río Serrano; see "Getting There & Away" under "Parque Nacional Torres del Paine," below.

WHERE TO STAY

It seems that anyone and everyone who owns a home large enough to rent out a few rooms has decided to hang a HOSPEDAJE sign above their door. These simple, inexpensive accommodations can be found everywhere, but higher-end (and more expensive) options are to be had as well. The high season in Puerto Natales is longer than in any other city in Chile, generally considered to run from October to April, and the price range shown reflects this. At press time, two new upscale hotels were in the works; one is owned by Hotel Altiplanico in San Pedro, the other will be designed by the same architect who sketched the plans for the Explora hotels. At press time, a new upscale hotel was in the works; owned by Hotel Altiplanico in San Pedro de Atacama. The Altiplanico del Sur is slated to open its doors in September 2005, so verify its status at the lodge's website, www.altiplanico.cl or check www.torresdelpaine.com.

EXPENSIVE

Hotel CostAustralis ⋆⋆⋆ While many hotels in the area claim to have renovated since the last edition of this book, few have done so with the same level of class as the CostAustralis. This hotel has long been considered the most upscale hotel in town, and now they've overhauled the entire lobby lounge and have expanded to a new fourth level. Floor-to-ceiling windows face out onto the sound, which means that whether you're in the bar, the restaurant, or the lounge, you always have sweeping views and a splendid evening sunset. It is a large hotel, but it retains a certain coziness, with deep couches and soft lighting. Spacious doubles come with a sea view or a somewhat depressing view of the buildings in the back; the 28 rooms on the fourth floor, though priced the same, are entirely new, with marble bathrooms and plenty of closet space, so ask for one. The price is fairly high, even by U.S. standards, and, therefore, might not be appealing to anyone who plans to arrive late and leave early. The hotel has combined what were once two restaurants into one formal dining area (see "Where to Dine," below). This hotel is popular with European tour groups.

Pedro Montt 262, Puerto Natales. © 61/412000. Fax 61/411881. www.australis.com. 74 units. $147–$181 double. Rates include buffet breakfast. AE, DC, MC, V. **Amenities:** 2 restaurants; bar; room service; laundry service. *In room:* TV.

MODERATE

Aquaterra 🐟🐟   It is a fantasy many of us have, to open a small inn in a place we fell in love with while traveling. The three owners of Aquaterra did just that, trading the bustle of Santiago for this windy, quiet town, and travelers should be thankful, as the hotel is one of the best lodging options in town. The rooms are not huge, but they feature comfortable beds with marshmellowy down comforters accented with colorful woven throws. Five rooms have shared bathrooms, 10 are en suite, and all rooms are flooded with light. The hotel's restaurant and tiny lounge with a wood-burning stove are cozy places to relax and read. What really stands out here is the pleasant, friendly service; there are also on-site massage services.

Av. Bulnes 299, Puerto Natales. © 61/412239. www.aquaterrapatagonia.com. 15 units. $68–$90 double. DC, MC, V. **Amenities:** Restaurant; lounge; massage. *In room:* No phone.

Hostal Los Pinos 🐟 *Value*   The Hostal Los Pinos is a great value for the price. It's tucked behind two cypress trees, across from the local high school and 3 blocks from the plaza. The friendly owners make you feel at home, especially while relaxing in the ample living area. Oriental rug runners lead to squeaky-clean rooms with enough details here and there to bring this hostal to a step above most moderate accommodations found in town. The bathrooms aren't huge, but they'll do, and the newer mattresses are not the foam variety normally found in most economical lodging.

Philippi 449, Puerto Natales. © 61/411735. Fax 61/411326. 12 units. $32 double. Rates include continental breakfast. No credit cards. **Amenities:** Lounge. *In room:* TV.

Hotel Cisne Cuello Negro 🐟 *Kids*   This hotel sits a 3km (1¾-mile) taxi ride outside town, and it's ideal for those who want to be surrounded by a bit of greenery and history. The Hotel Cisne is in the old mutton-canning and wool plant that once operated as a collection and export site for various sheep ranches. The old wooden buildings provide great places to walk and explore, especially if you have kids. The hotel itself is a three-story white building with red tin awnings, and it fronts a grassy slope that leads into the sound. After a fire burned part of the building, they rebuilt an airy restaurant lit by a plant-filled atrium. Rooms are spacious and comfortable, with good beds and sunny views. There are two large suites surrounded by floor-to-ceiling windows. Much of the time the hotel sells packages to guests that include transportation from Punta Arenas, 3 nights' accommodations, a 1-day tour through Torres del Paine, and a catamaran journey to Parque Nacional Bernardo O'Higgins and Serrano Glacier.

Road to Torres del Paine, northeast of Puerto Natales, Km 3. In Punta Arenas, José Menéndez 918. © 2/235-0252. Fax 61/248052. www.pehoe.com. 39 units. $110 double. Rates include buffet breakfast. AE, DC, MC, V. **Amenities:** Restaurant; bar; laundry service. *In room:* TV.

Hotel Lady Florence Dixie ⚐ *Value* This hotel is about as downtown as downtown gets in Puerto Natales, located on bustling Avenida Manuel Bulnes. Guests enter the wooden gate and find a courtyard and a motel-like setup that's nicely designed, with wooden banisters and trim. The rooms are comfortable, and it's one of the few hotels in this price range that has cable TV, if that's important to you. You might consider one of the pricier front rooms because they are newer, with gleaming bathrooms, and they have soundproof windows. The two women who run the place are very accommodating.

Av. Manuel Bulnes 655, Puerto Natales. © 61/411158. Fax 61/411943. Florence@chileanpatagonia.com. 19 units. Oct–Apr $82–$92 double; May–Sept $66 double. AE, DC, MC, V. **Amenities:** Lounge. *In room:* TV.

Kotenk Aike Cabañas These cabins are about 2km (1¼ miles) outside of town on an exposed grassy slope, and they're a good bet if you're looking for your own room with a kitchen. The German-style A-frame *cabañas* sit apart from each other, and each has two upstairs bedrooms, one with a full-size bed and one with three twins; all are brightly lit. There's a tidy kitchen with a burner, a microwave, and a table. The distance from town means you'll have to walk or take a taxi (costing about $1), but the all-embracing views are worth it.

Costanera (Pedro Montt), northeast of Puerto Natales, Km 2. © 61/412581. Fax 61/225935 (in Punta Arenas). 5 *cabañas.* $64 *cabaña* for 5. MC, V. *In room:* TV, kitchen.

INEXPENSIVE

Casa Cecilia *Value* Casa Cecilia is a budget favorite in Puerto Natales, consistently garnering rave reviews from guests for its full range of services, pleasant rooms, and delicious breakfasts. The front lobby acts as a travel agency of sorts, providing information, arranging excursions, and renting camping equipment; beyond that is a common area and a kitchen that guests can use—and they do. Rooms are stacked on two floors and encircle an atrium; some come with private bathrooms, some shared, and they are a good value for the price. However, rooms are lit by the interior atrium, not from the outside. The Swiss-Chilean couple (she's Cecilia) speak several languages and are very friendly. This hostel is popular with a wide range of ages and types.

Tomás Roger 60, Puerto Natales. ©/fax 61/411797. redcecilia@entelchile.net. 15 units. Nov 15–Feb $35 double, $21 double with shared bathroom; Mar–Nov 14 $20 double, $14 double with shared bathroom. Rates include full breakfast. AE, DC, MC, V.

Concepto Indigo *Finds* The Concepto Indigo is a hip, outdoorsy hostel/restaurant located along the Costanera. It's a shingled barn of a building with a rock-climbing wall, so you won't have any trouble spotting it. The rooms are inexpensive but remarkable only for the tremendous view of the sound seen through giant windows—especially the corner room, which has a full-size bed and a twin. Only three rooms come with a private bathroom, but there are several bathrooms, so you most likely won't find that sharing is a problem. The best thing about Concepto Indigo is its restaurant downstairs, with wraparound views, stacks of magazines, and a few couches to kick back on. When the wind picks up (which it usually does), the place really whistles and shakes.

Ladrilleros 105, Puerto Natales. © 61/413609. Fax 61/410169. www.conceptoindigo.com. 8 units. $40 double; $28 double with shared bathroom. MC, V. Closed May–Aug. **Amenities:** Restaurant; bar.

WHERE TO DINE

Along with the following restaurants, there are several that serve inexpensive fare, such as **RePizza,** Blanco Encalada 294 (© 61/410361), a popular place for pizzas, and **El Cristal,** Av. Manuel Bulnes 439 (© **61/411850**), which has sandwiches, meat and seafood dishes, and a daily set lunch for about $5.

Concepto Indigo ✪ VEGETARIAN   This cozy and happening eatery is one of the few in town with a water view. The simple menu here is heavy on the vegetarian side and is hit or miss; some options, like the Indigo Salad, are overpriced. That said, the sandwiches are served on wagon-wheel bread and are hefty enough for a dinner. There's also a good wine selection. Concepto Indigo has a better atmosphere than it does food, with hip decor and candlelit tables, good music, and an evening slide-show presentation of Torres del Paine. The bar is a good place for a late-evening drink, and there's a computer with Internet access in the adjoining lounge.

Ladrilleros 105. © 61/413609. Main courses $3.50–$7. AE, DC, MC, V. Daily 11am–11pm; bar closes at 1am. Closed May–Aug.

El Living ✪✪ *Finds* CAFE/VEGETARIAN   If you're looking for a friendly, comfortable place to kick back and spend the evening, then look no further. At El Living, run by a British expatriate couple who have lived in the area for more than a decade, you can lounge on a comfortable sofa with a pisco sour or have an excellent vegetarian dinner at one of their handmade wooden dining tables. The menu is simple and inexpensive but fresh and delicious. The Sweet and Sour Red Salad is a perfect mix of beetroot, red cabbage, kidney beans, and onion; the veggie burger is delicious and served on a whole-wheat baguette. This is one of the only places in Chile that serves a peanut-butter-and-jelly sandwich. There's also French toast with fried bananas, and a variety of cakes baked daily. A full bar and wine list round out this excellent place.

Arturo Prat 156. © 61/411140. Main courses $2.50–$3.75. No credit cards. Daily 11am–11pm.

Hotel Capitán Eberhard ✪ *Kids* CHILEAN   Like the CostAustralis (see below), this restaurant features a lovely view of the sound, but the difference is the Eberhard is cozier and full of old-fashioned Puerto Natales charm. Nothing has changed in this dining room since the hotel's inception 30 years ago, including the unique notched wooden ceiling. The menu features typical Chilean fare and very good salmon dishes, such as salmon with a creamy seafood sauce. Try the abalone in salsa verde appetizer. There's also a kid's menu. The bar is handsomely designed, with a black bar and tables offset by cinnamon-colored wood. The fixed-price menu is a steal at $9 and includes a soup or salad, a main course, and dessert. The restaurant has a Patagonian-style barbecue annex, but they open only for groups. If you have a large enough one, you may inquire as to whether they will prepare the barbecue for you.

Pedro Montt 58. © 61/411208. Main courses $7–$11; 3-course fixed-price menu $9. AE, DC, MC, V. Daily 7–10am, 12:30–2:30pm, and 8–11pm.

Hotel CostAustralis ✪✪ *Moments* INTERNATIONAL   Recently expanded, this is the only restaurant approximating fine dining in Puerto Natales, with tasty cuisine and a wonderful ambience. The sunset views from the picture windows in combination with your candlelit table make for a sumptuous environment. The new chef is very talented and tries hard to maintain the regional angle in the menu. A good example is the lamb and potato stew typical of this region but not easy to find in restaurants. Salmon and conger eel are usually the fresh catches of the day. Other specialties include wild hare marinated in red wine and herbs, and pork loin with mustard and whiskey. Top off your dinner with the apricots and peaches stewed in syrup and served with cream of wheat, or minty pears poached in wine with chocolate ice cream.

Pedro Montt 262. ℭ 61/412000. Main courses $8–$13. AE, DC, MC, V. Daily noon–3pm and 7:30–11pm.

Vitrola ℛℛ CHILEAN/SEAFOOD   Focusing on fresh ingredients and quality service, this new eatery has a bistro feel to it, with the catch of the day scribbled on a board outside. The pasta dishes are recommended, and their roasted lamb is as delicious as their salmon, probably the freshest in town. The dining area is decorated with the works of Chilean artists.

Ladrilleros 209. ℭ 09/571-7398. Main courses $5–$9. No credit cards. Daily 7–11pm.

PUERTO NATALES AFTER DARK

Little more than a few years ago, the only nightspot in Puerto Natales was a brothel. Now there are several bars where the party doesn't wind down until about 5am. **El Tunel,** at the corner of Eberhard and Magallanes streets, is a playful mix of casual (swing seats) and sophisticated (they boast one of the longest wine lists in Southern Chile). Often the basement level here doubles as a disco. **The Pub El Bar de Ruperto,** Bulnes 310, has pool tables and loud music; down the street is the newest hip nightspot for a cocktail. **Chil-e,** Bulnes 315, is in a converted old home with a main lounge area, separate rooms for groups of friends, and frequent live DJ music. **Kaweshkar,** Eberhard 161, is a lounge that serves food, cocktails, and natural juices; and **Pub Indigo,** Ladrilleros 105, is a quiet spot for an early drink and views of the sound.

3 Parque Nacional Torres del Paine, Chile ℛℛℛ

113km (70 miles) north of Puerto Natales; 360km (223 miles) northwest of Punta Arenas

This is Chile's prized jewel, a national park so magnificent that few in the world can claim a rank in its class. Granite peaks and towers soar from sea level to upward of 2,800m (9,184 ft.). Golden pampas and the rolling steppes are home to llamalike guanacos and more than 100 species of colorful birds, such as parakeets, flamingos, and ostrichlike rheas. During the spring, Chilean firebush blooms a riotous red, and during the autumn, the park's beech trees change to crimson, sunflower, and orange. A fierce wind screams through this region during the spring and summer, and yet flora such as the delicate porcelain orchids and ladyslippers somehow weather the inhospitable terrain. Electric-blue icebergs cleave from Glacier Grey. Resident gauchos ride atop sheepskin saddles. Condors float effortlessly even on the windiest day. This park is not something you just visit; it is something you experience.

Although it sits next to the Andes, **Parque Nacional Torres del Paine** is a separate geologic formation created roughly 3 million years ago when bubbling magma began growing and pushing its way up, taking a thick sedimentary layer with it. Glaciation and severe climate weathered away the softer rock, leaving the spectacular Paine Massif whose prominent features are the *Cuernos* (which means "horns") and the one-of-a-kind *Torres*—three salmon-colored, spherical granite towers. The black sedimentary rock is visible on the upper reaches of the elegant Cuernos, named for the two spires that rise from the outer sides of its amphitheater. *Paine* is the Tehuelche Indian word for "blue," and it brings to mind the varying shades found in the lakes that surround this massif—among them the milky, turquoise waters of Lagos Nordenskjold and Pehoé. Backing the Paine Massif are several glaciers that descend from the Southern Ice Field.

Torres del Paine was once a collection of *estancias* and small-time ranches; many were forced out with the creation of the park in 1959. The park has since grown to its present size of 242,242 hectares (598,338 acres), and in 1978 was declared a World Biosphere Reserve by UNESCO for its singular beauty and ecology. This park is a backpacker's dream, but just as many visitors find pleasure staying in lodges here and taking day hikes and horseback rides—even those with a short amount of time here are blown away by a 1-day visit. There are options for everyone, part of the reason the number of visitors to this park is growing by nearly 10,000 per year.

In February 2005, a careless backpacker camping in a non-designated site in Parque Nacional Torres del Paine ignited a raging fire after accidentally knocking over his stove, eventually burning nearly 15,000 hectares around the Laguna Amarga and Laguna Azul areas of Torres del Paine. Although the park's major highlights (such as the Towers, Horns, and Glacier Grey region) were left unscathed, the scorched hills and forests at the Laguna Amarga entrance are a bleak welcome for visitors to the park. Also, backpackers on the Circuit trail will spend a full day or more passing through the tragically blackened remains of wilderness from just beyond Hostería las Torres until just before the Dickson Glacier area. For this reason, visitors may consider foregoing the Circuit trail for the "W."

ESSENTIALS
WHEN TO COME & WHAT TO BRING
This is not the easiest of national parks to visit. The climate in the park can be abominable, with wind speeds that can peak at 161kmph (100 mph) and rain and snow even in the middle of summer. It is not unusual for visitors to spend 5 days in the park and never see the Towers. On average, the windiest days happen between late November and mid-March, but the only predictable thing about the weather here is its unpredictability. Spring is a beautiful time for budding flowers and birds; during the fall, the beech forests turn colors, which can be especially striking on walks up to the Towers and to the glacier. The winter is surprisingly temperate, with relatively few snowstorms and no wind—but short days. You'll need to stay in a hotel during the winter, but you'll practically have the park to yourself. Summer is, ironically, the worst time to come, especially from late December to mid-February, when the wind blows at full fury and crowds descend upon the park. When the wind blows, it can make even a short walk a rather scary experience or just drive you nuts—just try to go with it, not fight it, and revel in the excitement of the extreme environment that makes Patagonia what it is.

I can't stress enough the importance of bringing the right gear, especially waterproof hiking boots (if you plan to do any trekking), weatherproof outerwear, and warm layers, even in the summer. The ozone problem is acute here, so you'll need sunscreen, sunglasses, and a hat as well.

VISITOR & PARK ENTRANCE INFORMATION
Your visit to Torres del Paine will require logistical planning, unless you've left it up to an all-inclusive tour or hotel. Begin your research at www.torresdel paine.cl, an English-language overview of the park and its surroundings, including maps, activities information, events, photos, hotel overviews and links, and more. The park service, Conaf, has a relatively unhelpful Spanish-only website at www.conaf.cl.

The park's administration and visitor center can be reached at © **61/691931;** it's located at the southern end of the park. The park is open year-round from

8:30am to 10:30pm. The cost to enter is $13 for adults, 75¢ for kids; during the winter, the cost is $7.50 adults, 55¢ kids.

GETTING THERE & AWAY

Many travelers are unaware of the enormous amount of time it takes to get to Torres del Paine. There are no direct transportation services from the airport in Punta Arenas to the park, except with package tours and hotels that have their own vehicles, or by chartering an auto or van (try **Viaterra, ☎ 61/410775; www.viaterra.cl**). The earliest flight from Santiago to Punta Arenas arrives at around noon; from there it's a 3-hour drive to Puerto Natales. The last bus to the park leaves at 2:30pm for the 2-hour journey to the park—however, this is likely to change with the opening of the new access route to the park that will shorten the journey to about a 45-minute to 1-hour drive (slated to open in late 2005). If you're relying on bus transportation (as most do), it's only logical that you will need to spend the night in Punta Arenas or Puerto Natales. If you've arranged a package tour or hotel stay that picks you up at the airport, remember that the trip can be very tiring if you factor in a 4-hour flight from Santiago and 5 hours in a vehicle.

BY BUS   Several companies offer daily service from October to April. During the low season, only two companies, Bus Sur and JB, offer service to the park. Buses to Torres del Paine enter through the Laguna Amarga ranger station, stop at the Pudeto catamaran dock, and terminate at the park administration center. If you're going directly to the Torres trail head at Hostería Las Torres, there are minivan transfers waiting at the Laguna Amarga station that charge about $3 one-way. The return times given below are when the bus leaves from the park administration center; the bus will pass through the Laguna Amarga station about 45 minutes later.

JB, Arturo Prat 258 (**☎ 61/412824**), leaves at 7am, 8am, and 2:30pm, and returns at 1, 2:30, and 6:30pm; **Bus Sur,** Baquedano 558 (**☎ 61/411859**), leaves daily at 7:30am and 2:30pm; **Fortaleza Aventura,** Arturo Prat 234 (**☎ 61/410595**), leaves at 7am and 2pm, returning at 2 and 6pm; **Turismo María José,** Av. Manuel Bulnes 386 (**☎ 61/414312**), leaves at 7:30am, returning at 2pm; and **Andescape,** Eberhard 599 (**☎ 61/412592**), leaves at 7am, returning at 12:15pm. The cost is around $7 one-way.

BY TOUR VAN   If you don't have much time to spend in the park or would like to get there at your own pace, check into the minivan tour services that plan stops at the Salto Grande waterfall and carry on to Lago Grey for a walk along the beach to view giant icebergs (see "Tour Operators & Adventure Travel Outfitters," under "Puerto Natales, Chile," earlier in this chapter).

BY CAR   Heading north on Pedro Montt out of town, follow the dirt road for 51km (32 miles) until you reach Cerro Castillo. From here the road turns left and heads 47km (29 miles) toward the park (keep your eyes open for another left turn that is signed TORRES DEL PAINE). You'll come to a fork in the road; one road leads to the Lago Sarmiento Conaf station, another to the Laguna Amarga station. If you are planning to head to the Torres trail head and Hostería Las Torres hotel complex on your way out, then take the Lago Sarmiento entrance; it's faster, and you'll get to view the blue, blue waters of Lago Sarmiento. You can park your car at the Hostería Las Torres, the park administration center, the Pudeto catamaran dock, or the Lago Grey ranger station. As of press time, an alternate route to the park (faster and more direct from Puerto Natales) had yet to open but plans to in 2005. Check with the park service at www.conaf.cl or your rental-car agency for updated information.

CROSSING LAGO PEHOE BY CATAMARAN   Day hikes to the Glacier Grey trail and backpackers taking the W or Circuit trails will need to cross Lake Pehoé at some point aboard a catamaran, about a 45-minute ride. The cost is $16 one-way. Buses from Puerto Natales are timed to drop off and pick up passengers in conjunction with the catamaran (Dec–Mar 15 leaving Pudeto at 9:30am, noon, and 6pm, and from Pehoé 10am, 12:30, and 6:30pm; in Nov and Mar 16–30 from Pudeto at noon and 6pm, and Pehoé at 12:30 and 6pm; in Oct and Apr, from Pudeto at noon, from Pehoé at 12:30pm; closed May–Sept but may expand service—check with Conaf). Hikers walking the entire round-trip Glacier Grey trail can do so only taking the 9:30am boat and returning at 6:30pm from December to March 15.

GETTING TO THE PARK BY BOAT   Relatively few people are aware that they can arrive by a zodiac-catamaran combination that takes visitors from Puerto Natales through the Ultima Esperanza Sound and up the Río Serrano, or vice versa. This is a highly recommended way to do one leg of the trip rather than ride both ways in a vehicle, but it's an all-day affair. Also, you'll need to arrange transportation with your hotel to or from the administration office. Along the winding turquoise river, visitors are taken through territory that rivals Alaska, past the Tyndall and Geike glaciers, and eventually to Serrano Glacier. Here they disembark for a walk up to the ice, then board another boat for a 3½-hour ride to Puerto Natales. The one-way ride costs $85 per person, depending on the season. You can also do a round-trip journey leaving from and returning to the park for about $60. See "Tour Operators & Adventure Travel Outfitters" under "Puerto Natales, Chile," earlier in this chapter for more information. **Onas** is the oldest-running company with zodiac service, leaving daily at 8:30am from the administration office (they'll pick you up from longer distances for an extra charge). **Aventour,** Av. Espana 872 (© **61/241197;** www. aventourpatagonia.com), also takes guests down the Río Serrano in a covered boat; however, Onas's zodiac is more adventurous, and their guides are a lot more fun. **Aventour** can include a stay at its **Monte Balmaceda** lodge (doubles with a view $103) near Serrano Glacier; however, I recommend it only for travelers with a lot of time or those who seek low-key activities.

Active travelers will be interested in following the same Río Serrano route but by **kayak,** about a 3-day journey. This trip is suitable for travelers on their way back to Puerto Natales, to take advantage of the river's downward current; at night, travelers camp out on shore. **Bigfoot Expeditions** out of Puerto Natales offers this excellent journey (Bories 206; © **61/413247;** www.bigfootpatagonia.com).

WHERE TO STAY & DINE IN TORRES DEL PAINE
HOTELS AND HOSTERIAS

Hostería Lago Grey ✦   This spruce little white *hostería* is tucked within a beech forest, looking out onto the beach at Lago Grey and the astounding blue icebergs that drift to its shore. It's well on the other side of the park, but the view is better here than at the Hostería las Torres, and they have a transfer van and guides for excursions to all reaches of the park. The 20 rooms are spread out from a main common area, a thoroughly enjoyable place to relax, with a restaurant, outdoor deck, and lounge area. The price suggests more luxurious rooms, but the walls are a tad thin and have little decoration. Also, when the wind whips up, this side of the park is colder. On the plus side, there are plenty of trails that branch out from here, including the stroll along the beach out to the Pingo Valley and the strenuous hike up to Mirador Ferrier. The transfer van will pick you up from anywhere in the park.

Office in Punta Arenas, Lautaro Navarro 1061. ℂ 61/229512. 20 units. Oct–Apr $199 double; May–Sept $95 double. Rates include buffet breakfast. AE, DC, MC, V. **Amenities:** Restaurant; lounge; tours.

Hostería Las Torres 𝒦𝒦 (Kids) This *hostería* sits at the trail head to the Torres on an *estancia* that still operates as a working cattle ranch. Accordingly, the complex includes a low-slung, ranch-style hotel, and there's a large campground and a hostel—meaning a fair amount of traffic coming in and out daily. In the afternoon, horses and the odd cow graze just outside your hotel room door, meaning it's a fun place for kids. The *hostería* is a decent value for its standard rooms, which are far lower in price yet nearly identical to the newer, "superior" rooms. This is an ideal lodge for horseback-riding enthusiasts due to their on-site stables, and its access to the Towers is convenient; however, it is a long drive to the other side of the park. The *hostería* now offers expensive packages that include guided tours, meals, and transportation, much like Explora, and excellent off-season trips to little-explored areas (their 4-night package is just $200 cheaper per person than Explora, so comparison-shop beforehand). Packages are run from 3 to 7 nights, or you can pay separately for day trips. Try spending 2 nights here and 2 at Hostería Grey, thereby avoiding the steep price of an excursion there. Las Torres recently inaugurated a small spa, with mud therapy, massage, and sauna. The buffet-style restaurant is above par, but pricey at $30 a person for dinner.

Office in Punta Arenas, Magallanes 960. ℂ/fax 61/710050. www.lastorres.com. 56 units. $118–$209 double superior; $89–$149 standard. Rates include buffet breakfast. 4-night packages per person, double occupancy, are $1,803. AE, DC, MC, V. **Amenities:** Restaurant; lounge; tour desk; horseback riding; room service; laundry service.

Hostería Mirador del Payne 𝒦 This *hostería* is part of an antique *estancia* just outside the park, and it boasts a commanding view of the Paine Massif rising behind a grassy field and Lake Verde. If you really want to get away from crowds, this is your hotel, although it doesn't put you directly near the park's trail heads. The rooms are in a unit separate from the main lodge, which has a restaurant, bar, and fireside lounge. The *hostería* offers horseback-riding opportunities that include a chance to corral cattle and assist with other ranch duties. Access

---

(Tips Advance Planning

Due to the soaring popularity of Torres del Paine, it is recommended that travelers book well in advance if planning on visiting the park between late November and late March. Nearly every business now has a website or, at the very least, an e-mail address, so trip planning is easier than ever. Hotels can be booked directly, and often they offer their own transportation from the airport or, at the very least, can recommend a service to call or e-mail. One-stop agencies such as Path@gone Travel, Eberhard 595 in Puerto Natales (ℂ 61/413291; www.pathagone.com), is a good place for refugio reservations, horseback-riding trips, or camping equipment rentals, and they can sometimes offer lower hotel rates at *hosterías* in the park. They can also solve tricky transfer problems. Turismo Comapa in Punta Arenas is another all-around company that can book tours, refugio stays, and more (Magallanes 990; ℂ 61/200200; www.comapa.com).

to the *hostería* is via one of two ways: by a road that branches off before arriving at the park or by a moderate 2-hour trail that leads to the park administration center. Guests arrive by road, but more than a few opt to end their stay here with a horseback ride to the park administration center to continue on to another hotel within the park's boundaries.

Office in Punta Arenas, Fagnano 585. ✆ **61/228712**. www.miradordelpayne.com. 20 units. Nov–Mar 15 $152 double; Mar 16–Oct $90 double. AE, DC, MC, V. **Amenities:** Restaurant; bar; lounge; tours; laundry service.

Hostería Pehoé ⭐

This is the park's oldest hotel, built before Torres del Paine was declared a national park. It is located near the Explora Hotel, on an island in Lake Pehoé, and it enjoys the same dynamite view of the Cuernos Formation. However, none of the rooms here comes with the view because they are located behind the main building in a grove of beech trees. It's an awesome location nonetheless, and it is situated in the middle of the park, cutting down on driving time to either end (the reason for its one star). The guest rooms have been spruced up a bit recently, but they are still too run-of-the-mill for management to charge $160 for a double during high season. This is the only hotel in the area with satellite TV in rooms. Guests normally take their meals in the hotel's restaurant, which offers so-so fare at above-average prices.

Office in Punta Arenas, Jose Menendez 918. ✆ **61/244506**. www.pehoe.com. 25 units. $160 double. AE, DC, MC, V. **Amenities:** Restaurant; bar; lounge; tours; laundry service. *In room:* TV.

Hotel Explora Salto Chico ⭐⭐⭐ *Moments*

Explora in Patagonia has garnered more fame than any other hotel in Chile, and deservedly so. Few hotels in the world offer as stunning a view as does Explora, perched above the milky, turquoise waters of Lago Pehoé and facing the dramatic granite amphitheater of the Cuernos formation. It is terribly expensive, but worth the splurge if you can afford it. Explora's style is comfortable elegance, and its handsome interiors belie the rather bland exterior: Softly curving blond-wood walls built entirely from native deciduous beech are a soothing ambience in which to relax after a long hike. A band of picture windows wraps around the full front of the building, and there are large windows in each room—even the bathrooms come with cutouts in the wall so that while you're brushing your teeth, you can still have your eyes on the gorgeous panorama. The furniture was handcrafted using local wood, and the crisp guest rooms are accented with Spanish checkered linens, handsome slate-tiled bathrooms, and warming racks for drying gear. Explora recently expanded to include 20 new guest rooms, meaning it is easier now to get a reservation than before, but the hotel has, in the process, lost a bit of intimacy that it had at 30 rooms.

Explora is all-inclusive, with prices that cover airport transfers, meals, open bar, and excursions. Every evening, 5 of the 20 full-time guides meet with guests to discuss the following day's excursions, which range from easy half-day walks to strenuous full-day hikes. There are about 15 excursions to choose from, including horseback rides and photo safaris. In the morning, a fleet of vans whisks guests off to their destination and back again for lunch; guides carry picnic lunches for full-day hikes. The set menu is limited to two choices, generally a meat and vegetarian dish, and it must be said that the food quality has at times been uneven—never bad, but not as outstanding as one would expect from a hotel of this caliber. Americans make up a full 50% of the guests, who typically leave thrilled with their visit. Note that the first-day arrival to the hotel is around 6pm, time for a short hike to a lookout point only, and the last day isn't really a day at all, as guests leave after breakfast for the drive back to the airport. Guests will want to consider Explora's new "Viajes," add-on journeys to Chaltén and the Fitz Roy National Park and Calafate, both in Argentina.

In Santiago, Américo Vespucio Sur 80, 5th floor. © 2/395-2533. Fax 2/228-4655. www.explora.com. 51 units. Packages per person, double occupancy: 3 nights/2 days $1,546; 4 nights/3 days $2,060; 7 nights/6 days $3,250. Rates include all meals, transportation, gear, and guides. AE, DC, MC, V. **Amenities:** Restaurant; bar; lounge; large indoor pool; outdoor Jacuzzi; sauna; massage.

REFUGIOS & HOSTALS

Five cabinlike lodging units and one hostel, all with shared accommodation, are distributed along the park's Circuit and W trails, and they are moderately priced sleeping options for backpackers who are not interested in pitching a tent. Although most have bedding or sleeping bags for an expensive rental price, your best bet is to bring your own. The price, at $22 on average per night (about $47 for room and full board), may seem steep; however, it is a far cry cheaper than many shared accommodations in national parks in the U.S. All come with hot showers, a cafe, and a common area for hiding out from bad weather. Meals served here are simply prepared but hearty, or alternatively, guests can bring their own food and cook. Each *refugio* has rooms with two to six bunks, which you'll have to share with strangers when they're full. During the high season, consider booking weeks in advance; although many visitors have reported luck when calling just a few days beforehand (due to cancellations). All agencies in Puerto Natales and Punta Arenas book reservations and issue vouchers, but the best bet is to call or e-mail (shown below). There is a scrappy *refugio* near the park administration center, with two rows of sleeping berths that I do not recommend except in an emergency situation! This *refugio* is on a first-come, first-served basis.

The first three refugios are owned and operated by Fantástico Sur, a division of the Hostería las Torres. They can be booked by contacting ©/fax **61/710050;** albergue@lastorres.com.

- **Refugio Chileno.** This is the least-frequented *refugio* because it is located halfway up to the Towers (most do the trail as a day hike). Hikers will find it more convenient to stow their stuff in the campground at the *hostería,* but, then again, this *refugio* puts you away from the hubbub below.
- **Albergue Las Torres.** This *albergue* (lodge) is the largest and most full-service *refugio* in the park; it sits near the Hostería Las Torres. You may dine in the hotel or eat simple fare in the *refugio* itself. Horseback rides can be taken from here.
- **Refugio Los Cuernos.** This may be the park's loveliest *refugio,* located at the base of the Cuernos. The wood structure (which miraculously holds up to some of the strongest winds in the park) has two walls of windows that look out onto Lago Nordenskjold.

The first two *refugios* below can be reserved at ©/fax **61/412877;** andescape@ terra.cl. The Lodge Paine Grande can be booked at © **61/412742;** contact@ verticepatagonia.cl.

- **Refugio Grey.** Tucked in a forest on the shore of Lago Grey, this log-cabin *refugio* is a 10-minute walk to the lookout point for the glacier. It's a cold but refreshing setting, and it has a cozy fireside seating area. Spend a day here and take a walking tour on the glacier (see "Excursions Around Glacier Grey," below).
- **Refugio Dickson.** One of the loneliest *refugios,* due to its location well on the other side of the park (part of the Circuit trail). There are a lot of mosquitoes

in the summer, but you can't beat the rugged location on a grassy glacial moraine, facing Dickson Glacier.

• **Lodge Paine Grande.** This hostal-like "lodge" replaces the old *refugio* Pehoé, at the busiest intersection in the park. It is the hub for several of the trail heads to the park administration center, Glacier Grey, and French Valley, as well as the docking site for the catamaran. Utilitarian in style, the hostal has 60 beds, two lounges, and a cafeteria that can serve 120 people. Days walks to Glacier Grey and French Valley can be taken from here.

CAMPING IN TORRES DEL PAINE

Torres del Paine has a well-designed campground system with free and concession-run sites. All *refugios* have a campground, too, and these and other concession sites charge about $6 per person, which includes hot showers, clean bathrooms, and an indoor dining area to escape bad weather and eat under a roof. The site at Las Torres provides barbecues and firewood. Free campgrounds are run by Conaf, and they can get a little dingy, with deplorable outhouses. Beginning in March, mice become a problem for campers, so always leave food well stored or hanging from a tree branch. The JLM hiking map (available at every bookstore, airport, kiosk, and travel agency, and at the park entrance) denotes which campgrounds are free and which charge a fee.

TRAILS IN TORRES DEL PAINE

Torres del Paine has something for everyone, from easy, well-trammeled trails to remote walks through relatively people-free wilderness. Which path you choose depends on how much time you have and what kind of walking you're up for. If you have only a few days, I suggest you stick to the major highlights. If you have a week or more, consider a horseback-riding trip to the base of Mount Donoso, or a bird-watching trip through the Pingo Valley, or a walk to the Valle de Silencio beyond the Towers. The best way to plan a multiple-day hike is to begin at Hostería Las Torres, reached from the Laguna Amarga ranger station, although it is just as feasible to start at Lago Pehoé by catamaran and start the trip up to the glacier or French Valley. Pick up one of **JLM's Torres del Paine maps** (sold everywhere), or download a map from **www.torresdelpaine.com** to begin planning your itinerary. Walking times shown below are average. The minimum number of days shown assumes walking 4 to 8 hours a day; plan for extra days if you want to take it easy, and factor 1 or 2 days for bad weather.

LONG-HAUL OVERNIGHT HIKES

The Circuit   The Circuit is a spectacular, long-haul backpacking trip that takes hikers around the entire Paine Massif. It can be done in two ways: with the W included or without. Including the W, you'll need 8 to 11 days; without it, from 4 to 7 days. The Circuit is less traveled than the W because it's longer and requires that you camp out at least twice. I don't recommend doing this trail if you have only 4 or 5 days. This trail is for serious backpackers only because it involves several difficult hikes up and down steep, rough terrain and over fallen tree trunks. You'll be rewarded for your effort, however, with dazzling views of terrain that varies from grassy meadows and winding rivers to thick virgin beech forest, snowcapped peaks, and, best of all, the awe-inspiring view of Glacier Grey seen from atop the John Garner Pass. If you're a recreational hiker with a 4- to 6-hour hike tolerance level, you'll want to sleep in all the major campgrounds or *refugios*. Always do this trail counterclockwise for easier ascents and with the scenery before you. If you're here during the high season and want to get away from crowds, you might contemplate walking the first portion of this trail, beginning at Laguna Azul. This is the old trail, and it more or less parallels the Circuit, but on the other side of the river, passing the gaucho post La Victorina, the only remaining building of an old *estancia*. At Refugio Dickson, you'll have to cross the river in the *refugio*'s dinghy for $4. To get to Laguna Azul, you'll need to hitchhike or arrange private transportation.

Approximately 60km (37 miles) total. Beginning at Laguna Amarga or Hostería Las Torres. Terrain ranges from easy to difficult.

The W   This segment of the Paine Massif is so called because hikers are taken along a trail that forms a W. This trail leads to the park's major geological features—the Torres, the Cuernos, and Glacier Grey—and it's the preferred multiple-day hike for its relatively short hauls and a time frame that requires 4 to 5 days. In addition, those who prefer not to camp or carry more gear than a sleeping bag, food, and their personal goods can stay in the various *refugios* along the way. Most hikers begin at Hostería Las Torres and start with a day-walk up to the Torres. From here, hikers head to the Los Cuernos *refugio* and spend the night, or continue on to the Italiano campsite near the base of the valley; then they walk up to French Valley. The next stop is Pehoé *refugio*, where most spend the night before hiking up to Glacier Grey. It's best to spend a night at Refugio Grey and return to the Pehoé *refugio* the next day. From here, take the catamaran across Lago Pehoé to an awaiting bus back to Puerto Natales.

Approximately 56km (35 miles) total. Beginning at Hostería Las Torres or Refugio Pehoé. Terrain ranges from easy to difficult.

DAY HIKES

These hikes run from easy to difficult, either within the W or from various trail heads throughout the park. Again, the times given are estimates for the average walker.

Glacier Grey   This walk is certainly worth the effort for an up-close look at the face of Glacier Grey, though warm summers of late have sent the glacier retreating. There aren't as many steep climbs as the trail to Las Torres, but it takes longer to get there (about 3½ hr.). I recommend that hikers in the summer walk this lovely trail to the glacier lookout point, then take the boat back to Hostería Grey (see "Excursions around Glacier Grey," below). The walk takes hikers through thick forest and stunning views of the Southern Ice Field and the icebergs slowly making their way down Lago Grey. A turnoff just before the lookout point takes you to Refugio Grey.

3½ hr. one-way. Difficult.

Lago Grey (Moments)   Not only is this the easiest walk in the park, but it is one of the most dramatic for the gigantic blue icebergs that rest along the shore of Lago Grey. A flat walk across the sandy shore of the lake takes visitors to a peninsula for a short hike to a lookout point with Glacier Grey in the far distance. This walk begins near the Hostería Lago Grey; they offer a recommended boat ride that weaves past icebergs and then takes passengers to the face of the glacier (see "Excursions Around Glacier Grey," below).

Departing from the parking lot past the entrance to Hostería Lago Grey. 1–2 hr. Easy.

Lago Pingo (Finds)   Lago Pingo consistently sees fewer hikers and is an excellent spot for bird-watching for the variety of species that flock to this part of the park. The trail begins as an easy walk through a pleasant valley, past an old gaucho post. From here the trail heads through forest and undulating terrain, and past the Pingo Cascade until it eventually reaches another old gaucho post, the run-down but picturesque Zapata *refugio*. You can make this trail as long or as short as you'd like; the return is back along the same trail. The trail leaves from the same parking lot as the Lago Grey trail.

Departing from the Lago Grey parking lot past the entrance to Hostería Lago Grey. 1–4 hr. one-way. Easy/moderate.

Las Torres (The Towers)   The trail to view the soaring granite Towers is a classic hike in the park but certainly not the easiest. Those who are in decent shape will not want to miss this exhilarating trek. The trail leaves from the Hostería Las Torres and begins with a steep 45-minute ascent, followed by up-and-down terrain for 1½ hours to another 45-minute steep ascent up a slippery granite moraine. Midway is the Refugio Chileno, where you can stop for a coffee or spend the night. Don't give up—the Torres do not come into full view until the very end.

3 hr. one-way. Difficult.

Mirador Nordenskjold   The trail head for this walk begins near the Pudeto catamaran dock. This trail begins with an up-close visit to the crashing Salto Grande waterfall. Then it winds through Antarctic beech and thorny bush to a lookout point with dramatic views into the French Valley and the Cuernos, looking over Lago Nordenskjold. This trail is a good place to see wildflowers in the spring.

1 hr. one-way. Easy.

Valle Francés (French Valley)   There are several ways to hike this trail. From Refugio Pehoé, you'll pass by the blue waters of Lake Skottsberg and through groves of Chilean firebush and open views of the granite spires behind Los Cuernos. From Refugio Los Cuernos, you won't see French Valley until you're in it. A short walk through the campground leads hikers to direct views of the hanging glacier that descends from Paine Grande, and enthusiastic hikers can continue the steep climb up into the valley itself for a view of French Valley's enormous granite amphitheater.

Departing from Refugio Pehoé or Refugio Los Cuernos. 2½–4½ hr. one-way. Moderate/difficult.

OTHER OUTDOOR ACTIVITIES IN THE PARK
HORSEBACK RIDING
A horseback ride in Torres del Paine can be one of the most enjoyable ways to see the park, especially from the Serrano Pampa for big, bold views of Paine Massif. Both Hostería Las Torres and Explora have their own stables, but only the *hostería* has daily horseback rides, even to the Refugios Chileno and Los Cuernos; its Punta Arenas office is at Magallanes 960 (©/fax **61/226054**). The full-day trips cost $75 per person, and they leave from the hotel. **Path@gone Travel** in Puerto Natales, Eberhard 595 (© **61/413291;** pathgone@entelchile. net), can arrange a wide variety of trips across the Serrano Pampa to Lago Grey and excursions around the Laguna Amarga and Laguna Azul sectors, leaving from the park concession near administration. The cost depends on the number of riders (10 maximum) but averages $28 to $50 per person for 1- to 3-hour rides. Your hotel can reserve a horseback ride leaving from the concession-run stable near the administration center, too. For longer, multiday horseback-riding trips, contact **Chile Nativo Expeditions,** Eberhart 230 (© **61/411835;** www. chilenativo.com). Chile Nativo can plan custom-made journeys within the park

and to little-known areas, some of which include an introduction to the *gaucho* and *estancia* (ranching) way of life. Most trips require prior experience.

EXCURSIONS AROUND GLACIER GREY

A surprisingly accessible and electrifying excursion in the park is taking a crampon-shoed **walk across Glacier Grey.** Trips begin from the Refugio Grey with a 15-minute zodiac boat ride to the starting point on the western arm of the glacier. The excursion is a full-day trip, so the only way of participating is to lodge at the *refugio.* Guests are provided with full equipment, including crampons, ice axes, ropes, and harnesses, and are given basic ice-climbing instructions. Visitors who have taken this hike have consistently given rave reviews for the chance to peer into deep blue crevasses and explore the glacier's otherworldly contours up close. **Bigfoot Expeditions** runs this concession (Bories 206; © **61/413247;** www.bigfootpatagonia.com), and reservations are necessary (though if you're in the area, check for last-minute spaces). The cost is $60 per person, which includes a snack (ask about food because it may not be enough for lunch); credit cards are accepted at their concession site at Refugio Grey.

Now that the glacier has receded, the best way to view it up close is to ride **Hostería Grey's half-day boat ride,** which takes passengers past floating icebergs and directly to the face of the glacier. Passengers ride round-trip from the shore at Lake Grey; however, hikers can take the Pehoé ferry, walk approximately 4 hours to the Grey *refugio,* and then ride back on the Hostería Grey boat ($45 one-way), and transfer to the administration center and wait for a bus to drop them back at their hotel (though most hotels will arrange pickup for this excursion). The price is $60 round-trip and $45 one-way, and there are two trips leaving daily, at 8am and 3pm. Best of all, the journey runs year-round. Reservations are imperative, as are transfer reservations from the administration center; contact the *hostería* at © **61/229512;** www.austrohoteles.cl. Travelers who are not lodging at the Refugio Grey may take the early boat from the Hostería Grey, participate in the glacier walk (see above), and head back with the late boat.

4 El Calafate, Argentina ★★

222km (138 miles) south of El Chaltén; 2,727km (1,691 miles) southwest of Buenos Aires

El Calafate is a tourist-oriented village that hugs the shore of turquoise Lago Argentino, a location that, combined with the town's leafy streets, gives it the feel of an oasis in the desert Pampa of this region. The town depends almost entirely on its neighboring natural wonder, Perito Moreno Glacier, for tourism. Thousands of visitors come for the chance to stand face to face with this tremendous wall of ice, one of the few glaciers in the ice field that isn't retreating.

The town was named for the calafate bush found throughout Patagonia that produces a sweet berry commonly used in syrups and jams. As the economy in Buenos Aires deteriorated, many Argentines fled to the countryside and some came here, to El Calafate, which had suffered from a tourist trap mentality for years. Thankfully, this tendency is waning as more migrants head south to set up businesses that are meant to really serve visitors. The town itself is quite a pleasant little place, but you won't find many attractions here—they are all within the confines of Los Glaciares National Park. What you will find, however, are several good restaurants and a charming main street lined with boutiques boasting fine leather goods and shops selling locally manufactured chocolates, jams, and delicious caramel cookies called *alfajores.*

ESSENTIALS
GETTING THERE

BY PLANE   El Calafate's **Aeropuerto Lago Argentino** (no phone) has dramatically changed transportation options here in the past few years; before you would have to fly into Río Gallegos and then take a long bus ride across the flat Pampa. Service is from Argentine destinations only: **Aerolíneas Argentinas/ Austral** (ⓒ **11/4340-3777** in Buenos Aires; www.aerolineas.com.ar) has daily flights from Buenos Aires and flights from Bariloche, Trelew, and Ushuaia several times a week. New in 2005 are 747 flights arriving directly from Ezeiza International Airport in Buenos Aires during the high season (before, most flights left from Aeroparque, downtown). Be sure to specify which airport you'd like to fly from. **Southern Winds** (ⓒ **0810/777-7979**) flies from Buenos Aires and Bariloche three to four times a week.

Aerovías Dap (no phone; www.aeroviasdap.cl) has a morning flight to Puerto Natales (mid-Nov to mid-Mar Mon–Fri) aboard a seven-seater Cessna propeller, but that service is frequently canceled due to high winds. The airline companies don't have offices in El Calafate, but any travel agency can book tickets for you. From the airport, **Aerobús** (ⓒ **02901/492492**) operates a bus to all the hotels in town for $3; they can also pick you up for your return trip if you call 24 hours ahead. A taxi into town should cost no more than $9 for up to four people. There's also a Hertz Rental Car desk (no phone; www.hertz.com) at the airport.

BY BUS   El Calafate has a bus terminal located on Julio A. Roca, reached by taking the stairs up from the main street, Avenida del Libertador. To and from Puerto Natales, Chile: **Buses Sur** (ⓒ **02901/491631**) and **Turismo Zaahj** (ⓒ **02902/411325**) have five weekly trips leaving at 8am, as does **Cootra** (ⓒ **02902/491444**). The trip takes 5 to 6 hours, depending on how long you get held up at the border. To get to El Chaltén, take **Chaltén Travel,** which leaves daily at 8am and returns from Chaltén at 6pm (ⓒ **02902/492212**); **Caltur** (ⓒ **02902/491842**); or **Interlagos Turismo** (ⓒ **02902/491179**). The latter two leave daily at 7:30am and return from El Chaltén at 5pm.

BY CAR   Ruta 5, followed by Ruta 11, is paved entirely from Río Gallegos to El Calafate. From Puerto Natales, cross through the border at Cerro Castillo, which will lead you to the famous RN 40 and up to the paved portion of Ruta 11. The drive from Puerto Natales is roughly 5 hours, not including time spent at the border checkpoint.

GETTING AROUND

For information about transportation to and from Perito Moreno Glacier, see "Parque Nacional Los Glaciares & Perito Moreno Glacier," later in this chapter. If you'd like to rent a car, you can do so at the new **Europcar** office at Av. del Libertador 1741 (ⓒ **02902/493606;** www.europcar.com.ar). Rates begin at $40 per day, including insurance and taxes. There's a brand-new Hertz Rental Car desk (no phone; www.hertz.com) at the airport as well.

VISITOR INFORMATION

The city's **visitor information kiosk** can be found inside the bus terminal. They offer an ample amount of printed material and can assist in planning a trip to Perito Moreno Glacier; open October through April from 8am to 11pm daily and May through September from 8am to 8pm daily (ⓒ **02902/491090**).

A good website to check for information is www.elcalafate.com.ar.

If you require help arranging any aspect of your trip, a very helpful agency to contact is **SurTurismo** ★★, 25 de Mayo 23 (ⓒ **02902/491266;**

suring@cotecal.com.ar). They can secure everything from airport transfers to hotel reservations at discounted rates. They also provide private and licensed guides for treks and tours of the region.

WHAT TO SEE & DO IN EL CALAFATE

El Calafate serves mostly as a service town for visitors on their way to visit the glaciers (see "Parque Nacional Los Glaciares & Perito Moreno Glacier," later in this chapter), but it does present a pleasant main avenue for a stroll, and as expected, there are lots of souvenirs, bookstores, and crafts shops to keep you occupied. Heading out of town on Avenida del Libertador, you'll pass the **Museo Municipal** (no phone; free admission), open Monday through Friday from 8am to 1pm and 3 to 9pm, with a collection of farming and ranching implements, Indian artifacts, and historical and ethnographical displays. It's worth a stop if you have the time. And that's about it here in El Calafate, although if you are interested in bird-watching, you could take a short walk to the Bahía Redonda at the shore of Lago Argentino to view upland geese, black-necked swans, and flamingos.

ATTRACTIONS & EXCURSIONS AROUND EL CALAFATE

For information about visiting the glaciers and the national park, see "Parque Nacional Los Glaciares & Perito Moreno Glacier," later in this chapter.

HORSEBACK RIDING   Cabalgata en Patagonia, Julio A. Roca 2063 (✆ **02902/493203;** cabalgataenpatagonia@cotecal.com.ar), offers two horse-back-riding options: a 2-hour ride to Bahía Redonda for a panoramic view of El Calafate ($12) and a full-day trip bordering Lago Argentino, with an optional stop at the Walicho Caves, where one can supposedly view Indian "paintings," which are billed as real but are really reproductions. This tour costs $15 per person and includes lunch. Book directly or with a travel agency.

VISITING AN *ESTANCIA*   **An interesting option worth looking into is one of the several *estancias,* or ranches, that have opened their doors to the public, offering day activities, restaurant services, and even lodging, should you opt to spend the night. Perhaps the most exclusive and well known is the **Estancia Helsingfors, open from October to March and located on the shore of Lago Viedma about 150km (93 miles) from El Calafate. Helsingfors offers lodging, horseback riding, overflights, bird-watching, boat trips, and fine dining. For more information, contact their offices in Río Gallegos at Av. del Libertador 516 (✆/fax **02966/420719**).

All of the following *estancias* offer lodging, a restaurant, horseback riding, trekking, vehicle excursions, and transportation from El Calafate. The closest to El Calafate is the **Estancia Huyliche** (✆ **02902/491025;** teresanegro@cotecal.com.ar), about 3km (1¾ miles) from downtown, open from October to April; they also offer boating excursions. **Estancia Alice El Galpón** (✆ **02902/492290;** info@elgalpon.com.ar), open October through April, is 20km (12 miles) from El Calafate on RP 11, and offers activities that lean more toward ranching, including sheep-shearing and wool-packing demonstrations, sheep round-ups, and maintenance of the animals, as well as bird-watching. **Estancia Alta Vista** (✆ **02902/491247;** altavista@cotecal.com.ar), at 33km (20 miles) from El Calafate on the dirt road RP 15 near the beautiful area of Lago Roca, is open October through March and offers ranch activities and fishing. **Estancia Nibepo Aike** (✆ **02966/422626;** nibepo@internet.siscotel.com.ar) is pic-turesquely nestled on the southeast edge of the national park about 60km

(37 miles) from El Calafate, and it's also near Lago Roca, offering fishing and ranch activities October through April.

WHERE TO STAY
EXPENSIVE

Hotel Kosten Aike ★★ *Value*   This charming newer hotel offers modern and attractive accommodations paired with high-quality service. The Kosten Aike is priced lower than its competitor, the Posada Los Alamos (see below). The Posada's design is buttoned-up conservative, while the Kosten Aike is fresh and stylish. Both the architect's and the designer's good taste saved the Kosten Aike from the cookie-cutter style usually seen in new hotels. Furnishings and artwork imported from Buenos Aires include matching drapes and bedspreads in rust and beige accented with black geometric squiggles, papier-mâché lamps, iron and rosewood tables and chairs, and petal-soft carpets, and all rooms feature sumptuous bathrooms. Some rooms have bay windows and are very large; they aren't any more expensive, so ask for one when booking. The airy lobby is inlaid completely with gray stone. The Kosten Aike has a chic restaurant off the lobby that serves contemporary regional and Argentine fare.

Gobernador Moyano 1243, El Calafate. ⓒ **02902/492424,** or 11/4811-1314 (reservations). Fax 02902/491538. www.kostenaike.com.ar. 80 units. $88–$150 double. AE, DC, MC, V. **Amenities:** Restaurant; wine bar; fireside lounge; exercise room; gym; spa; game room; concierge; business center; room service; laundry service. *In room:* TV, dataport, minibar, hair dryer, safe.

Hotel Posada Los Alamos ★★ *Finds*   The Posada Los Alamos is as conservative as a Brooks Brothers suit. Because of the low-key design of the "complex" and the slightly aloof service, you can't help the feeling that you're in a private country club. The style is classic: a red-brick exterior fringed with the hotel's namesake alamo trees, plaid carpet, old English furniture, and windows with wooden, triangular eaves. Downstairs is a comfortable lounge, and the lobby's large windows look out onto an expansive lawn. Rooms have ample space, and each has a slightly different color and style. Ask for one that looks out onto the quiet, grassy backyard instead of the dusty dirt road. The hotel's excellent restaurant, La Posta, is reviewed under "Where to Dine," below.

Gobernador Moyano and Bustillo, El Calafate. ⓒ **02902/491144.** Fax 02902/491186. www.posadalosalamos.com. 144 units. $92–$158 double; from $158 suite. AE, MC, V. **Amenities:** Restaurant; bar; lounge; golf course; tennis court; tour desk; room service; massage; laundry service; dry cleaning. *In room:* TV, minibar, safe.

MODERATE

Hostería Sierra Nevada ★ *Finds*   This charming *hostería* is a 15-minute walk from all the shops and restaurants. It's the only recommended property right on the lake, and every room comes with a water view. Built in 2000, the two-story building has a pleasant expansiveness to it, and the rooms are fresh and modern, with wrought-iron furniture, firm mattresses, and beautiful granite-tiled bathrooms and showers. Large French doors in each room slide open to reveal the garden and the lake just beyond. Most of the guests here are South American, so the staff members don't speak much English, but they're friendly and pleasant and will try their best.

Libertador 1888, El Calafate. ⓒ **02902/493129.** Sierranevada@cotecal.com.ar. 18 units. $58–$76 double. Rates include buffet breakfast. MC, V. **Amenities:** Restaurant; bar. *In room:* TV, safe.

Hotel Kapenke *Value*   This hotel is a good option for moderately priced lodging in El Calafate. The Kapenke underwent a minor renovation in 2000, installing new wallpaper and, in the hallway, lemon-yellow paint. The bathrooms are cramped, but the rooms are decently sized and come with a large chest of drawers and comfortable beds—ask for a room on the second floor, as they are brighter. Apart from a few corner sitting areas spread about each floor, there is a large lounge with lots of padded wooden chairs. The staff isn't as energetic or as helpful as one would hope.

Av. 9 de Julio 112, El Calafate. (C)/fax **02902/491093**. www.kapenke.com.ar. 32 units. $52–$70 double. MC, V. **Amenities:** Restaurant; bar; lounge; room service. *In room:* TV, dataport, hair dryer, safe.

Michelangelo Hotel The Michelangelo is very popular with traveling foreigners, especially Europeans. The well-maintained hotel sits about a 2-block walk from the main street and is cater-cornered from the phone center, a convenient yet quiet location, and is recognizable by its A-frame porticos. Probably the best thing about the Michelangelo is its excellent restaurant (reviewed under "Where to Dine," below) and its comfortable rooms, although they're not especially noteworthy. Rooms are average size, with white walls, dark beams, and little decoration; new mattresses were added in 2002. The softly lit lounge has a handful of chairs, a banquette, and potted plants. The staff is exceptionally friendly and helpful here, and they speak passable English.

Gobernador Moyano 1020, El Calafate. (C) **02902/491045**. Fax 02902/491058. michelangelohotel@cotecal. com.ar. 20 units. $58–$74 double. AE, MC, V. **Amenities:** Restaurant; bar; lounge; room service. *In room:* TV, minibar.

INEXPENSIVE

Hostal Lago Argentino Like Los Dos Pinos (see below), the Hostal Lago Argentino offers different options for budget travelers. There are $7 beds in two-bunk, shared rooms in one wing and, across the street in a pink-and-blue building, modest yet tidy doubles with private bathrooms that for $24 make for a great value in El Calafate. The rooms aren't huge, but there's a small seating area, should you need a little space. The *hostal* is about a block from the bus terminal.

Campaña de Desierto 1070, El Calafate. (C) **02902/491423**. 8 units. $24 double. No credit cards. Closed July to mid-Aug. **Amenities:** Lounge.

Los Dos Pinos The Los Dos Pinos has just about every and any combination for budget travelers. At the bottom of the rung is the grassy campground, which comes with barbecue pits and costs $3 per person; next up is the $12 option for a bed in a six-bunk room that you might or might not have to share with strangers during the high season. There are several cabins and a few rooms that come with a kitchen. One floor has three rooms and a hall that leads to a shared kitchen and bathroom. The *cabañas* have Kelly green cement interiors and two bedrooms with one single and one bunk bed and a shared eating area and kitchen. The "deluxe" rooms are simple doubles with a private bathroom but no kitchen, and are a good deal for the price. The hostal sits at the end of a gravely dirt road about a 4-block walk to the main street, not exactly a choice location, but peaceful. Also, the surrounding grounds are unattractive because the lot seems to be in a perpetual state of half-completed construction.

Av. 9 de Julio 358, El Calafate. (C)/fax **02902/491271**. losdospinos@cotecal.com.ar. 25 units. $22 double; $12 per person *cabaña*. MC, V. **Amenities:** Lounge.

WHERE TO DINE

If you're just looking for a pleasant place away from the main street crowds in which to unwind with a cup of tea, then try **Kau Kaleshen,** Gobernador Gregores 1256 ((C) **02902/491188**). Located in a charming house on a side street, this tea house is open daily from 5pm to midnight and offers a "Te Completo" for $6 that includes your choice of either tea or specialty coffee, along with homemade breads and jam, a selection of pastries, and toasted sandwiches. Credit cards are not accepted.

MODERATE

La Posta 🌟🌟🌟 ARGENTINE   Although it's in a building separate from the Posada Los Alamos, the La Posta is considered to be part of that hotel. This is El Calafate's most upscale restaurant, serving great cuisine and choice wines in a cozy, candlelit environment. The menu, printed in four languages, offers well-prepared dishes that effectively blend Argentine and international-flavored fare, like filet mignon in a puff pastry with rosemary-roasted potatoes, king crab ravioli, almond trout, or curried crayfish. Desserts are superb. If you're staying at the hotel, a lovely breakfast buffet is served here every morning, and the service both morning and night is exquisite.

Gobernador Moyano and Bustillo. ✆ 02902/491144. Reservations recommended in high season. Main courses $7–$13. AE, DC, MC, V. Daily 7pm–midnight.

INEXPENSIVE

Casablanca CAFE/BAR   The Casablanca is the local hangout for a beer and a quick meal, and one of the few places around where you can grab a meal at odd hours. There's a wooden bar and a dining area with tile floors and metal chairs and tables, and an elevated TV that's usually on. The menu is mostly pizzas, sandwiches, and empanadas, with one special and a popular steak-and-fries plate for $4, but sandwiches are your best bet here. This is a good spot for writing out postcards and sipping a cold beer on a warm afternoon.

Av. 21 de Mayo and Av. del Libertador. ✆ 02902/491402. Main courses $4–$6; sandwiches $1.50–$3. No credit cards. Daily 10am–3am.

Casimiro 🌟 *Moments* REGIONAL   This sleek wine bar and restaurant has quickly become the number one hot spot in El Calafate. The chic and modern black-and-white decor, thick tablecloths, flickering candles on every table, and young and energetic waitstaff make this place a winner. You can sample one of the many wines while enjoying an appetizer platter of regional Patagonian specialties such as smoked trout, smoked wild boar, and a variety of cheeses. Main courses change frequently but usually range from a simple steak to an elaborate pasta with salmon, cream, and capers in white-wine sauce; there's always a chicken and seafood offering as well. If you're celebrating a special occasion, this would be an excellent place to try a glass of dry Argentine sparkling wine.

Av. del Libertador 963. ✆ 02902/492590. Main courses $6–$11. MC, V. Daily 10am–1am.

El Rancho PIZZA   El Rancho's brick interior, with its white lace curtains and old photos, is cozy and inviting, but the restaurant's tiny size means you might have to wait for a table on busy evenings. There are 32 varieties of pizza on offer here and 5 varieties of hefty empanadas. Also on the menu are fresh salads and a couple of steaks. They also deliver, free of charge.

Gobernador Moyano and Av. 9 de Julio. ✆ 02902/491644. Pizzas $2–$6. DC, MC, V. Tues–Sun 6:30pm–midnight.

La Cocina 🌟 *Value* BISTRO   This little restaurant serves bistro-style food, including fresh pastas such as raviolis and fettuccine, fresh trout, and meats that are prepared simply but are quite good. Try the crepes stuffed with vegetables or combinations such as ham and cheese, or meat items such as steak with a pepper and mustard sauce. Of all the restaurants on the main street with a similar appearance, such as the Paso Verlika, La Cocina is without a doubt the best.

Av. del Libertador 1245. ✆ 02902/491758. Main courses $3–$5. MC, V. Tues–Sun noon–3pm and 7:30–11pm.

La Tablita ★★ *Value* STEAKHOUSE Carnivores need not look any further. La Tablita is all about meat, and it's one of the local favorites in town for its heaping platters and giant *parrilladas* (mixed grills) that come sizzling to your table on their own minibarbecues. The *parrilladas* for two cost $12, but they really serve three diners, given the size and assortment of chicken, sausage, beef, lamb, and a few innards you may or may not recognize. The filet mignon is incredibly tender here and, at $6, is one of the least expensive filets that we've ever had. The sunny, airy restaurant can be found on the other side of the bridge that spans the Arroyo Calafate, about a 2-minute walk from downtown.

Coronel Rosales 24. ✆ 02902/491065. Main courses $3–$7. AE, MC, V. Daily 11am–3pm and 7pm–midnight (Wed closed for lunch).

Michelangelo *Finds* ARGENTINE The Michelangelo Hotel's restaurant is as popular with the public as it is with its guests. The semielegant dining area is very pleasing, with low ceilings, stone-and-mortar walls, and candlelit tables. The Michelangelo has added more exotic fare to its menu than La Posta, such as wild hare and smoked venison. The lamb in red-wine sauce with roasted potatoes is quite good, as are other meat dishes, such as filet mignon, or chicken with a balsamic and tarragon vinaigrette. The fresh pastas and fish dishes are light and simple, as are the salads.

Gobernador Moyano 1020. ✆ 02902/492104. Main courses $5–$8. MC, V. Daily noon–3pm and 8pm–midnight.

Parrilla Mi Viejo STEAKHOUSE Mi Viejo is another local barbecue favorite, with enough variety on the menu to satisfy everyone. Mi Viejo (My Old Man) seems to refer to the crusty character manning the lamb barbecue spit at the restaurant's front entrance, serving up weighty, delicious cuts of meat. Three to five diners could eat from a $10 *parrillada* meat assortment, depending on their hunger. The menu also offers trout and salmon dishes and a few interesting plates such as pickled hare. The restaurant is located on the main drag, and its dining room is warm and pleasant.

Av. del Libertador 1111. ✆ 02902/491691. Main courses $3–$6. MC, V. Daily 11am–3pm and 7pm–midnight.

Pura Vida ★ *Finds* VEGETARIAN/REGIONAL The friendliest place in town is a short walk from downtown but is worth finding. Set in a woodsy location overlooking the lake, this is the best place in El Calafate for home-style cuisine that favors vegetarians. Try the delicious pumpkin soup or the gnocchi in saffron sauce. If you want to try a regional specialty, then go for the *cazuela de cordero* (hearty lamb stew with mushrooms). For dessert, both the rice pudding and the pumpkin ice cream are delicious. Fresh fruit shakes, sandwiches, and afternoon tea with homemade rolls and jams are also offered. The service is laid back, the crowd is young and relaxed, and the view of the lake is divine.

Av. del Libertador 1876. ✆ 02902/493356. Main courses $4–$7. No credit cards. Thurs–Tues 4pm–12:30am (to 1:30am Fri–Sat).

Tango Sur DINNER/SHOW The Porteño owner of this restaurant/nightclub has brought tango to the south of Argentina. The Tango Sur, in a lovely raspberry-colored building made of old brick, serves light meals and features a nightly tango show of crooning and dancing. The interiors are crammed with memorabilia and antiques such as a megaphone, records, microphones, and anything related to tango that the owner could find. The menu is brief, serving grilled steak, beef *milanesas* (breaded filets), and sandwiches—better to order a drink and an appetizer platter.

Av. 9 de Julio 265. (ⓒ) **02902/491550.** Main courses $4–$8. No credit cards. Tues–Sun 7pm–5am.

PARQUE NACIONAL LOS GLACIARES
& PERITO MORENO GLACIER ✫✫✫

The Los Glaciares National Park covers 600,000 hectares (1.5 million acres) of rugged land that stretches vertically along the crest of the Andes and spills east into flat Pampa. Most of Los Glaciares is inaccessible to visitors except for the park's two dramatic highlights: the granite needles, such as Fitz Roy near El Chaltén (covered in "El Chaltén & the Fitz Roy Area, Argentina," below), and this region's magnificent Perito Moreno Glacier. The park is also home to thundering rivers, blue lakes, and thick beech forest. Los Glaciares National Park was formed in 1937 and declared a World Heritage region by UNESCO in 1981.

If you don't get a chance to visit Glacier Grey in Torres del Paine, Perito Moreno is a must-see. Few natural wonders in South America are as spectacular or as easily accessed as this glacier, and unlike the hundreds of glaciers that drain from the Southern Ice Field, Perito Moreno is one of the few that are not receding. Around 1900, Perito Moreno was measured at 750m (2,460 ft.) from the Península Magallanes; by 1920, it had advanced so far that it finally made contact with the peninsula. Each time the glacier reached the peninsula, which would occur every 3 to 4 years, it created a dam in the channel and the built-up pressure would set off a calving explosion for 48 to 72 hours, breaking the face of the glacier in a crashing fury. The phenomenon has not occurred in many years, but Perito Moreno is usually reliable for a sending a few huge chunks hurling into the channel throughout the day.

What impresses visitors most is the sheer size of Perito Moreno Glacier, a wall of jagged blue ice measuring 4,500m (14,760 ft.) across and soaring 60m (197 ft.) above the channel. To give you some perspective of its length: You could fit the entire city of Buenos Aires on this glacier. From the parking lot on the Península Magallanes, a series of vista-point walkways descend, which take visitors directly to the glacier's face. It's truly an unforgettable, spellbinding experience. There are opportunities to join an organized group for a walk on the glacier, as well as boat journeys that leave from Puerto Banderas for visits to the neighboring glaciers Upsala and Spegazzini.

GETTING THERE & ESSENTIALS

At Km 49 (30 miles) from El Calafate, you'll pass through the park's entrance, where there's an information booth with erratic hours (no phone; www.calafate.com). The entrance fee is $10 per person. If you're looking for information about the park and the glacier, pick up an interpretive guide or book from one of the bookstores or tourist shops along Avenida del Libertador in El Calafate. There is a restaurant near the principal lookout platform near the glacier and a good, though expensive, restaurant inside the Los Notros hotel (see "Lodging Near the Glacier," below).

BY CAR Following Avenida del Libertador west out of town, the route turns into a well-maintained dirt road. From here it's 80km (50 miles) to the glacier.

BY TAXI OR *Remise*   If you want to see the glacier at your own pace, hire a taxi or *remise* (a private taxi). The cost averages $50 for two, $75 for three, and $100 for four, although many taxi companies will negotiate a price. Be sure to agree on an estimated amount of time spent at the glacier.

BY ORGANIZED TOUR   Several companies offer transportation to and from the glacier, such as **Interlagos,** Av. del Libertador 1175 (© **02902/ 491175;** interlagos@cotecal.com.ar); **City Tour,** Av. del Libertador 1341 (© **02902/492276;** morresi@cotecal.com.ar); **Caltur,** Av. del Libertador 1177 (© **02902/491368;** caltur@cotecal.com.ar); and **TAQSA,** in the bus terminal (© **02902/491843**). These minivan and bus services provide bilingual guides and leave around 9am, spending an average of 4 hours at the peninsula; the cost is $30 to $50 per person, not including lunch. For a more personalized tour (a private car with driver and a bilingual, licensed guide), contact **SurTurismo,** 25 de Mayo 23 (© **02902/491266;** suring@cotecal.com.ar); they can arrange for a half-day trip costing $60 to $75 for two people (prices vary with the seasons).

OUTDOOR ACTIVITIES

There are several exciting activities in this region, including a "mini trek" that takes guests for a walk upon the glacier. The trip begins with a 20-minute boat ride across the Brazo Rico, followed by a 30-minute walk to the glacier. From here guests are outfitted with crampons and other safety gear, then spend approximately 1½ hours atop the ice, complete with a stop for a whiskey on the thousand-year-old "rocks." This great trip gives visitors the chance to peer into the electric-blue crevasses of the glacier and truly appreciate its size.

Solo Patagonia, Av. del Libertador 963 (© **02902/491298;** www.solo patagonia.com.ar), offers visitors navigation trips through the Brazo Rico to the face of Perito Moreno, including trekking to the base of Cerro Negro with a view of Glacier Negro. Both Solo Patagonia and **Upsala Explorer** ⚓, Av. 9 de Julio 69 (© **02902/491034;** www.upsalaexplorer.com.ar), offer a variety of combinations from Puerto Banderas to Los Glaciares National Park's largest and tallest glaciers, respectively, the Upsala and Spegazzini. Upsala Explorer makes a stop at the Estancia Cristina for lunch and offers optional trekking and 4×4 trips to the Upsala Lookout. Solo Patagonia offers similar journeys, including a stop at the Onelli area for trekking, as well as navigation-only journeys. Both companies charge $90 to $125 for this all-day excursion.

LODGING NEAR THE GLACIER

Los Notros 🏵🏵🏵 *(Moments*   Few hotels in Argentina boast as spectacular and breathtaking a view as Los Notros—but it doesn't come cheap. This luxury lodge sits high on a slope looking out at Perito Moreno Glacier, and all common areas and rooms have been fitted with picture windows to really soak up the marvelous sight. Although the wood-hewn exteriors give the hotel the feel of a mountain lodge, the interior decor is contemporary. Each room is slightly different, with personal touches like antique lamps and regional photos; crocheted or gingham bedspreads; lilac, peach, or lemon-yellow walls; padded floral headboards or iron bed frames; and tweedy brown or raspberry corduroy chairs. Bathrooms are gleaming white, and premium rooms in the newer wing have whirlpool baths. The older "Cascada bungalow" rooms have very thin walls; if you're a light sleeper, be sure to request a top-floor room or a room in the newer "Premium" (and more expensive) wing.

Inside the main building is a large, chic, and expansive restaurant renowned for serving creative regional cuisine. Upstairs is an airy lounge area with chaise longues positioned in front of panoramic windows; here you'll find a TV room with a selection of nature videos. Guests at the Los Notros must opt for one of the multiple-day packages that includes airport transfers, meals, box lunches for expeditions, nightly discussions, guided trekking, boat excursions, and ice walks. Although Los Notros offers 4-night packages, you might find that length of time too long unless you're looking to get away from it all for a while. Note that prices jump substantially during Christmas, New Year's, and Easter week. One-night stays are on request only and are sold only subject to availability; the hotel prefers to sell its rooms to those buying their all-inclusive packages before releasing the rooms to those seeking just an overnight stay.

Main office in Buenos Aires: Arenales 1457, 7th floor. ℂ 11/4814-3934. Fax 11/4815-7645. www.losnotros. com. 32 units. $930 per person for 2-night package Cascada bungalow; $1,060 per person for 2-night package in double superior; $1,270 per person for 2-night package in double premium. Rates include all meals and transfers. Room-only rates available by request only, depending on availability. AE, DC, MC, V. **Amenities:** Restaurant; bar; lounge; tour desk; room service; laundry service. *In room:* Minibar.

5 El Chaltén & the Fitz Roy Area, Argentina ⟨★⟨★

222km (138 miles) north of El Calafate

El Chaltén is a tiny village of about 200 residents whose lifeblood, like El Calafate's, depends entirely on the throng of visitors who come each summer. This is the second-most-visited region of Argentina's Los Glaciares National Park and quite possibly its most exquisite, for the singular nature of the granite spires that shoot up, torpedo-like, above massive tongues of ice that descend from the Southern Ice Field. In the world of mountaineering, these sheer and ice-encrusted peaks are considered some of the most formidable challenges in the world, and they draw hundreds of climbers here every year.

Little more than 5 years ago, El Chaltén counted just a dozen houses and a hostal or two, but the Fitz Roy's rugged beauty and great hiking opportunities have created somewhat of a boomtown. The town sits nestled in a circular rock outcrop at the base of the Fitz Roy and is fronted by the vast, dry Pampa. Visitors use El Chaltén either as a base from which to take day hikes or as an overnight stop before setting off for a multiple-day backpacking trip.

ESSENTIALS
GETTING THERE
BY PLANE All transportation to El Chaltén originates from El Calafate, which has daily plane service from Ushuaia and Buenos Aires. From El Calafate, you need to take a bus or rent a car; the trip takes from 3 to 3½ hours.

BY CAR From El Calafate, take RN 11 west for 30km (19 miles) and turn left on RN 40 north. Turn again, heading northwest, on RP 23 to El Chaltén. The road is unpaved.

BY BUS Buses from El Calafate leave from the terminal, and all cost about $30 round-trip. **Chaltén Travel,** with offices in El Chaltén in the Albergue Rancho Grande on Avenida del Libertador (ℂ **02962/493005;** chaltentravel@cotecal.com.ar), leaves El Calafate daily at 8am and El Chaltén at 6pm. Chaltén Travel can arrange private tours and day trips to outlying destinations such as Patagonian ranches, as well as summer-only transportation up RN 40 for those crossing into Chile. **Caltur,** which leaves from El Chaltén's Hostería Fitz Roy at Av. San Martín 520 (ℂ **02962/493062;** caltur@cotecal.com.ar), leaves El Calafate daily at 7:30am and leaves El Chaltén at 6pm. **Los Glaciares,** San

Martín 100 (☎ **02962/493063;** www.losglaciaresturismo.com), leaves El Calafate daily at 8am and returns at 5:30pm.

VISITOR INFORMATION

There is a $10 fee to enter the park. El Chaltén also has a well-organized visitor center at the town's entrance—the **Comisión de Fomento,** Perito Moreno and Avenida Güemes (☎ **02962/493011**), open daily from 8am to 8pm. Here you'll find maps, pamphlets, and brief interpretive displays about the region's flora and fauna. In El Calafate, the **APN Intendencia** (park service) has its offices at Av. del Libertador 1302, with a visitor center that is open daily from 9am to 3pm (☎ **02902/491005**).

OUTDOOR ACTIVITIES

TOUR OPERATORS   Fitz Roy Expediciones 🐾🐾, Lionel Terray 212 (☎/fax **02962/493017;** www.fitzroyexpediciones.com.ar), offers a full-day excursion trekking through Valle de Río Fitz Roy combined with ice climbing at Glacier Torre. No experience is necessary, but they do ask that you be in fit condition. They can also arrange for you to make the descent back to the base on horseback. Fitz Roy Expediciones offers a variety of trekking excursions, including a complete 9-day circuit around the backside of the Fitz Roy and Cerro Torre peaks, for $950 per person, all equipment and meals included, as well as 2 nights' lodging in an *albergue.* **Alta Montaña,** Lionel Terray 501 (☎ **02962/ 493018;** altamont@infovia.com.ar), also offers summer-only day-trekking excursions. There are several resident mountaineering and trekking guides who speak English and can be hired on a freelance basis, including Alberto del Castillo (☎ **02962/493017**), Jorge Tarditti (☎ **02962/4993013**), and Oscar Pandolfi (☎ **02962/493016**).

HIKING & CAMPING   If you're planning on doing any hiking in the park, you'll want to pick up a copy of Zagier & Urruty's trekking map, *Monte Fitz Roy & Cerro Torre,* available at most bookstores and tourist shops in El Calafate and El Chaltén. You'll also need to register at the park service office at the entrance to El Chaltén. You won't find a well-defined circuit here as you do in Torres del Paine, but there is a loop of sorts, and all stretches of this 3- to 4-day loop can be done one leg at a time on day hikes. Trails here run from easy to difficult and take anywhere from 4 to 10 hours to complete.

One of the most spectacular day hikes, which can also be done as an overnight, 2-day hike, is the 19km (12-mile) trail to the **Mirador D'Agostini,** also known as Maestri, that affords exhilarating views of the spire Cerro Torre, another mountain peak. The hike takes 5½ to 6 hours to complete and is classified as easy, except for the last steep climb to the lookout point. It's possible to camp nearby at the D'Agostini campground (formerly Bridwell). Leaving from the Madsen campground, a more demanding, though beautiful, trail heads to several campsites and eventually the Laguna de los Tres, where there is a lookout point for views of Mount Fitz Roy. This walk is best done as an overnight trip; it's too much to undertake in 1 day. Campgrounds inside the park's boundaries are free but do not have services; paid campgrounds (outside the park) have water, and some have showers.

HORSEBACK RIDING   There's nothing like horseback riding in Patagonia, and two outfitters offer several day excursions: **Rodolfo Guerra,** Las Loicas 773 (☎ **02962/493020**), has horseback rides and a horsepack service for carrying gear to campsites. Also try the **El Relincho,** Av. del Libertador s/n (☎ **02962/ 493007**).

WHERE TO STAY IN EL CHALTEN

Finally, a much-needed luxury option is coming to Chaltén. But not until mid-2005. The owners of the drop-dead-gorgeous Los Notros (that faces Perito Moreno glacier) are building **Los Cerros,** a small deluxe inn with grand views over the mountains. Expect rustic luxury and an all-inclusive program very similar to Los Notros. Rates will begin at $585 per person for 2 nights in a standard room and go to $1,116 per person for 4 nights in a premium room. The rates include transfers from El Calafate or Los Notros, meals, taxes, and a choice of several guided excursions, including treks, hikes, and 4×4 rides. For more information, contact their Buenos Aires reservations office (© **11/4814-3934;** info@loscerrosdelchalten.com).

El Puma ⚐ Until Los Cerros opens (see above), El Puma offers the most comfortable accommodations in El Chaltén. The owners of this hotel work with the outfitter Fitz Roy Expediciones, which has an office next door. The hotel sits back from the main road and faces out toward snowy peaks, although without a view of Fitz Roy. Inside, warm beige walls and wooden beams interplay with brick and are offset with soft cotton curtains and ironwork. Although the common areas have terra-cotta ceramic floors, all rooms are carpeted. The rooms are well designed and bright; the lounge has a few chairs that face a roaring fire. There's also an eating area with wooden tables and a small bar. Service here is very friendly.

Lionel Terray 512, El Chaltén. © **02962/493095.** Fax 02962/493017. Elpuma@videodata.com.ar. 8 units. $90 double. Rates include buffet breakfast. No credit cards. Closed Apr–Oct. **Amenities:** Restaurant; bar.

Hostería El Pilar *(Finds* The Hostería El Pilar is the most popular lodging option in the area. True, the hotel's location 15km (9¼ miles) from El Chaltén toward Lago del Desierto does put guests far from restaurants and shops, but then lovely, peaceful surroundings are what many guests look for when they come to visit the national park. The yellow-walled and red-roofed El Pilar was once an *estancia;* now it's tastefully and artistically decorated with just enough detail to not distract you from the outdoors. The lounge offers a few couches and a fireplace, and is a comfy spot to lounge and read a book. Rooms are simple but attractive, with peach walls, comfortable beds, and sunlight that streams through half-curtained windows. Guests normally take their meals at the hotel's restaurant, which serves great cuisine. The hotel offers guided excursions and is located next to several trail heads. If you're driving here, keep an eye open for the sign to this hotel because it's easy to miss.

Ruta Provincial 23, 15km (9¼ miles) from El Chaltén. ©/fax **02962/493002.** 16 units. $90 double. MC, V. Oct–Apr; rest of the year with a reservation. **Amenities:** Restaurant; bar; lounge.

Hostería Fitz Roy This mint-green hotel is spread out somewhat ranch style, with a popular restaurant and regular bus service to El Calafate. The hallways are very dark, but the rooms receive decent light; none has a view of much of anything. The rooms at the Fitz Roy are simple but clean. If by chance you're traveling with five people and you all want to sleep in the same room, they've got one to fit you. This hotel is a decent value, but the service could use a smile.

Av. San Martín 520, El Chaltén. © **02962/493062,** or 02902/491368 (reservations). Fax 02902/492217. www.elchalten.com/fitzroyinn. 30 units. $82–$114 double. Rates include buffet breakfast. MC, V. Closed June–Aug. **Amenities:** Restaurant.

Hostería Los Ñires This *hostería* offers unremarkable but clean and comfortable accommodations. In one wing are rooms with a private bathroom; the other is a hostel setup with shared bunks and bathrooms and a common area with a kitchen. The rooms have white walls and no decoration other than a view of the Fitz Roy peak, and a wide variety of combinations, including several quadruples. If it's fairly slow in the hostal, they'll make sure you don't have to share your three-bed room with a stranger. The main building has a roomy restaurant and lounge. Breakfast is not included for guests in the hostal.

Lago del Desierto s/n, El Chaltén. ℰ 02962/493009. Losnires@sanjulian.com.ar 12 units. $38 double with private bathroom; $12 bunk with shared bathroom. MC, V. **Amenities:** Restaurant; laundry service.

Posada Poicenoit & Albergue Rancho Grande   These two jointly owned lodging options sit next to each other. The Posada Poicenoit is a tiny, attractive hotel built of wood with just three rooms: two doubles and a quadruple, all with private bathrooms. There's a small foyer with high ceilings, filled with several wooden tables for breakfast or snacks. The rooms are simple but comfortable and sunny. Next door, an equally attractive hostal caters to a predominantly back-packer crowd. Each room has two bunk beds, and rooms are shared if you don't have three friends to help you fill one. The restaurant and eating area is a great place to unwind, with long wooden tables, a lofty ceiling, and broad windows. Guests, including guests from the Posada Poicenoit, may use the *albergue*'s kitchen.

Av. del Libertador s/n, El Chaltén. ℰ 09262/493005. chaltentravel@cotecal.com.ar. 3 units, 8 dormitory-style rooms. $24 double; $9 per person dormitory. AE, MC, V. Closed May–Sept. **Amenities:** Restaurant; lounge; kitchen.

WHERE TO DINE

During the winter, only one restaurant valiantly stays open: **La Casita,** Avenida del Libertador at Lionel Terray, in the pink building (ℰ 02966/493042). La Casita offers average, home-style fare, including sandwiches, meats, pastas, stuffed crepes, and absent-minded service; it accepts American Express, Master-Card, and Visa. At other times of the year, the best restaurant in town for food and ambience is **Patagonicus,** Güemes at Andreas Madsen (ℰ 02966/493025). Patagonicus serves mostly pizza and enormous salads in a woodsy dining area; no credit cards accepted. Another good restaurant can be found inside the **Hostería Fitz Roy,** Av. San Martín 520 (ℰ 02966/493062), which serves Argentine and international fare such as grilled meats and seafood, pastas, and more in a pleas-ant dining area with white linen-draped tables; it accepts MasterCard and Visa. For sandwiches, snacks, coffee, and cakes, try the **Albergue Rancho Grande,** Av. del Libertador s/n (ℰ 02966/493005); no credit cards accepted.

6 The Far South: Puerto Williams, Chile

Puerto Williams is the southernmost town in the world, though it functions pri-marily as a naval base with a population of less than 2,500 residents. The town occupies the northern shore of Isla Navarino in the Beagle Channel, an alto-gether enchanting location framed by towering granite needles called the "Teeth of Navarino." As a destination, it is surpassed by its Argentine neighbor Ushuaia and its burgeoning tourism infrastructure. Argentines, in fact, like to say that Ushuaia is the southernmost city in the world, but then Argentines make a lot of false claims in Patagonia, such as ownership of the Southern Ice Field (the majority lies in Chile). Apart from a few hiking trails and a museum, there's not a lot to do here, but adventurers setting out for or returning from sailing and kayaking trips around Cape Horn use the town as a base. And really, there is a certain cachet to setting foot in this isolated village and knowing you're at the end of the world. The best way to visit Puerto Williams is via the *Mare Australis* cruise ship, or any other ship that allows for an afternoon or 1 day of exploring this far-flung locale. The Yamana culture, who so perplexed the first Europeans in their ability to withstand the harsh environment with little clothing, is long gone, but visitors may still view the last vestiges of their settlements and a well-designed anthropological museum in town.

GETTING THERE

BY AIR **Aerovías DAP,** O'Higgins 891 (© **61/223340** in Punta Arenas, 61/621051 in Puerto Williams; www.aeroviasdap.cl), flies to Puerto Williams from Punta Arenas on Tuesday, Thursday, and Saturday from April to October, and twice a day Tuesday through Saturday from November to March; the cost is $64 per person. Contact DAP for information about occasional flights from Ushuaia to Puerto Williams. DAP also has charter flights, and overland flights to Cape Horn from Punta Arenas.

BY BOAT The cruise ship *Mare Australis* makes a stop here; for information, see "Cruising from Punta Arenas to Ushuaia" under "Punta Arenas, Chile," earlier in this chapter. The passenger and cargo ferry **Transbordadora Austral Broom** offers cheaper passage to Puerto Williams with a 34-hour journey from Punta Arenas (Av. Bulnes 05075; © **61/218100;** www.tabsa.cl). During the summer, the ferry leaves Punta Arenas four times a month on Wednesday and returns on Saturday; sleeping arrangements consist of reclining seats ($120 adult one-way) and bunks ($150 adult one-way). Kids receive a 50% discount. **Victory Adventure Travel,** based out of Puerto Williams at Teniente Munoz 118, #70 (© **61/621092;** www.victory-cruises.com), specializes in sailing journeys around the Beagle Channel and Cape Horn, and as far away as Antarctica. The schooner-style ships are not luxurious, but they are warm and comfortable, and their small size allows for a more intimate, hands-on journey than the *Mare Australis.* A 7-day trip starts at $198 per person, per day. **Sea & Ice & Mountains,** in Puerto Williams (office located in the Coiron Guesthouse; © **61/621227;** www.simltd.com), is a German-run agency with a six-passenger yacht that takes visitors on 5- to 7-day journeys around Cape Horn and past the Darwin mountain range; contact the agency for prices. For general travel agency needs, including city tours, airline tickets, and hotel reservations, contact **Turismo Akainij,** Uspashum 156 (© **61//21173;** turismoakainij@hotmail.com).

WHAT TO SEE & DO

The **Museo Maurice van de Maele,** Aragay 01 (© **61/621043**), is open from 10am to 1pm and 3 to 6pm (closed Fri and Sun), featuring a good collection of Yaghan and Yamana Indian artifacts, ethnographic exhibits, and stuffed birds and animals. The museum's docent is an anthropologist, naturalist, and all-around expert in the region; he is usually on hand to provide tours in the area. About 3km (1¾ miles) southeast of Puerto Williams on the main road, at the La Virgen cascade, is a medium-level **hiking trail** with an exhilarating, sweeping panorama of the Beagle Channel, the Dientes de Navarino mountain range, and Puerto Williams. The hike takes 3 hours round-trip. One of Chile's best backpacking trails, the **Dientes de Navarino Circuit,** is here, thanks to an Australian who blazed the trail in 1991. The circuit is 53km (33 miles) in length and takes 4 days minimum to walk, with a difficulty level of medium to high. The trail is open only from late November to April; otherwise, snow makes this walk dangerous and disorienting. The best map is JLM's *Tierra del Fuego* map, sold in most shops and bookstores.

WHERE TO STAY & DINE

The pickings are slim but reasonably priced; however, note that travelers will not find luxury in Puerto Williams. Basic, clean accommodation can be found at the **Hostería Camblor,** Calle Patricio Cap Deville (© **61/621033;** hosteria camblor@terra.cl), which has six newer rooms for $12 to $18 per person, and some rooms come with a kitchenette. The Camblor also has a restaurant that occasionally serves as the local disco on Friday and Saturday nights, so noise could be a problem. Another simple but comfortable place is the **Hostal Yagan,** Piloto Pardo 260 (© **61/621334;** hostalyagan@hotmail.com), with doubles for $15. For dining, try the convivial **Club de Yates Micalvi** (© **61/621020**), housed in an old supply ship that is docked at the pier, which serves as the meeting spot for an international crowd of adventurers sailing around Cape Horn. Or try the Hostería Camblor's restaurant or **Los Dientes de Navarino** (© **61/621074**), on the plaza. Also try the **Restaurant Cabo de Hornos,** Ricardo Maragano 146 (on the second floor; © **61/621232**), for Chilean specialties.

7 Tierra del Fuego: Ushuaia, Argentina ★★

461km (286 miles) southwest of Punta Arenas; 594km (368 miles) south of Río Gallegos

The name *Ushuaia* comes from the Yamana Indian language meaning "bay penetrating westward," a fairly simple appellation for a city situated in such a spectacular location. It's the southernmost city in the world (although the naval base and town Puerto Williams is farther south across the channel). Ushuaia is encircled by a range of rugged peaks and fronted by the Beagle Channel. It was first inhabited by the Yamana Indians until the late 1800s; then it became a penal colony until 1947. The region grew as a result of immigration from Croatia, Italy, and Spain, and migration from the Argentine mainland, with government incentives such as tax-free duty on many goods being part of the draw. Today the city has about 40,000 residents. Ushuaia is a great destination with plenty of activities, and many use the city as a jumping-off point for trips to Antarctica or sailing trips around Cape Horn.

ESSENTIALS
GETTING THERE

BY PLANE   There is no bus service to town from the Ushuaia Airport, but cab fares are only about $4; always ask for a quote before accepting a ride. **Aerolíneas Argentinas/Austral,** Roca 116 (© **02901/421218;** www.aerolineas. com.ar), has two to three daily flights to Buenos Aires, one of which leaves from Ezeiza and stops in El Calafate. Air service frequency increases from November to March, when there's also a daily flight from Río Gallegos and twice-weekly flights from Trelew. **Aerovías DAP** now has air service to and from Punta Arenas for $100 one-way (plus $6 airport tax), leaving Tuesday and Friday; its offices are at Av. 25 de Mayo 62 (© **02901/431110;** www.aeroviasdap.cl). During high season, DAP increases flights from Punta Arenas to five weekly, in addition to a daily flight from Cape Horn.

BY BUS   Service from Punta Arenas, Chile, costs $21 and takes about 12 hours. **Tecni Austral** (© **02901/431407** in Ushuaia, or 61/222078 in Punta Arenas) leaves Monday, Wednesday, and Friday at 7am; tickets are sold in Ushuaia from the Tolkar office at Roca 157, and in Punta Arenas at Lautaro Navarro 975. **Tolkeyen,** Maipú 237 (© **02901/437073;** tolkeyenventas@arnet. com.ar), works in combination with the Chilean company Pacheco for trips to Punta Arenas, leaving Tuesday, Thursday, and Saturday at 8am; it also goes to

Río Grande, with three daily trips. Both companies take the route to Punta Arenas via Bahía Azul. Techni Austral offers service to Punta Arenas via Porvenir for the same price, leaving Saturday at 6am. **Lidded LTD,** Gobernador Paz 921 (© **02901/436421**), Techni Austral, and Tolkeyen all have multiple day trips to Río Grande.

BY BOAT The company **Crucero Australis** operates a cruise to Ushuaia from Punta Arenas and vice versa aboard its ship the M/V *Mare Australis;* departures are Saturday from Punta Arenas and Wednesday from Ushuaia, from late September to April. If you have the time, this is a recommended journey for any age, and it's covered in the box "Cruising from Punta Arenas to Ushuaia," under "Punta Arenas, Chile," on p. 428.

GETTING AROUND

BY CAR Everything in and around Ushuaia is easily accessible via bus or taxi or by using an inexpensive shuttle or tour service, so renting a car is not necessary. Rentals, however, are very reasonable, from $30 to $55 per day. **Avis,** Avenida del Libertador and Belgrano, drops its prices for multiple-day rentals (© 02901/422744; www.avis.com); **Cardos Rent A Car** is at Av. del Libertador 845 (© 02901/436388); **Dollar Rent A Car** is at Maipú and Sarmiento (© 02901/432134; www.dollar.com); **Localiza Rent A Car** is at Av. del Libertador 1222 (© 02901/430739); and **Seven Rent A Car** rents 4×4 Jeeps with unlimited mileage at Av. del Libertador 802 (© 02901/437604).

VISITOR INFORMATION

The **Subsecretaría de Turismo** has a helpful, well-stocked office at Maipu 505 (© **02901/423340;** fax 02901/430694; info@tierradelfuego.org.ar). They also have a counter at the airport that is open to assist passengers on all arriving flights. From November to March, the office is open daily from 8am to 10pm; the rest of the year, it's open Monday through Friday from 8am to 9pm, weekends and holidays from 9am to 8pm. The national park administration office can be found at Av. del Libertador 1395 (© **02901/421395;** open Mon–Fri 9am–3pm).

FAST FACTS: USHUAIA

Currency Exchange Banco Sud, Avenida del Libertador and Godoy (© **02901/432080**), and **Banco Nación,** Av. del Libertador 190 (© **02901/422086**), both exchange currency and have 24-hour ATMs.

Laundry Los Tres Angeles, Rosas 139, is open Monday through Saturday from 9am to 8pm.

Pharmacy Andina, Av. del Libertador 638 (© **02901/423431**), is open 24 hours a day.

Post Office Correo Argentino is at Avenida del Libertador and Godoy (© **02901/421347**), open Monday through Friday from 9am to 7pm, Saturday from 9am to 1pm; the private postal company **OCA** is at Maipú and Avenida 9 de Julio (© **02901/424729**), open Monday through Saturday from 9am to 6pm.

Travel Agency/Credit Cards American Express travel and credit card services are provided by All Patagonia, Juana Fadul 26 (© **02901/433622**).

WHAT TO SEE & DO IN & AROUND TOWN

The best way to get oriented and get a feel for the landscape is to take a walk to the city park and up to the **Punto Panorámico,** a great lookout point where you get sweeping views of the city and the channel. The trail begins at the southwestern end of Avenida del Libertador and is free.

Ushuaia

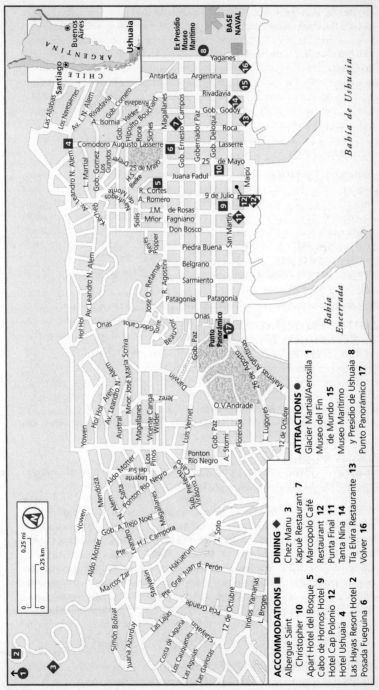

ATTRACTIONS ●
Glacier Martial/Aerosilla 1
Museo del Fin
 de Mundo 15
Museo Marítimo
 y Presidio de Ushuaia 8
Punto Panorámico 17

ACCOMMODATIONS ■
Albergue Saint
 Christopher 10
Apart Hotel del Bosque 5
Cabo de Hornos Hotel 9
Hotel Cap Polonio 12
Hotel Ushuaia 4
Las Hayas Resort Hotel 2
Posada Fueguina 6

DINING ◆
Chez Manu 3
Kapué Restaurant 7
Marcopolo Café
 Restaurant 12
Punta Final 11
Tanta Nina 14
Tía Elvira Restaurante 13
Volver 16

473

Glacier Martial/Aerosilla *Finds* Glacier Martial is a pleasant excursion that sits in Ushuaia's backyard. Avenida Luis Fernando Martial winds 7km (4¼ miles) up from town to the base of a beautiful mountain amphitheater, where you'll find a chair lift that takes visitors to the small Glacier Martial. It's a long walk up the road, and there are no buses to take you there. Visitors usually hire a taxi for $2 and walk all the way back down, or arrange for the driver to pick them up later. At the base of the chair lift, don't miss a stop at **La Cabaña** *♣* (*①* **02901/ 424257**), an excellent tea house with a wraparound outdoor deck and mouth-watering cakes and pastries.

Av. Luis Fernando Martial, 7km (4¼ miles) from town. No phone. Admission $2 adults, $1 children under 9. Daily 10:30am–5:30pm.

Museo del Fin de Mundo *♣* The main room of this museum has an assort-ment of Indian hunting tools and colonial maritime instruments. There's also a natural history display of stuffed birds and a "grandfather's room" set up to resemble an old general store, packed with antique products. But the strength of this museum is its 60 history and nature videos available for viewing and its ref-erence library with more than 3,650 volumes, including a fascinating birth record. Its store has an excellent range of books about Patagonia for sale.

Maipú 175. *①* **02901/421863.** Admission $2 adults, 60¢ students, free for children under 14. Daily 10am–1pm and 3–7:30pm.

Museo Marítimo y Presidio de Ushuaia *♣* *Moments* Ushuaia was founded primarily thanks to the penal colony set up here in the late 1800s for hundreds of Argentina's most dangerous criminals. The rehabilitation system consisted of forced labor to build piers and buildings, and creative workshops for teaching carpentry, music, tailoring, and other trades—all of which, coincidentally, fueled the local economy. The museum offers a fascinating look into prisoners' and prison workers' lives through interpretive displays and artifacts. There's a restaurant here, with "prison" meals and other theme items.

Yaganes and Gobernador Paz. *①* **02901/437481.** Admission $2 adults, $1.50 seniors, 70¢ children ages 5–12, free for children under 5. Daily 10am–1pm and 3–8pm.

OUTDOOR ACTIVITIES

BOATING Navigation excursions are very popular here, with several compa-nies offering a variety of trips. The most popular excursion is a half-day trip cruising the Beagle Channel to view sea lions, penguins, and more. You'll find a cluster of kiosks near the pier offering a variety of excursions. **Motonave Bar-racuda** (*①* **02901/436453**)leaves twice daily for its 3-hour trip around the channel for $21 per person, visiting Isla de Lobos, Isla de Pájaros, and a light-house. **Motovelero Tres Marías** (*①* **02901/421897**) also leaves twice daily and sails to the same location; however, they have a maximum of nine guests and add an hour's walk, crab fishing, cognac, and an underwater camera to the package, which costs $28 per person. **Tierra del Sur** (*①* **02901/421897**) combines a bus/boat trip, visiting Estancia Harberton (see below) first, then embarking for a 1½-hour sail to a penguin colony during penguin season from November to April. **Motovelero Patagonia Adventure** (*①* **02901/421897**) has an 18-pas-senger maximum and leaves daily; it visits the sea lion colony and includes a walk on the Isla Bridges for $20. This company also works with the Aventuras Isla Verde in the park for a full-day sail; inquire at their kiosk.

FISHING For a fishing license and information, go to the **Club de Pesca y Caza,** Av. del Libertador 818 (no phone). The cost is about $10 for foreigners per day.

SKIING   Ushuaia's ski resort, **Cerro Castor** (© **02901/422244;** www.cerro castor.com), is surprisingly good, with more than 400 skiable hectares (988 acres), 15 runs, three quad chairs and one double, a lodge/restaurant, and a slope-side bar. Day tickets cost $18 to $26, depending on low or high season, and the resort is open from June 15 to October 15. To get there, take the shuttle buses **Pasarela** (© **02901/433712**) or **Bella Vista** (© **02901/443161**); the fare is $5.

TOUR OPERATORS

All Patagonia Viajes y Turismo, Juana Fadul 26 (© **02901/433622;** allpat@ tierradelfuego.org.ar), is the local American Express travel representative and acts as a clearinghouse for everything—if they don't offer it themselves, they'll arrange an excursion with other outfitters, and they can reserve excursions in other destinations in Argentina and Chile. All Patagonia offers three glacier walks for those in physically good shape, scenic flights over Tierra del Fuego ($50 per person for 30 min.), and treks and drives in its Land Rover with nature guides. If you're not sure what you want, start here. **Canal Fun & Nature,** Riva-davía 82 (© **02901/437395;** www.canalfun.com), is a great company with excellent guides who provide 4×4 trips and walks culminating with a barbecue, as well as kayaking and nighttime beaver-watching, and they'll custom-build a trip for you. **Rumbo Sur,** Av. del Libertador 350 (© **02901/430699;** www. rumbosur.com.ar), and **Tolkeyen/PreTour,** Maipú 237 (© **02901/437073;** tolekeyenventas@arnet.com.ar), are two operators that deal with larger groups and arrange more classic excursions, such as a city tour and guided visits to the national park and Lagos Escondido and Fagnano.

EXCURSIONS AROUND USHUAIA

One of the most intriguing destinations around Ushuaia is the **Estancia Harber-ton,** the first ranch founded in Tierra del Fuego. It is now run as a museum. The ranch is located on the shore of the Beagle Channel and can be reached by road or boat. The entrance fee is $3 April through October and $5 November through March. Transportation to the *estancia,* 90km (56 miles) from Ushuaia, is provided by most travel agencies in town, for an average cost of $50 per person plus the entrance fee, provided you are a group of four or more. Roughly from October to April, several tour companies offer a catamaran ride to the *estancia,* a 6-hour excursion for $75 per person; try **All Patagonia,** Juana Fadul 26 (© **02901/433622**). Tour groups will also arrange a boat excursion to a **penguin colony** from the *estancia,* an add-on excursion that costs about $26 per person.

After the turnoff for Estancia Harberton, RN 3 begins to descend down to **Lago Escondido,** a beautiful lake about 60km (37 miles) north of Ushuaia that provides a quiet spot for relaxation or fishing the mammoth trout that call the lake home. The lake is home to a stately, gorgeous lodge, the **Hostería Petrel** (© **02901/433569**). The wood-and-stone lodge has nine rooms, and seven splendid wooden cabins have just been constructed on the shore. Each cabin has one bedroom and a trundle bed for two more in the living room, with folksy fur-niture made of thin tree trunks, and an ultrapeaceful front deck for kicking back and casting a line. The cabins cost $62 April through October and $85 Novem-ber through March; double rooms in the lodge are $45 to $70 for the same dates. The cabins do not come with a kitchen, but the lodge has a restaurant; they also have a gift shop and Jacuzzi, and they hire a summer-season fishing guide.

PARQUE NACIONAL TIERRA DEL FUEGO

Parque Nacional Tierra del Fuego was created in 1960 to protect a 63,000-hectare (155,610-acre) chunk of Patagonian wilderness that includes mighty

---

A Ride in the Park

If you don't feel like walking but would like to take in the sights at Parque Nacional Tierra Del Fuego, you can take a ride on **El Tren del Fin del Mundo,** a vapor locomotive that is a replica of the train used to shuttle prisoners to the forest to chop wood (© **02901/431600;** www.trendel findelmundo.com.ar). The train departs from its station (which houses a souvenir shop and cafe) near the park entrance four times daily; the journey is 1 hour and 10 minutes round trip and costs $17 adults ($33 for first class), $7 kids.

---

peaks, crystalline rivers, black-water swamps, and forests of *lenga,* or deciduous beech. Only 2,000 hectares (4,940 acres) are designated as recreation areas, part of which offer a chance to view the prolific dam building carried out by beavers introduced to Tierra del Fuego in the 1950s.

The park's main claim to fame is that it's the only Argentine national park with a maritime coast. If you've been traveling around southern Argentina or Chile, chances are, you won't be blown away by this park. Much of the landscape is identical to the thousands of kilometers of mountainous terrain in Patagonia, but the park offers easy and medium day hikes to get out and stretch your legs, breathe some fresh air, take a boat ride, or bird-watch. Also, there are areas where the road runs through thick beech forest and then abruptly opens into wide views of mountains whose dramatic height can be viewed from sea level to more than 2,000m (6,560 ft.). Anglers can fish for trout here in the park but must first pick up a license at the **National Park Administration office,** Av. del Libertador 1395 (© **02901/421395;** open Mon–Fri 9am–3pm), in Ushuaia. The park service issues maps at the park entrance showing the walking trails here, ranging from 300m (984 ft.) to 8km (5 miles); admission into the park is $5. Parque Nacional Tierra del Fuego is 11km (6¾ miles) west of Ushuaia on RN 3. Camping in the park is free; there are no services, but potable water is available. At the end of the road to Lago Roca, there is a snack bar/restaurant. At Bahía Ensenada, you'll find boats that take visitors to Isla Redonda, where there are several walking trails. The cost is about $8, or $15 with a guide. All tour companies offer guided trips to the park, but if you just need transportation there, call these shuttle bus companies: **Pasarela** (© **02901/433712**) or **Bella Vista** (© **02901/443161**).

WHERE TO STAY

Accommodations are not cheap in Ushuaia, and quality is often not on par with price. Below are some of the best values that can be found here.

VERY EXPENSIVE

Las Hayas Resort Hotel *Finds* Ushuaia's sole luxury hotel is located on the road to Glacier Martial, and if you're looking for elegant accommodations, this is for you. This imposing hotel sits nestled in a forest of beech, a location that gives sweeping views of the town and the Beagle Channel. It's at least 3km (1¾ miles) from downtown, however, so you'll need to take a cab, hike, or use one of the hotel's summer-only transfer shuttles. The sumptuous lounge stretches the length of the building; here you'll find a clubby bar, formal restaurant, and fireside sitting area. The rooms are decorated with rich tapestries, upholstered walls, and bathrooms that are big and bright. The ultracomfortable beds with thick linens invite a good night's sleep. A glass-enclosed walkway leads to one of Ushuaia's few swimming pools and an indoor squash court; the hotel also offers automatic membership at the region's golf club. The owner of Las Hayas promotes an air of genteel exclusivity, making the hotel not entirely suitable for children. The hotel's gourmet restaurant changes its menu weekly but specializes in black hake and king crab dishes. Downstairs, there's a more casual restaurant and an indoor garden dining area.

Av. Luis Fernando Martial 1650, Ushuaia. ℂ 02901/430710. Fax 02901/430719. www.lashayas.com.ar. 102 units. $185–$230 double. Rates include buffet breakfast. AE, DC, MC, V. **Amenities:** 2 restaurants; bar; lounge; indoor swimming pool; exercise room; Jacuzzi; sauna; concierge; room service; massage; laundry service; dry cleaning. *In room:* TV, hair dryer, safe.

EXPENSIVE

Hotel Cap Polonio   This hotel is a good choice for its central location and bustling, adjoining restaurant that essentially forms part of the hotel's entrance lobby. The hotel has a bright yellow-and-red exterior and sits on busy Avenida del Libertador; for this reason, you'll want to request a room in the rear of the hotel to avoid the noise. The rooms here at the Cap Polonio are some of the better rooms in town, but the shag carpet and frilly bedspreads are a little dowdy. Also, as with most hotels in town, a single bed is laughably narrower than a twin and might be uncomfortable for anyone over the age of 10; ask for a double instead.

Av. del Libertador 746, Ushuaia. ℂ 02901/422140. www.hotelcappolonio.com.ar. 30 units. $72–$95 double. AE, MC, V. **Amenities:** Restaurant; bar; room service. *In room:* TV.

Hotel Ushuaia   This hotel is another that offers sweeping views; however, it is only an 8-block walk to downtown—convenient for anyone who wants to be closer to restaurants and services. In this price range, the Hotel Ushuaia is one of the city's better values, offering very bright interiors and comfortable, spacious rooms, although everything is aging fast. From the vine-draped reception area, long hallways stretch out on both sides; centered in the middle is a second-story restaurant with a lofty, V-shape ceiling from which hang about 100 glass bubble lamps, a style that is somewhat 1970s, but attractive nevertheless. All doubles cost the same but range in three sizes; when making a reservation, ask for the largest double they have, which they'll also give to singles when they're not full.

Lasserre 933, Ushuaia. ℂ 02901/423051. Fax 02901/424217. 58 units. $68 double. Rates include buffet breakfast. AE, MC, V **Amenities:** Restaurant; bar; lounge; room service; laundry service. *In room:* TV.

Posada Fueguina 🏠🏠 *Finds*   This is one of our favorite hotels in Ushuaia, full of flavor and cozier than anything in town. The Fueguina has hotel rooms and a row of inviting wooden *cabañas* (no kitchen) on a well-manicured lot, and their freshly painted cream-and-mauve exteriors stand out among the clapboard homes that surround them. Inside, Oriental floor-runners, dark glossy wood, and tartan curtains set the tone. Everything is meticulously maintained. Most rooms are spacious; the second and third floors have good views, and the three rooms on the bottom floor are brand new. Bathrooms are sparkling clean; many received new fixtures in 2002. The cabins do not have interesting views, but they're so comfy you won't mind. The hotel is a 3-block walk to downtown.

Lasserre 438, Ushuaia. ℂ 02901/423467. Fax 02901/424758. www.posadafueguina.com.ar. 23 units, 5 *cabañas*. Nov–Feb $130 double; Mar–Oct $96 double. Rates include buffet breakfast. AE, MC, V. **Amenities:** Bar; lounge. *In room:* TV, minibar, hair dryer.

MODERATE

Apart Hotel del Bosque *Value*   The Apart Hotel del Bosque gives guests a huge amount of space, including a separate living/dining area and a kitchenette.

However, the kitchenette is intended more than anything for heating water, not cooking—for that reason, they include breakfast, which is not common with apart-hotels. The 40 guest rooms are spread out much like a condominium complex, each with a separate entrance and maid service. The exteriors and the decor are pretty bland but very clean. Inside the main building there's a cozy restaurant with wooden tables where they serve fixed-price meals. The hotel is located in a residential area about a 3-minute walk from downtown.

Magallanes 709, Ushuaia. ©/fax 02901/430777. www.hostaldelbosque.com.ar. 40 units. Apr–Sept $50 double; Oct–Mar $80 double. Rates include continental breakfast. AE, DC, MC, V. **Amenities:** Restaurant; room service; laundry service. *In room:* TV, dataport, minibar, hair dryer, kitchen.

INEXPENSIVE

Albergue Saint Christopher This fun, inviting *hostal* is for those who are looking to spend a lot less, but you'll have to share a room with strangers if you don't have your own group. Rooms have two to three bunk beds and are not always separated by gender, but they'll try to find you a same-sex room if you ask. The *hostal* attracts a vivacious crowd that ranges in age from 20 to 40 years of age. The staff are entertaining, and the common area is a great place to hang out and chat. Guests have use of the kitchen facilities, and the *hostal* is packed with information about excursions around the area.

Gobernador Deloqui 636, Ushuaia. © 02901/430062. hostel_christopher@yahoo.com. 5 shared units. $12–$19 per person. No credit cards. **Amenities:** Lounge.

WHERE TO DINE

A dozen cafes can be found on Avenida del Libertador between Godoy and Rosas, all of which offer inexpensive sandwiches and quick meals. The most popular among them is **Tante Sara,** San Martín 137 (© **02901/435005**), where a two-course meal of salad and ravioli or gnocchi costs $6. A block away, the Tante Sara Café is the place to sip coffee with locals in the afternoons. In addition to the restaurants listed below, you might consider the Hotel Las Hayas's **Luis Martial** (© **02901/430710**). It offers great views and gourmet dining, as well as fixed meals and weekly changing menus.

Chez Manu *Finds* SEAFOOD/FRENCH The Chez Manu offers great food and even better views seen through a generous supply of windows. The two transplants from France who run this restaurant, one of whom was once the chef at the five-star resort Las Hayas, stay true to their roots with a menu that offers French-style cooking using fresh local ingredients. Dishes include black hake cooked with anise and herbs, or Fueguian lamb. Before taking your order, the owner/chef will describe the catch of the day, usually a cold-water fish from the bay such as Abejado or a Merlooza from Chile. The side dishes include a delicious eggplant ratatouille, made with extra-virgin olive oil and herbes de Provençe. The wine list includes several excellent regional dry whites.

Av. Fernando Luis Martial 2135. © 02970/432253. Main courses $5–$9. AE, MC, V. Daily noon–3pm and 8pm–midnight.

Kapué Restaurant ARGENTINE FINE DINING This is undoubtedly the best restaurant in Ushuaia, for its superb cuisine, lovely view, and warm, attentive service. The menu is brief, but the offerings are delicious. Don't start your meal without ordering a sumptuous appetizer of king crab wrapped in a crepe and bathed in saffron sauce. Main courses include seafood, beef, and chicken; sample items include tenderloin beef in a plum sauce or a subtly flavored sea bass steamed in parchment paper. Kapué offers a special "sampler" with appetizers, a main dish, wine, dessert, and coffee for $30 per person. The extensive gourmet wine list ranges in price from $6 to $38; there's also wine by the glass. Finish it all off with a sorbet in a frothy champagne sauce. Kapué's dining area is cozy, and candlelit tables exude romance.

Roca 470. ℂ **02901/422704.** Reservations recommended on weekends. Main courses $7–$12. AE, MC, V. Nov 15–Apr 15 daily noon–2pm and 6–11pm; rest of the year dinner only 7–11pm.

Marcopolo Café Restaurant INTERNATIONAL   This stylish restaurant is a good place for lunch, for both its varied menu and its atmosphere. The softly lit dining area has warm yellow walls and beige linen tablecloths, both of which are offset with artsy ironwork knickknacks, colorful candles, and watercolor paintings. The menu will satisfy most tastes, as it includes creative renditions and simple, familiar items such as chef salads and shrimp cocktails. Try a local specialty, such as trout stuffed with king crab or Fueguian lamb in a flaky potato pastry. There's also fresh, homemade pasta with a choice of six sauces. The Marcopolo is open early for breakfast and also has a cafe menu that offers sandwiches, soups, and pastries, which can be ordered all day.

Av. del Libertador 746. ℂ **02901/430001.** Main courses $3–$8. AE, MC, V. Daily 7:30–10:30am, noon–3pm, and 8pm–midnight.

Punto Final (Ꝯ *Moments* CLUB/INTERNATIONAL   Punto Final is one of the more hip and happening places in Ushuaia. The location couldn't be better: right on the waterfront with fabulous bay and mountain views from the large windows that wrap around the entire building. The atmosphere is much like a big city club, with leopard-print fabric upholstery on the booths and bar stools. Techno music plays in the background during the early evening when full meals are served. You'll find dishes such as sliced melon with ham, grilled steaks, chicken breast with white-wine and cream sauce, and a simple trout with butter sauce. Most of the trendy people who come here come for drinks and, after midnight, to dance. This place is a zoo from midnight to 3am, and even later on the weekends. If you're looking to live it up with young Argentines, then this is your place for the night.

Maipú 822. ℂ **02901/422423.** Main courses $5–$9. AE, MC, V. Daily 11am–4am (to 5am Fri–Sat).

Tante Nina (Ꝯ *Finds* SEAFOOD/ARGENTINE   For the best atmosphere and water views in the center of town, Tante Nina is your best bet. The elegant dining room has huge picture windows overlooking the bay, handsome wooden chairs, and white tablecloths. This place is becoming very popular since it opened a year ago, and many of the local elite choose to dine here. Specialties are the seafood casseroles (known as *cazuelas*), most of which come with fresh king crab (all for $12). There's a delicious Hungarian-style cazuela with king crab, tomatoes, cream, and mushrooms; a long list of fish prepared many different ways; and, of course, grilled chicken, tenderloin, and the very interesting pickled Patagonian rabbit, for the terribly adventurous. For dessert, try the homemade almond ice cream or the luscious lemon sorbet. Service here is refined, if slightly aloof, and the diners tend to be on the older side.

Gobernador Godoy 15. ℂ **02901/432444.** Reservations recommended for dinner in high season. Main courses $7–$12. AE, MC, V. Daily 11am–3pm and 7pm–midnight.

Tía Elvira Restaurante ARGENTINE BISTRO   Tía Elvira is part restaurant, part minimuseum, with walls adorned with antique photos of the region and various artifacts its owners have collected during its 30 years in business. The menu features fairly straightforward Argentine dishes such as grilled meats, but the restaurant serves mostly simply prepared seafood, including king crab, trout, sea bass, and cod in a variety of sauces, such as Roquefort or Parmesan. There's also a list of homemade pastas, including lasagna and stuffed cannelloni. The restaurant is on the waterfront, with up-close views of the canal and the pier, and caters mostly to foreign tourists.

Maipú 349. ℃ 02901/424725. Main courses $4–$8. MC, V. Daily noon–3pm and 7–11:30pm.

Volver ARGENTINE   Even if you don't eat here, don't fail to stop by just to see this crazy, kitschy restaurant on the waterfront. Volver is inside a century-old yellow tin-pan house. Old newspapers and signs wallpaper the interiors, which are also packed with oddball memorabilia, photos, gadgets, trinkets, and antiques. The food is pretty good, too, serving regional dishes such as trout, crab, lamb, plus homemade pastas. King crab is served in a dozen different ways, including soups, casseroles, or naturally with a side sauce. The desserts are primarily crepes with local fruits like calafate. One complaint: Service can often be absent-minded or hurried.

Maipú 37. ℃ 02901/423977. Main courses $5–$8. MC, V. Daily noon–3pm and 7:30pm–midnight. Closed for lunch Mon.

8 Antarctica

It may be the coldest spot on the planet, but it's a hot destination for travelers seeking the next great adventure. Antarctica is its own continent, but the hook of the Antarctic Peninsula is closest to the tip of South America, and, therefore, the majority of people depart for Antarctica from Ushuaia.

Antarctica is home to exotic wildlife and landscapes that are equally savage and beautiful. Be prepared for ice like you've never seen it: monumental peacock-blue icebergs shaped in surreal formations, craggy glaciers that crash into the sea, sheer ice-encrusted walls that form magnificent canals, and jagged peaks that jut out of icy fields. A major highlight here are the penguins—colonies of several hundred thousand can be found nesting and chattering away throughout the area. Humpback, orca, and minke whales are often spotted nosing out of the frigid water, as are elephant, Weddell, leopard, and crabeater seals. Bird-watchers can spend hours studying the variety of unique seabirds, including petrels and albatrosses.

Most important, Antarctica sits at the "End of the World," and this reason alone is enough to compel many people to travel here. Like the early explorers who first visited this faraway continent in the 1800s, travelers today revel in the chance to venture to a pristine region where relatively few humans have stepped foot before. But Antarctica's remoteness comes with a toll: No matter how you get here, it's not cheap, and the tediously long traveling time and sometimes uncomfortable conditions are also part of the price you'll pay. Nevertheless, many of Antarctica's 14,000 yearly visitors would agree that the effort is worth it.

A BRIEF HISTORY

The history of exploration and the discovery of the Antarctic continent are littered with claims, counterclaims, tall tales, intrigue, and suffering. Captain James Cook discovered the South Sandwich and South Georgia islands (a part of Antarctica, these islands are a British possession) in 1773, but he never spotted the Antarctic continent. He did, however, set off a seal-hunting frenzy after providing reports of the large colonies he found there, and it's estimated that sealers discovered around a third of the islands in the region. Two sealers were the first to actually step foot on the continent: the American John Davis at Hughes Bay in 1821, and the British James Weddell at Saddle Island in 1823.

Antarctica

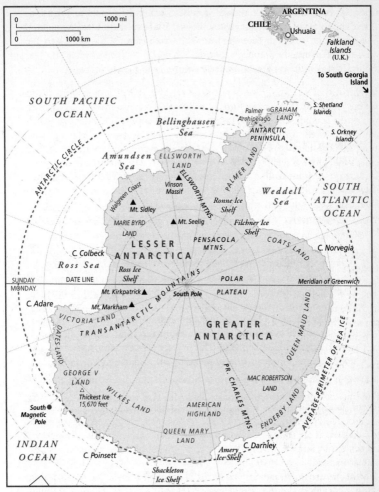

During a scientific expedition in 1840, the American navy lieutenant Charles Wilkes finally concluded that Antarctica was not a series of islands and ice packs, but rather a contiguous landmass.

The South Pole was not reached until 90 years later, on December 4, 1911, by Norwegian Roald Admudsen and his well-prepared five-man team. Though Amundsen's arrival at the pole accounted for one of the most remarkable expeditions ever to be completed by man, his feat at the time was eclipsed by the tragic finale of an expedition led by his rival, the British captain Robert Scott. Scott arrived at the pole 33 days later, only to find Amundsen's tent and a note. Scott and his party, already suffering from scurvy and exposure, finally froze to death on their return trip, just 18km (11 miles) from their ship.

No other destination has held such an adventurous cachet for explorers. One of the greatest adventures ever recorded was in 1915, led by the Irish explorer Ernest Shackleton, who pronounced Antarctica "the last great journey left to man." Shackleton attempted to cross the Antarctic continent but never achieved his goal: Pack ice trapped and sank his boat. The entire party miraculously survived for 1 year on a diet of penguin and seal before Shackleton sailed to South Georgia Island in a lifeboat to get help.

Today 27 nations send personnel to Antarctica to perform seasonal and year-round research. The population varies from 4,000 people in the summer to roughly 1,000 in the winter. There are a total of 42 stations that operate year-round, and an additional 32 that operate during the summer only. The stations study world climactic changes, and in 1985, researchers at the British Halley station discovered a growing hole in the ozone layer.

PLANNING YOUR TRIP TO ANTARCTICA
VISITOR INFORMATION
A number of websites offer helpful information about Antarctica. A few of the best include:

- **www.iaato.org**: This is the official website of the International Association Antarctic Treaty Organization, the only governing body in Antarctica (although it is more akin to a gentleman's treaty among all nations with bases here). It is important that your tour group be a member of the IAATO, International Association of Antarctica Tour Operators. Most cruise operators are members. Membership in the organization ensures a safe and environmentally responsible visit to Antarctica. Statistics, general information, and news can be found on this website.
- **www.70south.com**: This site includes links to other Antarctica-oriented websites, as well as weather and event information and message boards.
- **www.antarcticconnection.com**: This site offers travel information, tour operator links, and Antarctica-related items for sale, including maps and videos.

ENTRY REQUIREMENTS
No single country claims Antarctica as its territory, so visas are not necessary, but you will need a passport for unscheduled stops and your first stop in either Argentina or Chile (see chapter 2 for information about entry requirements).

WHEN TO GO
Tours to Antarctica are conducted between late November and March—after March, temperatures dip to lows of –100°F (–38°C) and the sun disappears until September. The opposite is true of the summer (Dec–Mar), and visitors can expect sunlight up to a maximum of 18 to 24 hours a day, depending on where you are in Antarctica. Summer temperatures near the Antarctic Peninsula vary between lows of 5°F to 10°F (–15°C to –12°C) and highs of 35°F to 60°F (2°C–16°C).

What you see during your journey to Antarctica may depend on when you go. November is the mating season for penguins and other birds, and visitors can view their offspring in December and January. The best time for whale-watching is during February and March.

SAFETY
EXTREME WEATHER Cold temperatures, the wind-chill factor, and perspiration all conspire to prohibit the body from keeping itself warm in Antarctica's conditions. Travelers, therefore, need to outfit themselves in the highest-quality outdoor clothing available. Tour operators are constantly amazed at how underprepared visitors to Antarctica are, and they, therefore, will provide you with a packing checklist. Ask your tour company if it provides its guests with waterproof outerwear or if you are expected to bring your own. Additionally, the thin ozone

layer and the glare from snow, water, and ice make a high-factor sunscreen, a hat, and sunglasses absolutely imperative.

SPECIAL HEALTH CONCERNS   *Everyone* should bring anti–motion sickness medication on their trip to Antarctica. If you suffer from a special health problem or are taking prescription medication, bring a signed and dated letter from your physician for medical authorities in case of an emergency. Delays of up to 4 weeks have been known to happen on guided trips to the interior, so visitors should seriously consider the extremity of such a trip, submit themselves to a full medical exam before their departure, and bring the quantity of medication necessary for a long delay.

MEDICAL SAFETY & EVACUATION INSURANCE   All passenger ships have an onboard physician in the event of a medical problem or emergency; however, passengers should discuss an evacuation policy with each operator. Emergency evacuation can be hindered by poor weather conditions, and anyone with an unstable medical condition needs to keep this in mind. Also, check your health insurance to verify that it includes evacuation because it can be unbelievably expensive—from the Shetland Islands alone, it costs $35,000 to evacuate one person.

GETTING THERE
BY SHIP

Few would have guessed that the collapse of the Soviet Union in the early 1990s would be the catalyst to spawn tourism in Antarctica. But when Russian scientific ship crews found themselves without a budget, they spruced up the ships' interiors and began renting the vessels out to tour operators on a rotating basis. These ships (as well as others that have since come on the market) are specially built for polar seas, complete with antiroll stabilizers and ice-strengthened hulls. A few of these ships have icebreakers that can chip through just about anything.

Before you go, it helps to know that a tour's itinerary is a rough guide of what to expect on your journey. Turbulent weather and ice conditions can cause delays or detours. Wildlife sightings may prompt your group to linger longer in one area than the next. The ship's crew and the expedition leader of your tour will keep you informed of any changes to the program.

Typical Itineraries

A journey's length is the determining factor for which stops are made. Tour companies offer roughly similar trajectories for cruises to Antarctica, with the exception of a few over-the-top cruises. (Got 2 months and $50,000? Then Quark Expeditions conducts a full circumnavigation of Antarctica.) Apart from the destinations listed below, cruises attempt a landing at research stations when convenient. Most Antarctic cruises leave from Ushuaia, Argentina, although a tiny fraction leave from New Zealand. The Ushuaia departure point is the quickest way to reach Antarctica. Although Chile used to be a departure site for Antarctica, few (if any) travelers now leave from Chile; those who do, make the journey aboard a military ship. Plan to leave from Ushuaia.

Remember to factor in 2 days (4 in total for the return trip, if traveling to the Antarctic Peninsula) to cross the Drake Passage, during which time you'll not do much more than hang out, relax, take part in educational lectures, and suffer through occasional bouts of seasickness. Cruises typically last 8 to 13 days for the Antarctic Peninsula, and 18 to 21 days for journeys that include the Subantarctic Islands. Seasoned travelers have frequently said that 8-day trips are not much of a value; consider tacking on 2 extra days for a 10-day trip.

THE ANTARCTIC PENINSULA This is the easiest site to visit in Antarctica, and due to its rich variety of wildlife and dramatic scenery, it makes for a magnificent introduction to the "White Continent." If you have a short amount of time and/or a limited budget, these trips are for you.

All tours stop at the **South Shetland Islands.** Historically, sealers and whalers used these islands as a base; today they're home to research stations, colonies of elephant seals, and a variety of nesting penguins and sea birds. Popular sites here are **King Island, Livingston Island,** and **Deception Cove,** a collapsed, active volcanic crater with bubbling pools of thermal water.

Tours continue on to the eastern side of the Antarctic Peninsula, with a variety of stops to view wildlife such as Weddell and leopard seals and vast colonies of Adélie, chinstrap, and Gentoo penguins. At the peninsula, sites such as the **Lemaire** and **Neumayar** channels afford camera-worthy views of narrow, sheer-walled canals made of ice and rock. At **Paradise Harbor,** calving icebergs theatrically crash from the harbor's main glacier, and throughout the area, outlandishly shaped gigantic icebergs float by. Other popular stops include **Port Lockroy,** a former British base that is now run as a museum; **Cuverville** and **Rongé** islands, with their penguin colonies; and **Elephant Island,** named for the huge, sluglike elephant seals that inhabit it.

THE POLAR CIRCLE Ships with ice-breaking capabilities can transport guests past the Antarctic Circle and into the zone of 24-hour sunlight. The highlight here is **Marguerite Bay,** with its abundant orca, minke, and humpback whales, and multitudinous Adélie penguins. These cruises typically stop for a fascinating tour of research stations, both ultramodern and abandoned ones.

THE WEST SIDE & THE WEDDELL SEA Longer tours to the peninsula might include visits to its west side, known as "iceberg alley" for the mammoth, tabular chunks of ice floating slowly by. Stops include the rarely visited **Paulet Island,** an intriguing crater island, and **James Ross** and **Vega** islands, known for their nesting colonies of Adélie penguins.

An even longer trip (or simply a different itinerary) takes travelers to the distant **Weddell Sea,** which is blanketed with a vast expanse of pack ice, looking much like a frozen sea. But that's just one of the highlights here; the real reason visitors pay extra time and money to reach this white wonderland is because of the colonies of emperor penguins that reside here. Rugged mountains and glaciers are also part of the view.

SUBANTARCTIC ISLANDS Tours to the Subantarctic Islands begin or end with a trip to the Antarctic Peninsula and the Shetland Islands, which is the reason these tours run 18 to 21 days. A few of these faraway islands are little-visited by tourists, and they instill a sense of adventure in the traveler for their remoteness and fascinating geography, not to mention their important historical aspects.

The first stop is usually the **Falkland (Malvinas) Islands,** to view bird life, especially king penguins, and to tour the Victorian port town of Stanley. Some tours fly directly from Santiago, Chile, to the Falklands and begin the sailing journey there.

South Georgia Island is surely one of the most magnificent places on Earth and is, therefore, a highlight of this trip. The island is home to a staggering array of wildlife and dramatic landscapes made of rugged peaks, fiords, and beaches. South Georgia Island is also subject to unpredictable weather, and, therefore, trip landings here are at risk of being canceled far more frequently than at other sites. Some tours tack on visits to the **South Orkney Islands** (with their dense area of Antarctic hairgrass—an indigenous flowering plant) and the actively volcanic **South Sandwich Islands.**

Tour Operators

Prices vary depending on the length of the trip, the company you choose, and the sleeping arrangements you require. A 9-day journey in a room with three bunks and a shared bathroom runs about $3,500 per person, and a 21-day journey with lodging in a corner-window suite runs between $12,000 and $15,000 per person. Shop around to find something to suit your needs and budget.

Prices include passage, meals, guides, and all excursions. Some tours offer scuba diving, kayaking, overflights, or alpine trekking, usually at an additional cost. When researching trips, also consider the size of the ship: Tour companies offer space for anywhere from 50 to *600* passengers. Most travelers like to share their space with fewer people; although some enjoy the camaraderie of a crowd, more than 100 to 150 guests is just too many. The International Association Antarctic Treaty Organization limits landings to 100 people, meaning large ships must conduct landings in turns.

A few well-known tour operators include:

- **Abercrombie & Kent,** 1520 Kensington Rd., Suite 212, Oak Brook, IL 60523-2141 (© **800/544-7016** or 630/954-2944; fax 630/954-3324; www.abercrombiekent.com). Like Quark, A&K offers deluxe journeys, with trips that run from 14 to 18 days.
- **Aurora Expeditions,** 182A Cumberland St., The Rocks, NSW 2000, Australia (© **02/9252-1033;** fax 02/9252-1373; www.auroraexpeditions.com. au). This is an Australian company with a variety of educational, photographic, and climbing tours for small groups.
- **Geographic Expeditions,** 2627 Lombard St., San Francisco, CA 94123 (© **800/777-8183** or 415/922-0448; fax 415/346-5535; www.geoex.com). Tours vary between 11 and 28 days, with small boat cruising, trekking, and climbing options.
- **Lindblad Expeditions,** 720 Fifth Ave., New York, NY 10019 (© **800/397-3348** or 212/765-7740; www.expeditions.com). This venerable Swedish-run company was the first to bring tourists to Antarctica. It offers 11- to 28-day tours, with trekking.
- **Mountain Travel Sobek,** 1266 66th St., Emeryville, CA 94608 (© **888/687-6235** or 510/594-6000; fax 510/525-7710; www.mtsobek.com). This well-respected company has been operating Antarctic tours for 15 years. They offer 11- to 21-day tours, with zodiac rides.
- **Oceanwide Expeditions,** 15710 JFK Blvd., Suite 850, Houston, TX 77032 (© **800/453-7245;** fax 281/987-1140; www.ocnwide.com). This Dutch company operates a variety of journeys aboard its own ship.
- **Peregrine Adventures,** 258 Lonsdale St., Melbourne, VIC 3000, Australia (© **1300/854444** in Australia, or 03/9662-2700 outside Australia; fax 03/9662-2442; www.peregrine.net.au). This Australian company is the only operator that doesn't charge solo travelers a single supplement.
- **Quark Expeditions,** 980 Post Rd., Darien, CT (© **800/356-5699** or 203/656-0499; www.quarkexpeditions.com). This highly esteemed company offers the industry's most outrageous trips.

BY PLANE

Apart from working for a research station, one of the few ways to get out and really explore the Antarctic continent is by plane, and there are a handful of

---

> ### *Tips* Last-Minute Reduced Fares to Antarctica
>
> Several travel agencies in Ushuaia offer reduced fares for last-minute bookings made about 15 to just a few days before a cruise's departure date, with prices 10% to 50% lower than the advertised rate. Two agencies to try are **Rumbo Sur,** Av. San Martín, Ushuaia, Argentina (© **2901/ 421139;** fax 2901/434788; www.rumbosur.com.ar); and **All Patagonia,** Juana Fadul 26, Ushuaia, Argentina (© **2901/433622;** fax 2901/430707; www.allpatagonia.com). Note that the best deals on discounted rates tend to occur in late November and early December, before the onset of the high travel season in Southern Argentina.

---

companies that offer a small selection of astonishing and out-of-this-world journeys to the Antarctic interior and beyond.

Flights to the Antarctic can be divided into two distinct categories: flights that access man-made airstrips on certain islands close to the peninsula, and flights that penetrate the frigid interior, relying on natural ice and snow runways for landing areas. The logistics involved in flying to the Antarctic are complicated, to say the least, and fuel becomes an issue. Make no mistake, air travel to the Antarctic is a serious undertaking; however, the rewards can be unforgettable.

From Punta Arenas, Chile, King George Island on the peninsula is the preferred destination. The island houses a number of research stations, some of which can be visited, and it boasts extraordinary wildlife and sightseeing opportunities. The average stay is 1 or 2 days, but weather delays can alter itineraries.

The severity of the landscape and the remoteness of the interior of the Antarctic continent call for special considerations when planning and preparing for an unexpectedly prolonged stay. All travelers attempting a trip to the interior should be aware of the extreme climatic conditions. Travel delays caused by severe weather are the norm. These trips, however, represent adventure travel in its purest form.

Tour Operators

Prices vary depending on the company and the destination. In general, flights to the peninsula are much cheaper than those to the interior. As expected, these all-inclusive trips can cost anywhere from $12,000 to $30,000 per person, depending on the destination. Logistical support for extended expeditions can easily run to over $40,000. Prices typically include transportation, meals, and guides.

- **Adventure Network International,** 4800 N. Federal Hwy., Suite 307D, Boca Raton, FL 33431 (© **866/395-6664** or 561/347-7523; fax 561/347-7523; www.adventure-network.com). This company began as a private plane service for climbers headed for Vinson Massif, the highest peak in Antarctica. They now include several 7- to 22-day tours, such as flights to the South Pole and the Transantarctic and Ellsworth mountain ranges, an emperor penguin safari, and a 60-day ski trip to the South Pole. Activities planned during these trips can include hiking, skiing, and skidoo trips; overnight camping; and ice hockey, igloo building, and just about anything else related to ice.
- **Aerovías DAP,** O'Higgins, Punta Arenas (© **61/223340;** fax 61/221693; www.aeroviasdap.cl). This small Chilean airline specializes in charter flights to the peninsula, in particular King George Island.

Index

FROMMER'S® COMPLETE TRAVEL GUIDES

Alaska
Alaska Cruises & Ports of Call
American Southwest
Amsterdam
Argentina & Chile
Arizona
Atlanta
Australia
Austria
Bahamas
Barcelona, Madrid & Seville
Beijing
Belgium, Holland & Luxembourg
Bermuda
Boston
Brazil
British Columbia & the Canadian Rockies
Brussels & Bruges
Budapest & the Best of Hungary
Calgary
California
Canada
Cancún, Cozumel & the Yucatán
Cape Cod, Nantucket & Martha's Vineyard
Caribbean
Caribbean Ports of Call
Carolinas & Georgia
Chicago
China
Colorado
Costa Rica
Cruises & Ports of Call
Cuba
Denmark
Denver, Boulder & Colorado Springs
England
Europe
Europe by Rail
European Cruises & Ports of Call

Florence, Tuscany & Umbria
Florida
France
Germany
Great Britain
Greece
Greek Islands
Halifax
Hawaii
Hong Kong
Honolulu, Waikiki & Oahu
India
Ireland
Italy
Jamaica
Japan
Kauai
Las Vegas
London
Los Angeles
Maryland & Delaware
Maui
Mexico
Montana & Wyoming
Montréal & Québec City
Munich & the Bavarian Alps
Nashville & Memphis
New England
Newfoundland & Labrador
New Mexico
New Orleans
New York City
New York State
New Zealand
Northern Italy
Norway
Nova Scotia, New Brunswick & Prince Edward Island
Oregon
Ottawa
Paris
Peru

Philadelphia & the Amish Country
Portugal
Prague & the Best of the Czech Republic
Provence & the Riviera
Puerto Rico
Rome
San Antonio & Austin
San Diego
San Francisco
Santa Fe, Taos & Albuquerque
Scandinavia
Scotland
Seattle
Shanghai
Sicily
Singapore & Malaysia
South Africa
South America
South Florida
South Pacific
Southeast Asia
Spain
Sweden
Switzerland
Texas
Thailand
Tokyo
Toronto
Turkey
USA
Utah
Vancouver & Victoria
Vermont, New Hampshire & Maine
Vienna & the Danube Valley
Virgin Islands
Virginia
Walt Disney World® & Orlando
Washington, D.C.
Washington State

FROMMER'S® DOLLAR-A-DAY GUIDES

Australia from $50 a Day
California from $70 a Day
England from $75 a Day
Europe from $85 a Day
Florida from $70 a Day
Hawaii from $80 a Day

Ireland from $80 a Day
Italy from $70 a Day
London from $90 a Day
New York City from $90 a Day
Paris from $90 a Day
San Francisco from $70 a Day

Washington, D.C. from $80 a Day
Portable London from $90 a Day
Portable New York City from $90 a Day
Portable Paris from $90 a Day

FROMMER'S® PORTABLE GUIDES

Acapulco, Ixtapa & Zihuatanejo
Amsterdam
Aruba
Australia's Great Barrier Reef
Bahamas
Berlin
Big Island of Hawaii
Boston
California Wine Country
Cancún
Cayman Islands
Charleston
Chicago
Disneyland®
Dominican Republic
Dublin

Florence
Frankfurt
Hong Kong
Las Vegas
Las Vegas for Non-Gamblers
London
Los Angeles
Los Cabos & Baja
Maine Coast
Maui
Miami
Nantucket & Martha's Vineyard
New Orleans
New York City
Paris

Phoenix & Scottsdale
Portland
Puerto Rico
Puerto Vallarta, Manzanillo & Guadalajara
Rio de Janeiro
San Diego
San Francisco
Savannah
Vancouver
Vancouver Island
Venice
Virgin Islands
Washington, D.C.
Whistler

FROMMER'S® NATIONAL PARK GUIDES

Algonquin Provincial Park
Banff & Jasper
Family Vacations in the National
  Parks

Grand Canyon
National Parks of the American
  West
Rocky Mountain

Yellowstone & Grand Teton
Yosemite & Sequoia/Kings
  Canyon
Zion & Bryce Canyon

FROMMER'S® MEMORABLE WALKS

Chicago
London

New York
Paris

San Francisco

FROMMER'S® WITH KIDS GUIDES

Chicago
Las Vegas
New York City

Ottawa
San Francisco
Toronto

Vancouver
Walt Disney World® & Orlando
Washington, D.C.

SUZY GERSHMAN'S BORN TO SHOP GUIDES

Born to Shop: France
Born to Shop: Hong Kong,
  Shanghai & Beijing

Born to Shop: Italy
Born to Shop: London

Born to Shop: New York
Born to Shop: Paris

FROMMER'S® IRREVERENT GUIDES

Amsterdam
Boston
Chicago
Las Vegas
London

Los Angeles
Manhattan
New Orleans
Paris
Rome

San Francisco
Seattle & Portland
Vancouver
Walt Disney World®
Washington, D.C.

FROMMER'S® BEST-LOVED DRIVING TOURS

Austria
Britain
California
France

Germany
Ireland
Italy
New England

Northern Italy
Scotland
Spain
Tuscany & Umbria

THE UNOFFICIAL GUIDES®

Beyond Disney
California with Kids
Central Italy
Chicago
Cruises
Disneyland®
England
Florida
Florida with Kids
Inside Disney

Hawaii
Las Vegas
London
Maui
Mexico's Best Beach Resorts
Mini Las Vegas
Mini Mickey
New Orleans
New York City
Paris

San Francisco
Skiing & Snowboarding in the
  West
South Florida including Miami &
  the Keys
Walt Disney World®
Walt Disney World® for
  Grown-ups
Walt Disney World® with Kids
Washington, D.C.

SPECIAL-INTEREST TITLES

Athens Past & Present
Cities Ranked & Rated
Frommer's Best Day Trips from London
Frommer's Best RV & Tent Campgrounds
  in the U.S.A.
Frommer's Caribbean Hideaways
Frommer's China: The 50 Most Memorable Trips
Frommer's Exploring America by RV
Frommer's Gay & Lesbian Europe
Frommer's NYC Free & Dirt Cheap

Frommer's Road Atlas Europe
Frommer's Road Atlas France
Frommer's Road Atlas Ireland
Frommer's Wonderful Weekends from
  New York City
The New York Times' Guide to Unforgettable
  Weekends
Retirement Places Rated
Rome Past & Present

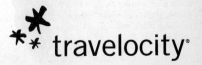

MAY 2006

Travel Tip: Make sure there's customer service for any change of plans — involving friendly natives, for example.

One can plan and plan, but if you don't book with the right people you can't seize le moment and canoodle with the poodle named Pansy. I, for one, am all for fraternizing with the locals. Better yet, if I need to extend my stay and my gnome nappers are willing, it can all be arranged through the 800 number at, oh look, how convenient, the lovely company coat of arms.

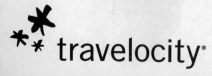

travelocity®

1-888-TRAVELOCITY / travelocity.com / America Online Keyword: Travel